ABRAHAM KUYPER

Collected Works in Public Theology

GENERAL EDITORS
JORDAN J. BALLOR
MELVIN FLIKKEMA

AbrahamKuyper.com

COMMON GRACE

GOD'S GIFTS FOR A FALLEN WORLD

Volume 2: The Doctrinal Section

ABRAHAM
KUYPER

Edited by Jordan J. Ballor and J. Daryl Charles

Translated by Nelson D. Kloosterman
and Ed M. van der Maas

Introduction by Craig J. Bartholomew

Common Grace: God's Gifts for a Fallen World
Volume 2: The Doctrinal Section

Abraham Kuyper Collected Works in Public Theology

Lexham Press, 1313 Commercial St., Bellingham, WA 98225
LexhamPress.com

Originally published as *De Gemeene Gratie.* Tweede Deel. *Het Leerstellig Gedeelte.*© Boekhandel voorheen Höveker & Wormser, 1902.

This translation previously published by Christian's Library Press, an imprint of the Acton Institute for the Study of Religion & Liberty, 98 E. Fulton Street, Grand Rapids, MI, 49503.

Print ISBN 9781577996699
Digital ISBN 9781577996958

Translators: Nelson D. Kloosterman, Ed M. van der Maas
Acton Editorial: Jordan J. Ballor, Stephen J. Grabill, Timothy J. Beals,
Paul J. Brinkerhoff, Eduardo J. Echeverria, Andrew M. McGinnis, Dylan Pahman
Lexham Editorial: Brannon Ellis, Justin Marr, Stephen Kline
Cover Design: Christine Gerhart
Back Cover Design: Brittany Schrock
Typesetting: ProjectLuz.com

CONTENTS

GENERAL EDITORS' INTRODUCTION

In times of great upheaval and uncertainty, it is necessary to look to the past for resources to help us recognize and address our own contemporary challenges. While Scripture is foremost among these foundations, the thoughts and reflections of Christians throughout history also provide us with important guidance. Because of his unique gifts, experiences, and writings, Abraham Kuyper is an exemplary guide in these endeavors.

Kuyper (1837–1920) is a significant figure both in the history of the Netherlands and modern Protestant theology. A prolific intellectual, Kuyper founded a political party and a university, led the formation of a Reformed denomination and the movement to create Reformed elementary schools, and served as the prime minister of the Netherlands from 1901 to 1905. In connection with his work as a builder of institutions, Kuyper was also a prolific author. He wrote theological treatises, biblical and confessional studies, historical works, social and political commentary, and devotional materials.

Believing that Kuyper's work is a significant and underappreciated resource for Christian public witness, in 2011 a group of scholars interested in Kuyper's life and work formed the Abraham Kuyper Translation Society. The shared conviction of the society, along with the Acton Institute, Kuyper College, and other Abraham Kuyper scholars, is that Kuyper's works hold great potential to build intellectual capacity within the church in North America, Europe, and around the world. It is our hope that translation of his works into English will make his insights accessible to those seeking to grow and revitalize communities in the developed world as well as to those in the global south and east who are facing unique challenges and opportunities.

The church today—both locally and globally—needs the tools to construct a compelling and responsible public theology. The aim of this translation project is to provide those tools—we believe that Kuyper's unique insights can catalyze the development of a winsome and constructive Christian social witness and cultural engagement the world over.

In consultation and collaboration with these institutions and individual scholars, the Abraham Kuyper Translation Society developed this 12-volume translation project, the Abraham Kuyper Collected Works in Public Theology. This multivolume series collects in English translation Kuyper's writings and speeches from a variety of genres and contexts in his work as a theologian and statesman. In almost all cases, this set contains original works that have never before been translated into English. The series contains multivolume works as well as other volumes, including thematic anthologies.

The series includes a translation of Kuyper's *Our Program* (*Ons Program*), which sets forth Kuyper's attempt to frame a Christian political vision distinguished from the programs of the nineteenth-century Modernists who took their cues from the French Revolution. It was this document that launched Kuyper's career as a pastor, theologian, and educator. As James Bratt writes, "This comprehensive Program, which Kuyper crafted in the process of forming the Netherlands' first mass political party, brought the theology, the political theory, and the organization vision together brilliantly in a coherent set of policies that spoke directly to the needs of his day. For us it sets out the challenge of envisioning what might be an equivalent witness in our own day."

Also included is Kuyper's seminal three-volume work *De Gemeene Gratie*, or *Common Grace*, which presents a constructive public theology of cultural engagement rooted in the humanity Christians share with the rest of the world. Kuyper's presentation of common grace addresses a gap he recognized in the development of Reformed teaching on divine grace. After addressing particular grace and covenant grace in other writings, Kuyper here develops his articulation of a Reformed understanding of God's gifts that are common to all people after the fall into sin.

The series also contains Kuyper's three-volume work on the lordship of Christ, *Pro Rege*. These three volumes apply Kuyper's principles in *Common Grace*, providing guidance for how to live in a fallen world under Christ the King. Here the focus is on developing cultural institutions in a way that is consistent with the ordinances of creation that have been maintained and preserved, even if imperfectly so, through common grace.

The remaining volumes are thematic anthologies of Kuyper's writings and speeches gathered from the course of his long career.

The anthology *On Charity and Justice* includes a fresh and complete translation of Kuyper's "The Problem of Poverty," the landmark speech Kuyper gave at the opening of the First Christian Social Congress in Amsterdam in 1891. This important work was first translated into English in 1950 by Dirk Jellema; in 1991, a new edition by James Skillen was issued. This volume also contains other writings and speeches on subjects including charity, justice, wealth, and poverty.

The anthology *On Islam* contains English translations of significant pieces that Abraham Kuyper wrote about Islam, gathered from his reflections on a lengthy tour of the Mediterranean world. Kuyper's insights illustrate an instructive model for observing another faith and its cultural ramifications from an informed Christian perspective.

The anthology *On the Church* includes selections from Kuyper's doctrinal dissertation on the theologies of Reformation theologians John Calvin and John à Lasco. It also includes various treatises and sermons, such as "Rooted and Grounded," "Twofold Fatherland," and "Address on Missions."

The anthology *On Business and Economics* contains various meditations Kuyper wrote about the evils of the love of money as well as pieces that provide Kuyper's thoughts on stewardship, human trafficking, free trade, tariffs, child labor, work on the Sabbath, and business.

Finally, the anthology *On Education* includes Kuyper's important essay "Bound to the Word," which discusses what it means to be ruled by the Word of God in the entire world of human thought. Numerous other pieces are also included, resulting in a substantial English volume of Kuyper's thoughts on Christian education.

Collectively, this 12-volume series will, as Richard Mouw puts it, "give us a much-needed opportunity to absorb the insights of Abraham Kuyper about God's marvelous designs for human cultural life."

The Abraham Kuyper Translation Society along with the Acton Institute and Kuyper College gratefully acknowledge the Andreas Center for

Reformed Scholarship and Service at Dordt College; Calvin College; Calvin Theological Seminary; Fuller Theological Seminary; Mid-America Reformed Seminary; Redeemer University College; Princeton Theological Seminary; and Southeastern Baptist Theological Seminary. Their financial support and partnership made these translations possible. The society is also grateful for the generous financial support of Dr. Rimmer and Ruth DeVries and the J. C. Huizenga family, which has enabled the translation and publication of these volumes.

This series is dedicated to Dr. Rimmer DeVries in recognition of his life's pursuits and enduring legacy as a cultural leader, economist, visionary, and faithful follower of Christ who reflects well the Kuyperian vision of Christ's lordship over all spheres of society.

Jordan J. Ballor
Melvin Flikkema

Grand Rapids, MI
August 2015

EDITORS' INTRODUCTION

Abraham Kuyper's doctrine of common grace is one of the most significant, and controversial, aspects of the great theologian's legacy. This multi-volume translation of his exhaustive treatment of the doctrine is intended to provide deeper insights into the motivations for, reasoning in, and implications for Kuyper's understanding of this crucial, and oft-misunderstood, element of divine action.[1] For Kuyper, common grace was clearly grounded in Scripture and was taught but not fully developed in the historic Reformed faith. In addition to these biblical and historical reasons for articulating his teaching on common grace, there were doctrinal and apologetic reasons as well. In doctrinal terms, common grace was necessary for a full understanding both of special, saving grace as well as for the underlying continuity of God's faithfulness to his creation. At the same time, common grace also served an explanatory function, helping us to understand how there can so often be such genius and goodness in the world of unbelievers. These diverse foundations of common grace lead to an understanding of the moral significance of common grace as well, which involves the natural law, civic righteousness, and social order.

1. For more on the motivations and methodology for these translations that hold for these latter two volumes as well, see the editors' introduction to *CG* 1.

FOUNDATIONS OF COMMON GRACE

First and foremost, for Kuyper the doctrine of common grace was biblical, and like Reformed theologians before him, Kuyper was determined not to be silent where Scripture provided positive witness.[2] Calvin, when discussing the grace that characterized God's general relationship to his fallen creatures, refers to Matthew 5:45, which says God "makes his sun rise on the evil and on the good, and sends rain on the just and on the unjust."[3] This verse is significant as well for Kuyper, but the main biblical foundation for Kuyper's exposition of common grace is the Noahic covenant, which Kuyper describes as the doctrine's "fixed historical starting point."[4] The fact that Kuyper's biblical exposition of common grace begins with Noah rather than Adam underscores his understanding that common grace is a post-fall necessity, and thus a kind of divine action that is only possible in light of sin.

As the first volume of this trilogy focuses on the biblical foundations of the doctrine, the second takes its point of departure in the historical grounding of the doctrine. That is, Kuyper defends his attention to common grace, which passes three quarters of a million words over the three volumes, by pointing out that the Reformers recognized and affirmed the reality of common grace, but given their context did not develop and fully explicate it. An important element of the second volume is thus Kuyper's articulation of a precedent for his understanding in the writings of the Reformers and Reformed confessional standards, particularly the Canons of Dort.[5] Even though he thought the treatment of common grace in the era of the Reformation was underdeveloped, Kuyper understood that it was this way for a legitimate reason. As he put it, the controversy at the time had more to do specifically with the doctrines of salvation and special grace, and so it was natural for the Reformers to spend much of their

2. This is the reason, for example, that Calvin defends inclusion of the doctrine of predestination in his work. See *Inst.*, III.31.3, p. 924: "For Scripture is the school of the Holy Spirit, in which, as nothing is omitted that is both necessary and useful to know, so nothing is taught but what is expedient to know."
3. See *Inst.*, III.25.9, p. 1004.
4. *CG* 1.2.1, p. 10. For background on the Noahic covenant as a general covenant for the preservation of all of creation in the Reformed tradition, see Jordan J. Ballor, *Covenant, Causality, and Law: A Study in the Theology of Wolfgang Musculus* (Göttingen: Vandenhoeck & Ruprecht, 2012), 46-57.
5. See, for example, *CG* 2.2.

energy developing and debating the topics that were of the most salience at the time. "Every period cannot do everything at once," contends Kuyper, "and it was entirely correct that in the days of the Reformation, theologians saved their time and strength for elucidating those contrasts that were of primary importance in that period. Had they acted differently, they might have misjudged their calling for the time in which they lived."[6]

In his own time, however, Kuyper judges that it is past time for more attention to be paid to common grace. This should be, in part, the natural outworking of focus on special grace, which can only fully and rightly understood within the context of common grace. Because of the relationship between the work of God in creation, the age of human fallenness, redemption and restoration of the world, and the consummation of God's providential purposes, the work of special grace which involves regeneration and reconciliation must be connected to God's original purposes in creation. These purposes have been maintained and preserved, even in the midst of corruption and sin, through common grace. Thus, observes Kuyper, speaking of this gift of preservation, "It also appears that the grace extended to our race that had fallen into sin consists not in the gift of something new, nor in the re-giving of something we had lost, but exclusively in the continuation of something that lay at the foundation of our creation."[7] Special grace has a specifically remedial purpose, as the prophet Isaiah puts it, in the day of redemption: "Then the eyes of the blind shall be opened, and the ears of the deaf unstopped; then shall the lame man leap like a deer, and the tongue of the mute sing for joy" (Is 35:5-6). So while the restorative and reconciling work of special grace and the preservative and sustaining work of common grace need to be properly distinguished, they are best understood as complementary. Special grace depends on common grace, for if humankind were no longer existing after the fall into sin, there would be no one to save.

There is also a critical explanatory function that common grace serves, specifically, to help us understand how what is good or true or beautiful in some sense can be said to exist in the non-Christian, fallen, and sinful world. There is, in fact, some virtue that can be found among the unregenerate, even if it is not goodness in its fullest sense, or entirely free from impurities, or soteriologically significant. On one level all that fallen human beings

6. *CG* 2.12.4.

7. *CG* 1.55.1, pp. 485-486.

do falls short of the glory of God and merits punishment. But on another level, everything is not as bad as it could be, and there are degrees of corruption, impurity, and evil that allow for some relative and comparative discernment. So among sinners it is not the case that everything is as evil as it could possibly be. And among Christians, because sanctification is a temporal and progressive reality, what is done continues to be marred by imperfection, vice, and sin to a greater or lesser degree. In this way, it would be natural for someone to conclude, when comparing the confession of the church against the reality of the lives of its members, "the world turns out to be better than expected and the church worse than expected."[8]

This point about the virtues of unbelievers, often described in terms of civil or moral good as opposed to Christian or salvific good, underscores a salient aspect of Kuyper's treatment of common grace as it relates to the moral order and civil society. That is, Kuyper connects the doctrine of common grace to the broader natural-law tradition, with implications for a proper understanding of civil virtue and the functioning of the social order.

COMMON GRACE AND THE MORAL ORDER

Common grace is a multifaceted concept for Kuyper. Indeed, it reflects the diversity and scope of all of God's creation itself. A critical aspect of that creation for our theological understanding, however, is the moral order. God has created human beings in his image, and this means in part that human beings are moral agents. In its essence, moral agency entails instructions and responsibilities. Humans have been placed as stewards over creation, and their responsibility includes adherence to the moral order that God has instituted.

A classic way of articulating this dynamic in Christianity is the rich and diverse tradition of natural law. God has created human beings in a certain way, with a particular set of powers, talents, skills, and habits, aimed at corresponding goods and ends. There is a law that governs the natures that God has created, a law that is fitted to and appropriate for all these different creatures, from stocks and stones to human beings and angels. A good way of understanding the natural law is as "the moral aspect of the penetrating arrow of general revelation."[9]

---

8. *CG* 2.2.1.
9. J. Daryl Charles, *Retrieving the Natural Law: A Return to Moral First Things* (Grand Rapids: Eerdmans, 2008), 130.

All of this holds true for the state of humanity in its integrity, before the fall into sin and corruption. The fissure that sin creates affects every aspect of human existence, but it does not impact the moral demands that are placed upon humans by their nature and by God. That anything continues to exist of humanity after the fall is an act of grace, and that the moral obligations that govern human nature are not completely lost or eradicated is likewise evidence of God's ongoing gracious activity. In this way, Kuyper writes that "thanks to common grace, the spiritual light has not totally departed from the soul's eye of the sinner. And also, notwithstanding the curse that spread throughout creation, a speaking of God has survived within that creation, thanks to common grace."[10] Here Kuyper stands in line with Calvin, who, notwithstanding a strong accent on human depravity, can nevertheless insist that recognition of moral reality is "implanted in all men."[11] Moreover, the seeds of moral discernment in the human heart remain in effect even in the midst of the vicissitudes of life; neither war nor catastrophe nor theft nor human disagreement can alter these moral intuitions. Even those who "fight against manifest reason" in their unjust actions "do not nullify the original conception of equity" that is implanted within.[12]

We may therefore understand the existence and acknowledgement of natural law after the fall as an aspect of God's broader sustaining and preserving grace.

This is a significant, and often controversial, teaching.[13] And although Kuyper and the later neocalvinist tradition has often been described, and

10. *CG* 1.55.5, p. 490.

11. *Inst.*, II.2.13, p. 272. Calvin is here mirroring the Pauline declaration that "since the creation of the world his [God's] invisible attributes are clearly seen" so that human beings are "without excuse"; this moral state of affairs exists because all people show the moral law to be "written in their hearts" (Ro 1:20; 2:15a).

12. *Inst.*, II.2.13, p. 272-73.

13. For a study of Protestant antipathy towards natural law, which is largely at odds with the early centuries of the magisterial Protestant traditions, see Stephen J. Grabill, *Rediscovering the Natural Law in Reformed Theological Ethics* (Grand Rapids: Eerdmans, 2006). See also Jordan J. Ballor, "Natural Law and Protestantism—A Review Essay," *Christian Scholar's Review* 41, no. 2 (Winter 2012): 193-209; J. Daryl Charles, "Burying the Wrong Corpse: Protestants and the Natural Law," in *Natural Law and Evangelical Political Thought*, ed. Jesse Covington, Bryan McGraw, and Micah Watson (Lanham: Lexington Books, 2013), 3-34; and Charles, *Retrieving the Natural Law*, 111-55.

understood by its own devotees, as in opposition to natural law, Kuyper himself is quite clear: natural law is a manifestation of God's common grace.[14]

As Kuyper well understood, moral law is the gracious means by which God governs the universe. Kuyper frequent speaks of moral law by using the grammar of "divine ordinance." Expressing itself through various divine ordinances, the moral law is woven into the fabric of creation. In *Our Program*, Kuyper speaks of the "natural knowledge of God" accessible to all human beings and "universal moral law" that "was ingrained in man before his fall" and which, "however weakened after the fall, still speaks so sharply, so strongly, so clearly among even the most brutalized peoples and the most degenerate persons that Paul could write: 'For when the Gentiles, which have not the law, do by nature the things contained in the law, these, having not the law, are a law unto themselves, even though they do not have the law. They show that *the work of the law is written in their hearts*, while their conscience also bears witness, and their conflicting thoughts accuse or even excuse them.'"[15]

This, of course, is none other than the language of natural law. Thus it is that Kuyper can speak of "the ordinances of God" which direct and preserve all of human life and form the underpinnings of common grace. These laws or ordinances, in turn, facilitate what Kuyper referred to as *soevereiniteit in eigen kring*, what we call "sphere sovereignty" or "structural pluralism,"[16] developed at some length in his third Princeton lecture, "Calvinism and Politics." Common grace, supported by divine ordinances, makes civil life possible, based on moral principle and shared morality. At bottom, justice

14. See, for example, James W. Skillen and Rockne M. McCarthy, eds., *Political Order and the Plural Structure of Society* (Atlanta: Scholars Press, 1991). On the connection between common grace and natural law, see Vincent Bacote, "Natural Law: Friend of Common Grace?" in *Natural Law and Evangelical Political Thought*, 153-164.
15. Abraham Kuyper, *Our Program: A Christian Political Manifesto*, ed. and trans. Harry Van Dyke (Bellingham, WA: Lexham Press, 2015), §63, pp. 76–77. See also Kuyper, *Our Program*, §§29, 31, and 327.
16. On the equation of "sphere sovereignty" and "structural pluralism," see Simon P. Kennedy, "Abraham Kuyper: Calvinist Anti-Revolutionary Politician and Political Thinker," *Australian Journal of Politics and History* 6, no. 2 (June 2015): 169-83; James D. Bratt, *Abraham Kuyper: Modern Calvinist, Christian Democrat* (Grand Rapids: Eerdmans, 2013), 130-48; Kent A. Van Til, "Subsidiarity and Sphere-Sovereignty: A Match Made in...?" *Theological Studies* 69, no. 3 (2008): 610-36; and James W. Skillen and Rockne M. McCarthy, "Sphere Sovereignty, Creation Order, and Public Justice: An Evaluation," in *Political Order and the Plural Structure of Society*, 397-417.

is impossible without the moral law; in Kuyper's thinking, justice derives from divine ordinances.

Lest he be misunderstood, Kuyper puts the matter of the natural moral law in perspective by understanding it in relation to human sinfulness:

> Therefore the situation after the fall, also according to the testimony of the apostle, is not that this darkening changed all at once into pitch-black night, and all religious and moral awareness was totally deadened in sin, but to the contrary, that this otherwise necessary final impact of sin has been restrained, and thanks to that restraining there remains in people a consciousness of good and evil, an awareness of justice and injustice, a certain knowledge of what God wants and does not want. However dense and heavy the mists may be in which people are enveloped as sinners, the light did not abandon the struggle but continued to penetrate those mists.[17]

In discussing the connection between common grace and the moral order Kuyper often relies on the traditional language of "light" and "darkness," which connects both with scriptural witness as well as classical natural-law thinking.

Kuyper is not, however, averse to explicit invocation of the language of natural law, which is characteristic of so many later Protestant figures. Part of the reason that the specific language of *natural law* in its moral sense fell into disuse among Protestants in this and following eras has to do with the rise of naturalism and rationalism. *Nature* came to be identified with that which was other than human, and even taken in materialistic or naturalistic dimensions. Thus, when Kuyper sometimes distinguishes between "natural laws" and "moral and spiritual law," he can be understood to be referring to the "laws of nature" in their natural scientific sense rather than their moral and theological sense.[18] In this way Kuyper notes in his Stone lectures that "as a Calvinist looks upon God's decree as the foundation and origin of the natural laws, in the same manner also he finds in it the firm foundation and the origin of every moral and spiritual law." He distinguishes here between natural laws referring to the laws that govern non-human existence, and

17. *CG* 1.55.4, p. 488.
18. See for instance, Abraham Kuyper, *Lectures on Calvinism* (Grand Rapids: Eerdmans, 1931), 115; and *CG* 2.79.1.

the moral and spiritual laws that govern humans as moral and spiritual beings. Such distinctions are not to be radically opposed, however, as he continues to describe them as "both these, the natural as well as the spiritual laws, forming together one high order, which exists according to God's command, and wherein God's counsel will be accomplished in the consummation of His eternal, all-embracing plan."[19] When we understand that it is part of human nature to be a moral and spiritual being, we might likewise recognize how speaking of laws of nature with respect to humanity is also legitimate.

Because there is such a close connection between the natural, moral law and common grace, Kuyper often catachrestically uses the terms interchangeably. But more technically in Kuyper's understanding we should recognize the ongoing preservation of human beings as morally responsible agents is a manifestation of his larger conception of common grace and not simply identifiable with it. Apart from the terminology, however, the substance of the connection between common grace and the moral order is explicit, as Kuyper affirms "a knowledge of God and of his justice that persisted in spite of our sin, and that was and is still maintained, due not to our efforts but despite our unrighteousness, by the common grace of God."[20]

COMMON GRACE AND CIVIC RIGHTEOUSNESS

The knowledge of God and his justice, even as it is incomplete, fragmentary, and error-prone, preserves the existence and enables the flourishing of unregenerate humanity. There exists among unbelievers incredible genius, awe-inspiring artistry, and striking virtue. The truth of this "is immediately evident from the undeniable fact that in people like Plato and Aristotle, Kant and Darwin, stars of the first order have shined, geniuses of the highest caliber, people who expressed very profound ideas, even though they were not professing Christians. They did not have this genius from themselves, but received their talent from God who created them and equipped them for their intellectual labor."[21]

---

19. Kuyper, *Lectures on Calvinism*, 115. See also *CG* 2.39.3.
20. *CG* 1.55.6, p. 490.
21. *CG* 3.63.2. See also Abraham Kuyper, *Wisdom & Wonder: Common Grace in Science and Art*, ed. Jordan J. Ballor and Stephen J. Grabill (Grand Rapids: Christian's Library Press, 2011), 53.

As we have seen, whatever goodness there is among non-Christians exists because "the sinner still knows the justice of God, and the revelation of God in the human heart and in creation still continues to function even after the fall."[22] From this reality it follows that there is some level of goodness or righteousness that is possible for sinners to achieve on the basis of common grace. By definition this righteousness is not salvific. Common grace refers to that which is preserved and sustained in the face of sin, but not to that action of God which redeems, renews, and reconciles. That is the realm of special grace. Kuyper is at pains to show that whatever goodness perdures in the sinful world, it does not reach to what is truly good; hence, the identification of good works in the Heidelberg Catechism of those "which proceed from true faith, and are done according to the Law of God, unto His glory, and not such as rest on our own opinion or the commandments of men."[23]

And yet there is some virtue or righteousness that is realized in the life of fallen humanity. Thus Kuyper affirms that "in the unconverted, all kinds of powers certainly function, albeit only partially in the direction ordained by God."[24] In part this aspect of the doctrine of common grace refers back to that explanatory function of the doctrine in Kuyper's thought. It helps Christians to understand that when they look out into the world and examine history they find examples of what appears to be morally virtuous activity among sinners. The connection between common grace and civil righteousness enables Christians to affirm that there is good *in some sense* that is manifest in the life of the nations without confusing or conflating this with good in its fullest, most robust, or ultimate sense.

At the same time, the moral significance of this civic righteousness is ambiguous. The moral aspect of common grace is sufficient to allow there to be some expressions of civil good and social life, but its soteriological significance ends with human beings left "without excuse" (Ro 1:20). As with all good things, whatever good is in such civic righteousness is in the final analysis to be attributed to God rather than to human initiative. And because of the pervasiveness of fallen humanity's sinfulness, Kuyper holds to the fundamental Reformed conviction that of its own accord humanity would increase in sin rather than in virtue. "Common grace is still continually at

22. *CG* 1. 55.6, p. 491.
23. Heidelberg Catechism LD 33, Q & A 91.
24. *CG* 2.39.5.

work to partially redirect into the right direction all kinds of powers and activities within him," writes Kuyper of unregenerate man, "that left alone would head entirely into sin."[25]

So while Kuyper is sure to recognize and celebrate that there are some vestiges and elements of goodness or righteousness that persist among sinful humans, he is likewise keen to properly categorize and relativize such goodness. Civic righteousness truly exists, but it is not salvific; it is a result of God's divine graciousness rather than innate human goodness; it falls short of true virtue and Christian righteousness; and it is rather less common than we might wish. There is this consistent dynamic: God continues to graciously offer and give good gifts to his creatures, even while those creatures persist in making ill use of those gifts and turning those gifts to bad ends: "The light of truth has definitely not retreated altogether but has *continued* to shine. It is strictly due to us that the light does not penetrate to our soul's eye."[26] Or as Kuyper concludes: "Common grace is present, but we have rejected it."[27] It is true that not all those uses and ends are as bad as they could possibly be; they may even be considered relatively good in some sense. And yet we must ultimately recognize that this situation cannot continue forever.

COMMON GRACE AND SOCIAL ORDER

One of Kuyper's great insights in his treatment of common grace is that even in the midst of such ambivalence, amidst the good and the evil that exist in this life, some degree of not only individual virtue but also social development is realized. God's preserving work of common grace helps us explain both civic righteousness and the ongoing realities of social life. Common grace makes individual life as well as social flourishing possible, even if these are constrained by sin and cannot reach their eschatological fullness.

The final volume of his trilogy on common grace focuses specifically on working out the implications of these realities for social life. For Kuyper, the realities of family and work are embedded in the creation order. As such, they are preserved in the context of sinfulness, but are not brought into existence anew. Likewise, the church could in some sense be said to be present wherever there are children of God, whether in the state of

25. *CG* 2.39.5.

26. *CG* 1.55.4, p. 489.

27. *CG* 1.55.4, p. 489.

integrity or after corruption. But the church as an institution specifically formed around special grace is a feature of the post-fall situation. Similarly for Kuyper, there may be a sense in which political life could be said to exist in the primal condition, but it is only after the fall in sin that government takes on its distinctive character as a coercive power for the administration of civil justice.[28] The state is, in this sense, the institution of common grace *par excellence*. It provides a curb on social evil, and a check on sinful ambition.

This role is essential for all of human society, whether characterized as Christian or not. This is why the state is an institution of common grace: "The essential character of government as such does not lie in the fact that canals are dug, railways built, and so forth, but in the sovereign right to compel subversives by force and if necessary subdue them with the sword."[29] For Kuyper the state is a necessary institution for the preservation of social life in the fallen world. But as his distinction between sphere sovereignty and state sovereignty indicates, even if the government is a particularly salient example of a common-grace institution, it is not itself identical with all of social life and is in fact sharply limited by the legitimate and warranted functions and roles of other institutions.[30] Two examples of special notice are the family and work, realities which are embedded in the nature of creation and reaffirmed in the curse and promise.

In a remarkable treatment of Adam and Eve's fall into sin and the divine discourse in Genesis 3, Kuyper underscores the fundamental functions of procreation in marriage and co-creation in work. When God demurs from striking down Adam and Eve immediately, he preserves them in life in the face of death. As Kuyper observes, "Over against death stands life; and for life two things are necessary, namely, the emergence of life and the maintenance of life."[31] Family and procreation represent the basis for the emergence of human life, while work and co-creation represent the basis for the maintenance of life.

28. One of the elements of political life that is changed after the fall is the possibility and legitimacy of an organically unified, global political entity. See Kuyper, *Calvinism*, 100-101. On the state and church as institutions formed within the context of sin, see *CG* 3.4-5.

29. *CG* 3.7.1.

30. As Kuyper once put it, "Sphere sovereignty defending itself against State sovereignty: that is the course of world history even back before the Messiah's sovereignty was proclaimed." See Abraham Kuyper, "Sphere Sovereignty," in *AKCR*, 469.

31. *CG* 1.31.2, p. 273.

In an incisive treatment of the curse and promise to Eve and Adam, Kuyper highlights the foundation of grace that provides for the ongoing existence of and care for human life. To the woman God says, "in pain you shall bring forth children" (Ge 3:16). The element of the curse is present with the imposition of painfulness; but the element of grace is present in the promise: "you shall bring forth children." Despite their sinfulness and the threat of death that they deserve, Adam and Eve will have children and humanity will continue to exist. The woman becomes Eve, mother of all the living, a promise of life in the face of sin, death, and damnation. "Had absolute death set in," writes Kuyper, "then the mother in Eve, from which our entire human race had to come, would be closed forever. And behold, the opposite happens: the womb of all human life is opened up. The Lord says, 'You shall bring forth children.' This, if you will, is the word of creation to which we and everyone called human owe our being. Here, therefore, life instead of death is at work."[32]

The same is true for Adam and the productive labor that is necessary for the maintenance of human society. God says to Adam, "By the sweat of your face you shall eat bread" (Ge 3:19). The element of the curse is present in that work now has become toilsome and troublesome, painful and difficult. But the element of grace shines through in the promise: "You shall eat bread." So just as God works through procreation to guarantee that human beings will continue to exist, God promises that through work human beings will get their daily bread. As Kuyper observes, "Hunger brings death, but bread maintains life. To him who is about to die, it should be said, 'Bread will be taken away from you and hunger shall become your death.' But now the opposite is said: 'You shall eat bread.' And what does this say other than that life will not immediately drain away into death, but that it will be *nourished* and *maintained*."[33]

Through spheres like the state, family, and work God's common grace is present to preserve, protect, and promote social life.

CONCLUSION

The continued existence and provision for humanity after the fall into sin is a critical argument in favor of Kuyper's doctrine of common grace. We

32. *CG* 1.31.2, p. 274.
33. *CG* 1.31.2, p. 274.

might explore this as a basic, and from Kuyper's perspective undeniable, point of departure for the validity of the doctrine.

After the fall into sin, it is on the one hand clear that humanity continues to exist, but that it does so not on the basis of any inherent merit or desert. God deigns to forbear, and his patience is an unmerited gift. It seems entirely appropriate to describe this divine preservation as *grace*. "In the day when Adam and his wife ate of the forbidden tree, they did not die, which would have happened if no grace had been granted them," concludes Kuyper.[34] Likewise, this grace is not limited to a chosen few. It applies to everyone who lives, whether or not they will ultimately be saved or damned. It again seems entirely appropriate to identify the extension of such graciousness to everyone as *common*.

Acknowledgment of the cogency of such reasoning does not entail that one accedes to every aspect of Kuyper's own exposition of the doctrine of common grace, however. And in fact Kuyper's treatment, both in general and in its specifics, has engendered a significant amount of controversy, even becoming the occasion for ecclesiastical split. Along with the transmission of Kuyper's extensive work on the doctrine a number of other important materials—critical, constructive, as well as corrective—are coming into availability in English as well.[35]

---

34. *CG* 1.31.1, p. 272.

35. Significant articulations and criticisms of common grace include: Herman Bavinck, "Common Grace" [1894], trans. Raymond C. Van Leeuwen, *Calvin Theological Journal* 24, no. 1 (April 1989): 38-65; idem, "Calvin and Common Grace," trans. Geerhardus Vos, *Princeton Theological Review* 7, no. 3 (1909): 437-465; Klaas Schilder, *Christ & Culture*, trans. William Helder and Albert H. Oosterhoff (Hamilton, ON: Lucerna, 2016); Cornelius Van Til, *Common Grace* (Philadelphia: Presbyterian and Reformed, 1947); Cornelius Van Til, *Common Grace and the Gospel*, 2nd ed., ed. K. Scott Oliphant (Philadelphia: Presbyterian & Reformed, 2015); S.U. Zuidema, "Common Grace and Christian Action in Abraham Kuyper," in *Communication and Confrontation* (Toronto: Wedge Publishing Foundation, 1972), 52-105; Henry R. Van Til, *The Calvinistic Concept of Culture* (Grand Rapids: Baker, 1959); Joachem Douma, *Common Grace in Kuyper, Schilder, and Calvin: Exposition, Comparison, and Evaluation*, trans. Albert H. Oosterhoff, ed. William Helder (Hamilton, ON: Lucerna, 2017); Richard Mouw, *He Shines in All That's Fair: Culture and Common Grace* (Grand Rapids: Eerdmans, 2001); Cornelis van der Kooi, "A Theology of Culture: A Critical Appraisal of Kuyper's Doctrine of Common Grace," in *Kuyper Reconsidered: Aspects of his Life and Work*, ed. Cornelis van der Kooi and Jan de Bruijne (Amsterdam: VU University Press, 1999), 95-101; and John Bolt "Herman Hoeksema was Right (On the Three Points that Really Matter)," in *Biblical Interpretation and Doctrinal Formulation in the Reformed*

The goal of this current translation project is to expose new audiences to Kuyper's many-faceted thought. Kuyper's broader project with respect to common grace may not demand assent; it does demand attention. Much of his treatment is constructive, speculative, and in some cases idiosyncratic. Some of the ways he explicates his understanding of common grace is particularly marked by his own context, biases, and presuppositions. Indeed, affirmation of the general thrust of Kuyper's purposes in his treatment of common grace does not mean that there must be adherence to every jot and tittle of his thought. Regardless of what we find today to be valuable, debatable, or detestable about Kuyper's thought, his work in these volumes demonstrates his genius and why it has been found to be so inspirational for more than a century. Kuyper's vision is comprehensive and compelling, and one that has deep lessons for us today. Common grace works as far as the curse is found:

> Common grace extends over our entire human life, in all its manifestations. There is a common grace that manifests itself in order and law; there is a common grace that manifests itself in prosperity and affluence; there is a common grace that becomes visible in the healthy development of strength and heroic courage of a nation; there is a common grace that shines in the development of science and art; there is a common grace that enriches a nation through inventiveness in enterprise and commerce; there is a common grace that strengthens the domestic and moral life; and finally there is a common grace that protects the religious life against an excessive degeneration.[36]

This is a refreshing and bracing perspective, especially in a world where the disagreements between different confessions and creeds are

---

Tradition: Essays in Honor of James De Jong, ed. Arie C. Leder and Richard A. Muller, Grand Rapids: Reformation Heritage Books, 2014), 295-318. The present translation has occasioned renewed criticisms from historical opponents of common grace, including David J. Engelsma, *Christianizing the World: Reformed Calling or Ecclesiastical Suicide?* (Grandville: Reformed Free Publishing Association, 2016). For more on the development of the Protestant Reformed Churches, see Herman Hanko, *For Thy Truth's Sake: A Doctrinal History of the Protestant Reformed Churches* (Grandville, MI: Reformed Free Publishing Association, 2000).

36. *CG* 1.56.5, pp. 497-498.

increasingly pronounced. Common grace can help us remember that amidst all of the dynamic and sometimes dizzying diversity in human existence, there exists a deep unity and solidarity that defines us as human beings created in the image of God. This vision offers a corrective to idols and ideologies of our day that threaten to overwhelm or enslave us, and provides a constructive way forward as faithful disciples of Jesus Christ.

Jordan J. Ballor
J. Daryl Charles

VOLUME INTRODUCTION

NOT SO COMMON

Abraham Kuyper's *Common Grace* is a vast, rich work comprising three parts. The volume you now hold, the second, is aptly titled "Doctrinal." Here we see Kuyper in his element. His academic training was as a theologian, and among his many other roles he taught theology at the Free University of Amsterdam. Kuyper's major academic work was his three-volume *Encyclopedia of Sacred Theology*, an extraordinary piece of writing through which we see his rigor and creativity as a theologian. It is well known that Kuyper's gifts and calling took him into virtually every field of practical and academic life; there is hardly anything about which he did not write. However, it seems that the role of theologian remained central to his identity, and we certainly witness that dimension in volume 2 of *Common Grace*, in which he covers the theology of common grace.

DOCTRINE BY WAY OF SCRIPTURE

As we move into the second volume of *Common Grace* it is worth remembering that it is preceded by another volume—a Scripture-focused one. The first volume, though called "Historical," could easily be titled "Biblical," because it deals with the biblical story from creation to the second coming.

The importance of this can easily be missed. We live in a day when many works of theology and Christian scholarship engage only minimally with Scripture, if at all. Not so with Kuyper. His entire first volume is devoted to the biblical foundations for common grace, and he insists on taking that journey before setting forth the doctrinal framework. Even in the second volume of *Common Grace*, the reader will be impressed by Kuyper's constant return to Scripture. His is a model we need to recover. If we believe with Kuyper that Scripture is God's authoritative Word for all of life, then his constant moving back and forth to and from Scripture must be essential in our project of Christian scholarship. As Kuyper asserts, "A man walks a straight path only if, gratefully accepting the light God has given, he accepts as dogma or doctrine what God has revealed to us in his Word concerning … mystery."[1]

The reader will encounter in volume 2 of *Common Grace* discussions of a number of different doctrinal points. These range from divine action and the distinction between immediate and mediate action by God, to the transcendence and immanence of God. Kuyper also presents a thought-provoking discussion of God's providence and how common grace should influence that doctrine. The doctrines of creation and the fall are in the foreground. Kuyper is fascinating in that he traces the origins of the fall to the spirit world and then explores the role of the spirit world in common grace, noting that "these millions and millions of spirits are instruments God uses in his governance of this world."[2] He is also refreshing in the emphasis he places on the incarnation. And since common grace enables the progress of history, it is not surprising that eschatology enters into the debate. Though he (perhaps wrongly) holds to the idea of the destruction of everything before recreation, he nevertheless rightly affirms a strong doctrine of continuity between the old and the new creation: "And when at the end of the ages that healing process will have run its full course, then it is not the *first* world that will be destroyed in order to be replaced by a *second* world, but it will be the age-old world of Adam, created by God once long ago, and corrupted by us, saved in Christ, that will appear to have carried within itself such hidden powers that this very world itself will one day stand before God in glory, to magnify his majesty."[3]

1. *CG* 2.1.2.
2. *CG* 2.53.1.
3. *CG* 2.23.4.

While Kuyper never confuses doctrine with a living relationship with the Creator, he takes doctrine—what we believe about God and God's relationship to his world—with the utmost seriousness and rightly believes that it can direct us in our lives and in our complex, modern societies. In his words, "Dogmas, after all, are not the result of clever arguments, but doctrines that provide an explanation concerning the mighty issues at the foundation of our human existence that impinge irresistibly upon anyone who thinks and reflects and refuses to close his or her eyes to reality."[4] He does not lose sight of the glory of God as the focus of all of life and creation, and in keeping with that vision he clearly articulates the characteristic Reformed emphasis on the sovereignty of the triune God. Romans 11:36, which reads "From him and through him and for him are all things. To him be the glory forever! Amen" [NIV], could easily serve as an epigraph for the work of Kuyper. Creation finds its meaning in the glory of God, and as this is taken seriously, creation is illumined so that we can see God working through his handiwork.

To rightly understand creation, however, special revelation is necessary. John's Gospel tells us that Jesus is the light of the world. Johan Georg Hamann, a great Christian philosopher who was a contemporary and perceptive critic of Immanuel Kant, asserted that, "All the colors of this most beautiful world grow pale once you extinguish its light, the firstborn of creation."[5] Kuyper would have said a hearty "amen!" to this. As Kuyper writes, "Everything in all of creation that lives or breathes is placed in service to the self-glorification of the triune God."[6] He was well aware that much in life will remain mysterious, but he still devoted considerable energy toward allowing the light of Christ to shine as fully and intensely as possible on the world around him. In the second volume of *Common Grace*, he brings every major locus of doctrine into play, relating all of these to the titular topic. Yet he also regularly slips into application. One gets a sense of Christ and Scripture as a floodlight illuminating the entire field of creation. Thus it is natural that Kuyper can't stay away from practical application. Indeed, there are discussions of topics ranging from education, art, clothing, to insurance and—surprisingly—smallpox vaccinations!

---

4. *CG* 2.4.1.
5. J. G. Hamann, *Writings on Philosophy and Language*, trans. and ed. K. Haynes (Cambridge: Cambridge University Press, 2007), 65.
6. *CG* 2.15.1.

PUBLIC THEOLOGY FOR THEN AND NOW

Kuyper's writing manifests what we might call a contextual sense of doctrine. He recognized that different times call for different emphases doctrinally. Though he had no interest in adjusting doctrine to the *zeitgeist* of his day, neither did he have any interest in a petrified Reformed Christianity stuck in the sixteenth century. Kuyper sought to preserve the heart of the Reformed tradition while taking *semper reformanda* seriously. At several points in volume 2 of *Common Grace*, he notes the deficiencies of earlier Reformed theologians, especially in relation to common grace, and proposes ways to develop Reformed doctrine further. This is not to suggest that he believed truth changes, but rather that it needs to be contextualized for different times and places. Kuyper himself wrote a book on the angels of God, a topic discussed several times in this volume, but he himself noted that in his day there was no longer the same interest in angels that there was in the medieval era.

On the other hand, a robust doctrine of common grace was needed in Kuyper's day. He lived when modernism was sweeping across Europe, and he recognized that its comprehensive vision could only be met by a correspondingly comprehensive Christian vision. Central to such a vision for Kuyper was a theology of common grace. In this belief Kuyper was undoubtedly correct, and it is at least as true in our day as his, though we, unlike him, live amidst the unravelling of modernism. Many of the fault lines in the modernist geography are working themselves out in our fast-changing, bewildering global context. Mark Lilla, in his important book *The Stillborn God: Religion, Politics, and the Modern West*, notes that the twilight of the idols—or what has been called the "death of God"—has been postponed. Religion has made a remarkable and unexpected comeback in our modern world. Lilla argues that the actual choice we face today is not between past and present but between two great traditions, two antithetical ways of viewing the human mystery. The one is modernism; the other is that of Christian political theology.[7] The problem, according to Lilla, is that we have forgotten just what the tradition of Christian political thought entails.

Though Kuyper does not use the language of political theology, the parallels between his work and Lilla are remarkable. Kuyper, his predecessors, and his followers never ceased to confront their hearers with the choice

7. Mark Lilla, *The Stillborn God: Religion, Politics, and the Modern West* (New York: Vintage Books, 2008), 13.

between the French Revolution's ideals and the gospel. Lilla speaks comparably of a great separation in the West. What Lilla notes of other theologians is certainly true of Kuyper: "To think that the West could produce its own political theology, in a thoroughly modern vein, is surprising and unsettling. More unsettling still is the fact that these new political theologians produced original and challenging works not to be dismissed lightly."[8]

This publication of Kuyper's major public theology works in English is a significant contribution toward helping the West recover its legacy of Christian public thought. The issues we struggle with in what Lilla calls the postponement of the twilight of idols are precisely the issues that Kuyper wrestled with in his Dutch and European contexts—issues like the public role of religion, genuine societal pluralism, justice for all, faith-based initiatives, and education. Kuyper can help us not only to recover our memory, but also to find resources with which to explore the pressing issues of our day in fresh and compelling ways.

And it is important to note that Kuyper does this from a firm base in Christian doctrine. Ernest Gellner perceptively observed in 1992 that, "In North America, religious attendance is high, but religion celebrates a shared cult of the American way of life, rather than insisting on distinctions of theology or church organization, as once it did."[9] He damningly notes that, "Christian doctrine is bowdlerized by its own theologians, and deep, literal conviction is not conspicuous by its presence."[10] On the other hand, he also noted one thing that resisted (and still resists) secularization: "But there is one very real, dramatic and conspicuous exception to all this: Islam. To say that secularization prevails in Islam is not contentious. It is simply false. Islam is as strong now as it was a century ago. In some ways, it is probably much stronger."[11] Kuyper, unlike the theologians Gellner refers to here, holds fast to Christian doctrine in his writing and unpacks it critically in relation to modernism. Thus, Christ and culture are integrally related in his work. Kuyper also develops a Christian, pluralist societal philosophy that resists secularization; yet it is one markedly different from Islam. Kuyper does all this by journeying at length through the doctrine of common grace.

8. Lilla, *The Stillborn God*, 11.
9. Ernest Gellner, *Postmodernism, Reason and Religion* (New York: Routledge, 1992), 5.
10. Gellner, *Postmodernism, Reason and Religion*, 5-6.
11. Gellner, *Postmodernism, Reason and Religion*, 5.

It may seem laughable in our present media-dominated context to imagine that a long, three volume exposition of doctrine, written by a thoroughly orthodox Reformed theologian in another place and time, might hold vital clues for life today. Indeed, *Common Grace* was written as newspaper articles, published week by week over six years in his newspaper, *De Heraut*, and some perseverance is required to work through them. But this says far more about our context, dominated as it is by tweets and short attention spans, than it does about Kuyper's thought. Nevertheless, *Common Grace* makes for compelling reading, and not least this second volume. As Kuyper synthesizes the biblical data doctrinally, volume 2 becomes, in many ways, the heart of *Common Grace*.

WHAT DOES COMMON GRACE ENTAIL?

Kuyper's creativity as a theologian is remarkable. Readers may be surprised at how many areas he engages with in his articulation of the doctrine of common grace. His work cries out for serious dialogue. But what does common grace really entail? It means that God relates to the whole of his good, but fallen, creation with grace. In Dutch, as in English, *common* can have pejorative connotations, but that is not the meaning Kuyper aims for. *Common* can also mean *universal* or *general*. Grace—undeserved mercy—relates to the whole of creation. Hence the title of this introduction: "Not So Common!"

Evil Restrained

The engine of a Christian worldview is its understanding of how nature relates to grace, and Kuyper rightly asserts that, "Common grace touches on the relationship between *nature* and *grace* or, if you will ... the relationship between *church* and *world*, between *theology* and secular *scholarship*, between our *old man* and our *new man*—or also, if we may express it thus, between our *self* and *Christ*, between our self and *us ourselves*."[12] Common grace alerts us to the fact that after the fall and despite the curse under which the creation languishes, God never for a moment gives up on his creation. By his grace, he restrains its tendencies toward evil and sin. Kuyper never blurs the boundary between the believer and the unbeliever, between regenerate and unregenerate. Regeneration comes from God's *particular*

12. CG 2.25.1.

grace; the division between saved and unsaved is absolute. Yet Kuyper never makes the mistake of drawing the dividing line of antithesis—the great struggle between the kingdom of God and that of darkness—between the church and the world. The antithesis runs through every aspect of life, and the struggle it represents is at work in *every* human heart and in *every* human institution. Particular grace changes the direction of what Kuyper calls the "core" of the self so that a person may live in faith, but there is more to the self than its core. A person can be regenerate without grasping the functions of faith for all dimensions of his or her life. Such a person can continue to enact pre-conversion perspectives in areas of life.

Thus Kuyper can reflect honestly and openly on why non-Christians sometimes behave far better than Christians and why Christians often fail to live up to their confession. Consider the years of apartheid in South Africa: At least sixty percent of the country claimed to be Christian, but many white South Africans were, in practice, racist. At the same time the struggle against apartheid was often led—sacrificially—by non-Christians or even atheists. How was this possible? Such things are possible because of God's common grace, grace extended to all people and to the whole creation. This can also be attributed to the fact that Christian conversion is only a *beginning*, not an end. It needs to be followed by sanctification, which Christians reach to varying degrees.

We further see that God never gives up on his purpose for creation or ceases moving it toward the goal he set for it when he made it. History has a purpose, and Kuyper unashamedly articulates this in terms of progress, advocating for a positive view of cultural advancement. Sin may and does distort this in myriad ways—and indeed, Kuyper's view is itself problematic at points, especially concerning his racial prejudices—but common grace ensures that there is normative development in history as the world moves toward the goal God set for it. Common grace thus not only holds back evil but simultaneously enables progress.

A remarkable aspect of this volume is Kuyper's exploration of the contrast between the curse placed on creation and God's continual grace shown toward the same creation. With Kuyper we might reflect on whether this is a contradiction. Kuyper rightly argues that it is not. Evil requires punishment, but death, the symbol of the curse, remains the great enemy for both God and humankind. Indeed, redemption is God's project to erase evil from his creation and to lead it to the destiny he intended for it. For

Kuyper, common grace is the indispensable background that makes such redemption possible.

The Church in the World

Kuyper repeatedly urges us to use all legitimate means and opportunities provided through common grace to combat sin and misery, and thereby to acknowledge God wherever we find his grace in operation. Thus we must not, for example, neglect the university, for it is one of the major ways of advancing common grace and reducing misery. Combating sin and misery is a comprehensive calling; it includes the raising of children, ensuring people have adequate clothing, health care and housing for all, fostering neighborliness and vibrant, rich community. Everything that common grace puts at our disposal—farming, industry, trade, everything that adds to the quality of life and makes it more noble—must be appropriated to oppose sin and misery.

In Kuyper's writings we note a resistance to a purely individual account of sin, evil, and common grace. An organic metaphor is central to much of Kuyper's thought and he rightly insists that we think of humans not merely *individually* but also *corporately*, as an organism. On the *imago dei*, for example, Kuyper affirms that each individual is created in the image of God but also argues that such is God's greatness that we are all needed to genuinely image God in his creation. So too with suffering. Some suffering is indeed related to personal sin, but much is not. One of Kuyper's arguments in favor of insurance is that it helps alleviate much unnecessary and undeserved suffering that results simply from being part of humanity. The Kuyperian tradition is well-known for setting up Christian institutions such as schools, political parties, labor unions, and so on. This is a truly missional vision of the people of God contributing to the flourishing of all, and it is one that we need to recover. Indeed, one of Kuyper's great concerns is to allow the leaven of the gospel to penetrate every aspect of our lives. If God never gives up on his creation, how can we?

Kuyper is insightful in his recognition that there are a number of different Christian perspectives on the relationship between Christianity and culture—whether Anabaptist, Roman Catholic, or Reformed—and he realizes that these differences matter. They profoundly shape Christian thought and practice, especially in the public domains of life. Yet for Kuyper, the doctrine of common grace creates a barrier against any view that would restrict

Christian involvement to the sphere of the church. Christ governs common grace, and "this judges every perspective that sees Christianity as a religion floating atop the waters of history like an oil slick; as if the Christian church had to hide itself in this world like a hermit, without maintaining a connection with the life of that world."[13] We find Kuyper's historically sensitive philosophy of sphere sovereignty, for example, in his statement that, "What we today mean by the church—that is, an organization separate from the household, the family, and civil society and hence independent with its own boundary and enclosed within its own sphere, with its own offices and ministries, with its own law and regulations, with its own property and its own symbol—did not come into being until after Jesus' ascension, ... the church does not emerge as independent *world church* until *after* the day of Pentecost."[14] Some Kuyperians denigrate the institutional church, but this is not an emphasis we find in his writings. He is rightly sensitive to the unique role of the institutional church and its importance for the other spheres of life: "Only those who return continually to the tent of their God to be anointed anew with fresh oil can go out from that tent into the world to glorify their God there and to bless that world."[15] At the same time, he is alert to sphere universality or what Herman Dooyeweerd calls *enkapsis*—the interlacement of societal spheres—and notes of the Christian school that, "Our school is not a Christian school if the Word and prayer are not there, if it does not promote the knowledge of the truth, if the sound of Jesus' call does not go out from it, and if the particular grace [that flows] from baptism does not make itself felt there."[16] Kuyper wants us to take church seriously so that we can genuinely contribute to culture.

CRITICALLY ENGAGING KUYPER

A feast awaits the reader of this volume, and the reader is encouraged to savor it, learn from it, and live it. However, it is worth raising two ways for critically engaging with Kuyper. The first is his Eurocentrism. Though history progresses beneath the hand of God's providence, looking back from our time we can see more clearly than Kuyper how hard it is to trace that progress. Kuyper tends to see the Europe of his day as the high point

13. *CG* 2.23.4.
14. *CG* 2.22.2.
15. *CG* 2.46.3.
16. *CG* 2.46.4.

of cultural progress. He speaks, for example, of Germany as moving into its highest period of flowering, whereas during major parts of the twentieth century it turned out to be the exact opposite. Kuyper is also quick to denigrate continents like Africa and makes some distinctively unhelpful comments about Jews.[17] As much as we grant him leniency for being a product of his times, we should not follow him in these areas. We need a far more nuanced and chastened view of historical progress.

The second is Kuyper's articulation of the relationship between common and particular grace. Kuyper himself is aware of the danger of a duality between the two, but even so he fails to fully reconcile them. Kuyper speaks of particular grace as having to do with the salvation of the soul whereas sanctification and action in the world are always in the realm of common grace. Kuyper was criticized for his view of their relationship by A. A. van Ruler, and in a lengthy article S.U. Zuidema accepts the validity of much of Van Ruler's critique.[18] Kuyper does speak of the independent purpose of common grace, he does think of common grace as the ground of possibility of particular grace, and there is a tension in his thought in these respects.

On the other hand, Zuidema points out that van Ruler does not take into account Kuyper's resolution of some of the tension in *Common Grace* especially in *Pro Rege*, which Kuyper wrote later in life. According to Zuidema, Kuyper began by defining the purpose of particular grace too narrowly,[19] but as he came to emphasize the antithesis in common life he breaks through to "*the confession that truly Christian action is possible also in the domain of common grace. The fear of the Lord, not distinguishable from the confession and experiencing of Jesus Christ as our Lord and King, is totalitarian in that it embraces not only the mystic life of the inner soul and not only the life of the hereafter but embraces no less our life 'in all areas of life' in the present dispensation.*"[20] This is a complex discussion and an area that English-speaking

---

17. *CG* 2.
18. S.U. Zuidema, "Common Grace and Christian Action in Abraham Kuyper," trans. Harry Van Dyke, in S. U. Zuidema, *Communication and Confrontation* (Toronto: Wedge, 1972), 52-105, 53. Article translated by Harry Van Dyke. Republished in Steve Bishop and John H. Kok, eds., *On Kuyper: A Collection of Readings on the Life, Work and Legacy of Abraham Kuyper* (Sioux Center, IowaIA: Dordt College Press, 2013), 247-286.
19. Zuidema, "Common Grace and Christian Action in Abraham Kuyper," 53.
20. Zuidema, "Common Grace and Christian Action in Abraham Kuyper," 96. Emphasis original.

Kuyper students will need to revisit in detail as more and more of Kuyper becomes available in English.

CONCLUSION: TAKE AND READ

English speaking readers now have the immense privilege of having available more of Kuyper's work in English than ever before. We live in what might be called "a Kuyperian moment"—not only in the sense that so much Kuyper is now available in English, but also because we and our world need Kuyper's pointed insights at this time. There is a great deal at stake in how we receive Kuyper's legacy, and readers must not make the mistake of reading this introduction rather than reading Kuyper *himself*. Be immersed in *Common Grace*, both this volume and others in this series. A feast awaits and we need to be fed by this rich food.

Craig G. Bartholomew

ABBREVIATIONS

GENERAL AND BIBLIOGRAPHIC

AKB	Kuipers, Tjitze. *Abraham Kuyper: An Annotated Bibliography 1857–2010.* Translated by Clifford Anderson and Dagmare Houniet. Brill's Series in Church History 55. Leiden: Brill, 2011.
AKCR	*Abraham Kuyper: A Centennial Reader.* Edited by James D. Bratt. Grand Rapids: Eerdmans, 1998.
CCS	Calvin, John. *Calvin's Commentaries Series.* Edited by John King. 45 vols. Edinburgh: Calvin Translation Society, 1844–56.
CE	*The Catholic Encyclopedia.* Edited by Charles G. Herbermann, Edward A. Pace, Condé B. Pallen, Thomas J. Shahan, and John J. Wynne. 15 vols. New York: Robert Appleton, 1907–12.
CG	Kuyper, Abraham. *Common Grace.* Translated by Nelson D. Kloosterman and Ed M. van der Maas. Edited by Jordan J. Ballor and Stephen J. Grabill. 3 vols. Bellingham, WA: Lexham Press, 2015–.
CO	Calvin, John. *Ioannis Calvini Opera Quae Supersunt Omnia.* Edited by Guilielmus Baum, Eduardus Cunitz, and Eduardus Reuss. 59 vols. Corpus Reformatorum, 2nd ser., 29–87. Brunswick: Schwetschke, 1863–1900.

DLGTT	Muller, Richard A. *Dictionary of Latin and Greek Theological Terms*. Grand Rapids: Baker, 1996.
ESV	English Standard Version
Inst.	Calvin, John. *Institutes of the Christian Religion* (1559). 2 vols. Edited by John T. McNeill. Translated by Ford Lewis Battles. Philadelphia: Westminster, 1960.
KJV	King James Version
LW	Luther, Martin. *Luther's Works*. 55 vols. American ed. Edited by Jaroslav Pelikan and Helmut T. Lehmann. Saint Louis: Concordia; Philadelphia: Fortress, 1955–86.
LXX	Septuagint (Greek translation of the OT)
NIV	New International Version
NSHE	*The New Schaff-Herzog Encyclopedia of Religious Knowledge*. 13 vols. Edited by Samuel Macauley Jackson. Grand Rapids: Baker, 1949–50. Originally published in 12 vols., 1908–12.
NT	New Testament
OT	Old Testament
PRRD	Muller, Richard A. *Post-Reformation Reformed Dogmatics*. 4 vols. Grand Rapids: Baker, 2003.
RD	Bavinck, Herman. *Reformed Dogmatics*. 4 vols. Translated by John Vriend. Edited by John Bolt. Grand Rapids: Baker, 2003–8.
SV	*Statenvertaling* ("States Translation" of the Dutch Bible, 1637)

OLD TESTAMENT

Gen	Genesis
Exod	Exodus
Lev	Leviticus
Num	Numbers
Deut	Deuteronomy
Josh	Joshua
Judg	Judges
Ruth	Ruth
1–2 Sam	1–2 Samuel
1–2 Kgs	1–2 Kings
1–2 Chr	1–2 Chronicles
Ezra	Ezra
Neh	Nehemiah

Esth	Esther
Job	Job
Psa (Pss)	Psalm(s)
Prov	Proverbs
Eccl	Ecclesiastes
Song	Song of Songs
Isa	Isaiah
Jer	Jeremiah
Lam	Lamentations
Ezek	Ezekiel
Dan	Daniel
Hos	Hosea
Joel	Joel
Amos	Amos
Obad	Obadiah
Jonah	Jonah
Mic	Micah
Nah	Nahum
Hab	Habakkuk
Zeph	Zephaniah
Hag	Haggai
Zech	Zechariah
Mal	Malachi

NEW TESTAMENT

Matt	Matthew
Mark	Mark
Luke	Luke
John	John
Acts	Acts
Rom	Romans
1–2 Cor	1–2 Corinthians
Gal	Galatians
Eph	Ephesians
Phil	Philippians
Col	Colossians
1–2 Thess	1–2 Thessalonians
1–2 Tim	1–2 Timothy

Titus	Titus
Phlm	Philemon
Heb	Hebrews
Jas	James
1–2 Pet	1–2 Peter
1–3 John	1–3 John
Jude	Jude
Rev	Revelation

OTHER ANCIENT WRITINGS

b. Sanh.	*Babylonian Sanhedrin* (Talmudic Tractate)

CHAPTER ONE

THE PURPOSE OF THIS DOCTRINAL INQUIRY

What is man that you are mindful of him, and the son of man that you care for him?

PSALM 8:4

Our first series studied the rise of common grace and traced its course until Bethlehem, on the basis of holy Scripture. Our second series then sought to determine the meaning common grace has already gained from the first to the second coming of Christ—which still lies in the future. It further examined what, according to the apocalypse of the New Testament, common grace will mean for the end itself and for what comes after the end. Together both series thus constituted a bird's-eye view of the course of common grace in the history of our race and of our world, from the fall until the restoration—or, if you will, from paradise to the parousia. This is a process that crosses centuries; its course is necessarily divided into two parts by the first coming of Christ. § 1

It is now necessary for us to examine common grace doctrinally so that it can be better understood as a mystery, and so that it can be understood in relation to other doctrines or dogmas.

To orient our readers, we must immediately point out that dogma possesses not only an aspect that points toward heavenly things, but also an aspect that is turned toward what is earthly. Each dogma or doctrine springs from the root of religion, such that any point in any dogma that we no longer sense as relevant to our religion withers in our consciousness and fades from our faith. We see this in the history of the doctrine of angels. Originally this doctrine was woven into everyone's religious consciousness, because all people realized that angels had to be taken into account in their own religion and for the life of their own souls. But since the world of angels became entirely divorced from many people's own religious consciousness, and because it retained no other significance than that of a piece of heavenly life that dissolved before us in poetry, this doctrine ceased to be part of the content of people's faith. Thus, doctrine or dogma always has an aspect that is directed upward and an aspect that is directed downward. This is true such that our Belgic Confession does not hesitate to declare concerning the dogma of the holy Trinity, "All this we know as well from the testimonies of Holy Writ as from their operations, and chiefly by those we feel in ourselves."[1] Here it is stated plainly that the doctrine of the Trinity also has an aspect that is turned toward us and that explains a portion of the life of our own soul. And when we consult the Heidelberg Catechism, we find that the confession of Father, Son, and Holy Spirit connects in an even narrower sense with three moments in our personal existence: the confession of God the Father with our creation, the confession of God the Son with our redemption, and that of the Holy Spirit with our sanctification.[2] Furthermore, Lord's Days 1–33 speak of faith under this threefold division, and only then follows the discussion of the law and of prayer.

§ 2 That this must be so, and cannot be otherwise, lies in the nature of religion. In religion there are two things—God and man. The right communion of man with his God lies in religion. For now we leave aside the question of the various relationships in religion that concern knowing God, trusting God, submitting oneself to God, fearing him, loving and honoring him, and being his child in all these things. For our present purpose, it is enough if it is recognized that everything not relevant to religion falls outside dogma. If people realize that religion is always aimed on the one hand toward God

1. Belgic Confession, Art. 9.
2. See Heidelberg Catechism, LD 8, Q & A 24.

and on the other hand toward man, then every doctrine must also always be viewed from these two aspects.

Regarding the side turned toward man, in the manifestation and life of man, on the one hand, we are dealing with what falls under our observation and can therefore be determined without the help of dogma; but on the other hand, we also are dealing with a hidden aspect of man and of human life. Relative to that, we can adopt only three positions: (1) agnosticism, (2) hypothesis, or (3) revelation. Agnosticism—that is, the system of *not* knowing—acknowledges that there are enigmas in man and that man walks amid riddles, but it forgoes the attempt to allow light to shine on those riddles. The agnostic acknowledges that there is a mystery but he lets it be a mystery and considers every attempt to unlock it to be pointless and hopeless.

The man of hypotheses judges differently. He likewise begins by determining that in man and in his life we are faced with a mystery, but he also claims that we certainly have the means at our disposal to penetrate that mystery: the manifestation of man's being and life in the visible world. He investigates these manifestations. For him, those are what is known. From the known data he now seeks to arrive at the solution of the unknown. He does this by assuming suppositions or hypotheses and investigating whether the assumptions would explain the unknown—if what he assumes is true. If he does not succeed, he rejects the supposition and takes refuge in another hypothesis. On the other hand, if he considers his assumption to be able to explain the unknown, then he declares that he has found the key to the mystery and announces his hypothesis as the result of science. In this way the system of materialism found acceptance for a while, and with much ado it was peddled as science. But at present people, even in unbelieving circles, have almost universally come to the conviction that the hypothesis of materialism is foolish.

The third way, finally, is that of dogma or doctrine, and is taken by those who, just like the preceding two types of persons, acknowledge the existence of mystery within man and within human life; but these people confess that light can fall upon this mystery only if God lets light fall upon it. For that reason, since God gave us his revelation, we sin if we posit with the agnostic that there is no light, since this would be a repudiation and ungrateful denial of God's love that comes to our aid. But we sin equally if—like the man with the hypothesis—we deliberately close our eyes to this God-given light and sit in our own artificial light, peering at what we do not understand anyway, and by closing the shutters keep out the light that God wants to let shine through our windows. A man walks a straight path only if, gratefully accepting the light God has given, he accepts as dogma or doctrine what God has revealed to us in his Word concerning this human mystery.

§ 3 If we ask which mystery the dogma of common grace sheds its indispensable light upon in man and in human life, it will not be difficult to perceive it clearly and plainly. We observe two powers in man and in human life: on the one hand the power of sin, and on the other hand the power of what is good and beautiful. If we follow the course of sin in our own heart and in the life of the world, then all is dark and somber, ashen-gray and deathlike, and ultimately leads to death in its manifold forms. Then there can remain no room for anything in man and in human life that is good and lovely. If, on the other hand, we leave sin out of consideration for a moment and look at all kinds of refreshing things in man and in human life that enthrall us, then human life still offers us so much that is lovely and so much that fascinates us and strikes us as beneficent, that we could almost ask ourselves if the whole notion of the depravity of our nature through sin does not rest on legend and illusion.

We encounter contradictory phenomena here. At times we become pessimists and see the world appear before us in devilish form, such that there is nothing good in it. At other times, however, we become optimists and feel delighted by the abundant display of noble sentiment, robust resilience, and earnest intent that we observe in life around us. This contradiction can weaken us. We almost reach the point where we despair because of sin and assent to the *ex profundis* of wailing humanity, but then life fascinates and charms us so much that we might begin to see sin as a force virtually conquered, and concurring with the panegyric of humanism, might burn our incense to humanity. As we alternate between the two notions and dispositions of the soul, we discern more and more that we stand before an enigma. If we follow the one route, we end up being contradicted by the facts of the good and lovely in humankind and in human history. But if we take the relative good as our point of departure and try to follow our route from there, we similarly end up being contradicted as we encounter the dreadful manifestation of sin. Therefore neither the one nor the other *leitmotif* proves to be correct. We grope about, and we feel that there must be a third something since both routes lead us in the wrong direction. We detect the presence of that third something, but we do not see it and do not know it. And so that third something becomes for us the mystery that lies hidden here.

This mystery becomes even more obscure and enigmatic for us when §4
we take into account the grace that struggles against sin. We confess that this grace is not from man but from God. We acknowledge that this grace operates only through faith and that therefore a separation enters life between those who want this faith and those who go counter to this faith. From this perspective the fact is simply that believers and unbelievers stand over against one another in the world. We will forgo for the moment a more precise distinction. We take *belief* and *unbelief* in the most general sense. There are those who believe in Christ, and there are those who do not believe in Christ at all. This causes life to be divided into two streams: those who believe, and those who want something else, intend something else, and strive after something else. And if we belong to those who believe, no matter what charitable sense toward our fellow human beings inspires us, we come into conflict—involuntarily and without seeking it—with those others. We face conflict in the domestic, social, political, and—even more strongly—in the ecclesiastical sphere. But in our understanding, a higher jurisdiction stands above the dispute with unbelievers. Our faith claims to be indispensable in overcoming sin and making an honorable life possible. And now comes the unbelieving person who with evidence shows us how particularly in our circles, all kinds of sin are still active, whereas in the circle of the unbelievers all kinds of good and attractive manifestations of a nobler approach to life can be observed. That is why the unbeliever cannot understand the indispensability and effectiveness of our faith, and why we in turn begin to doubt the reality of the distinction between faith and unbelief. If within our group that has faith, there is so much to complain about, and so much in the unbeliever's group to be commended apart from faith, what then remains of the validity of the distinction that divides all of life? This continues on a personal level, as often as we catch ourselves sinning in spite of our faith, and conversely are so often put to shame by the elevated, noble sensibilities in the man without faith.

Here again, therefore, an unknown force is in play. We are convinced from history and the experience of our own soul that a world-conquering power is hidden in faith. Nevertheless, in life the relationship between believers and unbelievers does not correspond to the conclusion we would draw from this power of faith. On the other hand, we know from both history and self-knowledge what evil power lies in sin—including the sin of unbelief. And yet, also herein the outcome again and again does not correspond to the conclusion we were compelled to draw. There must therefore be a third something that interferes here. We can detect but not explain this third something. And from that angle as well, we stumble upon a mystery for whose unveiling we keep calling.

§ 5 This same mystery appears even more starkly in the contrast between the kingdom of grace as embodied in Christ's church, and the kingdom of nature as manifested in the life of the world. Here again we take the concepts *church* and *world* in their most general sense. But under whatever form we take this distinction and contrast, it would follow from our confession that the light would radiate from our church and the shroud of darkness would hang over the world. That which is pure, holy, pleasant, and harmonious should be sparkling in our church in an eye-catching manner. By contrast, the shroud of the impure, sinful, and less noble should be hanging over the world. Yet the facts are *not* in agreement with this. Already in the days of the apostles there were instances of terrible sin in the church of Christ, and in century after century the life of the church has supplied something that gave legitimate cause for complaint. By contrast, in the life of the world so much has developed that is interesting, so much that is beautiful, and so much that is attractive that we sometimes have felt a struggle well up in us to turn away from the church and to seek our place in the life of the world. The sharp line of demarcation our confession drew between church and world turned out to be unable to withstand the test. And we saw how in order to escape from this disappointment, the one person simply retreated into his church, refused to hear about the world, and—to avoid being hindered by this disappointment—ultimately became a spiritualist; whereas the other person, in order to cast off any notion of narrow-mindedness, became in effect a child of the world and either let go of his church or made his church worldly.

Here again we have the same struggle. On the one hand, we have the fact of history and the confession of our own heart that the church is the salvation of the world. And on the other hand, we have the facts before our eyes that the church remains so far below its own standard, while the life of the world appears to supply so much more than what apparently could be expected from it. Here again, there must be a third something that can provide an explanation of this apparent contradiction. This is a mystery we encounter without it being immediately unveiled for us.

When giving direction to our own life and steering our own life's course, § 6
we run into the same uncertainty. If our human nature is depraved to such a great extent and the world so far sunk under the curse that from that world and from our nature in that world nothing can come that can survive when weighed in the scales of the holy; and if, by contrast, the gospel is the only salt that prevents decay; and if the church of Christ is the sole creation of God that bears the mark of eternal permanence—is it not then reasonable that we withdraw our talent, our vigor, our time, our efforts from that world and direct them wholly toward the church and the gospel? Yet this is not possible. A rare individual may be able to find his life's work as a preacher in this country or as a missionary sent out among pagans or Muslims. Another who is independently wealthy may direct all his vigor toward philanthropic work. But what is impossible in any case is that *all* members of the church could devote their earthly existence entirely to spiritual matters. Each mother already has an entirely different calling in the home. This includes the requirements of day-to-day living, food preparation, taking care of clothing and entertainment, as well as the upbringing of children and preparing them for life in civil society. And besides, where would the thousands who have no money but must earn their own bread and their family's bread find that bread if they did nothing throughout their entire life but be directly occupied in the kingdom of Jesus? Paul himself functioned as apostle in the evening after having sat with canvas on his lap working in the tentmaker's shop in the morning and afternoon. This means that for the vast majority of believers in Jesus, the larger portion of their strength and time is spent in labor—and not in the kingdom but in the world. And it means that they can take delight in activity of a holy character primarily only on Sunday and then only in the morning and evening hours.

This also does not correspond to the contrasting valuation of life in Christ's church and life in the world. If the life of the world flows away toward perdition and into nothingness, and if only the life of Christ's church possesses the mark and guarantee of eternal permanence, how then can the world give a child of God satisfaction? And how can he be in harmony with his life conviction if he actually devotes nine-tenths of his life to what passes away and has no purpose, and is left with at most one-tenth for that which has value for his heart? According to his confession it should be different; according to the demands of life it cannot be any other way. Here again a third something must play a role that modifies this implication of his faith. And he does sense and notice that third something, but he cannot bring it to light. It is and remains a mystery to him.

§ 7 We could continue pointing out the same contradiction in virtually every area of life, between on the one hand the consequence of what we confess, and on the other hand what we find before us in real life. We cannot deny these facts, nor can we surrender our confession—yet the two do not fit together. To be sure, if we weaken the concept of sin, blur the distinction between nature and grace, let church and world merge, and consider our work in the world and in the sacred realm as being identical in kind, then we do not encounter this problem. But what does this mean other than surrendering our confession, going over to the camp of the Moderns, and thus accepting the standard of the world as *the* standard?[3] Or by closing our eyes to the profundity of things, we could also float along on the surface, half unthinkingly, and say that we don't worry about these contradictions as long as we do not feel them and are not bothered by them. But what does this mean, other than that we fall asleep and close our eyes and escape from the riddles of life by not truly living? If we say, on the other hand, "I hold fast to my confession, the contrast between grace and nature exists, sin is a force in life, and I do not close my eyes to the struggle this causes in our human life, but I stand with an observant, inquiring, and questioning eye and I search for the solution to the mystery that has me in its grip"—then it is impossible for us not to have personally discerned that disturbing contradiction on each of the points we discussed.

Indeed, we would go still further. When the Moderns in this country thought for a time that they had wiggled out of the grip of these enigmas by erasing the boundary, they merely dreamed a beautiful dream from which all too soon they awoke to bitter disappointment. Even though they had surrendered the contrast between nature and grace, they nevertheless held on to the contrast between the sacred and the profane, between what is noble and what is ignoble. And behold, even in this weakened form, the revived contrast immediately confronted them again with similar enigmas,

3. Modernism was a theological movement associated with thinkers like J. H. Scholten (1811–85), one of Kuyper's teachers. It viewed the progress of history as culminating in the moral primacy of the state, which had surpassed and replaced the church as the main locus of meaning and significance. Added to this was a corresponding derogation of the authority of confessional standards and the rigor of doctrinal affirmation. Originally attracted to Modernism, Kuyper later turned toward orthodoxy, which placed him in opposition to the movement.

which have led to very diverse solutions in their own circle and which still continue to divide attitudes among them. This is what is brought about by sin, that terrible force against which they consider themselves honor-bound to do battle. But that very battle is inconceivable without the ranks and battle arrays surfacing again and again, where friend and foe become entangled. Initially their whole battle was against us. Now they have come to the point of realizing that they must look for their enemy elsewhere, and that in their efforts to overthrow the enemy they have to come back to much of what we held and to the things in us that they were contending against.

CHAPTER TWO

THE PROBLEM TO BE SOLVED

He turns rivers into a desert, springs of water into thirsty ground, a fruitful land into a salty waste, because of the evil of its inhabitants. He turns a desert into pools of water, a parched land into springs of water.

Psalm 107:33–35

§ 1 The battle between our understanding and the reality we sketched in our previous chapter, based on the life experience of many and drawn from life itself, could be formulated succinctly this way: *the world turns out to be better than expected and the church worse than expected.* Since we have been raised in a confession that, as generally understood, knows nothing of the world other than that it is bent on evil, and of the church little else than that it is the congregation of believers, we expect to encounter in the world sin upon sin, and to feel attracted in the church by an ideal, holy life of love. And a person who, expecting to find it so, goes out into the world at an adult age and has the good fortune of being allowed to find himself in more noble-minded worldly circles, after having heard of much censure and ecclesiastical vexation in church circles, will doubt the correctness of his confession; he will find the expression *the world was better than expected, the church worse than expected* to be a reflection of his own experience.

For the moment we deliberately leave aside the well-known fact that in quite a few other circles we find, even after our most somber imaginings, that the life of the world appears to be *worse* than we thought and that it sometimes allows a glimpse into the depths of Satan. Conversely, in the broad circle of the church we encounter silent, holy powers at work that are not merely to be compared with salt, but actually impede decay. For the moment our intent is only to make understandable how—both in the past and the present—the generally superficial public opinion has harbored the conviction that the world is better and the church worse than those from the Christian side have wanted people to believe in a theoretical sense. Public opinion, which since the advent of the printing press has bundled together its once-scattered forces, has become *the* force in the world from which the questions of life arise; to these questions it then seeks answers in terms of the then-dominant lifeview.

For the moment, therefore, we do not minimize in the least the contrast we have pointed out. We even put it deliberately in such a sharp, shrill form. Much can be leveled against this same contrast, but each of us continually encounters it somewhat in his own life and his own heart. And what we want to make concrete and understandable at this point is how a doctrine like that of common grace is not a speculative notion based on book learning. Rather, it reflects the attempt of Christ's church to provide an answer in light of God's Word, to an extremely important and indeed profound and complex problem—a problem with which every sensitive and reflective person is directly confronted at every moment in the world, in his church, in his surroundings, and in his own heart. Again and again we have the unavoidable sense of deadly sin that is everywhere, but present in such a way that the general condition is still not so bad. And on the other hand, we have the sense of a saving divine grace, but we see it in such a way that its fruit and effect disappoint us.

We are simply faced with this problem, with this dilemma, and it is not dismissed with the following statement that acknowledges something but not much—and in any case not enough—namely, that the world is bad and the church is good, but that the persons you encounter are sometimes better than their environment or worse than their doctrine. This is true, but it does not provide a solution, since those persons are also either children of the world or sons and daughters of the church. By isolating them individually from that world or that church, we cut the ties between persons and between generations, and we become incapable of presenting any worldview. That is, unless the worldview, by disconnecting everything into separate parts, is one that comes down to this: that everything depends only on the individual, and within that individual, everything depends on his free will. That would mean in point of fact that we have no worldview, but only the existence of endlessly divergent persons, or rather that we determine individualities for ourselves. With this partially true objection we would not advance a single step here. It does not change the facts of life. And as long as we hold fast to a confession that is directly contradicted by the endlessly recurring facts in life, one of two things has to happen: either we lose faith in our confession, or we hold fast to our confession but hang a veil in front of reality in order not to see it. Those who, with us, want neither the one nor the other but who hold fast to the confession and at the same time acknowledge that God's providential ordination is manifested in reality, therefore refuse to resign themselves to that contrast. They feel themselves compelled to think more deeply about the confession and to investigate it, with the facts of reality before them, to see how the confession holds up in the face of these facts. This leads us directly to the doctrine of common grace, because it is precisely this forgotten and neglected chapter of our confession that presents the solution to this point.

§ 2 The following statements of the Three Forms of Unity of the Reformed churches are relevant here:

1. Belgic Confession, Art. 14:

   "… And being thus become wicked, perverse, and corrupt in all his ways, he has lost all his excellent gifts which he had received from God, and *retained only small remains thereof …*"

2. Belgic Confession, Art. 15:

   "… Nor is [original sin] altogether abolished or wholly eradicated even by baptism; since sin always issues forth from this woeful source, as water from a fountain."

3. Canons of Dort, chapter 3/4, Art. 4:

   "There remain, however, in man since the fall, *the glimmerings of natural light*, whereby he retains some knowledge of God, of natural things, and of the difference between good and evil, and shows some regard for virtue and for good outward behavior. But so far is *this light of nature* from being sufficient to bring him to a saving knowledge of God and to true conversion that he is incapable of using it aright even in things natural and civil."

4. Heidelberg Catechism, Lord's Day 44, question and answer 114:

"Can those who are converted to God keep these Commandments perfectly?

No, but even the holiest men, while in this life, have only a small beginning of such obedience ..."

5. Canons of Dort, chapter 5, Art. 4–8:

Article 4: "Although the weakness of the flesh cannot prevail against the power of God, who confirms and preserves true believers in a state of grace, yet converts are not always so influenced and actuated by the Spirit of God as not in some particular instances sinfully to deviate from the guidance of divine grace, so as to be seduced by and to comply with the lusts of the flesh; they must, therefore, be constant in watching and prayer, that they may not be led into temptation. When these are neglected, they are not only liable to be drawn into great and heinous sins by the flesh, the world, and Satan, but sometimes by the righteous permission of God actually are drawn into these evils. This, the lamentable fall of David, Peter, and other saints described in Holy Scripture, demonstrates."

Article 5: "By such enormous sins, however, they very highly offend God, incur a deadly guilt, grieve the Holy Spirit, interrupt the exercise of faith, very grievously wound their consciences, and sometimes for a while lose the sense of God's favor, until, when they change their course by serious repentance, the light of God's fatherly countenance again shines upon them."

Article 6: "But God, who is rich in mercy, according to His unchangeable purpose of election, does not wholly withdraw the Holy Spirit from His own people even in their grievous falls; nor suffers them to proceed so far as to lose the grace of adoption and forfeit the state of justification, or to commit the sin unto death or against the Holy Spirit; nor does He permit them to be totally deserted, and to plunge themselves into everlasting destruction."

Article 7: "For in the first place, in these falls He preserves in them the incorruptible seed of regeneration from perishing or being totally lost; and again, by His Word and Spirit He certainly and effectually renews them to repentance, to a sincere and godly sorrow for their sins, that they may seek and obtain remission in the blood of the Mediator, may again experience the favor of a reconciled God, through faith adore His mercies, and henceforward more diligently work out their own salvation with fear and trembling."

Article 8: "Thus it is not in consequence of their own merits or strength, but of God's free mercy, that they neither totally fall from faith and grace nor continue and perish finally in their backslidings; which, with respect to themselves is not only possible, but would undoubtedly happen; but with respect to God, it is utterly impossible, since His counsel cannot be changed nor His promise fail; neither can the call according to His purpose be revoked, nor the merit, intercession, and preservation of Christ be rendered ineffectual, nor the sealing of the Holy Spirit be frustrated or obliterated."

§ 3 These excerpts from our Forms of Unity show clearly that our confession acknowledges two things: (1) that in the sinner—that is, in fallen man—there still remain small traces of the original glory, still a certain *light of nature*; and (2) that sin continues to be at work in believers as well, until death, and that as a consequence of this they too can fall into serious sins.

Thus our confession not only speaks of the absolute contrast between faith and unbelief, and sin and holiness; our confession also explicitly indicates a specific cause—both on the part of the sinner and on the part of the believer—explaining why in fallen man a certain good survived, and in believers a certain evil still produces aftereffects. Once we have determined this, our attention is then arrested by the fact that we cannot say lightly that the confession of our churches is in conflict with the reality of life. Rather, the reverse must be said, that confession and reality fit perfectly together as long as we do not take a few pieces of it in isolation but take the confession as a whole.

The world is not as bad as expected thanks to the light of nature, which God keeps burning within the fallen sinner. And similarly, the church is not as good as expected because of the fact we confess, namely, that sin still continues to produce aftereffects in the believer so that even the holiest persons in this life can never manifest anything but a small beginning of the true good. The church has confessed this on the basis of the virtues of the Gentiles that are acknowledged in Scripture and on the basis of the profound sins of believers, such as the sins of David and Peter that are clearly attested in Scripture, specifically in Romans 2:14–15. There we read, "For when Gentiles, who do not have the law [of Sinai], by nature do what the law requires, they are a law to themselves, even though they do not have the law. They show that the work of the law is written on their hearts, while their conscience also bears witness, and their conflicting thoughts accuse or even excuse them."[1]

Implicit in this significant statement is, first, that a Gentile, here meaning *fallen man*, has in his inner man a certain awareness of the good even when he lacks higher grace. Paul contrasts Jews and Gentiles here not in their national existence, but in the spiritual sense. For him, the Jews are the sinners who received higher grace, and the Gentiles are the fallen sinners who lack this higher grace. And whereas the Jews thought that they could elevate themselves above the Gentiles, Paul casts them down by pointing out to them their unfaithfulness, apostasy, and sinful existence. He elevates the Gentiles not because of what they are in themselves, but appealing to the common grace of God that is active in them. And this common grace manifests itself in the first place in this: they still have something written on their hearts. Not that the Jews did not have this. Originally they had this also; Jews and Gentiles are both fallen sinners, and it is in each of them as it is with all fallen sinners. But because the Jews looked down condescendingly upon the Gentiles, Paul brings the Gentiles to the forefront and says that the Gentiles are indeed fallen sinners, but God has not *entirely* withdrawn from the fallen sinner his original spiritual work in humanity. He has always left some divine handwriting on their hearts.

We must remember, if we are to understand this correctly, that original § 4
righteousness also included this: man had the law of God clearly and perfectly in his own soul's awareness. Neither Adam nor Eve had ever heard of the Ten Commandments. They had never had any instruction in the moral law. Nobody had given them the requirements of the law, and the only command they received externally was the prohibition against eating from the tree of knowledge. But this did not make them morally ignorant.

1. The insertion [of Sinai] is Kuyper's.

On the contrary, they understood God's will and law perfectly, because God had imprinted his holy will in their souls and written it on the tablets of their hearts. A healthy person breathes entirely according to the law of breathing, without ever having heard anything about that law, and only someone with a respiratory illness is bothered by it and calls in the learned expertise of a physician. So it was in this case as well. Adam had never learned to walk, but walked spontaneously, and in the same way Adam had never learned a moral law, but he possessed that law that was given in the awareness of his soul. Only sin caused a disturbance in this. Through sin this soul awareness became flawed. Thus the divine handwriting departed from the heart through sin. And in connection with this, the prophecy was given to Israel that one day man would no longer learn the law by external means, but God would once again write the law on his heart.

This apparently referred back to the covenant at Sinai. At the making of that covenant God had given his law, which was no longer clearly legible on the tablets of man's heart, externally on tablets of stone, so that man had to learn that at divine instigation: *externally*, coming to him from the outside, instead of *inwardly*, coming from within himself. And thus Jeremiah 31:33–34, referring back to this, says, "For this is the covenant that I will make with the house of Israel after those days, declares the Lord: I will put my law within them, and I will write it on their hearts. And I will be their God, and they shall be my people. And no longer shall each one teach his neighbor and each his brother, saying, 'Know the Lord,' for they shall all know me, from the least of them to the greatest, declares the Lord. For I will forgive their iniquity, and I will remember their sin no more."

§ 5 If we did not know anything more than this, we might first conclude that every trace of the divine handwriting was lost through sin and that nothing of it remained in the fallen sinner. But this is precisely what Paul argues against, stating that this is definitely *not* the case. He declares in so many words that in his day—that is, forty centuries after paradise—the Gentiles definitely still possessed a remnant of this divine handwriting in their soul: "They show that the work of the law is written on their hearts." [Rom 2:15]. Note that it does not say that they have the *law* itself written on their hearts, but "the *work* of the law," as if to indicate a practical impulse rather than a clear, pure knowledge. But whatever criticism can be brought against this, it clearly states that there is still something of God's original handwriting present in the fallen sinner's heart. Largely erased and having become illegible in its details, this divine handwriting remains even in the fallen sinner, enough that we can see that it once stood there and still can discern something of what it originally said.

There is an obvious reason why this is contrasted with the condition of the soul of the Jew. A capable shop owner knows by heart how many of each article he has in stock and where every article is. But someone who has a large store and owns stockrooms and warehouses can no longer keep everything in his head and therefore keeps books. His books then show him in which stockroom this lot is held and in which one another lot is kept, and also how much of each article he still has in stock. Thus he gets used to relying more on his books than on his memory, and in the end his books have become his one indispensable possession. Something similar also necessarily occurred in Israel the more it was directed toward the external law. Originally, before Sinai, Israel also lived exclusively by moral awareness—that is, by the knowledge of God's law that still remained imperfectly in their hearts. But when the Israelites received the law externally, and thus possessed the book of the law, the necessary consequence was that they placed more value on that law for their moral awareness, learned externally, than on the faint reflection of that law in their inner being. This very viewpoint of the Jews, therefore, also meant that they had moved from internal knowledge of the law more to external knowledge. In the case of the believing Jew this did not matter, because the Spirit of God interpreted the law spiritually for him and bound it upon his soul. But for the vast majority of Jews who lived outside the Spirit, this resulted in their descending in many respects below the level of the best of the Gentiles. And this is the reason that Paul—by in a certain sense elevating the best of the Gentiles above the vast majority of the Jews—says emphatically of the Gentiles in particular that they have the work of the law still written on their hearts.

In the second place, it follows from Romans 2:13–15 that this remnant of § 6
the law in the heart of the fallen sinner is to some extent kept alive in that sinner by divine grace. Paul continues by saying that "their conscience also bears witness"—that is, their conscience bears witness to this remnant of the law and still says "amen" to it. The conscience and the law of God are thus differentiated. The conscience is not, as many say, the *same* as the law of God. On the contrary, the conscience bears witness *with* the law.

This shows us that conscience and law are two distinct things. Does not the phrase "also bears witness" imply that there is first one that witnesses and that the other also bears witness along with the first? The law is therefore the witness of God in the soul. And the conscience is man's awareness that bears witness together with the witness of God. This is why there could be no conscience in Adam, because in Adam the law of God could not yet be distinguished from his own awareness; but conscience had to emerge in Adam immediately after his fall—namely, as soon as God's law and the consciousness of his soul diverged. In the same way, conscience will fall silent in the state of glory as soon as all conflict between the law of God and the consciousness of the soul is taken away. This is the reason we never read about conscience with respect to Jesus, and still today we hear discussion about conscience much more in the unbelieving world than in the church. It is therefore remarkable that Paul deals here with the conscience only in relation to the Gentiles and not in connection with the Jews. He says of this conscience that it is neither resisting nor silent vis-à-vis the remnant of God's law, but that it also testifies in support. And because this cannot come from sin, it follows that God not only left a remnant of his law in the heart of fallen man, but also works upon his conscience and forces him to say "amen" to that law in his consciousness.

§ 7 Third, it follows from Romans 2:13–15 that this work of common grace is not limited to the fallen sinner as an individual or as an isolated being, but also works upon man in society. Paul says that "their conflicting thoughts accuse or even excuse them"—that is, declare them not guilty. This refers to two things. It refers first to the opinion they form of one another amongst themselves, and second, to the public administration of justice. More succinctly, it refers to the passing of judgment on one another, privately and publicly. This private and public rendering of judgment persisted in the world, even as it still continues today. We form an opinion about all kinds of people around us. We speak with others about third parties, and we reach favorable or unfavorable conclusions. On a larger scale the general public gets involved, and thus opinions and notions about people are formed; one person is praised and the other reproached. And in addition to this private rendering of judgment we have the judge who renders public judgment on accusations that are brought before him. Both private and public judgment presuppose a standard used for judging. The judge acts according to the criterion of good and evil as indicated in the penal code, and individual and public opinion judges on the basis of a certain sense of good and evil that speaks communally in the hearts of all. This would not be possible if God had not preserved certain general notions about justice and injustice, good and evil, in human society as well. And in that sense the apostle points out how these private and public urges to render judgment also show that God has not entirely abandoned the Gentiles but continues to work his grace among them as well.

Fourth and finally, it follows from Romans 2:13–15 not only that this common grace allowed the continuation, preservation, and functioning of an awareness within the fallen sinner of what is honorable and dishonorable, of justice and injustice, of good and evil; it follows also that this common grace lends the fallen sinner strength to do what is good. Paul says, "when Gentiles, who do not have the law [of Sinai], *by nature do* what the law requires."[2] Thus they not only *know* but they also *do* the things of the law, and from the fact that they do them he draws the conclusion that they have knowledge of the law. Thus this *doing* even serves as the starting point of the apostle's argument. If it is certain that even a child of God confesses to being incapable of *thinking* any good on his own, let alone *doing* it, then it necessarily follows that the Gentiles as well do this good not of themselves or their own strength, but only because common grace prompts and equips them to do this. § 8

Therefore, the Reformed churches have said nothing in their Forms of Unity about the light of nature that they could not justify by holy Scripture. In fact, faced with the same phenomenon as we are (that the Gentiles so often are better than expected and the Jews so often worse than expected) Paul has provided us with the answer to this enigma of life by pointing us to common grace—the light of nature. This means nothing less than that God (1) left in the fallen sinner a continuing remnant of the divine handwriting of the law; (2) expresses this remnant upon the soul's awareness so that the fallen sinner bears witness to that remnant of the law; (3) presses for the rendering of judgment in society that uses this remnant as standard; and (4) in many respects effects powers within sinners to accomplish the good.

This also explains why in those days the Gentiles could be better than expected, even as also in our day the people of the world so often are better than expected. And if we ask why back then, Israel, like the church today, could so often be worse than expected, we must read and reread Romans 7 and remember only that one pleading exclamation to see also the obverse of the enigma solved: "Wretched man that I am! Who will deliver me from this body of death?" [Rom 7:24].

2. The insertion [of Sinai] is Kuyper's and emphasis added.

And if anyone should ask whether Paul judges the Gentiles too favorably, let it suffice to refer simply to Romans 1 where the terrible sinfulness of Gentile life is depicted in all its harshness; this should convince us that Paul certainly did not intend his statement concerning common grace to apply to Gentile life as such, but to the light that still shines in this sinful life.

But we will discuss this subject in a subsequent chapter.

CHAPTER THREE

THE PROBLEM FURTHER ELUCIDATED

But I see in my members another law waging war against the law of my mind and making me captive to the law of sin that dwells in my members.

Romans 7:23

In connection with our confession, we can point to four statements of holy Scripture that could solve the question of why people of the world are so often better than expected and believers in Christ are so often worse than expected. § 1

The two statements that explain why people of the world are better than expected are, on the one hand, Romans 3:12, "All have turned aside; together they have become worthless; no one does good, not even one"; and on the other hand, Romans 2:14: "Gentiles, who do not have the law, by nature do what the law requires."

Over against these stand two other statements that make us understand the contrast between ideal and reality among the believers in Christ. On the one hand, there is the elevated tone of Romans 8:1 (KJV): "Who walk not after the flesh, but after the Spirit."[1] On the other hand, we have Romans 7:23: "I see in my members another law waging war against the law of my mind and making me captive to the law of sin that dwells in my members."

These four statements are purposely taken from the same epistle to the church at Rome to ensure that they do not stand in contrast accidentally as the result of a different line of argumentation or a different point of departure. After all, there cannot be divergent conceptions in one and the same letter. Besides, in the epistle to the Romans the statements to which we pointed closely follow one another in pairs. The one pair is from Romans 2 and 3, the other pair from Romans 7 and 8; the latter are separated by only three verses.

Certainly only what we quoted from Romans 2 and 3 is directly related to common grace. But in this doctrinal exposition, we must pay attention from the start to the fact that both phenomena—the restraining of the sinner so that sin does not run rampant in him, and the believer being still embodied in the flesh—to some extent run parallel. There are two principles at work: the principle of sin against God, and the principle of grace against sin. There are two kinds of life: a life proceeding from sin and a life proceeding from grace—or, if you will, on the one hand life from the natural, and on the other hand life from the supernatural. In the one, the seed of destruction is at work, in the other, the seed of God. There are, the Apostle John says, "children of the devil" and "children of God," even as Jesus stated it: "Your will is to do your *father's* desires. He was a murderer from the beginning" [John 8:44]. Those thus are the children of the devil. Jesus states it as sharply as possible: "You are of your father the devil."

But while we must hold on to this contrast as absolutely as we can, it does not manifest itself quite this pointedly. This is because both life principles are impeded in their manifestation. In the sinner, sin does not manifest itself as strongly because it is restrained by common grace; but similarly, the life of grace does not manifest itself quite as strongly because it is still impeded in its development by the body of death. Fundamentally they stand over against each other like black and white. But in reality so much white is mixed in with the black and so much black still swirls through the white

1. This is generally considered to be a later addition found in the Textus Receptus, on which the SV and KJV are based. It is therefore omitted in the ESV and most other modern versions.

that it sometimes looks as though both flow together in a grayish tint. This is not so, of course. Water may swirl at the mouth of a river, tasting neither sweet nor brackish. The water is a mixture of sweet and salty; nevertheless, when we go back to the source of each, in the stream that ran down the mountain we find water that slakes the thirst of our tongue, and water rolling in from the ocean that increases and worsens the thirst of the tongue. And so it is here. A person who bears the stamp of the world and a person who is a sheltered child of God may confuse us and cause us to lose sight of the distinction. Nevertheless, when we go along the stalk down to the root of both their lives, we immediately can see that their roots are different: the root of the child of God springs from grace; the root of the child of the world springs from his own self.

Leaving the sheltering of God's seed for the moment and limiting our- § 2
selves for the time being only to the restraining of sin by common grace, we must now emphasize that we make a mistake and go astray if we think that the restraining of sin takes place uniformly in everyone. On the contrary, just as there is endless variation of degree in the area of *particular* grace, so too there is immeasurable variation in the working of *common* grace. The difference is clearly demonstrated by the Queen of Sheba who travels to Jerusalem to hear Solomon's wisdom [1 Kings 10], and the Rabshakeh who comes to revile the God of Israel at the walls of Zion [2 Kings 18–19]. In the present, on the one hand we are offended by brute sensuality, impudent pride, and criminal meanness in the world, while on the other hand we are attracted by noble sentiment and high ideals among the children of the world, often even to the point of shaming us. Comparing Romans 1 and 3 with Romans 2 clearly shows that holy Scripture intends this to be understood in no other way than as a result of common grace. In Romans 1 it says of the Gentiles that God has given them up to a debased mind and that they are sunk to the depths into unnatural and perverted sins. In Romans 3 it says that they all fall short of the glory of God, so that there is not one who does good. Romans 2, on the other hand, speaks of Gentiles who do what the law of God calls for—something imprinted on their hearts.

The divergent operation of common grace must therefore briefly be explained. With common grace there is never (as is self-evident) the operation of a pure, perfect, or saving good. Such a good must spring from true faith, be perfectly in conformity to the spiritual intent of God's law, and have nothing else in view than God's honor; this cannot be the case in the sinner apart from regeneration.[2] There is nothing in fallen man that can lead to salvation, not even under the strongest working of common grace. In that sense all sinners "have become worthless," and "no one does good, not even one" [Rom 3:12]. This must stand clearly in the foreground if we are to avoid misunderstanding. Common grace never has any function other than temporarily mitigating and restraining human self-destruction through sin.

But with this proviso it is certain that this mitigating function is not the same for all, nor the same for each individual at every moment. We see on every side how among the persons of the world the one is moderate, modest, and virtuous, while the other is a troublemaker, has a twisted heart, and is corrupt in his actions. There are all kinds of differences; there are more than just noble-minded and virtuous people standing over against the base and vile natures. Between these two extremes we find an endless continuum of imperceptible gradations.

In this context we must note that the original creation ordinance continues in the sinful situation and under common grace. The creation ordinance teaches clearly that the children of man were not uniformly foreordained by God. With respect to their nature as human beings they are one, but in all other ways individuals are as dissimilar as two leaves on a tree—never perfectly identical. Everything shows variegation, differences in tints, differences in temperament and disposition, talents, and gifts. Men and women differ most strongly, but also within each gender the variations are immense, even apart from the differences in age and the distinctions in occupation and work. One person has more will, another more intellectual power. One is more artistically talented, another more suited to practical life. One has a more sanguine temperament, and another is more phlegmatic or choleric. And to this must be added the powerful difference in nature and nurture. We sometimes speak of first-, second-, and third-class individuals, and generally this is applicable, but to be accurate we should distinguish a whole scale of classes, ranging from the man who kicks at stones on the path to spirits as outstanding as Plato or Calvin.

This diversity is neither created nor destroyed by common grace. Rather, common grace works in very different ways depending on whether it manifests itself in a man of very modest aptitude or a man of very great aptitude. What arises from creation is not annihilated by sin but influences the form

2. These are the marks of goodness according to the Heidelberg Catechism, Lord's Day 33, Q & A 91.

that sin adopts. Taken as male and female sinners, a man and a woman are not identical. A woman who sins is different from a man who sins. And thus sin will take a different form and follow a different course in the person with one talent than in the person with three or five talents; different in the sanguine person than in the choleric or phlegmatic person; different in the person of willpower than in the person of intellectual power; in short, as it permeates all the differences between individuals, sin will manifest itself in ever-different forms because of those differences.

Therefore, the harp that common grace plays is not a harp with strings § 3
of uniform thickness and length; all strings are different. That is the first distinction. But through this first distinction runs a second one that depends on whether the strings are touched with more or less force and are held for a shorter or longer time. Thus there can be two people who both possess, by virtue of the creation ordinance, the greatest talents and rich genius; and yet common grace has such an entirely different effect on them so that one, precisely because of his great talent, becomes an uncontrolled villain, a feared devil. The other could become a blessing for our race through the nobility of his word and his high-minded striving. Or, on a more modest scale, there can be two people in the same city, both gifted with courage and ingenuity, but in such a way that the one uses his gifts to agitate the city through bold thefts whereas the other, who is his equal in talent, uses this same talent to track down and capture the thief. The talents of a capable police commissioner and a notorious thief will always display a strong affinity.

God's sovereignty is therefore unmistakable in common grace. When one individual, carried by common grace, becomes a figure like Plato or Cicero, whereas another turns into a Cain or a Judas, it cannot be explained on the basis of the greater excellence of the former person. It can be explained only as God's ordination. It is he—our God—who in his omnipotence lets his common grace work on all; without that common grace a sinner would immediately be eradicated. But he also, according to his ordination (which is inscrutable in this case), causes the gifts of creation to bear noble fruit in one person while letting those same gifts in another turn into instruments of wickedness. In this manner the excellence of the gift of creation works toward God's honor and is a blessing for humanity, while at the same time the terrible character of sin is preached in living color.

In the same manner common grace differs in its effect not only between § 4
individuals, but also between nations. This is also definitely related to the

gifts of creation that have been bestowed on one nation in one way and on another nation in a different way—more to one and less to another. The constitution of the Babylonians stood far above that of the Elamites. The Greeks were superior to the Syrians and the Romans to the Carthaginians. And what an immeasurable difference exists today between the United States and Peru, between England and Portugal, and between the French and the Germans! It is therefore quite natural that the difference in the gifts of creation also manifests itself in sin. And it is equally natural that common grace functions very differently in different nations because of this original difference between one nation and another. Common grace is undoubtedly at work even among the wild native African peoples, but how weak it is when we compare their life with the operation of common grace among the European nations.[3] We leave aside the question of how much this has to do with deep national sins in the past. We are simply claiming that common grace works not only on individuals but also upon nations, and that its effect on the individual is dominated by its effect on the nation as a whole.

The same applies in the smaller units that we call tribes, generations, and families. There is no doubt that the tribe of Judah received a stronger working of common grace than the tribe of Dan, and a house like the house of Orange[4] more than many other royal houses. Every one of us can name a family in his neighborhood for whom the rule is a higher, more noble-minded way of life—even without an actual conversion. This contrasts sharply with another family who produces almost no good effect or influence. Anyone who knows many families knows very well that in each family a certain spirit prevails; the spirit in one family attracts, while in another it leaves us indifferent, and in a third it repels us. And these differences certainly relate not only to the difference in the creation ordinance as it pertains to those families, but no less to the difference in the functioning of common grace. Outside of any life of faith, in the civil and natural realm one family may be borne by a higher power than another.

The same must be said about differences in time periods. We speak of the spirit of a given century. Compare the spirit of the century of the Reformation with that of the French Revolution, or the spirit of the

3. For more on Kuyper's problematic judgments based on racial and ethnic stereotypes, see the volume editors' introduction to *CG*, as well as *CG* 1.12.10n4.

4. The royal family of the Netherlands.

eighteenth with that of the nineteenth century; when we do so, we sense immediately that this difference between one period and the next is indeed real. In the age of the Reformation, the things that today fill our heads and hearts would not have entered our thinking in the same way. What at that time drove the human spirit now leaves humanity cold. That zeitgeist, that temper of the times, definitely exerts an influence on the spirit of the nations, generations, and families, as well as on the spirit of the individual. And this difference in spirit from century to century is in turn directly related to the varying operation of common grace. This is done as it pleases God to leave one or another propensity of our nation, more or less, to the deadly impact of sin, or to remove it powerfully from that impact.

But this must not be understood as though divine sovereignty here is § 5
equivalent to arbitrariness. God does not, with his common grace, play a game with humanity like a boy who, sitting on a stool, lets a bird tied to a string fly away one moment and pulls it back the next as he pleases. This would fail to reckon with God's providence. His providence flows from his decree, and his decree about the world and its inhabitants is not like a weathervane that endlessly swings on its pole, but is rather like a plant that must go through a certain developmental process, or like a traveler who follows the proper path to a specific goal. There is a plan in the history of our human race. In that history a monumental building is being constructed according to definite specifications. All the parts fit together. It is not an endless repetition of the same, but a steady progress. And a golden thread runs through it all, one that is continually being spun further. It is one splendid work of embroidery that seems to be made only of loose stitches jumbled together; but when it is turned around we see the design that is gradually being completed through all these stitches.

Thus the course of common grace is tied to and determined by the providential plan that flows from the divine decree. It is not merely playing with brush and palette, now putting on thicker paint and then again using fainter colors. Rather, a guiding thought determines what the brush takes from the palette and the way in which the brush paints on the canvas. In all this there is steering, direction, a guiding principle, and progress. Common grace functions such that where sin would have thwarted and destroyed the human race's development, common grace advances that growth in spite of Satan. In spite of the changes brought about by sin, God's grand plan nevertheless continues. Humanity comes into being. It acquires its history. In that history it goes through a process, and that process must flower into something the creation ordinance produced only as a bud. Common grace is the holy instrument through which God brings this process to completion, in spite of sin.

And this is what causes us to cherish God's work through common grace—namely, its effect on individuals at their various ages, and the working of that same common grace in nations, generations, and families. Similarly, its effect on the spirit of the age, century after century, is so intertwined and interwoven that the one effect always fits in with the other, such that out of the totality of all these effects proceeds the *history of humanity*.

Without this common grace in its universal ramifications and differences in degree there would be no history. Sin would dissolve it, unravel it, end up in chaos, and in the end exhaust its strength in death. Only by restraining that fatal impulse of sin does a coherence continue to exist and the effect of the one upon the other can continue; a certain order is maintained and life continues to flourish upon the precipice of death. Thus it can be explained that while the nature of humankind is entirely depraved and that nothing but weeds could grow out of that depravity—no one doing good from his own impulse, not even one [see Rom 3:12]—the life of humanity, its history, and our experiences among humanity nevertheless display much that is rich and glorious that we are driven to worship. What grows from our race is never anything but divine gifts of creation—not made by us but sovereignly given to us. What we, apart from regeneration, accomplish on our own can only be a wish and inclination to rob God of or destroy those gifts. The fact that so much still can arise and in fact does arise from these gifts of creation is only because God's common grace restrains our sinful raging.

CHAPTER FOUR

THE SOLUTION ACCORDING TO UNBELIEVERS

We destroy arguments and every lofty opinion raised against the knowledge of God, and take every thought captive to obey Christ.

2 Corinthians 10:5

Two things clearly confront us because of our deeper investigation into the doctrine of common grace. First, we discover the well-known fact that when tested against the doctrine of our depravity through sin, the unconverted world is not as bad as expected, and when tested against the doctrine of regeneration, the church is worse than expected. And second, we find that in conformity with holy Scripture, the Reformed confession explains the first phenomenon by the fact that common grace curbs and tempers sin in its effect, while the other is true since the regenerated life remains hindered in its manifestation because of the lasting effects of our sinful nature, until death. We have included the parts from the Forms of Unity as well as from holy Scripture that indicate this. And as long as we clearly keep in view the tempering of sin by common grace, as well as the hindering of renewed § 1 life through the aftereffects of sin, we can readily explain how unbelievers both are better than expected and believers worse than expected.

At the same time, we must point out that others who were faced with the same problem have tried to solve it in an entirely different manner and in a wide variety of ways. Dogmas, after all, are not the result of clever arguments; they are doctrines that provide an explanation concerning the powerful issues at the foundation of our human existence, issues that irresistibly impinge upon anyone who thinks and reflects and refuses to close his or her eyes to reality. Dogmas do not provide answers that human ingenuity has discovered to the questions that arise from these issues; they provide answers that divine revelation has given us in holy Scripture. Precisely for this reason, however, it is obvious not only that the dogmas themselves deal with these kinds of questions, but also that all kinds of human considerations—wholly or partially divorced from Scripture—have tried various solutions to these issues again and again. And in the circles where they have been adopted, the solutions arising from these considerations exercise virtually the same authority as genuine dogma does among believers. In the former kinds of circles such solutions have the force and significance of pseudo-dogmas. They are assumptions that are accepted as axioms and become the point of departure for all reflection, and for which any further proof is considered superfluous. It is therefore not the case that the church starts from such dogmas but that the world does not. On the contrary, people in both the church and in the world start from such general fundamental tenets, and the only difference between real dogmas and pseudo-dogmas is that the dogmas of the church are based on divine revelation, whereas the pseudo-dogmas of the world are based on those human considerations of which the Apostle Paul says, "We destroy arguments and every lofty opinion raised against the knowledge of God, and take every thought captive to obey Christ" [2 Cor 10:5].

§ 2 The solution that the people of the world provide for the problem we are dealing with differs depending on the group for which the solution must possess validity. Among people of the world we can distinguish between people of practice and people of the academy. The former are satisfied with a rough, general solution that, guided by so-called common sense, is sufficient for practical life. The others, by contrast, dig deeper into the foundations of life and do not rest until they have arrived at a philosophical solution to the problem. Let us pause for a moment to look at the solution given in both of these groups, since the nature of our investigation requires it.

Among the practical people—those who function with so-called "common sense"—the solution to the problem lies in dividing the human race into three main classes. In the middle, in their view, stand the ordinary, normal, decent people, the kind of people they themselves are. On either side of this large middle group two abnormal classes of people are found: to the right are the precisionists, and to the left the scoundrels of all stripes.

Belonging to the class on the right—that is, the class of the precisionists, are all people who as believers presume to distinguish themselves from unbelievers and who dare to draw that line through all of life. It is absolutely not true that all *orthodox* persons count. Oh no—persons of whom rumor has it that they consider themselves to be orthodox, but who as ordinary people go along with the people of the world in associations, in society, in the area of education, as concerns science and art—they do not evoke resentment on the part of anybody and do not offend anyone, much like churches that do not let anyone know about their orthodoxy. These people are not considered to belong to the precisionists. But the world counts among the precisionists those who are open about their confession, who oppose the world with that confession, who order their lives differently on the basis of that confession, and who consequently demonstrate an aspiration of their own in all areas of life. Such people they call "the fanatics," "the night school,"[1] "the precisionists," and "the pious folk"—a class of entirely unmannered and disagreeable people.

1. This term (*de nachtschool*, here translated literally) was crafted in the middle of the nineteenth century by Otto G. Heldring (1807–73) to refer, with some nuance, to tendencies toward dogmatism and to confessional debates within Dutch Reformed Christianity at the time. Although he was not averse to addressing the importance and potential consequences of these developments as they came to influence both church and society, the term itself was often picked up by others as a slur to label all those, including Groen van Prinsterer (1801–76) and Willem Bilderdijk (1756–1831), who advocated Reformed teachings as they applied to church, state, and society. In 1864, Heldring began an article on "How the Orthodoxy of Our Day Contradicts the True Teaching of the Reformed Church" with these words: "When someone wants to make an everyday matter unpopular they exaggerate things. Caricature helps to make things look ridiculous, but when religious matters are embellished they become odious. In our time, on all sides, Reformed doctrine is misunderstood, mocked, and despised. What is currently being passed off as orthodoxy often completely contradicts the true orthodoxy of the Reformation. It piles misunderstanding upon misunderstanding and envelops Christianity in the dark of night, which moved me long ago to call this movement 'the night-school.' For some it has become truly midnight. This allows liberals great advantage and grounds to object, but also reason

And even as the class of the precisionists is thus set apart to the *right*, a separate group of people to the *left* is classified in the same way among the scoundrels. Among them are murderers, thieves, women (but not men) who abandon themselves to fornication, public drunkards who stagger along the streets and canals, hoodlums who beat people up or pull a knife, swindlers, loan sharks, con artists, cheaters, people who commit unnatural sins; as well as people of low, rough, and mean behavior; women with children born out of wedlock; and so much more. In short, they look down upon all the evil riffraff with the contemptuous condescension that proudly says, "I thank you that I am not like other men, extortioners, unjust, adulterers, or even like this tax collector" [Luke 18:11].

In the middle group, by contrast, stands anyone who honors himself as a "good and decent man" (to use the words of Haverschmidt).[2] Thus, beside these "good and decent men" stand on the one side the "disagreeable precisionists," and on the other the "evil riffraff." In the world's expansive field there is good seed that sprouts from the good heart, and mixed in with that good wheat all kinds of invasive plants and weeds—the invasive plants of the rabble and the weeds of the precisionists. "Invasive plants" and "weeds." They do realize that a precisionist individual is something quite different than a thief or a murderer, a whore or a cheat, but nevertheless the precisionist individual is condemned as a guilty person. His precision is pride, born from conceit and pretense. The precisionist individual is in part the victim of a narrow upbringing and ignorance, but his precisionism nonetheless is seen as spiritual moralism. And those people are still the best ones among them, while the mass of fanatics is far worse, since they are insincere and simply maintain a pious front. Fundamentally most of them are frauds who try to inspire confidence through their pious appearance, but then abuse that pious appearance to lie and deceive and to abandon themselves in secret to all kinds of sly tricks. The invasive plants—the evil riffraff—and the weeds of the strict ones are therefore fundamentally the

enough for everyday folks to scoff. And saddest of all, the truth itself is clothed such that she is unable to present herself as worth being recommended, accepted, and loved by all." See Otto G. Heldring, "Hoe de overgeërfde regtzinnigheid onzer dagen in strijd staat met de ware leer der Hervormde Kerk," *De Vereeniging: Christelijke Stemmen* 18 (1864): 525.

2. François Haverschmidt (1835–94), a Dutch pastor who wrote poetry under the pseudonym Piet Paaltjens. The quote comes from a poem called "Three Students" (*Drie Studentjes*).

same; the difference between the two lies only in this, that the evil riff-raff pursues more what the senses desire in the material world, whereas the strict ones indulge in all kinds of aberrations in the spiritual realm. Sensuality and pride are the two sins that spread rampantly, of which the one springs from the body, the other from the soul. On the basis of this simple distinction the ordinary people of the world can be said to follow more the sensual impulse of the body, the strict ones more the spiritual impulse of the soul. But both fall under the same judgment, that they are corrupted forms of the common type of people, and they are therefore a hindrance to the ordinary, good, worthy citizens.

This notion rests on the pseudo-dogma (according to the common claim § 3
that man himself is the measure of all things), that all people should be of the class of people to which a person himself belongs. Those who do not display the common characteristics of his type, whether to the left or the right, are no good. One's own kind is good and decent, and those who are unlike them are no good. But this perspective utterly denies the confession of the depravity of our human nature. There is no original sin. Man is in control of his own destiny and of his own situation through his free will, and that free will is a capacity ready for use and generally functions well—not that we are always and under all circumstances exactly the way we should be. No, everyone has his deficiencies, his shortcomings, and his peculiarities. Sometimes we do not function properly. But those things are tiny blemishes that do not affect the respectability of the person or the decency of his character. A person remains a good, decent, virtuous, respectable, honorable human being, even with all these minor faults. It is simply a fact that every human being has his weak side. That is part of our human essence. We tolerate this in others and we therefore want others to tolerate this in us. But it is inappropriate to have guilty feelings, to repent, to acknowledge that we have perverted our love for God. Occasionally, when one has done something repulsive, the conscience speaks, but is stilled again quickly. For such a good and decent man, it is out of the question that he should fall on his knees before God and acknowledge that in and of himself he is a lost sinner. That is fine for people who are in prison, for prostitutes and tax collectors, but it is out of the question for good people. They simply have no guilty feelings, and it therefore sounds like pure folly to them to take their refuge in a Redeemer. There is really nothing in them to find fault with. Their behavior is impeccable. Their heart is oh-so-good. They do not lack in generosity and love. What benefit would arise from all

this speaking of sin? Jesus has not come to call the righteous but sinners to repentance, and they do not belong among those sinners. Why would they repent?

This is how people guided by "common sense" account for human life. It is natural that the world is not as bad as expected, since the good, decent people set the tone, constitute the majority, and put themselves in the foreground everywhere. The fact that there is still so much rabble running around among the good people is the result of nothing but the wickedness of the wicked, for which decent people are not responsible. The fact that fanatics and moralists surface again and again is a kind of insanity that does not argue against the essential decency of our human race. It is only entirely natural that, as soon as the moralists gain the upper hand, the church *must* turn out worse than expected. What would such a church become other than a kind of asylum for credulous fools?

§ 4 We must add another thing to what has been said. These people of the world are not all of the same mind and not all identical in the tenor of their life. There are also different types among them. Space prevents us from describing all these various groups in detail. Let it suffice to point out that the good farmer, the quiet citizen of private means, the gilded youth,[3] the scholarly recluse, the artist, the hunter, the coffee house customer, the workman, the loafer, the woman, the man, the young man, and the young girl, all differ in this respect. Virtually all of these social groups therefore live with their own notions of what is moral. There is a very different conscience at the commodity exchange than in the farmhouse. It would be considered very immoral for a young girl to do what for a young man is called "enjoying life." Each one of these groups is different, even down to their lifestyles, the language they use, and the tone of their conversations. One considers cursing and ranting natural, whereas in many a fashionable family an unseemly word never passes their lips. Thus the precision of the moral sensibilities differs strikingly among all these groups, and among families in those groups, and among members within those families.

But all those differences are merely a difference of degree, not a difference in the perspective on life. One overlooks more, another less. One group is more permissive, the other less. But the main point is and remains that in

3. *Jeunesse dorée* was a name given to a group of young dandies in France who, after the fall of Robespierre, strove to bring about a counterrevolution. The term was later used for any young person living an affluent lifestyle.

all these groups the members of the group, including oneself, are counted among the normal, good, decent, and respectable people. People who stand below one's own group are considered a lesser sort—the sort of beings who have come down in life, people with peculiarities. But neither the fact that many have sunk below the normal level nor the fact that others have ended up with peculiarities can change anything in the fundamental perception these people have about human beings as human beings: human beings are good and decent, with minor faults and insignificant shortcomings, and the human heart in itself is by nature good. The consequence is therefore that the wisdom of these kinds of people consists in this: they want to elevate those lower sorts of people to their own level, or to cause those odd people to unlearn their peculiarities. This should happen (preferably) through coercion. They think that everyone should be trained in *their* school in order to be formed like them, and that those peculiarities should be rendered unlawful so as to compel them to abandon their oddities. The fact that those other people are not as good and not as decent as they are is merely the result of unwillingness or of a bad upbringing. Break that unwillingness and correct, under compulsion, that upbringing and nearly all people will become good and decent.

During the larger part of the previous century, this was in fact the prevailing and dominant opinion in our country as well. All people of "common sense" in higher and lower circles lived out of that pseudo-dogma of the decency of human nature. Even at the beginning of the previous century, when going to church was still a more common custom and people prayed at the table, when reading [the Bible] at breakfast was still in vogue, and when the dignified gentlemen—including non-preachers—still wore a white scarf, this was in fact the axiomatic dogma. The human heart was fundamentally good and most people decent. To the left were the candidates for the jail cell, and to the right the disagreeable obscurantists among the strict ones. "Oh, that all people were decent" was the recurring sigh that came from this false dogma. This practice of making people decent began with *Virtuous Henry* of the Society for Public Welfare and was later to be continued in the secular school by teaching "Christian and social virtues."[4] Then

4. Nicolaas Anslijn, *De Brave Hendrik, een leesboekje voor jonge kinderen* (Leiden: Du Mortier en zoon, 1809) became an enormous success. In time, however, the virtuousness of the protagonist became something to be derided and scorned. Today *brave hendrik* is used as a pejorative term for someone who is rather disgustingly

the generation of rascals would automatically be rooted out and destroyed, and the prisons, according to Opzoomer, could be sold and slated for demolition.[5] And as for the moralists, the first thing to do was to send the cavalry after them, and when that did not work, the system of exclusion was put in place. No "strict" individual should be helped to advance in this world. It was a matter of course that no precisionist came under consideration for an office or profitable job or a position of honor. No one who brings wheat into his barn wants to lug in a single sheaf of the invasive plants he had cut down or the weeds that were pulled up.

§ 5 Thus the pseudo-dogma stood over against the dogma of Christ's church, at least as long as people remained mired in general reflections and theories. But it became somewhat different when people talked among themselves about people who were not present, or came in contact with "real life" in the family or in business. When persons A and B talked about person C who bothered them or of whom they were jealous, then the pseudo-dogma of the "decent nature of man" suddenly fell completely by the wayside for A and B. This C was an insufferable person in whom no speck of good was left. He was always on people's lips, and the tongue increasingly became a lash of merciless criticism. He could not be given the benefit of a doubt because of good intentions. Everything needed to be explained in the blackest and nastiest terms possible. They merrily slandered C to their heart's content, and in the end it was a pleasure to apply the old church dogma of man's depraved nature to evil person C, without allowing him the benefit of the doctrine of common grace for even a moment. Thus it went on behind people's backs or in letters. The pseudo-dogma was abandoned and people stopped pretending, treating poor C as though the church dogma of the evil human heart still flowered and flourished.

It was no different when one opposed a bothersome individual in the family or business in-person. How often at such a time did the husband forget his entire dogma of the praiseworthy quality of our human nature vis-à-vis his "dear wife," or the wife forgot the drivel she had otherwise uttered about human decency regarding her husband. How much scorn was heaped in many a family on "those children who are simply unmanageable," and how often it came to a mudslinging match on the part of father and mother when in the course of child-rearing, they called their children

nice, a goody-goody.

5. Cornelis Willem Opzoomer (1821–92), Dutch theologian and lawyer.

good-for-nothings, apes, rascals, and the like! How sweet it was sometimes between oh-so-respectable "ladies" and the purportedly "decent" domestic servant girls! According to the demand of the pseudo-dogma you would have thought that those ladies when among themselves would have had nothing but appreciation and praise for the goodness and soundness of human nature as manifested in their cooks, seamstresses, washerwomen, and cleaning ladies—but the reality was different. There was almost never an expression of satisfaction; complaint after complaint almost always crossed their lips and was answered like an echo by a counter-complaint.

We also hear again and again, on the street and in front of the houses in our slums, the same outcry against the pseudo-dogma of man's good and innocent nature. We hear it in every altercation between the parties involved, whether in the office, the exchange, the store, and the workplace; in the barracks between corporal and soldier, and on the ship between those who must give orders and those who must obey; and over an inheritance among the heirs, at a public auction about a misleading sale, or in the market about the sale of a horse. Wherever you find people standing opposed to one another with conflicting interests, and the word or deed of the one decides the advantage or disadvantage of the other, there are always harsh words and sometimes blows. And when among those "good people" with their "innocent hearts" it comes to cursing and ranting, to taunting and insulting, or in more "respectable" circles it comes to caustic exchanges, the careful observer is struck by the strangeness of the situation: from that same world he first hears the crass objection to the foolishness of the church's dogma and immediately thereafter watches that same world literally exhaust itself in demonstrating the factual proof of that dogma's truth.

This sharp contrast has gradually become so clear over the past twenty years that the beautiful theory of "common sense" designating the good human heart as "innocent" has been discredited. It is still dominant in public circles. But reactions are emerging from all sides, and it now is beginning to become fashionable, going to the other extreme, to switch from "Virtuous Henry" to a hopeless wretch who could do nothing better than to disappear from the world stage as soon as possible.

CHAPTER FIVE

WHY IS THIS SOLUTION UNSATISFACTORY?

They go from strength to strength; each one appears before God in Zion.

PSALM 84:7

§ 1 The notion popular since the second half of the last century—namely, that our society consists of a large middle group of good, decent people, with a left wing and a right wing (on the left the "people from the slums" and to the right the "precisionists") has today run its course. It still lurks about and produces its aftereffects among the coarse lower classes, but it has already been abandoned in scholarly circles. From the philosophical schools another way of viewing life has now penetrated those higher circles not with one voice, but rather with a dissonant refrain. The view depends on whether people in those circles are more optimistic or pessimistic. Anyone who is cheerful about the future is considered optimistic, while anyone who views things as cloudy and dim is pessimistic. To correctly appreciate common grace, we must look at the claims of these two schools.

Chronologically the optimistic school had the floor first. Thus, allow us to begin by sketching its way of thinking.

As the older ones among us remember well, what is called Modernism emerged in the ecclesiastical, theological, political, and educational realms with a merciless critique of existing conditions. No less definite was the assurance that little else was needed than the strict implementation of its prescription, so that we could move into a more beautiful, blissful state—if not a golden age. The blame was laid on the stupidity of people. The fault was not their wickedness, but their ignorance; it was from their ignorance that all evil was born. What had been said about *sin* was at the very least grossly exaggerated. This could be seen clearly when one compared the higher with the lower classes. In the lower classes people were backward in knowledge and scholarship, and it was precisely those classes that supplied the unfortunate ones who populated the brothels and prisons. On the other hand, the light of knowledge and scholarship shone upon the higher classes—and how rarely did a man or a woman from those classes run afoul of the police! If, therefore, we could succeed in letting that same light of knowledge shine on the lower classes as well, then we might reasonably expect that sexual offenses and vice would gradually disappear from those classes as well.

This is an absurd claim, of course! This conclusion would have been valid only if more or less knowledge would have been the only difference between the two classes. But it was the pinnacle of folly, since the difference between the two kinds of social standing consisted in entirely different things—in poverty and wealth, in smaller or larger living spaces, in a more public and a more withdrawn life, in coarser or more refined work, and so forth. The test would therefore have succeeded only if people had succeeded in giving the lower classes not only more knowledge, but also more prosperity, better housing, a more sheltered life, less coarse labor, and so forth. But to think that only a bit of additional knowledge would transform the social position of this lower class, with all the rest remaining the same, was pure self-deception. Bitterly disappointing results have proven this more than convincingly.

But for more than a century people were deaf to this. The slogan became § 2
"knowledge is power." Knowledge was the effective medicine, and people set out to spread that greater knowledge in all kinds of ways. This brought the Modernist school immediately into conflict with orthodoxy. It was not as if orthodoxy joined in opposing the spread of that additional knowledge. Rather, this school could not do otherwise than accuse orthodoxy of deliberately keeping people ignorant in *spiritual* matters. They had the precious

Bible—what a marvelous book for nurturing our human race! But orthodoxy prevented people from seeing the preciousness of this book. It led people to believe that everything in this book was true. And that was absurd. There were no miracles. All such content was myth or saga. All that mattered in holy Scripture was the moral-ethical content. And to get a taste for this and to see the sublime in this Bible, it should be looked at in the way that they, the Modernists, did. Each individual book was spurious, all those miracle stories were made up, and only in this way would people come to love their Bible and learn to appreciate it. This was the promise published far and wide; evil orthodoxy, which systematically darkened this beautiful light, was tirelessly disparaged. And what then was the fruit of this modern action, perhaps not in the first generation but certainly in the second? Nothing less than that the whole Bible was shoved into a corner. Virtually nobody read it anymore, and already today we find in these circles educated men and women who are utter strangers to the content of holy Scripture.

Meanwhile, behind this modern viewpoint lurked a principle that still continues to work unrelentingly, long after Modernism came to be considered an outmoded perspective. This basic assumption is that man is a being that develops from lower to higher, according to a fixed law. At first the matter of how this development began was not discussed. The creation narrative was disavowed along with the narrative of the fall, but people initially did not have a clearly delineated notion of man in his original condition. That was left out of consideration and no urge was felt to penetrate deeper into this question. This changed when the "invention" of Darwin gained ascendance over people's minds. We all know of Darwin's system, which amounts to this, that no creatures were created, but that all kinds of beings gradually developed from one single being. This was claimed especially with respect to animals. And once it had been accepted that a snail and a bird of paradise, a starfish and a deer, ultimately came from one type, it was no longer a great mental leap to accept as well a relationship between a highly developed animal and an as-yet very low form of human. In this view a Khoi or a Bushman and an orangutan or chimpanzee do not differ so greatly from each other. If it was further assumed that a Khoi was still highly complex compared with the much lower forms of human life that had preceded him, then one was involuntarily swept along with the idea that the first man, in his lowest form of development, could well have been an exceptionally felicitously developed orangutan.

Once this conception of the origin of man gained acceptance, the logical conclusion was that the development of our human race was understood as a slow, steady climb from a very rough, almost totally animal condition to an ever higher form of life. Therefore, the later one enters this life, the better off one is, since then humanity would have progressed that much further in its development. Compared with all previous centuries, our century therefore stood highest. In the Middle Ages it still had been very dark. In the days of the Reformation only a faint half-light initially broke through. At the end of the eighteenth century the sun had finally broken through the clouds. And now, in our beautiful century, people walk in the most glorious light. And because the Roman Catholic Church wanted to take us back to the Middle Ages, and orthodoxy back to the morning dawn, both had to be resisted as taking us back from the light to darkness. A subsequent century would stand even higher than our century. And we could now already describe, as has been done, what kind of marvelous state of happiness was awaiting our human race then.

Returning to the main point, careful investigation in this vein has shown § 3
that humanity as a whole does indeed continually progress, but that not every human being has participated at the same pace. In one person, the animal instincts were still more powerful than in another person. There were highly developed people but also very backward people. Almost no two people were alike. And from that difference in degree of development emerged what we call "sin." Even the most advanced individual still felt something of the depravity of sin, but in him it was nothing but an urge toward the higher, from which his dissatisfaction with his present condition sprang. But sin, crime, and abomination essentially originated simply in the lower degree of development. The fact that someone does bad things means merely that he has not yet come far enough. This "sin" must therefore be combated by education and police—not because such a deed is bad but in order to help the backward person advance. It does no harm to continue speaking of "repentance" and "guilt," because it helps humanity advance, as long as we always keep in mind that all this is merely a manner of speaking. The final conclusion is that there is neither sin nor reason for repentance, since everything that irritates and disturbs the person in the higher class can be explained from the fact that the other people *have not yet reached their highest level.*

In the perspective of this optimistic school, the situation in our society must be understood approximately in this way—that in this century humanity as a whole has reached the level of development that befits its age. But keep in mind as well that in the generation now living, we must differentiate between the great mass of people in the middle who have—albeit by different steps—reached the level appropriate to our century, and the people at a lower level of development who are backward, who still have too much of the animal in them, and who therefore have a major struggle to keep up with humanity in its course of development. Above the middle class, on the other hand, another small group stands out: the group of the most highly developed who are ahead of their time. It is this small group of philosophers and thinkers who have the calling to lead humanity further. And what about the orthodox and moralistic people? Well, for them there is actually no place at all in this worldview. They stand outside the law. They are the criminals proper, since they knowingly suppress the light under darkness. This may not apply to the mass of the people who have been misled, but certainly to their leaders, who definitely know better but who act dishonestly in their desire for priestly dominance, and who deliberately keep the masses who follow them on the wrong track.

§ 4 And if, finally, we ask about the ultimate point of departure of this entire worldview, the answer can be nothing else than *pantheism*. This is because pantheism teaches a God who is not who he will eventually be, but who develops in the same way as man does. It teaches a God who at first does not know about himself; who first gradually awakens to a semi-conscious life and who gradually becomes more aware of himself as the world—and in that world, humanity—progresses. As long as man was still asleep in the animal world, God also slept. Only when man awoke did God also awake. And as man became clearer in his consciousness, God also became clearer to himself. God has no self-awareness outside of man, but only in man. Thus it is self-evident that God can be known much more in the more highly developed geniuses than in the common people who stand on a lower plane. And when on occasion an especially profound philosopher emerges who understands quite a bit more than most of his contemporaries, then such a man is one in whom God is especially present, especially manifests himself, and in a special way becomes aware of himself. It is from this pantheism, in fact, that Darwinism was born; from this the whole theory of the development from lesser to greater had its origin. In this way everything hangs together. It is the one thought that dominates heaven and earth and all of life on earth. "From lower to higher!" is the slogan. It still resonates in a manner that is far from Christian, even in the *Excelsior*.[1] It is also obvious that this school must be optimistic. Ever further, ever better! And amid all that is backward and disappointing we are comforted by the firm conviction that this evil too will soon pass.

It is a pity that all too soon such a beautiful dream foundered. On the §5
basis of historical considerations, Buckle came up with the claim that the form of life changes, but that there cannot be any moral progress in our life.[2] Rather, fateful causes unknown to us govern the course of life, so that year after year the same self-generated evil repeats itself with mathematical precision. It appeared that each year so many murders, so many suicides, involving so many men and so many women, yes, even down to the kind of suicide, was ultimately a fixed rule—so many each year by hanging, so many by drowning, so many by rifle, so many by poison.

On the other hand, Lombroso came up with the thesis that all atrocity and crime are the necessary consequence of physical condition, which in turn is determined by heredity and birth.[3] Proposals were even made to exterminate these wretchedly foreordained beings, or at least to prevent them from procreating. And worst of all, the beautiful expectation that increased knowledge would produce morality and decency was not fulfilled. Rather, crime crept upward into the cultured classes. The murderer who entered as a well-dressed gentleman was no longer a rarity. Deceit in business and fraud increased. The number of suicides, as well as the number of insane people, increased at an alarming rate. And immorality (taken in its common meaning) increased to terrifying proportions in connection with prostitution.

It therefore became apparent that this optimistic notion—one of a beautifully progressing development that soon would open paradise to us—ran aground on the facts of life. Orthodoxy had been accused of deluding the masses, and behold, here Modernism itself appeared to be guilty of deluding the masses. The consequence was that some serious thinkers returned to the once-spurned orthodoxy, while others made a turnabout from their earlier optimism to a pessimism that at present is starting to hang like a lead weight upon our entire society. Although this newly emerged lifeview

---

1. *Excelsior* is Latin for "greater" or "higher," and a common nineteenth-century motto.
2. Henry Thomas Buckle (1821–62) was an English historian famed for his unfinished *History of Civilization in England*.
3. Cesare Lombroso (1835–1909) was an Italian criminologist and physician.

is commonly attached to the name of Schopenhauer, let no one think that it originated with him.[4] This pessimism was rather a necessary reaction to the earlier carefree optimism of the Modernist school. It crept into the mind and filled the air until Schopenhauer finally provided it with a theory and expression. Thus people came to this confession of despair: our world is profoundly miserable. It is in fact the most miserable world imaginable—a world in which misery exerts a sovereign will against which knowledge has no effect and which can be resisted only through the will of the self that brazenly dares to defy the whole world and does not seek the world.

This of course totally changed the perspective on the composition of society. Man now appeared as the *victim*. The explanation of human misery, and thus also of sin, was no longer sought in man but in that will that drove everything. There was a difference in degree in the kind of misery different people fell victim to, but it was dominated by conditions against which people were powerless. One exception was the small group of people who grasped the essential situation and resisted that all-propelling will—through suicide if necessary. There was no cure for the misery of the masses. They were ensnared in all kinds of bonds from which they could not disentangle themselves, and they were dominated by influences against which they were powerless. There was a hopeless conviction that in the end gleefully extinguished every spark of hope that still glowed. It did this not as a game, but rather from the profound sense that people could only clearly and lucidly grasp the terrifying nature of this misery if they were able to awaken something in their will that through self-destruction enabled one to tear to shreds those harmful bonds.

As a result, the verdict on orthodoxy also underwent change. It was still seen as a phenomenon of deception, but it was just one of those miseries that also belonged to life, neither better nor worse than others. And nothing could be done about it. The dark cloud of orthodoxy simply had to hang over a portion of our society. Thus it had always been, thus it was now, and thus it would remain. And furthermore, even though orthodoxy was mistaken in allowing a beautiful hope for the future to shimmer, it also had this positive aspect, that from its position, it had also opposed *will* with *will*, and it had sought the means of salvation and escape in the energy of the will rather than in civilization and enlightenment. When we who are

4. Arthur Schopenhauer (1788–1860), German philosopher best known for his work, *The World as Will and Representation* (3rd ed., 1859).

orthodox encounter the leaders of this movement, we sense immediately that they no longer display any of the old spitefulness of the "enlightened ones." They do not concur with us, and sometimes they shrug their shoulders about us. But they understand that we are the way we are, and they don't even consider treating us unkindly.

Conversely, it must similarly be acknowledged that these new concepts spoke especially to Reformed Christians. While *predestination* was once the watchword by which the Reformed could be recognized among all other orthodox Christians, the term *foreordained* was also in the warp and woof woven by these pessimists. Granted, it was with an entirely different understanding; yet it still had the same conviction that life was not a Pelagian game of free will, but that a higher power pervades life, one that rules the course of life. By contrast, Reformed Christians had caused great irritation by confessing the absolute depravity of our nature by sin, and had continually placed in the foreground the consequences of sin as being *original sin* and *misery*, so it must have surprised them to find that now, from an entirely different corner, a similar acknowledgement of an inherited misery that dominates all of life was being defended against the men of the Enlightenment. We say *similar*, because we do not for a moment want to lose sight of the fact that the Reformed and the pessimists mean something entirely different by those terms. But what does become apparent is that while the men of the Enlightenment had branded us deceivers because we refused on the basis of God's Word to adopt their emerging worldview, their opponents now showed them how our perspective was much more in agreement with history and the facts than theirs.

Yet there is more.

Even if the lifeview of the pessimists continues to gain ground—indeed, even if they become dominant for a period of time—there can be no doubt that one day that lifeview will disappear. The human heart still experiences too much pure joy for such a morbid perspective to be able to disturb spirits for long. But even if this lifeview disappears, it will nevertheless have dealt a blow to the Modernist lifeview from which the latter will never be able to fully recover.

So, let us take a look at the development: first, the period of so-called "common sense" with the "Virtuous Henry" theory; then, the period of the men of the *progressive*-development view; and in the third period, which we have now reached, this lifeview has also been weighed and found wanting by the pessimists. The result can only be that we are strengthened in our most sacred faith and put the value of our confession in a light that is all the more clear. Even among us, virtually no thought was given any longer to the doctrine of common grace. It was no longer considered worth the effort of thought. But now it nevertheless appears in retrospect that precisely this common grace, along with our confession of sin and misery, promises nothing less than to resolve one of the great enigmas of life. It promises to explain to us how, in our society, on the one hand so much deep depravity stirs and must stir, yet on the other hand there is in that same society an indescribable number of things that fascinate us, elevate our heart, and cause us to savor human happiness. Without the confession of common grace, either our relative happiness will cause us to ignore sin, or our awareness of sin and misery will blindfold us to the joy of life. With that confession of common grace we have the understanding and the capacity to recognize both in their full value.

CHAPTER SIX

THE SOLUTION FROM THE ROMAN CATHOLIC SIDE

What then shall we say? That the law is sin? By no means! Yet if it had not been for the law, I would not have known sin. For I would not have known what it is to covet if the law had not said, "You shall not covet."

ROMANS 7:7

From the beginning of our discussion we have directed attention to how the Roman Catholic life- and worldview also occupied a curious position with respect to the important question that engages us. This is a position that, when compared with the practical school of common sense or the speculative thought of the philosophical schools, certainly contains much that appeals to us, but it cannot for that reason alone be our position. The learned author Mr. Th. Bensdorp of the Congregation of Redemptorists protested against our portrayal of the position under discussion,[1] and he did this in such a chivalrous manner that we are still looking forward to § 1

1. Th. Bensdorp, "Dr. Kuyper over her katholieke leerstuk der oorspronkelijke gerechtigheid," *De Katholiek* 110 (1896): 23–60; 300–329.

a suitable time to respond to what he has written. However, we must not and cannot do this in *De Heraut*, since Mr. Bensdorp has shifted the question to an area that requires us to go deeper into the history of the dogma, including an evaluation of the terms of the dogma, a discussion that falls outside the scope of a popular weekly magazine.[2] But allow us here an early brief rejoinder to the complaint of Mr. Bensdorp—namely, that we have presented the Roman Catholic Church doctrine incorrectly. We do assume that a Roman Catholic will never feel comfortable with our representation of the doctrine of his church any more than we Calvinists can find ourselves fitting into the representation that the most able and astute Roman Catholic theologians give of the Reformed confession. But that difference in nuance does not justify the charge that our representation is *formally* incorrect. For our part we have seriously attempted to do full justice to the Roman Catholic worldview. To this end we have literally copied the official church doctrine, and to the extent that the meaning of that church doctrine could be ascertained, we have referred to the literal statements of Bellarmine.[3] Can it then be said that the Roman Catholic doctrine is not correctly represented by us?

Here a distinction must be made. What is the Roman Catholic doctrine here? Not, of course, what one or another Roman Catholic teacher expounds, but only what has been officially settled on *by the church*. But in addition to this sober determination, which addresses only the main points, there has historically been a Roman Catholic theological exposition of their dogma that is *not* officially authorized. This exposition has progressed through different phases. It was still simple in Augustine's writing, began to develop more broadly in Alexander of Hales, was delineated more distinctly in Thomas Aquinas, and subsequently underwent all kinds of additional

2. Th. F. Bensdorp (1860–1917) was a Roman Catholic "Redemptorist" apologist. The Redemptorists are a Roman Catholic religious order originally founded in Italy in the eighteenth century for mission work among the poor in Europe. These chapters of *Common Grace* were originally written as weekly installments in *De Heraut*, columns to which Bensdorp frequently responded critically.
3. Robert Bellarmine, S.J. (1542–1621), was perhaps the foremost apologist, controversialist, and polemicist of the Roman Catholic (or Counter-) Reformation era. He was canonized in 1930 and named a "Doctor of the Church" (*doctor ecclesiae*) in 1931.

changes in its conception and in the expansion of its stipulations.[4] In the days when Calvinism was gaining influence, Bellarmine was prominent among the Roman Catholic polemicists who occupied themselves with this additional exposition. It is especially against his exposition of the Roman Catholic Church doctrine that this contrast has developed and in our view has become fixed in terms of dogma. This is why, when we had to make a choice, we stayed with the exposition of Bellarmine. And we are as yet unable to see that our approach would not be correctly demarcated. Or did not Gregory himself, who was pope at that time, appoint Bellarmine to deal with the controversy with Protestantism in the *Collegium Romanum*?[5]

We cannot entirely preclude a subjective element, either on our side or on the side of Mr. Bensdorp. Our esteemed opponent himself would not claim that the broad exposition of this church dogma that he has presented was already valid from, say, the days of Augustine, or was already officially accepted back then as church dogma. He must therefore also make a distinction here between church dogma and the *exposition* of that church dogma. The latter is always to some extent subjective in character and therefore lacks general unanimity. And to the extent that it was our purpose to establish a conception of the essential import of the Roman Catholic life- and worldview on the basis of both dogma and exposition, it could scarcely be otherwise than that our view would be different than that of a theologian of the Roman Catholic Church. For as we already stated above, any conception of the Calvinist life- and worldview from the Roman Catholic side often gives us the impression of being far from accurate. Strict objectivity is unattainable here. Even the clearest lens in our spectacles still colors our perception.

Only on one point can we already state an objection, without a detailed § 2
argumentation that would of course not be appropriate for the columns of this magazine.

Thus Mr. Bensdorp writes that we make an erroneous distinction between the essence and the nature of man, and that it will not do to posit

4. Augustine (354–430), bishop of Hippo (modern Annaba, on the coast of Algeria); Alexander of Hales (ca. 1185–1245), English Franciscan and scholastic; Thomas Aquinas, O.P. (ca. 1255–74), Dominican philosopher and theologian.
5. Gregory XIII (1502–85), pope from 1572, commissioned Bellarmine to lecture on controversial theology at the then-new *Collegium Romanum*, now known as the Pontifical Gregorian University.

with us that sin left man's *essence* undamaged but corrupted his *nature*. On this point the learned author says:

> Furthermore, we comment on the words [we have] quoted that Dr. Kuyper erroneously distinguishes *essence* from *nature*. Essence and nature are one and the same matter. The professor senses this himself; for he soon substitutes the "working of nature" for "nature." Thus he writes in the sentences just quoted, "sin did change the functioning of the *nature* of man [thus not the *nature as such*], but the essence of man has remained what it was, and will remain so," and so on. And a little further on: "In Satan as well, the essence of the angel remains unchangeably the same; only his nature has, with regard to its function [thus once again, not nature as such], changed completely into its opposite." Still somewhat further on, "What has changed is not his essence but the functioning of his nature." If in these three sentences we substitute *essence* for *nature*, then the meaning remains exactly the same. Clear proof that *essence* and *nature*, in the sense in which Dr. Kuyper uses the latter term here, have the same meaning. Over against the *essence* of a thing stands therefore not its *nature*, but rather the *accidental*, the *coincidental*, the incidental. Dr. Kuyper would have spoken correctly if he had written: "through sin man's essence or nature has not been changed in its *essential* but in its *accidental* aspect." But what he writes now of man, "*Undamaged* in his essence, he has become *depraved* in his nature," is a contradiction.[6]

In his *Dogmatic Theology*, Dr. Heinrich, who is undoubtedly also in the eyes of Mr. Bensdorp one of the clearest Roman Catholic thinkers of this century, posited almost the same distinction that we touched on. He declares, "While essence and nature are *formally* the same, *conceptually* they are distinguished to the extent that the substance as the principle of action is called *nature*, whereas in the word *essence* we think primarily of

6. Bensdorp, "Dr. Kuyper over her katholieke leerstuk der oorspronkelijke gerechtigheid," 55. [Compare *CG* 1.18.3].

the principle of being."[7] So too we also drew attention to the function to make the distinction between *essence* and *nature* apparent. And while it is entirely correct that we spoke of "the functioning of nature" in order to let the deeper unity of nature and essence not slip away, it is not so that in the three quotes the word *nature* can be replaced by the word *essence*. We could have reverted to substance as the unity of nature and essence, but the working of nature is not the same as the working of the essence. The *essence* is what *is*; nature is what *works*. And as often as we encounter the contrast between *being* and *action*, we must avoid confusing them. When the holy Apostle Peter states that "he has granted to us his precious and very great promises, so that through them you may become partakers of the divine nature" [2 Pet 1:4], our esteemed opponent will concede that we neither can nor must write instead: "so that through them you may become partakers of the divine essence." The doctrine of the incarnation also depends on a similar distinction. And although it would not be appropriate to insert a fundamental argumentation for the Reformed doctrine of sin into a study concerning common grace, we nevertheless continue to maintain unremittingly the thesis that the human essence remained human essence, but that the nature of man became so fundamentally depraved that only regeneration—the bringing the dead back to life [see Rom 4:17]—stems this ruin.

Nevertheless, let us say a brief word about the remark that it is not § 3
sufficient to make a distinction between what belongs to the sphere of human nature and what lay outside that sphere, but that rather a distinction should be made between natural, extranatural, and supernatural righteousness. The Roman Catholic theologians understand *natural* righteousness to mean that even without the *donum superadditum* of the *iustitia originalis*—that is, without the special gift of original righteousness—Adam had been able to arrive at righteousness from his created nature through struggle; not, of course, without God, but, so to speak, with no other help from God than the normal help which the creature always needs. *Extranatural* righteousness is, then, the righteousness that was added to him at creation so that he could maintain it without struggle under the constant influence of God. And *supernatural* righteousness, finally, is understood to mean the righteousness that receives its impetus not from man but from God, and because of that origin goes far above natural righteousness. No matter how

7. Johann Baptist Heinrich, *Dogmatische Theologie*, 10 vols., 2nd ed. (Mainz: Franz Kirchheim, 1881–1900), 5:370.

sharply delineated this distinction may have been developed on the part of the Roman Catholics in terms of the dogmas of church and merit that were later developed from it, this distinction starts from a false dualism whose very foundations we challenge. We refuse to allow in the ethical realm any holiness or any righteousness that has come into man as an element alien to his nature. Every combining within man of a natural and a non-natural element is and remains artificial. In the ethical realm there is no room for any artificial linkage. We can help a plant survive that otherwise would grow up puny and later perhaps would wither in the location where it stands, by *adding* fertilizer, adding water, pruning, getting rid of insects and parasitic plants, so that it flourishes and produces more fruit. But all this remains within the confines of the nature of the plant, because nature is geared to this. It belongs to a plant's nature to be nourished and watered, and getting rid of insects only removes what goes against its nature. In the same way, all that man receives from God to let what is dead and withered within him come back to life, to strengthen him, to nourish him, to provide him with water, to shine light upon him and to let him bring forth the delightful fruit—is not something that falls outside the limits of his nature, but is given in the ordinance for human nature in creation itself. Whatever exceeds or goes beyond these limits cannot be grace for him. When we on our part also speak of supernatural power and grace, we have only its *immediate* character in view; this is contrasted with the *mediate* character of all power of God that works through nature as instrument, and therefore works primarily in relation to the *depravity* of nature. In nature, which is fallen away from God, nothing can be brought to thrive or flourish except through an act of God that goes beyond the limits of nature and comes from outside. This implies most certainly a dualism, but a dualism brought about by sin. But what we are refusing to do is attribute that dualism to creation itself.

§ 4 The very creation of man in the image of God determines by sacred ordination that his nature has been designed for all of these things—fellowship with God, those divine powers that man receives, and reaching the ultimate goal for which he has been created. Nature is not understood in isolation from God—as if man, God's creation, would at a single point along his path be expected or able to do or produce anything from himself, apart from God. On the contrary, it is precisely by virtue of his creation in the image of God that it belongs to man's own nature to be all he is *from* God, *through* God, and *for* God. It is inherently sinful to think or desire even for a moment that man would be anything in himself over against or apart from God; that would introduce a dualism that is directly contrary to the organic relationship between God and the man created in his image. Even in the highest perfection, when once the saints, without spot or wrinkle, will sparkle in inalienable bliss like stars at the firmament, nothing will shine in them that goes beyond the limit of their nature as determined actively and passively in creation. Rather, the extent of those limits will have been reached. When medicine heals the sick person, it does not do so outside the limits of his nature, since expelling the illness through medicine belongs to the makeup of his nature. But even if we concede that in the state of depraved nature we may call the medicine of saving grace on the one hand *extra*natural and on the other hand *super*natural—not only with respect to its *immediate* origin but also with reference to that damaged nature—it still does not follow at all that we may make the same distinction already at and in creation. The followers of Scotus,[8] who sensed something of this, therefore maintained the distinction that the "original holiness" of Adam was not given in his creation, but only *thereafter*. When we look at it carefully, it is only this "original holiness" that is first qualified as "supernatural" by Alexander of Hales. Or as Bonaventure expressed it, "that the creature is consecrated as a temple of God, is received as his child, and is accepted as a child, this is an *addition* in every creature that goes *above* his nature (*hoc est supernaturale complementum omnis creaturae*)."[9]

We are opposing precisely this notion of the *complementum* (addition) § 5
that in the dogma of the church has become the *donum superadditum* (added gift), in contrast to the *pura naturalia* (mere nature). If Mr. Bensdorp considers it improper to deduce too much from the image of the "golden rein,"[10] what remains is the clear and plainly stated assertion that a distinction must be made between what God by virtue of the

8. John Duns Scotus (ca. 1265–1308), a Franciscan philosopher and theologian.

9. Bonaventure (ca. 1217–74), Franciscan theologian. The citation comes from *Sent.*, II, dist. 29, art. 1, qu. 1, "Whether apart from the gift of grace man would have been accepted by God in the state of innocence?"

10. "Golden rein" is a term used by Bellarmine to refer to original righteousness: "it is to be observed that Divine Providence, in the beginning of creation (initio creationis), in order to provide a remedy for this disease or languor of human nature, which arises from the nature of a material organization (ex conditione materiae), *added* to man a certain remarkable gift, to wit, original righteousness, by which as by a sort of golden rein the inferior part might be easily kept in subjection to the superior,

creation ordinance allocated man as his nature, and what he additionally gave him out of grace by means of a supernatural or extranatural gift. What we confess in relation only to the fallen and damaged nature is here being distinctly transferred to nature as it was created originally. After Thomism had driven back Scotism, when "original holiness" came to be considered more generally as a gift given to Adam immediately at his creation, a distinction was invented between what was posited in Adam as being his nature, and what God through grace added to him beyond these limits of the natural.

We are not playing here with the word *grace*. We know very well how from the Roman Catholic side it is acknowledged that even the undamaged natural man could not progress without God's help, since man is designed for the steady reception of divine help and support. But *that* grace is not in view here. The "original holiness" that was linked with the "original righteousness" refers not to a normal support of God, but a *donated* gift that went beyond the limits of the matter. In creation, man received two things from God: (1) his nature, with all that belonged to that nature; and (2) a gift of grace, *ultra terminus naturae*—that is, going beyond the limits of that nature—as Alexander of Hales was the first to formulate it. And it is this combination that we are opposing. Had human nature been designed for this higher development, then that *iustitia originalis*—that is, that original righteousness—also belonged to this nature in its completion and final end. And if this *iustitia originalis*, or original righteousness, was *not* something for which our nature was designed—something alien to it, something different, something that lay outside being created in God's image—then the nature of man will continue to differ from that higher grace also in nature and kind. Then one cannot merge organically with the other and we are left with a purely artificial connection; this dualism will continue into man's highest development.

§ 6 But we must not let ourselves be distracted from our subject. This point can be adequately dealt with only in a separate polemic, for which we hope to have time and opportunity in the future. Now this topic obstructs our path only to the extent that this Roman Catholic life- and worldview takes a path of its own in order to resolve in its own way what we explain with

and the superior to God." See Bellarmine, *De gratia primi hominis*, ch. 5, as quoted in William G. T. Shedd, *A History of Christian Doctrine*, 2 vols. (New York: Charles Scribner, 1863–69) 2:143.

"common grace." Once the distinction is accepted that original righteousness was not part of man's original nature but was added to our nature, then it follows immediately that the loss of this original righteousness as such left the nature of man unaffected. It is not as if Roman Catholics teach that our nature today would be the same as Adam's nature when it was created, apart from original righteousness. On the contrary—without desiring to further argue over the word *nature*—they also definitely teach that a *weakening* of that nature took place, that Adam's sin is a cause of evil in us, and that such evil was passed from generation to generation through original sin. But however much this may be confessed, there is no question of an actual depravity of that nature so that it could no longer produce anything good, not even in the area of civic righteousness. It could never produce any *saving* good, but it could certainly produce all kinds of *civic* good. And thus the contrast becomes this: we say that the depravity of our nature not only cuts off everything good, but even causes it to be able to produce nothing *but* evil. And it is only the tempering power of common grace that restrains this decay and still allows civic righteousness to manifest itself. From the Roman Catholic side, on the other hand, it is maintained that in spite of the appearance of sin, nature still has a certain power within itself to accomplish civic righteousness. Not—let it be clearly understood—that Rome would ascribe this to the *pura naturalia*—that is, *apart from* God's help; nevertheless, here that help from God means nothing else than a general support on God's part. This support is assumed to be necessary and indispensable in every creaturely realm, flowing as a matter of course from the dependence of the creature as such.

This distinction between Rome's perspective and ours dominates to no small extent the respective views on humanity and human life. Of course, § 7
this does not involve doing any good that merits salvation. According to Rome's teaching, by virtue of what man's nature allows, he is utterly incapable of doing that good; any capacity for doing salvation-meriting good comes into view only when, through the dispensation of the church, higher grace flows into the will. But if we restrict the focus to this life, pay attention to society only in its earthly existence, and ask only about what is called created righteousness among men, then in spite of sin man's nature is still quite capable of such civic good even after the loss of original righteousness and after the fall into sin. Often the sinner will succumb in the battle that must be fought to achieve this, but he will also prevail at times. And the phenomenon that we still see—namely, that so much in the world around

us is kind, uplifting, and noble—must be explained on the basis of this nature of man that is still so rich and is supported by divine help.

But standing over against this human society as we find it among the pagans, Muslims, and Jews, and functioning with the powers that still remain in our human nature, is the church as the guardian of the treasure of supernatural grace, and no higher light than the one she has lit shines either on the individual human being or on human society. Those two spheres of life lie separated alongside each other. On the one hand, there is human society apart from a higher power, functioning only out of the weakened *pura naturalia*; and on the other hand, there is the life sphere in which the light of the church radiates but which is then dominated by the church. And in that sphere, life is on a higher plane to the degree that it bears the church's stamp. The whole of life, from the cradle to the grave, is framed by the church: ecclesiastical guilds and commerce, ecclesiastical science, ecclesiastical art. In this way the church brings its heavenly powers and its heavenly radiance into the entire arena of human life. In this way the dualism that was allowed to enter the original creation at its starting point returns here at the end of the road. As far as the supernatural transcends the natural, just as far does human life in the life-sphere of the church stand above the life-sphere that develops outside this light of the church. And then even though the life of society that stems from the natural powers is treated kindly, when tested against the criterion of the church its value must be discounted, because it has no ideal significance.

§ 8 By contrast, we confess that the spiritual life in Adam was organically one with his nature at his creation; sin caused the working of this organic existence to turn into its opposite; and it was then that a dual grace of God entered: The one is common grace to restrain the full effect of this decay in death and misery. The other is particular grace that came to put right again the organic existence of man, both *potentially* in regeneration, and *actually,* now and already, partially in repentance and sanctification, and one day fully in glory. Consequently, for us, both ecclesiastical life and extra-ecclesiastical life stand under the influence of saving grace. Both what is manifested on the one hand as civic good, and on the other hand as saving good, we owe to the mercy of our God. We confess that in both of these, he is seeking the glorification of his own name and the maintenance of his own work over against Satan.

Through this, life outside the church receives its independent meaning, its own honor, its own goal and destination; yet furthermore it is included together with the church's life under one and the same perspective, derived from a single source, the one influencing the other, and aimed in its ultimate purpose at one and the same goal: the triumph of God over against Satan. We acknowledge without hesitation that from the Reformed side, this more correct perspective on life has not always been maintained. Through spiritualistic one-sidedness, many people among us have fallen into a dualism that has clouded their perspective—albeit in a different manner than Rome—and they have haughtily opposed God's work in the world. But this must not be attributed to our confession. This dualism is not from, but against our confession. With the rise of Calvinism this narrow-minded avoidance of the world was discernible only with the Anabaptists, but not among the true Calvinists.[11] And now that the dust has been blown off this confession once again, the unique life- and worldview that was ours originally has returned. From more than one angle it has demonstrated its power at the same time in the predilection for honoring both particular and common grace: just as much theoretically in our doctrine as it has practically in our conduct.

11. In general, Kuyper uses the term "Anabaptism" to refer to a manner of dealing with the problem of the relation of the Christian and the world, a position that expresses an excessive spiritualization, a version of otherworldly Christianity that is aversive to the world or culture. Historically, "the name 'Anabaptists' (meaning 'Rebaptizers') was given by their opponents to a party among the Protestants in Reformation times whose distinguishing tenet was opposition to infant baptism, which they held to be unscriptural and therefore not true baptism." See "Anabaptist," in *NSHE* 1:161.

CHAPTER SEVEN

THE REFORMED POINT OF DEPARTURE

Among whom we all once lived in the passions of our flesh, carrying out the desires of the body and the mind, and were by nature children of wrath, like the rest of mankind.

EPHESIANS 2:3

§ 1 In conformity with holy Scripture, Reformed churches confess that through what happened in paradise "our nature became so corrupt, that we are all conceived and born in sin," and this in the sense that we are "so depraved that we are wholly incapable of any good and prone to all evil." This condition cannot be changed "unless we are born again by the Spirit of God."[1]

We cannot say that this confession fits with our personal experience, nor with much else that we read in Scripture. It does not fit with our personal experience, since we encounter all kinds of things that strike us as attractive in the lives of people who are alienated from any kind of faith and in whom we cannot assume regeneration; far from being "prone to all evil," these attractive things rather run counter to that disposition. And also does

1. Heidelberg Catechism, Lord's Day 3, Q&A 7–8.

not fit with what we find elsewhere in Scripture. Abimelech even appears to put Abraham—the friend of God—to shame.

This contradiction is completely resolved by the confession of common grace. "Incapable of any good, and prone to all evil" expresses how each human being, apart from regeneration, would prove himself to be if common grace did not keep his evil impulse in check. Experience shows us how the power of the Lord largely renders "the evil nature" harmless behind the bars of common grace. "Incapable of any good, and prone to all evil" does not express what we find in the "born again" individual, nor what we find in everyday life in all those who have not been regenerated. Rather, it acknowledges what lies in our depraved nature and what would immediately proceed from it as soon as God ceased to temper this evil impulse through common grace.

And do not say, "Why then the confession of our depraved nature? By admitting to the actual situation, we encourage the conclusion of those who deny the depravity of our nature, and this confession of yours is then nothing but a generous supposition that falls outside of reality." Deeper reflection teaches us something different. As yet, some remain who appear not only *inclined* to all wickedness but who also *commit* it. Judas is not unique in history. David's dealings with Uriah remain horrendous. The cold-bloodedness with which time and again two or three people are murdered at the same time for the sake of insignificant loot is appalling. The Armenian murder scenes have made all of Europe shudder: a hundred thousand men, women, and children cut down with the saber by cowards.[2] And this is to say nothing of cannibalism in wild regions and of the cruelties of Dingane[3] with his own troops. In all this, and in so much more, "prone to all evil" is manifested in a deadly manner.

And what is the consequence if we do not confess the general depravity of our nature? Then we would ascribe all evil things to an exceptional wickedness in these particular individuals and elevate ourselves above

---

2. Kuyper is likely referring to the slaughter of Armenians before and during the Russo-Turkish War of 1877–78 in what is now eastern Turkey. Decades later, in 1915, in what is often referred to as the Armenian Genocide, the Ottoman Empire would expand its attempts to exterminate Armenians through the systematic starvation and killing of about 1.5 million people.
3. Dingane Zulu (ca. 1795–1840) was a Zulu chief who became king of the Zulu Kingdom in 1828, after his assassination of his half-brother, Shaka Zulu. During his reign there were massacres of Dutch Boers and the decisive Battle of Blood River between the Boer Voortrekkers and the Zulu, in which 3,000 Zulu were killed.

them as being much better. But if we acknowledge the depravity of our nature in general, then these horrors simply show us what springs from our nature as soon as God lets go of us, surrenders us to our natural impulses, and does not keep us in check through common grace. Then we do not elevate ourselves when we hear of all these terrible things, but we sense what would spring from our own heart too if God did not restrain us; this is precisely what drives us to seek greater nearness to the grace of our God. We realize how the seeds of all evil lie in each person's heart, and how the difference between one individual and the next springs only from the fact that this evil seed remains hidden in the one but germinates in the other; this gives us a sense of solidarity in guilt and teaches us to give thanks for the preserving grace of our God. In the refugee church in London, sometimes an illegitimate child was presented for baptism; the church did not want the honorable woman who was present at the baptism to think within herself how decent she was and how bad that girl was; rather, the church exhorted her to confess in prayer before God that this evil that manifested itself sprang from the common root of sin and that her own preservation [from this sin] was due only to the grace of God.

Second, the regenerated individual is absolutely not rid of the effects of his natural inclination. He too can fall deeply, and even if in his case it does not come to complete ruin, he daily encounters in the life of his own soul all kinds of evil that wells up from the contaminated spring. Denying the depravity of our nature will continually lead to spiritual despair, to doubt concerning our situation, and to surrendering the assurance of faith. On the other hand, if we confess this depravity, then there is a solution for this fearful riddle, and the sin that is committed immediately drives the child of God back to the grace of his God, with broken heart and contrite spirit.

Third, the confession of common grace makes us acknowledge that in this common grace God uses our human lot in life, our human upbringing, our human discipline, and so forth, more as the means to stem the evil that wells up. This confession therefore urges us to not sit back passively but to be intent on combating and fighting the evil, not on our own but in the service of God.

Fourth, and finally, it makes this remarkable difference: he who considers it the natural fruit of a nature that is not quite entirely depraved when he examines his own civic virtue and the many kinds of human attractiveness in other persons who have not yet been regenerated, must necessarily go searching again *within man* for his point of support. Conversely, he who acknowledges the total depravity of our nature but confesses that God tempers it through common grace, both in the civil realm and in the still bearable condition of our human society, glorifies nothing but the generosity of God.

We are not saying, therefore, that the appeal of our forefathers to holy Scripture to prove the depravity of our nature was always equally impeccable. We have specifically mentioned before that what we read in Genesis 6:5 is not a *general* statement about our human condition throughout the centuries, but rather a *particular* statement about the terrible explosion of evil just before the flood. For it says, "The Lord saw that the wickedness of man was great in the earth"—that is, that evil at that time had reached a pinnacle, which Moses expresses immediately thereafter in this way: "every intention of the thoughts of his heart was only evil continually." These words thus describe the terrible degeneration that had erupted back then because common grace had withdrawn itself to the utmost. But apart from this, the description that the holy Apostle Paul gives us in the first three chapters of his epistle to the Romans is such that we call it the definite demand of holy Scripture that we confess that our human nature is totally depraved in itself.

Meanwhile a secondary notion has crept in at this point that becomes § 2
highly dangerous when it goes beyond its legitimate boundaries but is certainly justified in part. It is often taught that the phrase "incapable of doing any good" did not mean that fallen man was no longer capable in himself of doing any *civic good*, but the phrase merely had in view his spiritual incapability and had in mind our powerlessness to accomplish any *saving good*. It then follows that good works are only those that strive only for the glory of God, from sincere faith, and in conformity with God's will. Man, it is then acknowledged, has been utterly incapable of doing such good since his fall. Rather, apart from regeneration, he tends to oppose faith, always challenges God's law, and in his best intentions had ulterior motives that aimed not at God's honor but at his own advantage or pleasure. In this way it seems that the drastic statement of holy Scripture about the depravity of our nature could be salvaged while at the same time making it quite understandable how so much in everyday human life could still be appreciated because it is "lovely and commendable" [Phil 4:8]. All kinds of civic and common natural good still sprang from our fallen nature, but this kind of good, however valuable for life on this earth, falls entirely short in terms of eternity and the exalted destiny of man. Fallen nature is entirely incapable of that spiritual good that counts toward and qualifies for [eternity]; saving grace has to come to our aid for this kind of good. For it was

acknowledged that civic good was not accomplished apart from God. But the assistance of God that has been provided for this purpose is nothing other than the divine assistance that is indispensable for every creature. Just as we cannot breathe without God perpetuating life in us, so too we cannot accomplish civic good without the same divine power sustaining and perpetuating our natural life.

This perspective, which is at its core Roman Catholic, leads in principle to the thesis that man *before* the fall possessed the saving good (then called "original righteousness and holiness") only as a gift of grace that was added to what was in his nature by virtue of creation. Thus a duality has been posited within the originally created man. First he possessed the human nature that was given him as a human being, with all the powers and capabilities that were in principle inseparable from that human nature. And second, he possessed the grace that was given him in addition to his nature—that grace consisted of original righteousness and holiness, the true spiritual and saving good. Thus a good was to be found in each of these two: human nature as such possessed a certain capacity for doing civic earthly good, and the donated grace given to man possessed the capability of the spiritual-saving good. There were two spheres, one of which was earthly, the other heavenly; human nature as such was for the earthly sphere, whereas the donated grace of original righteousness was significant only for the heavenly sphere. When in the fall original righteousness was lost, man lost through it his spiritual capacity for the saving good, and this could only be restored in him through supernatural grace. What he did retain, on the other hand, was what his human nature contained and was capable of in itself. It was conceded that these powers of human nature as well had not survived the struggle unscathed; nevertheless, this weakening was something quite different than total depravity. Thus civic good could still be explained on the basis of this weakened nature, and this weakened nature that still remained provided a point of contact for supernatural grace. It is not as if supernatural grace could spring from it. Without "helping grace" the sinner could do nothing. But the point of contact is there. The Roman Catholic doctrine runs along these lines and it does not make any difference whether subsequent Roman Catholic theologians expounded this in even greater detail and made it more plausible by means of even more precise distinctions.

How we assess this perspective depends on the relationship we posit between *essence* and *nature* on the one hand, and between the *natural* and the *supernatural* on the other. If we understand the nature of man to be the same as the essence of man, then we also concede that sin has left man essentially unimpaired, and that man's nature (now taken in the sense of *essence*) could not be totally depraved. The Lutherans have gone too far here, and over against the Lutherans we Reformed have always defended the thesis that the sinner is not like a "stock and block,"[4] but remained human, retained his human essence, and was and still is saved in his human essence.[5] Also over against the Anabaptists, we have continually defended this in our thesis that the rebirth is a re-creation and not a new creation. The sinner is not a rotten tree in whose root a new tree is created. It is the same tree that first became wild and was eaten away by rot, and whose essence is now freed from this decay and becomes capable, through grafting, of sprouting new branches and bearing good fruit.

We posit this not only with respect to the essence of man in general, but also with respect to the essence of each human being individually. One day each child of God will receive a white stone, and on that stone will appear a new name that no one knows except God and the one receiving it [see Rev 2:17]. That name will express the most intimate and unique aspect of his personal essence. It is also certain that that new name will express only the unique aspects that were put into his unique essence by virtue of creation. As a child of God, John is a very different being than Peter, and Peter a very different being than Thomas. The unique form of being a child of God in each of these three apostles is indissolubly related to the original stamp that God impressed upon the essences of these three men when he formed

4. See Canons of Dort, III/IV, art. 16: "This grace of regeneration does not treat men as senseless stocks and blocks, nor take away their will and its properties, or do violence thereto."
5. See The Formula of Concord, Part II, art. 2, point 24, pp. 525–526, in *The Book of Concord: The Confessions of the Evangelical Lutheran Church*, ed. Theodore G. Tappert (Philadelphia: Fortress, 1959): "But before man is illuminated, converted, reborn, renewed, and drawn by the Holy Spirit, he can do nothing in spiritual things of himself and by his own powers. In his own conversion or regeneration he can as little begin, effect, or cooperate in anything as a stone, a block, or a lump of clay could. Although he can direct the members of his body, can hear the Gospel and meditate on it to a certain degree, and can even talk about it, as Pharisees and hypocrites do, yet he considers it folly and cannot believe it. In this respect he is worse than a block because he is resistant and hostile to the will of God unless the Holy Spirit is active in him and kindles and creates faith and other God-pleasing virtues and obedience in him."

them at birth. To this extent there is therefore no difference. The essence of man in general, and of each human being in particular, remains intact. The most deeply fallen sinner remains a human being and can be saved only as a human being. Had his essence itself been lost, then there would not be redemption, but rather the disappearance of one human being in order for another human being to be put in his place by means of a new creation. The expression that we are a new creation, "created in Christ Jesus for good works, which God prepared beforehand, that we should walk in them" [Eph 2:10] has never been understood by the Reformed in any way other than in the sense of re-creation—the same being, first bound in sin and death, and now set free unto life and righteousness.

§ 4 But precisely for this reason we cannot concede that *essence* and *nature* may be taken here to have the same meaning. Earlier we pointed out that holy Scripture also ascribes a nature to God, and declares that the children of God may "become partakers of the divine *nature*" (2 Pet 1:4). This cannot be understood in the sense that we would become partakers of the *essence* of God. When Paul says "We ourselves are Jews by *nature*" (Gal 2:15 KJV), he apparently is not speaking of his essence, but of something special in which this essence manifests itself. *Nature* here stands over against *spirit*. And when in 1 Corinthians a *natural* body is distinguished from a *spiritual* body, it is not intended to mean that only the natural body reflects the essence of the body, whereas the spiritual body does not reflect the essence of the body. In the resurrection we receive the same body according to its essence. But *natural* body here means the essence of the body in a certain state. For our part we therefore distinguish between *essence* and *nature*, and furthermore in a still narrower sense, between nature *as such* and nature *in its ruined state*. When it is confessed, for example, that we are by nature "inclined to all wickedness," it means "in accordance with our depraved nature," and when "natural love" is mentioned, we understand this to mean the love that ignites its spark within human nature as such.

We make a distinction between *essence* and *nature* such that *essence* expresses that which constitutes our being human, and that *nature* indicates the activity—the working—that manifests itself on the basis of this *being* human. In this regard, the capacities and powers constitute the link that connects essence and nature. These capacities and powers have their foundation in the essence of man, and they operate in his nature. Love and hate are one and the same force, but at one time they operate on the positive side, at another time on the negative side. It is the same power that can direct itself toward God and against God; therefore sin is not something separate in human nature but only a switching of the direction in which the powers of man function. They work either upward, and then they are good, or downward, and then they are evil. The tongue remains one, whether it curses God or praises God, but in one person it will be inclined toward praising the Lord; in another it will turn toward cursing, even thoughtlessly and unintentionally. In sin there is no single power at work that does not belong to the essence of man, and also in eternal glory not a single power will manifest itself that does not have its foundation in the essence of man since paradise. But the direction in which those powers work can be opposite, and it is precisely by means of the direction of these powers that our nature, not our essence, is expressing itself.

But if we are to gain a clear insight, we must also make a distinction in this context between man's *self* and his *nature*. The powers created in man's *essence* function under a dual motive—on the one hand under the motive of his *self*, and on the other hand under the motive of his *nature*. One who abuses the power of his hand in a fit of anger to give another person a slap in the face acts under the motive of his *nature*; by contrast, the one who suppresses the surge of anger and extends his hand in reconciliation, causes the power of his hand to work against his nature, under the motive of his *self*. The character of our nature is thus fully understood only in contrast with our self. Our forefathers at the Synod of Dort confessed in the Canons of Dort that man was originally furnished not only in his understanding "with a true and saving knowledge of his Creator, and of spiritual things; his heart and will were upright, all his affections pure," but also that through sin he was not only darkened in his knowledge—distorted in his will—but also become "impure in his affections."[6] These emotions, these inclinations, are a power that must be distinguished from our *self*. Even if our self remains passive, there is still a working in us that drags our self along. We always lean to one side or the other. And this leaning, this inclination, causes the direction in which our powers will operate to be automatically given, unless our self opposes it or a higher grace turns it in a different direction.

This distinction is sensed most readily as soon as we move from human § 5
nature in general to the particular nature of the individual. Then it becomes clear how the nature of one person is inclined more toward a quiet and

6. Canons of Dort, III/IV, art. 1.

domestic life, and another toward an eventful, adventurous life; how the nature of one person inclines more toward the sensual, and the nature of another impels more toward pride; and similarly the nature of one person urges him to restless activity, whereas that of another causes him to enjoy a latent slowness. These then are not the proclivities that are arranged and caused by our self, but conversely are those that try to rule our self.

In the same way, within common human nature, as soon as an action has begun its course, there is also a certain inertia. In the state of glory this will be an inclination, a proclivity, a sure and firm leaning toward God. Our nature will then sparkle in unchanging holiness. But now, by contrast, that tendency of our nature is entirely in the other direction, away from God. At creation—that is, in the state of righteousness—this inclination was of course not yet present. Originally Adam's self stood free with respect to his nature. It was not his nature that determined the direction of his self; his self would through a fundamental act of the will determine once and for all the direction of his nature. If his self had at that point turned the powers of his essence toward God, then his nature would have received immediately the proclivity, the inclination *toward* God and with this it would have been assured of eternal life. But when in that first fundamental choice, his self chose *against* God, then through this choice he gave to his nature—and through his nature, to human nature in general—the inclination in the opposite direction. Through this choice, the disposition of our nature toward evil has been decided in such a way that our self no longer has the power to straighten out that nature inclined toward evil.

But against this a twofold grace is at work. First, *common grace* sees to it that the nature that is inclined toward evil does not go to the ultimate extreme—in effect overwhelming man's self. And second, through supernatural grace, *particular grace* brings about an opposite tendency in the *nature* of the born-again individual. Furthermore, this supernatural grace as it operates in the body of Christ makes this changed, re-created nature into a communal one under Christ as our head. But in the meantime, the *essence* of man as such remains one. It is and remains always the essence of man—as it was created by God; as it fell in Adam; as it became depraved after the fall in our common nature; as it was supported in that depravity of our nature by common grace; as it was re-created in the child of God into divine nature; and as it will one day radiate in a perfectly glorious nature with an inalienable crown in the state of glory.

CHAPTER EIGHT

THE TEMPERING OF SIN

> *Then God said to him in the dream, "Yes, I know that you have done this in the integrity of your heart, and it was I who kept you from sinning against me. Therefore I did not let you touch her."*
>
> GENESIS 20:6

The fact itself is thus settled for us. Common grace exists and functions; the fruit of this common grace is that the deadly decay of sin does not progress to its ultimate end in all that is called human, in the whole of creation. If we overlook this fact that dominates all of history, we either cannot acknowledge the depth of sin, or do not take seriously enough man's creation in the image of God. But where do we go from here? Do we merely have to acknowledge this fact, or is there information at our disposal that may help us to gain insight to some extent into the way in which this common grace operates? It is a question that must be asked circumspectly and answered even more circumspectly, because it takes us into the hidden realm of the mystical life. Yet it is a question that must be faced. In any case, this question is highly important. In general, the life of the world appears before us illuminated by the light from above, and our spirit perceives here and there some patches of light in the midst of this world that is sunk in gloom § 1 and darkness. These are patches of light that one person sees spread over all of Europe and [North] America, whereas another reduces these to the small circles that take the confession of the Christ more seriously. A third person virtually shrinks these patches of light to points of light that shine from the heart of a few especially devout people.

The doctrine of common grace, on the contrary, shows us that *all* of creation, from the beginning until now, has been sustained by nothing but the grace of God—grace that in every nation and in every century has been at work in each generation and each person. And dimly shining through the darkness in which everything lies, we see a reflection of the saving, sustaining, preserving power of God. Without common grace, everything would collapse with a single, awesome peal of thunder and sink into hell. The fact that everything is still standing, and that as it stands it still manifests much beauty, is not because sin is not so terrible or the curse not so awful, but because God's common grace is so omnipotent.

But how does this working of common grace take place? When Abraham deceived King Abimelech of Gerar using Sarah—saying that Sarah was his sister—the danger of adultery emerged. Abimelech had taken Sarah, who in his eyes was a marriageable woman, into his harem; thus the way was paved for him to unintentionally and unwittingly have illicit intercourse with the lawful wife of Israel's progenitor. But it did not come to that. The evil was stopped. And in what the Lord himself said to Abimelech, we are told that it was definitely God who prevented this evil: "It was I who kept you from sinning against me. Therefore I did not let you touch her" [Gen 20:6]. This was not, as everyone will concede, a work of particular grace toward Abimelech, even though this act touches indirectly upon the work of God's particular grace in Abraham and Sarah. Here there was an inclination or proclivity toward sin *against God*, as the Lord explicitly declares. The occasion was also prepared. The sin was about to be committed. And yet it did not take place. It did not progress to the end but encountered an obstruction. It was stopped by God. The commentators on the Dutch Bible translation surmised that Abimelech was suddenly made unwell—became ill—and thus was kept from perpetrating this evil.[1] But what we are told

1. Kuyper is referring here to the marginal notes of the Dutch *Statenvertaling* (lit., "States Translation," hereafter cited in the notes as sv). Published in 1637, the sv was the first Bible translation from the original biblical languages of Hebrew, Aramaic, and Greek into Dutch, commissioned by the States General of the Netherlands.

amounts to this, that in the very night after Sarah was led into Abimelech's harem, God appeared to him in a dream and revealed to him that Abraham's story about Sarah being his sister was not true. In that dream God said to him, "Behold, you are a dead man because of the woman whom you have taken, for she is a man's wife" [Gen 20:3]. These words do not allow for any other interpretation than that Abimelech had no longer any desire to sin and that it was God who deliberately had taken away this desire. That this was so is confirmed by two facts: (1) by what is reported in verse 4, "Now Abimelech had not approached her," and (2) that God himself declared to Abimelech, as we already saw in verse 6, that this taking away of his desire had been the work of God. He had prevented it. He, the Lord, had not allowed it to happen.

Thus we have here a direct working of God on the person of Abimelech, whereby a sinful urge was curbed, a compelling sin was restrained, and a premeditated evil was thwarted. It was thus a direct working that affected Abimelech's senses as well as his soul, took away the sensual urge in his body, and broke the lust in his soul. We had to go into some detail on this because holy Scripture presents us here, in more detail than usual, the working of common grace. And it is expounded and explained by God himself. What happened with Abimelech is all the more striking because it clearly shows that common grace did not function *ethically*. This means that the restraining was not the result of better or more pious thoughts that God had generated in Abimelech—as was the case, for example, with Joseph when Potiphar's wife tried to seduce him [Gen 39]. There was no such working on the conscience involved here. On the contrary, Abimelech was not at all aware that he was about to sin against God. He said frankly, "In the integrity of my heart ... I have done this," and he asked boldly, "Lord, will you kill an innocent people?" [Gen 20:4–5]. There is therefore no sense of guilt mentioned. Abimelech did not understand in the least that what he was about to do would have been sin against God. Yet that is very definitely what it would have been. The Lord states it explicitly: "It was I who kept you from sinning *against me*." The working of common grace thus bypassed entirely the personal moral sense of Abimelech. What took place was not a moral working, but a working of power. It was God who intervened with his omnipotent hand in the personal life of Abimelech, in his senses and his soul. It was God who broke the power of sensuality and extinguished the lust in his soul. It does not matter at all whether this happened, as the commentators on the Dutch Bible translation suspect, through an illness.

Such an illness that suddenly overtakes someone still is and remains a working of God's power on his person. For now we leave the question entirely open as to whether we must think of this illness as the result of observable causes, such as catching a cold or something similar, or that God cast this illness immediately and without mediate causes upon his body.

§ 2 We read elsewhere in Scripture about a similar act of God that prevented sin. It says in Genesis 31:4–7, "So Jacob sent and called Rachel and Leah into the field where his flock was and said to them, 'I see that your father does not regard me with favor as he did before. But the God of my father has been with me. You know that I have served your father with all my strength, yet your father has cheated me and changed my wages ten times. But God did not permit him to harm me.'" Here too evil had been planned; the inclination was present, but God prevented it. He had not permitted Laban to harm Jacob. In the same vein we read in Psalm 105:14–15, "He allowed no one to oppress them; he rebuked kings on their account, saying, 'Touch not my anointed ones, do my prophets no harm!'" The "doing no harm" did not consist in prohibiting but in preventing his anointed from being harmed. And although we have here only a few isolated instances, Romans 1 shows us that this effect of arresting sin has a much more general character. When it says that the Lord God "gave them up to a debased mind," [Rom 1:28] which became the cause of humanity's sinking progressively further into sin, it automatically implies that a period preceded this in which God did *not* let them go and did *not* give them over; he thus kept them in his hand, stopped and restrained them on their path, and preserved them. The hardening that is constantly threatened is therefore not an infusing of deliberate sin into the soul, but only the withdrawal to a greater or lesser degree of that grace through which up this point the terrible outbreak of evil had been prevented. As long as God covers us with his wings, no hardening comes and we are protected; but when God withdraws and the continued effect of sin is released, then the hardening comes automatically. In a northwesterly wind a ship runs aground on our coast—not because the helmsman steers toward the coast, but because he ceases to steer away from the coast. Thus when the rudder ceases to function, the ship speeds swiftly toward the coast and is smashed against a sandbank. Another ship might not run aground, not because the ship is better or because the forces of wind and tide have no effect on that ship, but only because the helmsman in that case is able to counteract the forces of wind and tide with his rudder.

And so it is here. The sinful force that seeks to run our soul aground through wind and flood, smashing it into the shore, is present and works upon every soul; it is God who turns the rudder in the little ship of our soul with his omnipotent hand and thus prevents it from being cast up on the shore. And thus God the Lord does not cease to wrest that rudder in our soul against wind and flood—otherwise the rudder would suddenly be thrown about, our heart would turn and slide backwards, and the shipwreck of our soul would certainly follow.

Thus when the righteous complain, "O Lord, why do you make us wander from your ways and harden our heart, so that we fear you not? Return for the sake of your servants, the tribes of your heritage" [Isa 63:17], it does not mean in the least that the Lord deliberately incited his people to unbelief and apostasy. Rather, quite the opposite: it means that his people, if he lets go of them for even a moment, incline with irresistible pull toward evil; it means that everything is kept from sliding down this slope only by God's restraining and preserving grace. The complaint therefore amounts to this: You, O God, who until now have preserved us, kept us in check, and curbed the evil proclivity in us—why did you cease to preserve us in this way, since you knew that this had to lead to our straying from your ways and our departing from the fear of your name?

It is in the nature of things that holy Scripture speaks of preserving grace almost exclusively in relation to the children of God—the Lord's people, his inheritance—and that it therefore discusses common grace almost solely as it is intertwined with particular grace. What we read about Abimelech was an exception. But to the extent that it is interwoven with particular grace, common grace always possesses the same character, namely, that it keeps from sin, and in that sense it preserves from evil. Our conclusion can therefore be no other than that sin presses and incites by using creation's powers that have been corrupted. It is God as Creator who limits and breaks the strength of the incitement and pressing toward evil of these forces he placed in the creature and maintained in the creature.

In the entire universe there is no single power at work other than those § 3
ordained, created, and maintained by God from moment to moment. To the extent that these forces are spiritual in nature and have been created in reasonable creatures, he has also determined the direction in which these powers should operate. But this determination of their direction is not a natural necessity. Moral forces do not operate like gravity. A stone

that is released *must* fall and cannot go upward. A helium-filled balloon *must* go up and cannot come down as long as the gas does its work. But in the moral realm, every force is governed by a tiller, and depending on whether the tiller is moved to the left or the right, the force works, say, to the north or to the south. Or in terms of ethics, the force works upward or downward, toward what is holy or toward the unholy, toward virtue or toward sin, for good or for evil. Sin is therefore not the creation of a new force, but the directing of the forces of creation against God's ordination and in the wrong direction. In no single sin can a new force ever work that was not created by God. From what source would such a force have come into being, and who would have created it?

If, after having created these forces, God had given them an independent existence so that they thereafter existed outside of him, then their further functioning would have been left to these forces themselves; they thus would constitute an isolated sphere within creation. But this is not how it is. No one possesses, in his blood, in his nerves, in his muscles, and equally in his will or his intellect—even for a single moment—a force that can rest in itself; if God ceased to maintain all this in himself, nothing would be left of all these powers, nor would they exist anymore. To put it strongly: God himself supported and strengthened the muscles in the hand of Rome's soldiers when their evil hands drove the nails into Jesus' hands and feet, and if at that same moment God had withdrawn his power from their muscles, their hands would in that very moment have been paralyzed and grown rigid; then no one could have harmed Jesus. Thus all this has not only been permitted, in the sense that God did not act against it, but it could happen only because God maintained the powers that made it happen.

§ 4 No matter how terrible it is to think about, no sin is ever committed except with the powers created and maintained by God, even in the very moment when the sin was committed. holy Scripture occasionally presents a conception that seems to suggest that in a few cases God deliberately incites and stirs to sin, and it therefore appears to us dualistically—as though sin operates independently, on its own initiative and by its own powers, as if it were God who first needed to incite the independent possessor of these sinful powers to use them for sinful purposes. But in such narratives we do not find any development of doctrine, no revelation of truth, but only a report in human form, and the *analogia fidei* demands that we explain all such conceptions in light of the intentionally given revelation.[2] When we read that God "repented" of something, then the *analogia fidei* requires that we interpret this in accordance with the intentional rule of revelation: God "is not a man, that he should have regret" [1 Sam 15:29]. With him "there is no variation or shadow due to change" [Jas 1:17]. This method is the only true one. holy Scripture generally places narratives, reports, and announcements in the framework of our human notions, but if we are to penetrate to the true background, those notions must always be interpreted on the basis of the absolute notion that is given to us in the definite revelation of truth. So too, when it states: "O LORD, why do you make us wander from your ways?" [Isa 63:17] or when it indicates that God incited David to count the people [see 1 Sam 24:1], then that notion must be understood as a human one. Thus it must be interpreted according to the rule that all power is God's and that the sinful working of divine power within human beings can either be given free rein or be curbed by him.

Strictly speaking, therefore, we cannot say that common grace is supernatural. It may certainly be called this insofar as it proceeds from God toward our human race. Fallen nature left to itself—that is, working with nothing but the powers God has embedded within it and also without these powers exercising any authority other than what proceeds from fallen man—would shoot as swiftly as an arrow into the abyss of destruction. There is thus certainly an intervening act of God that in its motive works not in mediated form, but without mediation. The working would be mediate if the motive—that is, the moving willpower—proceeded from the human self, but it is here immediate insofar as God leaves the working of the forces not to the impulse, not to the urge, not to the sway of the sinful self and the inclination of sinful nature, but arrests and stops the continued sinful effect by means of intentional power. This is like the wagon driver going down a steep mountain, who knows that the wheel of his cart, once it begins to roll, will cause the wagon to fly down at an ever-accelerating speed until the wagon loses all control and crashes into a ravine. For that reason he puts an iron groove with a chain around the wheel so that the progress is slowed and the wagon glides downward slowly. God does the

2. *Analogia fidei*, or analogy of faith, is the principle that "individual doctrines are to be understood in light of the whole understanding of Christian faith." See Donald K. McKim, *The Westminster Dictionary of Theological Terms*, 2nd ed. (Louisville: Westminster John Knox, 2014), 11.

same with his common grace. He knows how the wheel of the sinful life, governed by nothing but the axle of the sinful self in man, will turn ever faster, and in that ever more rapid turning it will corrupt all of man and must ultimately lead him into the abyss. Now God slows that wheel of life by slinging the groove of common grace around it and anchoring it with the iron chain of his divine will. To this extent we therefore concede that also in common grace there is a supernatural, unmediated act of God, an intervention in the course of the wheel of sinful life, an acting outside of man's self—bringing the impact of his divine will to bear not only *through* man's will, but even *against* it.

§ 5 But even though that fact is indisputable, the initial impulse of the working of common grace is not supernatural. This is clear even in the illustration of the wheel above. The wagon driver on the mountains does not keep the iron chain of the brake in his hand, but hooks it to the wagon itself, and it is the wagon itself that keeps the wheel from turning more rapidly. And so it is here. All working of common grace happens through powers that are present in the nature of man. Viewed superficially it seems to be otherwise. When God allows the evil powers more rein in one person than in another, it gives us the impression that God—if we may put it this way—exerts more pressure on the one than on the other. But this is merely appearance, stemming only from the fact that we always imagine man as working apart from and outside of divine power. If instead we perceive clearly that all forces at work in man, regardless of whether they function for good or for evil, are supported and maintained from moment to moment by God, and that they would be annihilated immediately if God ceased even for a moment to support them and to allow them to work—then it becomes clear that if God the Lord lets these forces work more strongly in the one individual, more weakly in the other; then that working remains entirely within the sphere of the creaturely, natural, and sinful life.

We sense the truth of this most clearly when we pay attention to how *differently* God allows this force to work, even where there is no sin in the picture at all. Imagine two people with poetic talent—take, for example, Bilderdijk and da Costa.[3] Neither in one nor in the other did the force of their poetic talent ever function except through divine impulse. And yet, what a difference between the one hundred fifty collections of poems Bilderdijk

3. Willem Bilderdijk (1756–1831), was a poet and founder of the *Reveil*. Isaäc da Costa (1798–1860) was a poet and friend of Bilderdijk, and is generally recognized as Bilderdijk's successor among Dutch poets.

has left us, and the relatively small poetic legacy of da Costa. One poetic talent thus received a much stronger impulse from God than another. This phenomenon appears in all kinds of areas.

If conversely we think of such human powers directed toward evil, then it is clear how a ruler such as William III and one such as Napoleon could have the same talent to rule and to conquer the world and to enforce their will through the force of arms; nevertheless, in Napoleon that talent could be unleashed in such an unbridled fashion that he became in many ways a scourge of humanity, whereas in William III such talent, because it was restrained and guided, could become a blessing for Europe.[4]

Pride is the power of self-control turned into its opposite through sin. God created power in our spirit that must be directed toward maintaining our character, our personality, and the uniqueness of our essence, as well as toward letting the light that can radiate from us shine as much as possible, for his glory. In the sinner, by contrast, this human power is inverted and becomes pride, conceit, haughtiness. In this sin as well, therefore, nothing but a sacred force is at work in us, created in us by God and belonging to our human essence, but now turned in the opposite direction and applied in its opposite working. Thus sin and the passion of pride come to life in us. But just as apart from sin we can imagine a difference of degree in the intensity with which this power would work for good, so too is a difference of degree conceivable in the intensity with which this same power would progress toward evil. In Pharaoh this degree of intensity was raised to its most extreme height—quite different, for example, from Rezin, the king of Damascus.[5] If God permits this intensity to continue at a high level, then sin breaks out in a terrible way; but when he restrains this intensity, then sin remains more moderate in its workings. Depending on whether that intensity increases or decreases under his divine ordination, the working of common grace also increases or decreases. When the chain in the hanging clock breaks, the whirring of the gears stops suddenly with a rattling sound; but as long as there is a restraining function, the gears run down slowly, and if the clock is not re-wound, their movement comes to an end only when the weight has reached the bottom.

---

4. Napoleon Bonaparte (1769–1821) was a French military and political leader who led France in the Napoleonic Wars against a series of European coalitions. William III (1817–90) was king of the Netherlands.
5. Rezin ruled Damascus during the eighth century BC until King Ahaz of Judah invaded Damascus, killing him (see 2 Kgs 16:7–9).

CHAPTER NINE

THE ANABAPTIST SOLUTION

I know and am persuaded in the Lord Jesus that nothing is unclean in itself, but it is unclean for anyone who thinks it unclean.

Romans 14:14

§ 1 The Anabaptists have their own position with regard to the question occupying us as well. For them the world as such lies in evil; the world is unclean, and all that comes from the world or belongs to the life-sphere of the world is unclean. Consequently, even the government that carries out its duties in the sphere of the world is considered unclean, and the child of God who has received an entirely other, new, heavenly life would degrade himself and go against his heavenly calling if he devoted energy and time to a government office. The true disciple of Christ stands outside the world and over against it. He must tolerate the world but must not devote himself to it. And so on this point, the entire confession of the Anabaptists has ultimately shrunk down to the approach known as avoidance—the conviction that a regenerated person must be in the world yet outside the world. The world must be avoided not only in this negative sense, as the apostle exhorts us that we should "not love the world" [1 John 2:15], and as it is accepted among all Christians that we should not follow worldly manners and amusements;

but the world must also be avoided in the absolute sense, such that *world* must be understood as the entire life sphere of the world—all of natural life. For that reason, a child of God must also avoid the offices of judge, of mayor, and so forth. All those things are worldly matters, and a Christian should stay away from them.

This Anabaptist perspective, which is still being defended in many circles that go under the name Reformed, would never have been adopted if the confession of common grace had continued to live among the churches. The Anabaptist doctrine of the avoidance of worldly things is nothing but the natural fruit of the dualism that had taken root through the Roman Catholic notion of original righteousness. This notion not only persisted but even intensified among the Anabaptists and continued to have an impact even among the Lutherans; it was fundamentally vanquished only on the part of the Reformed.

This is felt most clearly when we pay attention to the meaning of exorcism. It was understood that the world of evil spirits took possession of the souls of people, and that the evil spirit had to be expelled from the soul through a solemn incantation in the name of Jesus. According to the Gospel narratives this indeed happened frequently in Jesus' day. Jesus himself points to the casting out of demons as a hallmark of his messianic office. He gives to his disciples the power to cast out demons, and others outside the immediate circle around Jesus also succeeded in doing this [see Luke 9:49]. Yet it occurs as an exception, as a disaster that befell a few, one that manifested itself more frequently in Jesus' day as a reaction of the world of the devils against his incarnation. But instead of acknowledging this phenomenon as an exception, this possession has been generalized and, following the rabbinic example, the thesis came to be accepted that everyone born of a woman began by being subject to the rule of the evil spirits, and therefore the evil spirit had to be exorcised from every human being who came to Jesus, or from each infant that was presented for baptism. This exorcism then could be performed by two kinds of people: either by exceptional people who had received an extraordinary gift for doing this, or by office holders who did this by authority of their office. This expelling of the evil spirit was called *exorcism*; the person performing the exorcism was the *exorcist*; and among these a distinction was made between "exorcists by grace," who had been raised up by Jesus for this purpose, and "exorcists by virtue of their office," who had been appointed by the church or who performed this ministry as part of their regular office. At infant baptism this

§ 2

took place through the so-called exsufflation and insufflation. The exsufflation served to cause the evil spirit to leave the person being baptized, and the insufflation served to have the Spirit of grace from the treasury of church enter him. The rule for this was presented to the catechumens literally as follows: *The priest shall blow three times in the face of the one being received and say once: "Go out from him, evil spirit, and make room for the Holy Spirit, the Comforter." Then he will blow crosswise upon his face and say, "Receive the good Spirit through this insufflation and through God's blessing. Peace be with you."*[1]

Two separate things were therefore being confused in this exorcism. It was patterned after the casting out of demons that is reported in the Gospels as something that took place in the case of a few but certainly not all people. However, it was applied to the severing of the tie that exists between Satan and *all* non-sanctified people. As a consequence of the sin to which Satan tempted Adam, Adam was a slave of sin and thus an instrument of Satan. All his descendants share with him in that fate. Christ, who had come to destroy the works of the devil, broke these bonds. And thus it had to be made clearly manifest that a transition from the kingdom of Satan into the kingdom of Jesus Christ was occurring at this point. And because the "evil spirit" rules in the former, and "the good Spirit" in the latter, exorcism was intended not only to depict this exchange of spirit and Spirit symbolically, but also to bring about this exchange of spirit and Spirit in actuality. In the church, as the mystical body, the good Spirit dwells. Therefore the good Spirit can be granted to the sinner only from that church. And the priest who baptizes is that church's lawful representative through whose act the good Spirit passes from that church into the one being baptized.

Linked with this as well is the distinction between consecrated and unconsecrated soil. The influence of Satan extended not only to the person of Adam and his descendants, but also to his body and his world. The curse rests on this earth since the fall, and consequently this material world also lies in evil. The church is like an oasis in that barren wilderness. Where the church is, there is consecrated soil. Outside the church the soil is ordinary. This gives rise to the necessity of consecrating the land where a church will be built. A cemetery must also be consecrated as well as everything to be used in the sacred liturgy. It even became such that things used in everyday

1. Here Kuyper relates a common liturgical formula, with antecedents in the patristic period.

life were purified through exorcism, including farmland and fruit standing in the fields. In various regions in Russia, the so-called Fruit Festival is celebrated, a day on which the priest pronounces the exorcism formula over the orchard.[2] Until that day no one dares eat of that fruit for fear of ingesting something of the evil spirit, but once that day has passed, all danger has vanished and the harvesting begins.

Here too we encounter a rather general view. It is judged that the world, as well as the persons and the things in it, lie under the power of the evil one; that the kingdom of Christ is inserted into this world as a separate creation; and that exorcism and consecration are the means to effect the transfer of a person and the transfer of soil from that evil world to the kingdom of Christ. Not—it must be understood clearly—that no deeper causes contributed at this point; but exorcism and consecration are nevertheless two indispensable acts to complete the transfer. It was not the Lutheran Church but the Reformed Church who from the very beginning took a principled position against this perspective. The question whether these exorcisms should be continued even became one of the characteristic points of difference between the Lutheran and the Reformed denominations. At the end of the sixteenth century in Germany, the continuation of exorcisms was even enforced through imprisonment, and as late as 1822 it was incorporated in the new Berlin court liturgy, although it must be said that also on this point, Germany is gradually beginning to acknowledge the better and clearer insight of the Reformed.[3] At the same time, the influence and aftereffects of these old German-Lutheran notions have still been so strong among the Ethical theologians that it is known that at the inauguration of a certain school, those in attendance went from room to room to kneel in each room and to exorcise the presence of evil from each room § 3

2. See *The Protestant Theological and Ecclesiastical Encyclopedia: A Condensed Translation of Herzog's Real Encyclopedia*, vol. 2, trans. by J. H. A. Bomberger (Philadelphia: Lindsay & Blakiston, 1860), 255, s.v. "Exorcism": "In Russia there is a special festival for the consecration of fruits by the priest, and before that day no one durst eat; after, he may devour ripe and unripe indiscriminately, and if any one becomes dead-drunk he has the consolation of knowing that it was not caused by demoniacal influences."

3. In *The Lutheran Cyclopedia*, ed. Henry Eyster Jacobs and John A. W. Haas (New York: Charles Scribner's Sons, 1899), s.v. "exorcism" it is noted that "it is remarkable that the *Berlin Court and Cathedral Agenda of 1822* revived [the practice of exorcism], in the words, 'Let the spirit of the unclean give place to the Holy Ghost;' but its example has been followed by none."

though prayer. This is how long and how widely such a notion can continue to have an effect.

Even though the Reformed resist all consecration and exorcism, even to the extent that they do not want to speak at all of the consecration of a church, let no one suppose that the Reformed would therefore deny the spiritual truth that underlies these actions. Granted, in our day many are alienated from this deeper view, but this was certainly not the case in the days of our forefathers; a careful reading of the beautiful first question and answer of the Heidelberg Catechism will provide concrete proof of this. This question deals with the state of the Christian both in life and in death, and the answer includes reference to the entire human personality, body and soul. And what does the catechism affirm concerning the full human personality thus understood? First, that the sinner was under the power of the devil, so that Satan was his master and he was Satan's slave and servant, and his whole existence was confined within Satan's bonds. Second, that the sinner who has become a Christian was released from this dominion [of Satan] and has been redeemed from every power of Satan. Third, that he now stands under the power of King Jesus and has become his servant or slave. And fourth, that this redemption from Satan's power has been accomplished, not by consecration or exorcism, but through Christ himself, and is confirmed by the Holy Spirit. There is therefore nothing superficial here. The power of Satan over the sinner is understood as a reality. He who commits sin is a servant of sin. He who would stand free in Christ must come out from under the power of Satan and transfer to the power of Christ. We are transferred from the domain of darkness to the kingdom of his beloved Son [Col 1:13]. A breach occurs—a break with the power of Satan in order to come under the power of Christ and to remain under it. But this transition—this transferring from one realm to another, from kingdom to kingdom, from power to power—is not brought about by the act of a human being, or by an act of the church, but by the work of grace that proceeds from God; even the sacrament of baptism can do nothing but affirm this act of Christ.

The fact that Christ and his disciples had cast out demons was therefore not denied but maintained: possession was something entirely different from the sinner's being under the curse. The latter was something that related to all human beings before their regeneration, whereas demon possession involved only a few individuals. This being under the curse referred to the indwelling of the evil one, while demon possession referred to the impact of the evil spirit in the soul. Consequently, a demon-possessed person could be delivered from an evil spirit without having any part in Christ, in such a way that he still remained in the kingdom of Satan. Conversely, the person redeemed from the curse and power of Satan became a free man in Christ and could no longer be robbed of the freedom of God's children.

The most important objection to this confession of the Reformed churches was derived from the Old Testament, of course, and the subject requires that we take a deliberate look at this objection. It cannot be denied that in the ministry of the tabernacle and the temple, practices were used that were similar to those still observed in the Roman Catholic, Greek Orthodox, and Lutheran Churches. What was said to Moses from the burning bush, "Take your sandals off your feet, for the place on which you are standing is holy ground" [Exod 3:5], was not fiction but reality. It was the presence of the Lord God who had established on this guilty earth a distinction between the world outside him and the world under him. And insofar as the Lord caused his presence to dwell in the tabernacle and later in the temple, the sites of the tabernacle and the temple were also holy ground, and all that was used in the ministry in that sacred location was consecrated to him and was in an exceptional sense *holy*. Indeed, to an extent the shadow of the Lord's presence stretched over the whole camp in the wilderness, and in Palestine over the entire land and its people so that—albeit to a lesser degree—the whole camp and the whole land of Canaan were considered one holy area, distinct from the unholy terrain of the wilderness and the unholy territory of the Gentiles. To the extent that uncleanness came forth from human life and thus entered the holy land, this uncleanness had to be removed from the midst of the people. Especially death, and in equal measure whatever had to do with our sinful birth, caused this uncleanness to enter the land; hence the many laws given to Israel to restore the Levitical purity after all kinds of contamination by a corpse, by carrion, through birth, and through what related to sexual life. Already long before John the Baptist came on the scene, proselyte baptism had introduced the rule that anyone from the Gentiles who joined Israel had to immerse himself in the baptismal water in order to rise from the water, cleansed thanks to that baptism of any Gentile taint in Israel. § 4

Taking this as the starting point and in view of this example, people have wondered whether we must not maintain similar washings and cleansings in the New Testament era. Starting with baptism, this notion of cleansing or consecration through this sacrament was transferred to the whole sacred liturgy, even to the extent that before entering the house of prayer, people sprinkle themselves with holy water, as if to keep from bringing into the Lord's house the defilement, coming from the world, that always clings to us. Through long disuse we are now no longer accustomed to any such practices. In spite of that, we can still explain very well how, in the absence of deeper reflection, the copying and following of those God-given ordinances in the Old Testament imperceptibly gained ground not only among the Jewish Christians in the first century, but also later among those who read the Old Testament.

§ 5 Everything depends here on the central question: How are such actions understood: as instrumental or as symbolic? Or to put it in our own words: do we think that such actions make things clean and holy, or that they merely foreshadow and symbolize cleanness? Our answer to this question, together with the Apostle Paul, is that all such actions were not real, did not actually make holy, but only depicted cleanness and holiness. "Priests who offer gifts according to the law … serve a copy and shadow of the heavenly things" (Heb 8:4–5).[4] Even the distinction between clean and unclean things with respect to food or drink or special days was a shadow of things to come, and the body—the *reality* of these things—is only *in Christ* (see Col 2:16–17). On this basis we understand the purity laws in Israel, in their broadest sense, to have been shadow-like ceremonies that did not produce the reality but merely depicted and portrayed it. It was not a distributing of grace but, if we may put it so, a prophetic object lesson given by God to Israel. True, this does not deny that the many washings and cleansings also had the result that they promoted a certain material cleanliness, but we consider this to be an incidental consequence, not the goal for which they were instituted. Purity and cleanliness, if you will, of body and clothing and household goods certainly improved with prosperity, but this is not why these laws were instituted insofar as they pointed to the sacred.

This is sensed best when it comes to circumcision. In the judgment of physicians, this promotes cleanliness in eastern countries in more than one respect, and has therefore been adopted by other nations as well, and even today is in use among all Muslims. But no one would claim that this was the purpose behind God's decreeing it to be the seal of the covenant.

4. Kuyper assumes Pauline authorship of the epistle to the Hebrews, a view with precedent in the Reformed tradition. See, for instance, the Belgic Confession (1561), art. 4, which includes Hebrews among "the fourteen epistles of the Apostle Paul."

Today we still notice how the Jews who live among us lag by nature behind the Dutch nation in neatness and hygiene. When we enter a home in the slum in the Jewish district, we sense immediately that here not the same habits are followed when it comes to neatness and hygiene as among us.[5] This must have been even more obvious in the warmer country where they lived. Undoubtedly the purification laws and the many ablutions that the law prescribed also had a social significance among such a people. The epidemic skin diseases that were so common among the surrounding nations occurred less frequently in Israel, and stringent rules had been instituted especially against lepers; these facts must most definitely be explained from the additional purpose of the law to promote cleanness and neatness of the body, of clothing, and of the home. But even if we concede this without reservation, it is nevertheless clear that the *religious* meaning of these purification laws, in contrast to their social purpose, could not be *real*. Levitical purity was not spiritual purity. A less-than-neat Jew in Jerusalem could be more devout and God-fearing than a worldly, extremely neat lady of Jerusalem.

These symbolic, foreshadowing practices that constituted these conse- § 6
crations and ablutions in the Old Testament were furthermore no less prophetic in nature. We must pay attention to this. A symbol can have three kinds of meaning. It can be prophetic, explanatory, or commemorative, depending on whether it looks to the future, the present, or the past. When in the marriage ceremony the bride and groom give one another before God the right hand of fidelity, it is an explanatory symbol because it serves to confirm the mutual declaration that they take one another as husband and wife. Thus also the handshake closing a sale, and so forth. Wearing the ring of a deceased father or mother throughout life intends to perpetuate thereby the memory of father and mother. Such a symbol is therefore commemorative in nature, just like the stones that were erected in all kinds of

5. Here Kuyper compares Jews in the slums with the Dutch in society at large. The statement could equally be reversed: the Dutch in the slums lag behind in hygiene by the Jews outside the slums. See Auke van der Woud, *Koninkrijk vol sloppen: achterbuurten en vuil in de negentiende eeuw* (Amsterdam: Prometheus, 2010), which shows on the basis of detailed documentation that in the latter half of the nineteenth century the conditions in the slums were deplorable and filthy, primarily due to urbanization and overcrowding. This had nothing to do with ethnicity except that perhaps the Jews were proportionally overrepresented in the slums because they had in the past been barred from many occupations.

locations in Israel were symbols of remembrance. The manna in the ark and Aaron's staff that blossomed had a similar meaning [see Exod 16:33–34; Heb 9:4].

On the other hand, the symbolic ministry of the offerings and all the solemnities that went with it generally had a prophetic character, according to the testimony of the Apostle Paul. They were shadows, not of things present, nor of things past, but of things to come. They foreshadowed what would come in Christ. All prophetic symbols disappear when that which the symbols prophesied appears. A railway crossing arm raised while the train is a long distance away must be lowered when the train approaches. This then is also the great truth Paul defended so emphatically over against the Jewish Christians. All these symbols are now antiquated and obsolete and near disappearing. They no longer have any point. And wanting to maintain them anyway would in fact be a denial that their realization has come in Christ.

From this it follows that in the church of Christ, we neither can nor may maintain these symbolic actions. Those symbols were shadows of things to come; the substance—that is, the reality—of these things has come in Christ. Thus the symbols fall away. The only remaining question would be whether, now that the prophetic symbols have fallen away, an entirely different set of explanatory symbols could be introduced in the church of Christ. In itself there would be no objection to this. Baptism and the Lord's Supper are in part symbolic signs instituted by Christ himself. It would therefore in principle not be impermissible to give an illustrative expression to other ecclesiastical actions if people felt an urge and a need to do so. Folding hands and closing eyes for prayer is already such a symbolic action. And this system could certainly be expanded still further. Let us simply observe that the symbol merely supports the spiritual act, and therefore the spiritual act stands on a higher plane if it rejects this assistance. People in southern regions will feel a greater need for such symbols than people who live in cold regions. But the introduction of too many explanatory symbols was especially checked by the fear that they then would be copied after the Old Testament, thus giving the impression that the ministry of shadows was still being maintained, as if this whole ministry of shadows had not been done away with in Christ's sacrifice when the curtain of the temple was torn in two.

CHAPTER TEN

THE UNBRIDLED OPERATION OF THE CURSE

Cursed is the ground because of you.

GENESIS 3:17

Those who, during the first half of the sixteenth century, went along with the religious movement of the time had thus been brought up with notions that drew a dividing line through life, a boundary that separated a holy realm from an unholy realm. By nature, the whole earth with its earthly life was unholy. Only the church of Christ through its presence constituted a holy oasis in this wilderness, one that expanded this holy, sacred circle through consecration and the shedding abroad of grace. There were differences in this holy realm because of degrees in holiness. The priestly life stood above the life of the common layperson, and among those laypersons the "*bon catholique*" [good Catholic] stood above the mere followers. The monastic life was considered especially holy, and at the pinnacle of holiness stood those who were later canonized and thus taken up into the order of the saints. But apart from these differences, the entire realm of the church, that is, all those among the people who had been baptized and everything in § 1 the material area that had been consecrated—stood with a character of its own over against what was merely of the world. According to the notions of the time, even those who had received nothing but a heretical baptism, though they had not yet received grace, had at least received the sanctified character; with this they had become suited for saturation with grace later. Starting from the fact that original sin had desecrated our human race and the curse had defiled the material world, people maintained the conviction that only the church could check both the defilement and the curse, doing this for sanctification by means of emanating grace, and doing this for the removal of the curse by means of its consecrations.

Only when we clearly realize how most of those who later would go along with Anabaptism were raised with these notions, do we get a correct insight into Anabaptism. The Anabaptists also remained stuck in this two-sided or dualistic perspective and changed it only to the extent required by their altered view of the church. From the outset they harbored two kinds of impulses that, depending on their differing instincts, conducted a very different opposition to the church: they either protested against the church from a desire to be free of the clergy, or they separated from the church out of an aversion to its externalization of the sacred. The former were people who called for freedom above everything else. The others, quieter and more devout by nature, moved from the external to the spiritual. These latter, the most religious ones, are the ones who left their imprint on the Anabaptist movement. These spiritually inclined people—or rather, these one-sidedly spiritual or excessively spiritual individuals—confessed along with the church of that time that the human race was unholy through sin, and the earth was desecrated by the curse. Yet they claimed that the church had the power neither to sanctify human beings by imparting grace nor to remove the curse from earthly life by means of consecration. They were convinced that only a direct work on God's part could bring salvation at this point. So they placed the *immediate* working that went out from God through the Holy Spirit over against the *mediate* working that thus far had been thought to operate through the instrumentality of the church. It was God, and not the church, who directly seized the souls internally through the Holy Spirit, created new life in the individual, and shone new light within them. But only that new life and that new light constituted the oasis in the desert of this human life and in the wilderness of this earthly life.

Driven by the desire to envision a radical contrast between the natural-earthly life and the spiritual-heavenly life especially sharply,

Anabaptism came to abandon the notion of *re-creation* and replaced it with the notion of *new creation*. Christ could not have taken on the same flesh and blood as our flesh and blood, but created for himself in Mary's womb new flesh and blood that was similar to ours and thus conformed to our human nature; but it was nevertheless not taken from the human nature as once created. They also held that the human being conceived and born in sin was not re-created into a new human at regeneration, but that a new human being was created within that person through the Holy Spirit. In this way they denied any organic connection between the existing life of the world and the heavenly life of grace. Any bridge leading from the one to the other was demolished. The "worldly life" and the "life of grace" were placed opposite one another without any connection, as two entirely divergent spheres of human life. Hence their system of avoidance. Anyone who had received new life and new light no longer belonged in the old world, but had to flee and avoid it. Hence their system did not allow holding an office in government, because among the "saints" no government was needed. The government existed only to control public sin, and a child of God who undertook this kind of task was surrendering himself afresh to that life from which God had cut him off. For this reason the Anabaptist did not swear an oath, since among the saints the truth did not need further affirmation. Their yes was *yes*, their no, *no*. The oath served only to maintain the truth within the arena of the lie, and for that reason it might serve unregenerated persons but could not serve the children of God. They must be taken at their word. For them, swearing an oath would have been denying their holy and high character. Hence their unwillingness to bear arms in combat, because war also arose from sin. War was imaginable only in the sinful world. For the saints, peace on earth had already been proclaimed in the fields of Bethlehem [see Luke 2:14]. Therefore, by girding themselves with the sword they would become entangled once again in conditions that were in conflict with their nature and character.

Even the later excesses that devolved into the most brazen antinomianism were related to this dualistic standpoint. Granted, a law was given on Sinai, but that law was fitted to unholy life in the world. In that unholy world the wild animal raged; that wild animal had to be tamed; the law was given to tame it. How then could this law still apply to God's free-born and liberated, holy children who lived only out of the Spirit? They no longer were in the wild nature in which they were born. They had put off that wild nature. The wild vine had become a noble grapevine. Who would lock up behind bars in an iron cage a hyena that had been changed into a gentle lamb—that was no longer a hyena at all, but rather a soft and gentle lamb? The bars would be suitable for a hyena but would be absurd in the case of a lamb. A ewe lamb behind locks and bars becomes ridiculous. In the same way, the law no longer applied to them. More strongly still, by putting themselves under the law they would be as foolish as a lamb that would crawl back into a cage with bars. The lamb does not belong in that cage but must graze in the open meadow. Or if you prefer a human image, say that the madman must certainly be rendered harmless, if need be under lock and key and in the straitjacket; but we must realize with equal clarity that the madman who has totally recovered and has come to be fully in his right mind would dishonor himself if he voluntarily crept back behind lock and key. And yet, for human beings, that lock and key is the law of Sinai.

In this way, in the overstraining of his one-sided spiritual notion, the Anabaptist came to cast off the law, began to live deliberately outside that law, and on that basis abrogated property and marriage, and replaced it with communal property, including women. Even the nudists in Amsterdam emerged from the same principle.[1] In paradise, before sin, neither Adam nor Eve wore clothing to cover their shame. But after they fell, they discovered that they were naked and grabbed a covering of leaves. If a child of God is like Adam before the fall, then it follows that he also does not know shame, that clothing does not befit his spiritual state, and that nudity is obviously required of God's saints. It is therefore not only under John of Leiden in Münster[2] and in the case of the nudity in Amsterdam that such horrific thoughts arose and were implemented. Throughout history we repeatedly witness the rise of sects that end up committing such excesses. Even in the previous century groups of men and women were known in the Netherlands, in South Africa, and in Brazil who, not on the street (since the police prevented this) but at their communal gatherings, let the clothes fall from their bodies and made a mockery of all God's laws.

---

1. In the early years of the Reformation a group of radicals ran naked through the streets of Amsterdam proclaiming God's judgment.
2. John of Leiden (1509–36) was an Anabaptist leader who along with Jan Matthys expelled Catholics from Münster in 1533 in an attempt to establish an Anabaptist theocracy. During the subsequent siege by Catholic forces, van Leiden instituted polygamy and took sixteen wives. In 1535 starving Münster residents opened the gates and Catholics retook the city, executing van Leiden in 1536.

Of course, their view of the church was also related to this. Certainly there was a church, but only a mystical one, the hidden body of Christ. It was a misunderstanding of the spiritual nature of this body of Christ to make any attempt, either in this depraved world or in the visible shape of her life, to bring that body of Christ to visible manifestation. There *was* no visible church, or rather, the church was not visible to the physical sense of sight. Only the spiritual eye saw it. The only thing one could have on earth, therefore, were groups, assemblies, of regenerated individuals who then admitted newly regenerated individuals and examined them spiritually. There could therefore be no leadership office among them. Study was unnecessary, because it was worldly. Whoever read God's Word, and had the Spirit, saw and understood the meaning of the Word by the higher light. In fact, even that Word was ultimately dispensable. It was a ladder for climbing to the pinnacle of the temple, but once there, a person lived only by the higher light. In their meetings or assemblies, therefore, only he who was prompted by the Spirit—and he alone—must speak. § 3

They also wanted baptism, but then only as a kind of proselyte baptism—that is, as a sign that a person had come over from the evil world into the holy company. Hence they considered baptism as nothing, and infant baptism especially had to be combated as an evil. They could not acknowledge the baptism administered in the established church, since acknowledging it would imply the recognition of that church itself, and that church could not be acknowledged without surrendering one's entire confession of a company of saints gathered by God. Only the saints could evaluate whether someone was born again, and only the saints could then administer baptism to the regenerated. Their entire lifeview, therefore, really did find expression in *rebaptism* or *anabaptism*. They did not teach that one was allowed to or even could be baptized twice. That would have been an illogical thesis from their perspective. They rather intended to say that neither the ecclesiastical baptism nor infant baptism was or could be true baptism. They therefore were not allowed to honor these as baptism; the individual thus baptized was still unholy. Only through the baptism of the saints could they take a person into the assembly of the saints.

In this way it is clear how the entire Anabaptist system can be understood through the adoption of the basic position of the Roman Catholic Church of that time concerning the relationship between the natural and the spiritual. The only change they made was that as instrument of grace, the church is replaced by the assembly of the saints as those newly created § 4 and enlightened by God himself. The Anabaptists, and even Menno Simons, did not realize this and acted as if they were arguing merely on the basis of holy Scripture and the spiritual experience of life.[3] But this was self-deception. All interpretation of Scripture requires an *analogia fidei*—that is, the norm of the confession of faith, or as we would say today, a confession of the foundational notions, the principles and dogmas that rule the whole of our life- and worldview. The Anabaptists had not derived their dogma from Scripture when it came to the relationship between natural life and spiritual life; rather, they had found this in the old church and brought it into the assembly of the saints. Their appeal to Scripture was therefore nothing but pretense and self-deception. Hence they continually appealed to one series of statements from Scripture while overlooking and silencing the other more foundational series that stood over against it.

Among Dutch Christians, Guido de Brès as well as à Lasco and Micron, along with so many other scholars, have with infinite patience taken the trouble to combat their false doctrine concerning the incarnation of the Word, but none of them has made the least headway.[4] This is not because the Anabaptists were dishonest people, but because the foundational theses they had taken over from the Roman Catholic Church preceded their searching of Scripture and could not be verified by Scripture. This foundational thesis about the relationship between nature and grace found a corrective in the Roman Catholic understanding of the church. But when it was transferred into Anabaptist circles, this corrective was lost, and the result was not gain, but loss—not, of course, where it concerned the personal life of the earnest and devout Anabaptists or Mennonites, but rather as it concerned the influence on confession, ecclesiastical structure, and civic life. Contemporary Anabaptists in our country, who do not speak of their church but of the "Mennonite Association,"[5] of course no longer understand anything of the original contrast under which they emerged,

3. Menno Simons (1496–1561) was a significant leader among Anabaptists and the forebear of Mennonites.
4. Guido de Brès (1522–67) was a native of the Low Countries who studied in Geneva under John Calvin and Theodore Beza and was the author of the Belgic Confession; Johannes à Lasco (1499–1560) was a Polish Reformer who exercised great influence on the Netherlands; Marten Micron (1523–1559) was a native of Ghent and a collaborator with à Lasco.
5. The *Algemene Doopsgezinde Sociëteit* had been formed in 1811.

but their history shows how they have been eminently capable of creating room for themselves in commerce and industry, and thus have acquired a rather powerful financial influence, while at the same time their confessional position has gradually been lost altogether, and their association as such may be said to have been lost entirely to modernism. It even has come to the point that the more devout elements no longer could feel at home and have sought out other fellowships.

We must also draw attention here to a secondary point. In the so-called § 5
consecrating of unconsecrated ground, of a building, of water, of unction, of clothing, and so on, we hear the conviction that something unholy clings to matter; and that the word of the priest, a blowing with the lips, a sprinkling with holy water, and so forth, can have the power to exorcise the unholy. In our previous chapter we were reminded about how these kinds of consecrations are an imitation of what was decreed in Israel for the purpose of maintaining Levitical purity, and that they were already manifested in the days of the flood in the distinction between clean and unclean animals. At the same time we gave the reason why it had to be this way in Israel but why it is improper to transfer it to our circumstances. Why not accept *declaratory* symbols, as long as they do not lead to superstition? But we should not accept symbols with magical powers.

But now we must expound on this point at a more fundamental level. Holy Scripture speaks throughout of a blessing and a curse, two mystical concepts that can never be fully explained by our thinking intellect; yet the devout heart senses their reality with definite certainty. To put it succinctly, *blessing* is when we have our God with us, and the *curse* is when we have our God against us. Blessing leads to life, but a curse leads to death. This distinction is therefore based on the conviction that God sustains and works all things, and that we in turn and in our own way work within this work of God. Two cases are then conceivable. Either we seek and intend something with our work with which the work of God co-operates, and it therefore succeeds and leads to the final goal. Or we seek and intend something that is in conflict with what God is doing, so we are knocked back, hurt our hands, and in the end pursue not the life of glory but of death and misery. We take nourishment, but before we take it to us we pray for God's blessing upon it, intending thereby that the food may truly serve to strengthen our vitality, promote our well-being, and renew our energy to serve our God in the work he has entrusted to us. If that is indeed the effect of the food you ate, then God has blessed the food.

So it is with all things—your work, your endeavors, your choice of occupation. Not as though there could never be adversity mixed in as well. Steady prosperity is not in the least a sign of blessing. Then the brothel owner who later becomes rich would share excessively in that blessing. No, blessing extends over our life, our being, our comings and goings as a coherent whole. To be able to speak of blessing we must not look at the success of this or that individual matter. Rather, we must look over the totality of our life in its overall connectedness, even in connection with the life of our children in a later generation, and then ask whether our inner and outer life serve to bring us and our children personally closer to God and serve to give us assurance of eternal life—indeed, whether, while being under that grace, we lead a life that promotes the things of God and leads to the coming of his kingdom. When things are in accordance with the six petitions of the Lord's Prayer, there is blessing; when things go against those petitions, there is a curse.

§ 6 But in this context this important question arises: whether this principle relates only to the spiritual aspect of our existence or also to the physical, material, and external. And this is what the Anabaptist denies. No, he finds blessing and curse only in the spiritual sphere. Any connection and relationship between the spiritual and the physical, between the visible and invisible, between the internal and external, escapes him. He has neither eye nor ear for this. This is evident most clearly in the sacraments. In every sacrament there are two things: something that is believed and something that is seen, whether real or symbolic, and the mystical element consists precisely in the organic connection that is established between the two. As human beings we consist of soul and body, not tripartite but bipartite. We cannot deny that we must distinguish between soul and spirit, but not in the sense that they are two separate constituent parts of our human essence. There not three, but only two foundational elements: the material and the spiritual, and what is therefore quite absurd is not the distinction between the spiritual and the natural, but rather to conceive of body, soul, and spirit as three independent constituent parts of our human existence. But although we are body and soul, matter and spirit, these two are not placed disconnectedly side-by-side, but exist in an organic bond. Not through the nerves, since the nerves are matter, but at the point unknown to us where the nerves touch on the soul and the soul grasps the nerves. We must therefore not confuse body and soul, nor merge them together. The soul is not a sublimate of matter, nor the body a sediment of the soul in us. Even as the invisible stands over against the visible and is distinct from it, so too body and soul are two; yet they have been linked by God in our creation by a mystical bond—a bond that may dissolve temporarily in death, because death is a punishment for and consequence of sin—but a bond that God's omnipotence will restore in the future. And so it is also with the invisible and visible life of the world. There is a mysterious bond between the spiritual and the material nature as well.

Hence sin brings about not only the death of man but also the curse on the earth. God says it clearly to Adam: "Cursed is the ground because of you" [Gen 3:17]. Anabaptists understand this to mean that now a certain mysterious substance is spread over the earth and that the curse consists in that evil substance, so that by removing that evil substance the curse can also be removed from the earth. In reality, the curse, even sin, is not something independent, something tangible, or something material. The blessing is not a kind of dye that injects a good thing into creation, and the curse a kind of dye that spreads a sinister thing across creation. Both sin and curse are original creation forces that have been inverted. Through the curse, the earth brings forth thorns and thistles. A brand new creation of thorns and a new intentional creation of thistles did not occur, but the forces present in nature were diverted and transmuted so that what once was a good plant has now been transmuted into a thorn or thistle, just as Isaiah 55 teaches us that one day the thistle shall become a myrtle and the thorn a cypress [see Isa 55:13]. Although we must admit that the thorn and thistle are mentioned here more by way of illustration, and that this curse extends over all of life in nature, in no case may we say that the curse is a kind of unholy substance that adheres to things, something we can make disappear through a certain magical formula. The curse still rests on all of nature. Christ has not taken away the curse against nature. The only thing that may be confessed is that the curse can vary in degree, and that both common grace and particular grace contribute to the tempering of that curse.

CHAPTER ELEVEN

COMMON GRACE GROUNDED IN CREATION

This was to fulfill what was spoken by the prophet: "I will open my mouth in parables; I will utter what has been hidden since the foundation of the world."

MATTHEW 13:35

§1 Opposed to the more-or-less dualistic relationship between nature and grace as it was already fixed from the Roman Catholic side and thereafter mistakenly intensified by the Anabaptists, the Reformed confession maintains the conception of a correspondence between nature and grace that is grounded in creation itself, and thus also in the creation decree as such. As Matthew 13:35 tells us, the symbolism—that is, the symbolic correspondence between the life of nature from which Jesus derives his parables, and the mysteries of the kingdom that he conceals in those parables—arose *before the foundation of the world*. In the same way, according to our Reformed confession, there is also an original relationship and an original connection between the *nature* that God has assigned to us and the *grace* he has granted us. Even as our ear is designed for the world of sounds, and the world of sounds for our ear, so also do nature and grace fit together. And even though the quinine that must extinguish the fire of fever in our blood has been extracted from a tree and is administered to us externally, this medicine would bring us no benefit if there were no connection between the medicine and our nature, and between our nature and the medicine.[1] This principle governs our confession of humanity in the state of righteousness, a humanity in which we cannot presume a duality. Thus we deny that by nature humanity would have received a life corresponding only to the phenomena of this earthly existence, while in the meantime suitability for heavenly life would have been added to human nature as something higher. And this same principle governs our confession of common grace as well, in which we state that our human nature is not mutilated but corrupted; this means that the powers and capacities that originally indwelt human nature have not been taken away, but have been partly condemned to inaction and, as concerns their working, have been partly turned into their opposite. Hate is not a force other than love, but the same force turned into its opposite.

Meanwhile, these powers that have been turned into their opposite remain subject to God, even in their sinful state. He can keep the working of these powers in check, curb them, temper them, and arrest them, or he can allow them to continue functioning unhindered and unimpeded. The doctrine of common grace expresses that it has pleased God in general—that is, among humanity as a whole, and in each human being individually—not to allow the unholy working of these powers that have turned into their opposite to continue unhindered, but to temper and restrain them. And it is in this sense that we teach, on the one hand, the total corruption of our nature by sin; this means that in its corruption, our nature, if left to itself, would immediately surrender itself as prey to eternal death. And we teach, on the other hand, that in the actual life of humanity we have our eyes open to the continuing rich development of which humanity proved capable and to so many beautiful things in humanity that come to manifestation. The dogma of the corruption of our nature through sin tells us what would become of us if God let go of us; the dogma of common grace tells us what can and does still flourish in our human race because God preserves us.

We learn from holy Scripture that such a restraining and tempering of §2
the corruption that stirs within us has taken place. For if the holy apostle

1. The genus *Cinchona* refers to a group of flowering plants famed for their medicinal uses, including the production of quinine, which is a natural painkiller, antimalarial, and anti-inflammatory.

tells us that when the children of man abandoned him more and more, God "gave them up to a debased mind to do what ought not to be done" [Rom 1:28], then this clearly implies that originally this was *not* so, and that this giving up was preceded by a period in which God preserved the children of man in a stronger sense. We learn as well that in the case of nations and of groups where it did not come to such an outpouring of unrighteousness as Paul describes in Romans 1, this can be explained only by the fact that they were preserved by God. For us this doctrine of common grace also follows from the fact that what happened after the fall was not what had been announced before the fall as the necessary consequence of sin. The necessary consequence would have been that Adam and Eve would have perished body and soul in eternal death on the very day when they ate from the forbidden tree. Instead, we find that this consequence did not immediately take place in such dreadful finality, but was postponed until after they had departed from this life, in part even until after the day of judgment. By contrast, Adam and Eve's life on earth was lengthened to almost thirty generations, their vitality was maintained, shame about their sin gripped them instead of pride, and a rich human life developed from them throughout a series of centuries.

This cannot be explained either, except by the fact that God himself restrained the consequences and continuing effects of sin. Moreover, examples we have quoted, such as Abimelech, show how and in what way this restraining or hindering of sin takes place. What holy Scripture teaches us about the hardening [of the heart] can be explained only on the basis of the withdrawal of tempering and preserving grace. Likewise, the history of our human race shows clearly how, on the one hand, an evil, displaying a hellish and demonic character, rages in our human race, and how nevertheless within that same human race a human life flourishes that, even outside the realm of particular grace, often strikes us as ennobling. And finally, the testimony of our own heart tells us that an unholy fountain of sin still wells up within our hearts, and that it was only the preserving grace of our God that kept us from the gross erupting of that sin, even when we did not yet know our Savior. Scripture, history, and the experience of our own soul thus compel us to continue struggling to hold unswervingly to the dogma of common grace.

§3 For us, common grace is also directly related to our creation—namely, in the sense that our human nature must already have been designed at our creation to make such a working of common grace possible. It makes some sense that in popular understanding the acts of God in his *creation* and in his *grace* are two successive, separate acts. But if we keep to Scripture we must not for a moment put up with this notion, not even when it comes to particular grace. With holy Scripture before him no one can nor may affirm that God first created the world, then waited to see how it would go in that world, and only then, when he saw that it had fallen, thought of a plan, a decree of salvation to save the fallen world. According to holy Scripture, every plan, and every decree, and every intention of God *always began before the foundation of the world*. The decree of the Almighty stands from eternity before the fall and before the creation, not after the creation and after the fall. This is what the entire Christian church in all its diversity confesses. There may be disagreement as to whether in this decree the knowledge of the fall was foreseen or predetermined. But there is no difference of opinion about the fact that God's decree bears an eternal character and existed before creation, indeed, before the foundation of the world. Jesus himself declares that one day he will say to the saints, "Come, you who are blessed by my Father, inherit the kingdom prepared for you *from the foundation of the world*" [Matt 25:34]. From his glory as Mediator he declares in John 17:24 that they were given to him "*before the foundation of the world*." And the holy apostle also declares that "he chose us *before the foundation of the world*" (Eph 1:4). No divergent viewpoint is even thinkable here. Those who stand on the foundation of holy Scripture confess all this with us. And yet it is quite striking that, as often as it reveals this thought, holy Scripture does not speak of "before the *creation* of the world" but explicitly of "before the *foundation* of the world," since these two expressions absolutely do not state the same thing. *Creation* refers to the moment of coming into being; *foundation*, on the other hand, points to the thought that determined the plan of creation with the intent of implementing it.

Job 28 clearly expresses this distinction. In that well-known chapter, Job first speaks of the calling that man received from God to make manifest the hidden mysteries of God's creation. God enclosed gold and silver, all precious metals and precious stones, in the heart of the earth, and if there had been no human beings to bring these treasures to the surface, and to let the luster of the gold shine and to bring out the brilliance of the diamond by cutting it, then God would never have received the honor and praise for these, his more delicate creations in the mineral kingdom. But man, Job says, has been ordained so that there might be "a mine for silver, and a place for gold that they refine." The dust is removed from the ore, and the copper is smelted from the ore. Man brings up the sapphire, and climbs paths where no bird of prey reaches, in order to look for the crystal (vv. 1–11). In short, man has been designed and intended for digging up what God has hidden in the earth and for glorifying the greatness of God through doing this. But, Job continues under the influence of the Holy Spirit, "where shall wisdom be found? ... Man does not know its worth." And then he switches to the train of thought that we know in such a rich and powerful way from Proverbs 8, which unveils before our eyes the mysteries that lie behind the creation, when God "drew a circle on the face of the deep, when he made firm the skies above, when he established the fountains of the deep, when he assigned to the sea its limit." Thus Job declares how in and with all this, wisdom was the counselor of the Lord, and how in the very *foundation* of creation, eternal wisdom expresses itself; for all things, as the apostle affirms, are "through him" and "without him was not any thing made that was made" [John 1:3].

§4 The expression "before the foundation of the world," therefore, compels us to go behind the creation, back to this holy plan for creation, and if the mysteries of the kingdom are linked with "the foundation of the world" by Jesus himself in his parables, how then could we be free to close off the sphere of the *natural life* from the sphere of the *life of grace*, as if the one had nothing to do with the other? A master builder who puts up a monumental building or a tower whose top reaches into the clouds was involved in the plans, and when he made those plans, he had in mind that those who came after him might have to make repairs, and thus he allowed for the possibility of these repairs being successful by planning the original construction in such a way that the restorer would be able to access all parts and sections of palaces, cathedrals, or towers. An architect who simply put up walls and towers as it pleased him, but gave no thought to possible repairs, so that when problems came up, no one could get to the affected spot, would rightly be condemned as careless and thoughtless. And how could people make us believe that the Lord God, the Master Builder and Artist of his marvelous universe, had allowed the foundation and the creation of his world to take place thoughtlessly, without any provision in case restoration had to be done? This provision cannot be separated from the counsel of creation. And precisely because the thought of this provision is made manifest in the foundation and the creation itself, Scripture always points back behind the foundation of creation itself in relation to all this gracious provision.

It is not difficult to realize how we must understand these provisions. §5
Something can be created in such a way that it is amenable to restoration, but also in such a way that, should anything go wrong, restoration is out of the question. We know this distinction from everyday life. An elegant Chinese porcelain plate that slips out of our hands and breaks into three or four pieces, is simply gone. For no matter how much we clamp and glue, the fractures and cracks remain, and the broken plate can never be restored to its original flawlessness. You may be able to have a new copy made, but you cannot restore the broken plate to what it was before it broke. But it is entirely different when it comes to fusible metal. When treated with care, a gold chain that has broken can be restored in such a way that the break disappears altogether. Porcelain and metal are thus quite different. What is made of porcelain resists restoration; what is made of metal invites restoration. And this distinction between porcelain and metal does not come later, but is grounded in their respective creations, indeed, in the foundation of each one's nature. The nature of the fine clay from which porcelain is baked is different from the nature of fusible metals. The divergent natures of the two are not accidental, not without purpose, but have been thought out by God and willed in the foundation of things. The fact that a gold stylus, a gold chain, a gold cup can be restored is not something that is added to the nature of the gold, but it is an intrinsic property. The nature of gold is intended and designed for the possibility of restoration. Broken gold jewelry cannot restore itself. Only the hand of a skilled artisan that is added to the gold makes the restoration a fact. But this does not deny that the greatest artist would be powerless when faced with a damaged piece of gold jewelry if the nature of the gold had not been designed for the possibility of restoration.

If we transpose this to spiritual creatures, we immediately realize its significance for restoring fallen nature through grace. For from God's Word we know of two kinds of spiritual creatures, one of which turned out to be restorable after the fall, the other not. Angels and human beings stand in contrast to one another in precisely the same way as porcelain and gold. The angel is a holy being, but if he falls, it is impossible for him to get back up. Scripture nowhere indicates with even a single word that there would be a way of escape for the fallen angel. It says nothing about reconciliation for the sin of angels, nor about the rebirth of a dead angel. The angels either are good or they are evil. Those who are good have never been sinners; those who are evil can never become good. It is the same as with porcelain, which is high in value, but once it breaks, it is lost forever. So too the angels are not salvageable once the plate of their glory breaks. Man, by contrast, is like gold. He too can fall, and when fallen, he too would remain lying in his broken condition without a restoring hand from the outside. But with man it is fully possible that the break in his heart may be healed and that, through the conflagration of a purifying fire, what appeared lost may be restored to its former glory, indeed, to a higher splendor than originally. But from this it also follows, then, that this salvageability and restorability of man cannot have come to him from the outside after his fall, but that it must have been grounded in the foundation of his human nature itself. If he had received a spiritual nature like that of the angels, man's salvation would also have been unthinkable.

But now that the possibility of man's restoration and redemption has been proved, it also appears indirectly that it had already been taken into consideration in the foundation of his nature, that already in the ordination of the creation of man this factor of restorability was included. This means that common grace as well as particular grace find their point of contact in the nature as well as in the essence of man. Even as the broken piece of gold jewelry cannot restore itself, so of course the fallen human being cannot raise himself up and re-create himself. The saving hand of the artist is indispensable for both the broken gold and the fallen man, and therefore we confess that only the saving hand of God can raise him up from his fallen state. But God would not be able to do this if the capacities for this had not been created in human nature itself. God can save a fallen *human*, but not a fallen *angel*, and if our nature were the same as that of the angels, then God—and we say this with all due reverence—also would not be able to provide us with anything that would serve for our salvation.

This is not a restriction imposed on God from the outside, for it is God himself who has chosen it to be this way—namely, that human beings are created to be different from the angels. But then the possibility of our redemption and re-creation lies only in the fact that in his eternal plan God has conceived of our human nature differently, has willed it differently, and has ordained it differently. And for this reason it is and remains impermissible to sever the work of grace from the very creation of our nature itself. Both are fundamentally related. In our creation itself we are designed to have the possibility of being redeemed, re-created, and restored.

It is therefore not of secondary importance that Scripture again and again links election with the foundation of the world. For election, like predestination, would be totally inconceivable and impossible if the very creation of our nature had not opened up the possibility of the sanctification of the sinner.[2] Any salvation of the sinner is the result of two factors: first, what was put into our nature at the foundation of creation to make restoration possible; and second, what God did for his work of grace to make use of that disposition in our nature. This is exactly how it is with our medicines. The disposition in our nature certainly does not heal us; what heals is the medicine. But *that* the medicines have an effect on us and can heal us lies in the disposition of our nature. If this were not so, no medicine could benefit us. That it benefits us is only because our nature is designed for the medicine and the medicine for our nature. This can best be seen in the wretches who have ruined this disposition of their nature through a profoundly sinful life, so that in the end no medicine has any effect on them any longer, and every medicine refuses to do its work in their ruined nature.

If this is true of particular grace, and if the Reformed church therefore rightly confesses, in opposition to Lutheran excesses, that the sinner is *not* a "stock and block" but a redeemable human being—redeemable because in the foundation of his existence he has been designed for redeemability—the same applies to common grace, albeit in a modified manner.[3] Common grace does not find its image in the medicine of the physician, but in the §6

2. While *election* and *predestination* are sometimes used interchangeably, in a technical sense *predestination* is the broader term, inclusive of election and reprobation, while *election* is properly used in reference to those who are elected to glory. See the next chapter for Kuyper's more extended discussion of the two concepts and, in particular, his emphasis on the connection between the doctrines of creation and predestination.
3. The Formula of Concord (1577), a Lutheran confessional statement, reads, "But before man is illuminated, converted, reborn, renewed, and drawn by the Holy Spirit, he can do nothing in spiritual things of himself and by his own powers. In his own conversion or regeneration he can as little begin, effect, or cooperate in anything as a stone, a block, or a lump of clay could." See *The Book of Concord: The Confessions of the Evangelical Lutheran Church*, ed. Theodore G. Tappert (Philadelphia: Muhlenberg, 1959), 525–26. Similar phrases with somewhat different emphases are found in Reformed confessions, including the Canons of Dort (1618–19), Third and Fourth Heads of Doctrine, Art. 16, where it is stated that the "grace of regeneration does not treat men as senseless stocks and blocks, nor take away their will and its properties, or do violence thereto," and in the Second Helvetic Confession (1566), ch. 9, no. 2: "Secondly, we are to consider what man was after his fall. His understanding indeed was not taken from him, neither was he deprived of his will and altogether changed into a stone or stock."

marvelous art of the lion tamer, an art that finds a weaker manifestation in the talent with which the skilled rider controls his horse, as well as in the art with which man has tamed the originally savage nature in the wild animals that our pets once were. We encounter this restraining of the wild nature in animals in three degrees: (1) in the *domestication*, or making tame, of once-wild animals into pets, an effect that can best be observed by looking at a wild cat in the zoo and comparing it with our domestic cats; (2) in *training*—that is, the art of subjecting a strong animal not previously used to being dominated by our will; and (3) in the art of *taming*, which still remains a mystery and gives some individuals the ability to mesmerize carnivorous, wild animals.

We must look for the analogy to common grace in this broad realm of the threefold action exercised by humans upon animals. The sinner is a human being gone feral, and common grace is the holy art applied by God to subdue that feral nature in the sinner, whether in general, temporarily, or individually. For in the realm of common grace, there is *domestication*, as manifested in general among the civilized pagan nations. There is *training* as we encounter it in the preserving grace that we experience in our personal life. And there is a holy *taming* of our wickedness as is so often seen strikingly in the restraining of reprobates.

But in the case of animals, it is definitely not only the action of the one who tames that matters, but equally the disposition in the nature of the animal, the degree to which it belongs to his nature to *become tame*, to respond to *training* and *taming*. Not all animals can become pets, but only those animals that in their nature are suitable for this. Not all animals let themselves be trained, but only those animals to whose nature the possibility of being tamed was granted. And similarly not all animals can be tamed, or at least some animals only by way of exception. Ordinarily the lion and the bear can be tamed; the tiger and the hyena cannot. The brown bear can, the polar bear cannot. And thus it is with common grace when it comes to the restraining, tempering, taming of the feral character of fallen man. For then the question of whether taming will be possible also depends on the quite different question whether the capacity for this was present in the original nature—in other words, whether God originally created our human nature such that, after having become feral, it could be tamed again. There are persons in whom this is possible, others in whom it is impossible. There is here a boundary between possibility and impossibility, and it is this boundary that has been determined as far back as our creation.

CHAPTER TWELVE

COMMON GRACE AND PREDESTINATION

The times of ignorance God overlooked, but now he commands all people everywhere to repent.

ACTS 17:30

Common grace could not have an effect on our fallen nature if our original nature had not been designed for this possibility in creation. We cannot put nails into glass, but we can put them into wood. Thus we find that wood is designed in its nature to be nailed together again when it breaks; but glass does not have the nature required for such nailing. Therefore we must not present common grace as something that was thought up by God only after creation and not incorporated into God's plan until after the fall. Nor was common grace afterward applied to us externally and without any relationship to our nature, similar to how we can put a chain around a leaning tree to keep it from leaning even further. Common grace is not a bar in a cage that prevents the wild animal from hunting prey. It is not a chain put around the muzzle or neck of a brown bear to keep the angry animal from doing harm. Rather, common grace must be compared with a calming tonic that wards off and stems the overly strong stimuli of the nerves, and thereby prevents a flaring up of the blood erupting in anger and §1 rage. But this is precisely why here as well, as with all medicines, there is a necessary connection between the nature of the medicine and the nature of our nerves. For a substance that passes through our body without being absorbed in the blood has no effect.

It must therefore be strongly emphasized that both particular grace and common grace find the required disposition in our original human nature. And it is no counterargument that the working manifest in both these displays of grace is added to our nature from outside and cannot spring from our nature itself. Or do we not, in the physical realm, find it to be willed by God that man hungers and thirsts, and that the water to quench his thirst and the food to quiet his hunger do not spring from his nature but are added to his nature? Even though we do not overlook the difference between water and chamomile, or between bread and quinine, in that water and bread belong to man in his normal condition and chamomile and quinine only under abnormal circumstances, both correspond in this respect: (1) both water and bread as well as chamomile and quinine have been created by the same God who created our human body with its nature; (2) both come not from within man, but from outside him; and (3) both are suitable to be absorbed into our blood and through the blood to have an effect on our body. There are all kinds of liquids and substances where this is not the case, things that either bring us no benefit or that damage, poison, or ruin our body. Therefore, we cannot assume dualism here. There is most certainly a dualism between the nature of our human body and acetic or prussic acid, but not between our nature and the common foodstuffs or medicines we take.[1] Rather, nothing can be a foodstuff unless it is suited to our normal nature, and nothing can be a medicine unless it is suited to our sick nature. The high art of our physicians is to find what is suited to our sick nature.

§2 We do not deny that the Roman Catholic theologians as well as the serious thinkers among the Anabaptists have woven into their further elucidations much that softened the severity of the dualism they champion, but in our opinion, this dualism nevertheless continues to exercise its harmful influence. For one or the other must be true: either what comes to us from God after our creation, whether in the original or in the fallen state, is considered to correspond to our original nature, and then dualism must be overcome in predestination; or our human nature constitutes a complete

1. Acetic, or ethanoic, acid, is the primary component in vinegar. Prussic acid, or hydrogen cyanide, is highly poisonous and flammable.

whole, and first original righteousness and later saving grace were added. Then salvation and eternal bliss stand outside an organic relationship with our inner life, a bandage applied to the world, an ornament put around the neck. It must not be assumed that the proponents of the dualism between nature and grace intend this. On the contrary, we may assume that they too will not be at peace with a final result that lets grace float like a drop of oil on the surface of the waters of nature. They too will posit that it is ideal for the higher life of grace to become our own life. But to make this ideal possible, they must confess with us that our nature was designed for that higher grace—or, if you will, that our original nature contains the capacities and specifications that enable it to absorb this higher life of grace, these higher spiritual workings.

In this context we therefore consider it a definite error that in the doc- §3
trine of foreordination or predestination, the emphasis has until now fallen too one-sidedly on particular grace, and that common grace has not been included as well in predestination. We must go still further to raise the question whether our Reformed dogmatics is not also, to some extent, contrary to holy Scripture: it has almost exclusively viewed predestination as a decree of God concerning the eternal weal and woe of his rational creatures.

This fact cannot be denied.

No matter which of the larger works on "systematic theology" from the Reformed perspective we open, we always find the notion that predestination serves only to provide the background for election and reprobation. Therefore, the distinction between predestination and election is generally not very pronounced. And virtually all of those authors who deal with both subjects separately end up in superfluous repetition. For the most part they discuss under both topics the same claims, the same objections, and the same conclusions. This could not be otherwise. As long as in our thinking we abandon the rest of God's creation and focus only on human beings and angels, and the only question we ask is what the final end of people and angels will be, then we will be moving in a separate sphere and letting go of the organic bond between the rational creature and God's creation as a whole. In this perspective the salvation of the elect then becomes the main issue. That is the goal on which everything is focused. And the whole work of grace appears as nothing but an aid that God uses to bring the elect to salvation.

In that line of thought, the fate of the lost is a side issue, insofar as nothing happens to them other than that the spiritual pestilence from which they suffer continues to work in them until eternal death. Nothing can be said about them other than that they are *not* saved, and for the rest they are brought up only as a reminder. The elect, by contrast, call for a broad undertaking on God's part. They are conceived in sin, and yet they are elect and thus must be led to glory. For this purpose, the power of grace that emanates from God will seek to put forth its highest effort. For this purpose, the Mediator is appointed, the Word becomes flesh, and the holy Passover Lamb is sacrificed on Golgotha; Immanuel rises on the third day; Christ ascends to heaven; the Holy Spirit is poured out; and Christ's church goes out into the world.

Thus everything that is expressed and revealed in holy Scripture as great and glorious appears as *means*, and the only *goal* that is targeted is concentrated in the salvation and glorification of the individuals elected by God. It is therefore *they* who stand in the foreground in the treatment of the doctrines of predestination and election. The final end of *their* existence is the pivot on which everything turns. And the impression is given that Christ and his mysteries had no other character than that of performing an emergency service so that the elect might receive their portion in the kingdom. This one-sided treatment in dogmatics then automatically results in an equally one-sided treatment of these mysteries in preaching. And it was no less understandable that wherever the official ministry taught in this way, the same detached, instrumental understanding of predestination and election found entrance in the congregation. This evil had an even more insidious effect in that the elect generally were not even viewed in their solidarity, as members of one body and together as bearers of the human race, but were rather viewed one by one, as separate individuals.

Thus in the end this twisting of one of the most profound truths has robbed the church of all comfort, undone every connection, ruined the common life of the church, promoted unhealthy mysticism, and not infrequently cultivated vainglory and pedantry among the few who dared call themselves elect. And this could not have been otherwise. The aggregate of God's truths is one, and his decree over his whole creation is one; all parts stand in an organic bond with each other, and each finds its ultimate goal in the self-glorification that Almighty God seeks in his work. But when we tear asunder what God has thus joined, and when we take a profound doctrine like that of predestination separately and on its own, and when we relate it only to the ultimate fate of rational persons, then our soul will injure itself on the fragments, and the blessing it contains will not accrue to us.

We do not say this with the intent of pushing humanity into the background in the doctrine of predestination, or of rebuking the authors of our Reformed dogmatics for beginning by putting humanity, and more specifically elect humanity, in the foreground. This is most definitely not the case. The elect will always have a place of honor in predestination. Our Reformers could not have begun except in the way they did. They adopted the doctrine in the main from the Roman Catholic Church and made only those changes that required the banishment of human free will, and did so again later also over against the Remonstrants. Every period cannot do everything at once, and it was entirely correct that in the days of the Reformation, theologians saved their time and strength for elucidating those contrasts that were of primary importance in that period. Had they acted differently, they might have misjudged their calling for the time in which they lived. Therefore a rebuke is in order only for the fact that rather than further spinning the thread that was handed to them by the Reformers, the best Reformed theologians have become spiritually sluggish, and have placed their theological thinking in an idle mode. §4

For almost two centuries they have done almost nothing but copy what others had written, without even suspecting that so many other profound questions still lay behind what they so faithfully transmitted. Pick any handbook of that nature from the period after the Synod of Dort, and the author wrote (sometimes verbatim, mostly painstakingly and faithfully, always in his own way) about what his predecessor had in turn already taken over. There is no trace of development, of clarification of theological insight. Theology has come to a standstill. And thus it continues, until the times of relaxation set in, when semi-Remonstrant pursuits become acceptable again and later authors become intent on what is called sharpening the finer points.[2] Thus we can understand that, after having been mentioned very occasionally in connection with predestination, common grace soon gets entirely silenced in the treatment of that doctrine, so that even the phrase no longer appears. People sensed and knew, therefore, that a certain connection existed, but that connection, that link, was never mentioned again in connection with predestination. It was mentioned, for example, in the question as to whether or not the Noachian covenant belonged to the dispensation of particular grace too; and later also when combating

2. Kuyper apparently refers here to a renewal of Remonstrant thought that would reinvigorate Reformed theological reflection concerning predestination.

or defending so-called prevenient grace;[3] occasionally also in connection with the doctrine of the *external* covenant of grace. But no one discussed common grace as part of predestination itself.

§5 Yet it requires no profound contemplation to perceive immediately that common grace is totally indispensable for the construction of the doctrine of predestination. For even when taken in its most common formulation, predestination presupposes that the elect are conceived and born—and yet, without common grace, Adam and Eve would have had to die on the day they ate of the forbidden tree, so that none of the elect would have seen the light of life.

Predestination also presupposes that in elect individuals, before their regeneration and conversion, sin does not have its full effect—and yet, without common grace, sin would immediately have continued exerting its effect in each individual until the very end, even as in the world of angels, where no common grace restrains and each fallen angel is an absolute demon.

Predestination presupposes that human life takes shape under a certain constraint and order, so that as the church of God goes out into the world she may find a place to stand—and yet, without common grace, the general degradation would long ago have surpassed the degeneration found before the flood, so that any existence of God's church would have been impossible.

Predestination presupposes that there would be a centuries-long preparation of a nation from which Christ could be born—and yet, without common grace, a more tranquil development such as took place along the shores of the Mediterranean Sea, which alone made the existence of Israel possible, would simply have been unthinkable.

Predestination presupposes that when Christ has appeared and his church goes out into the world, everything in that world would have been prepared, arranged, and foreordained for receiving the gospel; the outcome has indeed taught exactly how the conditions in the Greek and Roman world of that time allowed the church to be accepted—and yet, without common

3. Prevenient grace refers to grace that must precede conversion. It is understood as necessary "since mankind is universally sinful and incapable of salvation or of any truly good work without the help of God. A fully monergistic theology, Augustinianism or Calvinism, must assume that this grace is irresistible, whereas a synergistic system, semi-Pelagianism or Arminianism, will hold prevenient grace to be resistible." See *DLGTT*, s.v., *gratia praeveniens*, p. 132.

grace, such a living environment in which the church of Christ could make its appearance simply could not have existed.

Indeed, to mention nothing else, in individual persons and in individual families, predestination ensures that everything that the elect of the Lord needs to be led to his Savior will be present—and yet, without common grace in the world of Christendom as well, that enlisting of the generations, as the covenant requires [see Deut 7:9], would be unthinkable.

All of this shows, therefore, that particular grace *presupposes* common grace, and that common grace is the broad pedestal on which particular grace is erected. Consider how in our Christian educational system both elements mesh like the teeth of two gears.

Nevertheless, common grace went virtually unmentioned in the doctrine §6
of predestination. Without linking it to the life of the world and of humanity, of the generations and of families, the decree was applied directly to the elect persons. Everything that lay between the decree and the individual was lost from view. This was a lacuna that necessarily obstructed any clearer insight into predestination. To name but one example, it became the reason why the doctrine of the covenant and the doctrine of predestination were regarded as the starting points of two conflicting themes. Meanwhile, the cause of this incompleteness lay deeper. In thinking about predestination, people jumped over creation and thereby failed to pay attention to the link between the grace of God that comes to us and the nature originally given to us by God. That link was indeed discussed in connection with the doctrine of sin, and in connection with the doctrine of regeneration and sanctification, but it was omitted when it came to the doctrine of predestination.

This is a common mistake of our entire dogmatic theology: it did not take theology as an organic unity but rather as a collection of disparate and independent doctrines. Thus there was a doctrine of God, and a doctrine of Christ, and a doctrine of holy Scripture, and a doctrine of the church, and so forth. But insufficient attention was paid to the mutual connection that tied these various doctrines together. A particular custom was handed down whereby theologians got used to classifying the immense series of various questions that arose for discussion in dogmatics into groups under these different headings. People knew under which doctrine each question had been treated up to this point, and they continued to follow that ancient practice. This was implemented to the extent that the doctrine of regeneration, for example, which certainly deserves a separate discussion, was discussed for a long time partly under *faith* and partly under *the church.*

Once such a doctrine or question came to be treated customarily under another dogma, then no one would think of taking this into consideration in connection with the doctrine of predestination, and thus virtually no attention was paid to the link between creation and re-creation when this doctrine was discussed.

§7 Creation was mentioned in connection with the doctrine of predestination from only one perspective—namely, when the question arose whether to take the side of the infralapsarians or the supralapsarians. How, it was asked, did God, when he made the decree of predestination, view the persons before him: as persons who had already been created and had fallen, or as persons who had as yet to be created? This is an extremely important question, but the way it was posed did not help either to advance discussion or to permit a resolution. Without a moment's hesitation, anyone looking at this issue from a human perspective had to view election, along with Walaeus, as election from among fallen sinners.[4] Conversely, anyone looking at it from God's perspective simply had to understand election, along with Gomarus, as a decree made before the foundation of the world that governed the creation ordinance as well.[5] All the disputes that have been waged between the parties have not brought the church one step further, for the simple reason that the parties begin from opposite starting points. One party stood squarely on the flat plains below, while the other viewed the dispute from the mountaintop, and for that reason they could not understand each other. It is therefore absurd to identify a theologian in our day as a "supralapsarian," or to identify oneself as an "infralapsarian" in opposition. This is so unthinkable simply because this profound issue has acquired an entirely different form in our century. Those in our country, and in America, who have opposed the author of the present work as if he were reviving the reasoning of Gomarus, have shown that they have understood neither the state of the question nor the intent of the author. For there has been no other intention than to show that those who think that Walaeus had avoided the reef they were in danger of hitting are mistaken, and conversely, to show that Gomarus's system was pointing, as if with his forefinger, to a matter of very serious importance that should not be

4. Antonius Walaeus (1573–1639) was a Dutch Reformed pastor and theologian who was among the contributors to the Leiden *Synopsis purioris theologiae* (1625).

5. Franciscus Gomarus (1563–1641) was a Dutch Reformed pastor and theologian at Leiden University and a noted opponent of Jacobus Arminius (1560–1609).

neglected. That importance lay in the fact that the connection between predestination and the decree of creation must not be misunderstood.

Here we mention only two of the many points that must be considered. In the first place, we must point to the fact that the covenant promise to "you and your offspring" [see Gen 9:9; Acts 2:39] does not permit us to lose sight of the *creation ordinance of the birth of children* in relation to election. For predestination entails determining from which father and mother and in what environment the elect will see the light of life, even as God spoke to Jeremiah, "Before I formed you in the womb I knew you" (1:5). If the birth of each of us is connected with the work of creation, and with the ordinances that govern and maintain creation, then it is obvious that the decree of creation and the decree of election are inseparable. This is in the first place.

Second, not all people are identical. There are kinds of people, types with different natures, people with different aptitudes and very diverse talents; people are also classified in terms of temperament. Of course, it is absolutely not an indifferent matter for eternal glory whether the assembly of the perfectly righteous will be a gathering in which *all* these varieties and kinds of talents and temperaments find their place, so that the full and rich life of humanity can shine gloriously, or whether that assembly will include all those who belong to only one type or two types, to the exclusion of all others. In the latter case, glorified humanity would be a mutilated humanity, and the larger part of God's creation in our human race would be lost forever. If the latter is impossible, and we must therefore assume the former, then it follows that predestination enjoys a most intimate connection with creation, and therefore in the doctrine of the decrees, justice must be done to the connection between the decree of creation and the decree of predestination.

CHAPTER THIRTEEN

PREDESTINATION IN CONNECTION WITH "ALL THINGS"

A plan for the fullness of time, to unite all things in him, things in heaven and things on earth.

EPHESIANS 1:10

§1 Common grace, no matter how fervently championed, gets lost again as long as we fail to include it in predestination or, if you will, in the eternal decree. Only what has its roots in predestination can find its rightful place in the dogma of the church and in theologians' study. Common grace, after having been confessed so decidedly by Calvin and having always been appreciated in its import from the Reformed side, nevertheless has come to be neglected almost entirely both in the Reformed confessions and in Reformed dogmatics; this sad fact must be attributed in no small measure to the exclusion of this doctrine from predestination. Virtually the only thing that was seen in predestination was particular grace that concerned the elect and the lost, and consequently common grace wandered outside the gate, unable to find a place of its own. If this is to change, and if in the future development of our theology the full weight of common grace is to be placed in the scales, then it is urgently necessary to correct this indisputable error at a foundational level. But this cannot very well be done without first presenting a more general discussion of the nature of predestination to the extent that it also governs the view of common grace.

When we carefully examine the many expositions of the doctrine of predestination in the writings that have come down to us from the days of our forefathers, we cannot come to any other conclusion than that predestination was viewed at that time only as *the decree of God concerning the eternal fate of creatures gifted with consciousness*. It was expressed in this way so as to also include the angels, but the angels were mentioned only very much in passing, and in the end the doctrine amounted almost exclusively to the decree of God concerning the eternal fate of each of us human beings individually. The angels could be discussed in this context only in passing because predestination encompassed the foreordination of the means of grace toward reconciling and sanctifying the sinner, and such means of grace were of course not decreed for the angels. A fallen angel is not saved, and the angels therefore could not be included here other than to the extent that they would exist in blessedness and be preserved from falling into sin, or conversely to the extent that they fell prey to doom and therefore were given over immediately and irrevocably to that doom. This might possibly still be called the *election* of the good angels and the *reprobation* of the bad ones, but predestination as such was not applicable to them except in a very indirect sense. Predestination thus remained in the main the decree of God concerning the eternal result in which the life of human beings, each individually, would end.

As proof that we are not overstating our case here, we present by way §2
of example what the well-known theologian Petrus van Mastricht wrote on this subject in his otherwise eminent *Dogmatics*.[1] He wrote,

> This predestination is nothing other than the decree of God concerning the revelation of his particular glory in the eternal condition of rational creatures. It is called a decree because it contains God's definite statements and feelings, to be executed

1. Petrus van Mastricht (1630–1706) was a German-Dutch theologian and professor of Hebrew and practical theology at Frankfurt and, later, Utrecht. His major work is the *Theoretico-Practica Theologia*, 2 vols. (Amsterdam: Henricus & Theodorus Boom, 1682–87). It appeared in Dutch as *Beschouwende en praktikale godgeleerdheit*, 4 vols. (Rotterdam: Hendrik van Pelt, 1749–53).

through a firm and certain policy and plan. Therefore, all that has been said in the preceding chapter concerning the decree of God in general recurs again to be applied to the foreordination. In addition to other things, we find in predestination the following in particular: In the first place, a conception of the end—the display or manifestation of God's glory, not of all God's glory in general but of his particular glory, namely, first of God's power and rule to make known his power (Rom 9:22 as well as verse 21). Or does not the potter have power over the clay? For [he does] to the extent that he can suit his creatures, no matter how free they are, to such uses as he himself wants to, and make from one and the same lump, purely as it pleases him, this one a vessel of wrath, that one a vessel for honor and glory. Second, the glory of his grace and mercy (Eph 1:6): to the praise of his glorious grace, insofar as he decided to restore the creature that deserved nothing but wrath and eternal damnation not only to eternal life but [to do this] even through the death of his own and only-begotten Son. Third, the glory of his avenging justice (Rom 9:22): he wants to prove his wrath, namely, in the just condemnation and damnation of the obstinate creature.

Second, there is in predestination a notion and conception of the means and, we might say, an understanding of them in relationship such that God should choose from these means the most appropriate ones. These means are, first, the gracious salvation, and a just condemnation or damnation; for God has determined to reveal in these the glory of his grace and righteousness. Second, the general creation of the whole human race; the establishment of the covenant of works with created humanity, the abandoning of that covenant, or allowing the fall, so that he might have an object in whose gracious salvation and just damnation he would reveal the glory of his mercy and of his wrath. All these things converge into one and the same means in the doctrine of predestination. Third, from all created human beings the election of particular persons in whom specifically God's mercy and wrath would become manifest.

Third, there is an intent and ordering of the means by which the gracious salvation of some and the just damnation

> of others would be brought about and provided: namely, the restoration of some through the Son as Mediator and the leaving and abandonment of others in their sins. We will speak more of this in the appropriate place.
>
> The object of predestination, through which this aspect of the doctrine also differs from the decree in general, is the rational creature: angels and humans, each in particular, namely, because they are subject to an eternal state, in which God's particular glory can and must be manifested and revealed through their salvation and damnation.[2]

This leaves nothing to be desired in clarity, and fully confirms what we maintained: predestination is viewed almost exclusively as a determination concerning the future of the individual human being.

Thus also à Marck: "This predestination is, in short, God's decision concerning the human beings who will over time fall in and through sin, to redeem them in part through Christ and faith in him and save them, to the honor of his grace and mercy; and to show his severe righteousness by leaving them in part in their misery and damning them."[3]

À Brakel writes, to mention only one more: "Predestination is an eternal, volitional, and immutable decree of God to create some men, concluding them in the state of sin, and bringing them unto salvation through Christ, to the glory of His sovereign grace. He simultaneously decreed to create other men, also concluding them in the state of sin, to damn them for their own sin, to the praise of His justice."[4]

This limiting of predestination to the election or reprobation of the individual human being did not begin with these Reformed theologians. §3
Rather, we may say that they did little else here than follow the approach

---

2. Mastricht, *Beschouwende en praktikale godgeleerdheit*, 1:691–92.
3. Johannes à Marck (1656–1731) was an influential Dutch Reformed theologian and church historian in Leiden, whose major works included the *Compendium theologiae Christianae didactico-elencticum* (Amsterdam: Wetstenios, 1722). Here Kuyper cites a Dutch edition of that work, *Het merch der christene got-geleertheit* (Rotterdam: Topijn, 1730), 170.
4. Wilhelmus à Brakel (1635–1711) was a Dutch Reformed pastor and theologian of the Dutch "Second" or "Further" Reformation (*Nadere Reformatie*). His major work cited here is *Logikē latreia, dat is Redelijke godsdienst*, vol. 1 (Leiden: D. Donner, 1893), 171; ET: *The Christian's Reasonable Service*, trans. Bartel Elshout, ed. Joel R. Beeke, vol. 1 (Grand Rapids: Reformation Heritage Books, 1992), 214.

they found ready-made in the old school of theology as it had received its imprint under the influence of the scholastics. We already find the same limiting of predestination to the predestination of the eternal fate of man and angel in Thomas Aquinas, although it must be conceded that Thomas still felt the connection between predestination and the providence of God more strongly than came to be the case later.[5] In general we must therefore never forget that our Reformers and the theologians who came after them did not want to create a new theology, but rather took over what had been taught up to that point in the schools, correcting only what they had come to see as error on the basis of the Reformation principle. In the early writings on dogmatic theology we can therefore distinguish two very different components. On the one hand, there are a number of sections that have been totally reworked and put together anew because they came into conflict with the very principle of the Reformation. But on the other hand, there are also a number of equally important topics that were not involved at that time in the conflict and consequently were adopted without criticism or correction from the books of the Roman Catholic scholastics. The following is a striking example: According to the doctrine of the Roman Catholic Church, regeneration in the sinner is brought about by baptism. Consequently, regeneration was discussed in times past exclusively under the doctrine of baptism or the doctrine of the church, wheres the doctrine of salvation was discussed exclusively under the chapters on *repentance* and *faith*. Our Reformed theologians, of course, could not adopt this view of regeneration. Regeneration was for them not a fruit of the action of the church in baptism, but the result of a direct working of the Holy Spirit in the soul of the sinner. What they should have done was to transfer regeneration to soteriology and discuss under that topic the matters of *regeneration* and *conversion* in turn. But this is not what they did. Accustomed to the old framework, they continued to discuss only *repentance* and *faith* under soteriology. It is due to this that the doctrine of regeneration in fact did not come to development and that the questions it involved were discussed instead under the *capacity for faith*.

Therefore it should not surprise us in the least that the doctrine of predestination continued to be treated in the old manner and in the traditional sequence, as focusing primarily on the salvation of the elect and the

5. See, for instance, Aquinas, *Summa Theologiæ* I-I, Q. 23.

damnation of the lost. A conflict about this profound doctrine (indeed, a great deal of conflict) erupted, of course, in the days of the Reformation too. But that conflict revolved almost exclusively around the independent character of predestination and its absoluteness. Conflict arose over the question of whether or not God the Lord in his decree of predestination had been dependent on something in man, so that God's decree had in fact been determined by a foreseen faith in man. And on the one hand, it was also maintained that the decree was *absolute*—that is, that it firmly determined the means as well as the complete outcome, down to the individual persons. Others maintained, on the other hand, that the decree did establish certain conditions and appointed certain means, but that the final outcome vis-à-vis the individual was *not* included in the decree. Our forefathers battled at that time on principle over these two points, with the Roman Catholic theologians on the one hand, and with the Remonstrants on the other. They insisted that a dependent and non-absolute decree of God was *not* a decree, and they consequently have elaborately worked out both these aspects of truth in their dogmatics, sometimes even three times in succession: first under *predestination*, then under *election*, and finally under *reprobation*. But precisely because all their attention was focused on the discussion of these two questions, they did not enter into a further elaboration of this doctrine. They had neither the time nor the strength to do so; all their efforts were required for banishing Arminianism.[6] And when at the Synod of Dort the victory over the Arminians had been won, a period of fatigue and slackening followed, in which little was done except simply copying the work of the men who had come before Dort.

There was also a second cause. For the church of God and for the individuals in the church, and thus also for preaching, it was precisely *this* aspect of predestination that not unnaturally worked itself into the foreground. The awakened soul looks first and foremost to his personal salvation, and he seeks as a matter of preference such preaching as gives him decisive answers and sheds light on that aspect concerning his personal §4

6. The term *Arminianism* derives from the Dutch theologian Jacobus Arminius (1560–1609) and refers to his understanding of the relationship between predestination, grace, and atonement in salvation. Among other things, Arminius "taught conditional predestination," and "his followers expressed their convictions in the famous five articles which they laid before the States as their justification. Called Remonstrants from these *Remonstrantiæ*, they always refused to be called Arminians." See "Arminius, Jacobus and Arminianism," in *NSHE* 1:297.

salvation. We must remember well that in the battle with the Remonstrants the church members themselves had participated in this spiritual struggle for years. In all kinds of circles this was a main topic of conversation, and every good Reformed Christian saw himself continually called upon to defend the truth of predestination in contrast to the deception of Arminianism. And because in the church this battle was almost always engaged in *personally*, the natural result was that predestination was spoken of almost exclusively in its application to the eternal fate of individuals. Thus it began and thus it has continued to be in the church, and we may safely say that the lack of the assurance of faith, and the fretting until death over one's eternal destiny that has to such a large degree broken the power of faith, was a direct result of this one-sided perspective on the matter.

And what finally must also be considered is that holy Scripture itself never gives us dogmatics, but rather always gives us the revelation concerning the truth in direct relationship to the conditions under which the prophets and apostles worked. As a result [we find] also in holy Scripture [that] far and away most places in which predestination is spoken of present it in a rather close connection with man. And because back then the custom of arguing on the basis of proof texts still held sway, it cannot be thought remarkable that eyes remained closed to the much further-reaching meaning of predestination. In God's decree man is indeed the highest creature, and this is what leads so easily to letting all of predestination revolve around man as the center.

§5 There was one point, however, on which our Reformed forefathers broke through this one-sided notion—namely, to the extent that, when questioned about the "highest end" of all things, they placed *Soli Deo gloria* unconditionally in the foreground, and so too with this doctrine, they never let the salvation of the elect take anything but second place.

They maintained this view in relation to predestination as well, and none of our forefathers has dealt with this topic without also stating firmly that God the Lord was seeking first and foremost his own honor in this decree of his. All the rest, including the salvation of the elect, was declared to be subordinate to that highest goal. It was a pity that they did state this forthrightly in the opening sentences but failed to do it justice in their further development. This can be explained primarily from the fact that, holding fast to the statements of the holy Apostle Paul in Romans 9:22–23, they were of the opinion that they had said everything when they pointed to the revelation of God's mercy and his severity as the goal of election and reprobation. The consequence of this has therefore been that under the doctrine of predestination they included Christ, his incarnation, his death, his resurrection, his ascension, and his sitting at the right hand of God, but presented them only as "ordained means of grace" for the realization of the salvation of the elect.[7]

It is against this one-sided and limited notion of the decree of predestination that we must lodge our protest, not least in the name of holy Scripture itself. For in this way we isolate humanity from the rest of creation. People set man apart and let the rest of creation go. In this manner the unity of God's creation, the coherence in his holy decree, is broken, and what God has united is torn asunder. The world is not merely a silver bowl on which golden apples have been placed for a moment, only to be removed later. Or, using a different image, the world is not a stage on which man appears temporarily, only to have the whole stage torn down later and after which only man is retained. The world God created, and the humanity he put into that world, constitute a single organic whole. God created "the heavens and the earth" [Gen 1:1], and these heavens and that earth together constitute the instrument of his glory. That earth and these heavens are not conceivable without humanity, and humanity is not conceivable without that earth and these heavens. Even as the eye alone reveals the radiance of the soul but is nevertheless one with the whole body, so too man, having been created in God's image, is the richest manifestation of God's creative omnipotence, but even so is not conceivable without that world, of which he is the member and priest. He is related to the animal kingdom, related to the plant kingdom, related to the mineral kingdom.

Heaven and earth are concentrated in man as in a single focal point. Granted, God created two separate things—first the universe, and then man in addition to and within that universe—but he nevertheless created that universe and man as a single whole. If we call that universe a mighty mystical body, then within that body man is the heart in which life beats, the mouth through which the universe breathes, the eye with which the universe sees. But no matter how high the central place may be that man occupies in the universe, we must neither separate man from that universe nor that universe from man. Man is not a creature in the universe akin to someone on a ship who steers toward the haven of eternal rest and says

7. See, for instance, Belgic Confession, Art. 21; Heidelberg Catechism, Lord's Day 12, Q&A 31.

farewell to the ship once he has arrived in that haven—that is, then turns his back on the universe and henceforth exist onlys spiritually with his God. On the contrary, heaven and earth have been created by God as a single mighty whole in order that in that whole, in that majestic, complete work of creation, the name of our God would be glorified for all eternity.

§6 It is in this sense, then, that the apostle reveals to us God's "plan for the fullness of time, to unite all things in him, things in heaven and things on earth" [Eph 1:10]. Earlier we have already explained at length that this "uniting all things" here means restoring "*in its organic unity* under one head." Implicit in these words, therefore, is the fact that earth and heaven constituted one organic whole at creation; that the two were dislodged from this organic unity; and that God's honor now depends on both of them once again shining in their organic unity as the one great, glorious creation. This then leads us to the entirely different notion that the goal of predestination to give God the certainty that nothing of the full self-glorification that he sought through and from his creation will elude him but will accrue to him undiminished and fully intact. This purpose of creation was in danger of being thwarted by Satan. And predestination then must be distinguished from the decree of creation by—and solely by—the fact that the decree of predestination appoints and determines the means that must lead with absolute certainty to the end that God, in spite of sin, will nevertheless at one point receive full self-glorification from his creation. The Christ has been appointed for this purpose, so that under this Christ as the new Head the pieces of heaven and earth that had been broken apart might be restored to one organic whole according to God's initial intent.

Thus the decree of predestination encompasses all of history, the entire course that earth and heaven will take, and is aimed toward ultimately giving God his glory from that whole creation and from that whole universe. And only when this is clearly understood and acknowledged without any reservation, is it also clear, second, how in this foreordained plan man had to be in the foreground. For even though he is only a piece, a part, a member, an instrument of this world, he is also its *main instrument*, and it is only through man that God can be given that glory on behalf of, and from, and through his whole creation. Man is the mouth, man is the heart, man is the living eye of the whole of creation, and therefore God could not receive glory from his creation if that mouth fell silent, that heart ceased to beat, and that eye grew dark. Therefore it must be certain that man is saved, that man will be restored to new life, and that one day man in his blessedness will sing praises to God. Precisely because predestination wants to ensure that God will receive his praise and honor *from his entire creation*, the certainty of man's salvation must also be fully incorporated in that predestination. And also because humanity in general does not mean anything as long there is no certainty about the question who these people will be, predestination cannot be complete except in *personal* predestination and thus also in *personal* reprobation. As our forefathers expressed this, *the King cannot be without subjects*.[8]

8. Belgic Confession, Art. 27: "The church has been from the beginning of the world, and will be to the end thereof; which is evident from this that Christ is an eternal King, which without subjects He cannot be."

CHAPTER FOURTEEN

THE CONNECTION BETWEEN PREDESTINATION AND CREATION

For from him and through him and to him are all things. To him be glory forever.

ROMANS 11:36

§1 Predestination thus points to the final result of *all things*, and not merely to the final fate of angels and humans. "All things" is even the fixed expression holy Scripture uses for this. We speak of "the universe." Our Dutch version does not know this word; it speaks only of "the world." But when holy Scripture wants to express even more clearly that it is referring not only to this earth with its atmosphere, but to the whole creation of God, it expresses this through the phrase *all things*. Thus it says of the creation: "*All things* were made through him, and without him was not any thing made that was made" [John 1:3]. And in the same way, including not only the *coming into being* but also the *existence* and the *purpose of its existence*, the apostle tells us that "from him and through him and to him are *all things*."

Only when we take "all things" together do we have the whole work of God before us. God did not create angels and humans and in addition all kinds of superfluous things. In God's creation nothing is secondary, nothing is superfluous, nothing can be dispensed with. To put it strongly, not a speck of dust too many has been created, not a drop of water beyond what was required, and thus there is among the thousands of stars not a single diamond in the Milky Way that could be missed. It is all one; it all constitutes a single whole; it all together makes up the great organic universe of the Lord our God—that is, the world in which he delights—better still, the appointed instrument of his glory.

"To the praise of his glorious grace" [Eph 1:6] did God call into being all things that were not. This is even repeated as many as three times in the hymn of predestination that Ephesians 1 leads us in singing. First in verse 6, then in verse 12, and finally in verse 14. Not our glory but the glory of our God is the highest goal. And the goal of the way of God is not merely that this glory *be*, but that this glory *be praised*. "To the *praise* of his glory." In Ephesians 1 the holy apostle does not limit this lofty goal to humanity but expands it to the whole of creation; this is evident not only from his statement that God will "unite *all things*" but also from what he adds in verse 11: "who works *all things* according to the counsel of his will." We can, we must, therefore not exclude from predestination the rest of creation outside of man. Nature and grace are two kingdoms, but under one King, and the rule of that King of kings extends over all that is "*on* the earth, *above* the earth in heaven, and *under* the earth" [see Phil 2:10; Rev 5:13]. Just read and reread it in the profound, all-encompassing passage of Colossians 1:16–20 that organically puts it all together: "For by him *all things* were created, in heaven and on earth, visible and invisible, whether thrones or dominions or rulers or authorities—*all things* were created through him and for him. And he is before *all things*, and in him *all things* hold together. And he is the head of the body, the church. He is the beginning, the firstborn from the dead, that in everything he might be preeminent. For in him *all the fullness* of God was pleased to dwell, and through him to reconcile to himself *all things*, whether on earth or in heaven, making peace by the blood of his cross."

Even the question that is being discussed so often in our day as well, whether the Christ would have come even if humanity had not fallen, loses its importance through this. For we must most certainly protest against the false doctrine, promulgated since the days of Origen, that holds that an incarnation of Christ would have occurred even if humanity had remained sinless.[1] The holy Scriptures know nothing of an incarnation of God in Christ *apart from* sin, and all of Scripture continually confesses that Christ has come to save sinners and to preserve a world created by God and still loved by him as the work of his hands. What the Ethical theologians in our day have championed and preached in this regard has been a result of pantheistic philosophy and must be rejected in the name of holy Scripture.[2]

But the notion that the incarnation of the Word was secondary and fortuitous must equally be rejected. It has not been uncertain or doubtful even for a moment whether Christ would come, and no one must say that it was in man's power to prevent the entire revelation of God's glory in Christ. God did not have two plans for the world, one in case man remained standing and the other for the possibility that he fell. God's counsel is from eternity, not conditional but firm in itself, and it is *that* counsel of God which *alone* exists and will exist for eternity.

There is one counsel, therefore, in which there is no other world than this world that fell into sin and is preserved by the love of God in Christ. The decree of *creation* and the decree of *predestination* are therefore not two decrees that stand side by side, connected but in essence separate. On the contrary, there is nothing but one single decree, and when we nevertheless speak of several decrees, it is only because we distinguish the rich contents of the eternal counsel in its parts, according to the need of our small and limited understanding. But in itself it is and remains one, and what we call predestination is in this decree only that part in which it was decided *that* and *in what manner* God the Lord achieves his one and eternal goal with his creation, in spite of sin. The fact that in this decree of predestination humanity stands in the foreground is only because in the origin of all things as well, humanity is the crown of the whole of God's creation. Humankind is a little lower than the angels in origin but destined to judge even the

1. Origen (184/185–253/254) was an Alexandrian exegete who exercised massive influence on the development of patristic theology.
2. Rooted in the theology of Friedrich Schleiermacher (1768–1834), the "Ethical" modern theologians prioritized the personal experience of faith over dogmatic concerns, particularly regarding the doctrine of election. J. H. Gunning (1829–1905), a Dutch Reformed minister, is an important example of this in Kuyper's context.

angels one day. [We are] the heart, the core, the apex of God's creation; its instrument, its priestess, its vicegerent under God. It is therefore Christ's place to appear before God as the Head of *that humanity*, it is his calling as Head of that humanity to subject *all things* to himself, and it will one day be the ultimate pinnacle of his eternal glory to hand over the kingdom to God and the Father, that God may be all in all.

If this is how we must view predestination, then we will also sense §2
immediately why we should not say that although some people will be saved from the masses, humanity [as such] will perish. This has been taught and is still often taught. There can be no objection to this perspective, and we fully endorse it, as long as what is intended is that "many are called but few are chosen" [Matt 22:14], and that being called applies to specific individuals known by name by God, and that all these—and these alone—will be saved. But if it is taken beyond this, to refer to a few who are taken as "a brand plucked from the fire" [Zech 3:2] and [to claim] that the human race as such is lost forever before God, then we must strenuously protest against this wrong notion.

In this context we must already warn against the expression "a brand plucked from the fire." A brand is a piece of wood that has been brought into the house from the field or from the woods for the purpose of maintaining a fire. Once such a brand has been placed on the fire, it is allowed to continue to burn and no one will pull it back out, simply because doing so would serve no purpose. The Dutch Bible therefore renders not "a brand" but "firewood" in Zechariah 3:2, which is apparently intended to mean that something had been put in the fire by mistake, already had caught fire, and would quickly have burned up had it not been *plucked* from the fire in time and thus been *preserved* from burning. But this is merely in passing. The main point here is that when we speak only of the salvation of a few individuals and view humanity, mankind, the human race, as something that passes and will be lost, then we show that we do not understand what *mankind* is and, in general, fail to understand what an *organism* is.

A few roots, a few branches, a few leaves, and a few flowers do not in any way make a plant. They constitute a plant only when they have all sprung together from one seed and are interconnected in a living being. The same is true of an animal. Some blood, muscle, nerves, bone, and skin together most certainly do not constitute an animal. On the contrary, when the butcher has displayed such an assortment of pieces in his shop, it is neither a cow nor a calf that hangs there; the cow and the calf are gone. The animal was present only as long as these pieces were joined together as members of one living body. It is absolutely not the same whether I say, "Here are some branches, some leaves, some flowers, but the tree is gone," or "There stands the tree that still has some branches, some flowers, but all the rest has been trimmed off." The owner of an orchard who is told that in his orchard there still lie a few branches heavy with apples, but the trees themselves have been cut down and are lost, would know immediately that he has lost his orchard and that those few branches with apples have barely any transient value for him. And thus we must not say that God the heavenly Gardener planted a trunk[3] of humanity and that this trunk is lost, but that this does not matter because a few branches of the tree have been spared. The trunk, the tree, the plant is something quite different from the branches, the leaves, and the fruit. The trunk surpasses in value all incidental branches by far. And when we know of the continued existence of a few flowers but consider the plant to be lost, we do have a bouquet, a spray, but we have lost the plant. We are impoverished. And thus we allow God to be impoverished through Satan if we posit that God, who created mankind as a trunk, as a race, as a single plant, as a mighty organic whole, allowed that humanity to be wrested away from him while he as God would be left with nothing but a few stems and a few cut flowers of the plant of his creation. True, this is not how it is intended, but it is implicit in it, and to speak in this way about the salvation of the few shows a lack of consideration.

A bouquet of elect persons will not one day spread its fragrance before God, but rather the *plant* of saved humanity itself will flower before God for all eternity. holy Scripture clearly shows this when it calls the elect the members of one organism and presents us all together as constituting one body, whose head is Christ; and also when it shows us elect humanity, not as a bundle of severed vines but rather as branches *in the vine*. Or when it testifies that those who have life have become one plant with Christ. This must not be understood to mean that these persons were first cut off from the original body of humanity and now have been put together as a new body under Christ. How could we think such a thing? A plant from which we cut a few branches and flowers in order to put together a new plant from those cut-off branches and flowers? Imagine the body of an animal or a human being from which you cut some members in order to make

3. In Dutch, *stam* is both "tree trunk" and "tribe, race."

from those members again a body, with a new head. We cannot make or put together a plant or a body. The unmistakable characteristic of each organism is precisely that it grows from a seed and is and remains a unity within itself. This is why Paul teaches in 1 Corinthians 15 that the resurrection is the sprouting anew of life from the dying seed. And after first applying this to the resurrection of our *physical* body, he then applies it directly also to the "body of humanity" when he says,

> It is sown a natural body; it is raised a spiritual body. If there is a natural body, there is also a spiritual body. Thus it is written, "The first man Adam became a living being"; the last Adam became a life-giving spirit. But it is not the spiritual that is first but the natural, and then the spiritual. The first man was from the earth, a man of dust; the second man is from heaven. As was the man of dust, so also are those who are of the dust, and as is the man of heaven, so also are those who are of heaven. Just as we have borne the image of the man of dust, we shall also bear the image of the man of heaven. (vv. 44-49)

Precisely for this reason Christ did not borrow a human body for the years of his time on earth, but entered *into our race*, and has sprung forth from us as a child of man—or, if you will, he came forth from humanity as the Son of Man.

In full agreement with this, Christ affirms in Matthew 13:30 that it is not §3
the *elect* who are separated from humanity, so that humanity perishes and only those few are saved, but rather the reverse: the *lost* are separated. Certainly, there are sheep and goats, and the shepherd separates those. But when it comes to deciding whether the goats must go and the sheep remain, or the goats stay and the sheep go, Matthew 25:34 emphatically states that the sheep *remain* and inherit the kingdom, and the goats are told that they must get out: "*Depart from me*, you cursed" [Matt 25:41]. Similarly, the good branches remain in the vine, and the branches that are pruned away and thrown into the fire are the evil and useless ones.

The Lord even teaches the same thing in Matthew 13 extensively and in deliberately chosen images. In his explanation of the parable of the weeds and the wheat, the Lord says in so many words: "The one who sows the good seed is the Son of Man. The field is the world, and the good seed is the sons of the kingdom. The weeds are the sons of the evil one, and the enemy who sowed them is the devil. The harvest is the end of the age, and the reapers are angels. Just as the weeds are gathered and burned with fire, so will it be at the end of the age" (Matt 13:37–40). And in verses 41–42 there follows, "The Son of Man will send his angels, and they will *gather out of his kingdom all causes of sin* and all law-breakers, and throw them into the fiery furnace. In that place there will be weeping and gnashing of teeth." Thus the lost are gathered and removed from his kingdom. They go away and are thrown into the fiery furnace. Not so the others; they *remain*. And Jesus teaches the same thing again in the parable of the net, where he says at the end in verses 49–50: "So it will be at the end of the age. The angels will come out and *separate* the evil from the righteous and throw them into the fiery furnace. In that place there will be weeping and gnashing of teeth." Here too the righteous are the ones who *remain*, and *the evil ones are separated out of the midst of the righteous*. Thus also there was a "trunk of David"—that is, the Davidic house that was cut down to a stump—and all the wood it had sprouted was cut off, but the stump remained alive in the ground, and from that stump of Jesse a shoot came forth [see Isa 11:1].

In the vision of Isaiah's calling, the Lord also said to Isaiah that the nation of Israel would be cut down to its root but a tenth would be spared, and that thereafter that tenth part would be cut off too, so that all that remained would be the stump. But nevertheless in that stump the holy seed would *remain* and this holy seed in the stump would be the support and would carry in it the prophecy of the future (Isa 6:13). And in this way the Lord clarifies to Isaiah that the situation with this people would be as with an oak tree, or a terebinth, that, when cut down, nevertheless sprouts again from its trunk. Thus it says in verses 12–13, "'The LORD removes people far away, and the forsaken places are many in the midst of the land. And though a tenth remain in it, it will be burned again, like a terebinth or an oak, whose stump remains when it is felled.' The holy seed is its stump." Thus we see here also the destruction of what is lost while the stump remains and sprouts anew.

To this we add that Paul speaks also in Romans 11 of saved humanity as a tree *from which branches are broken off*. Thus we also do not have here the notion that the tree is removed while a few branches are saved, but the reverse: the tree remains and branches are removed. Indeed, those who are saved from elsewhere must be grafted into the tree that remains. On these grounds we reject as unscriptural any notion that would have us believe that the tree, the stump of humanity, will disappear and that the believing branches are broken off. No, in our humanity as well as in our human race the fixed rule of *all* organic life persists: the tree, the stump, remains, but the wild shoots and the rotten branches are removed. To put it differently: humanity itself is renewed, our human race as such is re-created, and what is not elected to life is broken off, separated from it, removed.

It is as in the days of Noah. Of the millions of people then alive only *eight* §4
people were saved in the ark, yet no one denies that in that ark *our human race* was saved. Otherwise we would have to say that after the flood there has no longer been a human race. There, too, the stump of humanity remained in the ark, and the millions of unbelieving branches were broken off. And what the flood did back then, baptism does today as the sacrament of regeneration. This is something to which the holy Apostle Peter points so emphatically when he speaks of the days of Noah and says, "They formerly did not obey, when God's patience waited in the days of Noah, while the ark was being prepared, in which a few—that is, eight persons—were brought safely through water. Baptism, which corresponds to this, now saves you, not as a removal of dirt from the body but as an appeal to God for a good conscience, through the resurrection of Jesus Christ" (1 Pet 3:20–21). In a statement such as this, the superficial reader sees nothing but a quotation, but those who search the Scriptures learn and know more. It is the indication of the correspondence between what happened back then and what happens now. Then, all the rest was separated, was cut off, perished, but our race was saved in the ark. And thus also now, the people with an evil conscience perish, but the people with a good conscience are *saved through the water of baptism*. Not through the power of the water, but through the power of the *resurrection of Christ*, for it is precisely in this resurrection of Christ that the resurrection, the re-creation, of humanity is given in principle. And therefore it says of Christ in verse 22, "[He] has gone into heaven and is at the right hand of God, with angels, authorities, and powers having been subjected to him." Thus we find the reborn, the re-created, the renewed humanity under Christ as its Head, which again is not humanity *outside* the rest of creation but [humanity] in connection with all things, with the whole universe. "All angels, authorities, and powers are subjected to him."

Thus when our forefathers came to the prayer in the Form of Baptism, referred to Noah and his eight souls, and taught the churches to pray, "O Almighty and eternal God, Thou, who hast according to thy severe judgment punished the unbelieving and unrepentant world with the flood, and hast according to thy great mercy saved and protected believing Noah and his family,"[4] they did not burden the prayer with a superfluous recollection but confessed a holy, all-encompassing truth that expresses the whole destiny of the church. Just as back then the unrepentant world perished, and yet the essence of the world and the essence of our human race was saved, so too now God preserves, through baptism (that is, through re-creation, renewal, and rebirth, of which baptism is the symbolic image), the family tree of *our human race*, created by him and intended for his own glory, and along with that human race his *entire* original creation or, if you will, "all things," even though the reprobate will be removed from it and will perish forever.

§5 And when we understand predestination therefore as the unconditioned decree of God to one day separate all sin from his divine creation, all that leads to sin, all that is reprobate and lost; to lead the creation thus purified, with the human race as core and center, to eternal glory; and to glorify himself in that glorification of his handiwork—with this proviso that it be firmly determined which individuals will constitute that reborn humanity and which will not—then it is immediately clear that common grace cannot be excluded from that decree of predestination. For without that common grace there would not have been a development of our human race, but our whole race would already have been cut off in eternal death with Adam. Without common grace there would not have been a place for God's church on earth to emerge and develop. And also without that common grace, all prevenient grace would have been lacking for the elect themselves, which makes us Arminian if we understand such grace as *particular*; and that [prevenient grace] has a right and reason to exist only as part of common grace.

4. A source for this language is the Dutch Psalter of 1566, edited by Petrus Dathenus (ca. 1531–88). Luther's earlier Form of Baptism of 1523 is quite similar and influential on later Reformed formulations. See *LW* 53:97 and Hughes Oliphant Old, *The Shaping of the Reformed Baptismal Rite in the Sixteenth Century* (Grand Rapids: Eerdmans, 1992), 230. The English text appears in the CRC *Psalter Hymnal* (Grand Rapids: Christian Reformed Church, 1934), 84.

CHAPTER FIFTEEN

TRIUMPH OVER SATAN

But who are you, O man, to answer back to God? Will what is molded say to its molder, "Why have you made me like this?"

ROMANS 9:20

We think that we have in fact succeeded in making clear in our previous three chapters the organic relationship between common grace and the rest of the body of dogmatics. Until now, dogmatics stood on its own, in the perspective of many, and common grace was a *supplement* to it. Common grace was an appendix, an addendum, an act of grace that should not be forgotten but that was isolated from the rest of the administration of grace. But now this has radically changed. If all things flow from God's decree, then common grace also had to be given its proper place in that decree. Thus, together with particular grace, it flows as a unique yet equally refreshing and clear stream from the mountains of God's holiness to the plain of earthly life. But even this was not enough for us. In the decree that is always one, we are accustomed to segregating the decree of predestination and considering it in isolation. But as soon as predestination is separated out, then the final end of the universe, the ultimate glory of our God, and in that glory the salvation and the glory of the people of his favor too, depend upon §1 it. Thus even if it were conceded that common grace flows from the *general* decree, it nevertheless continued to wander outside the gate as long as it was not assigned its own essential place within the decree of predestination. Dualism would then persist. Then, particular grace alone touched on the holy things of God; what became of the rest of creation, or what happened to the Gentiles and the lost on earth, lay outside particular grace, became secondary, and scarcely captured our attention.

But now, by contrast, it has been shown how common grace is woven into predestination itself. And it is woven in not as a homeless person for whom an emergency spot is cleared under the roof of particular grace, but rather as an indispensable link in predestination and absolutely inseparable from it, a necessary component that must be incorporated, acknowledged, and valued as a housemate. We even refused to accept the always somewhat demeaning role it has been assigned, as if it alone served among the many means that had to work together toward the salvation of the elect. We rejected that entire notion. With regard to the self-glorification of God, everything, without distinction, comes to mean: Also the incarnation, the resurrection of Christ, his redemptive work, and thus also common grace. This, however, is entirely different from the usual understanding. Everything in all of creation that lives or has breath is placed in service to the self-glorification of the Triune God. But this transcends by a great distance the limited notion that one creature was put into the service of bringing another creature to its goal. And from this perspective it also became apparent to us that common grace is to be understood from the lofty perspective of the glory that God seeks for himself.

§2 The difference between this notion and the commonly accepted one is understood best if we listen to those eccentric groups that live strictly and severely on the basis of election, but only after they have pried election loose from the whole of God's counsel. For in those groups the confession of election often does not result in making the human heart tender and humble, but elevates it and at the same time makes it callous. The elect in those groups then walk around with a very high opinion of their own excellence, not because of what is in themselves but because of the favor of their God that rests upon them. And furthermore, they now view the rest of humanity as absolutely secondary, as having come into this world only to perish, and as serving no other purpose than serving them. Then the image of the wheat and the chaff is beloved: What matters is the wheat, not the chaff. The elect are the wheat, but in order that the wheat might come, the chaff first had to develop in the stalk and ear. But once the wheat has been threshed, the chaff has served its purpose and has no further use than to be thrown into the fire. And thus children dared say of their unbelieving father or mother, "They have been my chaff to allow me to become wheat, but otherwise there is nothing to them." Put this next to Paul's awesome language, "For I could wish that I myself were accursed and cut off from Christ for the sake of my brothers, my kinsmen according to the flesh" [Rom 9:3], and look for the word that you yourself would use to characterize such a sinful language of spiritual self-exaltation. Nevertheless, we lack the right to reproach such people for this, for they in fact did nothing but draw the correct and accurate conclusion from what you yourselves have taught them. For if it is true that everything that stands outside particular grace serves only as a means toward the salvation of the elect, on what basis can we challenge their right to apply this notion to themselves as well?

But if instead we realize the error of this notion and acknowledge that the creation and common grace have been placed in the service of God's self-glorification, then such a derisive thought vis-à-vis one's father and mother would never have entered the mind of such a child, but rather the realization that these too are lost creatures of God, who in the great and mighty ordination of the Lord of lords must serve his glory. God created heaven and earth and all that is in them for his glory. Satan set out to deny God the glory from his work. And the whole of predestination is nothing but the pure, clear, entirely sovereign, and absolutely all-determining expression of God's will, designed not simply to thwart this intent of Satan but rather to use Satan's intent to enlarge even more the glory he must derive from his work. For note well that grace not only restores the breach and heals the wound, but it applies the evil of Satan and the sin of man, directly against the will of Satan and the design of man, as a means to raise the self-glorification of God to an even higher level. And this being the case, the creature, including then the elect, must never insert itself as *goal* in the series of means and say, "This is for my sake!" No, it is never for our sake, but everything always revolves around God, and God alone. And thus we are and exist, together with all the rest, only and solely for the sake of our God.

To that lofty perspective we now lift up common grace. Certainly, common grace was indispensable for the manifestation of Christ's church, under both the old and the new covenant. Leave common grace entirely out of the picture, and already long before the flood our human race would not only have been totally dehumanized, but would have perished in insanity, suicide, and complete bestial brutality. Without common grace Noah and his family would have been massacred long before the flood, and no ark would ever have floated on the waters of salvation. And equally we can and must confess that neither in the days of the patriarchs, nor in the land of Goshen, nor in Palestine could the people of the Lord have emerged and maintained themselves if the nations around them had not been tempered by common grace in their evil, but had sunk another ten or twenty degrees below the moral level of the cannibals of New Guinea or the interior of Africa.[1] As the common expression says, it is entirely true that apart from common grace the church of God would have "found no place to set her foot" [Gen 8:9]. And it is equally true that each elect individual knows in his own life the sustaining grace of his God, through which the effect of evil in him has been tempered and the sprouting of all kinds of seeds of sin in his heart has been arrested. Once in a while a rank villain may still come to conversion before his death, but this is generally not the way of the Lord with his elect.

As a rule, preserving and prevenient grace intervene and cut off the most shocking abominations. And this was one of the reasons why in the generations belonging to the covenant, more noble sensibilities developed over the centuries. And thus we readily concede, in the third place, that without common grace the incarnation of Christ would have been unthinkable and that all preparations would have been lacking that now, in the fullness of time, have brought about precisely in such miraculous ways the expansion of Christ's church among the Gentiles in the pagan world. But even though we do not take away anything from these three effects of common grace—indeed, even if we are prepared to raise each of these three to the highest level of importance—we nevertheless resist the notion that the purposes for which God brought about common grace were limited to these three.[2]

§3 No, God Almighty seeks most of all in common grace the self-glorification of his name as well. In that common grace as such there already lies, apart from all further motive, a triumph of God over Satan, a radiance of his own glory. What Satan set out to do in paradise was to deliver the ultimate blow to God's whole creation, and to deliver the fatal thrust to the man whom

1. For more on Kuyper's racial and civilizational judgments from his Eurocentric perspective, see *CG* 1.12.10n4; 1.41.1n3.
2. That is: the restraint of sin, advancement of civilization, and preparation for the incarnation.

God had made. His goal was to have all of this sink all at once into death and darkness. God himself had said: "In the day you commit this sin you will surely die" [see Gen 2:17]. Well, Satan invoked that death. He pierced the dike that kept at bay the stream of death and doom, and he reveled in the demonic thought of how the flood of death and perdition would soon devastate and destroy everything. Adam had to die; Eve had to die. And then the human race would be finished. There would come no other human race. And all that God in his creation decree had envisioned bringing about in and through that human race in terms of gifts of heart and head and spirit, would forever be buried under that evil flood. Such was Satan's intent, an absolutely and totally evil intent. His desire was not to pilfer a few souls from God. No, much bolder and much greater, his plan was to frustrate the entire building when the first foundations barely stood above the ground, in this way to render the building and to ensure that the Great Builder and Artist would stand shamefaced at the failure of his own work.

And this is what common grace has prevented. The construction that God undertook has *not* been arrested and *not* been thwarted. In spite of Satan, the Lord our God has continued for all these centuries with the further building and implementing of his original plan. The human race was not smothered in Adam, nor was it stifled in Eve, but it has come into being through Adam and Eve in untold numbers of millions upon millions. In that human race, there was certainly a worm, so that on the branches the fruit ripened in which that worm-hole would be manifest. Yet in spite of that worm-hole the beauty, the glowing ripeness, the fragrance of the fruit could be admired. In a broad branching out into all kinds of peoples and nations, tongues and languages, God has managed, with very different levels of development, to bring out all the treasures he had embedded in our human race. Among those nations he has raised up geniuses and heroes, profound thinkers and artists who would pass on to the human race what he had given them, so that century after century the spiritual assets of humanity would increase in significance and value. In addition to those heroes and geniuses, he has also brought forth morals and ordinances, customs and laws that brought to development bravery and courage, a sense of civic-mindedness and moral earnestness.

From this gold God has fashioned all the jewels he had intended in his own mind and has displayed them before an admiring humanity. And precisely through the contrast with the exceedingly rich luxuriance in the external life he has all the more clearly thrown into relief how much poorer and more meager the deficiency of the inner life is, the spiritual desolation and the deterioration of the soul that destroyed our race inwardly. Thus two goals were achieved simultaneously. God has established his own miraculous work, which was inherent in the swaddling clothes of creation, in spite of Satan's evil intent. And at the same time he has made manifest all the more fearfully the inner emptiness and profound depravity of the human heart. Thus common grace has come about in the first place for God's sake, to show his glory and majesty in the life of humanity and in the life of the nations. In his decree there lay a history, prepared for our race. Satan wanted to thwart this history for our race. And in fact, thanks to common grace this history of our race came anyway, and still continues solemnly and stately toward its completion. And at the same time God has placed this same common grace in service to his plan of salvation for his elect, but the salvation of the elect is here only an intermediary link. The link that anchors the whole chain is ever again and ever only the glory God seeks for himself.

§4 Does this mean that the whole riddle is solved and that it has pushed aside the veil shrouding the profound divine mystery? Not in the least. Jesus himself pointed as with a finger to that unfathomable mystery when he said of Judas, "It would have been better for that man if he had not been born" [Matt 26:24; Mark 14:21]. Well, *who* caused him to be born? Who said to him, "Judas, come forth"? Was it not God the Lord himself? And do we not have to agree that Judas was also created by God and that he did nothing but what had been written beforehand would happen? Indeed, can you imagine the reconciliation of the world without a Caiaphas who condemns Jesus, without a Judas who betrays him, without a Pontius Pilate who gives him over to the death on the cross, without soldiers who cause his sacred heart-blood to flow? And when Jesus then nevertheless says, "It would have been better for that man if he had not been born," can this mean that Judas was responsible for his own birth, and does the question not appear to be instead whether God should have allowed this individual to be born? We feel the profound implications of this question. For what applies to Judas applies to all who do not attain to eternal life, and thus the question is involuntarily transmuted into the much broader question: Why did God not prevent all these lost children of man from being born? After all, he is also their Creator and they came into being only through his creative will. Assume that only those other human children who will go on to salvation had sprouted on the trunk of humanity: would not the history of mankind have been more transparent to us? We understand why Abel was born, but why did God create Cain, who murdered Abel and brought forth an entire depraved race from his own loins? We can compress the whole profound mystery we are faced with here, in that one fearful, bitter question.

We can answer that the creation and generation of individuals is not something isolated but hangs together with the whole ordination of God for our human race, and that this human race *had* to be this way and *could* not be otherwise in accordance with God's ordination over all of creation. But with this we have given no answer at all, because we have only shifted the mystery. For then the question we have avoided is immediately replaced by another one: Why has God ordained and created the world to be this way and not otherwise? Would it not have been possible to create another world, a world Satan could not have attacked, in which no sin could have entered, a world that would have grown steadily from a pure seed to highest glory? The pessimists in our day try to convince us that the existing world is the worst imaginable. As recently as the past century, a philosopher tried to demonstrate that the existing world is the best possible.[3] And the question cannot be repressed: Was the creation of *this* world necessary? Could not a world without sin, death, and destruction have been created? Indeed, why was Satan created if God knew that this once-so-glorious angel would become a Satan?

Now comes the infralapsarian who says, "This is precisely why I assume §5
election to have been out of a fallen humanity, as God saw us before him as fallen human beings in his eternal perspective." And we unhesitatingly agree that with this the infralapsarian is defending a part of the truth that we also defend forcefully. We even add that the supralapsarians have not infrequently defended their own, opposite, system in a way that harmed moral awareness, sense of guilt, and repentance with respect to sin. And this must never be. For if one thing is certain on the basis of holy Scripture and our own conscience, then it is that the culpability is ours, that there is not a grain of culpability that we may or can shift away from ourselves, and that our conscience, above all when enlightened by grace, honors and reveres God more and more as just in his condemnation of all sin. Any

3. Gottfried Wilhelm Leibniz (1646–1716) was a German philosopher whose *Theodicy*, originally published as *Essais de Théodicée sur la bonté de Dieu, la liberté de l'homme et l'origine du mal* (Amsterdam: I. Troyel, 1710), argued that God would necessarily create the best of all possible worlds.

notion that the present author rejected the seriousness of infralapsarianism *in that sense*, is little less than theological libel.

No, our objection to infralapsarianism was of a quite different nature. We commented that in our opinion we would speak thus to the adherents of this outmoded system: Your system does not achieve what it presents as its goal. You are under the illusion that the mystery of God's plan has been solved for you if you posit that in his eternal view God saw man as fallen, and then elected a small number [of individuals] from that fallen humanity. But this does not bring you a single step further. It *would* bring you further, and you would have explained the riddle, if it were certain that God had *had* to create this humanity, which he saw beforehand would fall. But this is precisely *not* how it is. God is under no necessity. He is eternally the Sovereignly Omnipotent One. And so if we say "God knew and foresaw (1) that humanity would fall, and (2) that if men were thus created, the stream of sin and suffering would begin to flow," then the same question returns in this new form: Why, if he knew this, did God not refrain from bringing this creation into being and why did he not create something entirely different?

A ship owner who knew that if he let this ship sail with three hundred souls on board it would certainly be shipwrecked, but who also thought, "I will take measures to keep thirty souls alive in this shipwreck"—would such a ship owner be acquitted of blame if, instead of not sending out the ship, he let it take sail anyway? And are we therefore here not also faced with the question: If God knew that the head angel would become a Satan, and that Adam would fall; and that such terrible, such untold misery, yes, that curse and death would come over creation—was he virtually not under an obligation to decide (we say this with trembling reverence) *not* to create this world in this form, *not* to create that future Satan, *not* to let that weak Adam be born? At least according to Jesus' statement, it would have been better if that Judas, and thus also that Satan, indeed, that Adam had not come into being. And thus we sense immediately that the infralapsarian deceives himself when he thinks that his system solves the problem. Indeed it does not—with his system he remains equally dumbfounded and perplexed, faced with exactly the same awesome problems—at least if he has the intellectual powers to be consistent in his thinking and the courage to penetrate to the bottom of these things.

And with this we arrive at the same question that the holy apostle wrote down with these words: "Will what is molded say to its molder, 'Why have you made me like this?'" [Rom 9:20]. Although this does not resolve the question, the right to ask the question is disputed and denied. Let this be clear: we cannot escape thinking about this question, but because there is no apparent basis for the right to ask it, we are not justified in doing so. The answer to this question lies too high; we cannot reach it. And even if all the geniuses of the world were to unite their talent to seek the answer to this awesome question, they would never be able to do anything but stammer, and in that stammering confess their own ignorance. Only the person who bows down and worships here is wise. The fear of the Lord is the beginning of wisdom [Ps 111:10; Prov 9:10]. After all, and note this, because he is God, a necessary limit has been imposed on the omnipotence of God in his work of creation: God cannot create gods. That would have meant canceling out his own being God. Thus a contrast, specifically a contrast of subordination, of inferiority, of a lower order, had to remain between God and his highest creature. Only in *the image* of God, not *as* God, could the rational creature be created. And it is from this contrast between God and the creature as *not*-God that all the anxiety of the broken moral life emerges. Here lies the solution to the mystery. However, we can point to the place where the solution lies, but we will never be able to remove the veil from it.

CHAPTER SIXTEEN

HE DWELT AMONG US

... and dwelt among us.

JOHN 1:14

§ 1 Having placed the connection between common grace and the doctrine of predestination in the necessary light, we now must ascertain to what extent the doctrine of common grace also relates doctrinally to the confession concerning Christ. We must not wander down the wrong path of Christo-*centrism*,[1] which ends up in the practically pantheistic notion that the divine-human in Christ stood above what is only divine and not also human in the Father. Yet our apprehension toward this heretical mysticism must never make us overlook the central significance that the dogma of the incarnation occupies in dogmatics. In essence there can never be another center for all things than God himself, and it is precisely in this regard that the apostles of the Christo-centric theology have defrauded, albeit unthinkingly, the honor and majesty of the divine Being.[2] But when it is a matter, not of the essence of things but of the orderly development of our thoughts

1. Note by author: *Christo-centric* is an expression used by the Ethical theologians and means Christ *at the midpoint* or *in the center*.
2. As Bratt observes in his biography of Kuyper, "Ordinary Christians pray first for themselves, then for their neighbor, and finally for the adoration of God, he observed; the order should be just the reverse. Evangelicals and Ethicals were merely

in dogmatics, then all threads of the fabric most certainly converge in the mystery of the incarnation, simply because our dogmatics sheds light on the connection between God and a world *sunken into sin*, and because this connection does not proceed outside of Christ at any single point. When we reverse these two, we end up confused. As decidedly and definitely as the Christo-centric notion has to be rejected whenever the *essence* of *things* is involved, equally undoubtedly the question "What do you think about the Christ?" must remain the linking element that keeps the various parts of dogmatics in their mutual relationship.

We therefore must also ask ourselves with regard to the doctrine of common grace where and how the threads that show us the connection between this doctrine and the "mystery of the Christ" [see Eph 3:6] are being woven into the fabric of dogmatics. Our point of departure here is the declaration of the Apostle John, "And the Word became flesh and dwelt among us" [John 1:14], because it is precisely in the contrast and mutual connection of both these statements that we find the indication of what we are seeking. In the incarnation as such, common grace does not appear as a necessary link. The conception of Christ by the Holy Spirit is a complete and absolute miracle—there is no gradation. It is the conception, not by the will of a man but by the Holy Spirit, that severs all communion between the Christ and the life of sin of our human race. And even though we do not deny that the Virgin Mary was a "prepared vessel," and even though our confession "born of the Virgin Mary" feels to us just as comforting as, conversely, the mere sound of reading "born of Herodias" would offend us, nevertheless we must never seek the *cause* of the Messiah's holiness in the essentially *relative* difference between these two women. Causally, the Messiah owed this holiness exclusively to his deity and instrumentally to his conception by the Holy Spirit. This miraculous conception is what cut off all communion with the original guilt of Adam and thus also all communion with original sin. It therefore makes no difference as such whether this cutting off took place in the organism of a more noble person such as Mary or in the organism of a woman of less noble origin and personality. When we separate white milk from another colored liquid using an impenetrable glass barrier, we achieve the same result regardless of whether

Christocentric; real Calvinists were Trinitarian, with a special relish for God's secret counsel." See James D. Bratt, *Abraham Kuyper: Modern Calvinist, Christian Democrat* (Grand Rapids: Eerdmans, 2013), 179.

we use that glass partition to separate the milk from jet-black ink or from sunny, sparkling wine. As long as the glass partition lets *nothing* through, the milk remains equally white, regardless of whether there is a dark black or a light-colored liquid on the other side.

Similarly, in principle it was immaterial for the conception of Christ whether the sinful element was tinged darker or lighter in the woman in whom he was conceived. As long as it was certain that he could not have even a hint of communion with this sinfulness in the woman who received him, the degree of sinfulness in the character of that woman did not affect his holiness. We do not deny the fact that the Virgin Mary stood on a relatively higher plane, and we certainly are aware of the meaningful significance of this, but that significance does not lie in the conception itself, as if the more noble development of this virgin added anything whatsoever to the holy conception of Christ. The origin of an absolute distinction can never be found in a relative difference. And here the distinction between Christ and all human children is absolute. We all are conceived under original sin; only Christ stands outside original sin, solely because of his conception by the Holy Spirit.

§ 2 It is also apparent in a different way that this cannot be otherwise. There are hereditary defects and hereditary sins that we sometimes see being inherited from father to child over three or four generations. And although it must be conceded that many of these defects and sins must be attributed to upbringing and similarity in living environment, it never must be said that lineage does *not* a play a role in such hereditary sins. Indeed, certain distinct, sinful inclinations are passed on, even down to the formation of the body and the intermixing of blood. Therefore, had such hereditary sins and defects played a role in the mystery of the incarnation, then we certainly would have to confess that it would have made a very great difference from which race, from which family, and from which individuals the child was born. For in what we call "hereditary sins," the difference between one family and another, between one mother and another, certainly plays a role, even if we think only of those peculiar sins in which character is manifested. But we are not speaking here at all of those kinds of "original *sins*"; we are speaking of "original *sin*" [singular], which is something entirely different. For original guilt and original sin do not come to us through our mother, but through Adam. Consequently, this original guilt and original sin are entirely the same for all who are born of Adam. "Therefore all men are conceived in sin, and are by nature children of wrath, incapable of saving good, prone to evil, dead in sin."[3] Whether therefore John the Baptist was born from Elizabeth, or the princess who danced so sinfully before Herod was born from Herodias, neither added or subtracted one whit from the transmission of original guilt or original sin. This was the same for both. And because in the incarnation of the Christ the question concerning hereditary family sins is not relevant, but only the question concerning the original guilt and the original sin that accrues to us because of our tie with Adam, it is striking how in this way too the moral condition of the Lord's mother could add nothing to nor subtract anything from his being conceived *outside of* original guilt.

Even if we consider the Virgin Mary the holiest mother relatively speaking, even her child would not have been conceived except in sin and therefore would have been subject to damnation if the miracle of the conception by the Holy Spirit had not intervened. From this it follows equally that this miracle would have had quite the same effect even if that mother had personally been involved in many hereditary and actual *sins*. The fact that the Messiah stood outside original guilt and therefore also outside original sin must be explained, at least instrumentally, not from the spiritual or moral condition of the mother of Jesus but exclusively from his conception by the Holy Spirit. We say "at least instrumentally," for viewed from an even higher perspective, all essential communion between Christ and our original guilt was cut off by the fact that he was God. Because he himself was God, he could not enter into any essential communion with any guilt or sin. And because he could not, he was conceived by the Holy Spirit, and any other conception was unthinkable in the case of the Christ.

The attempt to shed clearer light on this conception by excluding the § 3
Virgin Mary herself absolutely from any communion with sin either *in* or *after* her conception, goes deeper than the notion that the cause of Jesus' sinlessness could lie in Mary's *relative* holiness, but it also appears to fall short of its goal. Realizing that nothing could be achieved with a difference in degree, it has been attempted to posit an *absolute* holiness in Mary, as we will later show in more detail. Mary's conception was not put on a level with that of Christ; rather, it was conceded that the conception of Mary was through the will of man, so that in her origin she partook of original guilt, and her salvation also could not be complete without the atoning

3. *Canons of Dort*, III/IV.3.

sacrifice of Christ. But it was assumed that she was already sanctified in her mother's womb and, ultimately, that this sanctification of the Virgin Mary already had taken place before life had entered her.

Not all concede this latter point, and Thomas Aquinas even considered it unthinkable, yet this notion ultimately gained the upper hand. It was still conceded that the *fomes peccati*, or what our Confession calls a "woeful source," was still potentially present in Mary but fully restrained, so that no sin sprang from it.[4] But here too the notion tended increasingly toward the absolute, in order that the presence of the "woeful source" might be denied. But however this was argued, the goal remained that of precluding any contact with the sinful on the part of Christ. And to the extent that this was focused on his mother, it was seen correctly that staying with the *relative* was not enough, but that there had to be an ever sharper and more determined progression toward the *absolutely* holy nature of Mary. Any communion between Mary and sin remained a stumbling block, and the goal would be reached only if that communion could be denied entirely.

But precisely this goal could never be achieved and, therefore, has not been achieved. The fact remains that Mary was born by the will of a man, and thus the tie that binds her to original guilt remains. For if this last link were severed (and only then would the objective have been achieved), the whole work of redemption would have become superfluous. For if it had been possible for Mary to be conceived and born by the will of a man and yet apart from all contact with original guilt, then all God would have had to do was to let the children of Adam and Eve be born in the same way in order to destroy the consequences of the fall, entirely apart from the entire work of redemption. The problem here, therefore, is that in order to achieve the goal, *any* connection between the Virgin Mary and sin must be *totally* nullified, and this is impossible without rendering the entire incarnation superfluous. In the meantime we do not have to enter further into this issue, since Thomas Aquinas himself asserts that holy Scripture does not teach us anything about the presumed sinlessness of Mary.[5] This would mean

4. Belgic Confession, Art. 15. The *fomes peccati* is "literally, *the tinder of sin*; i.e., the fomenter of sin or source of sin; the inborn concupiscence (*concupiscentia*, q.v.) of the newborn child which ultimately will issue in sin." See *DLGTT*, s.v. "fomes peccati."

5. In his treatment of the question of "the sanctification of the Blessed Virgin," Aquinas writes, "Nothing is handed down in the canonical Scriptures concerning the sanctification of the Blessed Mary as to her being sanctified in the womb; indeed, they do not even mention her birth." See *Summa Theologiæ* III, Q. 27, Art. 1.

positing a second source of mystical truth beside Scripture, something we are not allowed to do. Suffice it to say that the preceding clearly shows that in this way too, common grace as such could neither add to nor detract from the essential holiness in the conception of the Christ. The holiness of that conception flows essentially from the deity of the Christ and its realization through the conception by the Holy Spirit, and from this alone.

But it is quite a different matter when John asserts, in the second place, that the Word not only became flesh *but also dwelt among us*. To understand this simply as merely saying that Jesus temporarily took up residence in Nazareth (and in Capernaum, and so on) would be entirely contrary to the spiritual intent of this entire first section of John's Gospel—indeed, contrary to the very words he chose in the original. Literally, he says, "He has *tabernacled* among us; he pitched his *tent* among us, lived among us as *in a tent*." "House" and "tent" indicate a readily grasped contrast: a person dwells in a house as in a fixed place where one has to live; in contrast, one pitches a tent where one stays only temporarily. Thus Peter calls the body a tent: "As long as I am in this *tabernacle*" (2 Pet 1:13 KJV), where the same word is used as in John 1:14. And also in 2 Corinthians 5:1 and following, this same word *tent* or *tabernacle* is used for our earthly body. Here we live in a tabernacle; after our resurrection we will have in our *glorified body* "a *building* from God, a *house* not made with hands, eternal in the heavens" [2 Cor 5:1]. The tabernacle is to the temple as a tent is to a house, which is why the tabernacle is also called "the tent of meeting." And the basic thought behind this contrast is that someone who dwells in a tabernacle or tent is there only *temporarily*, whereas one who lives in a building or house is there *permanently*. Thus when John says of the Christ, "The Word became flesh and tabernacled among us, lived among us as in a tent," it is not the same as "he dwelt among us *permanently*." Christ will not dwell permanently among us until the kingdom of glory. His dwelling among us in the days of the apostles continued to be temporary in character. It was not a matter of his being absorbed into our community of life, but rather a temporary joining of our community, establishing a connection with it, manifesting himself in it. John therefore continues, "And we have seen his glory, glory as of the only Son from the Father, full of grace and truth" [John 1:14]. § 4

We must pay attention to *both*. On the one hand, this implies that Jesus entered into our *community*, but on the other hand, it points to the fact that Jesus' entering into our community still bore an incomplete character. The question now arises, Which community is intended here? Two kinds of answers can be given. It can be understood to refer either to just the community of the *spiritual* life in the children of God, or to the community of our *human* life as such. The former would be the only correct view if, after his birth, Jesus had remained isolated from the everyday society of Israel and had been locked up, as it were, within the restricted company of the saints and involved only with the spiritual element in that group. Then the words "and dwelt among us" could not refer to anything other than his dwelling among *the children of God*, and specifically in the *spiritual* sense.

But this contradicts the entire gospel. Jesus does not lock himself up within the restricted company of believers, but he goes out into the full marketplace of life and lives among the crowds. He seeks the sinners and tax collectors. And not only that: far from seeking only the spiritual as point of contact, he also heals the sick, gives food to the hungry, and involves himself with the restricted company of his followers in their daily work and life. Thus the fact that the Word did not merely become flesh but also dwelt among us points to a manner of entering into our community that encompasses the human element in its broader sense. The Word becoming flesh is indeed the starting point for dwelling in this community, but by itself the incarnation would not have led to genuine community. The incarnation itself would have been undeniable as fact, but it would not have been observable to the world. It would have occurred outside the foreknowledge and awareness of the children of men. The sun must not only be actually present behind the horizon; it must also rise above the horizon to enter into our lives with its rays. Only then do we see its radiance as part of God's glory. And in this way the incarnation did not remain isolated but was manifest among humanity. Only then could the glory of the only begotten Son be seen.

§ 5 Furthermore, justice is done to John's entire prologue only when this deeper meaning is assigned to the words "and has dwelt among us." If in those first heavenly sounds of his Gospel the apostle had confined himself to the *spiritual*, we still could think that, as he was transitioning to Christ in the flesh, John wanted to try to shed light on him only from his spiritual side. But John does not do this; on the contrary, he begins instead by pointing to the creation of all things and emphasizing how Christ was already the light of men from creation. All connection with John's majestic introduction would be severed if, having come to his testimony concerning the incarnation, he nevertheless ignored our human life as such and retreated exclusively to the spiritual. Indeed, the stark assertion that the Word became *flesh* prohibits this. It is especially that expression that points to the long-awaited moment when the dividing wall between the spiritual and the physical, the visible and the invisible, would be taken away, so that the full glory of God now could radiate, no longer from Sinai but in grace, and no longer in the shadows but in truth and reality. "The Word became flesh and dwelt among us ... *full of grace and truth*" [John 1:1, 14].

If the apostle wants to indicate by this that what began with the holy conception of Christ continued in his manifestation among men by entering into their life-community, then it would be extremely superficial and arbitrary if this community were considered merely external and understood only in terms of his actual sojourn on earth. When traveling in a foreign country, you actually can move among the walking crowds in the street without there being any kind of life-community whatsoever. What binds and unites us with others are numerous invisible bonds, all kinds of relationships and connections that cause something similar to happen in your heart and theirs, such that at many points the manifestations of your life flow together with theirs in a common channel. You experience this in your own home with the members of your own family. And it also manifests itself in the small circle of those who appear to be like-minded with you. This can be so strong that you sometimes wonder whether the individual members of the family, or the separate individuals in that group, still live a life of their own. But even if outside your own home, and among those who are less close to you, this pull of the ties of community, that communal life of being as one and feeling as one, is less conspicuous, the life-community nevertheless extends there too, even though realizing this takes more effort. What an enormous difference shared language makes, to the extent that you share it with your environment in the same country—or, conversely, when you experience language arising as a barrier between your thought world and that of the people around you. If we are therefore to understand Jesus' entering into the life-community of Israel of that time, it is necessary that precisely those invisible bonds be set in full relief here, because it is precisely in those ties between people that common grace manifests itself.

CHAPTER SEVENTEEN

HE DWELT AMONG ISRAEL

And the child grew and became strong, filled with wisdom. And the favor of God was upon him.

LUKE 2:40

§ 1 The line of demarcation has thus been drawn distinctly and clearly. There are two matters: First, there is the mystery of the *incarnation* as such, and common grace has nothing to do with this, not even as concerns the Virgin Mary. But second, after the incarnation follows what John calls the *dwelling among us*, and this cannot be explained apart from common grace. When we consider Jesus' birth as well as his manifestation among Israel, danger threatens from two sides. On the one hand, people are inclined to explain Christ only from the absolute miracle, without taking into account the conditions of human life under which he appeared. On the other hand, the connection between Jesus and his environment can be so one-sidedly emphasized that in the end people think Christ can be explained entirely on the basis of his descent and environment, and they do not rest until the absolute miracle involving Christ has been denied. By giving in to the former tendency, we are left with nothing but a divine manifestation that stands out sharply against all that is human around him and therefore also remains outside our own life. But if we go down the other erroneous path, then in the end *everything* about Christ becomes human and we lose the Son of God and are left with nothing but the rabbi from Nazareth. We must surrender therefore to neither the one approach nor the other. The strained, one-sidedly *supernatural* approach leaves us with Christ but takes Jesus from us, whereas the weak *human* approach deprives our soul of Christ and leaves us nothing but a particular Jesus. But it cannot be surprising that how the Mediator was viewed tended to lean alternatingly first in the one direction and then in the other. The neglect of the doctrine of common grace also contributed to this, and only by applying the doctrine of common grace to the Christ of the Gospels does it become possible to do justice, on the one hand, to the absolute miracle of his incarnation and, on the other hand, to his entering into our community, or if you will, his *dwelling among us*.

On the believing side it was mostly the former error that was committed. The absolutely divine side of Christ's person was worshiped, together with the equally absolutely divine side in the miracle of his incarnation, but scant attention was paid to his connection with our human community. In the brief sketches of the Savior's life that were presented in various places, all the emphasis fell on the miracles he performed and the divine oracles that were heard from his lips. Thus little else was done than to present a brief excerpt from what the evangelists tell us, an excerpt that was dry, bare, and lifeless, one that often resembled more a list of events than a vivid portrait of life. Others therefore took the other, still much preferable way of integrating the narratives of the four evangelists, as chronologically as possible, from which the harmonies or synopses of the Gospels were born. Catechism classes often used the kind of books with questions and answers that fragmented even further what was already not very coherent, causing the loss of any sense of a coherent whole. In the meantime, fortunately, the congregation itself still diligently read the Gospels and absorbed the living portrait of Christ. The inadequate, one-sided treatment of Christ's life ran counter to the *actual* appearance of the Lord to such an extent that when it says in Luke that Jesus "increased in wisdom and in stature and in favor with God and man" [2:52], many actually did not know what to do with these words. So they preferred to skip over them, and, if these could not be evaded, they in effect set them aside by giving them an artificial interpretation.

On the unbelieving side, by contrast, another approach was traditionally § 2
preferred. Even if people did not yet dare to brazenly deny the absoluteness

of the miracle involved in Jesus' person and presence, this miracle nevertheless was increasingly placed in the shadows, and the effort was made to "humanize" Jesus, as it was called, and to explain him in terms of his human environment. But people gradually grew bolder, and especially in this century people have endeavored to write biographies of Jesus. What then was produced under the title *Life of Jesus* by Strauss and by Renan, and in our country by Meyboom, to mention only the best-known names, is also well known in our churches—if not from personal reading, then by hearsay.[1] Just as people wrote a life of William the Silent, or a life of de Ruyter, or a life of Napoleon, so too now the life of Jesus had to be portrayed.[2] And because a good biography strives especially to show the development of the character of its protagonist and to explain his behavior and actions on the basis of that development and his environment, the focus in these "lives of Jesus" was primarily on explaining Jesus' actions in terms of his people, his descent, his upbringing, the then-prevalent conditions in Israel, the ideals and dreams of his community, and the persons in his environment. Ultimately, *everything* had to be explained. Thus imagination was brought in to assist, and these works devolved into what may be called, without exaggeration, the historical novel. A process continued and did not come to rest until *everything* miraculous had been rendered ordinary, until everything supernatural had been made natural, and finally Jesus was made to *dwell among us*. But this was done by making him into our image, instead of our being changed into the image of the Son of God. The result was that in this way, Jesus became like one of us, a human being who deluded himself and thus was sinful too.

This was not the case for every life of Jesus that saw the light. In our country the late professor van Oosterzee[3] made a noble attempt to place in contrast to this falsified representation a life of Jesus as demanded by

1. David Friedrich Strauss, *Das Leben Jesu, kritisch bearbeitet*, 2 vols. (Tübingen: Osiander, 1835–36); Ernest Renan, *Vie de Jésus* (Paris: Michel Lévy Fréres, 1863); Hajo Uden Meyboom (1842–1933) was a professor at Groningen known for his radical historical criticism.
2. William the Silent (1533–84) was a leader in the Dutch revolt against Spain and the ancestor of the Dutch monarchy; Michiel de Ruyter (1607–76) was a Dutch naval hero; Napoleon Bonaparte (1769–1821) was emperor of the French from 1804 to 1814/15.
3. J. J. van Oosterzee (1817–82) was a professor of biblical and practical theology at Utrecht and author of, among many other works, *Geschichte oder Roman? Das Leben Jesu von Ernst Renan vorläufig beleuchtet* (Hamburg: Rauhen Hauses, 1864).

the Gospels, and we owe him and his like-minded colleagues abroad who made such counterefforts our thanks for that excellent intention. But we should not let the excellence of the intent tempt us in the direction of the errant path on which they strayed. For they in fact also tried to be biographers, and writing from this perspective they could not prevent their work from continuing to be overshadowed by that of their opponents. Those who wanted a biography of Jesus were much more satisfied with the efforts of Strauss and Renan, genuine biographies and explanations of the life of Jesus that tried more or less to satisfy the demands of a normal biography. What van Oosterzee and others offered by contrast as an antidote pretended to be biography but was not, or at least was so only half-heartedly and in part. The supernatural that refuses all explanation was placed side by side with the natural, which was then explained aphoristically. Thus it failed to create unity. People received pieces of a portrait, but not a portrait of the beauty of unity, and the sad result was that those who tended toward unbelief were not cured of their unbelief, while those who initially still stood firm in their faith gradually became used to a notion of Jesus' life for which they sought a different solution than what van Oosterzee and his like-minded colleagues offered.

Here we see people once again falling into the old error of all apologetics that rides roughshod over principles: they let themselves be lured into the territory of the enemy, and in *his* territory they lost the battle. An organically explanatory biography of Jesus is incompatible with the believing acknowledgment of the supernatural in him. Even the biography of a Christian man or woman in whose life a considerable breach was made by a poignant conversion is conceivable only up to a certain point. But things must go totally wrong when this approach tries to apply its method to him who was the image of the Father; he *cannot* be explained on the basis of our human community, because he did *not* arise from our human race and human life. Whoever wants to explain him on this basis is in fact denying his mission to the world. It is not we who can explain him. He explains us.

It is therefore understandable that the believing church, led by spiritual § 3
instinct, has turned from the lives of Jesus with a measure of revulsion, and it is to be applauded that the attempt to produce such a biography from the orthodox side was abandoned and now is condemned more and more on principle. But it does not follow in the least that nothing better remains for us than to return to the old, stiff rigidity in representing Jesus. The

struggle of the spirits that came to light in these lives of Jesus left behind fruit for the Lord's people, and theological scholarship owes it to Christ no less than to his church to profit from that fruit for the knowledge of his name. And this is in fact possible if the meaning of common grace is allowed to be placed in the correct light for the whole of *Christ's dwelling among us*.

It goes without saying that particular grace did not accrue to Christ. Particular grace saves the sinner, not the Holy One of God. When Luke 2:40 states that "the grace of God was upon him" [KJV] and Luke 2:52 says that he grew in grace or "favor with God and man," then in neither instance must we think of particular grace. In the first statement, "grace" must be understood only as the special grace of God that is the joy of the angels and also rested on Adam in paradise before the fall. In the second, the addition of "with God and man" by itself indicates that nothing else could be meant here but favor that is elicited and evoked. If all particular grace is therefore excluded in the case of Christ, then the indwelling and inner working of the Holy Spirit in the Mediator, along with the fact that he is given the Holy Spirit "without measure" [John 3:34] and whatever else is said in the Gospels in this regard, can never be explained in any other way than either as an anointing for his task or as an expression of personal communion. This communion of Jesus' human existence and human consciousness with the divine life and divine knowledge must not be compared with the way in which we as born-again children of God enjoy communion with the eternal Being in this life; this communion can only be compared to the communion Adam possessed before the fall, which the angels possessed apart from the fall and the saved individual will possess in the eternal kingdom after glorification. This comparison never holds completely true, of course, for the communion *with* and the knowledge *of* God arose in Jesus from his personal union with the Father and the Holy Spirit, and therefore this communion remains entirely unique in its mode of existence. We may therefore point to this comparison only to the extent that it gives us a notion of a communion between our spirit and the Spirit of God apart from any interference of sin and thus without particular grace.

§ 4 But whereas there can be no work of particular grace in Jesus, common grace is an altogether different matter. An angel never shares in particular grace either, simply because a fallen angel cannot be saved and a blessed angel is never fallen. But when an angel is sent to minister, and thus is manifested in human life, it is not insignificant for that angel in which environment he appears.

To clarify this, compare the actions of the angels in Sodom, in the midst of the iniquity that had broken out there in terrible form, with the appearance of the angels in the fields of Bethlehem to proclaim in their heavenly chorus God's pleasure with man. In Sodom everything was repugnant. There was nothing but abomination and human disgrace. In the fields of Ephrathah, by contrast, there was the enchantment of the beauty of nature, appealing scenes of human life; there was nothing repulsive, and everything was attractive. Even an angel, in his fleeting appearance, benefited from what peace and joy common grace preserved among human beings, if we may express it thus. And the very same now applies, to a much higher degree, to our Savior. It is the varying degree to which common grace impacts human life, restraining its iniquity and tempering its misery, that causes living conditions to be very different in one nation from those in another, and within the same nation it diverges widely, depending on time and social environment. Even now, nineteen centuries later, the living conditions among the primitive tribes of New Guinea are quite pitiful when compared with the social environment in which Jesus appeared. That difference was not at all insignificant for the accomplishing of our Savior's mediating work. Imagine our Savior appearing among a tribe where cannibalism was still practiced: the emergence of the church of the new covenant would simply have been unthinkable. We therefore are not dealing here with something secondary or incidental, but with a distinction that was of the utmost importance for Jesus' ministry. Living conditions with a very weak working of common grace would have been entirely unsuitable for the Savior's ministry. His ministry could be a blessing only if he ministered in a land and among a people and in a social environment in which the fruit of common grace was quite remarkable. And thus we may say, without a hint of exaggeration, that in a very considerable measure Jesus benefited from common grace for the fulfillment of his office of mediator.

The character of common grace, in contrast to particular grace, makes it possible to benefit from the fruit of common grace where there is also total separation from sin, as was true with Jesus' holy personality. Particular grace is *personal*, and common grace is *general*. Consequently, particular grace touches exclusively the core of the inner life of the soul, but common grace extends to all of human life in all its manifestations. The silt of common grace settles down into the entire bedding of life, into the morals and customs, into the general conditions of a nation, and thereby constitutes the channel through which the stream moves. Thus anyone who lives among such a people shares in the good things that common grace brings and that are present in the communal conditions, regardless of one's individual condition or personal qualities. A land where there is safety for persons and property displays a higher degree of common grace than a tribe where each individual lives by the sword. But once such a desired condition of order and national peace has been achieved, its benefits also accrue to the thief and the scoundrel, as long as his crime is not discovered. The personal life of individuals is not in view, because where common grace brings about a desired national condition, that desired condition offers its fruit to anyone who lives in such a nation. And on that basis it must be said that we cannot speak in any way of particular grace in connection with Jesus, but we must insist that the fruit of common grace accrued in no small measure to him as well.

§ 5 Indeed, we must go further. This fruit of common grace cannot have been an accidental benefit for the Son of God's appearing. The child of God already rejects any notion that there might be anything secondary or unimportant in the entanglements of his own life; rather, he confesses out of a deep conviction that God's *most special* providence has ordained, governed, and arranged all things and all circumstances, down to the smallest details, in such a way that it altogether had to be the way it is for the execution of God's plan with him.[4] And since this applies to each child of God, and thus also with regard to the fruit that common grace brings to each child of the Lord, we are naturally forced to confess that this also, indeed, even more strongly, must hold true in the case of the *supremely special* providence of God that surrounds the whole life and ministry of Jesus.

The stream of common grace moved from paradise through the life of the nations, not as in a playful game, but following the line God had set out for it; and as this stream pushed along, it dug the channel God had ordained for it. Only in this way did a history emerge for the nations. If the appearance of Christ is the center of that history, at which all lines from the past converge and from which the lines of all that follows radiate, then there also must have been a link between that process of common grace and the ministry of the Savior—a link not only in the result, but already in God's

4. See, for instance, the affirmation of special providence in the Heidelberg Catechism, Q&A 1, which reads in part that Jesus Christ "so preserves me that without the will of my Father in heaven not a hair can fall from my head; indeed, that all things must work together for my salvation."

providential ordination. Christ did not simply adapt to the environment existing at that time because common grace had brought about these conditions in Palestine; on the contrary, the conditions adapted to Jesus because the working of common grace had been ordained in terms of his coming and ministry as their goal. Thus Jesus did not simply *accept* it because this is how it was, but it *was* thus because it had to be that way for Jesus' appearance. This whole development was aimed at him; he was its goal; it culminated with him, and in him found its reason and cause. Then the whole social environment in which Jesus ministered was precisely how it had to be to serve his appearing and his ministry, and Jesus found the life-community that he joined precisely as it had to be to enable this connection.

Note well that each environment and each condition in which someone acts is *special*, and has an *individual, special* character. There is no such thing as a general human situation, and a general human community does not exist and is inconceivable. In those days things were different in Israel than in any other nation, and also different than they had been in that same nation in the past. Indeed, it was different in Galilee than in Judea, different in Jerusalem than in Bethlehem. No matter how completely Jesus has adopted general human nature and ministers in the full meaning of Redeemer and Mediator for all peoples, nations, and ages, he could not do anything else than join that one particular national environment as it presented itself at one particular point in time. Thus he did adopt our general human nature, but *his dwelling among us* could not help but bear a very special character, the character of the situation as it prevailed at that time. Only in the forms of the life of that day, in that specific land, did he manifest himself and reveal his glory, and from there the rumor of that glory has come to us. Precisely this precludes any notion of the coincidental and secondary. And our seeking soul only rests in its reaching for the portrait of Jesus when we firmly believe that in the course of the development of common grace, those forms and conditions of life that prevailed in Palestine at that time had become such as God had ordained them from eternity for the appearance of his dear Son on earth.

CHAPTER EIGHTEEN

BORN OF A WOMAN

But when the fullness of time had come, God sent forth his Son, born of woman, born under the law.

GALATIANS 4:4

§ 1 The fruit of common grace did not accrue to Jesus only after his birth. The connection between Christ and common grace was already functioning between the time of his conception by the Holy Spirit and his birth of the Virgin Mary. We must even note that we find precisely here the point that we encounter in the consistent heresy of the Anabaptists. Faithful to their point of departure that the work of salvation remains supernatural until the end, they maintained that the Christ did not take his flesh and blood *from* the Virgin Mary, but that an infant body had been prepared in Mary through a new creation. In that perspective, nothing came from Mary; her blood and her essence were not involved. The only role she had was to carry this newly created infant body inside her, analogous to a cage in which a bird is hatched. In fact, this body also could have been prepared elsewhere, even outside Mary. Whether she or another woman carried it during those months makes no difference. This newly created body descended into her, rested in her, and left her again, so that it merely passed through.[1] From

1. The Anabapist doctrine of Christ's heavenly or "celestial" flesh was characteristic of a number of early figures in the radical Reformation, including Caspar Schwenkfeld

that perspective, the first contact of the Son of Man with the life of humankind took place only after his birth, and even after his birth this contact remained a purely external one. But with such a newly created body, Christ then stood *outside* our race. The Word did become *flesh,* but not *our* flesh. He was a being that resembled us, but he never was our brother according to the flesh. A blood other than ours flowed through his heart. And not our blood, but a foreign life-fluid coursed through his veins.

In opposition to the Anabaptist heresy that cuts off the entire Christian confession at the root and makes all of salvation's work pointless, the Christian church erects the conviction that our Savior did not bring his flesh and blood *into* Mary, but received them *from* Mary, and that thus the one born from Mary not only seemed to be but in truth was "the Son of Man," the same as us in every respect—except for sin [see Heb 4:15]. But with this it is also unquestioningly confessed that already long before his birth, indeed, immediately after his conception, Christ came into contact with the fruit of common grace as found at that time in Israel and, more specifically, in Mary. We cannot unveil here all mystery behind which the first formation inside the body of our own mother is hidden, even though it goes without saying that only a complete uncovering of this mystery would give us a clear insight into the relationship of the Christ to common grace. In Psalm 139:15–16 David has given thought to that hidden coming into being of life as it appears before God's eye, and David envisions how he was formed as an "unformed substance" in what he calls the "depths of the earth." Paul joins in with this expression in Ephesians 4:9 with Christ in view, and contrasts the Christ's descent into "the lower regions, the earth," with his ascension, and the primary import of Psalm 139 also refers to Christ. And apparently what is written in that psalm about being "intricately woven" in the pregnant woman is perceived with such breadth and depth, and drawn so elaborately, that it transcends the personal import of David's own birth by far and finds its commensurate dimensions only when we look beyond David to Christ.

We stand here before a world of wonders, with repeatedly new questions § 2
at every new turn. What is born always contains what will become visible later, as well as what always will remain invisible. There is a seed from which the organic whole will develop. There is the purely material that is absorbed by this seed in order to develop. And there is the life-urge that

(1489/90–1561), Melchior Hoffman (ca. 1495–ca. 1543), and Menno Simons (1496–1561), and was associated particularly with Dutch Anabaptists.

manifests itself in this development. All this is *at first* one with the mother, not only through resting inside her but through the circulation they share. Nevertheless, it will be separated from her later, not only by coming out into the light of life, but also by having the shared circulation cut off. And beyond this there is under and through all of this the communion of the newborn with the woman who bears the child. This includes not only physical communion but sometimes communion reaching as far as character and temperament, and virtually always communion in ethnic distinctives, national distinctions, facial types, and family characteristics. This is a communion that not only moves ahead in the newly born but also goes back into a hereditary line of many generations. And this communal and unitive aspect nevertheless undergoes the change and influence of the personal element in the person who was born. There is a personal variation that is not immediately evident but sometimes lies dormant for twelve years or more, only then to leave its stamp on the new person who is now growing and soon will be an adult.

§ 3 But even if we could sharply delineate and delimit all these various factors within ourselves or within our own child, the results of which manifest themselves in our own life or in the life of our child, and even if we could determine their relative importance and significance, it would not follow in the least that we could succeed in achieving such a precise explanation in connection with the incarnation of the Word. But since it is impossible to make such an assessment of these various elements in connection with one single human being, and since we cannot say, either in general or in particular, how and in what way these various factors operate in the formation of the ordinary human being, it is a matter of course that in connection with the person of the Savior, whose conception was quite exceptional, we must abandon any attempt at coming up with a correct explanation. Our Catechism has indeed placed emphasis on one of these factors by affirming that the reason Christ was born as a child and did not appear as an adult was that he "with His innocence and perfect holiness covers, in the sight of God, my sin, wherein I was conceived";[2] but the very words in which this confession is formulated sufficiently indicate that we

2. Heidelberg Catechism, Lord's Day 14, Q&A 36.

have here a statement involving the panorama of redemption and not an analysis of the gestation of Christ.

This forces us at this point in our inquiry to let the specifics rest and to limit ourselves to those general lines that present the various factors in general. And then the Christian confession definitely requires that we not assume in Christ a hereditarily determined character. What we call an individual character in ourselves and others is always one-sided, an individual "wrinkle" found only in us and not in others, so that this one "wrinkle" is well-developed in us whereas we lack the other "wrinkles." It is not until we assemble a large crowd of human beings, each with a clearly developed character, that we obtain an impression of the full richness of the *human* character as such. Were we to try to conceive of such a clearly delineated character in Christ, then Christ would become limited and one-sidedly defined, and he would no longer be the "Son of Man." But neither must we say that there was therefore no character in Christ. Lack of character is generally felt to be a defect, but there was no defect in Christ. The only thing we can say therefore is that in Christ not only one aspect, not merely one "wrinkle" of the fullness of human character stood out, but that the full human character shone in him in organic unity. Not just a single ray, but all rays together. And that fullness of rays in a perfect harmony of splendor, in a perfectly pure balance of hues. But precisely from this it follows that Christ could not owe his *human* fullness specifically to Mary. Mary possessed only one piece of the human character, and because Christ adopted human character in all its aspects, he did not receive it specifically from Mary, nor did he bring it with him when he entered Mary as the Son of God, but he appropriated it from the general human nature that had come to Mary from Adam and passed from Mary to Christ. § 4

Thus the first requirement to be fulfilled here was that through all the centuries since paradise, the undamaged human nature was preserved in such a way that in the fullness of time it could be transferred to Christ. And precisely this would have been inconceivable if the ravages of sin after the fall could have continued unrestrained and unbridled and had not been arrested by common grace. If the long-suffering and tolerance of God had not intervened to temper the conflagration of the fire of sin that we had started, even though it had to continue smoldering, then adopting the undamaged human nature on the part of the eternal Word many centuries after the fall would simply have been impossible. If death had run its full course in our race immediately after the fall, there simply would have been no offspring. And even if we do not take this preservation into account, but assume that the degeneration of our human nature would have gone untrammeled toward its conclusion, even as it reaches that state in hell, then this alone would have resulted in the degeneration and corruption becoming a general mutilation and violation, and thus the adoption of our human nature on the part of Christ would have been inconceivable. The intermediate situation in which we humans find ourselves on earth consists precisely in sin having been arrested, so that our nature left to itself is absolutely helpless, yet there is left the possibility of its restorability. By leaving it open to restorability, this situation protects all core essences and data of our nature from destruction to such an extent that they could still be seized by Christ, personally in his own incarnation, and as far as we are concerned, in our incorporation into his marvelous body.

§ 5 Thus the fundamental connection of Christ with the fruit of common grace lies in the fact that throughout the centuries after the fall, common grace has preserved human nature from complete degeneration, mutilation, and destruction, and has thus brought it about that Christ, so many centuries later, would be able to adopt from a human being the undamaged human nature in the fullness and completeness of its capabilities. We have not taken this from the side of the *flesh*, but from the side of the human *character*, not, of course, to separate the character of our human nature from the nature of the human flesh and blood, but because it is clear that flesh and blood serve our higher nature, and not the converse. It is certain that the differences between flesh and flesh, blood and blood, with regard to peoples, nations, and tribes, are linked to the diversity in character and type, but this must never be understood in the spirit of materialism, as if the difference in nature and type, in character and attitude, were only the accidental result of the different mixings of blood. On the contrary, the spirit is served by the blood, and therefore when Christ adopted our human nature, attention first had to be focused on the undamaged state of our human nature in its highest perspective. What common grace preserved is not in the first place our flesh and blood, and therefore not the robustness, sturdiness, and beauty of the body. Common grace defends man, human nature, and the treasure of the higher human life against total degradation and destruction. Hence the impressive characters, the noble personalities, the towering talents we see century after century appear among pagans as well. And thanks to common grace, the eternal Word could associate itself with human nature that was preserved, spared, and safeguarded against damage and mutilation.

But having placed this decisively in the foreground, with equal resoluteness we now add that this saving and sparing of the *higher* aspect of our human nature would not have been conceivable if the human aspect of our *physical* appearance had not been spared at the same time. A noble character is reflected in a noble visage, and a noble family that has excelled century after century through robust characters is displayed with a beautiful exterior. Among the nations we already see how profoundly the physical appearance of people can be oppressed when sin continues rampantly, and how nobler sentiments can lift up and elevate a people's outward appearance. This difference continues, on the one hand, through the generations, and on the other hand, through the people, and when we now study the descendants of Shem, not in our Jewish quarters but in the opulent East, and among the Arabs in the desert, and among the more pure Jewish types who recently traveled through our country from Russia, we are involuntarily touched by the dignity of the human appearance and the noble facial features that are characteristic of this people. Especially the beauty of the man comes strongly to expression among the pure descendants of Shem, and even now when we compare a regal Bedouin head or a noble Jewish head of pure heritage with that of the Chinese or Japanese, the Khoi or Congolese of today, we savor and sense the common grace that has maintained in Shem's pure and noble descendants the dignity of human nature in their external appearance.[3] We note this not to emphasize what is called human beauty, but rather to accentuate how also in the external form of our human nature a dignity survived, not among all peoples, not in every race, but to a very high degree especially in the line that descended from Shem, and how this external dignity was linked with human nature in a higher sense.

Thus two things were saved by common grace: first, every feature and part of our human nature in its higher aspect, and second, what was required for the manifestation of that human nature in its physical presence. Moreover, it was not at all accidental that Christ's birth was already linked to Shem's progeny through Noah's prophecy. In all this there is one continuous holy ordination of God's most special providence. Common grace thus operates according to fixed rules, in anticipation of Christ, and

3. For more on Kuyper's racial and civilizational judgments from his Eurocentric perspective, see *CG* 1.12.10n4; 1.41.1n3.

particular grace caused Christ to make his entrance precisely at the point where common grace reached the intersection with particular grace. And both, this common and this particular grace, met in the virgin Mary.

§ 6 If we knew more about Mary, and if we were able with the help of psychological analysis to write a complete, satisfactory biography of this blessed one among women, going back into the life of her father and her mother, there undoubtedly would be more than enough opportunity to marvel at the exquisiteness of God's work in bringing forth this mother of the Lord. Although we resist the tendency that, under the leadership of Rome, found entry in such a considerable portion of the Christian church and that, at least among the unthinking masses, threatens to put Mary ahead of Christ, the Reformed nevertheless also confess wholeheartedly that the virgin Mary was a vessel chosen by God and that the woman chosen in his eternal decree to carry the Son of Man close to her very heart was prepared for this calling of hers and was conceived, born, raised, and enabled by her God both physically and spiritually.

The person, the disposition, the will and inclination, the character and the temperament, and the entire human constitution of the woman who was to become the mother of the Lord were in no way a matter of indifference. We must not say that any other unmarried young woman could equally have been mother of the Lord or that the infant Jesus could have nursed at the breast of any other woman. Even though the conception of the Lord was absolutely from the Holy Spirit, already during the period of pregnancy such a variety of influences passed from Mary to her holy child that it would be worthless to think for even a moment that these influences would have been the same if they had come from any other woman. Jesus took her blood into his veins; the flesh of Jesus' body was formed from her flesh; for many months the pulsing of the blood in her heart was the pulsing of Jesus' lifeblood. And even though it is not given to us to draw the boundary line between this particular element that Christ received from Mary, and those general human traits that he received through Mary from Adam, it nevertheless would be a shocking superficiality to totally discount those particular features of Mary's person.

§ 7 Even holy Scripture prohibits this. Although holy Scripture puts Mary in the shadow to such an extent that when we remain faithful to the Scriptures we are cut off from any danger of letting the child hide behind the mother, nevertheless holy Scripture does not portray Mary as an isolated individual young virgin, but instead it shows us Mary at the endpoint of a holy lineage that starts with Eve; continues through Seth and Enosh, diverges in Shem; and then finds its further definition in Abraham, Isaac, and Jacob; and finally in Judah and David. To some extent we might even say that as far as the generations are concerned, it is as if the whole history of the old covenant pursues only one goal: to bring forth Mary, and then from Mary, Christ.

The refinement or, if you will, this shielding from degeneration, takes place all along this long line by means of isolation and separation. Thus the descendants of Seth move away from the Canaanites; the Shemites from the Hamites and the Japhethites; Abraham's line from his blood relatives in Ur; Isaac from Ishmael; Jacob from Esau; Judah from Simeon and the rest of Jacob's sons; and then again, in the house of David, Jesse's tribe from the rest of the Judeans. This selection process continued thereafter, of course, in the dynasty of David, albeit with a skipping of generations, although we cannot trace this in detail. And thus at last the living line came to Mary, in order that through her, the God-ordained and God-prepared and hence eminently suitable instrument could appear, through which both the human nature that came from Adam and the fruit of common grace would be prepared at its richest and purest condition for the incarnation of the Word.

It remains to be noted that it is not always easy for us to keep the line of common grace separate from the line of particular grace in this context. Shem's election, Abraham's calling, and David's anointing belong to the latter and must not be confused with the activities of common grace, even though those vary in degree from nation to nation. But against this stands the reality that, apart from the salvation of the elect, the working of particular grace also has aftereffects upon common grace. Ishmael receives a fruit, a blessing, a promise that flows from the particular position of Abraham but also enters the common life of the nations through Ishmael. And in the same way, the preserving work of common grace is reinforced continually through the lateral effect of particular grace, even as we still see how the common human life in Christian countries, even for those thousands who live and die entirely outside of particular grace, stands on a visibly higher plane than in countries where Islam or Buddhism reigns.

CHAPTER NINETEEN

JESUS' INCREASE

And Jesus increased in wisdom and in stature and in favor with God and man.

LUKE 2:52

§ 1 It goes without saying that Jesus' contact with the fruit of common grace is manifested for us much more clearly after his birth. That contact certainly occurred during the weeks and months between his conception and his birth, and common grace passed from Mary to Jesus, but this is not open to our observation. After his birth, however, this contact occurs in the visible realm. As a child, Jesus lives under the care of Mary and Joseph. Until his twelfth year he lives virtually only in a domestic environment, and after that he lives in the flow of public life in Israel. Thus he grows up to be a youth and a man, and only when he is thirty does he manifest himself to the Baptist and undergo his initiation into the office of messiah at the Jordan River.

Of that long thirty-year period we know very little. We know something of the first year of his life on earth, then of a single incident from his twelfth year, but everything else remains in obscurity until his baptism at the Jordan. This of course is not by accident; God has willed it thus. And what has been recorded of the tradition about Jesus' childhood is so insignificant, and in part so unworthy of his holy person, that the knowledge of it brings us pain rather than making us long for the larger story. The evangelists show clearly that they do not attach value to a knowledge of those first years of his life—or rather, that for the church of all ages it is more important to get to know its Savior only at the manger and then immediately at his baptism, than to be able to follow the development of the Savior over those thirty long years. It does at times incite our holy curiosity to be able to imagine the child Jesus at the first development of his consciousness, his behavior as a boy in the family, his learning to read, his contact with other children, and so forth. But God has drawn a curtain over this, and the Spirit of the Lord does not want us to concern ourselves with this. What must speak to us is twofold: the gift of God's Son to the world when Jesus is born, and thereafter the coming of Jesus to the world when he reveals himself to John the Baptist.

To this extent we therefore might say that Jesus' contact with the fruit § 2
of common grace during the years of his upbringing and development is even more shrouded for us in the mists of mystery. And this is indeed the case if we want to point exclusively to facts and encounters. But this does not alter the fact that we know two things with certainty. First, Jesus grew up in Nazareth on the shore of the Sea of Galilee; from his twelfth year on, he participated in the worship in the temple of Zion; and he was already skilled in the Scriptures at that time, and later, as teacher in Israel, had knowledge of all religious, political, and social relationships in Palestine. This shows that the child Jesus did not grow up isolated from the world, did not live apart from the life of his people, and did not segregate himself from his contemporaries in spiritual solitude, but lived among his people and with his people and was, we might say, fully integrated in his contemporary environment.

This is the first definite fact; the second is that from the Gospels as well as from other sources, we know the social, political, and religious situation in Israel at that time to have been a situation that owed its existence only to common grace. Of course this was not solely due to common grace, for in Israel it was especially the work of God's particular grace that left its imprint on the nation. But no matter how broad a significance we assign to particular grace, we cannot deny that the influence of particular grace at that time was definitely no longer what it had once been in the days of David and that, on the contrary, all kinds of alien influences from Assyria and Babylon, from Egypt and Arabia, and from Greece and Rome were at work among Israel. The situation Jesus encountered when he appeared in Israel was therefore most definitely not a situation of general degeneration, nor a situation that manifested itself directly and entirely as the fruit of particular grace. It was one that also, and in no small part, was a result of common grace as it made itself felt both in Israel itself and in these other influences.

If we take these two facts together—that Jesus lived for thirty years among Israel and entered into the life of Israel, and that the condition of the nation at that time was due in no small measure to the effects of common grace—then it follows automatically that Jesus came into very extensive contact with the fruit of common grace, not just at disparate points, but in the entire development of his human life. It is from this environment, as the Lord found it in Israel, that he derived his illustrations and images. It is in connection with the everyday life of that time that he revealed the things of the kingdom to us. It is the language of the Israel of that time that he spoke, the customs of the Israel of his day that he followed. It was the questions that at that time stirred the emotions that he experienced. Therefore, although we lack the data to expound all this in detail, there can be no difference of opinion about the fact as such. The contact with the fruit of common grace, as it manifested itself at that time in Israel, did exist for Jesus and functioned for many years and on a very broad scale.

§ 3 The confession of Jesus as "God over all, blessed forever" [Rom 9:5] must not blind us. Of course every Christian confesses that the knowledge belonging to God's Son was omniscience, that his being was self-sufficient, and that nothing can be added to either his omniscience or his self-sufficiency. No increase or growth in these was conceivable.

In the case of the Son of God, who is to be worshiped as God with the Father and the Holy Spirit, there can be no development, no nurturing, no increase in knowledge. If we take anything away from this, we destroy in a single stroke the deity of Christ. But entirely separate from this is the question of how we must interpret the consciousness of him who made himself nothing and took on the form of a servant [Phil 2:7]. We can already understand that among people there is rich knowledge inside a person, and that nevertheless at a given moment, or through special circumstances, this person lacks command of this knowledge. Let us imagine a man who has a rich thought-world, a broadly encompassing mental development, and exceptional willpower. While he sleeps, his knowledge is not gone, his thought-world is still within him, and his willpower still hides inside him, but as he lies there sleeping, they do not show or manifest themselves. And even in a long, serious illness that affects the whole body, the mental organs may be temporarily nonfunctional to such a degree that later, as he recovers, he only gradually recovers his memory and grows again into his own thought-world. There is therefore nothing contradictory in confessing that while the infant Jesus lay in the manger, this perfect divine knowledge and this divine fullness of power were already present in him, and yet that all this was nevertheless hidden, not apparent—indeed, that even in his completed human nature it could never manifest itself other than very partially. *Finitum non capax infiniti*—that is, "The finite can never grasp the infinite"—is the decisive maxim our forefathers always defended, and it must therefore never be presented as if the human nature of Jesus, which was *finite*, was ever capable of revealing his *infinite* deity.[1] The pure light was in Jesus, but it could never radiate out through the prism of his human nature other than to the extent that his human nature allowed it to pass through, and in the tint that the prism of his human nature gave to it.

If it is a fact that our human nature goes through a process of growth and development and can reach its full dimensions only through that growth and development, then it follows that, in order to be in fact and in truth one of us, Son of Man, Jesus had to subject himself to that growth and that development in obedience to the Father and out of love for God's world. This did not happen out of powerlessness but rather out of the fullness of the power of divine love. The image of the sleeping philosopher we just presented falls short here, because the thinker is passive in his sleep, and the Son of God was active in both his incarnation and his human development. This is how he himself wanted it. He himself entered into this condition. It did not happen to him, but he sought it as such. He sought the flesh and blood of infants. He sought our human nature, and thus also the God-imposed limits and ordinances for that nature. And he sought all of this because he sought the elect of God. It was a descending to us in order to reveal in us the glory of his Father.

Growth and *development* automatically imply that one who grows and § 4
develops takes something from the outside into oneself and, by doing so, matures. If we therefore acknowledge that Jesus took on human nature, and that growth and development are inseparable from human nature, we also acknowledge that Jesus took into himself many things from the outside and, through growing up, reached maturity.

1. See *DLGTT*, s.v. "Finitum non capax infiniti": "*The finite is incapable of the infinite*; i.e., the finite or finite being is incapable of grasping, comprehending, or receiving the infinite or infinite being; an epistemological and christological maxim emphasized by the Reformed in debate with the Lutherans."

With respect to the body this is immediately clear. Each of us confesses that Jesus took into himself the flesh and blood of our nature from Mary's blood, and that only in this way could he reach full term and be born. And everyone equally agrees that, once he was born, Jesus nursed at Mary's breast and thereafter also took solid food and quenched his thirst by drinking. We can add that like each one of us, he inhaled and exhaled air, such that in this way his body was maintained and grew through what he took into himself from the outside. And no less does everyone concede that Jesus was not born with adult stature but was first a small infant, and that only by growing did he become a youth and a man, something that is conceivable only by means of taking into himself food and drink and air. This is why our forefathers attached such importance to the fact that we read that Jesus had hunger at Sychar [see John 4:5–6] and had thirst on the cross, because precisely this hunger and thirst showed that Jesus' body was not a body *in appearance only* that maintained itself automatically, but a body like ours that was maintained only by taking food and drink into itself. We do read that Jesus fasted for forty days in the wilderness, but even apart from the fact that other people have also fasted for long periods, the story of this fasting concludes with the statement that at last he became hungry, and being hungry always points to the need for taking food and drink into oneself.

When we move from Jesus' body to his spirit, however, many hesitate to reach the same conclusion. This hesitation must be resisted, however. For Jesus took on not only a human body, but also a human soul, and thus in that soul also the capacities of the human soul, and thus also a human consciousness and a human will. He was not God in a human body, but rather God revealed in our whole human nature, and in Jesus that spiritual nature of man was also real and actual. It was not just seemingly human, but human in accordance with all the stipulations that God himself had ordained for human nature when he created man. Here too we must ask ourselves what the content of that creation ordinance of God for our human nature is, whether our spiritual nature comes into the world completely adult, or instead develops. Further, we must ask whether it develops automatically or by taking things into itself from the outside. There can be no difference of opinion on this point. Everyone agrees that the creation of Adam and Eve as adult persons was not God's design for the race that would be born from them. On the contrary, each child also begins with being spiritually *un*developed. The child would never come to development if he were isolated from all other human beings. He only reaches maturity through contact with the human world around him. Here there is also a hungering for knowledge and a thirsting after learning, and this hunger is stilled and the thirst is quenched to no small extent from nature and the world of humans. It is not as if this were the only nourishment for the development of the spirit. For it is also from God himself, thanks to his revelation and the inner working of his Spirit, that man receives inner enlightenment and strengthening. But in most cases by far, even that revelation of God is tied to the service of and concourse with other people.

In any case, everyone will concede that, in addition to what is offered from the Word and through the Spirit, our spirit is also supplied with all kinds of things from nature and through our interaction with the world of humans who enrich us. It goes without saying that this does not mean that an adult spirit would be the product only of what it took in. This is not even true in the case of our body. If we do not have a healthy constitution, nourishment does not benefit us, and if we do not have the strength in us to enrich the blood from nourishment, the growth of the body does not occur. In the same way, the growth of man's spirit can never be the simple product of what it has taken in, but the spirit itself chooses what it will take in and make its own and processes what is taken in. Only this remains certain: according to God's design, the spiritual side of man's nature is also arranged in such a way that it must take in all kinds of nourishment from outside and that it forms itself in this way.

This being the case, we cannot help but posit one of two things in the case of Jesus as well: either he let his consciousness awaken apart from his environment (but then his nature was in this respect not a human nature), or, if he was truly human with respect to his spiritual nature as concerns the soul and its capacities, then a regular development must have taken place in his human consciousness, and that development must have occurred by taking into himself from nature, from the Word, and from the human world around him all kinds of notions, insights, and knowledge.

The Scriptures themselves attest that *Jesus also increased in wisdom*. This § 5
cannot have been from the inside, because with respect to his divine person his was the *perfect* divine wisdom that, because in itself it is eternally perfect, cannot increase. It therefore must have been an increase through taking into himself things from nature, from the Word, and from the world around him. There is no dispute that this taking into himself of that knowledge, and his developing through that knowledge, took place in an entirely unique manner in Jesus; on the contrary, it follows from the uniqueness of

his personality. It is sufficient for us that the absolute fact remains that Jesus developed, and that this development to full maturity occurred by taking in things from the outside. If we were to deny this, we would be assigning a human nature to Jesus, not as it should be according to God's design, but an *imaginary* human nature that would cut off for us any communion with Jesus.

If this is established, then what we posited at the beginning of this chapter is also completely established—namely, that in this too, common grace yielded a fruit for Jesus. It is not just the fruit that comes under consideration here; what holy Scripture has been for Jesus, none of us will ever fully understand. The distance between the child Jesus in the temple and the gray-haired scribes whom he questioned already proves this. And we can only guess by approximation how the service in Zion's temple served to deepen his insight into the sacred. If already among us human beings one person may receive a much profounder impression of sacred things than the impression that another receives, then with what depth and richness must Jesus have received this impression. Nor must we argue about what the Holy Spirit *without measure* has been for Jesus in the spiritual development of his human consciousness. All this is not merely added in the development of the human consciousness of Jesus, but it also points us to the main factors.

All this does not deny, however, that Jesus also absorbed the rich wealth of nature and also took into himself the language, the forms of consciousness, the notions, and the human and spiritual development he found in his environment and among his people. Jesus did not speak in the language of angels or in the language of paradise, but in the imperfect language of the Jews of that time. How else could they have understood him? And Jesus did not bring this language with him into the world, but he learned it from his mother. But a language cannot be learned without acquiring thoughts and concepts and ideas of which the language is an expression. And those concepts, in turn, Jesus could not make his own without entering into the development of life in his environment. Assume for a moment that Jesus had been born among a backward people that lived at a very low level; then the thought world in which Jesus grew up would have been a much poorer one. The fact that he grew up in the midst of a people where human life, through common grace, existed on as high a plane as it did, and was as rich as it was in Israel at that time, did not happen by accident but according to the wise ordination of God, and this was in order that Jesus' human consciousness would achieve precisely the development necessary for his role as messiah. And thus the fruit of common grace was given to Jesus in precisely the form and in the measure that in God's ordination were required for his divine mission.

CHAPTER TWENTY

JESUS' ENVIRONMENT

Consider the lilies of the field, how they grow: they neither toil nor spin, yet I tell you, even Solomon in all his glory was not arrayed like one of these.

MATTHEW 6:28B–29

§ 1 We also owe to common grace everything beautiful, everything good that still remained in the *kingdom of nature*. As far as nature is concerned, the law of sin threatened us with the curse that we would not inhabit paradise, but an earth that produced only thorns and thistles. But common grace consists precisely in that this curse has been arrested, and that although thorns and thistles did sprout and destruction did permeate nature in every other area, this destructive element did not gain the upper hand, and we have been left with an earth that offers an abundant, richly furnished wealth of nature. When Jesus came, he found in Palestine, which had not yet deteriorated, an Oriental opulence, a Levantine beauty in nature, whose language he captured and interpreted for his disciples. He did not close himself off from the nature that surrounded him. We do not find in Jesus the slightest trace of the trait that sometimes manifests a super-spiritual piety, that closes itself off spiritually and is blind to the beauty of nature. We encounter the Savior more outdoors than indoors, and every page of the Gospels proves that he did not walk through the valleys of Palestine with a distracted eye, but with eyes that were open to the beauty of nature. For he derives his metaphors from the life of nature, and from the life of nature he derives his parables, and it is strikingly clear over and over again that in what Jesus says about the things of natural life he does not rely on what others told him, but he observed everything with his own eyes.

There is more in this than superficially would seem to be the case.

The imagery derived from nature is not accidental. On the contrary, if Jesus had not had this imagery, if its subject matter had not existed and the Savior had been compelled to convey the truth of God only in abstract concepts, we would not have been told the half of it, and half of what he did tell us would not have been grasped by the disciples, by the crowds, and by later generations. And when we look at what still remains of the gospel even in those circles that have strayed from the truth, then what survives is a parable or a metaphorical saying, or one of those moving references to things such as the birds of the air or the lilies of the field. If none of this had been at Jesus' disposal, or if he had spoken exclusively in conceptual language, as John does in the prologue to his Gospel, then the preaching of the kingdom of heaven immediately would have been impeded, would have been absorbed by only very few people, and then only very partially. It never would have found its way to those thousands upon thousands who are averse to concepts and who live with images.

And this too is far from accidental, but is linked directly to the creation ordinance of God. All of nature is symbolic; that is, all of nature bears a symbol of the spiritual. There are two lives: a spiritual, invisible life and a sensory, visible life. And God created that life of nature and that life of spirit in mutual relationship. The one bears the image of the other. The spiritual mirrors itself in the natural, as the trees on the shore mirror themselves on the quiet, still surface of the water. On an even more profound level, God created nature not in order that there might be fruit and flower, but to reveal in nature his own wisdom and omnipotence. The virtues of our God shine through in nature, not by accident, but because God radiates them in nature. God's thoughts in the realm of nature allude to God's thoughts in the spiritual kingdom. And where we humans, who exist in soul and body, participate in both the invisible and the visible life, nature is aimed at explaining the spiritual to us, and the spiritual has been created to give the realm of nature its meaning for us. This carries over even to our human language. The sounds that cross our lips belong to the realm of nature, but the thoughts, perceptions, and emotions that we express to others in these sounds are unseen and invisible in character.

§ 2 From this it follows that the revelation of the kingdom of God cannot do without the language of nature that penetrates our sinful world. It is as the Apostle Matthew says: Jesus revealed in his parables things that were hidden from before the foundation of the world [Matt 13:35]. Indeed, God put into nature reflections of the things that would accrue to us in the kingdom of heaven. If the destructive effect of the curse had continued, and the language of nature had been erased for us, or if this epistle of nature been overgrown entirely with thorns and thistles, then there would have been no means to reveal the kingdom of heaven to us. And even if it were assumed that Jesus could have known that language of nature, what use would it have been if we human beings had not understood the language? Would he then have spoken, without our having understood him? Thus, if Jesus had to be able to reveal the things of the kingdom of heaven to us in the language of nature, it was indispensable for him (1) that nature would have been arrested in its destruction, so that it could still reflect the spiritual; (2) that Jesus would come to know nature in a land where it still spoke its own language sufficiently clearly; and (3) that the crowds who heard him speak would be accustomed to the same language of nature. And this is indeed how it occurred. Common grace has in general restrained nature's degeneration into one large field of thorns and thistles. There is destruction. Some regions of the earth are even totally degraded. Nevertheless the earth still offers very broad regions where nature's life flourishes richly.

The development of nature is much richer and more opulent in the Orient than in the north. Cold drives people indoors; the coolness of summer drives people outdoors. Consequently, people in the Orient live much more in nature, whereas the inhabitants of Greenland barely dare to venture outside even briefly. This is why the language of nature can be learned so much better in the Orient than in the north. Living regularly in the open air makes one receptive and susceptible to understanding the language of nature. This colors all language that is spoken in the Orient. Children are accustomed to it from an early age. The life of nature is absorbed to an extent that is alien to us. And it is therefore beyond dispute that we especially must be in the Orient to fully absorb the beauty of the starry sky and the opulence of nature. Correspondingly, we see that Jesus did not appear in Sweden or Norway, let alone among the Eskimos in Siberia, but in an Oriental land with a nature laden with Oriental opulence. Even beyond this, the whole earlier revelation that prepared Jesus' coming and formed the spiritual language prior to his manifestation, was from the beginning concentrated in the Orient. And the long line that runs from paradise to the manger of Bethlehem does not for a moment leave the Oriental world.

Yet there are still distinctions in this Oriental world. In the tropics, and thus also in our East Indian colonies, the life of nature is Oriental in character but not free in its development. The heat is too oppressive there. That makes colors too strong, which causes a leaning toward another extreme, bringing about what might be called Oriental one-sidedness. Nature then is Oriental in an exaggerated fashion and consumes those soft variegations and wealth of forms that make nature so *expressive*. The life of nature therefore stands higher in what is called the Levant—that is, the lands along the eastern half of the Mediterranean Sea, than in the common Oriental life. In fact, almost all countries that were prominent in the development of humanity before Christ lie in close proximity there: Egypt, Greece, Rome, Palestine, and beyond this, at the same latitude, Babylon. If we now ask in which part of the globe Jesus should have appeared to find nature in a form most suitable to expressing the things of the kingdom, no other answer can reasonably be given than that the Levant was the obvious region. Only here is nature rich, yet tempered, displaying its full beauty, while at the same time remaining free from the heavy, sultry, and oppressive character of life in the tropics. Thus it is common grace that in general arrested the destruction of nature, that arrested it *more* in the Orient than in the north, and that arrested it in the most desirable fashion precisely in a country like Palestine. Thus we may and must acknowledge that in the most literal sense it was common grace that made nature manifest itself before Jesus' eyes in such forms as made nature most suitable for reflecting the things of the kingdom. § 3

As a final fruit of common grace we must add that Jesus automatically encountered in this Levantine nature, and more specifically in Palestine, a population that from birth was designed to understand this language of nature. The Jewish people had always lived in either Egypt, Palestine, or Babylon, and it was therefore an Oriental people in the full sense of the word, but particularly a people of the Levantine stamp. This was part of God's ordination. God himself had called Abraham from the more out-of-the-way Ur to Palestine alongside the Mediterranean Sea. Israel's appointed homeland was there; Israel had formed its poetic spiritual language there; Israel had established the relationship between its life and the life of nature there. And it was the fruit of this appointing of Israel's dwelling place, as well as of its past, as well as of the formation of its language, that Jesus, who appeared at that time and among that people, could gather hearers around him who were no strangers to this language of nature.

§ 4 Thus the fruit of common grace was brought forth to the Mediator between God and man: first, in being from the line of David; second, in growing up among such a highly developed people; and third, in the symbolism of nature. But there is still more. The goal of Christ's appearing in the flesh was certainly not simply to manifest himself to us, to walk among our race, and in this course of events to proclaim to us the words of eternal life. He was also called to intervene in the existing life that he encountered, to engage it in battle, and not to rest until he ostensibly perished in it, that he might triumph precisely in that apparent demise. Jesus was, if we may express it in this way, an element of fermentation in the world in which he appeared. He compelled others to holy sympathy or repelled them in deadly antipathy. Contrasts existed between him and the human life in which he appeared, and he had to make the demand that this human life adapt itself to *him* and allow itself to be assimilated through *his* life. And when the world refused to do this, the only possible result was that a battle should ensue. Either the world had to triumph over him, or he had to triumph over the world.

From this it follows that Jesus did not walk through life avoiding and evading, but he seized life and engaged in wrestling with it. This is shown in his miracles when he heals the sick, releases the demon possessed, commands the winds, subjects the sea to his will, takes regal control over the nourishing properties of bread, and intervenes in existing conditions and transforms them according to his pleasure in so many other ways. But in the end that same battle had to be engaged with organized human life, as it appeared in fixed form in the schools of the scribes, in the hierarchy of the priests, and among the government of the country. Initially and by way of preparation, he conducted this battle by means of disputation and denunciating sermons, but in the end this struggle had to lead to a life-or-death conflict. The power of the hierarchy and national government had to yield to him or prepare itself *against* him and formally dispute the advance of his cause.

For us who believe, there resides in this the mystery of the work of reconciliation and of satisfaction, and we therefore confess with all of Christianity that the Son of Man took our sins upon himself and has taken them to the cross, and thus has borne the penalty for our sins through his death on the cross. But one thing is self-evident: neither the Sanhedrin in Jerusalem nor the Roman governor understood it in this way. In the days when this terrible legal action was carried out in Jerusalem, there was no one who thought of the self-sacrifice of the Lamb of God. Neither the Sanhedrin nor Pilate saw it this way, and even the thoughts of the disciples were focused on quite different things. It was a struggle between Jesus with his influence on the crowds and his miraculous power, on the one hand, and the hierarchy along with the imperial rule, on the other. And in that struggle Jesus perished on the cross, only to triumph later over both of these powers in his resurrection.

There are therefore two things here: the mystical background of the atonement sacrifice, and the apparent struggle between Jesus and the two powers of his time. And of course, it is inappropriate simply to combine those two sides of the conflict separately and entirely externally. On the contrary, precisely in the struggle between those two life powers of hierarchy and imperial rule the process of divine justice was executed, and it is therefore striking that our apostolic confession, when it comes to the death of our Savior, is in fact silent about the atoning sacrifice and mentions only the sober fact that he died "under Pontius Pilate." What, we might ask, does this have to do with our redemption from sin, and what does it matter whether Jesus died under Pontius Pilate or died some other death? For it is his death, his violent dying, his shed blood alone, in which our hope rests.

Our Catechism, meanwhile, emphatically points out that his being con- § 5
demned to death by *the temporal judge* gives his death the power to gain acquittal in God's judgment, and then maintains that his death under Pontius Pilate was *not* something secondary but was required by the world-atoning character of his death.[1] The mystery of reconciliation and the external course of events in the process surrounding Jesus are thus, according to our Reformed confession, definitely related. This relationship is confessed in the declaration that Jesus came into conflict with the temporal administration of justice as it developed under government authority. We must therefore take this as our starting point and confess that the reconciliation of our sin could be effected only if the Mediator came into contact with the temporal judge and was condemned to death by him. It is then immediately striking that in that contact, how the temporal judge acted

1. See Heidelberg Catechism, Lord's Day 15, Q&A 38: "That He, being innocent, might be condemned by the temporal judge, and thereby deliver us from the severe judgment of God, to which we were exposed."

and under which administration of justice the death sentence on Jesus was pronounced were of the utmost importance.

What is this temporal administration of justice? Is it a fruit of particular grace or of common grace? We hardly need to point out that it is a product of grace. An administration of justice is inconceivable in a hellish state, for all administration of justice envisions the triumph of justice over injustice, and in a hellish state, the point of departure is the triumph of injustice. We also see how, under completely degraded conditions, virtually all administration of justice collapses and only raw violence rules. Wherever the administration of justice deserving of its name may rule, we must welcome this administration of justice as a favor, a grace that God Almighty bestows upon us in this sinful world, against our merit. For the administration of justice is not a matter of arbitration. It is not a pronouncement on the part of knowledgeable, wise men based on what they consider to be fair and just. No, the administration of justice is a power that acts on its own authority to avenge the violation of the law and, if necessary, to avenge it with death. Even if this is usually presented today in a different manner, and even if the administration of justice today has an entirely different basis, it remains in the universal testimony inseparable from the character of the administration of justice that this justice acts against crime without being asked or called upon to do so, and punishes by means of compulsory implementation. If we believe in God, it follows that the right and power to do this have been given by God to the human judge, since without the divine ordinance man cannot have power over the person and life of his fellow human being. All administration of justice therefore flows from a God-instituted power that is ordained to put the rule of a moral principle in place of the power of raw violence. This is why Scripture presents it as a punishment when God takes away the judges, and teaches us to see a blessing, a favor, a grace in God's having mercy and giving us judges again as in the beginning. Thus Isaiah 1:26–27 says: " 'And I will restore your judges as at the first, and your counselors as at the beginning. Afterward you shall be called the city of righteousness, the faithful city.' Zion shall be redeemed by justice, and those in her who repent, by righteousness."

§ 6 The administration of justice cannot be viewed as belonging to particular grace. For the administration of justice was found not only in Israel but also among all peoples that are not utterly degenerated. The administration of justice existed not only in Christian countries but also among the pagans and Muslims. There is therefore no question that the administration of justice must be placed in the realm of common grace, and our Catechism very correctly points this out by speaking of the "temporal judge." For in Israel too, there was an administration of justice, and specifically the administration of justice by the Sanhedrin had a mixed character in Jesus' day, but the Sanhedrin's verdict on Jesus was not final. Our Apostle's Creed in fact does not mention the verdict of the Sanhedrin, and refers not to Caiaphas but to Pontius Pilate as the judge responsible. Thus it is confirmed from all sides that the administration of justice under which Jesus was condemned to death was not particular to the Jews but general to the world, and that what was manifested in that system of law and administration of justice must be viewed as having sprouted from the root of common grace. And we must not say that this fact, far from bringing Jesus a fruit of common grace, instead brought Jesus an evil counterfeit of that common grace. For as we will show in more detail, once we understand that the work of the Mediator could not be accomplished except as the result of a life-or-death conflict with the temporal administration of justice, we implicitly agree that the presence of such an administration of justice was indispensable for the Mediator's work, and that thus in this respect as well, common grace cooperated in accomplishing God's counsel.

CHAPTER TWENTY-ONE

JESUS AND ROME'S ADMINISTRATION OF JUSTICE

Zion shall be redeemed by justice, and those in her who repent, by righteousness.

Isaiah 1:27

§ 1 Common grace as exhibited in Pontius Pilate requires further elucidation. As the Heidelberg Catechism indicates, his name is of secondary import here; his importance lies in the fact that he functions as the "temporal judge."[1] There are also "spiritual judges," and it was in this character that the Sanhedrin functioned. But the verdict, the sentence, of this "spiritual judge" was immaterial, and the gate of justice is opened because Jesus let himself be condemned not by the spiritual, but only by the "temporal judge." In addition, if he had to be judged before an earthly court, then nowhere in the world could an administration of justice be found that more seriously intended to maintain justice than the jurisprudence that had developed among the Romans. In this connection we want to elucidate two points:

1. See Heidelberg Catechism, Lord's Day 15, Q&A 38.

(1) all administration on earth is a manifestation of God's common grace, and (2) the development of jurisprudence among the Romans offered this common grace in its richest development.

Our human life, as God ordained and created it, is characterized by having two aspects: the one physical, the other spiritual. Between these two, the order has been established that the soul should rule the body, and the body serve the soul. The material must then be nothing but medium and instrument, and the spiritual must guide and rule and order all things. It follows that there are two kinds of forces in human life: those forces that find expression in the "strong arm," and the forces of deliberation and will. According to this creation ordinance, an invisible order must therefore rule in the world of the children of man, one that is maintained invisibly and imperceptibly. This is precisely the difference between our status and that of the animal world, and even more strongly, between that of the plant kingdom and inorganic nature. In the world of animals there is an invisible force that again and again manifests itself in the mother hen who risks her own life to save her chicks, in the bird who sits days on end to hatch her eggs with a faithfulness that often shames us, and so forth. But all this is instinct; it is a working of God in the animal that only operates through the animal and works in it. Otherwise, all order in animal society is based on power and sensuality. The animal robs, murders, tears in pieces, and the only thing that restrains the animal is the fear of being torn to pieces itself, whereas the gentler nature of domestic animals is the result of human guidance. Similarly in the plant kingdom, one plant crowds out the other, the great tree sucks nutrition away from smaller plants, the parasitic plant creeps up the trunk to rob the tree of its strength, and the thorn squeezes life from the weaker plant. And within inorganic nature, the stronger force even more decidedly and absolutely pushes aside what is weaker. The order that is present is determined by the sum of the addition and subtraction of forces. Only in man, by contrast, do we find an invisible force at work that emerges from man's nature itself and creates an order in life that is the result of *spiritual* factors.

That was the issue in paradise. Would Eve allow the invisible, spiritual § 2
factor that tied her to God and his ordinance to dominate, or would she let the sensual factor of the lust of the eyes and the other senses predominate? Her fall and Adam's fall involved turning the appointed order upside down. The spiritual factor bowed and yielded, and the sensual factor triumphed. Of course, this does not exhaust the nature and significance of the fall.

There was also the Satanic element, as well as the yielding of the higher spiritual factors to the lower spiritual factors. But for the point that occupies us at present, it is sufficient to have identified the reversed order, in which, as a consequence of the fall, the visible and the invisible factors in human nature came to stand opposed to one another.

When human life began to develop into a multiplicity of individuals, the result had to be that the human order would be lost and the animal order would penetrate human life, which means that the *right of the strongest* came to rule. We see this in Cain: Abel annoys him, and with one blow he gets rid of Abel. If this evil process had continued undisturbed and unrestrained, human society would not have reached a higher level. The invisible, spiritual order would have gradually disappeared, to be replaced by a purely physical order. Lust and cunning, using the stronger arm as an instrument, would have determined all human relationships. Everyone would have lived by the sword, and after a short time, human society would have become identical to the social life of animals in the forest. We may state this all the more definitely because from of old there has in fact existed—and still exists—a kind of human society in some regions that bore a remarkable resemblance to this. When Scripture says that justice will dwell in the desert one day, it presupposes that precisely in the desert, life is generally lawless and depends only on the sword of the strongest. And today we still find in Africa entire regions where one tribe continually goes to war against another in order to destroy it by force of arms; after the victory is won, the victors kill the able-bodied men, rob all possessions, violate the women, and take the children for themselves. If we ask whether among such nomads in the desert, and among such native tribes in Africa, all common grace is absent where *justice* is concerned, the answer must be that common grace is lacking between one tribe and another, but not among the members of the tribe themselves. Among themselves they certainly have a system of justice, but between their own tribe and the tribes surrounding them, they do not know relationships based on principles of justice.

It is God's common grace that nevertheless ensured, despite man's sinful nature that urges him to give up the human order and to desire an animal order, so that in general a certain human order survived among human beings and even developed further. Man has not saved himself from destruction, but God the Lord has protected him from himself, including where temporal life is concerned. This saving act of God's common grace follows two paths in this respect: the one in man, the other between people;

the first internal, the other external. The internal path in man consisted in the fact that God restrained his wild passion, stimulated a need for peace and rest in him, and caused more gentle inclinations to arise in his heart. And the external path between people was that God forced man to abandon the wild, nomadic life, to settle in fixed locations, and to find subsistence in farming, commerce, and trade. For this quieter life, tied to fixed abodes, automatically brings with it, as it were, the need to feel oneself protected in the possession of one's home and property by an orderly power. The one who sows must have the assurance that he himself will be able to harvest, and that another will not come and steal his harvest. And when in this manner the spirit of man was prepared internally and externally to adopt a regulating order in society, God instituted government, and in this government the high moral character of the human social order was embodied and sealed.

After all, the question was not merely whether people could guarantee one another the quiet possession of life and property, but something quite different: whether the awareness would dawn that how we wanted to live together did not depend on us, but that we all had to bow together under an ordained arrangement that God had instituted for our human life. The conviction had to be awakened that justice is not a product of our whims, but an ordinance of God to which we have to submit ourselves. And precisely from this should arise the elevated notion that the transgressor had to be thwarted, not because he had harmed us but because he had violated the God-instituted rule of law. Only in this way could the rule of physical strength and human viciousness be destroyed, or at least tempered, and the rule of an invisible, spiritual rule of law among humans be restored. And this is what God gave us in the government that *he* ordained, that was *his* servant, and in this way he put a holy stamp on human justice. Justice would not be a negotiation between doves and hawks, no matter how willingly or otherwise they would be able to stick it out together; rather, it would be the ascendancy among people of the social order God had ordained for them. In addition, government had to be provided with a power stronger than the right of the strongest among its subjects. If necessary, the government should be able to break the strongest arm in order to implement justice and avenge, as well as be able to protect the weakest against the strongest. In all acts of violence the animal order of justice reared its head, and therefore the government had to be clothed with such an absolutely superior power that it was generally able to keep in check the strong one who wanted to commit evil, doing so by virtue of the grandeur of its majesty, thereby removing fear from among the weakest.

§ 3 This institution, of the *ordering and maintaining of justice* by the government through common grace, undoubtedly has not brought about an ideal situation, neither immediately, nor everywhere, nor enduringly. Common grace tempers the effects of sin, but it does not destroy sin, and since the government functioned through human individuals who themselves were also sinners—and often deeply sinful—this power of the government has often enough been abused to turn justice into injustice. The ordering of justice was often very flawed, the administration of justice quite unsatisfactory, which often made a mockery of justice rather than honoring it in the way that transgression was investigated or later punished. The examples are readily available of the innocent or injured party suffering wrong and the villain or violent criminal triumphing through the courts. But all this is the result not of common grace, but of the sinful nature it came to restrain. And even where the administration of justice is at the lowest possible level and leads to the most repulsive cases of injustice, the mere fact that a power of justice is active and that there is a form of justice that is stable over time is nevertheless in itself such a great gain that through this alone, a nation or tribe towers above any lawless society that functions through arbitrariness and violence.

We may therefore safely say that among the many mercies of God that have accrued to us through common grace, it is the institution of government that stands at the head of the line, not because the government also regulates some societal interests, but because in the first place it establishes justice, maintains justice, and has a power that is prepared to cast down anyone who resists its rule of law. Even waging war and instituting the force that this requires fall in principle under the same perspective. Because neighboring tribes or peoples try to violate the rights of the people over which a king rules, the king must have the power to resist them and, if necessary, to enforce the rights of his people. And even though this right of war has been abused most outrageously to make injustice triumph instead of justice, the truth is not obviated that in principle waging war finds its justification only in the *rights* of the people. Government and justice are then so intimately related that, as we have demonstrated in detail earlier, the command in Genesis 9:6 to punish by death anyone who shed man's blood, which in this way points exclusively to the judicial function, is actually a divine pronouncement that sanctions the functioning of the government as the servant of God.[2]

From the preceding it follows that the death sentence of our Savior in an ordered judicial administration, on which our salvation depends, was possible only because God's common grace had pushed back the raw violence in our sinful human society and made the functioning of a "temporal judge" possible. But additionally, in the second place, it follows that it was not at all immaterial under *which* judge's verdict Christ perished. As we already noted, temporal jurisprudence exists among virtually *all* peoples. But there is a difference between various forms of temporal jurisprudence. Among the Africans this jurisprudence is on a much lower level than among the Chinese, yet the best Asian jurisprudence stands far below the administration of justice among the more highly developed nations. This was also the case in ancient times, and without fear of contradiction we may maintain that among no people did the administration of justice stand on a higher plane in those days than the Romans. We must say this even if we include Israel, though we do not have the space to enter in more detail on this latter point. The Egyptians most certainly did not stand on a lower level of development, and the Greeks undoubtedly were in many respects the tutors of the Romans. But when it comes to justice and the development of justice, then the unique sense of the Roman people for a well-ordered, sharply delineated legal order providing sound safeguards towers so high above the administration of justice among all peoples of that time, that it is clearly evident how God had imposed upon *this* people, among other things, the extremely important calling of making clearly apparent the significance of justice for human society and of finding an appropriate embodiment for the pure, strict administration of this justice. § 4

In this respect the Romans are not only the teachers of their contemporaries but also the teachers of the world, and even though at present Roman jurisprudence is being increasingly abandoned in substance, the notions about the administration of justice that came to fruition among them still dominate our understanding of jurisprudence. Therefore, when the question was raised, apart from history, before which court Jesus had to be put to death in order to bring the legal battle between him and the world to the clearest decision, any expert would immediately have answered, before a

2. See *CG* 1.11.

Roman judge. This is what our Apostles' Creed expresses when it mentions Pontius Pilate by name. That he was "crucified under Pontius Pilate" means that the legal battled involved here has been brought to the clearest possible decision, because Jesus stood trial before a *Roman* judge.

Shall we then say that this high development of justice among the Romans was accidental? Of course not. God's ordination manifested itself in this as well, and it was his common grace for our fallen race, not only that law could take precedence over violence, but also that among this particular people the development of law should be most perfect. And if this is the case, then it shows how, by putting Palestine at one time into the hands of the Romans and thereby causing the administration of Roman law to exist in Jerusalem too, God the Lord ordained all things in this way so that at this point as well, common grace would serve Jesus' mediatorial office.

§ 5 Something must be added here to avoid misunderstanding. Undoubtedly, the development of jurisprudence among the Romans stood on a high plane in terms of form. But it absolutely does not follow from this that the moral order itself, which was maintained in human society through that jurisprudence, was also the true, genuine jurisprudence willed by God. On the contrary, all moral world order and societal cohesion that had been impregnated by this jurisprudence was at its root unholy and untrue. And because of the false premises they chose, nothing could proceed from the world ruled by this law other than that false moral world order which was embodied in the emperorship of Caesar Augustus, the ruler who was worshiped as *god*. Jesus placed the moral world order of the kingdom of God in opposition to this false moral world order. That is, over against a legal order that started from the sovereignty of the individual and therefore was bound to come into conflict both with the social element in our life and with the sovereignty of God, Jesus placed the only true judicial order of the kingdom of God, which finds its anchor in the epitome of the commandments—in loving God above all and our neighbor as ourselves. As a contrast to *falsity* Jesus placed *truth*; that is, over against a false view of life, which was in conflict with the order restored by God, Jesus placed the true confession of a moral world order that was in accordance with God's ordinances and would be realized in his kingdom. Hence he said to Pilate, "For this purpose I was born and for this purpose I have come into the world—to bear witness to the truth" [John 18:37]. These words would of course have no meaning if they are taken to mean that Jesus intended to say he had come into the world to reveal God's love for sinners, or, as Pilate took it, to solve a philosophical conundrum. He spoke of the kingdom. He had come into the world to be King, and the truth of which he spoke thus referred to the judicial order of the kingdom of God, which he posited as truth against the profound lie of a pseudo-moral world order established in Roman law, which found its culmination in Emperor Augustus. Ultimately the confrontation is between the God-anointed King and the emperor worshiped in Rome. The cry "We have no king but Caesar" is truly the cry with which Israel pronounces self-condemnation upon its own existence. And when Pilate finally succumbed to the fear that an acquittal of Jesus would violate the imperial majesty, both his verdict and the superscription above the cross indicated that he too viewed the perilous conflict as nothing but an elevated spiritual struggle between Jesus' claimed kingship and the actual emperorship of Augustus.

Since this could not be ascribed to formal justice, to the extent that no higher court of law was conceivable than that of the Roman emperor, the truth of the God-willed world order came to stand in opposition to the lie of the world order of unconverted human nature. Jesus could not be acquitted unless Pilate surrendered the mendacious root of his own judicial system and was converted to that root of truth from which the kingdom of God arises. But this would not have availed either. Pilate would have been recalled, and soon another governor would have sat as judge over Jesus. And this would have continued until Augustus himself rejected being worshiped and fell on his knees before Jesus to honor him as his Lord and his God. And even this would have been to no avail if it had remained limited to a *personal* conversion; it would only have achieved its goal if all of Roman society surrendered its false principles in order to adopt the true principles, making them the foundation for its jurisprudence. If we think it through to its conclusion, in this process against Jesus, the battle was fought to the end between the order of life that unconverted human nature had produced from itself by its highest level of development, and the other order of life that had been ordained in paradise and, embodied in Christ, now functioned as the central nerve of the kingdom of God. Therefore the world condemned itself in the death sentence pronounced upon Jesus. It had arrived at the pinnacle of legal development reached at that time, to be seen functioning in the Roman temporal judge; yet standing before the Son of God and the Messiah of the Lord, that world, because of its *untrue* premise and *false* principle, could do nothing but condemn him for being guilty of *lèse-majesté*—while making themselves guilty of violating the majesty of God.

CHAPTER TWENTY-TWO

JESUS AND THE PREPARATION OF THE WORLD

In those days a decree went out from Caesar Augustus that all the world should be registered.

LUKE 2:1

§ 1 Thus it is the most special providence of God that, in its ordained arrangement for the Mediator, ensures that the Mediator finds already prepared for him, as a fruit of [God's] common grace (1) "the flesh and blood of the children";[1] (2) the environment in which he grew up and "increased in wisdom and in stature and in favor with God and man" [Luke 2:52]; (3) the social environment that provided him with the form of living, thinking, and speaking in which he could reveal himself to Israel, and through Israel to the world; and (4) a most highly developed administration of justice before whose forum the legal battle between God and the world could be settled. Now we must add a fifth point: it is also thanks to common grace that *after*

1. See Belgic Confession, Art. 18.

his ascension the world appeared to be in a position to make room for his gospel and to make room for the world church.

Christ appears on earth in order to leave it again. He who descended ascends again. But this going away is not a disappearing. There is a trail of light that remains. We can even say to some extent that Christ first put on his *physical body* from the flesh and blood of children, and after that, he formed his *mystical or spiritual body* from all nations and peoples. When he left, he left nothing behind on earth, either in the circle of his disciples or among the Jewish nation, that could wrest itself from the impression left by his appearing. And what is more, when he goes away, his going away is not a separation, not a surrendering of this world, not a return to the situation where earth and heaven were two. Rather, from heaven he now impacts the earth, establishes a mystical communion with that world through the Holy Spirit, and continues his work, only *seeming to be* interrupted, by steadily and unceasingly exercising his influence in this world through his mystical body.

A [mere] reminder suffices here, since argumentation would be superfluous. For the whole tenor of Jesus' addresses, before and after the institution of the Lord's Supper, as well as the whole treasure of the writings his apostles left us, not in the least the book of Revelation, are designed as it were to cut off any notion that with the ascension everything was finished, and to make clear and plain in every way that once Christ was seated at the right hand of the Father, he continues the work that he once began by exerting influence on our earthly circumstances. It is not even an exaggeration to say that for the world in the broad sense, the work of the Mediator *began* only after his ascension. Until that time he had enclosed himself in Israel on the principle that his hour had not yet come to take the bread of the children and throw it before the "dogs"—that is, the Gentiles. That dam was not breached until the day of Pentecost, and it was not breached as a secondary consequence of his incarnation, but rather as the main goal of the incarnation. For in the clearest language we are told repeatedly that God did not give his Son to Israel but to the *world*, and that he had ordained the Mediator out of love for that world. Jesus is absolutely not a reconciler for Israel's sins alone, but for the sins *of the whole world*. And when he leaves the earth from the Mount of Olives, his command to his disciples is to go and *teach all nations*. We therefore stand here before a second work of Christ, but now a work performed from heaven, a work that is just as essential as the work he performed while still on earth. One of the more serious drawbacks that came in the wake of the so-called lives of Jesus was that they closed the church's eyes to this second part of Jesus' life; they ended Jesus' life with his ascension and ignored the extremely important fact of that second part of Jesus' life that does not begin until his ascension. Those who live outside Jesus are not bothered by this, but those who know from the experience of their own soul what the work of Jesus means in their own life sense immediately how in this way the entire significance of his mediatorship is misjudged and falsified.

§ 2 Nevertheless we must not dwell on this personal dimension; all attention must now be focused on the work of Jesus after the ascension *for the world in general*. The operation through which Jesus has accomplished, still performs, and will one day complete this second work is undoubtedly partly *mystical* in nature. Influences, powers of the kingdom, impulses, the fostering of love, consolations, inspirations, and guidance, all of which eschew any analysis and can only be observed, emanate from Christ through the Holy Spirit. These operations belong entirely and exclusively to the realm of particular grace and have nothing to do with common grace. However—and this must not be lost sight of for a moment—this *vertical* working joins a *horizontal* working across the breadth of the earth. The working of the Spirit is from above, but the working of the Word extends across the breadth of the earth. And it is only from the cooperation of these two that the great work of the exalted Mediator is accomplished among the nations. From this it automatically follows that it cannot be a matter of indifference in what situation, in what connection, in what mutual relationship, in what spiritual condition the peoples and nations of this world found themselves at the moment that this work began. This condition of course depended exclusively on what the ordained arrangement of common grace had brought about. And for this reason Christ was also entirely dependent for this second part of his work as Mediator on what he found on earth as the fruit of common grace. For as long as Christ lived only in Israel and worked only among Israel, he repeatedly encountered conditions among the people that, at least in part, were not ruled by common grace alone but equally by particular grace. But as soon as the stream of life that went out from him broke through the dam of Israel and flowed over the fields of the world, that entwining of particular and common grace ceased, and at that point everyone could grasp and see that we now are dealing with conditions that were *exclusively* the fruit of common grace.

Note this well: the church has existed since the beginning of the world because from paradise on, throughout all ages of history, God has had his elect on earth, and these elect have glorified his name on earth in one way or another. Our King was never without subjects. But it absolutely does not follow that the church throughout the centuries functioned as a body of its own, having its own form of existence, and as a separate organization. On the contrary, until Abraham, the life of this church was one with common human life. It is the father of the family, the king of the land (like Melchizedek later) who performs the worship of the Lord. There is no indication of a church outside the family or outside the life of the people. No trace of this can be found. Anyone who said, "Where is the church? Show me the church!" would have been dismissed with a shaking of the head.

After this the hidden life of the church withdraws into the patriarchal tent of Abraham. But we still do not note any independent, separate functioning of the church distinct from the patriarchal life itself. There are no ecclesiastical offices. There is no separate organization. We find no trace of this even among the Jews during those four centuries in Egypt. And when Moses finally leads the people out of Egypt and God places the people under rules and organization in the wilderness, we see offices and ministrations and rules emerge, concentrated in the tabernacle, yet in Israel the life of the people and the church remain intertwined. The nation is the church and the church is the nation. And although in Israel at that time the true church of God—that is, the totality of his elect—was something quite different from the total number of circumcised Jews, the church did not yet consist of those elect gathered together, even if mixed with a few hypocrites. Although millions fell away, so that there remained only seven thousand people as a whole who sought the Lord [see 1 Kgs 19:18], nevertheless all were circumcised and the boundary of the nation continued to constitute the boundary of the church. We may even say that Israel's national existence was deliberately called into being to provide the church of God with this form that was woven into the national life.

What we today mean by the church—an organization separate from the household, the family, and civil society and hence independent with its own boundary and enclosed within its own sphere, with its own offices and ministries, with its own law and regulations, with its own property and its own symbol—did not come into being until after Jesus' ascension, and in this sense *both* statements are true—namely, that the church has existed from the beginning of the world, and that the church does not emerge as an independent world church until after the day of Pentecost.

Prophetically speaking, this wholly unique significance of Jesus for the world, and conversely the high significance of the condition of the world at that time, is expressed thus in the opening sentence of the birth narrative in Luke: "In those days a decree went out from Caesar Augustus that all the world should be registered" [Luke 2:1]. That brief statement immediately places the manger of Bethlehem in historical relationship with the whole position of the Roman Empire of that time. The world empire had to dig the channel through which the stream of the world church would flow out. And we who confess Christ do not hesitate for a moment to confess with a loud voice that it was not Jesus who came to Rome's empire, but the Roman Empire that came to Jesus. This world empire existed because Jesus was to come. It arose to serve Jesus. And its task would be complete as soon as it had made the birth and establishment of Jesus' world church possible. The empire then perished, and what survived was not the throne of Emperor Augustus, but the kingdom of the Child who was born in the time of Emperor Augustus.

§ 3 The preparation of the Roman world of that time for the manifestation of the world church, and the beginning of the kingdom of Christ that manifested itself in the rapid spread of the Christian religion and in the equally rapid demise of paganism, constitutes such a unique event in the existing world that believing and unbelieving historians have tried very hard to explain this marvelous turn in the history of the world.

Mysticism provides no explanation for this. Why would the influence of the Holy Spirit, why would the inspiration that emanates from the exalted Mediator, be less now than back then? The mists may be thicker or thinner, and the light that our eye receives may therefore be dimmer or clearer, but the sun always remains the same sun, and its radiance does not decrease or increase, no matter how the radiance and glow of its light may vary on earth. So too now, therefore, the immense difference between the first miraculous rise of Christianity and the slowness with which it still continues to move in the Christian world, must never be explained on the basis of any activity on Jesus' part that has supposedly diminished since then; rather, it must be explained from the greater or lesser degree of density of the mists that in the life of the nations hinder or promote the breaking through of his light. The missionary, purposeful organization for the Christianization of the world certainly far exceeds similar action in the first century in scope, in financial support, and in the services of various personnel. Yet we fail to break through. We do not see anywhere among the pagan and Muslim peoples and nations an independent, strong Christian life emerge, and we already take comfort in the small triumphs that have been obtained on the South Sea islands, in Madagascar, in Minahassa,[2] and so on. We like to hide from ourselves the reality that the impact of this small gain is virtually nothing when viewed in the context of the world as a whole.

The four large segments of the world that lie before us in China and Japan, India, the Islamic world, and Africa dampen our Christian sentiments, and repeatedly the prayer and sigh arise within us that, going out as a Paul and Silas among these dark population groups, we might take the life of the nations for Christ by storm. Combined they far exceed a billion. Nevertheless we make no appreciable progress. Yet Christ lives and is the same now as then. Nor is there a lack of prayer for and commitment to missions. What does this show, other than that among these nations, in the course of their history, the *receptivity*, the hunger, that made possible such a miraculous rise of Christianity in the Roman world empire in the first century has not yet come about. And it is only in the light of this contrast that we learn to fully understand to what extent God the Lord by his common grace prepared the world of that time for the coming of Christ and the entrance of his church into the world. Holy Scripture speaks of "the fullness of time," and what does this mean, other than that *not* all times are equal, that there are times of preparation, times in which a certain process continues to work unnoticed? And then there also are times in which that process is completed, the fruit is ripe, and a condition has come about that is entirely geared to what God decided to accomplish in that "fullness of time." And because this sovereign ordination of God regarding the nations follows the trail of common grace from beginning to end, and became conceivable and possible only through common grace, we are not stating it too strongly when we venerate in the entire work of common grace a single divine administration that in the end caused all its rays to converge in the work of Christ as in a single focus. In that sense the cross of Golgotha is indeed the center of world history, to which all its streams flow as into a single ocean, so to speak, and conversely, from which all the brooks of history flow as from a fountain.

2. A peninsula in the northeastern part of Sulawesi in Indonesia.

§ 4 For its rapid progress in the world, the world church primarily needed three things: spiritual receptivity, historical ripeness, and community among the nations. It needed shared communication to be able to penetrate, historical ripeness to be able to manage the turnaround in the life of the nations, and spiritual receptivity to be able to find entrance into the heart. Now we offer a brief word about each of these three.

There can be isolation or community among the nations. Isolation exists when, as is now the case in Africa, tribe stands in enmity against tribe, peoples against peoples, when they close their borders and any communal trait is consequently lacking among the lives of all. But it is precisely this situation that the triumph of Rome's power put to an end. Rome had succeeded in binding together into one entity, not only the various tribes of Italy, but also all peoples of significance in Europe, and later part of Asia and Africa. The Roman eagle ruled from the borders of India and China to the west coast of the British Isles. That unity broke through all borders, not only with sword and law, but also by means of the community brought about by international trade. Thus one nation got to know the other. Roads were built, postal communication was established, and people began to make use of travel. People penetrated each other's thought-world, and the Greek language served as the vehicle to make the exchange of ideas possible for all those who were more highly educated. Thus for the first time a *life shared by the world* came into being. Before this time, there were households and families and tribes and nations, but it could not be said that *the world* in its totality had developed a life of its own. But now such a thing did exist. It was not of course a life shared by the *whole* world, for that is not the case even today. The world taken as a whole can be alive in its core and its head, even though the extreme parts and regions are in a state of petrification. Thus a household can live fully and strongly, even though the infants in the nursery cannot yet participate in the conversations. The Roman emperor of that time had united all of that contemporary world under his scepter, and in that immense empire he had made possible a certain community of life by means of an international government, through international communication and an international language. Hence the man from Tarsus, speaking that language, traveling those roads, living under that law, could disseminate in less than half a century the message of the gospel from Jerusalem to Spain and finally could boast that he had filled the whole world with the gospel.

But to this first power of common grace was added a second. In order to be able to occupy any position at all in the world, the entrance of Christianity had to occur in a period of *historical ripeness*. If Christianity had entered at a time when the furious struggle was going on between Rome and the Germanic, Greek, Asiatic, and African peoples, everyone's attention would have been distracted by this all-consuming struggle, and the fate of Christianity would have hung on the victory or defeat of the Roman arsenal. But now under Augustus, by contrast, a period of historical ripeness had indeed come about. Every great issue had been decided. Every mighty struggle had been waged. Rome no longer encountered resistance. A historical Sabbath, if we may put it this way, had begun. Peace ruled everywhere. Quiet rest was being enjoyed. People lived without a goal, without really knowing for what purpose. It was as if the process of history had come to an end. It was like an assembly meeting of nations where no one demanded the floor anymore, making it therefore eminently suitable to have everyone listen reverently when Christianity finally asked to be heard. If Christianity—if the world church—could not appear on the scene without bringing about a complete alteration in the history of the world, then precisely this is what the world had become ripened for in the days of the Roman Empire. History rested; it no longer had anything with which to be busy; and thus arose the time and opportunity to be occupied almost exclusively and undividedly with the *question Chrétienne*, the issue of Christianity, which before long came onto the agenda for discussion. § 5

And it is due to this twofold fruit of common grace that its third fruit, the *receptivity of temperament*, finally acquired its full significance. The missionary work of Christians is so difficult and so well-nigh hopeless among Muslims because the Muslim is entirely self-satisfied, elevates himself in his religious pride as being religiously superior to all, has smothered within himself all need for salvation, and has closed off for himself all access to a higher ideal. In some pagan countries we still find a similar situation, specifically among the Buddhists in India and China. And in the same way the worship of the gods in various countries that once constituted the Roman Empire was held in such high esteem that throughout long centuries it animated national life. But in those days God had not yet caused the Mediator to be born. That waited until the worship of the gods in Rome and in Greece had gone into decline, and higher needs were awakened by Plato and other philosophers. At that point, the worship of the gods no longer satisfied. The language of the philosophers could not satisfy the need of the heart. And then priests and priestesses were summoned to Rome from Egypt and the whole East, in order to satisfy the hunger of the heart through new rites and mysteries. Precisely because all religions had been strictly national, these rites no longer satisfied, now that a general *human* consciousness, a *world* consciousness, had been awakened, and thus all rites were mixed together to quench the international thirst. And when this attempt also failed and opulence brought boredom to the heart, and when sensual pleasures could not silence the cry of the human heart, then a general sense of dissatisfaction arose, and people sought something other and higher, as we see manifested in the Gospel narratives as well. Even some of the Roman officers did. And because Christianity did break through all national barriers and dams to be a *human* religion, to be a *world* religion, and as a world religion to satisfy the deepest wants and needs of the human heart, we may say without exaggeration that in the Roman world of that time, a channel had been dug along which the Christian faith simply had to flow outward.

Thus the condition of the world fit in with the work that Christ came to accomplish, not by way of a surprising coincidence, but because the same God and Father who so loved the world that he wanted to give it his only Son had prepared the world for the coming of that Son through the work of his common grace.

CHAPTER TWENTY-THREE

CHRIST AND WORLD HISTORY

They will bring into it the glory and the honor of the nations.

Revelation 21:26

In the meantime the attempt to trace the connection between the line of Christ and the line of common grace must not remain stuck at the first entry of Christianity into the world. The connection extends much further, running like a golden thread through all of the history that has transpired since Golgotha. But beyond this, the same connection must continue, as sure as the prophecy of Christ concerning the "close of the age" is certain and true, into the most distant future, until the hour dawns of which Jesus said, "Then the end will come" [Matt 24:14]. § 1

We can indeed observe a development—we might even say a miraculous one—of common grace also in regions and countries that so far have remained outside the stream of the Christian influence. But no matter how high that development climbed, it stood outside the historical development of our human race as a whole, and it is not through these countries and these peoples that the broad stream of common grace pushes on toward the end. We might think here not only of China and Japan, but also of the fairly high level of development that was found in the Americas when they were discovered, and no less of the high level to which India raised itself. No matter how much we discount the development of these population groups in the political, social, moral, intellectual, aesthetic, and religious areas, no one will dispute that they were able to create well-ordered and richly formed human societies entirely apart from the Christian religion. But it is also certain that, at least so far, they have not let the flow of their life converge with that of the life of higher civilization.

This is an irrevocable fact also for the truly high development that was reached by the original American population, especially in Mexico and Peru, since what once flowered there has perished forever, and the original population has partly been massacred and has partly disappeared. For India this is certainly somewhat different. The high level of development that India once reached, and that it still maintains in part in the isolated life of its people, has not remained without influence on the rest of the nations. However high the Himalayas may lie as a wreath along India's northern border, the mountain range was not a Chinese wall, and from long ago many relationships were established there between India and the Levant, not to mention the influence India had on China. Elements of Indian civilization most certainly were taken over in the early development of human life as we find it in the Levant and the western highland of Asia. And even now, the cultural power in India has been diminished to such a small degree that a new literary life has developed there instead. At the World's Congress of Religions, held in Chicago, the Indian swamis displayed a measure of self-confidence that their religion still had a great future before it.[1] We therefore cannot determine whether the root of the trunk may still be sound there and possibly be destined for new development that will bring renewed flowering. But to the extent that we refrain from guesswork and exclusively take into account the facts of history, we must conclude that the European-Christian influence that also asserted itself in India is moving with the momentum of a surging stream over ancient Indian life. There is no commingling or mixing of both developments. What existed in India from of old may be spared and saved, but it can no longer defend itself and

1. Kuyper refers here to the meeting of 1893. Swami Vivekananda's opening address indicated that he was "proud to belong to a religion which has taught the world both tolerance and universal acceptance." See J. W. Hanson, ed., *The World's Congress of Religions: The Addresses and Papers Delivered before the Parliament* (Chicago: Monarch, 1894), 39. See also Swami Vivekananda, "Hinduism as a Religion," in ibid., 366–76.

take the reins in hand. England is relatively small but rules over more than 300 million inhabitants of India with the calm majesty of the superior. If trouble comes, it will not be the original Indians but the Muslim tribes in the north that give the British army problems. And for the others, Indian life remains what it was. There is no acceptance of the Christian religion on the part of the masses, by any means. Some elements and products of European civilization are adopted—such as railroads, telegraphs, and so forth—but these remain altogether foreign elements that are inserted into Indian life but do not mix with it.

This is even more strongly the case in China and Japan. Human life, as § 2
it has established itself for centuries in these two powerful states, which comprise almost one-third of the human race, stands on a relatively high plane. There is order, and a high intellectual development has been achieved. Craftsmanship and the strong growth of the population proved that there was much prosperity. In addition, this was the effect of a *conscious* will, for everything bore a characteristic stamp. It was governed by a few leading thoughts. While the development it achieved may have been largely one-sided, nevertheless it was and remained of high significance. In hindsight it is now even more apparent that, due to the high level on which the life of these peoples stood, *personal* development has also progressed to such an extent that these people are capable, seemingly without much effort, to adapt unquestioningly to the much higher human development that the Europeans reached only after a struggle of many centuries. This manifested itself in Japan especially. Within living memory, Japan was virtually hermetically closed to Europe. Our country alone was allowed to conduct limited trade, under sharp supervision, on Dejima. It was not much more than forty years ago that an American squadron forced Japan to open its harbors to global trade,[2] and yet Japan already has succeeded now in introducing Western civilization on a broad scale in its government, the formation of its army and fleet, its administration, and so much more; as a result, supported by its strong fleet, it demands a voice among the naval powers. China is progressing much more slowly, but on occasion, as with the appearance of a man like Li Hongzhang,[3] it shows that a personal ripening is also

2. The policy of national isolation (*sakoku*) that originated in the seventeenth century was formally ended in 1866.
3. Li Hongzhang (1823–1901) was a leading statesman of the late Qing Empire and was generally recognized to be in favor of increased global development.

possible in China, one that makes affiliation with our Western, European civilization certainly conceivable.

The remarkable phenomenon emerges, however, that Japan and China imitate us (indeed, that they can imitate us in surprising ways and to some extent do as we do), but this connection with our life remains an altogether *external* one. In our East Indies the Chinese are fairly strongly represented, but for many centuries they have remained independent. In America, where many Chinese are currently emigrating, they remain entirely separate from the rest of the population. And when we observe the latest developments in Japan, we are struck by the curious phenomenon of a society that at its core is still genuinely pagan but is covered with a European veneer. Thanks to common grace, their own development has developed their skill and acumen, and kept their spirit *awake*, if we may put it this way, and to that extent it has prepared them to some degree for the adoption of an entirely different civilization.

Otherwise all that they owe to their own past is a cloak that must be discarded, not reconstructed. There is no organic connection between what has been developed among these people themselves and what they take over from Christian Europe. In every respect they appear to have a high aptitude. That aptitude has not been blunted by their own development, but has in many respects remained fresh. But to the extent that they now begin to imitate us, there is no continued spinning of the same thread nor a weaving of a new thread into the old fabric. What they had must be discarded and cleared away, to be replaced by what they took over from Europe. On this basis it must be said of the past development in Mexico and Peru, as well as of the current development of the people of Japan and China, that the fruit of common grace among these peoples was abundant, but its fruit remained confined to these peoples themselves and did not benefit our human race as a whole. Further, this power of common grace, where it comes in touch with our higher development, appears not to yield any permanent gain but rather to die away.

§ 3 The same must be said, albeit with some limitation, of the development that the Islamic faith provided for the life of many nations. Our conviction that Muhammed was a "false prophet" need not blind us to the undeniable merit of Islam in this respect. Islam was not limited to one nation but has traveled from nation to nation and ended up bringing a number of nations under its influence. And although the Levant was the seat of its primary power, Islam has managed to assert its sway deep into India, into the Indian

Archipelago, into the regions in the interior of Africa, and even beyond the Caucasus, in Russia. It must also be acknowledged that wherever Islam penetrated, this counterfeit revelatory religion left its own unique stamp on the life of the nations. By imprinting its own stamp on all of human life, it was able to introduce an entirely unique view of life that supplied the impetus for a major development in domestic, social, political, scientific, and even aesthetic areas. Islam was once even ahead of Christianity and lit a brighter light at its Asiatic universities than the one that illuminated the nations in the Christian world. It did not last long, but there was a time when Islam was the teacher of Christian Europe. Those who venture into Christian missions among the Muslims without clearly realizing this fact and still live more or less with the misapprehension that in Islam we have a common, low-level idolatry will harvest little else in the disappointment their work brings than legitimate punishment for their ignorance and superficial judgment. It must even be acknowledged that wherever Islamic development entered pagan countries, it brought about a turn in the people's consciousness by the implacable extermination of all image worship, which prepared these peoples for a much higher development. But—and this is shown by the lessons of history and the judgment of all experts—the development that Islam brings is a limited one that, as soon as it has achieved certain results, stops and cannot go on, causing ossification to set in. The collapse is greatest today in the oldest Islamic countries. The spirit that once was stimulated is now dozing. Thus in Tunis and Algiers, even as in Asia Minor and Bosnia, conditions have become increasingly miserable. Islam appears to bring a development that flourishes for a short time, but far from bearing a prophecy for an ever richer future, it lies under the doom of petrifaction and death.

At this point we cannot enter into a consideration of whether Islam owed its relative strength to elements of truth that it absorbed partly from Israel and partly from the earliest Christian developments. Such a miraculous development in the history of nations as Islam demands a much broader discussion than this cursory discussion can offer.[4] In this context we must only establish the fact that Islam has a much greater significance for world history than the Indian, Chinese, or ancient American civilizations,

---

4. Years later Kuyper would later provide just such discussions in the opening chapters of his three-volume work, *Pro Rege*, as well as in his reflections on Islam during his journey around the Mediterranean Sea, appearing in this series as *On Islam*.

and that the great distinction between Islam, on the one hand, and other civilizations, on the other hand, lies precisely in the fact that those other civilizations remained almost entirely outside any contact with the life of divine revelation; Islam, however, emerged only after the Christian religion had already conquered the Levant, and Islam found the areas for developing its power precisely in regions where the Christian church had already scored its triumphs. In the centuries prior to Golgotha no powerful religious development had ever come out of Arabia. It was only after the Christian religion had impacted Arabia as well as the Levant as a whole that Islamic activity appears to have emerged from the fermenting of all these elements. Such activity stimulated Arabia to this demonstration of power and caused it to gain ground because the Levant was prepared for this new phase in the development of the people. However high our estimation of the significance of this development that Islam brought about, Islam also appears to be a stream that silts up, a religion that has neither the power nor the calling to lead the general human development of our race. Islam is an intermezzo, albeit a very interesting and very broad intermezzo, but that is all. The main bedding along which the development of our human race moves is not formed by Islam, but by the cross of Golgotha.

§ 4 We must pay close attention to this distinction. We must distinguish between two rich operations of common grace. On the one hand, there is an isolated working of common grace that, limited in time and place, blesses a few groups of people but only has a limited power of development, and once the limit of that power has been reached, it either stands still or declines and ossifies. The characteristic of this isolated working of common grace is, therefore, (1) that it is *place-bound* and does not spread over the whole world, (2) that it is *time-bound* and has significance for only a few centuries, and (3) that it reaches is full growth after a short time and then cannot continue. In contrast to this stands the line of a quite different kind of common grace that supports the life of our race *as a whole race* and as such furthers our race in its development. The fruit of this activity of common grace is a human development that does not attach itself to a single population group, but is intended to bless all nations. It is a development that is not tied to a specific century, but steadily progresses over the course of all centuries. And finally, it is a development that is not tied to a certain limit of development but ever continues to progress and make giant steps forward in each new century, not in one area but in every area of human life.

To the first kind of activity of common grace belongs what we see in ancient America, in China, in Japan, in India, and partly within Islam. To the second kind of activity of common grace, conversely, belongs the human development that began in Babylonia and Egypt, came to a provisional flourishing in Greece and Rome, was taken up by Christianity, and since then has already progressed for eighteen centuries in Europe and America under the auspices of the cross of Christ. Stated succinctly, we might call the first the *special* activity of common grace in the service of a few peoples and times, and the second, the *general* activity of common grace in the service of the development of our human race. Once we accept this distinction, we are faced with the fact that those special developments take place outside the Christian religion, whereas the general activity of common grace is aimed at the appearance of the Christian religion and has come to powerful flowering only through the Christian religion.

If we keep clearly in view that Christ's program does not end with his ascension from the Mount of Olives, but truly commences only with his being seated at the right hand of the Father, then it becomes clear how for this, his second work, if we may identify it this way, Christ was bound entirely to this *general* line of common grace, and how, conversely, this general activity of common grace is governed entirely by Christ. From this perspective we must judge every view of Christianity as a religion floating atop the waters of history like an oil slick—as if the Christian church had to hide itself in this world like a hermit, without maintaining a connection with the life of that world, or as if the entire work of particular grace ran like a separate stream alongside the stream of common grace, so that their waters never mix or mingle.

Something else that lies judged by this is the dualism that divides nature and grace from each other like two separate spheres, which fails to understand that it is one work of God being accomplished both in particular grace and in common grace. It is one work of God in both, which finds its link in the Mediator between God and man, a link warranted and explained by the fact that the Lamb of God who bears the sin of the world is also the eternal Word through whom that world and everything in it were created. Particular grace does not create its own unique world to exist separately in the midst of the ancient world, letting that ancient world first perish and go under, only in order to replace it later with a newly created life. But it is and remains the same ancient world, created by God once long ago, maintained by common grace and restored in the core of its life and purified from the cancer in its root. And when at the end of the ages that healing process has run its full course, then it is not the *first* world that will be destroyed, to be replaced by a *second* world. Rather, it will be the ancient world of Adam, created by God once long ago and corrupted by us, saved in Christ, that will appear to have carried within itself such hidden powers that this very world itself will one day stand before God in glory, to magnify his majesty.

§ 5 This allows us to explain that after Rome and Greece all perished, following Babylon and Egypt, the leadership of the nations was entrusted to the world church of the New Testament, and for the first time from that moment on, common grace entered the new, rich paths that were opened up to it under the Christian religion. What we currently call the Christian world in Europe and America shows us the highest development of the human race yet known throughout the centuries, and everything prophesies that this development is destined to progress further and further for a long time to come. We cannot say yet whether the apostasy that has entered Christianity will persist, or whether the terrible struggle that will mark the end of the present era is already approaching. Were this the case, then the progress of our human development would already have reached its turning point. But we do not base our judgment on this. For then we would face an impending catastrophe, and history itself would be near its end point.

But without wanting to peek behind the curtain that hides this future from our eyes, the result of history is certain to us: the general activity of common grace, as it arose from Babylon and Egypt, from Greece and Rome, was taken up by Christianity, and under the leadership of Christ it has ascended for the first time to that general human development. This last development allows us to say that the history, not of the individual nations, but of *humanity* has truly begun. And thus we may say that common grace has been prepared by the Father for the Son, not only to make his incarnation possible, but to have him live among us as "Son of Man," to offer him the form and language for his gospel, to bring about his work of atonement through death under Pontius Pilate, and to open up for the Christian church its marvelous entrance into the Roman Empire. But we must say far more than this. That same common grace was prepared by the Father for the Son to make possible the general development of our human race—indeed more than that, a history of *humanity* in the rich, profound sense of this word—only in and through Christ.

CHAPTER TWENTY-FOUR

THE FULLNESS OF TIME

As a plan for the fullness of time, to unite all things in him, things in heaven and things on earth.

EPHESIANS 1:10

At this point, the significance of God's common grace for both the *incarnation* and the *work* of the Mediator may be considered to have been sufficiently clearly and completely elucidated in its various parts. Returning from our discussion of these parts to the whole, we still must add two more things in general to this more detailed discussion. § 1

The first concerns the clear revelation that Christ has come, and could only have come, in *the fullness of time*. This expression is derived from holy Scripture. The holy Apostle Paul says in Galatians 4:4, "But when the fullness of time had come, God sent forth his Son, born of woman, born under the law," and again in Ephesians 1:10, "As a plan for the fullness of time, to unite all things in him, things in heaven and things on earth." Saying this implies that the Word could not have become flesh at any arbitrary time, that not every era was suited for it; that the incarnation had to wait until time had been added to time, until finally the process of the time destined for it had run its course; and this in the sense that there was in fact only one year, one day, one hour in which Christ not only *could*, but also *had* to be born, and that this moment is called the "fullness of time." It is an image derived from filling a cup. While drop is added to drop, the cup is continually being filled, but *fullness* is achieved only when the last drop has been added. Immediately after that, the cup begins to overflow, and that one moment of fullness has passed. "Fullness of time" points to the fact that the past continually ripens, that the moment of full ripeness is finally reached, but also that immediately after that, the fruit falls from the tree and the ripening process is over. The fruit cannot progress any further. In the same way, there cannot be a Christ who just as well could have come immediately after the fall, or could have been born in Noah's day, or could have seen the light of day in Abraham's tent. However much Abraham desired to "see his day" [see John 8:56], the patriarch did not see it because *the day of Christ* had not yet arrived. There was only one day on which his appearance was possible, and that was the day of Bethlehem during the reign of Augustus.

Instead of a flexible determination of time we must hold to a firm temporal determination, and the past that lies before Bethlehem must be measured according to a fixed requirement and not arbitrarily. It must not be measured, of course, in the sense that this determination lay in a specific number of the year or in the name of Augustus; rather, from paradise a thread was woven that first had to be spun out to the end to make the birth of Christ and the success of his work as Mediator possible. It is precisely through this that the past that lies *before* Bethlehem acquires its *raison d'être*. God did not merely postpone the coming of Christ, wait around with it, and let his faithful on earth wait for it. No, there had to be a past before the manger, a history that constituted a firm and well-defined whole. Before Christ came, a work had to be completed that was indispensable for his coming. First, a process in which not a single link could be lacking had to run its course. A firm result had to be obtained that could not be incomplete in any of its parts. The "times" are merely the forms in which events manifested themselves, but the content consists of the events themselves, which like individual pearls are part of a single strand and like individual links are part of a single chain. When the final pearl has been added to the strand, and the final link has been attached to the chain, only then, the "fullness of time" has arrived and the coming of Christ is near.

§ 2 Understood in this manner, the history of the world that precedes Bethlehem acquires an inner, dynamic force; a fixed measure; and a predetermined end. But then it also speaks for itself that the fruit of this past must have a necessary connection with the appearance of Christ. It must not be understood in the sense that this past had its own boundaries and firm course, such that the incarnation of the Word was added to it *externally*. No, since the past progressed toward the fullness of time, and since Christ had to be born in the fullness of time, there also must exist an inner connection between that past and the coming of Christ. And the reason why that past lasted so long, and followed this course, and led to this result, must have resided in the fact that only in this way could a condition arise for the coming of Christ and the success of his work as Mediator that was precisely such as the coming of Christ required. From this it also appears that our exposition, in which we showed how Christ and his work relate at each and every point to the fruit of common grace in the past, rests on the supposition that holy Scripture itself affirms for us on God's behalf in its teaching of the "fullness of time."

The ordination indicated in this—in the fact that Christ could neither appear immediately after paradise nor in the days of Noah or Abraham, but instead had to wait until the "fullness of time" had come in due course—confirms in and of itself the thesis that there is a connection between Christ and the common grace that preceded his coming. If we imagine all this without common grace, and if we imagine the world being left to its own self-destruction in sin and the curse, then each century that passed after the fall would have made the coming of Christ increasingly more *impossible*, and the coming of Christ would have been conceivable only in the very moment when God in paradise called Adam to himself again. For without common grace, the line that proceeded from paradise would have been a continually descending line. Sin would have brought ever more terrible devastation, the curse would increasingly have wrought its destruction, and the end would have been such that very soon any sign of *humanness* would have disappeared from human society (assuming that this society would still be possible at all).

Fullness of time, on the other hand, presupposes a course of time, a course of centuries in which humanity progresses and a condition ripens in the world that makes it suitable to receive Christ. But this is possible only if sin and the curse cannot recklessly develop their full strength, only if God himself stops that ominous development and thus brings about a historical development that can lead to the desired result. This is precisely what we owe to common grace.

§ 3 We add here another comment that is no less important. Within confessing Christianity a tendency has continually manifested itself to short-change the true human nature and the true human character of Jesus' actions, his appearance, and even his being. That tendency was not the result of a lack of belief in the incarnation, but arose when heresy took control of the understanding of Jesus' human nature by short-changing the full, integral deity by placing a one-sided emphasis on the *human* aspect of Christ. For virtually all heresies that have arisen have tampered with the full confession of Jesus' deity. Initially it was claimed that his deity was confessed in the full sense, but soon it became apparent that a less worthy game was being played with the Word of "God," for what was meant was either an influence of God yielding a very high character in the man Jesus, or that Jesus' divinity was replaced by assigning a divinely high character to his human virtues and excellences. It goes without saying that the sad consequence in both instances was that the confession "My Lord and my God," which the whole church sang in imitation of the Apostle Thomas [see John 20:28], was in fact destroyed.

In our century the fraying of the dogma of Christ began in the same way. The "dumb orthodox" had lost their way.[1] They did not understand the humanity of Christ. The theologians themselves therefore would place more emphasis on that humanity, and precisely by doing greater justice to the *humanity* in Christ they would also make his *divine* nature more and better understood. But, after gaining the support of many through this siren song, they soon showed their real intent by abridging in many ways the essential divine nature of the Mediator. Once past this point, people strayed further and further from the confession of the truth. Even among preachers who call themselves orthodox, little remains of the confession of Jesus' deity other than that Jesus' *God-consciousness* stood at the highest level and that God revealed himself most perfectly in Jesus. But the vast majority have already left this phase far, far behind them, and most common among theologians now is the notion that we must actually see in Jesus nothing but a human being, [albeit one] more pious than any other person, and to that

1. In Dutch, *domme fijnen*. Elsewhere Kuyper describes "precisionists," who are particularly concerned with orthodox doctrine, even to the detriment of practice; in this case, according to their critics, the confessional concern about proper Christology led them to practically devalue Christ's humanity.

extent we must indeed honor him as a religious genius, but other than that, he did not triumph, even in the moral sense, over all the temptations of sin.

In contrast, the church of the living God has always held unswervingly fast to the confession that whoever even minimally infringes the deity of Christ cuts off the plant of the Christian religion at its root. All religion calls for fellowship with God, and the Christian religion alone can be the true one only if it is concerned with the mystery of a God revealed in the flesh, that is, that he has come near to us in our own human nature. It is therefore quite understandable that the church, seeing how many times it has been misled, ultimately refused to listen to the dulcet tones of those who came to it with the story that we must place more emphasis on the human nature of Christ. They were not wrong to fear that such words were merely the overture to a preaching that would finally lead once again to assaulting the deity of Christ. This apprehension may be considered short-sighted on the part of the church, but the responsible cause of that narrow-mindedness does not rest with the church at all, but with the learned theologians who repeatedly have misled the trusting and obedient church.

This apprehension may also explain why the church has so little concern § 4
for what the apostle reveals to us concerning the *fullness of time*. Hearing that something had to precede the coming of Christ, and that before Christ could come something had to be *prepared*, the church feared that all this concealed a snake in the grass, so it began to teach at this point a kind of "preparatory grace," from which Christ later could be explained, if not completely, then at least in part. If Christ is explained, even only partially, from the past that came before Bethlehem, then, as we immediately concede, the full being of God has already been shortchanged. For Christ's being God cannot be split up into parts and can never be explained from any cause other than *from God himself*.

We therefore put great stock in clearly bringing to the fore the fact that the apostolic teaching of the fullness of time does not serve in any way to explain Christ in his divinity even in the smallest part from the past or from the situation that preceded that past. Not *Christ himself* but exclusively what Christ *took upon himself* was prepared by that past and came to ripeness in the fullness of time. Christ *took upon himself* the form of a servant and *took on himself* the seed of Abraham (Heb 2:16 [KJV]). But what a person takes upon himself is not from him; he takes it from outside himself. For Christ to be able to take this upon himself, it had to have been present before he came. It had to stand ready, so to speak, at his coming so that he could adopt it.

And it also had to be ready in a form and a manner necessary for the incarnation. This happened under God's direction and was not our doing, but the end result had to be that at the moment of Jesus' conception, two things were given: *the Son of God*, who would adopt our human nature, and the *human nature* that would be adopted by him. Because the Son of God is unchangeable and remains eternally identical to himself, he could not prepare himself and adapt to our human nature. But if there was to be a connection, human nature would have to prepare itself for him and adapt itself to him. And it is this work of preparation that God himself accomplished in the progress of common grace and completed in the fullness of time.

It is the same distinction that we observe in growing wheat. This too involves two things. There is the *seed* that takes in substances from the soil and from the air in order to let the stalk, blade, and ear come forth; and there is the *soil*, a field, a piece of land that must be prepared so that the seed can take its nourishment from the soil. The farmer must therefore do two things. First, he must prepare the soil by plowing it, adding nutrients, and plowing furrows. And second, he must drop the seeds in the furrows of that prepared and loosened soil. And thus God the Lord has done two things. He first plowed the soil of our human life and made it fertile and thus prepared it and made it ready. And when this work was finished and that preparation was completed, in the "fullness of time" he sent his only Son down into that loosened and plowed soil of our human life. The first, the preparation of the soil, happened for the whole world through common grace, and in Israel's soil through particular grace; and the second, the sending of the Son into the world, was an act of divine mercy that is wholly concentrated in particular grace.

§ 5 If this is clear, then we can conclude from this how it is precisely the doctrine of common grace that cuts off Pelagianism and brings honor to the work of God.[2] For what hindered the devout soul in thinking about this

2. Pelagianism refers to a doctrine associated with Pelagius, a monk in the early fifth century identified "as the author or promoter of a heresy which sought to undermine the ancient faith by assailing the doctrine of divine grace." Pelagianism is at odds with the orthodox understanding of grace (particularly as articulated and defended by Augustine) through its denial of original sin and its consequences, and in its emphasis on a rigorous moral code as foundational for realizing salvation through one's natural, unaided powers. See "Pelagius, Pelagian Controversies," in *NSHE* 8:438–39.

preparation in the past was precisely that it created the impression that something had come from man after all, as if we humans had contributed something from ourselves to the incarnation, and as if Christ was the result of a dual working (we say this reverently): on the one hand, the act of God, who sent us his Son, but on the other hand, also an act by us humans, who offered him our human nature in a thoroughly prepared form. And then, of course, salvation would not be from God alone but from God and man jointly—in other words, Pelagianism.

But precisely this is utterly cut off in the Reformed confession by the doctrine of common grace. According to the dogma of common grace, we confess that the preparation of Christ's human nature, the result of which was brought about in the fullness of time, was not a work of man but solely a *work of God*. Indeed, it was such a work of grace that God has brought it to completion against the will and doings of man, in spite of them, in spite of their resistance and opposition. What each child of God confesses in relation to himself (namely, that he has received grace, not *due to* his cooperation but *against* his own intentions and aspirations) then becomes the glad and joyful, but also profoundly shaming, confession of the church in relation to Christ. The confession does not say, "We humans had developed so far in the days of Emperor Augustus, and had come so far in our own power, that at that point the appearance of Christ became possible." It is just the opposite: we humans had completely corrupted our way, and this earth would never have been prepared for the coming of Christ if God in his common grace had not countered our sin; had not arrested the devilish, continued working of sin; and had not brought about, due to this his common grace, a situation from which Christ could adopt human nature and continue his work as Mediator.

This sufficiently shows the supreme importance of the confession of §6
common grace especially for the doctrine of Christ. For without common grace, the entrance of Christ into this world remains entirely unconnected to the past and therefore becomes unhistorical and leads automatically to Anabaptist dualism—either that, or his coming becomes historically linked to the past, only to let the Pelagian poison creep in at that point, to explain Christ in part on the basis of ourselves, and finally to assault the confession of his being God. Justice is done to the pure confession of the incarnation of the Word, as adoption of our human nature by the Son of God, only if we also honor nothing other than God's activity in what preceded Bethlehem, in his act of mercy to our race, and an act of grace that contravened our

intentions, by arresting the working of sin through common grace. In any other view it is as if God, after expelling us from paradise, left the world to its own devices, to demonstrate his mercy again finally at the manger in Bethlehem, to restore what we had destroyed and spoiled. Then even the interlude in the ark, in Abraham's tent, and in Israel remains without significance. Why let believers look forward in vain, century after century, to the coming of the Messiah, if that coming could have been equally conceivable in Noah's day? If, on the other hand, we agree that there was a good reason for this, that there was nothing arbitrary in it, but that the coming of Christ had to be preceded by a preparation in Israel, then this alone is an acknowledgment that there was a work of God before Bethlehem, a work that was aimed at Bethlehem, was geared and suited to it, and was therefore indispensable for Bethlehem.

And if this is clearly understood, a second question automatically arises, namely, whether the history of Israel was a drop of oil floating atop the water—that is, whether Israel lived and developed without any connection with the outside world, or, conversely, whether what happened in Israel was connected in all kinds of ways with the development of the whole human race. The history of Israel shows that the latter was indeed the case. Although Israel sprang up from its own holy seed and grew from its own root, the whole history of Israel from the days of Abraham on shows that its past was continually interwoven with the history of the other nations, and that the empires of Egypt, Babylon, Greece, and Rome successively dominated the situation in Israel in all kinds of ways.

And this being the case, we must therefore acknowledge one of two things. Either we acknowledge that what took place outside Israel fell entirely outside God's gracious ordination, in which case the formation of Israel was in part due to us humans; or we acknowledge that the influences that were at work from outside Israel could only be part of God's ordination. But then we also confess that the grace of God must have benefited our human race in the life of those other nations as well. From this reality the conclusion directly flows that the incarnation of the Word is due entirely and undividedly to the grace of God alone, if we confess equally both that his particular grace worked in Israel and in Mary, and also that his common grace pursued its own goal, which it achieved in the fullness of time in the life of the surrounding nations.

CHAPTER TWENTY-FIVE

COMMON GRACE AND THE LIFE OF GRACE

So now it is no longer I who do it, but sin that dwells within me.

Romans 7:17

Now that we have finished our investigation into the significance of common grace for Christ and his work as Mediator, we begin a similar investigation in relation to the Christian and how he is brought to eternal life. Again, the confession of common grace on this point did not receive a complete exposition in the century of the Reformation. We therefore will point to facts that nobody disputes or denies, but that nonetheless were not given their due place in dogmatics. They are nevertheless extremely important for the self-knowledge and self-abasement of the child of God. In the devotional literature, and sometimes in poetry too, the experience of the soul found expression in this regard; but neither in the Catechism nor in the books on dogmatic theology, nor in catechetical explanations and sermons, was common grace sufficiently taken into consideration when it came to the matter of bestowing eternal life. In individual doctrinal studies various points came up for discussion, yet they did not bring the matter to an independent, well-rounded unity. Calvin led the way in confessing common grace as a fact and in assigning it a place in the outlines of the § 1 doctrinal structure, but there was no further elaboration. And those who came in the wake of Calvin have followed his example on this point. The fact that at present, the newly awakened Reformed theology attempts to make up for this damage does not in the least signify indulging in the desire to rap "the forefathers" on the knuckles; nor does it signify retouching to the best of our ability a disproportionality in the doctrinal structure out of an exaggerated sense of aesthetics. Rather, this is demanded by the sad experience of the church and theology resulting from this lacuna.

Let us begin by briefly elucidating this latter issue. Common grace touches on the relationship between *nature* and *grace* or, if you will (for this amounts to the same thing), the relationship between *church* and *world*, between *theology* and secular *scholarship*, between our *old man* and our *new man*—or also, if we may express it thus, between our *self* and *Christ*, between our *self* and *us ourselves*. There is an old life and a new life. The contrast is never expressed more strongly than when Paul wrote, "If I do what [is sinful], it is no longer I who do it, but sin that dwells within me" [Rom 7:20]. [The parts of] this dual life that is portrayed so beautifully in Article 35 of the Belgic Confession are sharply distinguished and yet related.[1] The result was, and still is, that the spiritual life sometimes manifests itself so strongly as new that it gives the impression that it stands outside all connection with the natural and has come about through a fundamentally new creation, and therefore stands alongside, independently of, parallel to the natural. The need to express it in this way was even so strong that the holy apostles did not hesitate at all to speak of a "workmanship" of God, as "created in Christ Jesus" [Eph 2:10], based on the thought stated by Christ himself, that in this new life we are in fact dealing with a second *birth*. Understood in this way, it therefore seems as if any connection with what preceded it should be cut off, and as if consequently all connection with the aftereffects of the natural life for this new life could be denied.

But opposite this stands, with equal rights, an entirely different perspective. For it is true that Jesus causes this new life to spring from a second birth, yet he does not contradict Nicodemus' comment that the same person of

1. See Belgic Confession, Art. 35: "Now those who are regenerated have in them a twofold life, the one corporal and temporal, which they have from the first birth and is common to all men; the other spiritual and heavenly, which is given them in their second birth, which is effected by the Word of the gospel, in the communion of the body of Christ; and this life is not common, but is peculiar to God's elect."

the first "birth" would enter again, as it were, into the mother's body and be born for the second time. Taken in the spiritual sense, this means that it is and remains one and the same life, but it is a life that repeats its birth. The same thought is expressed in the broad revelation about the resurrection. What is, dies, but it does not die to be destroyed and replaced by something new; rather, having gone through death, it awakens as a human being of a higher life. Thus the unity between the natural and the spiritual birth is strictly maintained. The old man does not, on the one hand, disappear to let a new man take its place, but it is and remains the same human being, who is first old and then becomes new and thus appears in its new life to be the product, not of a second creation that would be identical to the first, but of re-creation. The old man continues to exist and produce its effects even after that re-creation, and it is precisely from that continued existence of the self in its first form, along with its aftereffects, that so many painful issues are born for the life of God's child, of the church, and of Christian society. The same truth finds expression in the doctrine of the covenant of grace. For the covenant of grace links the new life to the genealogical course of the natural life, not in an absolute sense but nevertheless in such a way that the spiritual connection between God's saints converges with the genealogical connection in the natural realm, according to the formula "you and your seed" or "you and your children" [see Acts 2:39].

From this it is clear that the single matter of the new life, or the life of grace, can be viewed from two very different sides. Either we can feel an urge to emphasize the new aspect of this life, and then to let this stand out as prominently as possible, or there can be reason to focus attention on the fact that this new life is the same as the old life, but renewed at the root. Whoever argues the former will push the connection with the old into the background as far as possible; conversely, whoever wants the second will make as much as possible of this connection. From this the danger emerges that the former position ultimately closes its eyes entirely to the connection between the new self and the old, while on the other hand, the second perspective easily leads to letting the old stand out so strongly that ultimately the old self seems to be the force from which the new came into being. This has in fact led to the situation that in the Christian arena two opinions, two views, two fundamental insights have continually struggled with one another. § 2

On the one hand, the struggle arose in the days of the Reformation in terms of the Anabaptist position, which understood the new life as a second formal creation. It understood the flesh and blood of Christ as being created from heaven into this world. Thus, it severed any connection between God's child and the world, and it excluded the Christian entirely from civil society through so-called shunning and the rejection of government positions. This is spiritual dualism.

On the other hand, a contrasting approach tried to maintain itself at about the same time, adopting the character of Arminianism and attaching so much value to the old self that ultimately the new life was considered to have sprung from the will of the old self. This ultimately led to the destruction of God's almighty grace and the denial of total depravity through sin.[2] If we see this clearly, we will immediately understand why our forefathers, when they opposed Anabaptism in their first struggle, came out very decisively with their confession of common grace; but also we see how in their second struggle, this time not with the Anabaptists but with the Arminians, they were silent about common grace and focused all their energy on maintaining the character of the new life as brought about by God *without* any involvement of the old self. And because the second struggle came later, and in this second struggle the dogmatic formulations were worked out successively, it can be fully explained how our Reformed fathers, who first had acted so bravely with their confession of common grace, nevertheless allowed this important doctrine virtually to disappear from their later dogmatic formulations.

But what happened after that? Once Arminianism was officially and ecclesiastically overthrown, not only through the spiritual force of the truth, but with the help of the government, Reformed theology laid down the sword, broke off the battle, and thought that it could then manage with endlessly repeating the old argumentation that had once been used against the Arminians. In contrast to this the spirit of the world, realizing that it had not been spiritually disarmed in its final defenses, tried again and

2. "Arminianism" derives from the Dutch theologian Jacobus Arminius (1560–1609) and refers to his understanding of the relationship among predestination, grace, and atonement in salvation. Besides other things, Arminius "taught conditional predestination," and "his followers expressed their convictions in the famous five articles which they laid before the States as their justification. Called Remonstrants from these Remonstrantiæ, they always refused to be called Arminians." See "Arminius, Jacobus and Arminianism," in *NSHE* 1:297. Among other things, Kuyper associates Arminianism with a more optimistic view of human capability after the fall than that of orthodox Reformed teaching.

again, albeit in a different form, to engage us in the age-old battle. Without suspecting it, Reformed theology almost allowed itself to be pushed into the Anabaptist dualistic corner, and in the church this even went so far that in England Calvinism survived only among the Anabaptists and the Baptists, while in this country everything relating to the covenant of grace, and thus pointing to a connection with natural life, sank almost entirely into oblivion. Infant baptism survived, but in the context of a spiritual view of life in which, in the final analysis, only adult baptism would fit. This ensured that theology at our universities did little else than either rework the old or deviate into heretical directions. From the church came the urge to cut off communion with the world and to withdraw into conventicles, not seeking in any way to maintain the fundamental character of our original reformation in new, continuing, and further-developed Reformed theology.

In less than half a century, this had two consequences: on the one hand, the theology at our universities broke entirely with the Reformed confession and brazenly switched to the paths of unbelief; on the other hand, all that still stood firm in the church declined into mysticism and thus also surrendered the Reformed confession, not in name but in fact. This was a sad course of events, which still has its effects in the present shape of Reformed churches and can be brought to an end only by a broadly conceived, and at the same time profoundly radical, theological study.

In the meantime, after the church had fallen asleep and Reformed theology had sunk into unconsciousness, the spirit of the world had the playing field to itself, in order to bring the old self to renewed dominance in the broad arena of science and social life. Soon this old self was viewed once again as undamaged and was even praised in its lofty excellence. Of course, the consequence of this had to be, and indeed was, that even the existence of the new self was presumptuously denied, in fact branded as the product of a fanatical imagination, and the fight against the precisionists as bumptious fools was no longer undertaken through serious discussion but rather with mockery and derision. No longer was there a search for the correct relationship between nature and grace. All grace was audaciously denied; nature had become the one and all, and everything had to be explained from nature. In addition, when research in physics had taken such an unprecedented flight in less than a century, and had led to such surprising results, it was no wonder that ultimately not only *grace* but all that was *spiritual* was pushed aside, and the day seemed close when materialism would triumph forever. § 3

Then, of course, it would have been the calling of the church and of theology to defend, against this hubris of the *old self* and the natural life, the sound claim of the *new self* and of the life of grace so proudly that ultimately the correct relationship between the two could once again be identified. But the church did not think of this. It did not think of it in its official form, for it was ossified. Nor did it think of it in its spiritual core, for part of that spiritual core went directly to what was later called "night school," or another part sang the song of the unreflective in the spiritual luxury of the *Réveil*, which thought to possess, partly in philanthropy and partly in childlike joy, the strength to ward off this tempest of the spirits.

Consequently the task of rescuing the spiritual and searching for the relationship between spirit and nature moved from the church of Christ to philosophy. Because the church did not perform its duty, philosophy took over its task at that point. No one listened to theology anymore, but everyone listened to philosophy. As a result, serious and thinking Christians who felt the importance of this spiritual struggle increasingly turned away from theology and came to live with the illusion that philosophy ultimately had to rescue Christianity. Schleiermacher was the first to sense this opprobrium of theology and to make an attempt to put theology back in the saddle, but he did this by no other method than to transmute theology in effect into philosophy. What he presented as theology was in fact a philosophical form in theological garb. Thus Schleiermacher created the school of the so-called mediating theologians, who in our country manifested themselves as the Ethical theologians.[3] This school was characterized precisely by the fact that they let philosophy determine the main questions about the relationship between nature and grace, and hitched an entirely altered theology to this. In opposition to this stood the representatives of the more positive schools. Some were Methodists, who had an eye only for praxis and did not concern themselves with the deeper questions. Others were ossified Reformed Christians, who held fast to the old confession with might and main but did not themselves recognize how they could engage, from the perspective of their confession, in this more powerful spiritual struggle.

3. After his conversion in the early 1860s, Kuyper came to see the danger that theological modernism posed to vibrant Christian faith. In this respect, he was especially critical of the modernist Ethical theology associated with figures like Friedrich Schleiermacher (1768–1834) and Albrecht Ritschl (1822–89).

All this would have taken an entirely different course if the Reformed church and Reformed theology had succeeded in working out and carrying through in every direction its confession of common grace and what was directly related to it, and its confession of the doctrine of the covenant. This would have led it to achieve a satisfactory solution of the connection—so complicated and difficult—between nature and grace, world and church, and it would have been fully capable of challenging philosophy's leadership in the dispute that emerged. Sadly, it has not done this. It has imagined that complete victory was already won when in 1618/19 at Dort it challenged the capacity of the sinner's free will—that is, the capacity of the old self to choose spontaneously for the good; and it did not see the necessity of persevering down to the general foundations of life in the fundamental battle that lay behind this issue. It sought the support of the government and thought itself safe behind its shield. We then see, immediately after Dort, how the resilience faded from our theology. Voetius penetrated more deeply, but he was not understood.[4] Our Reformed theology fell asleep, and only after years of idleness and opprobrium did it reach back to its splendid past; but now it had to undergo its deserved punishment in being initially greeted with distrust. Our Reformed theology may even consider it a special favor of God that this distrust was no more vigorous and soon replaced by increased sympathy. This was an unexpected success, erroneously appreciated with too little feeling by many a preacher who, standing before a congregation that was not in the least prepared for this turn of events, thought he could speak reprovingly and condescendingly, whereas strength could have been found for victory only in the winning of hearts and in searching for the gradual transition. § 4

Precisely for this reason, the doctrine of common grace is of such overweening importance at this present juncture. Between the life of nature and the life of grace a broad, deep chasm yawns that can be bridged only by common grace. A failure to build this bridge can lead only to the ancient imbalance that is again gaining ground, either focusing virtually exclusively on grace, only to leave nature to the world, or settling into the life of nature to such an extent that grace is in fact denied. Whether we want to or not, we cannot ignore the question of free will. The will, free or unfree, is only a capacity *in man*. Behind the will lies man himself, and that man does not

4. Gisbertus Voetius (1589–1676) was a major orthodox Reformed theologian in Utrecht.

float about in the air but is part of *the world as a whole*; and therefore, behind the issue of the will lies the issue of man, and behind the issue about man lies the issue of the world taken as a whole. This is why we never let our sounding line descend to the bottom of this ocean as long as we have not penetrated into the primordial grounds of the relationship of the world to God. And that relationship to God, not of a conceivable world but of an actually existing world, is entirely dominated by the question of common grace. For in the world that actually exists, there is sin, and in that world the effects of sin are at work. And everything is thus epitomized in the question of how a sinful world can be blessed by God in so many ways without jeopardizing his sovereign holiness. And no answer can be found to this all-dominating question except in the confession of common grace.

§ 5 The whole conflict rages once again between the natural and this higher aspect that cannot be explained from nature but nevertheless manifests itself in the midst of the life of nature. The very same riddle confronts us when we see *Jesus* manifest himself in the midst of humanity, or the *church* function in the world, or *faith* operate in the midst of human deliberation and policy, or a *miracle* occur in the course of events, or *grace* inhabit the unholy heart. Again and again, what matters in these contrasts is the relationship in which the two stand vis-à-vis one another. All these relationships must possess the same foundation, have the same starting point, and fall under the same rule. This contrast as such already exists between God and the world, between this earthly existence and eternal existence, between heaven and earth, between what is spiritually invisible and what can be observed by our senses. But this relationship that as such already exists is now further focused and intensified because sin drives the already existing pairs even further apart, and the grace that opposes sin gives still higher expression to the spiritual. Rebirth is *more* than birth, resurrection is *more* than life, and the perseverance of the saints is *more* than the state of righteousness in paradise. Therefore, wherever the world, the natural, and the visible sink deeper through sin, there grace occupies a higher position than the original spiritual creation.

Even so, the chasm has widened from two sides. The world is weakened through sin, and the spiritual power has climbed to a higher position through grace. This still-deeper chasm therefore threatens to rupture all unity, all connection, all coherence, so that ultimately the born-again individual does not want to have anything to do with the world, and the world begins to deny all higher life, theology bans all science, and science denies theology any authority; and the church acts as if there is no world, and the world does not take the existence of the church into account. We encounter, on the one hand, mysticism that shuns the light, and on the other hand, a defiant unbelief. Here we have the church as a spiritual body that evaporates into thin air and lacks any embodiment, and in contrast to it we have the soulless world that no longer acknowledges any heaven above it. If this is to be opposed, and if it is our calling to restore to the awareness of our century the correct relationship between church and world, between theology and science, between rebirth and nurture, and between the old man and the new man, then no formulaic solution will avail any longer. No salvation can be found in any compromise. At that point the truth, the reality of existing nature that impinges upon us from all sides, both within man and outside man, must be faced. And this is precisely what we cannot do, unless in each of these contrasts we take into account the existence of common grace and the manner of its existence.

CHAPTER TWENTY-SIX

PREPARATORY GRACE

So the tribune came and said to him, "Tell me, are you a Roman citizen?" And he said, "Yes." The tribune answered, "I bought this citizenship for a large sum." Paul said, "But I am a citizen by birth."

ACTS 22:27–28

§ 1 If now we have arrived at the significance of common grace for the child of God, then we are immediately faced with the issue of the *gratia praeveniens et praeparans*—that is, prevenient and preparatory grace.[1] In Reformed circles it is not popular to speak of "preparatory grace," and this is understandable. For "preparatory grace" usually refers to a measure of preparation, not in common grace, but in particular grace. It is thus understood as a preparation that either bears a general character or that has arisen from man. In this way people ended up straying on the semi-Pelagian path, and this is precisely what brought discredit to the phrase "preparatory grace." It is not difficult to grasp the state of the question. The starting point lies

1. See *DLGTT*, s.v. "gratia praeveniens": "*prevenient grace, the grace that 'comes before' all human response to God.* A special term is given to the grace that necessarily precedes *conversio* (q.v.), since mankind is universally sinful and incapable of salvation or of any truly good work without the help of God. A fully monergistic theology, Augustinianism or Calvinism, must assume that this grace is irresistible, whereas a synergistic system, semi-Pelagianism or Arminianism, will hold prevenient grace to be resistible."

in the condition of man after the fall. In the Reformed confession, the condition after the fall is that man's *essence* could not be corrupted by sin, but his *nature* is so totally depraved by sin that he has become utterly incapable of anything good before God. This fateful effect of sin unavoidably would have led, in each and every person, to a hardening that would continue to its ultimate end had not common grace intervened, arresting the terrible destruction of sin and bringing about a certain capability for what is called *civic righteousness*.

But the sinner owes this civic righteousness not to himself but only to God. If God's common grace had not intervened, this civic righteousness would not exist; and if God were to withdraw his common grace, it would disappear. In addition, this civic righteousness alters man's condition but does not restore his nature, no matter how high a level it attains. A lion or tiger may become safe under the control of a trainer, and even perform orderly actions or tricks, but when the trainer is gone and the lion or tiger is let loose, the working of its wild nature returns immediately and it will throw itself on its prey and devour it. Sometimes even the trainer himself, in a moment of weakness of the will, becomes the victim.

The same also applies to man under the control of common grace. Now, and as long as God controls him through common grace, he is relatively tranquil and lends himself to performing orderly actions in civil society. But if God were to remove this restraining control, then it would become evident that his nature has remained the same, and that depraved nature would again bring forth evil with ever increasing intensity. This is why we never have the right to look down condescendingly from our presumed height on the evil of those who have fallen deeper. In principle, the same evil lurks in our own heart. We owe it only to divine grace (common grace) that it has not sprouted within us to that extent; and were this grace to depart from us, the same evil would sprout from our heart, depending on the occasion.

This Reformed confession, in the meantime, is still contradicted by oth- § 2
ers who claim that although our nature as such did indeed lose the adornment it had once received in original righteousness, as such it has remained untouched and can therefore, no matter how weakened, still obtain merit of congruity (*meritum de congruo*).[2] Still others maintain that a measure of

2. See *DLGTT*, s.v. "meritum de congruo": "*merit of congruity*; a so-called half-merit, or proportionate merit. In late medieval scholastic theology a distinction was made between a *meritum de condigno*, a merit of condignity or full merit, deserving of

depravity entered our nature, but this depravity did not penetrate so deeply that a certain ability for good did not still remain. This does not make any difference for the actual situation, as long as our opponents confess and acknowledge with us and we with them that, as commonly found among us, man possesses a certain capability for civic righteousness apart from regeneration and conversion. But we differ when it comes to how we must evaluate this capacity. For at that point, the one says that this ability comes from our weakened but not depraved nature, and the other argues that this ability springs from our *partially* but *not totally* depraved nature. In contrast, we Reformed say that the sinner owes this capacity, in spite of his nature being *totally* depraved, exclusively to the grace of God, who temporarily and to varying degrees arrests the consistent, continuing effect of depravity at the root of man's nature.

Applied to the entry into the soul of particular grace, this leads to the difference that, according to the Reformed confession, there is *nothing* in the sinner's nature, and *nothing* can emerge from the nature of the sinner, that could elicit or accept particular grace; on the contrary, *all* that springs from the nature of the sinner opposes and resists particular grace. Even a disposition prior to conversion (*dispositio praeveniens ad conversionem*) cannot be confessed by a single Reformed Christian. According to our confession, at the moment when God places his hand on the sinner to bring him life, there is and can be nothing in the sinner that, because it [would have to] proceed from his nature, stands in any other posture than enmity toward this act of God. What holy Scripture teaches about the enmity toward God in the sinner's heart must be understood entirely in this sense. It does not say that there cannot be among the unconverted a sense of reverence for the eternal Being; nor that when asked, the unconverted will always express himself in a wicked, hostile sense about the Father in heaven. On the contrary, it is entirely conceivable that the unconverted will also sing praise hymns to the God of love. But this does mean that when particular grace comes to demand that he confess his eternal death, the unconverted person will try to persist in opposition to God, rather than surrendering and wanting to die, and in his haughtiness and pride he will make himself instead an enemy of the God who seeks him and wants to save him.

---

grace, and a *meritum de congruo*, a half-merit or act not truly deserving of grace, but nevertheless receiving grace on the basis of the divine generosity."

If this is the case, it follows automatically that in the Reformed arena there never can be any thought of *anything*, no matter what, in the sinner through which, from his end, he would approach the work of God with anything that would help achieve, in cooperation with God, the great work of God's bringing him to life. The sinner not only does not contribute anything to that great work, but from his end he tries to *thwart* it. Even if there is in him a certain thirst for eternal salvation, he will still think up all kinds of alternative ways of salvation, but he will never acknowledge defeat and choose the way of salvation ordained by God. He is not *for* it, but *against* it. No one enters the narrow gate of his own accord. The broad way beckons all, without distinction. And if God left man to his own devices, merely offering him grace and pointing out the narrow gate to him, not a single sinner would enter through that narrow gate. Without distinction or exception, everyone would say that God was wrong with his narrow gate and that they, with their usually broad ways, knew much better. It is still the very same situation as in paradise.

Taken in that sense, Scripture therefore denies all "prevenient" or "preparatory grace" on our part, even where this still presents itself as essentially *grace* and is to that extent prepared to give God the glory. See the difference here. Two things can be argued: either the suitability for being converted that precedes conversion works from the natural inclination of man, apart from God's grace, or man by himself never possesses any suitability, but a guidance of God, a certain preceding work of grace, brings him to the point that when the cup of salvation is brought to his lips, he does not reject it, but takes it in hand and drinks. There is certainly a difference here. In the first case, the sinner is presented as suitable by himself to willingly go through the narrow gate when it is opened to him. In the second case, this is denied and it is argued that he will go through only when a measure of prevenient grace enables him to do so. But no matter how far these two opinions diverge, ultimately they both come to the same point. From both sides it is confessed that at the moment the sinner is offered salvation, *his will decides* whether to accept that salvation. He who then accepts salvation, accepts it himself, but he also could have rejected it. And thus in the final analysis the answer to the question of who will be saved is handed over to the arbitrary choice of the will of man, whether it be the choice of the will of the man who has set himself to do so, or the choice of the will of the man who was suited to it by prevenient or preparatory grace. Not a few people then expand the latter to the extent that in § 3 fact this predisposing grace is imparted to a very wide circle (at least to all those who have been baptized) and that it is now up to each individual's choice whether he will enter into life. Some then make the additional mistake of calling this grace that is imparted to all persons who have been baptized "common grace." And thus the beautiful doctrine of "common grace" is ultimately torn entirely from its root, weakened, and even misused *against* the truth.

This, then, has made Reformed Christians, to the extent that they are theologically more informed, reticent to hear of either a preparatory grace or a common grace. They cannot free themselves from the fear that all such doctrines will ultimately shortchange the perfection and irresistibility of God's work in saving grace. As far as they are concerned, a snake always lurks in the grass in all such doctrines and, because they do not feel themselves capable of drawing clearly and accurately the correct line between truth and error, they prefer to choose the safest option and declare simply that they want nothing to do with preparatory or common grace. They don't even remotely realize that they unwittingly have moved from Reformed to Anabaptist territory. Yet this is the case. For by wanting to leave out of account absolutely all differences in the condition of those who are converted, they close their eyes to the providential working of God insofar as it addresses the sinner *before* his regeneration and is connected with the ordination of regeneration. They take into account only the time from regeneration on. Everything that lies before or outside regeneration is none of their concern. And even the question about the identity and condition of the person in whom regeneration occurs does not concern them. They are interested only in what is *new* in the sinner through regeneration. This, therefore, is precisely Anabaptist dualism. And because we cannot observe what exists as regeneration before conversion, *regeneration proper* then ultimately ceases to interest them. They see in fact nothing but the act of *conversion*, and are more and more inclined to let the work of God begin for the first time with conversion itself. Thus the distinction between regeneration and conversion is increasingly lost, and as a result, for them infant baptism loses its true meaning, and they actually would consider it more reasonable if baptism came after conversion. Again, this is precisely the Anabaptist position.

§ 4 It is therefore necessary to remove this fundamental misunderstanding and to set forth the confession of this doctrine again in such a way, and to elucidate it in such a manner, that we can maintain two things simultaneously and with equal firmness. On the one hand, we must affirm the truth that whatever element is present in the sinner at the moment he is brought to life remains in every respect incapable of accepting salvation and is rather fundamentally antagonistic toward any acceptance of salvation. Thus the acceptance of salvation never depends on the free choice of the will of man, and when it comes about, it never comes from man, and when God wants to accomplish it, it can never be refused by man. On the other hand, however, we also acknowledge the truth that in God's ordination his providential guidance of the elect never falls outside their future conversion; rather, from the very beginning it was aimed at this, so that the result of regeneration and conversion depends not only on God's grace manifest in both acts, but also on the condition of the person in whom the two are accomplished.

For this, it is necessary that we correctly perceive the distinction between the working of God on our *person* as such, and the working of God on our *consciousness*. The distinction between these two is sometimes also called the supernatural and the rational workings. However, people are no longer familiar with these terms, and it is therefore necessary to cast the distinction between the two in such a form that it can communicate to us again. A person can go insane either because he starts to brood or because an abnormality develops in his brain that either gradually or suddenly confuses his thinking. In the first case, an unhealthy development of the mind arises in his consciousness. He has worries. He no longer sees a way out. He begins to brood, and the burden of thinking becomes too heavy. He is trapped. Thus he falls into the grip of false notions and false imaginings. Normal reasons no longer have an influence on him. He withdraws within himself. And thus finally his conscious power of thought, which was not designed for such suffocation, succumbs. Here the evil came about because of what happened *in his consciousness*, via all kinds of ratiocinations in which he entangled himself.

But it can also happen very differently. He could develop a physical disorder, either in the brain itself or in the nervous system that affects the brain. Through this, a certain pressure could be exerted in the brain itself that prevents its normal functioning. That impediment would then affect his consciousness. And thus the result could be that in the midst of the happiest of circumstances, without anything that weighs him down or causes him anxiety, he falls into the grip of false notions that in the end results in insanity.

The two kinds of insanity are quite distinguishable. In the case of the latter, the question will be whether the disturbance in the diseased brain or nervous system can be removed; if this is successful, then the patient will recover with virtually only medical or surgical treatment. But if the insanity is of the first kind, medical treatment will be effective only to the extent that it attempts to counteract the abnormal element from the confused mind that had an effect on the body; otherwise, a *spiritual* medication will be necessary. What is meant by psychiatry today seeks in effect only to free the spirit by removing physical disturbances. But the Christian side maintains that the first kind of insanity also requires spiritual medication, and that even the second kind, though it cannot be healed spiritually, can at least be ameliorated spiritually.

§ 5 However this may be, the difference between these two causes of insanity and the resulting difference in treatment is obvious. The first kind relates almost exclusively, or at least primarily, to the *consciousness*; the second relates to what is unhealthy in the *person* of the individual and only secondarily affects his consciousness. This same difference also manifests itself in the moral insanity that wields destruction in and through sin, and consequently also in relation to the spiritual medication that redeems and sanctifies the sinner. Does sin first emerge, as the Pelagian teaches, in the *conscious* life, or is the infant already conceived and born in sin? In the former case, sin is not part of his nature, but only of his rational consciousness. Man is then born without sin. There is no disorder in his nature. But as he grows up and comes to awareness, he sees evil examples that seduce him. He gives in to them. And thus he ends up sinning. But precisely because sin is not in his *nature* but only in his *consciousness*, he can quit sinning again at any moment. And after he quits sinning and repents, he can return to sinning. There is no background in his nature from which a certain continuity of his moral life springs. At any given moment his moral life is therefore what he himself, as a conscious being, wills it to be at that moment.

The matter is quite different, however, if he is conceived and born in sin. In this case the core of sin lies in his person; there is a disorder in his nature. As soon as he comes to *consciousness*, that disorder in his nature will have an effect on his consciousness and show it to be sinful. As a result of the depraved nature, neither his mind nor his will is able to function properly. And because evil works out *from his nature*, he will not be free at any given moment to do any one thing or the other, but because of the evil inclination and unholy urge that spring from his nature, he will be compelled unless that evil nature is tempered medicinally. And the working of evil will not allow him to stop before that nature itself can be healed of the indwelling depravity.

Thus the Pelagian and the scriptural diagnoses of sin are diametrically opposed. And many kinds of intermediate systems have been thought up that we can properly designate as semi-Pelagian and that are intended to smooth the sharpness of this contrast, but if we want to gain clear insight, it is necessary to leave these intermediate systems out of consideration for the time being, and contrast Pelagianism, which seeks sin not in our *nature* but in our *consciousness*, with the revelation of holy Scripture as the Reformed confession accepts it, which teaches us that our nature itself is depraved, and that therefore sin is present long before there is any awareness in the infant. Sin arises in our awareness from our nature, but the difference is and remains that according to Pelagianism, sin does not reside in nature but finds its origin in the conscious life, whereas according to the statement of God's Word, sin is rooted deep in our nature and therefore has already affected the child long before consciousness awakens, even when the child dies early and consequently never achieves awareness in this life. In that sense we compared the moral insanity of sin with mental insanity, and there too we found both cases standing side by side. On the one hand, there is the insanity that arises from a disturbance of *nature*, and on the other hand, the insanity that finds its cause in a confusion of *consciousness*.

If we clearly understand this twofold perspective of the nature of sin, § 6
then it follows automatically that the healing of this moral illness—that is, redemption from sin—must be entirely different depending on whether we make the first or the second diagnosis. If we say with the Pelagian that sin lies not in our nature but only in our consciousness, then we can apply no other means for healing *than those that work on the consciousness*. The Pelagian will exhort, advise, entice, and goad, but whatever he does, it will always be aimed at changing the consciousness and at effecting this change in consciousness through the sinner himself. He will neither want nor be able to know of any other medication or healing method than what proceeds *rationally*—that is, one that tries to work on the rational awareness through exhortation.

On the other hand, when we acknowledge with David that we are conceived and born in sin [Ps 51:1], or with the Reformed liturgical Form for Baptism that "our children are conceived and born in sin, and therefore are children of wrath,"[3] and that therefore the origin of sin lies not in our consciousness, but much deeper, in *human nature* itself—then we will understand immediately that a moral and rational medication—that is, a medication that comes to man from the outside—will be without any effect. For us then no other healing for the sinner is conceivable than a healing that attacks evil where it resides—that is, *in our nature itself*. This nature lies not in front of, but behind our consciousness. The disorder lies in the fact that nature itself lies. The disorder must therefore be removed from that nature. And only when that disorder in our nature has been removed can the healing of our nature and from our nature also affect our consciousness. Rational means can then be useful, and Reformed Christians also respect the rational medication, but *only in the second stage*. First, the spiritual psychiatry must remove the disorder in our nature. Once that has happened, and only then, can the external and reasonable medication perform its work, and not before. Consequently, Scripture teaches, and the Reformed church confesses, that God himself has to intervene first; that by means of the supernatural act of regeneration God must remove the disorder in our nature; and that only where this has happened can a change in consciousness occur. But that act, by which God turns around our nature, depends on God alone and cannot depend in any way on the choice of man's will. Only when, as a result of the removal of the disorder from our nature, our consciousness also turns around and comes to faith, can the born-again sinner himself also want what God wants.

Those Reformed Christians who still continue to be inclined to put most emphasis on the *rational* means and to place the *supernatural* means more or less in the shadows, must then remember that by doing so, they are ultimately taking the depravity of our nature too lightly and are still tending more or less toward a false and superficial diagnosis of sin that is utterly contradicted by God's Word.

3. See "The Form for the Administration of Baptism to Infants of Believers," in *The Psalms and Hymns: With the Catechism, Confession of Faith, and Canons, of the Synod of Dort, and Liturgy of the Reformed Protestant Dutch Church in North America* (Philadelphia: Mentz & Rouvoudt, 1847), 59.

CHAPTER TWENTY-SEVEN

IMMEDIATE REGENERATION

You have been born again, not of perishable seed but of imperishable, through the living and abiding word of God.

1 PETER 1:23

In every further definition involving prevenient grace or, stated more correctly,[1] preparatory grace, we cannot and must not lose sight of the distinction between the sinner's *regeneration* and his personal *conversion*. For it cannot be denied that something precedes conversion, even if only the call to conversion, and that this call, even if understood in an entirely external sense, already is a proof of grace. But regeneration is not like this. Grace can lie behind regeneration, but it does not manifest itself as such, and even where it can be demonstrated, it has an entirely different significance and bears an entirely different character. If we intermingle regeneration and conversion into the discussion of preparatory grace, we are in great danger of ending up using the words *grace* and *preparatory* in an unstable, changing sense and thereby reaching a wrong conclusion. § 1

1. Note by the author: *Gratia praeveniens*, or prevenient grace, is, in contrast to the *gratia cooperans*, also used for the first act of bringing to life.

To avert this danger to which our exposition might be exposed, we therefore will discuss both concepts separately and look first at the question of whether there is a preparatory grace that precedes regeneration. This grace can be of two kinds: either a grace that makes the sinner receptive to regeneration, or a grace that helps to bring about regeneration in him. Two things can assist in the safe birth of a child: in the first place, the robust health of the mother, and in the second place, the reliable help of the midwife. Or if we would prefer to compare regeneration to an operation, we can say that the success of the operation can be prepared in the first place by bringing the constitution of the patient up to a healthy level, and on the other hand by using the best operating table, instruments, and surgical team available. In that sense we can also ask when it comes to regeneration, first, whether the condition of the sinner makes a difference, and second, whether something can be done beforehand to make regeneration succeed better.

The question must be limited in this way. Many other acts of grace on God's part precede regeneration, but these do not bear a *preparatory* character. Everyone concedes that the eternal election of the sinner precedes regeneration, and that regeneration necessarily follows *because* election preceded it. And thus the Reformed church also acknowledges that regeneration as a rule falls within the sphere of the covenant of grace in the link with preceding generations. But when we speak of preparatory grace, this is not in view either. Preparatory grace then would be involved with regeneration only if the act of regeneration were preceded by making a person receptive to that regeneration, or if, before regeneration were accomplished, something had preceded that introduced or assisted it. Two things are done before peas or similar vegetables are planted. The soil in which the peas will be planted is prepared by being loosened and fertilized, and the peas are soaked in water to stimulate their rapid germination. In this sense it would be conceivable that something happened *within* the sinner beforehand to make him susceptible to regeneration, and that something happened *within* or *for* him to make the regeneration more successful.

§ 2 But we must reject precisely in this sense any notion of preparation in or upon the sinner in regeneration, since everything pointed out in connection with this claim prepares for conversion but not for regeneration. In fact, any notion of preparation is contrary to the very character of regeneration. We must allow only two exceptions here. In the first place, we can truly say that if common grace had not intervened, the son who was to be reborn would not have existed: if no common grace had come in paradise after the fall, Adam and Eve would have died that very same day, and no human being would have come after them. And also, if no doubling of common grace had come to Noah's family, and our whole race had perished in the flood, no one would have been born after the flood, and whoever is not born cannot be reborn. This we do concede, but it is not what is generally meant by "preparatory grace."

And we also acknowledge, secondly, that insofar as we can judge, regeneration never occurs except under such circumstances that, due to all kinds of preparatory grace, conversion can follow. We speak here with caution, because not every regeneration is followed by conversion, and our church also accepts and confesses that there may be many children who die very young in whom we cannot deny the presence of regeneration, in whom we can even assume regeneration as a rule, but who leave this life too soon to be capable of conversion. It is therefore advisable to be cautious when making statements on this point. But with that proviso it must be acknowledged that in persons who will still come to conversion in this life, regeneration does not occur except under such circumstances as prepare the possibility of conversion. But this does not change anything in our thesis that there is absolutely no preparation for *regeneration itself*. No one knows when, in which moment, the regeneration of a convert among the heathen or Muslims occurs, but it can be said that where such a heathen man or woman is born again, God's providential ordination also causes the circumstances and means to be present that will serve him or her later to come to conversion through contact with Christians or the preaching of the gospel. But then as well, all this serves to prepare for conversion, but not for regeneration.

In order to prevent misunderstanding, we must add something about sin. It has been stated (entirely correctly) that regeneration is impossible unless it is preceded by sin. Prior to his fall, Adam was insusceptible to regeneration. Regeneration was also impossible in Christ's case. And once a person has been regenerated, so that the germ of sin has been killed in him, he cannot be the object of regenerating grace a second time. It is therefore certain that "being dead in sin" [see Eph 2:1; Col 2:13] is the indispensable prerequisite for being able to share in the grace of regeneration. And it must also be acknowledged that under God's wondrous ordination, a deeper fall into sin was one means through which God brought more than one individual to personal conversion. Think only of Augustine.[2] But everything that comes beforehand, and even must come beforehand, is not therefore *preparation*, and least of all preparatory *grace*. No one will say that falling and breaking a leg is a preparation for the surgery to repair the leg. Even if we concede that regeneration necessarily must be preceded by a fall into sin or by being conceived and born in sin, this has nothing to do with the preparation for regeneration.

§ 3 Under only two circumstances could we speak of preparation for regeneration: In the first place, a sinner—say the one who has fallen the deepest—might be as such unsuitable for regeneration and therefore not eligible. And second, from the human end, something might have been performed or some collaboration might have been involved in regeneration through which the rebirth was accomplished. If regeneration were understood in either way, then a certain preparation would have to precede it, at least in the case of those sunk deepest into sin, to make them suited to and receptive to regeneration. The field of their heart, if we may put it thus, would have to be plowed and harrowed beforehand. And also, if anything assisted in regeneration from man's end before it came to regeneration, this collaborating force would have to be introduced into man if it were lacking. Thus we would have to assume an essential preparation for regeneration, if not in all people, then at least in most, and the question would even arise as to what extent we humans could do something on our part to foster this suitability for regeneration in ourselves and our children.

But neither of these two possibilities will ever be acknowledged from the Reformed side. "Though your sins are like scarlet, they shall be as white as snow" [Isa 1:18], and no one from our side will at any time concede, with the gospel before him, that any sinner could ever be allowed to think, "My sins

2. In his *Confessions*, Augustine relates his wicked lifestyle preceding his conversion. On one occasion, Augustine says that along with his friends he delighted in the theft and wanton destruction of some pears. He writes: "We derived pleasure from the deed simply because it was forbidden. Look upon my heart, O God, look upon this heart of mine, on which you took pity in its abysmal depths. Enable my heart to tell you now what it was seeking in this action which made me bad for no reason, in which there was no motive for my malice except malice. The malice was loathsome, and I loved it. I was in love with my own ruin, in love with decay: not with the thing for which I was falling into decay but with decay itself." See Augustine, *The Confessions*, trans. Maria Boulding, part 1, vol. 1, *The Works of Saint Augustine: A Translation for the 21st Century* (New York: New City Press, 2005), 2.4.9, p. 68.

are too great to be forgiven." That is the sentiment of Cain, not the fundamental idea of the gospel. On the contrary, the fundamental sentiment of the gospel is precisely the reverse: the person who has fallen the deepest can find grace. We never have to despair about the conversion of even the sinner who has strayed farthest: indeed, it is those who "labor and are heavy laden" [Matt 11:28] who are called to the Savior. Hardening certainly can occur, but this is not part of our discussion here. For hardening never occurs except in the struggle against grace.

Our church could never teach otherwise by virtue of her confession of the character of sin in man. If she took the Pelagian position that in sin we take into consideration only our sinful *actions*, the situation would be different. But our church never taught this. It always sought, with holy Scripture, the original, decisive guilt in the fall of Adam. It took humanity, not as a collection of individuals but as a single whole, and therefore responsible as a unit. There is hereditary guilt, which is the same for all. And in that hereditary guilt lies the fatal consequence, since by virtue of our hereditary guilt, we are all conceived and born in sin. Hence our confession at the holy baptism of our children, when we declare the belief that these still-innocent "children are conceived and born in sin, and therefore are children of wrath" as well.[3] The question of how far this inborn sin will develop in various individuals is not pertinent to this issue. In the one individual this development can go very far, in the other it will be arrested by grace, but both stand fully equal before God with respect to their hereditary guilt and hereditary sin. "All have sinned and fall short of the glory of God, and are justified by his grace as a gift" [Rom 3:23–24]. "There is no distinction" [Rom 3:22].

On the basis of this confession, with holy Scripture before us, we must not seek to maintain that one person is a more suitable object for regeneration than another, and therefore we also must not maintain that preceding grace would bring the sinner the required receptivity to be born again. Nothing precedes regeneration except being born *in* sin and *under* condemnation.

Nor must we concede even for a moment the second point, as if man § 4
himself, or anything from the human end, could collaborate in bringing about regeneration or in making it more successful. If this were not so,

3. See "The Form for the Administration of Baptism to Infants of Believers," 59.

there certainly would have to be preparatory grace to make this collaborating element present in the person himself or in his environment. But precisely this is not so. In man, or among humans, nothing whatever collaborates toward regeneration. Rather, everything works against it from the side of man. No one can posit two kinds of regeneration. Regeneration is the same for all. We therefore cannot say that regeneration is different for a human child of a month or a year than it is for an adult human. It is one or the other: either we must exclude all innocent infants from regeneration, or we must acknowledge that in regeneration we cannot posit anything as a prior requirement that cannot also be present in the tiniest infant. And in a week- or month-old child there is simply nothing that can collaborate: not his will, for it does not yet function; not his intellect, for it still sleeps; not his feelings, for he does not yet perceive them; not holy Scripture or sermons, for he does not yet know them. There is nothing from his environment, for that environment still lacks any means to influence such a child spiritually. We may already pray for that child, but he does not yet hear that prayer. So far, such an infant leads a purely material existence. The child sleeps, stares, contorts his muscles, and nurses at his mother's breast. That is all. From this perspective it is already certain that there cannot be collaboration of any kind. What is even more convincing, if we pay attention to it, is that according to Scripture regeneration can already occur in the womb, which makes the exclusion of any human collaboration absolute.

This can be made clear from yet another perspective. In man we have to make a distinction as well between the center and the circumference of his life. In his life there is a core, a *center* from which all of life's dynamic goes forth, and there are *life dynamics* that receive from that core their impulse and drive. Regeneration does not occur in the circumference but in the center, in that core. There is in us a pivot around which our entire life revolves. This pivot has been moved and pulled askew through sin, and all of life's manifestations become wrong as a result. This cannot be otherwise. And in regeneration this pivot is set aright again, though not with the result that all of life's manifestations are also immediately set right. This cannot be, since the working of the pivot on the circumference also suffers from sin. But in any case, regeneration, as the setting aright again of the pivot, can occur only where that pivot is located—namely, in the most central point of our human being. If man himself, or others on his behalf, could impact that pivot, that core of his life, then it would be conceivable to still speak of collaboration. But this is not the case. Every expression of our own life or that of others occurs far from the center, in the circumference. No one can get to that pivot. It is within no one's reach. *Only God* has access to this inner pivot of our life. And thus it appears along this path as well, that even the faintest notion of any collaboration from man in regeneration, and also of preparatory grace in that collaboration, must be categorically rejected.

This is even clearer when we pay attention to two things that can be § 5
distinguished in the center of our life. We have our *existence* and we have *consciousness* of our existence. We are and we think. We don't know how these two relate. This alone is certain: in God is, first, eternal being, and second, the divine self-awareness of this eternal being; and man, having been created in God's image, also receives both *existence* and *self-awareness* of this existence. Note well that conversion occurs, of course, in the sphere of that self-awareness. A mentally impaired man, a lunatic, someone who has lost his mind, cannot be converted as long as he is in this condition. But regeneration is different. Regeneration must penetrate equally as deeply as sin did, and sin has not only falsified our consciousness but also made our nature depraved. When we go back to the pivot, the core, the center of our human existence, then both the core of our existence and our nature, as well as the core of our consciousness, lie in that center. Nothing manifests itself in the circumference other than what works out from that center. Thus both the source out of which our nature works, and the source of the light that causes our consciousness to light up, lie in that one center, and they do so in such a relationship that our *consciousness* follows our nature, and not our *nature* our consciousness. And because God has all manifestations of our nature, and specifically, all manifestations of our consciousness, under his sovereign ordination, it necessarily follows that, in order to make action on our part possible, the complete act of bringing us to life on God's part must have occurred first. Thus there can be collaboration on our part, either from the impulse of our nature or in our consciousness, only when regeneration as such has achieved its full claim.

We must be careful, however, not to fall into another extreme here and § 6
present regeneration as an entirely *independent* creative act. This too has happened, and still happens, precisely in order to defend all the better the absolute character of regeneration against all spurious reasoning from the side of man. The notion then in fact amounts to this: First, the person who was *born* falls away and another *newly born* person takes his place. [Then,] the corpse of that man born initially remains chained for some time to the

newly born man, but it does not concern him, and when he dies, the chain is released and, now freed, the person ascends to heaven.

This notion is utterly false, and we must not let ourselves be confused by the expressions of holy Scripture that we must "put on the new self" [Eph 4:24; Col 3:10] and that we are "created in Christ Jesus" [Eph 2:10]. Regeneration is not an act of a *new* creation but an act of a *re-creation*. Consequently, regeneration is certainly dependent on what it finds. A Solomon is a person with quite a different predisposition than a David; a John is an entirely different person from a Paul. This difference, this distinction between persons is determined entirely by the *first birth* and cannot be transformed by regeneration. Regeneration cannot make a Solomon from a David, or a David from a Solomon. Dependence on the first birth is therefore actually present, but this does not give us any right at all to speak of a collaboration of something in man, since the question of how someone is born—with what aptitude, with which character trait, with what disposition—did not depend on himself, and he was not asked about it, but it depended only on God's ordainment. The divine act in regeneration thus does not depend on human choice, but regeneration as a *second* divine act joins in with the *first* divine act: birth.

§ 7 Therefore regeneration is only accomplished through "the living and abiding word of God" [1 Pet 1:23], and re-creation in regeneration is also, like the first creation, *from* the Father, but at the same time *through* the Word and *by virtue of* the Holy Spirit. By this we mean that we must understand the notion that "all things have been created *by* the Word; and that nothing has been created apart from the Word" [see John 1:3] in this way: in each creature a thought of God is expressed, in each creature a thought of God is at work and is embodied, and because in the eternal Word the fullness and glory of the thoughts of God reside, nothing can be created other than *through* the Word and *from* the Father.

The same holds true for every human being as well. The divine Trinity has embodied the one thought of his divine image in various ways in the various human beings. We are not all the same but different. This is where the *manifold* wisdom of God lies, and therefore each child of God will one day receive on the white stone a name that no one knows but God and he himself [see Rev 2:17]. If regeneration were to bypass the diversity in each individual's nature, we might still be able to think that it came only from the Father. But this is not the case. Regeneration goes along with the person as he is, as he received it in his personal existence from God, a personal existence that he received from the Father but through the Word. And this is precisely why in the re-creation of this existing personality a divine working must occur that is also from the Father but through the Son. Thus in regeneration there is most certainly a collaboration and cooperation, not a collaboration between God and man, but a collaboration of the divine persons.

Those who sensed this—foremost among them Guido de Brès, the author of the Belgic Confession—have always understood the beautiful words from 1 Peter 1:23–25 to refer to the divine re-creating power that comes about through the "living and abiding word of God."[4] It is the re-creating address of this "living Word" that they have heard in the word of revelation, and that voice of God is what for them makes the gospel what it is: gospel. It is stated so richly and gloriously: "You have been born again, not of perishable seed but of imperishable, through the living and abiding word of God; for 'All flesh is like grass and all its glory like the flower of grass. The grass withers, and the flower falls, but the word of the Lord remains forever.' And this word is the good news that was preached to you."

But of course those who do not fully open their eyes to the truth that this re-creation is through the Son could not read this in these words, and therefore they always understood these words more or less in the sense that regeneration came about through the Bible—that is, through the content of holy Scripture read by them or preached to them by others. This of course was not clear and plain to them. Nor could they ever make clear what the Word (in this case, holy Scripture) contributed to regeneration. Nevertheless, they continued to accept *something* like this. And this made it appear as if there was a certain preparatory grace also for regeneration. To this we say, No!

4. See Belgic Confession, Art. 24: "We believe that this true faith, being wrought in man by the hearing of the Word of God and the operation of the Holy Spirit, regenerates him and makes him a new man, causing him to live a new life, and freeing him from the bondage of sin."

CHAPTER TWENTY-EIGHT

COMMON GRACE IN OUR GENEALOGY

For the promise is for you and for your children and for all who are far off, everyone whom the Lord our God calls to himself.

Acts 2:39

§ 1 We have averted any danger of seeking in common grace a kind of preparation for the transition from death to life. There are only two states, our forefathers used to say: a soul is either spiritually dead or spiritually alive. There is no in-between state of a soul that is still largely dead yet somewhat alive. Regeneration (the introduction of life, the circumcision of the heart, the transforming of the heart of stone into a heart of flesh, the resurrection of the soul, or whatever we want to call the first act of God to impart saving grace to our soul) is immediate, cannot be prepared by anything, and is the same in the most terrible villain as it is in the most adorable child. There can be no preparation here.

But—and now we enter an entirely different area—preparation is not only possible but even indispensable *in conversion*. A person comes to conversion himself. Not from himself, but nevertheless as himself. He must be just as active in conversion as he is passive in regeneration. We can even say that *to convert* [or *to repent*] is the highest action we can achieve in this life. The correct understanding of this has been lost through preaching that called regeneration conversion, looked upon both as if they were one and the same, and completely lost sight of the profound distinction between the two. But precisely this must stimulate us all the more to resolutely disentangle the two again and again, and to make it increasingly clear to others and to ourselves that a person must first be made alive from being dead in order to be *able* to convert, but that conversion is a task imposed on him. After all, Scripture nowhere says, "Give birth to yourself again," but it does say again and again, *Repent*. It never says, "Bring yourself to life," but to the one brought to life it says, *Stand up*.

Here lies the reason why preparatory grace is as inconceivable in regen- § 2
eration as it is indispensable in conversion. It is not only that the one who repents after being regenerated is stimulated and urged to do so by the Holy Spirit, and is supported in the act itself by the Holy Spirit, so that after the fact of his conversion he knows that he owes it to God; it is also that grace very definitely has to precede conversion. This grace that precedes conversion is of two kinds: in part it is particular grace, and in part it is common grace. The preceding particular grace consists in God sending his law and his gospel to the sinner who will repent: his law to bring an awareness of guilt and sin, and his gospel to make known his way of salvation. Many children of the world receive this law and this gospel, but not mixed with grace—as an *external* call, to be sure, but not as an *inner* call. And this knowledge of the law and gospel, mixed with that singular grace through which the regenerated individual who will repent hears the voice of his God calling to his soul, cannot be absent here. Whoever does not hear God commanding him, "Repent," will not come to repentance. Repentance is an act of faith, to be sure, but it is an act of the *obedience* of faith. Whoever does not hear himself called will not consider coming. For that reason, no repentance is conceivable without grace preceding the call of God.

This preceding particular grace that belongs to the calling can either be compressed in a short time or be extended over a longer period. In one case, perhaps the person to whom the call is extended has grown up *outside* the knowledge of the law and gospel and makes contact with the law and gospel for the first time as an adult, shortly before his conversion. His introduction to the law and gospel is then almost immediately mixed with summoning grace, so that he comes to conversion almost immediately. In other cases, perhaps someone has been instructed in holy Scripture from infancy, and has attended church for many years and often moved in pious circles, so that he has had a broad external knowledge of the law and gospel for a long time; but this knowledge has no hold on him, because it was not mixed with the grace of the inner calling. Only years later, the scales fall from his eyes, his ears are opened, and he hears God's voice and repents. Between these two extremes, of course, are all kinds of intermediate forms that do not allow for further description here. But whether this knowledge and this summoning grace are added to him only shortly before or long before his conversion, they cannot be absent. Without this preparatory particular grace not a single sinner whom God has regenerated has ever repented. Regeneration alone cannot of itself lead to conversion. Conversion requires a knowledge of the law and gospel, and regeneration does *not* provide this.

§ 3 But in addition to this preparatory *particular grace* there is also a preparatory *common grace* at work here, and it is the latter that we must now elucidate. We therefore will speak no longer of knowledge of Scripture and of the preceding calling, for these do not fall under common grace. Common grace is never something that is added to our nature but always something that works from within that nature as a result of the arresting of sin and destruction. By contrast, Scripture and the calling do not come from our nature but are added to our nature. Here as well, the discrete realms of particular grace and common grace remain distinct with an unblurred line of demarcation.

Common grace operates first of all in our origin. This origin relates to our birth, which in turn is connected with the whole line from which we have come. For that reason, we move here entirely in the realm of the natural life. holy Scripture tells us, and the outcome confirms, that God generally causes his elect to be born from elect parents or at least from those who have a genealogical link with elect persons. It does not proceed from one link to the next; often links are skipped. But a child of God who traces his genealogical descent will very rarely be able to go back two or three generations without finding children of God among his parents or forebears. "You and your seed" is the formula with which holy Scripture reveals to us this important matter.

It could have been otherwise. God is omnipotent, and nothing would prevent him from seeking the multitude of his elect one time in Europe, another time in Africa, a next generation from Asia, and so forth. But this is not how it is. The elect of God sometimes live for many generations among the same nation, on the same continent, sometimes entirely among the same peoples; other than on rare exception, we do not see someone come to grace from other nations, on other continents, among other peoples. Even in one and the same city, in one and the same village, we see one family remain entirely outside grace, while in another family grace is transmitted from grandfather to father, from father to child, from child to grandchild. This is not an absolute rule. There are families who, after being visited for a long time by grace, are abandoned. There are others who, after living for a long time in the dark, journey to the living waters. Sometimes a single individual even comes to Jesus from a barren family and remains the only one in his family. But as a rule, grace generally persists in the same families, and the formula remains: "You and your seed." Not always "you and your child," but "you and your seed," viewed over several generations.

This rule is so firm that without it, covenantal grace would be unthinkable and the propagation of the church would be ended. Infant baptism is based entirely on God's working in this way. If this rule were not generally applicable, then there would be no ground at all to baptize the little children of believers. We must never allow the *spiritual basis,* which in infant baptism lies of course only in the presumption of regeneration, to put the *judicial basis,* which can only be derived from the covenant, in the shadows. For we do not know whether an infant is born again; the church can judge only whether a child is born of believing parents, and in this fact—and in this fact alone—lies the judicial basis for the church to embrace infant baptism. This of course does not explain infant baptism sacramentally; in order to explain it sacramentally, we must always go back to presumed regeneration. But when the church is faced with the question of whether it will baptize an infant who is presented for baptism, the church knows virtually nothing of the sacramental ground, of the spiritual ground in the soul of that infant; it can only take into account the outwardly observable fact that the child is born of believing parents. Of course, if we trace the link between baptism and regeneration, we must conversely investigate especially the spiritual, the sacramental ground, as was done so nicely by Kramer, who was taken from us all too soon.[1] But the result of that inquiry neither must nor can add to or detract anything from the judicial basis of

1. Kuyper refers here to one of his doctoral students, Geerhard Kramer (1870–97), who died before his dissertation on infant baptism could be corrected for printing. See *AKB* 1897.10, page 276.

infant baptism in the church of Christ, and this can never lie anywhere but in the rule of the covenant—that is, the rule that God the Lord causes his elect generally to be born in a genealogical context.

§ 4 It is clear that in this lies a grace, an act of grace. For through this grace those who are elected to life are as a rule born in the church and grow up in the church. And being born into and being raised within this more tranquil and less worldly environment generally has several results, among them that sin does not break out in the elect so sharply, that there is a comparatively stronger arresting of sin in them, and that in this way common grace works more strongly in them so that they consequently have less to dismantle when they reach repentance. This does not in the least involve anything *salvific* as yet, but in the fearful struggle that breaks out for them in the hour of conversion, they have to break fewer sinful ties, and their turning to the Holy Spirit is less fearful—the latter of which no one will deny. For someone who came to kill and murder, the struggle in the hour of conversion is terrible, difficult to watch; among the children of believers, however, are those who from infancy lived so close to the kingdom that their entry into the kingdom in some cases took place in a manner and at a moment about which afterward they barely could render an account. But precisely this great difference must and can never be explained from the notion that this child, who grew up in a Christian environment, did not have to take exactly the same steps as the criminal. Rather, we must explain it from the fact that whoever has gone a lesser distance has a shorter road back. Both have been equally, completely dead. Both are even completely passively placed in this new life by God. But the one person, at the moment when he became aware of the new life, had strayed less far down the path of sin than the other. And this was not his doing but only the fruit of common grace that God had worked in him.

This common grace might accrue to us only *after* our birth, already *at* our birth, or even long *before* our birth. And especially this latter case is important here, since the generational connection gains significance for the covenant of grace only through this common grace that already works before birth. When a person is born into this world, we must distinguish between what he received as a human being from God and what he received for and through our human race as a member of that race. This distinction speaks clearly in the two parts of the Reformed confession: first, that one's self, one's person, has not been inherited from one's parents, but is God's direct creation; and second, that one's personhood, which is received purely from God's hand, has acquired original guilt and has been defiled by original sin. Both of these doctrines are firmly established among us. The first is the confession of creationism in contrast to traducianism as championed by the Lutherans.[2] The second is the doctrine of our relationship to our covenant head, Adam. And even though the confession of creationism (usually presented as creating a soul in the "lump of flesh" that has already been prepared) warrants revision with respect to the formulation of the terms as well as on the basis of holy Scripture, the Reformed churches will always hold fast to the substance being confessed with this term. One's self, one's personality, is not a fruit of common grace, but a special gift of God.

Taking this as our starting point, we must apply the same distinction to § 5
what common grace accomplishes within the covenant of grace. For we cannot seek that working in the fact that one human being has come from the hand of the Creator differently than another. We do not deny that this is the case. People most definitely do not all resemble one another in terms of their personality and temperament; instead, they differ in every respect. A factory produces entirely uniform products of the same model by the hundreds and thousands; God never does this. The work of our God does not know uniformity. His is a "manifold wisdom" [Eph 3:10] and hence a manifold creation. But what must be denied and disputed is that through these differences in the creation of our personality, one person might be predisposed toward salvation, another not. For if we accept this, we remove all possibility of guilt and of moral responsibility. A human being as human being can still be saved even when he falls, and the personal difference between one human being and another, insofar as it depends on our having been created by God's hand, does not introduce the least change into this reality. If it nevertheless is certain that already at birth there can be, and generally is, a very pronounced difference between the predisposition of one person and of another with a view to his later conversion, then it follows that this difference can be explained only from what this individual received not from God but from his human ancestry. The working of common grace that occurs here thus must not be sought in his personality as such, but must be sought exclusively in the wrinkles of his personality, if

2. Traducianism refers to the doctrine that the soul of the child is generated by the parents; creationism holds that the soul of the child is a new creation, directly created by God.

we may put it that way, that he received through his birth from a given set of parents and from a given family.

All of this occurs with a firm limitation: the difference cannot be found in a different relationship to Adam, for our hereditary guilt that stems from our covenant head is the same for all; rather, it must be sought in the later modification of our personality that stems from the descent and birth from a specific family and from specific parents. Where our descent from Adam is concerned, it must be the same for all, because common grace cannot begin until after the fall. But as soon as common grace goes into action, the differences also arise. And even if we only can trace our lineage back to Noah, it makes a difference for each one of us whether our descent is from Shem, from Japheth, or from Ham. At the individual level this may no longer be traceable, but the difference as such is undeniable. The children of Shem had some advantage *because* they came from Shem, and Ham's children had a disadvantage *because* they came from Ham. This undeniable distinction has been transmitted from generation to generation, simply because the working of common grace was stronger in Shem's offspring than in the offspring of the Hamites.

§ 6 If we were able to trace back to the sons of Noah the "book of the generations," as Genesis calls it, of each human child who is born, and if we could point out those in each generation who were and were not elected to life, then the providential care of God for his elect would shine through the whole course of the generations. But we cannot do this. It is already too difficult to do, even if we were to go back ten generations and to identify three or four generations who had and who had not converted to God. The vast majority of people cannot even do that. The great mass of people know only about their father and grandfather. What comes before these is generally hidden in darkness, or is so uncertain that it does not provide anything for one to grasp firmly. But even if our view of God's providential work before our birth is obscured, this much is nevertheless certain for almost everyone: namely, that their ancestors too belonged to the church of God and holy baptism reached back into past generations of their family; that in the circles of their parents the fear of the Lord was known; and especially that in the generation that came immediately before them, the Lord's name was remembered.

This changes the character of a family. As was recently reported from the Minahassa Peninsula that the Christian natives in the third generation show an entirely different and much higher human type,[3] so it is certain that before we were born, those generations in which the fear of the Lord was a "family asset," if we may put it thus, display changed inclinations, changed sensibilities, a lesser flowering of sin, and in all this, a higher moral type. This does not mean that splendid civil righteousness is never, almost atavistically, displayed in *unregenerate* families. But in those families it is then generally counterbalanced by an increase in human pride or a drifting into human sentimentality, whereas the more tender, more serious, more humble disposition generally became the possession only of those other families through whose genealogy ran a holy line of election.

By virtue of the connection between soul and body, and no less by virtue of the unpredictable force of habit, this modified form of life becomes fixed in such families. The whole human appearance undergoes a measure of change in such families. And when a child is born into such a family, the effect of this ennobling can also be detected in that child. In the second generation, this peculiar effect is even reinforced, and it passes on to the third generation in an even more enhanced form. This continues, on and on. The working of common grace upon one generation has aftereffects in the next generation, and passes on in an even stronger form to the third. And even though marriages with other families often interfere in this process, just as personal iniquities not infrequently disrupt that work of common grace in the generations, this must not cause us to close our eyes to this work of God that runs atavistically down through the generations.

When softer inclinations come to the fore in the circle of the covenant of grace, the passions rage less vehemently, much that is terrible fails to happen, and a more benevolent way of life takes root, then this is undoubtedly also due to the nurture, the environment, the influence of the church, and so much more. But it would be shallow and superficial, and contrary to all of revelation and Scripture, to limit our understanding to the influences that come *after* a person's birth. If God visits the sins of the fathers upon

3. As Theodor Christlieb (1833–89), a professor of theology at Bonn, reported in 1882 of missions in Indonesia, "In Celebes we find the crown of all the Dutch Missions in the region of *Minahassa*, which has now become a Christian peninsula." See Theodor Christlieb, *Protestant Missions to the Heathen: A General Survey of Their Recent Progress and Present State throughout the World*, trans. W. Hastie (Calcutta: Thacker Spink & Co.; Edinburgh: David Douglas, 1882), 13.

the children to the fourth generation, and if he keeps steadfast love toward thousands among the descendants of those who love him, then here too we must go back to the time of birth and before. We must acknowledge that being born within the covenant of grace always involves "you and your seed," and honor must be given to God's providential care for his elect that goes back to the origin of the generations.

CHAPTER TWENTY-NINE

COMMON GRACE IN OUR UPBRINGING

And he answered him, "Sir, let it alone this year also, until I dig around it and put on manure."

LUKE 13:8

As fruit of our previous argument, we may expect agreement with our claim that although genealogical descent and birth from specific parents may aid the work of particular grace, nevertheless what benefits us—namely, our descent and birth—does not itself belong to particular grace but to *common grace*. This automatically resolves the battle that so often has been fought between those who held fast to hereditary grace and those who correctly maintained that "saving grace" is not inherited. There is no saving inherited grace, but common grace is definitely found in the inheritance that we receive from our parents and ancestors. § 1

Yet it is far from superfluous to focus attention on the invariable distinguishing marks that allow us to decide whether something falls under particular grace or common grace. Both seem to flow together to such an extent that confusion occurs easily. Here is the distinguishing mark: particular grace is every grace that comes exclusively to the elect; common grace by contrast is every grace that unbelievers can share with the elect. The fact that a person comes from a good family, and is born into a relatively good and God-fearing family, certainly does involve a grace from God. But this is a good that comes not only to Jacob but also to Esau. Both have Abraham, the friend of God, as their grandfather; both were born from Isaac and Rebekah; and yet this grace flows only with Jacob into the line of election, not with Esau. "Jacob I loved, but Esau I hated" [Rom 9:13]. This is precisely what common grace means, after all: *common* to the elect and the nonelect.

Related to this, in the second place, is that through the same working by which common *grace* comes to us, a common *disgrace*, if we may express it so, can come to us as well. Descent and birth can be to our favor, but also to our disadvantage. They may bring a grace, as well as a disgrace. We read that Jephthah, one of the most outstanding men whom God raised up as judge over Israel, was "the son of a prostitute" [Judg 11:1], and in the sacred genealogy of Christ we encounter Tamar, Rahab, and Bathsheba. Thus the same relationship can be the carrier of common grace as well as the carrier of a destructive influence, and the latter can be equally as common to the elect and the nonelect as grace.

And in the third place, we must comment that common grace as well as common disgrace can be an impetus to ruin as well as an instrument for good. If God causes his elect to be born from a godless family and from evil parents, then the stimulus of the contrast is at work, which leads from profound sin to a conversion that is all the richer. And conversely, for someone born of a God-fearing family who hardens his heart, from his youth on the sacred becomes a tasteless meal that repels him. Rousing someone to conversion is most difficult in the case of a child from a devout home who ultimately rejects the Lord. He knows all about the subject, and your finest words don't have any impact on him. Taking these three together, we can therefore say that common grace can always be recognized by these features: (1) it can be common to elect and nonelect; (2) it works through an instrument that can bring about good as well as evil results; and (3) both evil and good can be means in the hand of God to bless as well as to harden.

§ 2 These same characteristics also remain true in the second part of the doctrine of common grace, to which we now come. After origin and birth come *upbringing* and *environment*. No matter how difficult this may seem, both of these are also at work in the child, at least initially, in such a way that the child himself cannot have any influence on it, and it is God who has willed this as well. He was the one who in unconditioned freedom ordained and created, and even as he created Adam all at once as an adult, he also could have caused each human child to begin life as an adult—not, of course, as a child born from parents, but as a newly created human being. Or just as God created Eve from Adam, but in such a way that she also was immediately an adult, so too the same God then could have brought a subsequent generation into the world from the preceding generation as adult beings. In that case, each newly created human could immediately have determined his own position, and there would not have been any upbringing. But God has not willed it to be this way. He freely chose a quite different manner of procreation: man would henceforth come into the world, not as an adult person but as a helpless infant, conceived and born from a father and mother and therefore entirely dependent on his father and mother for the first years of his life. At first the child himself would be part of his mother, her flesh and blood, sheltered in her being. Then he would come into the world, to be nourished at his mother's breast and held in his mother's lap. And only thus would the child, with very slow transitions, gradually grow up to independence, ultimately to leave father and mother, to get married himself, and then to repeat the same life process as that through which he himself was born.

Furthermore, God the Lord could have created the children of men or § 3
caused them to be born in such a way that in the first years of their life they would not be subject to influences, unable to absorb permanent impressions. In that case, man would have spent the first years of his life in a state of dependency, but these years would not have been decisive for his future. He then would have spent these years of training as if in armor. But God the Lord did not want this either. On the contrary, he causes man to be born with a heart as tender and soft as wax. The young child is extremely susceptible to impressions. What we imbibe with our mother's milk often stays with us our entire life and has an effect on the rest of our life. When we were small children, we stood powerless in the face of this. We didn't even know what was happening to us. We were subject to a process without knowing it ourselves. We underwent influences that perhaps would dominate our entire life, but we underwent them entirely *passively*. This influence is not usually discussed. It seems like a dreadful thing to be so dependent. And so it is completely understandable that an individual who later boldly hardens his heart wickedly boasts that it is not his fault but God's doing that he has become so evil. And although we know better, and although God's church confesses that the cause does not lie with God but rather in the fact that sin crept from generation to generation in organic

connectedness, the hard fact nevertheless remains that for many people, their upbringing has been a curse rather than a blessing. We can go even further and say that if the upbringing is not bad, but nevertheless leads down the wrong path, it can cause an entire nation to sink and degenerate. This danger has also existed in our country, and it is only due to the vigor of the free school[1] that this evil has partially been arrested and can be resisted with hope and good results in the future.

If this is the case, then common grace is here for the taking. There is distinction; there is contrast. In the mighty work of raising children we see noble forces at work for good, but also harmful influences for ill. We see this in all kinds of ways. Someone born in a nation that regulates the education of its people well shares in the fruit of that good. But someone born in a nation that has ruined the education of its people was exposed to harmful influences. If we are born in a group that is in the habit of banishing its small children to hired childcare so that the mother may rest and the father not be bothered, our first formation was left to hired help who could be damaging and who in any case did not foster natural ties. On the other hand, if we are born in a group where the rule is that the mother is in the first place mother and only secondarily the one who governs the affairs of the household, then we have experienced being cherished by motherly love since childhood, and the natural ties in us have been strengthened.

Added to this are all the differences flowing from the personal aspect in the disposition of parents or guardians. There are parents who get along well with one another, and there are those who get along only marginally. There are parents capable of giving, able to supply our upbringing with all that it demands, and there are those who because of limited income were unable to give us what their heart would like to have given us and what their insight considered necessary for us. There are parents with an understanding of raising children, with pedagogical skill and a strong will to raise children, and there are parents who were weak in character, who floated more on their emotions and did not consider the ultimate outcome. There are parents who stood on a high level themselves and therefore could give us the support that would enable us to climb upward, and there are parents who were not able to support us because they themselves were in need of support instead. Finally, there are parents with a fine and earnest

1. That is, a school not run by the state or government but rather a private or denominational school.

sense of responsibility before that God in whom their children were also baptized, and there are parents who scarcely took into account the baptism of their children and gave more weight to the opinion of friends or neighbors than to the opinion of God, at present in their conscience and later at his judgment seat.

Among all these relationships, then, are the lax, evil, and wrong impulses that come from nature, and there is that which steels and strengthens, elevates and builds up—all this is the fruit of common grace through which the ruin in our ancestors' nature was arrested. If then the "lines have fallen in pleasant places" [see Ps 16:6] in parental concern and in intentions that were a blessing to us, and if the effect of this is noticeable in our own formation—indeed, if this influence for the good has been a support for us, since we do not say in our regeneration (*that* is absolutely God's doing) but in the working out of our conversion—then in this sound essence of our upbringing lies a gift of God's mercy, a gift of his goodness, a full draft from the cup of his common grace. Why this good is granted to us and not to another of the same background is the unfathomable secret of his sovereignty, but this does not negate the fact. The fruit of common grace is evident, not only in our origin and birth, but also in an upbringing that is both devout and sensible, well-rounded and solid, consistent. At this point we leave aside the question of how the working of common grace that only arrests can elicit this good from our depraved nature; we will discuss it later under the topic of the working of common grace on the "new man." At this juncture on our path, we confine ourselves to pointing out that if you were permitted to grow up under godly, serious, well-thought-out guidance since childhood, then you received a blessing from God; and this blessing, even though it later supports your conversion, nevertheless does not belong to particular grace, but definitely to common grace. Thus it is according to this fixed rule that a sibling who does not come to repentance also shared in the same privileges of common grace with you.

In addition to upbringing we mentioned in the second place the environment in which the child becomes an adult. We admit that the line of demarcation cannot be drawn sharply, as was the case with origin and birth as well. After all, our parents themselves are part of our environment and for many years constitute virtually the only environment for many a newborn child. *Upbringing* and *environment* are nevertheless two distinct concepts. Upbringing exercises a purposed, deliberate, and intentional influence; the environment exercises its influence involuntarily. It is the § 4 same difference as the impact of a plane on wood and that of air on wood. When we shave a piece of wood with a plane, we intentionally remove something from the wood. Our word for refinement or culture [*beschaving*] comes from this word for plane [*schaaf*]. The air also can have a great impact on unpainted wood and can cause it to weather or decay, but the working of the air is quite different. There is neither will nor intent behind it. For outside our father and mother, in our broader environment there are persons who set out to contribute to our formation, either for evil or for good. But when a brother or sister or other family members or visitors are intent on this, they take part in our upbringing and no longer have an impact merely by being in our environment. What we absorb from our environment comes to us imperceptibly and is based on the law of imitation that lies in our nature. Even if it is entirely true that the working of our natural penchant for imitation often finds its opposite in the repulsive working of an example that is not sympathetic to us, those attracting and repelling effects nevertheless stem from the same principle.

This inclination toward imitation is strongly at work especially in the first years of life. The child imitates what he sees. What he hears, he parrots. What he observes, he copies. Almost all children's play has the same basis. Precisely because the child does not yet have a life of his own, he imitates the life of his environment. Even as a mirror reflects the images that appear before it, not as the real thing but as an imitation, so too the real life of the parents is reflected in the life of the child. Thus parents who, even in the most careful upbringing, do not pay attention to the environment of their child, often tear down with one hand what they have built up with the other. Even those who allow the wrong family members, [simply] because they are family, to be around their children too freely, have only themselves to blame if harmful effects show up later on. But even if we have the environment of our children to a certain extent in hand, we never have it completely in hand. Brothers and sisters must live and grow up together, and even the influence of brothers and sisters, especially of the older siblings on the younger, is uncommonly great. Furthermore, we cannot escape the influence of those who function in our home as domestic help, even though it truly would be good if, with the hiring of domestics, more thought were given to the children than is commonly the case. Outside our environment in the narrower sense we must also take into account the environment of family members, friends, acquaintances, store employees, and so forth. The environment a child chooses for himself, the boys and girls he spends time with, his schoolmates and those with whom he plays, are also important here. Finally, and not least important, the environment of the church to which the child belongs by baptism must certainly be considered. All these components of his environment have an influence on the child, an influence that is sometimes so strong that it not infrequently completely changes the fruit of the upbringing.

Here also it is true that all these influences coming at us from these very § 5
divergent persons in our environment can work for good as well as for evil. There are older brothers and sisters who bless the younger siblings, and there are those who corrupt them. There are family members who do good for the child, and those who do the child wrong. Friends, acquaintances, and also domestic help can elevate us, but also bring us down. Friends and playmates can move us away from evil, but also seduce us toward evil. And the church to which we belong can undermine the sacred in us or strengthen it. It is always the possibility of a twofold effect that causes us to sink or be elevated. If our lot fell in an environment that in every way exerted an influence *for the good*, an influence that made us serious, gave us an appetite for the sacred, fostered solidity of character in us, and directed our spirit to what is lovely and commendable, then we have received in this an uncommonly great privilege, a privilege received above many others who absorbed all kinds of poison from their environment, who were weakened in their inner being through this environment, and who felt their sensual, lower nature being stimulated by it. And when we ascertain how one single wrong person in our environment can become the devil for us, someone who develops the evil within us, we will praise the grace of our God if we were protected from these demons of temptation in our environment.

We cannot understand why others have experienced something different; this is the unfathomable mystery of God's sovereignty, just as it is in our descent and upbringing too. But anyone who can gratefully praise God that his environment has influenced him for the good, from his childhood on, can see in this nothing but a most excellent gift of God's common grace, as a result of which, with and in one's conversion, the fruit later can be so rich. There is no doubt that this gift of God's lovingkindness belongs most certainly to common grace and not to particular grace. For here too we find the invariable characteristic; for the brothers and sisters who grew up with us in the same environment, and thus enjoyed the same privilege, can still end up hardening their heart and choosing against the Lord.

§ 6 Yet we must look at the ordination of our God over us from another perspective. What we identified is not merely the *fruit* of common grace; it is also common grace *itself*. What we mean is that it is not only a fruit of common grace that God worked in others, but it is also the means by which common grace works in us ourselves. God's Word does not analyze the psychological working of common grace. We can only guess by approximation what happens in man when God arrests the passion of sin that pursues the goals of evil, and weakens and stops it in its working. But as extremely difficult as it is for us to get a clear notion of this hidden working of God in our heart, we can just as clearly understand that God uses influences from outside to counteract and oppose the development of sin in us.

A fire can be fed and hence fanned by combustible materials we bring into contact with it, but it can also be tempered by withholding oxygen and fuel, and even extinguished by water or nitrogen. Nothing provides us with as clear a picture as when we observe a raging fire. First the flame breaks out, and then the flame is extinguished. But in the meantime the fire is definitely not yet put out. Below the surface that is saturated with water, the burning mass still continues to glow and smolder. If we stir it with a stick or a rod, the flame immediately bursts forth again, and once again water must be poured on it. And depending on whether oxygen reaches it again or the oxygen from the air is kept from it, the fire either flames up or smolders only internally. And it is the same way with our heart. The blaze of sin is in our heart, and those flames either burst forth or are kept under control, depending on the influence our environment exerts on them. If that environment consists of nitrogen, the sin is suppressed; if it is oxygen, then sin flares up in us again. And precisely to the degree that the one or the other happens, common grace either is working or not working in us. Entirely apart from the mystical working in our heart that arrests the ultimate full working of sin, common grace also works through the external influences that come to us from descent and birth, from upbringing and environment. And if these combined influences work to the good of our person, then we must see all these things as *means* God uses to restrain sin within us. These means are the fruit of the common grace that has been at work in our ancestors, parents, and environment, but at the same time these means themselves are instruments God uses to arrest and tame sin in us through common grace.

CHAPTER THIRTY

VOCATION AND ONE'S LOT IN LIFE

Through sloth the roof sinks in, and through indolence the house leaks.

Ecclesiastes 10:18

How strongly our sinful nature brings sin to manifestation in us depends to a certain degree, as we saw, on (1) our descent from the families of our father and mother, (2) our birth from specific parents, (3) our upbringing, and (4) the environment in which we grew up from childhood to adulthood. Now we add our vocation and our lot in life—not, of course, in order to view these two factors in the formation of our person in the light of God's special providence, but in order to show how *vocation* and *lot in life* are also often means God uses to temper the poison of sin in us. Only by that tempering do both of these factors fall under common grace. § 1

Not everyone has it in his own power to choose his vocation, even to such a small extent that many people think that they do not have a divine vocation at all. This is especially true of young men without a permanent appointment, of people of private means, of retired people, and of unmarried women. And in a sense it must be acknowledged that in all those situations, the vocation is either not yet or no longer firmly delineated. Vocation in the narrower sense is understood as a daily recurring obligation to perform work that is directed toward a specific goal. An appointment is not a requirement. A storekeeper did not receive an appointment from anyone, yet he knows quite well that he has a definite vocation with a specific goal and constantly recurring work. In human society an immense amount of work of all kinds must be performed each day. This mass of work is distributed among those who live in society, and we find our vocation in that portion of the work assigned to us. Only custom has, even if wrongly, caused common usage not to take domestic life—and thus also domestic labor—into consideration. A storekeeper has his family and his vocation (that is, his store). A seamstress who spends a single day sewing for a family is considered to have a vocation, but according to this incorrect usage, the housewife who in that same family is busy every day from early morning until late at night does not have a vocation. This narrower conception has a twofold cause. First, when we say "vocation," we think more of the *man* than of the *woman*; and second, we think of vocation as a means to earn one's bread or make one's living. Yet the notion of vocation does not imply either the one or the other. A widow can also be the head of a store or a small factory if her husband did this in the past. And even though there are writers and artists who not only earned nothing with their labors but sometimes even suffered loss, they nevertheless could very well be writers or artists *by vocation*.

Surveying all of human life as such, excluding no one, we are thus fully entitled to understand vocation as all regular activity to which we must daily devote our strength and our time. And in that sense no one is without a vocation, and it is a fault of so many that they do not realize their vocation. "Right now I'm not doing anything, since I am waiting for a job." "I don't do anything right now because I am retired." "I have nothing to do because I'm living off my interest." "I have nothing to do because I still live with my father at home"—these are all expressions of a lack of a sense of calling and of a sense of duty. *Everyone* must work, must work every day, and must work with all his strength, whether for the purpose of increasing his own worth, or of assisting others, or of representing the neglected interests of others. And anyone who knows how incredibly much remains undone each day that still awaits completion, cannot sufficiently deplore the fact that because so many do nothing every day from morning till night, such an incredible wealth of human vitality is lost. Thus when we speak in this context of our vocation, we understand it in the sense of *all* regular activity to which we daily must devote our time and our strength, whether in a steady job, with or without wages, outside the home or within the domestic sphere.

This vocation is very diverse in nature, and very different for different people. But it exercises such a strong influence on the formation of the person of each individual precisely through this great diversity. This is so true that, looking at the broad picture, the main vocational categories even put their stamp on the external appearance of the individual. Among a group of people who travel together on a ship we can readily recognize, without knowing anyone personally, who is the preacher, who the notary, who the doctor, who the schoolteacher, and who the storekeeper of the town. Even though all wear ordinary clothing, nevertheless their facial expression, their manner of behaving, their manner of speech, and their bearing soon give away whom we are dealing with. A vocation generally also has a *moral* side. By this we mean that each vocation brings with it its own particular temptations, but it also offers its own particular protection against all kinds of sins. For example, a storekeeper must remain in his store the whole livelong day, so he does not have the temptation to go out much and to hang out in the bar. Conversely, his conscience struggles continually with the eighth commandment. A preacher is not distracted by his vocation from the external religious forms; but conversely, the danger of Pharisaism lies in his path. A seamstress who goes out to sew is faced less with the temptation to fritter away her time than the daughter of the house, but because she goes from one house to the next, she is exposed to the danger of gossip and the abuse of confidentiality. And thus we can say that each vocation brings with it, to varying degrees, a certain temptation *to* sin and a certain protection *against* sin. This generally has the effect that everyone is strongly opposed to the sin against which his vocation offers protection, but conversely considers less serious the sin that his vocation makes appealing. § 2

Yet it should be the reverse. We should arm ourselves doubly against that sin to which our vocation brings a certain temptation, while being relatively less vigilant toward the sin to which we are *less* exposed in our vocation. However this may be, the fact remains that our vocation has no small effect on our moral formation, understood as something apart from saving grace. This distribution of vocations among people is also in God's hand. It is God's ordination that David's first vocation was shepherd, after which he received the vocation of king. Confusion arises, in our opinion, only when it involves a vocation we had to choose for ourselves. "What should I become?" is the great life question that occupies every young man and often fills his parents' heart with distress. And even if the young girl asks this question less openly, her future hangs on this question too. And later as well, when one has entered an office, the same question returns whenever we are faced with the choice of either remaining where we are or changing location. Then we make a choice, and because of this choosing we forget that it is God who ultimately directs us. At that point we can only transcend this contrast between our choice and God's ordination in prayer. But when we are ten years further on and look back on that choice in our past, it will become clear to most that God chose *for* and *through* them. Starting from that truth, we therefore posit that it is God who, as all-governing King, has determined our vocation for us and related that determination of our vocation to our moral formation. If our life vocation serves to elevate us, to spare us temptation, to stimulate us toward what is lovely and commendable, so that the fiery blaze of sin is *tempered* rather than fanned within our depraved nature, then our vocation is in God's hand a means to cause common grace, which stems sin, to work in us.

§ 3 In general this can be said of any vocation. As a Dutch proverb says, "Laziness is the devil's pillow."[1] Our vocation is what provides work, work in a context, work that ties us to a measure of order and regularity. Such work bans idleness, suppresses capriciousness, teaches us to submit to a certain discipline in life, and is as such already one of the most powerful factors God uses to counteract the bursting forth of sin. Regular days off, when no work is done, are generally days of much coarser excesses than days of regular work. Immediately after the fall, work is imposed on Adam as a punishment—but also as a prevention. Work is the preventative means against the dominion of sin in our heart. Hard work often takes away the time to ponder sinning and to think about sin. Someone who had the fortune of being obligated to work hard from his youth received in that obligation an uncommon gift of common grace. And parents, guardians, and teachers who allow their children, wards, or students to "hang around and mess about," as we might refer to this ugly idleness, and do not accustom them from early on to do regular work, are guilty not only of wasting their children's future but also of contributing to their moral deterioration. The "discipline" to which the poet of Proverbs continually points is not least of all the discipline of regular work, and anyone who loves himself in the

1. Compare also the Latin proverbs *pigrita est diaboli pulvinar* [leisure is the devil's pillow] and *otium est pulvinar diaboli* [idleness is the devil's pillow], which appear, among other places, in the rule of the Franciscan order.

loftier sense will thank God, not when he has nothing to do, but when he is busy, for hard work is a shield against evil.

But apart from the common grace that resides in the work of all vocations as such, there is in some special occupations an extraordinary common grace, and we must thank our God if one of these is our lot. In a very large class of society the woman is far more safeguarded than the man. Take the bricklayer's assistant, who must leave his house each morning when the sky is scarcely turning light, stack bricks in a pile, lift them on his shoulder, and carry them up to the bricklayer for the whole day, not to return home until late in the evening when the day is done. Compare with this the wife of the bricklayer's assistant, who remained quietly at home, who did not lift bricks from a pile but rather lifted her children out of bed, washed them and dressed them, and was busy with various kinds of work. Think of how deadening those bricks were for the human heart, and how being quietly busy at home was able to form and develop the heart of that woman. Or consider two brothers, one of whom becomes a preacher and the other enters the army or goes into the merchant marine. Consider how many wonderful impressions from a higher sphere of life the one received, and to how many occasions for temptation the other was exposed. And thus we will find, going through life, how the one finds in his vocation a natural means to delight in, and be busy with, things that are high, holy, and humane; whereas the other is in danger of succumbing to the monotony of his physical vocation. And equally, we find that the one will be held to decency and virtue through his vocation, whereas the other will be exposed to all manner of immoral temptations precisely due to his vocation.

Here again is the mystery! What is the moving cause behind the fact § 4
that the one received such a happy calling and the other such a dangerous one, a difference that often ended with moral elevation for the one and moral ruin for the other? Here too God does not render account of his holy actions, and we must reverently bow before him in the dust. But it is certain that whoever has received a joyous vocation, a vocation that elevates and ennobles him, must see in this a gift from God, and owes it to his God to bring him an offering of thanks for this. It is, after all, this vocation that in God's hand works as one of the factors that will not allow his evil, depraved nature to come to full expression; on the contrary, it will suppress that latent evil within him, stem it, and tame it. And he who later as a child of God comes to see what he really is and breaks through to redemption will afterward praise and glorify his God that in his vocation too, God put the

bridle on the evil within his heart and preserved him from excessively deep debasement and from overly flagrant excesses. We are faced here indeed with a factor of common grace, which appears convincingly from the fact that such a supportive and edifying vocation is not reserved for his children but that also others, who are lost, were placed by God in the same vocation. Being a shepherd is a vocation that certainly elevates, yet not only David was a shepherd, but so was Nabal in his day. But David was supported and strengthened by this vocation, whereas Nabal was tempted by it into deeper sin.

§ 5 Exactly the same now applies to our lot in life. By "lot" we mean the happy as well as the less happy condition of the life in which we are placed, and the vicissitudes that befall us in our life. Our lot in general already differs greatly from person to person. Being born among the Afridi on the slopes of the Himalayan Mountains or in the flat regions of our Low Countries provides quite different conditions for our life.[2] Also, within our own country it makes a considerable difference whether we are born in the quiet countryside or as residents of our tumultuous cities. And in those cities and villages as well it means a very great deal whether we were born among the more highly cultured classes or among the lower classes with their afflictions and cares. Financial situation also cuts a deep chasm between people. There are families who must live on five guilders a week, and there are others who have a hundred guilders or more at their disposal.[3] A spacious house with a separate room for each person, or cramped housing where all must live together in one room, has a major impact on our entire formation.

We could continue sketching in this way the differences in living conditions and lot in life in all their appalling contrasts to make tangible how strong an influence this alone exerts on an individual for his entire formation. "Give me neither poverty nor riches; feed me with the food that is needful for me" [Prov 30:8] will probably appear to be a slogan of the highest wisdom at this point, to the extent that both poverty and riches bring much more temptation to sin than the moderate life without care. But whatever criterion we apply here, it cannot be denied that in our lot in life too—that is, the general condition of our life—we have one of those powerful factors that affect our *moral* development from all sides. One person is debased or

2. The Afridi are a tribe of Pashtuns, a native ethnic group in Pakistan and Afghanistan.
3. A Dutch guilder at that time had roughly the purchasing power of $12–$13 in 2015.

brutalized by his life condition; another is kept in line by it and focused on a quiet and virtuous life.

The same may be said of the changes and vicissitudes in our lot. Here we have a child who grows up as an only child and is spoiled like an only child; somewhere else we find another who in a large circle of siblings learned early on the demands of yielding to older people, of serving others, and of living with others. The one child retained his solicitous mother until he left home as an adult; the other has never known his mother, or lost her too early to ever be able to reciprocate her love. And this broad difference in vicissitudes continues throughout life. The one has a strong constitution, the other a weak and sickly one. The one rides his cart, as the saying goes, on a smooth path; the other must row against the current all his life. The one prospers; the other struggles until the end. Suffering piles up on the head of the one, whereas the other always walks along nothing but sunny paths. Grief, distress, and sorrow will make the heart of the one grow rigid, making him somber and embittered, whereas the other is cheered by never-ending prosperity. § 6

The influence of this on our moral formation is uncommonly great. It is not that prosperity has always lifted up and suffering has always weighed down, or conversely, that suffering has always sanctified and happiness consistently has made a person superficial. The effects are as varied as the varieties of character among people. But these vicissitudes certainly have an impact, and our personality is formed and determined to no small degree by all such far-reaching vicissitudes in our lot in life. If as a child of God we already encountered before our conversion a lot in which the cup of joy and the cup of suffering alternately were brought to our lips in such a way that the equilibrium, even though it had been disturbed, was restored each time, and joys and sorrows collaborated in the right proportion to make us sober-minded and to keep us from what is base and vile, but rather led us up to what is elevated and noble, then our heart involuntarily exults, when looking back upon that life, in thanksgiving and worship to our God and Father who gave us such a strengthening and uplifting lot in life. For here too the explanation of this difference in our lot lies only in him who allowed this to happen to us, and we cannot fathom the mystery that blessed us so much more richly than many others. But we feel all the more the urge to honor in thanksgiving and praise the love of our God, who moved toward us in such beautiful proportions. Nor is it doubtful that in the condition of our life and our lot in life we did not encounter particular grace but definitely common grace. For here too the invariable characteristic applies that the same lot in life and the same conditions we received were given to others as well, who nevertheless hardened their heart to the love of their God.

§ 7 The fact cannot be denied, no matter how terrible it seems to us, that through his condition in life and his lot in life, one individual is placed in circumstances that foster sin in him and make the flame of sin erupt, whereas conversely, another lived in circumstances that suppressed sin within him, fended off temptation, and provided him with an impetus toward the good. But it is just as certain that there are children of God who grew up in equally unfavorable circumstances, sometimes burst forth in awful sin, and later, through a strong reaction, came to a conversion that was all the more profound. On the other hand, there were children of God who, behind the shield of common grace in their condition and lot in life, were allowed to safely enter the way of salvation, almost without any coarse excesses in sin. The moral factor, which has come up for discussion here, is therefore in no way decisive for salvation. Common grace is merely a means of assistance, never anything more, never anything else. But the end result nevertheless shows that far and away most believers were prepared and guided along this path by common grace, and that it always remains an exception when an elect child of God first goes through the fearful paths of terrible sin in order to come later to a sudden, radical conversion in reaction against this sin.

It is therefore very wrong to want to make this path, which leads a person through a reaction against terrible excesses in sin to a radical conversion, into a rule for everyone. This path through reaction may be more remarkable to us and may demonstrate even more miraculously the omnipotence of God's grace than the path accompanied by a soft breeze, yet it is neither the most common nor the most familiar one. The most common and familiar path our God uses to bring his elect to salvation relates to the preceding working of his common grace. It is a common grace through which God reins in, tames, and restrains the evil nature in the life prior to conversion so that no strong reaction can set in, indeed, such that many who look back at their past and relive their past life still pray that they may discover the moment when their transition took place. And God works this common grace in a variety of ways through one's descent and birth, through one's upbringing and environment, but also through one's vocation and lot in life.

CHAPTER THIRTY-ONE

THE MEANS OF GRACE

For it is impossible, in the case of those who have once been enlightened, who have tasted the heavenly gift, and have shared in the Holy Spirit, . . . and then have fallen away, to restore them again to repentance.

HEBREWS 6:4, 6A

We now come to a complex question upon which the requisite light still has not been shed. After the preceding discussion, it may be accepted as certain that descent and birth, vocation and lot in life do have an important impact, not on our regeneration but certainly on the form of our conversion. Meanwhile everyone concedes that everything at work in these four factors belongs to the domain of common grace and not of particular grace. Continuing along this line, we are now faced with an entirely different question: How must we look at the working of the so-called means of grace to the extent that these precede conversion and go out to the elect as well as the nonelect? It must be admitted that in unequal measure, albeit in *some* measure, each child of God who did not come to conscious conversion until later in life underwent a certain influence of holy Scripture, of the church of Christ, of Christian ideas, and of persons who had been converted to Christ. And it was these effects and influences on his person that in the hour of his conversion served in no small measure as aftereffects in God's hand to lead him to Christ. Indeed, the influence of these effects on conversion § 1 was usually paramount, to such an extent that most individuals explain the form of their conversion as almost exclusively the result of these means.

It is therefore obvious that for conversion to break through, these kinds of means are absolutely indispensable. Even as we focus all these means on their center (that is, in the Word), everyone concedes that no conversion is conceivable without the Word. "Faith, understood as an act, comes from hearing, and hearing through the preaching of the Word of God" [see Rom 10:17]. The Word is so much in the foreground here that even if we were to combine regeneration, conversion, and sanctification under the single broad concept of *being reborn for heaven* (as was often done in the past), we could say with complete accuracy that the regeneration of our whole person for heaven occurs through the Word. We must not think that this includes only preaching; it also includes the reading of the Word and, not least of all, all the derivative effects of the Word in conversations and habits of life. If, on the other hand, we take regeneration in the narrower sense, to refer to the first imparting of the new life, then we must leave all influences out of consideration in regeneration proper; these influences returned all the more strongly and decisively in our conversion and our growth in Christ. Even in the Gentile world any transition to Christ is totally impossible without its being preceded by the stimulus of the Word, in whatever form. For a pagan, coming to Christ is unthinkable without contact with the church of Christ, through its writings, its reputation, its members, or its missionaries.

§ 2 We are not so bold as to say even a single word about regeneration in the narrower sense with regard to the pagans, and it appears to us that anyone who presumes to have an opinion on this crosses the boundary of what is permissible. À Lasco, the Reformer of our Dutch churches in England, wrote already in the sixteenth century: "I am not so cruel of heart, that I do not occasionally allow my thoughts to wander concerning those millions upon millions who are born outside Christ in the pagan world."[1] And earnest Christians who have not locked themselves inside their narrow walls have constantly let their reflections hover over this painful issue. Almost

1. Johannes à Lasco (1499–1560) was a Polish reformer who influenced the Dutch reformation from the German city of Emden in East Frisia and pastored the Dutch church in London. For Kuyper's earlier evaluation of à Lasco in relationship to the question of salvation among the pagans, see Jasper Vree and Johan Zwaan, eds., *Abraham Kuyper's* Commentatio *(1860): The Young Kuyper about Calvin, à Lasco, and the Church*, 2 vols. (Leiden: Brill, 2005), 2:343.

automatically a distinction was made between the little children who died without ever having come to clear consciousness, and older persons, who had reached adulthood. Many of those adults were inclined to count at least some outstanding pagans, such as Plato and Cicero, among those for whose salvation they dared hope. From the orthodox side, however, the response to this has always been that we lack the right not only to make this statement, but even to make any conjecture, because it leads to a direct contradiction of holy Scripture. If holy Scripture tells us that "there is no other name under heaven given among men by which we must be saved" [Acts 4:12]—namely, the name of Christ Jesus—then it is not up to us to make an exception for Plato or Cicero. This must be stated all the more emphatically because not a few people now are also applying the same theory to those among us who die outside of Christ, who denied, opposed, and objected to his deity as well as the atonement through his sacrifice. We Christians must carefully hew to *the Word*, and we lack any right to make exceptions to it. We therefore reject such exceptions, certainly not because we lack compassion or because of hardness of heart, but because we would undermine and damage our own faith if we posited the possibility of a second way of salvation apart from Scripture and in conflict with its clear statements.

But the question changed, of course, when it did not involve adult pagans but small children among the pagans, Jews, or Muslims who die before, say, their second year. The rule of Scripture that only those who call upon the name of Jesus are saved does not apply to these infants. For among us as well, there lies within such a small infant no semblance or shadow of a confession of Jesus. We therefore must do one of two things: either declare that the rule does not apply in this case, or include in salvation all our small infants who die early. No one [who is orthodox] does the latter, and people readily concede that such small infants can enter into salvation, even if they have never heard of Jesus. If they are nevertheless conceived and born in sin, and therefore subject to condemnation, as we are, then it follows that God must regenerate such infants in a way that is incomprehensible to us, endow them with the capacity for faith, and make them partakers in the gifts of salvation of Christ. And it is on this basis that not a few people today, especially in America, are inclined toward the thesis that all such children—not only among us but also among the pagans, Jews, and Muslims—are begotten to life by God before they die.

However much may appeal to our human heart in such a thesis, no Christian church has ever included this in its confession, and we cannot keep silent about the fact that no one can justify making such a claim. First, it has never been taught on our part that all infants among us who are taken away will be saved, but only the elect. This understanding does not exclude any infant, for they may all be elect, but it nevertheless does put the matter in a different light. Second, our churches confess that believing parents may have this hope if their infants die prematurely, but they definitely do not say the same about the "unbelieving parents." The statement of the church is related to the covenant and the grace of the covenant, which the pagans, Jews, and Muslims of course do not fall under. And in the third place, there is no direct indication in Scripture to justify our positing such a speculative thesis as definite truth. This does not imply that the opposite is certain. Anyone who maintains the opposite also says more than he can justify. After all, the possibility must be acknowledged that God can regenerate an infant, entirely independent of all intermediate means. This being so, no one can prove that God could not do this same miraculous work outside the covenant as well. The lovely nature of the thought is somewhat appealing. But we can and must go no further. No one knows what God does or does not do in secret, unless he reveals it to us himself; and in this matter there is no revelation that is even remotely definite.

It therefore continues to appear to us that on this point we must refrain from any statement for or against, and must leave this whole important doctrine in the hands of our God, whose unfathomable mercy so far transcends our deepest compassion. On the basis of holy Scripture we can and must speak definitely and decisively only where adults are concerned, and then invariably the rule applies that "only those who call upon the name of the Lord will be saved" [see Rom 10:13].

§ 3 Thus, because the preparatory workings of the means of grace are indispensable for adults to come to conversion, we now face the question of whether these means of grace must be considered part of common grace or of particular grace. This is an extremely difficult question that nevertheless cannot be avoided. For what is the case? These means of grace affect not only those who will one day come to conversion, but also, albeit in a different manner, those who will die *unconverted*. These are therefore means ordained and used by God that are not limited to those who will be saved, but they extend also to those who will *not* be saved. If only the grace that concerns "things that belong to salvation" [Heb 6:9] is particular, then the question cannot be avoided whether these means of grace, which most definitely do not always lead to salvation, and which those who will be saved often have in common with those who die unsaved, must in fact be counted among the means of common grace. The heart-wrenching pericope in Hebrews 6:4–6 especially lends this question such a serious character. For there it speaks of people who are lost and nevertheless (1) have been enlightened, (2) have tasted a heavenly gift, (3) have shared in the Holy Spirit, (4) have tasted the good word of God, and (5) have tasted the powers of the age to come. Here are five wonderful things that many a child of God confesses wistfully are not yet his portion in rich measure.

We must therefore confront this matter earnestly. It is not simply a question of a merely formal reading of Scripture, of coldheartedly sitting under the sermon, of having been raised half-recalcitrantly in a Christian family. We are standing before the working of these means of grace that lie outside of salvation yet penetrate very deeply and go very far. They go so far that we can understand how one person who read the words of Hebrews 6:4–6 came to abandon the "perseverance of the saints" and came to acknowledge that the passage concerns persons who were indeed truly converted and later lost the "new life." For us, verse 9 cuts off this possibility; there we read, "Though we speak in this way, yet in your case, beloved, we feel sure of better things—*things that belong to salvation*." For this shows that the previous workings of which the apostle speaks did *not* belong to salvation. But if we, as Reformed Christians, understand Hebrews 6:4–6 as speaking of those who were *not* regenerated, it nevertheless is our duty to take into account such facts and possibilities, and it definitely is not fitting for us to think, when it comes to those who will be lost, only of entirely external, purely formal influences of the means of grace.

We must distinguish among four things here. The common means of § 4
grace as well as certain spiritual gifts work, first, on those who are already born again, and they serve to bring the new life to development. They work, second, on those who have not yet been born again, but who will come to life sooner or later, and these means then still have a preparatory character in view of the coming conversion. They work, third, on people who, by all later appearances, will die unconverted, and in these persons they serve to put their guilt in stronger relief and to bring hardening. And fourth, they work on the environment in which Christ's church functions, and at that point they serve to advance the higher development of general human life.

We cannot come to clarity on this issue if we fail to distinguish these four workings. Generally speaking, if we consider only what directly relates to salvation, or what mediately belongs to salvation, to be part of particular grace, but subsume all workings and influences that stem the power of sin but do not relate directly to salvation under common grace, then clearly, the same workings of the means of grace and spiritual gifts bear the character of particular grace if they accrue to those who are already born again or one day will be. But for those who one day will die outside Christ, on the other hand, they do not go beyond the character of common grace.

Although it sounds quite strange, to mention only one example, when we hear for the first time that holy Scripture also falls within the framework of common grace, it will be perceived that this is correct if we give it some thought. After all, common grace and particular grace do not stand alongside or in opposition to one another as two separate kinds of medicine, but they differ in purpose and import, and for this reason they differ also in the means that are used to reach this goal. Particular grace has a *positive* goal: to awaken, maintain, and perfect new and higher life in those who were dead in their sins. Common grace, on the other hand, has only a *negative* goal—namely, to stem the full development of the poison of sin. The means are also in accordance with this twofold goal, in the sense that the means of common grace can never bring something *to life* within the *dead* sinner, but they can very well come into play at conversion. A villain and criminal in whom common grace has worked to a small extent comes to conversion with greater difficulty and in a different way than the young man from a more tranquil context who by common grace was kept from every terrible excess of sin. In this regard, common grace can serve the development of particular grace.

But conversely, much that is a means for particular grace can also advance the goal of common grace by arresting sin. Let us not be misunderstood here: particular grace advances the goal of common grace not by killing the core of sin, but by stemming the development and expansion of sin. In its origin, the law of the Ten Commandments belongs to the particular covenant of grace; yet who can trace the incredible power for the arresting of sin that has gone forth among the masses from those Ten Commandments? The great difference, acknowledged by everyone, between human society in a Christian nation and in a pagan or Islamic nation can be explained primarily from the influence of the Word. Yet we must agree that the many good things in which a Christian society rejoices do not properly belong to particular grace but must be considered to belong to common grace. Beyond doubt also the Word, the sacrament, and even the spiritual gifts of which Hebrews 6:4–6 speaks belong *in their origin* to particular grace, for they bear a positive character and do not spring from nature, but are supernatural. But even if this is established with respect to their origin and character, it does not keep God from using these ordained means to arrest sin within individuals and human society, even when there is no salvation involved.

Here we touch on a point that obviously requires clarification in order § 5
to avoid misunderstanding. We have frequently expressed the view that the minister of the Word in the congregation of Christ must view those whom he addresses as believers. The entirely incorrect conclusion has been drawn from this that we have thereby cut off the proclamation of the Word to others. This is absolutely not the case. We have only demanded that we be discerning on this point. In the church an "assembly of believers" has gathered. This is the unique character of the gathered church. To what extent individual persons fit into this category often cannot be decided, but this does not change the matter itself. There may be hypocrites in the congregation, but anyone who shows himself to be an unbeliever will be removed from the group. On that basis we posited, and still do posit, the demand that the ministry of the Word in the church of Christ be in line with this, and thus should not address the world but the "believers." At the same time, it goes without saying that preaching must also be aimed at (1) bringing to actual faith those who have as yet only the capacity for faith, and (2) making it more and more painful for the hypocrites to remain in the church of Christ. The rule remains, as Christ himself has stated seven times, "He who has an ear, let him hear what the Spirit says to the churches" [see Rev 2–3]. From the Reformed side, nothing that even remotely hints at proof has ever been adduced against this thesis.

But by pushing this thesis into the foreground, we have never asserted, and could never assert, that anyone who stands outside the assembly of believers should be left to his fate. Christ's command is relevant: preach the gospel (and thus also the law, for without the law as background there is no gospel); *preach the gospel to all nations and to all creatures*. Far from overlooking this, let alone disputing it, we have continually emphasized and pointed out how Paul's proclamation on the Areopagus and elsewhere bore precisely this character, and we have characterized this proclamation, in contrast to the ministry of the Word within the congregation, as the evangelizing proclamation of the Word.

Missions already proves the need for this. For all missions is evangelization among pagans, Jews, or Muslims. And alongside so-called foreign missions we have home missions [or evangelization] in full equality, as long as home missions does not act as if it functions *within* the church. For it is true that in the church too, such degenerate conditions occur that it is almost like encountering paganism; but then, of course, the situation in the church is bad. The church as such must be reformed, and people must attempt to bring about a thaw of what is frozen, through catechesis or by other means, and to separate from the church all those elements in which all living fellowship appears to have died off. And this is not the end of it, of course: here too the duty immediately surfaces to preach the law and gospel again through home missions to these degenerated groups of the population, albeit to do so with discernment.

A measure of reticence in the sacred things remains called for here, and the word of Jesus applies also to us: "Do not give dogs what is holy, and do not throw your pearls before pigs" [Matt 7:6]. But with the proviso of this limitation, the general duty applies both to the church and to the members of the church to make the law and gospel known to *all* creatures: to make them known through one's behavior, by one's example and way of life, by the distribution of reading material, by distributing Bibles, and by proclamation or direct evangelization. This is commanded (1) because Jesus placed the duty upon us, (2) because the church has the capacity for this proclamation and expansion, (3) because its influence arrests and binds sin, and (4) because it does provoke mocking and hardening. Yet although this is reason for caution, it does not discharge us from our duty.

CHAPTER THIRTY-TWO

THE EFFECT OF PARTICULAR GRACE ON COMMON GRACE

The times of ignorance God overlooked, but now he commands all people everywhere to repent.

Acts 17:30

Thus we are faced with the undeniable fact that there are workings of grace that find their origin in particular grace and never affect what falls outside salvation. These workings can properly be divided into three areas. First, there are workings that proceed from the presence of God's children in this world, the acting of believers in the midst of this world, or if you will, from the manifestation of the church in this dispensation. Second, there are workings that flow from the preaching of the Word, in a variety of forms, through hearing and reading. And third, there are workings like those discussed in Hebrews 6:4–6—that is, workings of the Spirit that grip the emotions and the consciousness of some natural people. § 1

The first kind of working operates spontaneously and unintentionally. Those in the second group are deliberately sought and produced by the members or the officials of the church. The third are wrought directly by

God in a manner hidden from us. And we must acknowledge that these threefold workings (1) affect those who are elect to salvation, (2) make those who do not repent more guilty and partially harden them, and (3) affect, apart from salvation or hardening, both human life in general as well as the lives of many individuals by the strengthening of common grace, both *negatively* by preventing the breaking out of sin, and *positively* by advancing the development of our natural powers in spite of sin. As far as our topic is concerned, these three workings originate from particular grace and operate upon the elect for the benefit of particular grace, although they do not remain confined to this but radiate their glimmerings into the world and therefore are means that God uses to advance the completely other goal that he had envisioned in the work of common grace.

§ 2 The latter is immediately sensed when we realize what should be understood by the idea of a Christian nation, a Christianized people, a Christian society, a Christian state, and so forth. The sense of these very common expressions can be understood best when we contrast "Christian" with "pagan" or "Islamic." The Christian world in Europe and America presents an entirely different scene than does the pagan world in Asia and Africa or the Islamic world in the Levant and its surroundings. What makes up this difference? Not something supernatural that clings to Europe or America. In Christian countries nothing is added to what is human. It is all human development, human ennoblement, human culture, human enlightenment, human progress. It is altogether the powers of human nature that we see flourishing in Christian nations. The seeds of these powers are present among the pagans and Muslims, but they also send up shoots that only momentarily break through the surface and then become scorched and wither. In Christian society, however, they grow, flower, and bear fruit. This is the reason why before Golgotha we cannot speak of a human development in a more general sense. There was at most a *national* flourishing that lasted a while, but even under the Roman Empire there was no *human* development that brought out those latent powers of human nature as such. Only where the gospel enters the world and the church of Christ appears, does this human development begin. And this development of the latent powers of our nature soon takes flight to such an extent that the difference between the Christian and the non-Christian world becomes increasingly apparent. It does not take long before the Christian portion of humanity is standing at the head of *all* human development, is opposing *all* resistance of the non-Christian world, and after a short while is holding sway over the *whole* world.

This has become clear in the last four centuries especially. Before that time, the crescent still powerfully offered resistance and the pagan nations maintained their independence. But since then, Islam has been conquered, and in Asia and Africa one nation after the other has come under the domination of one of the Christian powers. Only China remains an exception, but at present it too stands at a turning point. And anyone who thinks that Japan proves the contrary forgets that Japan has a measure of power at its disposal only to the extent that it has begun to imitate the Christian nations in its way of life. The Christian nations together constitute barely one-third of the earth's population, yet everyone knows that as soon as the Christian nations combine their powers, neither paganism nor Islam has any more sway.[1] The triumph of Christian Europe is total. Germany only has 55 million inhabitants, China more than 400 million, yet in the most recent conflict between the two countries, there was trembling in Beijing because of its impotence, and in Berlin the awareness of its own power was celebrated.[2]

What is the reason for the supremacy of the Christian portion of the §3
world? Can we say that it is because, in Europe and America at least, the great majority of the population lives out of faith, is incorporated into Christ, and bears Golgotha in its heart? Not at all. This was not true in centuries past, and it is not true now either. The vast majority of the masses today is Christian in name only. Thousands upon thousands have even openly turned against the Christian confession. Those who are prominent are more intent on oppression than on the promotion of the Christian faith. And wherever the faith courageously lifts up its head again, it must struggle and do battle to find a place to stand. We still get the impression that it is and remains a small flock, and only the core of that small flock possesses a faith that has the power of revival.

1. Kuyper would come to somewhat less triumphalistic conclusions later in life. See Abraham Kuyper, *On Islam*, ed. James Bratt, trans. Jan van Vliet (Bellingham, WA: Lexham Press, 2017); and *PR* 1.I.1.
2. Occasioned by the so-called "Juye Incident," in which two Roman Catholic priests were murdered in Shandong, Germany invaded Qingdao in 1897 and founded the Jiaozhou Bay colony.

And yet, even though the great majority stands outside personal faith, everyone still holds on to the Christian name. Everyone claims to be a "Christian" but wants to be a Christian in his own way. The struggle between what *calls* itself Christianity and what is *essential* Christianity is centuries old and has gone through all kinds of heresies and schisms, but in our century it has come to a fundamental decision. What you call believing Christianity, we are told, is an invention of the church, something that was built on top of the original Christianity but has nothing to do with the ideal appearance of the Son of Man. Christ was not a supernatural manifestation but a man in the ideal sense, and we are the true disciples of Christ to the extent that we pursue the same thing he strove for. In this case Christianity, through its indirect influence, has uncommonly strengthened the impact of common grace, and through that strengthening of common grace the latent human powers were awakened. And now, instead of acknowledging this, that awakened power of human nature puts itself in the place of Christianity and says, "I am the true Christianity." Christianity does not reside in the Bible; nor in the gospel; and even less in the church, its offices, or its dogma; but Christianity is general love for people, human sobriety, and the ennoblement of human strength. The child pushes the mother aside and ascribes to himself the life he now has. This is in fact the new phase in which this struggle becomes increasingly intense. There is no longer a battle about heresy, no battle about schism, but a fundamental struggle between supernatural Christianity and the higher development to which human nature has come through Christianity but that now appropriates for itself the privilege of the Christian name.

§ 4 However sad this result may be, and however tense the situation consequently has become, the result provides us with the conclusive proof that the supernatural gifts of particular grace have served and still serve in God's hand to strengthen common grace. For the goal of common grace is, after all, to temper and arrest the fatal effect of destruction in our nature in such a way that, in the first place, human life is possible, and, in the second place, the powers that God has implanted in our humanity do not remain buried beneath the earth but burst forth and display the luster of his original ordination. Common grace has achieved this lofty goal only very partially in the nations that were deprived of all supernatural gifts, and common grace has become strong in reaching that goal only among nations in whose midst the church has appeared.

There is therefore no doubt that the supernatural powers that became manifest in the appearing of the church brought about this strengthening of common grace and offered it the means to let human nature, in spite of its inherent depravity, flourish so powerfully, as we have seen happen especially in our century. We of course do not intend by this to shortchange the more immediate goal that these supernatural gifts have with a view to salvation in the sphere of particular grace. We only maintain that in addition to this immediate goal, they also have exerted, and still exert, an indirect working, and this indirect effect serves to elevate human life to a higher level, to make it richer, to ennoble it, and to cause it to attain full development. And this is not merely appearance, for apart from the terrible churning of sin and the external appearance many people gaze at, it must not be denied in the least that among the children of the world there also are found in no small numbers those who manifest through their earnestness and devotion a "civic righteousness" that is beautiful as such and transcends by far what earlier centuries have known.

In general it can be said that the line of demarcation between the moderns and the orthodox coincides with this difference in their conception of Christianity. The modern "Christians" (to grant them for the moment the name they value so much) know no other Christianity than what has developed in a human manner, from man, as an ideal of human life. A few of them still concede that behind this human development the impulse of the Infinite has been at work, and that the impulse of the Infinite still tingles in many hearts, but this is and remains for them the Unknown that never operates except through what is known to be human. There has never been a breach in that long process of human development. One condition evolved from the other. They can explain the fact that Israel displayed a finer sense in the religious realm on the basis of her penchant for being curious. And the fact that within the bosom of that people no one experienced the religious life more richly and deeply than Jesus was the result of his personality. And even if it is the case that both these factors (Israel's penchant as a people and Jesus' personality) were in turn the product of other factors, so that if we had all atavistic data we would be able to fathom every mystery, they say, for the time being we still lack a clear insight that we might never be granted. But the axiom is certain that both Jesus and Christianity are *human* not only in essence and nature, but also entirely human in origin, and had nothing but *human powers* at their disposal. § 5

By contrast, orthodox Christianity confesses (albeit in various forms) that the pure power of human development has been broken by sin, and that consequently neither Israel nor its Messiah, neither regeneration nor the church, can be explained from the evolution of the powers that originally were placed within man. We therefore posit two factors here: the divine and the human, and depending on whether this relationship is taken in a pure or an impure sense, it pulls orthodox Christianity either in the proper or the improper direction. In general we can say that orthodoxy was inclined to put the human factor too much in the shadow, and to this extent it called forth the reaction of modernism, in which the human factor avenged itself one-sidedly. Only Calvinism has not made itself guilty of this, due to its confession of common grace. For it is this doctrine of common grace that serves to shine the light on the human factor at every point along the path of history and at every point of the personal formation of God's children.

§ 6 We can only point to the hybrid perspectives here. They are by their very nature a highly varied mixture, and depending on whether the true or the false element predominates in the mixture, there exists either the hope that these strayed individuals will return, or the certainty that they must ultimately go completely astray. What are called the theologians of the Groningen school, older Ethical theologians, younger Ethical theologians, modern orthodox theologians, or mediating theologians,[3] they are all theological mutts, the product of mixing two fundamentally opposite views of Christianity. On the one hand, there is orthodox Christianity with its confession of the Trinity, of Christ as God's only begotten Son, of the redemption through his blood, of the holy Scriptures as the revelation of God's will, and of the sacraments as seals of the covenant. On the other hand, there is modern Christianity, which views all this as the products of ecclesiastical contrivance and therefore rejects those dogmatics and turns Scripture into a natural product and takes Christianity as a purely human phenomenon. At present the hybrid perspectives fall between these two opposites, mostly in three manifestations: philosophical, mystical, or historical.

These halfway schools began philosophically by association with Schleiermacher and, via Schleiermacher, with Schelling or with theosophists such as

3. German, *Vermittlungstheologen*.

von Baader.[4] Thus they left the dogmas in name for what they were and used almost exclusively orthodox terms and expressions but gave these a twist or a turn that in fact caused their theology to end up in unclear philosophy.

More common today is the mystical school, which forgoes any possibility of explaining the mystery, but acknowledges certain divine workings aimed at saving us, located within the stirrings of the soul's emotions, operating in the men of God of olden times as well as in pious people. In this way it holds onto the psychological mysteries of Christianity, while at the same time stripping holy Scripture of its sacred character.

Finally, a more *historical* school has been added, which is averse to the metaphysical and, realizing how dangerous our floating on the mysticism of the emotions can become, reaches back behind the church and behind the apostles to the Christ of the Gospels and now considers itself to be better able to explain Christ than the apostles could.

These three schools are also found in our country under what is commonly referred to as the Ethical theologians. This is a very mixed crowd, therefore, and all the more mixed because there are two kinds of men in each of these three schools: men who still have a bond with Jesus through faith, but whose view of the Savior has become darkened, and also persons of the world who in fact make common cause with the moderns but still wrap the many-colored coat of Joseph around their waists.

But under whatever names or different forms Christianity may present § 7
itself, the situation remains the same. In Europe as well as in America, we find a Christian culture that in all kinds of demonstrable ways differs from pagan and Islamic cultures; these differences are not accidental but have come about through the influence of Christianity. This is already apparent from the fact that these differences did not occur anywhere Christianity did not come, while they occurred everywhere among all nations where Christianity entered, and were immediately noticeable when Christianity gained a firm foothold somewhere. What has recently been reported about the turn in the social life on Sulawesi confirms this again.[5]

---

4. Friedrich Schleiermacher (1768–1834) is often seen as the father of modern, liberal theology. F. W. J. Schelling (1775–1854) was an influential German dialectical philosopher. Franz von Baader (1765–1841) was a German, Roman Catholic philosopher whose thought is associated with Idealism and theosophy.
5. See *CG* 2.28.6n14.

But even though we may and must call our society in that comprehensive sense Christian, it does not mean that this Christian character is pure only at the core and becomes weaker the closer we get to the periphery. In each nation the core comprises those known by the Lord. They are the ones who bear the holy vessels. It is in them where the powers of regeneration, faith, and sanctification are again and again fed anew from their source in God. In that center, Christ is King in his church. In that center, God the Holy Spirit works as the indwelling God. Next comes the circle of the visible church, already mixed with hypocrites and therefore increasingly impure. Then comes the broad circle of the so-called national church that still has many excellent elements in it but in its vast majority represents nothing but a Christianity in name only.

Then we also find the ever-shrinking and decreasing circle of people of the tradition, who still maintain a certain form of the ancient Christianity, who still pray, still often read the Bible, and go to church on feast days. But behind them comes the group of modern Christians who are open about the fact that they have broken with all that is ancient but nevertheless continue to find their ideal in Jesus. After these come the socially decent people who, however, have become complete atheists and want nothing to do with modern Christianity. And finally, we find at the outermost periphery that very wide circle of people who think about *nothing*, who care about *nothing*, but who are in fact also devoid of any influence on the life of society and who live only for their business, or lose themselves in pleasure seeking, or waste away in the cesspool of pauperism and crime.

§ 8 If we apply the distinction between particular grace and common grace, then it is clear that particular grace performs its work only at the center, and that all influence for the good that flowed from Christianity to the broad circle of society does not lead to salvation and is therefore not particular. Rather, it flows into the work of common grace, which, also apart from future salvation, serves to develop and ennoble human life here on earth by arresting the effects of the poison of sin.

Even the modernist Christians recognize something of this. For they concede that, in the midst of the darkness that once enveloped the life of our ancestors, the church of Christ has indeed kindled a light that has powerfully advanced the enlightenment and civilization of these peoples. They even greatly appreciate, therefore, the services rendered in this way to civilization through ecclesiastical Christianity, and they are gladly prepared to accept these services once again where that institutional Christianity is willing to take upon itself the initial education of the completely uncivilized people of Asia or of Africa by means of missions. However, in their opinion this influence must not go beyond the nursery. Once that initial education of these peoples is completed, they must go to the humanistic school. And only then will they, the moderns, educate those developing peoples to a so-called higher perspective—even as some people today do not mind their small children being raised orthodox, provided that, once orthodoxy has completed its services to the small children, they remain free to reveal to the children the untenability of all those foolish claims. But it is precisely against this that Christianity submits its well-considered protest. Even if the nations move toward a *higher* development, Christianity wants to continue to set the tone. Or to express it in practical terms, Christianity does not allow itself to be confined to grade school; it also demands access, and access with honor, to the courses of study at the high schools and universities.

CHAPTER THIRTY-THREE

THE CHURCH AS INSTITUTION AND AS ORGANISM

One God and Father of all, who is over all and through all and in all.

EPHESIANS 4:6

§ 1 What God works in his particular grace has also influenced the unconverted world to no small degree by tempering sin and bringing development. To mention just one example, science most certainly owes its current rich and free flowering to the influence of Christianity. A scientific development such as has been achieved at present has not been seen even remotely in any country and among any people outside of Christianity. The sin in science also has definitely been tempered to the extent that inertia in research has been conquered and dishonesty in drawing up the results has been overcome. And yet science in its present state of development belongs to the sphere of particular grace to such a small extent that instead, science turns in supreme conceit not only against the medicinal power of Golgotha but even against the confession of God Almighty. And as with science, so it goes as well with all kinds of other phenomena in life. It is therefore clear that the Christian religion, although it springs from particular grace, nevertheless powerfully impacts all kinds of realms of common grace, but nevertheless the fruits of common grace again and again turn against the church, against the Christian religion, and against those who decisively confess that religion.

This brings us to the contrast, generally acknowledged nowadays, between the Christian church as *organism* and the Christian church as *institution*. The obvious danger is that, especially in these workings of the particular means of grace within the realm of common grace, the church might come to be viewed as an organism, which would falsify the entire notion. Institute and organism stand in contrast to one another as what has been built stands in contrast to what has grown. All that has been put together from parts and pieces or is kept together by means of an external force is an institution. An organism, by contrast, unfolds all its members out of itself, and as it changes its form, it perpetuates and expands its own life.

Applied to the church of Christ, the church is therefore an organism if we take it in its hidden unity as the mystical body of Christ that is partly in heaven, partly on earth, in part still unborn. It has penetrated into all peoples and nations, having Christ as its natural and glorious Head, and living through the Holy Spirit, who as the life-generating and life-maintaining power vitalizes the Head and the members. Taken as institution, on the other hand, the church is an instrument, a local and temporary institution based on human choices, decisions, and acts of will; consisting of members, offices, and resources. It is a manifestation, therefore, in the external and visible and observable world. It is something we can see with our eyes, hear with our ears, and touch with our hands, but it has reality only to the extent that the mystical body of Christ stands behind it and reveals itself through it, even if imperfectly. Should this cease to be the case, then the institution will no longer be the church but a pseudochurch, a false church.

When we observe this sharp contrast, we seem to avoid any danger of § 2
confusing the church as organism with the influence of the Christian religion on common grace. But as soon as we move away from the individual persons to pay attention to the organic coherence of our human race as well, then this danger definitely appears to exist. Even as a plant does not come into being by joining together root fibers, stalk, leaf, and flower, so too the mystical body of Christ does not come into being by gathering together a few converted persons. In the visible part there is indeed a gathering of individuals, and that is what the Catechism means when it says that "the Son of God, by His Spirit and Word, gathers, defends, and preserves

for Himself unto everlasting life a chosen communion."[1] But behind this gathering lies incorporation into Christ, which the Form for Baptism asks believing parents to affirm as existing in their infants even before they can repent. And this incorporation into Christ is directly related in turn to their having been born into the covenant of grace, which is not composed of individuals but runs genealogically through succeeding generations. And the holy Apostle Paul finally points us to the counsel of God, existing behind that incorporation of that covenant of grace, through which all believers are elect in Christ before the foundation of the world [see Eph 1:4].

The connection and coherence, therefore, do not come about through individuals who come together; rather, the individuals enter a connection and an organic coherence that precedes their personal existence and for which they have been intended. There is the eternal *being in Christ* according to God's counsel; there is the *being included in the covenant* by our inclusion in the seed of our ancestors; there is the *being incorporated in Christ* through the working of the Holy Spirit that precedes this working; and finally, there is the *personal coming to Christ*, with all his saints.

Only that marvelous grafting in the plant world gives us a shadowy image of this mysterious penetrating into Christ before we come to him. It is like a shadow because it works in reverse. It is not the cultivated plant that tames the wild shoot grafted onto it; rather, the cultivated shoot that is grafted on tames the juices of the wild tree that flow upward. Consequently, this is the reverse image of what we are looking for. For here, the mystical body is the organism that grafts the individual person into itself and tames him, and not the individual person who, by being grafted into the body, causes the body to bear cultivated fruit. But leaving this difference aside, the grafting image shows us two things: (1) how a loose shoot can be organically bonded with an existing tree through grafting, and (2) how this is possible only because before the grafting there was a correspondence and botanical unity between graft and tree. The shoot could not be successfully grafted if, in God's ordinance concerning the plant world, a correspondence were not established between shoot and trunk such that when they come into contact with one another, both can make their common nature work. And this gives a somewhat shadowy image of what occurs in the body of Christ. For here too, the individual member is brought to the body only subsequently,

1. Heidelberg Catechism, Lord's Day 21, Q&A 54.

but the fact that both can thus bond organically is possible only because a unity of life and a solidarity already existed beforehand by virtue of God's ordinance. But then it follows that—as in the case of the grafting of the shoot in the trunk, when it comes to the incorporation of the member into the body of Christ—we not only need to observe the shoot and trunk (that is, the member and the body), but we also need to draw attention to the organic bonds that link shoot and trunk, or in this case, member and body.

The Epistle to the Hebrews speaks of those organic bonds in relation to § 3
our material body, when it says, "For the word of God is living and active, sharper than any two-edged sword, piercing to the division of soul and of spirit, of joints and of marrow, and discerning the thoughts and intentions of the heart" [Heb 4:12]. There is thus "the division of soul and of spirit," but there are also joints that connect both with the body in the "marrow." In Ephesians 4:16 the apostle relates the image of these organic connections or joints directly to the mystical body of the Lord, when he writes: "From whom the whole body, joined and held together by every joint with which it is equipped, when each part is working properly, makes the body grow so that it builds itself up in love." "Joined and held together" expresses this same thought: It is not a joining as with a wrapped dressing or bandage. There is no external joining; there is no gluing or stringing together. Rather, there is a growing together that is conceivable and possible only where the two parts that come together belong together, are designed for one another, and in fact had the same kind of life in common before they came together.

The two sides of the wound immediately grasp each other in love and grow together in such a way that soon there is no longer a noticeable wound, because the two pieces belonged together, carried an identical life in themselves, and were fundamentally designed for one another. A fiber, a thread that remains hanging between them hinders them from growing together because it does not belong organically but is alien. And we notice this same growing together when we put a piece of tissue from our arm on a wound on someone else's arm. Those two raw pieces of tissue immediately grasp one another in love and immediately grow together, even as in the case of our own wound. In this case they do so not because they were originally one; your arm and the other's arm remain distinct. They grow together because they nevertheless had a oneness and an original unity in the oneness of all human flesh, and that oneness does not reside in the material elements—there were other cells in your arm than in the other's arm—but it resides in the oneness of the nature of the *joints and organic connections*.

These work, pull, and absorb in our arm in exactly the same way as they did in the other's arm. We had this in common with him. Your original oneness, correspondence, and unity consisted in this. And it is through this that the piece of flesh from *our* arm fixes itself in the *other's* arm and grows together with it because they already had an organic unity without knowing it.

If this has made it clear that in the organism of the church as well, we must pay attention not only to the mystical body and the incorporated member, but also to the organic connections or joining elements, then the question arises as to what kinds of *joining elements* these are. And then it has already become obvious from the chosen image of the graft and of the healing of the wound that these properties that make joining possible must originally be present in the nature of plants and of flesh. Certainly, we can put a plaster cast around the wound, sew it together with silver thread, or wrap a bandage around it; that plaster, that thread, and that bandage keep things together. But keeping things together is not the same as their growing together. This keeping together serves only to bring the parts that are to be joined close together, and the growing together always happens entirely apart from the plaster, thread, or bandage, through the working of the blood and the cellular tissue. So too, in the case of the organism of the church, those organic connections therefore must not be sought in what binds together externally, such as institutional association, church discipline, ecclesiastical practices, and so forth. These are necessary, of course, and they serve to keep things together *so that* there may be a growing together, but they in themselves do not bring about the growing together. This growing together can occur only when the workings and powers that were originally put into the nature of our race are "electrified" anew and begin to work. And this then is the reason the Spirit of the Lord not only works in the mystical body as such, and in the member that is to be grafted in, but the same Spirit of the Lord also impacts those organic connections and joints of our human life that together constitute the background that is common to all individuals.

§ 4 It would take us too far afield to discuss at length this common background of all individual human life. For this area is virtually limitless, since it encompasses virtually our entire human life. We therefore will give a single example to elucidate our meaning. As individuals, we human beings have the need to speak and to be spoken to by others. This is not always the case: there are times when our spirit seeks rest. Nevertheless, a single day in which no word passed our lips and no word struck our ear would seem difficult for us. This is what is so frightening about solitary prison confinement. But in order to be able to speak and, conversely, to hear oneself addressed, and to be able to understand what is said, there must be organic connections. Without such organic connections any speech at all is inconceivable. The connections are of two kinds: material and spiritual. They are *material* to the extent that they involve our organs of speech and hearing and the air waves we cause to vibrate. But on the other hand, they are also *spiritual*. Sounds are produced by matter, plants, and animals too. The storm howls, the plant rustles, the lion roars, and these sounds make a deep impression on us. Yet all this does not give us the language to speak. That language emerges only when the same thoughts arise in the one who hears our sounds or words as our soul feels when we utter them. And so language must not only have (1) the material connection of the sound of our words, and (2) the spiritual connection between sound and thought; there must also be (3) that still-higher *organic connection* that this language is also the language of the other with whom you speak.

Do we create this language? Does each individual begin to deliberate within himself how he will reproduce some thought or other by means of some sound or other? Of course not. He finds that language. That language existed before he was born. And each compatriot with whom he speaks has received that language from his ancestors, just as he himself did. This language is therefore older than he, and yet that language is what expresses his thoughts because it has pleased God to have him come from the same tribe or people and to give him a common life with them. The organic connection of language thus possesses its deeper ground in the even more original organic connection with his people. He has been *added to* his people and at the same time has *come from* the body of his people. There is an addition, but it is an addition grounded in the original unity of life, and the consciousness of that unity of life expresses itself in the unity of language.

If human language, therefore, is one of the indispensable elements that join human life together, then it is necessary that the Christian religion also enter into that language, that it master that element of human joining, penetrate it, inspire it, make it its own instrument, and thus use the language to bring about the growing together of the body and its members and develop it to perfection. Even if we were to remove all children of God from the Netherlands, so that not a single born-again individual remained in our country, the Christian religion would still be present *in the language*. For in that language each Christian thought has found expression. In that language § 5 its treasures and riches have been expressed. Christianity is woven into that language, as it were, and can be brought forth out of that language again at any moment, not in reality but according to the expression for our human consciousness. Only through this language does preaching occur. Through that language prayer is expressed. In that language we sing. Through that language we carry on our conversations, express our love, and comfort one another. If faith is from hearing, then that hearing comes from preaching, and that preaching is possible only through that language. Even if all voices were to fall silent, language would still preserve for us the full richness of the Christian religion in the printed word.

But precisely for this reason the Christian religion has exerted its influence on this organic joining element of language. It has not left this language as it was but has changed, modified, impassioned, and to a certain extent, Christianized it. If we consider the language as it was before the gospel entered these regions, and the language as it has now become through preachers and poets, through people who pray and who sing praises, then we sense immediately that Christianity has put its stamp on that language. It has not done so on the whole language. This language still knows its unholy, unexpurgated, malignant form. But in the broader spheres of that language a sphere of light has come into being, within which that language has adopted a character more sacred, more consecrated; and in that sphere the language has been absorbed into the organic life of the church of Christ. If we thus want to get a conception of what the church as organism is, it is not enough to pay attention only to the mystical body of Christ and to the spiritual members of that body; we must also consider human language to be part of it insofar as it has undergone the baptism of Christianity. For in that language an organic connection between one human being and another is manifested, a joining together of the parts, and the Christian religion has put its stamp on this joining element as well.

§ 6 We have expounded this briefly in relation to human language, but we could show in the same way how, in addition to language, there are all kinds of other joining elements and organic connections that, according to the original creation ordinance, unite our human life into a whole and are used to promote the growing together of the body and its members, and to increase in that unity the glory of our God. Quite the same thing applies to our domestic life together; to our life together in society; to the general world of thought, of existing customs, of the expressions of life in business, art, and science; and so much more. All these are things that link us in our life as the human race. These are connections we do not create but find; they exist outside us and compel us, connections on which we exert a certain influence but that exert a much stronger influence on us. All of these are connections that fundamentally are thoroughly *human*, and therefore in the Christian arena too they cannot be denied, discarded, or ignored. And the Christian mind has laid claim to all of these connections and joining elements. It has penetrated them, has changed and modified them, and has made them subservient to its purpose. And to the extent that this has happened it must be confessed not only that the church as an organic national church consists of the mystical body as a unity, and the members as parts of this body, but also that to both of these belong the totality of those joining elements, to the extent that they have been infused with the Christian spirit.

It is therefore thoroughly wrong if, when speaking of the church (not as *institution* but as *organism*), we refer almost exclusively to the elect or to those who have been incorporated, while closing our eyes deliberately to those rich and many-sided joining elements that in the end bind the multiplicity of the members into the unity of the body. Paying attention only to the persons like this is the curse of the nominalism that still operates in current liberalism. More than anything, Christianity is *social* in nature; and more beautifully than anyone, the Apostle Paul has pointed us clearly and repeatedly to these three aspects: body, members, and joints. The church as organism has its center in Christ, it expands in his mystical body, and it individualizes itself in individual members. But it finds its unity also, and no less, in those original joining elements and organic connections that unite us humans into one human race, and it is on these joining elements that the spirit of Christ imprints his stamp. But even though those Christianized joining elements serve in common grace to stem sin and carry general development further, the origin of their Christianization lies in particular grace, and they find their original and primary goal in the propagation of particular grace.

CHAPTER THIRTY-FOUR

THE NATIONAL CHURCH

Fear not, little flock, for it is your Father's good pleasure to give you the kingdom.

LUKE 12:32

§ 1 This is the place to examine the notion and phenomenon of the national church. For what the proponents of the national church have always intended, and still have in view today, is directly related to the impact both of the Christian church and of its means of grace on common grace. Its advocates have always maintained that the church of Christ cannot and must not consist of "believers and their seed"[1] (along with any hypocrites who have crept in), but that it must consist, if possible, of all the sons and daughters of the nation. And they do not want this because they are blind to the unbelief that thereby enters the church, but because they think that

1. This is a common formula derived from the covenantal promises in the Old Testament (such as Deut 11:9) and applied within the context of baptism. See, for instance, the form for baptism in *A Directory for the Publique Worship of God, Throughout the Three Kingdoms of England, Scotland, and Ireland* (London: Tyler et al., 1644), 41: "the Promise is made to Beleevers and their seed."

only in this way can the church also bless the ordinary civic life in a broader sphere and have an educating effect on the great mass of people. Between them and us, therefore, there is no difference regarding the fact that the church of Christ with its means of grace covers a wider field than that of particular grace. It is mutually acknowledged that the church does two things: (1) it has a direct impact on the elect; it induces them to repentance, comforts them, edifies them, binds them together, and sanctifies them; but (2) it also has an indirect effect on the whole of civil society; it compels them to civic righteousness. But we differ on a point: to achieve this good goal they incorporate civil society into the church, whereas for this same purpose we place the church, like a city on a hill, in the midst of civil society.

At this point we are not making an issue of the terms being used. We are concerned with the matter itself. But it is certain that the aim of the national-church system is to incorporate as quickly and comprehensively as possible the whole population of a country into the church. The system that we advocate, on the other hand, serves to distinguish between church and civil society, to admit only "believers and their seed," and to tolerate the hypocrites only to the extent that they cannot be unmasked. From this relatively small circle then, there must radiate influence upon the unchurched (or, if you will, civil society). Thus the contrast, it appears to us, has been clearly delineated, in a way that avoids any misunderstanding and does full justice to the sentiments of our opponents. They and we acknowledge the truth that Christianity is called not only to bring the elect to salvation but also to have an impact on human life in state, society, and school. But in their eyes, the means to achieve this is that the church incorporate as much as possible all those who belong to the nation, whereas we say that the church must remain the assembly of believers (with their seed) and this more narrowly delineated church must exert the blessing of its influence on state, society, and school. This is a contrast that also makes clearly apparent how the notion of the national church is directly related to the aspect of common grace we currently are discussing.

Faced with this deeply divisive dispute, we must immediately confess § 2
that the notion of the national church dominates virtually all of church history. Wherever we see the Christian church manifesting itself in its progress through the world, it always strives to entice to holy baptism all persons who belong to the population, by means of being flexible and obliging, and after a relatively short period Christianity then becomes the religion of the whole nation. Until the conversion of Emperor Constantine,

this was different. But when he became a Christian emperor, the national church began to be actualized. And since then it has continued under almost all church forms. Rome wanted a national church; in the East the Copts, Nestorians, and Greek Orthodox wanted national churches. We find national churches in all Lutheran countries. After a brief struggle, a national church has become dominant in the Calvinist countries as well. The same is true in England as well as in Scotland, Switzerland, and most surprisingly, the United States of America. This is such an overwhelming fact that it takes seriousness, courage, and deep conviction to nevertheless rebel against the national church, especially when we pay attention to two more things.

In the first place, in the Calvinist countries in particular, the essential notion of the national church did not persist, but the same notion was nevertheless applied in modified form. It is self-evident that the national church as such wants to be *the* church of the *whole* nation, the church of national unity, the church that (apart from a few inconsequential exceptions) encompasses the whole nation. This is how it was under Rome in the Middle Ages. This is how it still is in Russia, in the Balkan countries, in Greece. This is how it is in the Lutheran countries, such as Denmark, Finland, Norway, Sweden, and northern Germany. The Calvinist countries broke with this pattern insofar as they also tolerated other churches. They tolerated them not with full honors, not on an equal footing, not as having the same rights, but nevertheless as a coexisting church form. This is how it has been in Switzerland. This is how it came to be in England. This is how it was originally in France, when the Huguenots were still powerful. This is how it was in our country. This is how it came to be especially in the United States of America. Indeed, in later times the notion of a privileged national church weakened to such an extent that in our country the constitution promises equal protection to all religious persuasions, and in the United States of America there is not one church that might be said to be viewed more than other churches as the national church. At most it can be conceded that in the United States, the various Protestant churches have a higher national ranking than the Roman Catholics or the Mormons, although even this contrast is gradually losing its force. But even though this had to be noted, it is certain that, apart from a few small sects, all these churches existing side by side nonetheless attempt to embody *together* a single concept of grouping together everyone who belongs to the nation among one or another of these various churches.

Leaving the Jews aside, all non-Jews must indicate to which Christian denomination they belong.

This same thought operates even in our own circles. All churches that practice infant baptism value retaining within their church fellowship everyone who has been baptized and born into their group, and it almost never is the case that baptized persons who later appear to be entirely alienated from the Christian confession and the service of the Lord are excluded from the church for that reason. This continues from generation to generation, and for this reason, the same idea of a national church continues to be cherished, not extensively but intensively. In America not a town springs up without the whole population being classified by church, and all segments of the town's inhabitants together constitute a Christian population. The only thing that can be said is that the mobility that causes the Americans to continually move from one location to another makes a bit of a breach in that unity, since people who move from place to place join a certain church at one time, then a different one at another time. Another point to remember is that in these American churches, a distinction is made between the external and the internal church. The external church includes all those who have been baptized, but the internal, spiritual, actual church includes only those who have made profession of faith and have been admitted to the Lord's Supper. And only the latter exert influence on the organization of the church and the filling of its offices. It also is clear that in the Calvinistic countries, the full notion of the national church has long since been broken, and that attempts have continually been made to embody a purer conception, but as yet this has not led to a clear result. The contrast between church and world cannot become manifest where belonging to some church or other (except among the Jews, of course) is the general rule.

Our second comment is that the more deliberate and persistent opposi- § 3
tion to the idea of the national church unfortunately has emerged almost exclusively from the spiritualist sects. Again and again we see in history how small groups isolate themselves when they do not want anything to do with the national church. But in their opposition they fall into the other extreme—namely, that of denying the covenant of God, abolishing infant baptism, tearing asunder nature and spirit, and letting the church exist exclusively for the sake of heaven, while simply turning their back on the ordinary, natural human life in spiritual one-sidedness and haughty pride. This itself constitutes the very essence of a sect. For people have applied the term *sect* to every group that separates itself from the national church,

but this is not its essential characteristic; otherwise, there would always be only one essential, real church, and all other Christian persuasions would be described as sectarian.

But this position, which leads to the position of only one saving church, cannot be the Protestant position. Lutherans and Reformed, Episcopalians and nonconformists, Methodists and Presbyterians have never seriously maintained that one cannot be saved in the other segments of Christianity. The Protestant confession stands clearly in direct opposition to the notion of a single ecclesiastical institution that alone can save. From the beginning it included the multiplicity of the churches in its bosom; it acknowledges that there are differences that should not be ignored but cannot therefore decide salvation or damnation. No, a group is a sect only when it places itself outside human life. It becomes a sect when a number of individuals place their association outside the life of humanity and view themselves as a little holy circle that still mistakenly remains on earth but in fact has nothing to do with life here on earth. Such a group is not a sect until it ceases to confess Jesus as *the Son of Man*. And since one cannot deny that precisely these sects have most strongly come to resist the national church, both as idea and as phenomenon, the national church has in no small measure derived strength from the fact that it could continually present a choice: "Stay with me, because if you don't, you become a sect." In our country as well, the men of the national church have continually thrown the reproach at us since 1834 and 1886 that we have no other intention than, in the manner of the Labadists, merely to form a sectarian group of a few saints, and when the Synod of the Hague in 1886 condemned and expelled Dr. Kuyper, the main charge against him was derived from a sentence in his *Confidentie*,[2] in which he offered a plea for the small flock in the midst of the world, but which falsified his intention as if he had pursued sectarianism.[3]

§ 4 Therefore, even though the struggle against the national church must be carried on under very unfavorable circumstances, the struggle must not

---

2. Abraham Kuyper, *Confidentie: Schrijven aan de weled. Heer J.A. van der Linden* (Amsterdam: Höveker & Zoon, 1873); ET: "Confidentially," in *AKCR*, 45–61.

3. Kuyper refers here to the two great church schisms in the Netherlands in the nineteenth century. The first, that of the *Afscheiding* or "secession," led to the formation of an independent denomination of churches in 1834; the second was led by Kuyper himself in 1886 and was known as the *Doleantie*, or the secession of those who were "aggrieved." The Labadists were a Dutch sectarian movement led by Jean de Labadie (1610–74).

be abandoned. But one is in a position of weakness as long as the battle is carried on only from the spiritual side. For it is entirely true that the church is "the assembly of *believers*" and that, no matter how elastic we may make this word, there is no place for unbelievers or nonbelievers; however, the confession of the covenant, which in turn relates to the organic coherence of the generations, causes tangible difficulties here. If we take a Pelagian position and, looking only at the individual persons, declare that only those who declare and confess that they personally believe in Christ as their Savior belong in the church, then this gives us the means to decide who does and who does not belong to the church. But we also come immediately into conflict with the covenant, with the coherence of the generations, and thus also with infant baptism.

On the other hand, if on the basis of holy Scripture we are convinced (1) that the covenant concept must not be surrendered, (2) that the link between believers and their seed is a sacred, organic link that must be honored carefully, and (3) that consequently a church with only adult baptism starts from a false premise, then this individualistic standpoint appears to be utterly untenable. And we furthermore are faced with the objection that according to holy Scripture, the church has significance for the world as well—for the development of its human life, for its civil society, and its natural treasures of life—a significance that in this manner is completely lost. Such a narrow circle of persons who mutually examine one another, outside any connection with their lineage, also comes to exist apart from any connection with the life of the world and closes itself off in spiritual one-sidedness. History has confirmed this again and again, and by virtue of the principle from which such a group arises, it cannot be otherwise. Those who have separated themselves under all kinds of names, such as the Plymouth Brethren, have vigorously and sharply combated the national church as a rank falsification of the real notion of the church, which in turn had led the church on satanic paths.[4] But by confusing "church" and "national church," they have fundamentally turned against *any* conception of "church," and they now want to form nothing but "sweet, pious societies." But the result shows how, precisely through this error, they have placed themselves outside the movement and are focused on sweet peace for their

4. John Nelson Darby (1800–82) was an early leader of the Plymouth Brethren, originally an Irish movement for a church independent of the Anglican establishment.

own soul, but for the rest they exist in isolation in every country and have robbed themselves of any influence on the course of events.

The battle against the national church, then, can be conducted with hope for better success only when a better, purer, more scriptural conception of the church is placed against the notion of the national church; when the covenant notion is given its due; when attention is paid not only to the individual but also to the coherence of people in the organic connection of the generations; and further, when it is clearly pointed out in what way the church of Christ, if it once again has the courage to honor its boundaries, can nevertheless be a blessing to common human life. And this is possible only from a Calvinistic standpoint, because only the Reformed have clearly recognized the distinction between particular grace and common grace. As long as people close their eyes to this distinction, they know grace only within the circle of the church, and then people become *obliged* to take, if possible, all their compatriots into the sphere of the church if civic life is not to be abandoned to demonic powers.

This latter is not an exaggeration. Sin brings about a curse, and where the curse rules, the devilish powers work without impediment. If only *grace* can turn away the curse and stop the dominance of the demonic, then clearly one of two things must happen: either grace must be at work outside the church, or all that stands outside the church and cannot be taken into it must remain devoid of grace and therefore remain unresistingly and powerlessly subject to the curse. So-called exorcism is the natural means the church uses to break this power and repeatedly to withdraw a piece, a part, of the world from the curse and bring it under grace. Even the ground must then be consecrated, for in terms of the ground too, the world consists of two parts: the one consecrated, the other unconsecrated. All that is not consecrated still stands outside of grace. But this all is canceled when we realize that there is grace at work outside the church of Christ too, that there is grace also where its working does not lead to eternal salvation, and that we therefore have to honor a working of grace through which curse and sin are arrested in the natural, human, civil life as well, even though there is no connection with salvation.

§ 5 Once this is confessed with clarity, then even the possibility that the purer conception of the church could ever lead to sectarianism disappears. For then we acknowledge that only God tests purely spiritually, and that we can and must test only on the basis of an observable distinguishing mark he has established. We then confess that after the first generation of

Gentiles and Jews entered the church, successive generations no longer have come into the church merely through a choice of their own will, but are in the church by birth and must leave only if they manifest unbelief. The great covenant notion of "you and your seed" [see Gen 12:7] then remains honored, which is also our God's pledge of faithfulness. And while on the one hand, the contrast between the assembly of believers and the world is maintained, on the other hand, it is wholeheartedly confessed that in the world there is a grace at work as well, the common grace of our God, and that the church of Christ that manifests itself in the midst of the world is one of the most powerful means through which God is pleased to lead common grace to its goal.

In this manner we stand strong in contrast to the national church, if only for a reason everyone can grasp. For the national church has the same thing in view. It also wants to avoid Pelagianism in the formation of the church. It wants to bring us into contact with the church, not through our own will but by God's ordination. It wants to maintain the connection. It wants to honor the coherence of the generations. It lives by infant baptism. It wants to bless the world, even in those manifestations of life that are not directly related to salvation. And it places all this on such a high plane that it sacrifices the purity of the church and takes comfort from the thought that it must tolerate even atheists in its midst; conversely, it had to persecute and expel many devout confessors who reacted against it. However—and this is absolutely natural—it then must always leave a considerable portion of ordinary human life *outside* the sphere of the church. Rome realized this and therefore has tried, insofar as it was at all possible, to take *all* manifestations of human life into the sphere of the church: art, science, the guilds, and so forth. But the Protestant national church did not do this. It excluded art and science, trade and business, from the life of its church and made these expressions of civic life independent. As a result, people got used to seeing in these expressions of life phenomena that were inimical to the church because they were weapons for unbelief. This was not a major problem as long as human, nonecclesiastical work preferred to busy itself with more-or-less spiritual phenomena such as literature, art, jurisprudence, political science, and so on.

But this changed when scholarship in our century preferred to focus on *nature* and succeeded in expanding and confirming in a truly excellent way the power of the human spirit over nature. This was not a hindrance for us, because we confess that the influence of the Christian religion is exactly what has strengthened common grace on this point as well, to the extent that it is precisely in the Christian parts of the world that mastery over nature has been restored to us in such a remarkable fashion. This mastery was given to us in paradise but then lost; it has been restored now not as an instinctual mastery, as in paradise, but one that comes as the fruit of labor "by the sweat of our face" [see Gen 3:19]. From our perspective, therefore, we applaud this expansion of human power over nature, we thank God for it, and we prophesy that it will go even much further. To us, all of this is the fruit of common grace, and we confess that this grace could continue to work so marvelously because the hidden power of the Christian religion has strengthened and preserved it in order to liberate the human spirit more and more from the curse. But this is entirely different, of course, from the perspective of the national church. Specifically, the development of the natural sciences falls entirely outside the scope of the church, and because it knows nothing of the grace existing outside the sphere of the church, it must do one of two things. Either, to the extent that it wants to hold on to the faith and remain heavenly in nature, it must view this development of our power over nature with distrust and stand hostile in opposition to it; or, to the extent that it lets go of the faith, it must deny that a curse rests on nature and deny, or at least weaken, the depravity of our human nature through sin.

CHAPTER THIRTY-FIVE

THE EFFECT OF THE CHURCH ON THE WORLD

And God blessed them. And God said to them, "Be fruitful and multiply and fill the earth and subdue it, and have dominion over the fish of the sea and over the birds of the heavens and over every living thing that moves on the earth."

GENESIS 1:28

The conceptions of the national church and the church as organism (as § 1
distinct from the church as institution) stand in much sharper contrast to one another than is generally assumed. The national church preaches the principle that an entire people, an entire nation, can be incorporated into the church of Christ by baptism, not because the whole population believes, or at least may be thought to believe. But this is preached in spite of the fact that unbelief breaks out in the most brazen way possible, not only among the members of the church but also among its office bearers and councils, and even though it is widely known by everyone that the true believers constitute no more than a painfully small minority of the great mass. The proponents of the national church defend this public lie in two ways. First, in the antinomian sense, they say that the responsibility for changing the

sinful condition does not lie with the individual who transgressed but must wait until God himself directly excises the sin. And second, they point to all the good that comes from the continued existence of such a mixing, not so much for the church as for the nation and its social life. The latter is here apparently the goal and main point, the former nothing but a pretext for being able to excuse their own conscience for resigning themselves to and arguing for such a false mixing.

Indeed, the advocates for the national church claim that they would like "to set the situation aright," to use the language of the national church; but no matter how hard they try, "it cannot be, it has never been otherwise, and it will never be different. It is a fatal law under whose domination we sigh, and that law says that *all that ferments in the fatherland must continue to ferment in the church*." It is therefore not the church of Christ, nor the gospel, that leavens the world like yeast, but rather the reverse: it is the principle of the world that ferments and must ferment in Christ's church. In the face of this fearful, fatal law they stand powerless. They no longer have a guiding principle in their church, no spirit that rules, and there is not even a center from which action can emanate. The church, taken as a body, is one inert mass, simply because the composition of the church conflicts with the ABCs of the fundamental church principle. By contrast, civil society (or if you will, the world) definitely remains in its element and is not hindered the slightest bit in its activity, and the fermentation of principles therefore definitely comes from the world. And where such a fermentation percolates from the life of the people—a fermentation that not infrequently goes directly against the gospel—nothing else remains for the dull, lackluster church than to allow this leavening to continue on its own turf. As in a damp, musty mist that covers everything, the entire life of the church, whether we want it to or not, is robbed of its color and luster by the vapors that rise from this fermentation process.

§ 2 Serious thinkers realize how terrible this is, but they do not dare go against it. They react in words of protest, yes; in cutting, biting criticism, yes. Oh, they think it a misery for which there are not enough tears. Also, they want to do everything against it—only, the main notion of the national church must remain untouched as the first article of the confession of faith. And because any forceful and persistent action must lead immediately and necessarily to the breaking up of precisely this notion of a national church, and cause the courageous witnesses to be thrown out of the synagogue of this church, they warn each other not to lift a finger. The consequences have been disastrous. The passive attitude adopted in the days of the Reformation on the part of the Erasmians,[1] and adopted afterward at every new attempt at reformation in the Protestant churches on the part of men of their ilk, therefore must not be understood in the sense that they would greatly desire something else, but in the sense that they restrain themselves deliberately in order not to endanger the national church.

In fact, what drives, inspires, and restrains them is a general notion, a far-reaching conviction, that the will that envisions the unity of life should not be broken. We might likewise say they refuse to accept the breach between Christ and the world. They cannot resign themselves to the fact that Christ would not bless *all* of society, the *whole* nation, with his divine power. At least in Christian Europe, and even more so in the Christian Netherlands, everything *must* be Christian, be called Christian, and otherwise become Christian. Christ's church must have an impact on the whole life of the nation, and in order to be able to do this, the whole nation must by preference be incorporated into a church, and the church must extend over the entire nation. The influence of the church, they imagine, functions almost exclusively through the ministers and other office holders; therefore, in order to be reached by the ministers, the entire nation must be located within the walls of the church. For even if the results show that this has no benefit, even if it is clear before our eyes to what desecration of the sacred this leads, and to what bitterness of soul against brethren who hold a different view it tempts, nevertheless they do not give up: the national church must be safeguarded before all things. After all, whatever is currently still in such a miserable state and condition can improve before long. Later we can make up for what has been sinfully squandered in the past.

And when we pose the question to them—not from the perspective of reasoning but from the perspective of a more tender conscience—of whether allowing such conditions, living in such unholy relationships, and tolerating in full awareness the desecration and the causing to be desecrated of God's covenant, is permitted, then they take refuge in the tents of antinomianism. Certainly, it must be improved; it must change. Such a sinful condition must not continue. Only, how will he who is himself the

1. Desiderius Erasmus of Rotterdam (1466–1536) was the leading humanist of his day and earned a reputation for tolerance, even as he worked for reform within the Roman Catholic Church and engaged in polemics with Protestants, most notably Martin Luther (1483–1546) on the freedom of the will.

guilty party dare stretch out the hand to end that sin? In order to break with sin, one must stand up like an Elijah, judge like an Isaiah, act like a John the Baptist, break through like a Peter and Paul—and who has the right to do this when the guilt lies partly within himself? And even if one did not participate personally to any extent, is then the guilt of our forefathers not also charged to our account, and does not that guilt of our forefathers alone deprive us of any right to speak out? Does not God punish sin with sin? And when God wants to punish our guilt and the guilt of our fathers along with the sin of the church in our day, who can turn it away? Besides, is not such a sinful and sinning church a cause of suffering for the more tender conscience? And is that suffering not felt best and most acutely by those who love Zion? And what right would we then have to end our suffering by taking away the sin? In that suffering lies a punishment, and we must submit to that punishment with our contrite spirit. One day the morning light will dawn in this night, but God has reserved for himself the honor of this work. And we sinful humans must keep our hands off.

Finally the question is then raised on what basis people are in favor of the national church, for only when our point of departure lies in God's Word, and only when our point of departure is anchored in that Word, can further conclusions be correct. Those less well versed are pointed to the Old Testament dispensation in the days after the exodus from Egypt. In the period from Moses to Christ, the church in Israel merged with national life. Indeed, it can be said that the nation existed only for the sake of the church, even as our body exists only for our soul, and even as the bark of the tree exists only to protect the system of capillaries hidden behind it that carry the tree sap upward. Then it is not difficult at all to adduce all kinds of events from the condition of the church under Israel that serve as proof that nation and church must act as one, and to voice all kinds of statements that justify the beloved system, and indeed justify it before holy Scripture. After all, it is from those holy scriptures that the knowledge of Israel's history has come to us. Only, this was not the case from Adam until Moses.

They withhold the fact that this was true only under Israel on account of the dispensation of shadows, and that Christ as well as his apostles have once and for all broken with this dispensation of shadows because it is obsolete since it has been fulfilled and therefore is ready to vanish away [Heb 8:13]. They try to hide this from those who would discover it for themselves. But precisely the passion with which this is argued, the way the conscience is violated, the false conceptions that are presented—all this is abundant proof that in the notion of the national church we are dealing with an immediate consequence of a special conception of life that dominates everything. Expressions of small-mindedness may shore up this system, laziness and a desire for domination may support it, yet this incidentally sinful aspect is never the main point. The main point is that these advocates acknowledge with us that the blessing of the gospel reaches *further* than the souls of the elect. They also believe in an influence that emanates from the gospel upon common organic human life, but they imagine that this blessing can be secured only by incorporating that human life to its full extent, and thus as national life, into the church.

Thus the system of the *national church* is diametrically opposed to the doctrine of the *church as organism*. For the proponents of the latter confess that we must not want to limit the influence of Christ to elect persons, as if nothing else of Christ were noticeable on earth except the work of the Holy Spirit in regenerate persons. Such nominalism is rejected by both sides, and the proponents of the church as organism as well as the men of the national church concede that the Christian religion also impacts the organism of our human life. But only those who speak of the church as organism, as distinct from the institution of the church, maintain that the blessing of God in that broader sphere can work as intended only if the institutional church organizes itself according to the requirements given in the Word, and if baptism, as a sacrament of the Lord, is administered only to the believers and their seed, and such under a constant purification by means of church discipline. They therefore distinguish between the church as institution and as organism, and they do this in order that justice may be done to both the sacredness of the covenant among those who confess Christ and the influence that must go out into this world outside this sphere. § 3

But precisely this is impossible if we adopt the position of the national church. For in that position there is only one sphere, and that sphere is the church as institution. The influence of the Christian religion stretches no further than that sphere, and for that reason, if the nation is to share in that blessing, *that entire nation must be in the church*. And in order for this to be possible, the essence of the church and the holiness of God's covenant are sacrificed for the interests of the nation. By contrast, we confess the reality of two spheres.

First is the sphere of confessing believers, or the objective church, the sphere of the covenant. As the Heidelberg Catechism states, baptism extends exclusively over this first sphere, that the baptized may be "distinguished from the children of unbelievers."[2] Only within that sphere is the Lord's Supper administered, and [only] in that sphere is an "assembly of believers" recognized. Only the church that coincides with this sphere possesses the hallmarks of the true church: the pure preaching of the gospel, the pure administration of the sacraments, and the practice of church discipline for correcting faults in both confession and life.[3]

But we do not stop here. This church as institution does not cover *all* that is called Christian. Even though the lamp of the Christian religion burns only within the walls of that institution, its light shines through the windows far beyond it and shines upon all those aspects and connections of our human life that express themselves in various manifestations of human life and human activity. Jurisprudence, law, family, business, occupation, public opinion and literature, art and science, and so forth—the light shines upon all of this, and that illumination will be all the more powerful and penetrating the more clearly and purely the lamp of the gospel is allowed to burn within the institution of the church.

In addition to the first sphere of the church as institution, and necessarily related to it, we are acquainted with a second sphere as well, determined by the length of the beam of light that proceeds from the institutional church out across the life of people and nation. Because this second sphere is not attached to specific persons, it is neither determined nor circumscribed by the registering of a certain number of members, nor does it have its own office bearers, but it is absorbed into the very life of people and nation; therefore, this influence that works outside the church as institution points us to the church as organism. For the church as organism exists prior to the institution; it always stands behind the institution; it is the only thing that truly lends that institution essential value. The church as organism has its center in heaven, in Christ. It encompasses all the ages from the beginning of the world to its end, in order after us to fill all eternity. And it is therefore this church as organism that can manifest itself where all personal faith is absent but where something of the golden luster of eternal life nevertheless is reflected on the common skyline of the grand edifice of human life.

§ 4 In fact, therefore, *both sides* desire the same end, but they part ways on the question of how we must think about and achieve the influence of the Christian religion beyond the persons of believers. The devotee of the

2. Heidelberg Catechism, Lord's Day 27, Q&A 74.
3. See Belgic Confession, Art. 29.

national church answers this question thus: "You cannot have an influence on who or on what is not incorporated into your ecclesiastical institution. And therefore the whole nation must be included within my church, and I baptize all who come into the house of baptism. The light is burning only in my church. Outside my church is nothing but the deepest darkness of night. My church has no windows. The walls do not let through any ray of light. And for this reason, I must extend the walls of my church so that everyone may find a place in it and may rejoice in the radiance of the light of the gospel."

By contrast, we say that as the Word of God and our Heidelberg Catechism say, baptism must separate believers from the children of unbelievers. In the first place we therefore must take care that the church as institution be recognizable by the marks of the true church, that it clearly manifest itself, identified plainly and with boundaries, in the midst of the people. We should try to attract every person into that church, but only to incorporate into that church those who believe with their heart and confess with their mouth that Christ is the Mediator of God and men, they and their seed. The Christian church must be on its guard that where hypocrites have crept in and betray themselves, they be separated from the gathering of believers. But although the sanctity of the covenant—and together with this, the essence of the true church—must be maintained in this manner, the church of God nevertheless does not know windowless churches. The light that burns in her midst on the candlestand does not exist under the bushel, but it radiates through the windows to the outside. That light spreads its hues on all that is human in the life of people and nation. And it is through an indirect influence that the church as institution blesses the whole people and the whole life of the nation. Indeed, far from wanting to withhold this blessing from our whole nation, we instead maintain that this blessing will be all the greater and all the more glorious the more brightly the light of the gospel shines in God's churches, and in those churches it will burn all the more brightly the purer the flame and the purer the atmosphere in which that flame ascends. Thus it remains according to the rule instituted by Christ himself: His church is a city on a hill that catches everyone's eye from afar. His church is salt in the midst of the life of the world to stem the corruption in that world.

If we clearly grasp the contrast between these two views, then it will also be clear how everything here depends on the correct distinction between particular grace and common grace. If nothing lies under the curse but the world, and in that world [there is] particular grace, then we only see two phenomena in life: a part of the world that is Gentile, Muslim, and Jewish; and a part of the world in which particular grace is at work. The church as institution reaches as far as Christianity extends, and beyond that church there is in fact nothing but sin and ungodliness. And this being the case, the only thing we can do is attempt to expand the sphere of particular grace, surrendering its holy character by incorporating our whole people more and more into our church. In the system of the Roman Catholic Church this works because Rome seeks the essence of the church not in the persons of believers but in the church as mystical institution that as such is the bearer of particular grace. That particular grace then is a treasure entrusted to her, and one can partake of that treasure by entering into fellowship with the church. But it is utterly incomprehensible how people want to maintain this system if they seriously confess to believe that the church as institution is the "gathering of believers in Christ," and thus still subscribe to articles 27–29 of our Confession and question 54 of our Catechism. No one has ever made a direct attempt to harmonize the foundational statements of our Forms of Unity with the system of the national church. This system is nothing but the nationalization of what for Rome is the world church. It has been taken over from tradition, out of spiritual laziness, but it has never been proved before the court of Reformed principles.

The matter becomes quite different when we open our eyes to the Reformed confession of common grace. For in this case there are not *two* but *three* spheres. There is not pitch-dark night in the pagan regions on the one hand and all that is called Christian being baptized and in the church on the other. But there is instead (1) the church as institution, with the lamp of the gospel burning clear and bright within its walls, as the gathering of believers; (2) that part of the world that in Asia and Africa has been given over by God in the negative sense and therefore still walks in complete darkness; and (3) that other part of the world in which the Christian church has manifested itself, the world on which radiates the light of the gospel that shines through the windows of the church. This light that shines out from particular grace serves as means and instrument of common grace, and in this way, beyond the church as institution, in the midst of the life of the nation, a Christian hue is cast over this national life, and in this sense the whole national life is Christianized, even in those spheres where the Christian name is decisively rejected.

If we want proof that this latter perspective alone not only maintains the proper essence of the church and its marks, but also is the only one capable of explaining the facts of life, then note the uncommon power that has been gained by humans over nature precisely in the part of the world that has thus been Christianized. We owe this to the natural sciences, and those sciences have not flourished in China or Japan, not in India or Turkey, but in Christian Europe and Christian America. We can therefore say with certainty that we also must see in the power of these natural sciences a blessing from the Christian religion. From our perspective this is entirely rational. Man was told in paradise that he *would have dominion over nature*. Adam did have that dominion, but through sin it has eluded us. But now comes common grace to stem and restore what would have been lost through sin. This is indeed what common grace does. The power and dominion over nature that is exercised in China and India, and no less under Islam, is far superior to the powerlessness vis-à-vis nature in which the indigenous tribes in Africa have sunk and are descended. But when in common grace the exponential impact that proceeds from the church of Christ and particular grace arrives, then this common grace is multiplied threefold in strength, and we see precisely in the Christian world man's power over nature increase in such an incredible way, and we thank God for it, and applaud this liberation of man. But the system of the national church runs aground here. For it may explain on the basis of its national church the influence that goes out to philanthropy, art, and domestic and social life; nevertheless, steam and electricity, chemistry and economics, fall outside it, and how then can these grand inventions be explained that have characterized our century especially and that increasingly dominate the life of the world?

CHAPTER THIRTY-SIX

A CITY SET ON A HILL

O God, from my youth you have taught me, and I still proclaim your wondrous deeds.

Psalm 71:17

§1 Precisely because the church, according to Jesus' statement, is a city set on a hill [Matt 5:14], its glow must radiate into the distance. Or, stated less figuratively, a sanctifying, cleansing influence must go out from the church of the Lord for the whole of the society in whose midst she arises. That influence must begin by arousing a certain admiration for the valor with which persecution and oppression are borne. It then must inspire reverence for the earnestness and the purity of life in the ecclesiastical sphere. But it also must generate sympathy through the glow of love and compassion that develops in the church. And finally, as a result of this, it must purify and raise general understanding, elevate public opinion, cause these principles to be accepted, and thus carry to a higher level the commonly accepted view of life in state, society, and family.

And this is in fact what has happened. The church of Christ has almost nowhere maintained itself in a sustained fashion without bringing about these changes in the common view of life beyond its circle as well. This did not happen immediately, because the church first had to struggle through a period of persecution. But once it gloriously had survived this period, its way of acting usually—almost without exception, we may say—has resulted in an elevated standard of living. Two things occurred: (1) the confirmation of the church as the "city set on a hill," and (2) a change in civic life beyond the church in an uplifting and cleansing direction. And in both of these lay the natural fruit of two kinds of grace. In the "city set on a hill" was the fruit of *particular grace*, and in the ennobled society was the fruit of *common grace*.

Here too we could impose the strictest demand of the highest ideal, and then raise nothing but complaints about the spiritual misery of the church and the steadily increasing degeneration of society. We would be the last to deny that there is often cause for such complaint. But devotion to our ideal must not tempt us to an unhealthy and dispiriting pessimism. Even the purest church, both elsewhere and in this country, undoubtedly leaves much to be desired. But compared with so many other churches—especially compared with other religious bodies—it still stands on an incomparably higher plane and gives us cause for fervent thanks. And thus we certainly also must complain that in our civil society one injustice is piled upon another and one abomination after another offends us. But when we put it side by side with a pagan or Islamic society, we immediately feel our superiority, sometimes on every point. Take marriage, for example: compare the position of the married woman under paganism and Islam with what it is among us, and the wide difference stands out. It is not as if sin has been exorcised from our midst. On the contrary, sin agitates against the purity of marriage in our society as shamefully as it does elsewhere, and we cannot think of any form of sin in this area that does not occur in every way. But however much we may complain in our country about the still-imperfect position of the married woman, when we compare her position in our society with that in China or Asia Minor, we cannot for a moment be in doubt about the great progress that has been made among us.

And it is the same in every area. As the church of the Lord has been manifested, leaven has been placed in three measures of flour, and this leaven thoroughly permeates and influences all of life's relationships. This is not only an influence that is definitely experienced by the confessors of the Lord, but also one that extends over all of society. It even exercises this influence in such a way that both the Jews and the unbelievers in our midst unknowingly experience this impact. But this is precisely what shows that it is wrong to view this as an element of particular grace. Particular grace always works toward eternal life, and what works here is entirely taken up in time and therefore must be considered as belonging to common grace.

§2 We cannot object to the fact that a society dominated by these influences is usually honored with the name of Christian society or Christianized society. This is not permissible from the perspective of the national church, for the national church starts from the notion that Christian influence is operative in Christian persons alone. If someone does not personally belong to the church, then he also stands outside Christian influence, and for this reason the aim is to enfold the whole mass of the people within the walls of the church. But this cannot be achieved except by acquiescing to appearances, by disregarding the notion of the church, by surrendering our confession, by allowing unbelief to enter, and by abandoning all church discipline. Those who are proponents of the national church and therefore want to herd the whole nation into the sheep pen, must be flexible. For every principle that is applied to unite [also] keeps out and excludes. And since the goal of the national church is to include all and preferably not to exclude anyone, in the end they must untie every bond.

This in fact is what happened and was manifested most strongly in the practical doctrinal freedom that increasingly arose. And where holy baptism still had to be considered indispensable, the logic of the facts necessarily led to abandoning this bond as well. In name, in appearance, the notion of the church is held high. Or do we not see how even the Dutch Reformed Church, which allowed the most unfettered doctrinal freedom and declared baptism not to be indispensable, still proclaims to the people through its teachers that the Three Forms of Unity are still the official confession of the church?[1] But the *appearance* keeps drifting further away from the *essence*. All binding influence on the essence of the church was abandoned, and after this inner dissolution of the essence they put nothing but an abstract formula that lacks any effectiveness. Thus the lie ends up crowding out the truth in the church of Christ, and it is only on the basis of that infamous lie that the pretense of being a church is maintained in name. By contrast, we can maintain on the basis of our position both the essence of the church and the Christian character of society by means of the simple distinction between the fruit of particular grace in "the flock of the Lord" [see Jer 13:17] and the fruit of common grace that is brought about precisely by the activity of the church. And we can do this by acknowledging that the activity of the church exercises a grace that strengthens the working of

1. The Dutch Reformed Church, or Nederlandse Hervormde Kerk (NHK), was the national church in the Netherlands from which Kuyper led a secession in 1886.

common grace in national life in an unusual way. For we do acknowledge that common grace is at work in the civil society of the pagan and Islamic nations too. How much deeper would they have sunk otherwise? But we maintain that, in addition to the common grace at work elsewhere, a *higher degree* of common grace is at work in our countries, and this higher degree enters common grace only when it is strengthened, ennobled, and affirmed by the influence of the church of Christ.

At present people are trying again to dismantle this influence of the church of Christ in civil society. We can see this in the attempts to put free love in the place of marriage, or at least to weaken the bond of marriage. We can see this in the attempts to weaken parental authority and to bring childrearing under the tutelage of the state. And we can see so many more of these kinds of things. §3

The church must be blamed for this. By manifesting itself almost everywhere as national church, it has had to tolerate the lie in its own midst, has therefore entered into all kinds of false relationships, and on account of this, can no longer exercise the natural influence that initially went out from it. Often the national church ties itself to the opponents of Christianity to obstruct those who plead for the exercise of Christian influence. Zealous advocates for the Christian character of state and society thus see themselves hampered in executing their duty, all the more so because there are still so many who cannot conceive of any other way to Christianize society except to gather all into one church and Christianize society institutionally. We can therefore exercise a force for good if we get it firmly into our mind that the church of Christ can never affect civil society directly but only indirectly through its influence, and that therefore we must always strive (1) to ensure that the church of the Lord will always have full freedom of action and the full power to maintain its own character; (2) to resist every attempt to replace Christian notions with pagan concepts and notions in the legislation of our country, in public opinion, and in public institutions; and (3) to steadily expand in every area of that civil society the dominance of nobler and purer notions by the courageous behavior of her members. Stated more succinctly, we advocate a rigorously confessional church, but not a confessional civil society, not a confessional state.

This secularization of state and society is one of the deepest foundational notions of Calvinism, although it goes without saying that Calvinism has not succeeded in immediately working out this foundational notion in its pure form. Acting in a world that for centuries had held, and brought into practice, a diametrically opposite notion, Calvinism could only gradually develop its new view of life. But the result shows that this foundational notion is increasingly gaining ground, and that the continuing development in the life of the nations increasingly does justice to this secularization of state and society. It cannot be contradicted that the false idea of the French Revolution temporarily inserted itself here, through which the foundational notion of Calvinism was falsified. But that does not deny the fact that Calvinism has cultivated from its own root the conviction that the church of Christ, because it must be strictly confessional and maintain Christian discipline, cannot be a national church, and that therefore the Christian character of society cannot be sought in the baptism of all members of the nation. Instead, that character must be sought in the influence that goes out from the church of the Lord to the whole nation and the whole organization of the native land. The church of Christ envisions through her influence on state and civil society only a *moral triumph*, not the establishing of confessional ties, nor the exercise of authoritarian dominance. The example of the United States of America shows how the various parts of the Christian church, as soon as they all adopt this same position together, not only give up the mutual contest of vying peaceably with one another in the area of faith, but also—especially because of that good mutual understanding—exert a much greater influence on the civil and national circumstances than the mightiest national church was ever able to accomplish.

§4 The contrast between the church and the world can be done full justice only in this way. At present either this contrast is a fiction or we must seek the world in the church. To a certain degree we can most definitely say that "the world" must be sought in the spheres of pagan, Islamic, and Jewish life, but we find that contrast only momentarily compelling. When holy Scripture shows us the church of Christ, as opposed to the world, and warns us against conforming to the world, it refers to a non-Christian quality of life with which we come into contact daily and whose temptation we experience daily. Where can we find this world? In response people point to worldly arenas, worldly associations, worldly amusements, worldly literature, and worldly institutions. However, when you check the persons who constitute these worldly arenas, you will find that virtually everyone has been baptized and admitted to the Lord's Supper and is a member of Christ's church. In this case there is no contrast between church and world. Instead, there is within the church a contrast between Christians who confess the essence of the church and nominal Christians who stand entirely opposed to the essence of the church.

But if we come to see that those thousands upon thousands of persons who really and truly do not believe in anything, who never consider repentance, and who ridicule the sacred do not belong in Christ's church; if we come to see that the church must separate itself from them and once again return to its roots; if we come to see that the church of Christ, reduced to that small proportion, has once again become the essential church—only then will the church be able again to exercise her influence on state and society; only then will the scriptural contrast between church and world return; only then will church and world become two entities; only then will the church of Christ possess its demonstrable boundaries; and only then will it make sense to call out to the church that it must not bend to the pernicious influence of the world, but must rather exercise a blessed, sanctifying, and refreshing influence on that world. Then it will be understood again what conformity to the world is.

From this our opponents see that they wrongfully lay claim to the privilege of being the only ones with a heart for *all* of society, for the *whole* nation, and for *all* of civil society. On the contrary, we share this in common. The difference between us and them emerges only when it comes to *how* the blessing of Christ's church must go out to that civil society—whether that blessing comes directly, by incorporating the entire nation, confessing or not, believing or not, into the bosom of the church; or indirectly, by letting the church stand as a city on a hill in the midst of civil society and allowing its influence to elevate and ennoble that society to proceed indirectly from the church to civil society.

Of course it also remains our desire and our prayer that we might bring all our compatriots to the full confession of the gospel. But this result, for which we pray, is never achieved. In earlier centuries as well as now, and now to an increasing degree, the result shows that the *greater* part of our compatriots are hostile toward the gospel or ignore it in lukewarm, Laodicean fashion [see Rev 3:14–22]. If the church of Christ only has room for those who "believe with the heart and confess with the mouth," as our Confession states, then for every person of Reformed heritage it has been determined that, whatever the future may bring, we must reckon for the time being with the fact that among our compatriots the smaller portion has its place in the church and the greater portion its place in the world.[2] This being the case, it does not help if we look for the blessing for our nation in the bringing into the church of all who continue to tarry and have not come in. No other way remains open but to bless our nation and country indirectly and mediately by making the church of Christ once again a city set on a hill, and by once again letting the influence radiate from her that stems the evil in the world and elevates the life of civil society by strengthening the working of common grace in the life of the world. This is not a church that, in order to appear grand, carries the lie in "the folds of its garment" [see Hag 2:12], but only a church of the Lord that keeps the covenant of God sacred and remains satisfied with more modest proportions, acts *morally*, and can thereby exert *moral* influence.

§5 This rather extended discussion of the national church was necessary here because such a considerable portion of the working of common grace remains invisible as long as the national church is erected around and over the common terrain of life. We therefore will pass by what else could be said in connection with the national church. Our only goal here was to reveal this aspect of common grace that is overlooked the most because it is hidden. We now return to the meaning of that element of common grace with repentance in view, a meaning that will be grasped immediately when we compare the conversion of a pagan in a pagan country with the conversion of a baptized child in this country.

In missions, the continual complaint rightly has to do with the incomplete way the Christian life and the Christian confession find expression in a converted native person. Those who go from our church to Java or Sumba and there encounter the Christian natives are bitterly disappointed.[3] In this country we often hear the complaint about a deficient knowledge of Scripture, about the lack of insight into the Christian truth, about poor spiritual sensibility, and about a less puritan earnestness of life. But what remains of all this when we apply to such a converted Javanese the same yardstick that we use in this country? Then we are involuntarily faced with the question whether everything rests on self-deception and deceit, and whether every thought of carrying out fruitful missions among these people must be permanently abandoned. This impression is natural. If we fail to take into account the entirely different conditions under which

2. Belgic Confession, Art. 1.
3. Kuyper refers here to islands in Indonesia.

a pagan in a pagan country, or a Muslim in an Islamic country, comes to repentance, and if we imagine that we will finds things on Java the same as on Walcheren, and on Sumba about the same as on Urk, then we *must* end up being bitterly disappointed and deceived.[4] We are in serious danger of the improper spiritual conceit of feeling ourselves far elevated above the Christian native, and we risk letting the love that should have gone out to them dissipate.

But this judgment changes drastically, and we look at the circumstances quite differently, when we pay attention to the very different help that common grace supplies in the work of conversion in this country and on Java. When Christianity first went out into the world, it initially did not manifest itself among the nations that stood on a lower plane, which had experienced the blessing of common grace only in very small measure. On the contrary, it was manifest among those nations of the Levant among whom the working of common grace had been strongest up to that time. Apart from the question of whether at that time some messengers of the gospel already had gone to the Scythians and Parthians, it is a fact that the Christian church first achieved a solid formation in Rome and in Athens, in Asia Minor and in Egypt—precisely in those regions where the Greco-Roman civilization had reached the highest form of life then known. A civilization in which men like Plato and Cicero could emerge stood at that time on an incomparably much higher plane, of course, than the social conditions in which we still find the native on Borneo and Java.

At this point we will not discuss any further the path along which the civilization of that time had climbed to reach that level, nor what influence for good had been exerted by the Jewish colonies (among others) that lay scattered across the whole Roman Empire. It is enough for us to establish the fact that the Christian church, to be able to make its entrance into the world, saw its appointed course among those peoples that at the time stood on the highest plane. Only after the Christian church had taken on a fixed form among these peoples did the gospel go out, two or three centuries later, to the less advanced Celtic and Germanic tribes. And if the penetration of the spirit of Christ was difficult even in this more highly developed Greco-Roman world, as is apparent from the apostolic epistles, then it goes without saying that the same difficulty must occur to a much greater extent where

4. Walcheren and Urk are islands in the Netherlands.

we try to bring the gospel through our missions to a society that exists on a much lower level, such as we find in our Dutch East Indies. Especially disappointing is the fact that what we can achieve for the time being must make an extremely painful impression if we compare it with what we find in the best circles in our country. It is therefore no minor error that in connection with the work of missions, people so rarely and so inadequately consider the various stages in which common grace works *in a preparatory manner* for the work of conversion.

§6 This is not suggesting in any way that conversion itself would ever be a product of common grace. Conversion is the result of regeneration and is possible and conceivable only in the born-again individual. To put it even more strongly, the result of regeneration in conversion and later in sanctification never comes about except through the working of the Holy Spirit and, since it aims at eternal life, belongs unconditionally to particular grace. It is entirely decisive for a plant in what kind of soil we let it grow. If the soil is fertile and suited to the nature of the plant, then the plant's growth in that soil will be secure and verdant. But if we put the same plant in poor soil that is stony and arid, then the plant will sprout but yield only a very meager result. Even our average farmer knows this very well, and therefore he makes a distinction between various types of land and knows exactly which crop will do best in one kind of soil and which in another. But is this why the crop comes up out of the soil? Certainly not. The plant comes from the seed or from the cutting, and that seed and that cutting are one and the same, whether the soil is poor or rich, suitable or unsuitable. Similarly, the seed of regeneration remains one and always comes from the outside. But when this same seed of regeneration falls one time on the well-prepared soil of a life of high standing, and the other time on the poor soil of a low-level commoner, then the results *must* be very different. The plant remains of the true sort, for the seed was the true seed, but the soil on which it fell differed greatly, and that difference between the kinds of soil came about through the differing degree to which common grace was allotted to the one nation or the other.

CHAPTER THIRTY-SEVEN

COMMON GRACE IN SANCTIFICATION

For we hear that some among you walk in idleness, not busy at work, but busybodies. Now such persons we command and encourage in the Lord Jesus Christ to do their work quietly and to earn their own living.

2 THESSALONIANS 3:11–12

We now come to the meaning of common grace in the work of sanctification. §1
What we have considered up to this point in our discussion of common grace and the Christian referred exclusively to our being brought to Christ through regeneration and conversion. In this discussion it appeared that the fruit of particular grace is used by God in countries where Christ's church was manifested, in order to make common grace uncommonly much stronger: negatively by stemming sin more strongly, and positively by advancing in completely miraculous ways the development of what was embedded in our race at creation. Comparing a non-Christianized country to a Christianized one shows clearly how Christ's church exerted this dual influence on national life. But in this context the question arose whether this was an influence that the church exercised in its own sphere (that is, in the sphere of particular grace) or an influence proceeding from the church that was exerted on nonecclesiastical life and thus benefited

common grace. The former was the assertion of the national church, which we disputed. The latter appeared to us to be the teaching of holy Scripture and was advocated by us. Nonecclesiastical life achieved independence in family, society, and state; and the influence for good that emanated from the church worked on everyone, believers as well as unbelievers. The fruit of this was that the person living in a Christian country who is awakened to conversion is supported in this by a richly saturated environment that can elevate him, whereas conversely, the person who is called to Christ in a pagan country or among Jews or Muslims is oppressed and pulled down by an environment that exists on a level so much lower.

But now the same question returns when we deal with sanctification. One who has been converted is neither lifted out of his environment nor transposed into another world, but remains (at least as a rule) in the same family, the same household, and the same occupation or business, in part even in the same environment. This is not stated in an absolute sense, as if someone's conversion does not cause a certain breach in his life. That breach is always present, mostly virtually unnoticeable but sometimes very strongly. A young man raised in unbelieving circles, who until now only had worldly-minded friends and who gave himself with them to the service of the world, will of course change friends when he converts, unless his old friends let themselves be enticed by him to come to Christ. If the latter happens, so much the better; then the circle of friends remains unbroken but is transposed to an entirely different sphere of life. But if the friends kick against the goads, laugh at his piety, and lament the fact that "such a decent guy" has become a fanatic, then of course the breach must come, and after his conversion the young man leaves his former circle of friends to find other friends among the believers in the Lord. Similarly, someone who has worked in a business or occupation might no longer be able to continue in this line of work as a convert to Christ; he too will try to leave and find another job.

We therefore wholeheartedly admit that someone who is converted in a Christian country might be constrained to break with his former surroundings and to move into another environment. But—and we must pay attention to this—the reason for this is only that he lived in a church that was not the way it should be. He was assumed to have been born and raised in an unbelieving, worldly circle. Well then, we find such families in the national church by the thousands, but they do not belong in the church of Christ. With the exception of hypocrites, all families that belong to the church of Christ are confessing families, and church discipline sees to it that in these families there can be no worldly life that manifests itself externally. Even though we admit that conversion may lead to breaches, including in our Christian country, we admit this only with regard to a *false* church, not a church of Christ as it must be. If the church is unfit, if the church has ossified or been poisoned by worldly sensibilities, then the spiritual guidance of the converted goes over into mystical or Methodist hands, and we end up with thoroughly false conditions like those found again and again in the national church.

Consider a family that in name belongs to the church, has been baptized and received into the church, but lacks any trace of faith or any urge to bear testimony, and lives wholly in the world. When in that so-called Christian family a young man or young woman converts to Christ, there certainly will be in that family no hymn of praise that the child has been brought to Christ, but a lamenting and complaining that it is impossible to live under one roof with such a fanatical child and that the child is lost to the family. These are conditions that cannot be condemned too strongly. And it is only these false conditions that compel us to admit that even in a Christian country and among baptized people, conversion can lead to such a tremendous breach with one's environment.

But if, on the other hand, we leave aside such thoroughly false conditions, §2
and if we assume a church that corresponds even to a small degree to the marks of the true church, so that it keeps God's covenant holy and church discipline involves confession and life, then such a tremendous breach cannot occur in the case of baptized children. Only Christian families can belong to a Christian church, and in a Christian family no lamenting and complaining can occur if a child of the family is converted. Just as it is among the angels of God, there will instead be jubilation and thanksgiving in a Christian family. Conversion will then lead, not to a breach, but rather to the reverse, to a closer spiritual bond. Nor is it likely that someone from a Christian household will find himself in an occupation or business that is sinful in nature, which therefore would have to be given up after conversion. The only thing that can happen is that a young man might have come from a Christian home but not been converted until [just] now. Perhaps he had ventured into a circle of friends and playmates who no longer fit in with him after his conversion; now he would have to leave them on that account. It *is* possible, however, that someone might have grown up in a Christian household that is spiritless, dull of tone and spiritually lackluster, and that

such a newly converted person might be offended at the spiritual dullness of his family. The truly converted will not see this as a cause for him to break with his household, but on the contrary, as an opportunity for having, under the grace of God, an inspiring and edifying effect on the heart of his loved ones. And sometimes such a newly converted person turns away from his loved ones to join exclusively with persons outside the home who are spiritually more alive, but this is definite proof that the conversion of such a person was not on the right track, that he underestimated the sacred bonds God had established, that he lacked an all-encompassing love, and that he was in danger of straying on paths of spiritual pride.

If we therefore assume normal, healthy church conditions and a conversion that follows a clear course, then no breach worthy to be called such will occur, and one will continue to live in the same environment after his conversion as before. For we may say that his conversion consists in the fact that he converts from the world to Christ. But if he belonged to a good and healthy church from his youth on, this conversion cannot apply to his domestic environment; otherwise, his household would have been serving the world, and that is unthinkable in normal, good church relationships. For the transition of such a person from the world to Christ does not consist in an external transition, by means of a visible breach, but in a banishing of the world from his heart, from his affections and his inclinations. Even so, it must be the case that in a healthy church anyone who undergoes conversion must achieve a closer bond with his church and grow more fully into the life of his church precisely through that conversion. And this is in fact how it is where the church can hold up its head with honor, and fulfills her calling.

We can even say that children who grew up in such a home environment come only very rarely to what is called a dramatic conversion. A transition from the kingdom of darkness can no longer occur in them, because they have indeed been conceived and born in sin, and were therefore subject to all miseries, even condemnation, but they also were sanctified in Christ and baptized as members of his church. Already as small children, as children of believers, they must therefore be distinguished from the children of unbelievers. They grew up in a Christian household. They have been accustomed to dealing with sacred things since childhood. They know God's Word and his commandments. And thus we see generally that the transformation of their sensibilities and mind and their more conscious coming to the Savior occurs not suddenly but more gradually, even to such a degree that more than one who has entered eternity with rejoicing can have a hard time determining when he converted to his God. That moment did occur. There was a moment when the scales tipped, but not everyone pays such close attention to the course of their spiritual life that they can speak about it in retrospect with certainty.

"Giving testimony" of being saved, as it is called, is extremely easy for those who came to Jesus from a dead, worldly sphere, but it is extremely difficult for those who grew up with the Word of God and never became entangled with the world. Later reflection, deeper insight into the terrible contrast between sin and grace, also will bring that person to clearer insight into his or her conversion, but this is something quite different from having consciously lived through it. A child several years old can have suffered shipwreck with his parents and have been saved as through a miracle; at that moment he neither knew nor comprehended anything of his suffering, but when he looks back at that terrible moment, he may realize in retrospect very well how he was saved from the jaws of death and thank his God for it. But for such a child the cause of this thanksgiving arises only *later*, not out of his own reflection but from what his own thinking tells him *must* have happened to him without his having lived through it himself with clear knowledge and insight. The application of this image is self-evident. The more sick and ill a church is, the more the transition will speak to those who convert. And equally, the more unspiritual the household was in which we grew up, the more strongly will the moment of conversion be etched in our mind. But conversely, the purer and higher our church lives are, and the higher the plane of the household is into which God caused us to be born, the less the burgeoning of genuine faith will be noticed in us. In an essentially Reformed church—that is, in a church that is Reformed and lives according to the Word of God—most of [the members] will live from infancy in the fear of the Lord, and with virtually no transition in their heart break with the world to serve their King and Savior.

If in this latter case the convert's environment remains the same as it was before, the same is true of his life outside the church. As we already stated, when he is converted, he is not removed from the people, his country, his society, his work, and his social environment, but he continues to live in the same circles. For we have to separate ourselves from a "brother . . . if he is guilty of sexual immorality" [1 Cor 5:11] and we must therefore as members of the church exercise church discipline, but the apostle adds emphatically that we cannot separate ourselves from all wrongdoers, since we "would need to go out of the world" [1 Cor 5:10]. "I pray," Jesus said in his moving supplication before he went to Golgotha, not "that you take them out of the world but that you keep them from the evil one"—that is, "that you preserve them in the world" [see John 17:15]. This touches on a principle: we must reject the notion of a national church that allows the world within its own bosom, to which belong all kinds of utterly unbelieving persons, a church composed of households many of which decry all true faith as fanaticism. But we must resist the Anabaptist notion that the church is a church purely of saints, saints who should place themselves outside the world. The one who repents does not leave the world, but as one who confesses the Lord, he must live *in the world* for Christ. The former is much easier, but we are charged with the latter.

A baptized person who converts will extend his heart to the world with something of the love with which God loved the world when he gave the world his only Son. The hour will come when that person will judge the world together with all God's saints, but in the present day of grace he will still embrace that world in the love of compassion, live in its midst, and try to be an influence for good in it, by fulfilling his calling to be a witness to Christ and to bring his gospel to all creatures too. For it is very easy to be enthusiastic about missions, and to give money, and to hold prayer meetings for a missionary endeavor in a pagan country or among Muslims—but this is nothing but cowardice if we think that by doing this, we are finished, and if we do not have the courage to act equally decisively and boldly in our own surroundings. Only the one who dares to act in his own surroundings in a variety of areas of life for his Savior and for the people of his Savior, is worthy to reach out his hand toward missions in those far-away countries. The Reformed therefore have always urged those who are converted to manifest zeal for the Lord first in their own immediate environment, in their own sphere of living, in the midst of their ordinary activities. If things are going well, we do not withdraw from life but enter into it and try to serve our Savior in that life, not as a quasi-preacher without credentials but as a citizen among fellow citizens, in the multiplicity of aspects of the life of society and according to the nature of that life. But then, it goes without saying, we also remain in constant touch with that environment, and conversely, a certain influence proceeds to us from that environment. If the path that we must follow from conversion until death is the path of *sanctification*, then this raises the question for us concerning what significance the environment in which a converted individual lives after his conversion has for his progress in sanctification.

The implication of this question is typically considered to be purely dubious and dangerous. The individual is converted, but the life of the world is still unconverted. He can exert influence for good on his environment, but conversely, the influence that the world exerts on him cannot be considered anything but very bad. The greater his influence on his environment, the better; the greater the influence of his environment on him, the worse for his spiritual welfare. Of course, we immediately admit this in part. To the extent that the world lives out of sin, is focused on itself and not on God, and withdraws from the eternal to be engrossed in what is before its eyes, the converted individual must resist it and arm himself against it. Waking, praying, fighting is the watchword here. But, and this is all too often overlooked, *sin is not the only thing at work in that world.* For a world in which only sin were at work would have to be deprived of all grace, and precisely this is not true. Grace is also at work in the world, and that grace is what we call common grace, a grace that is never salvific but most definitely arrests sin and promotes development.

This is the point where common grace also touches on our sanctification. §3
It is not as if sanctification in its root and impulse does not come from the indwelling of the Holy Spirit. But the form, the life form, in which sanctification manifests itself, and how strongly it breaks through, depends in so many respects on the degree, be it greater or lesser, to which grace works in our environment. A contrast that is not to be misunderstood comes to us from the apostolic age to clarify this. At the beginning of this chapter, we placed as Scripture the admonition of the apostle to the church of Thessalonica: "For we hear that some among you walk in idleness, not busy at work, but busybodies. Now such persons we command and encourage in the Lord Jesus Christ to do their work quietly and to earn their own living." Thus, in this Christian church many were guilty of "walking in idleness," of doing nothing but being busy with idle things, being busybodies. And despite the extent to which sanctification was powerfully at work—so that the apostle could even say, "We ought always to give thanks to God for you, brothers, as is right, because your faith is growing abundantly, and the love of every one of you for one another is increasing. Therefore we ourselves boast about you in the churches of God" [2 Thess 1:3–4]—yet *on this point* sanctification had not worked strongly enough, and not all, but at least some, were leading a life that among us is unthinkable for Christians. They were wasting their time, squandering their life, and not doing anything. They ate their family's bread and generally spent the whole day walking

here and there, participating in all kinds of conversations and pretending to be curious and occupied with many things and always being busy, thus vexing the more sober minded.

Would something like this have occurred in a church in Palestine, or in a village church that consisted mostly of farmers? Do we also read of such a temptation to sin in the epistles written to non-Greek churches? No. This evil could in fact rear its head virtually only in Greek cities. The young people there were used to this kind of idle life of doing nothing. The custom there was to leave the work to slaves and lesser people and to spend one's life in so-called higher spheres. Did conversion result in the Christians of Athens, of Corinth, of Thessalonica magically getting rid of this idle view of life and becoming industrious, serious citizens? This had not happened in every case, and we see from what Paul wrote to Thessalonica that there too, among the *converted* youth, the old evil was still active, and the apostle had to oppose this continuation of the old evil very sharply and earnestly.

§4 And just as with that walking in idleness, so too was the situation with sexual immorality and the other sins of lasciviousness. This sin was found in the church in Jerusalem and the rest of Palestine as well, of course, but not in the same measure by far as among the wanton Greeks. All kinds of sexual sins were prevalent in a terrible way, especially in the Greek cities, and public opinion lacked the moral resilience to stand up for decency. In this connection, we see that in his letters the Apostle Paul continually was compelled to draw attention to the insidious spread of this sin in the church of Christ in these Greek cities too, and to oppose this evil with uncommon severity and admonition. Here conversion had indeed occurred. The churches even bore all kinds of persecution and oppression with heroic courage. Their readiness to sacrifice in support of the churches in Palestine was even a cause of praise and thanksgiving for Paul. But this did not contradict the fact that among them sanctification had not yet overcome the sin of sensuality, and that there still occurred situations among them that would have been unthinkable in the Jewish churches. It was not much better with banquets. The Greek was a reveler by nature. There were constant feasts, banquets, and dinners. And thus the abomination occurred among them, although not in Palestine, of abusing the holy Lord's Supper as if it were a sacrificial meal in a pagan temple, "not discerning the Lord's body" [see 1 Cor 11:29]. We can no longer imagine this, but in Corinth there were those who had turned the Lord's Supper into a drinking bout and erased any distinction between the table of the devils and the table of the Lord.

Superficially we would say that all those who behaved this way were hypocrites, but Paul does not deal with the issue in these terms. He perceives that what was happening here is merely a lack of sanctification that can be explained entirely from the environment in which they lived, and that must be opposed therefore all the more vigorously.

These examples are coarse, disgusting, and offensive. But when we come to see how in the churches in Palestine *other* sins were rampant that were linked to the Jewish life, it shows that progress in sanctification, as least in terms of its form in daily life, most definitely depends on the way of life, customs, and public opinion that are dominant in the environment where the church of Christ functions. Common grace works more strongly and differently in one environment than in another. The form and degree to which sanctification manifests itself will correspond to how this action of common grace occurs in the country, among the people, and in the city or town where the church of Christ functions and where the conversion of the believers occurs. If this is the case, then it is important to pursue this discussion further, and in connection with our view of sanctification, to give greater consideration—more than has occurred thus far—to common grace.

CHAPTER THIRTY-EIGHT

THE GRAFTING OF THE WILD TREE

Therefore, if anyone is in Christ, he is a new creation. The old has passed away; behold, the new has come.

2 CORINTHIANS 5:17

§1 Already on the basis of the preceding brief remarks, the reader will readily agree that we must take common grace into account in the work of sanctification. It nevertheless is extremely difficult to elucidate the distinction between the work of saving grace and the work of common grace in this matter. It is not that there is any doubt as to the reality of that distinction, but we lack the words and formulations to clearly keep separate the relationships and workings of the inner life of the soul. We make do with metaphorical language and compare the soul with a plant, even as Jesus spoke of the evil tree that cannot produce good fruit, or compared himself to a vine and us to the branches; or we clarify the working of the Word upon the soul by means of the image of the sower. This helps us in the right direction. Nevertheless, it remains metaphor and neither perfectly nor completely expresses the essential, spiritual quality of what occurs in the soul.

But we cannot escape this. When we trace the origin of language, we find that ultimately every expression for something invisible in our existence or everyday life is always derived from something tangible and visible. Even common expressions such as "grasping" something, "comprehending" something, and "objecting" to something are all derived from taking something with our hands or throwing something in someone's way. These kinds of expressions allow for a relatively clear delineation because they express an action, but it becomes much more difficult when we come to words such as *soul*, *mind*, and *sensibility*. And any kind of clear comprehension or clear conception escapes us when it comes to expressions such as "inner growth," "inward struggle," and "joints," which Paul refers to. Hence it becomes so hopelessly confusing when we come to speak of "the old man" and "the new man," or when Paul states that "If I do what I do not want, ... it is no longer I who do it, but sin that dwells within me" [Rom 7:16–17]. Even competent, clever thinkers who are accustomed to choosing their words with care appear to be mistaken from time to time. What will be the result then if common folk, who are guided more by inner senses or impressions, attempt to analyze such mysterious statements?

And yet, even though speaking about everything that occurs in the recesses of our soul's life is so extremely difficult, not one of us doubts that there exist *two kinds* of life at our regeneration, as our Confession expresses it so beautifully: "the one corporal and temporal, which they have from the first birth and is common to all men." But "the other [is] spiritual and heavenly, which is given them in their second birth, which is effected by the Word of the gospel, in the communion of the body of Christ; and this life is not common, but is peculiar to God's elect."[1] In those who have been born again everything thus appears before us in a twofold way, assuming two kinds of form, with two distinct operations. This is further complicated by the reality that the area of the inner life is already so mystical. Therefore, speaking about the hidden life of the heart, which is already so difficult, becomes doubly problematic. We must realize this so that we may be careful in how we state things, and not lose ourselves in generalities.

It is therefore advisable to look first at the contrast between the two §2
kinds of life where it still manifests itself in unmixed form—that is, in very small children who are taken from us early through death. It does not need to be pointed out that among these children there are those who immediately prior to dying had two kinds of life within them. Everyone agrees with

1. Belgic Confession, Art. 35.

this. Otherwise we would fall into the heresy either that these children were not conceived and born in sin, and thus could be saved without regeneration, or that they would have to be excluded from all God's mercy. As Reformed Christians we do neither the one nor the other, and our confession therefore remains that "our children are conceived and born in sin, and therefore are children of wrath," but also that God is capable of raising such an infant to a new life and leading the child into his salvation.[2] In their case, there is of course no conversion, but there is regeneration. The dual life spoken of in article 35 of the Confession is thus present in them too, but neither the natural life nor the life of grace has reached any development in them.

While bodily functions may already work in such an infant, the functions of the soul of the natural life do not work yet. Nor is there any development of the life of grace in such an infant. Such an infant does not yet know what it is to believe, does not yet know a spiritual battle, has not yet scored victories in the battle against sin. Everything is still dormant in such an infant. There is life, but there are no manifestations of it yet. The sweet creature carries the seed of life in the soil of the soul, but that seed has not yet sprouted. But when such an infant dies, without having come to any development here on earth, the child nevertheless enters eternal life, and in dying the child dies forever to the sinful life that was received in his natural birth; his sanctification is suddenly completed at his death, and in the life of such an infant, the new life that was received at his second birth unfolds pure and untainted. In such an infant the distinction is therefore clear. The life of the soul that was received from his natural birth does not come to development but dies off; however, the life of the soul that was received in his second birth comes to unfolding in eternal life, without any admixture and with purity. Everyone can understand this.

But it becomes more complicated and difficult when such an infant does not die but grows up to become a boy, a young man, and an adult. For then the natural life of his soul begins to develop with its sinful nature and wrong inclinations, and side by side with the natural *life of his soul* comes the radically different development of his *life of grace*. This is clear as day in the life of a man like David. When he falls into his terrible sin and moves Uriah

2. See "The Form for the Administration of Baptism to Infants of Believers," in *The Psalms and Hymns: With the Catechism, Confession of Faith, and Canons, of the Synod of Dort, and Liturgy of the Reformed Protestant Dutch Church in North America* (Philadelphia: Mentz & Rouvoudt, 1847), 59.

out of the way in order to cover up his scandalous incident with Bathsheba, we see the terrible manifestation of his natural life [2 Sam 11:1–12:23]. And when that same David later falls down before God in sackcloth and ashes, and begs so movingly, "Have mercy on me, O God, hear my prayer,"[3] then we hear in Psalm 51 a man who now leads each child of God to sing in tones more profound than those that often would have come out of our own heart. Those two manifestations of such a different and divergent life are mixed together in the adult, and no matter how these two war with one another, they nevertheless are expressions of the same self. The consequence of this, then, is that a man like Paul can arrive in Romans 7 at confessions arising out of the experiences of his own soul that are still confusing when we read them and that for centuries have led to very diverse sentiments: on the one hand, that in Romans 7 he is speaking as someone as yet *unconverted*, and on the other hand, that here a child of God is speaking *after* his conversion.

Undoubtedly only the latter is correct. It is not the unconverted person who is speaking here. An unconverted individual cannot say, "I thank God through Jesus Christ my Lord." But even if this is certain, it is nevertheless understandable that a superficial reading of Romans 7 can lead one astray. Or who can give a clear explanation of each step in the sequence of thoughts when the apostle says,

> So the law is holy, and the commandment is holy and righteous and good. Did that which is good, then, bring death to me? By no means! It was sin, producing death in me through what is good, in order that sin might be shown to be sin, and through the commandment might become sinful beyond measure. For we know that the law is spiritual, but I am of the flesh, sold under sin. For I do not understand my own actions. For I do not do what I want, but I do the very thing I hate. Now if I do what I do not want, I agree with the law, that it is good. So now it is no longer I who do it, but sin that dwells within me. For I know that nothing good dwells in me, that is, in my flesh. For I have the desire to do what is right, but not the ability to carry it out. For I do not do the good I want, but the evil I do not want

3. See Psalm 51:1 in *Het boek der Psalmen, nevens de gezangen bij de Hervormde Kerk van Nederland* (Leiden: Hoogeveen, 1773), 129.

> is what I keep on doing. Now if I do what I do not want, it is no longer I who do it, but sin that dwells within me. [Rom 7:12–20]

Indeed, at first reading, we might involuntarily conclude that the man who wrote in this vein has lost himself in absurdities and contradictions. But if anything is clear here, it is that two kinds of life are involved: the one as it came from nature, and the other as it originated in regeneration. And if for the time being we stick with this firm result, there is no doubt that this new life lives out of particular grace, and that whatever good still remains in that old life can only be the fruit of common grace. But let us pay close attention, closer than we have to this point, to the twofold source from which grace flows toward both the new and the old life.

§3 If we ask holy Scripture whether this new life grows into the old life in such a way that it mixes with the sinful character of that old life, then the answer is definitely in the negative. "No one born of God makes a practice of sinning, for God's seed abides in him; and he cannot keep on sinning, because he has been born of God," says the Apostle John [1 John 3:9]. And he repeats it in 1 John 5:18: "We know that everyone who has been born of God does not keep on sinning, but he who was born of God protects him, and the evil one does not touch him." This is in quite the same spirit as when Paul says, "Therefore, if anyone is in Christ, he is a new creation. The old has passed away; behold, the new has come" (2 Cor 5:17). If the rest of the apostolic literature taught us that neither Paul nor John nor the Christians to whom they wrote had ever committed any sin, then this would not present a problem. It would simply lead to the conclusion that the Christians in those days were perfect "saints" and we, who are daily aware of sin, could conclude only that such statements do not apply to us.

But this is not the case. Paul himself confesses deliberately and openly in Romans 7 that he still is continually surprised by sin, and his rebukes and admonitions to the churches of that day provide conclusive proof that the stains and wrinkles were manifold and sometimes even quite major back then as well. Furthermore, their pronouncements are absolute and unrestricted: "*No one* born of God makes a practice of sinning." With this word before us, we who continually confess guilt and sin before God could come to no other conclusion than that either we are not God's children, since we still continually sin, or this word of the apostle is untrue and does not stand up empirically. But if, on the other hand, you confess these three things—(1) that the apostolic word is true, (2) that you are a child of God, and (3) that you still fall into transgression daily—then it follows that this word of the apostle must not be understood of your *composite* life, as it is still in part old, in part new, but that it is being said only about *the new life* in contrast to *the old life*. It then shows that here two plants are growing up intertwined; there are all kinds of evil fruits on the composite tree, but when we look closely from what root such fruit have sprung—that is, on which stalks the evil fruit grows—we will always find that these branches or stalks are still from the *old root*, and that from the root of the new life not a single branch or stalk sprouted that produced even a single rotten or evil fruit. Only the person who lives out of that new life is born of God, and thus it can truly be said that he who is born of God does not sin and cannot sin, because the seed of God remains in him.

But however transparent this may be as such, it may never lead to the doctrine of two persons in one individual. In the child of God there is no combining of two selves. It is not the old man into whom a new man has been inserted to dwell (so that the old man is the host and the new man the guest), for holy Scripture teaches us always that the person himself is born again and that it is the self that converts. The doctrine of the believer being two persons or two selves—one self from the old man from Adam and another self from the new man from the Holy Spirit—has never brought anything but ruin upon God's church. It is in this slogan that the antinomians always sought their strength. The old man, the old self, that old Adam, may curse and rage, and steal and commit adultery to his heart's content. It is the host who does all this, and the indwelling holy person or self has nothing to do with it. The host is doomed anyway, is lost anyway. It does not matter what sins he commits. Indeed, he can do nothing but sin. But in the meantime, the "new self" indwells that evil person, the child of God, and that child of God does not have to worry at all about the sin of his host. His account is clear before God, and he does not have to concern himself with the defiled account of his host. That false notion—that there are two selves that live quite independently of each other, the one his sinful life, the other his holy life—must be opposed in every way possible and eradicated from God's church. And no matter how unfathomable we may find the mystery of two lives in one person, and of one self that draws its life from two roots, it nevertheless is certain that this is how we must confess the matter. It is not Saul who cries, "Wretched man that I am!" [Rom 7:24], and Paul who affirms, "Thanks be to God through Jesus Christ our Lord!" [Rom 7:25]. It is one and the same Paul who in one breath, from the depths of one human heart, affirms, "Wretched man that I am! Who will deliver me from this body of death? Thanks be to God through Jesus Christ our Lord!"

§4 To explain this mystery, people have rightly pointed to the concept of grafting. And indeed, this notion, from the plant kingdom, of grafting a good shoot onto a trunk gone wild, provides us an image of great significance. In fact, we see before our eyes how a wild tree can be cut down and how then in the heart of that stump a graft from a tree that is not wild can be placed, and how then the wild tree is forced to direct all sap from its evil root to the grafted shoot. On the old stump a new crown develops that is fed from the sap of the old, wild tree but nevertheless bears good fruit. This provides much that gives us at least some notion by way of explanation. For in the plant kingdom as well, there are two kinds of trees, the one old and gone wild, the other young and cultivated. The old trunk is broad and massive, while the graft of the new life is small and tender. Afterward, both work together. The old trunk keeps growing on its root, and in the meantime the first small graft shoots up to form a crown. Thus grown together, it becomes one tree, with one life. Yet the difference appears to be so striking that at the bottom of the old trunk, evil shoots continually grow out, and the good, cultivated wood only begins above the graft. The old trunk continually wants to kill off the graft, and if the gardener does not carefully chop off the shoots that spring from the old trunk, in no time at all the old tree will have sprouted again and the graft will die. On the other hand, if all that sprouts from the old trunk is carefully chopped away, then the old trunk is powerless and is forced to supply all of the vital sap from its roots to the grafted shoot that, due to that steady supply of vital sap, rapidly shoots up.

No matter how remarkable and striking this illustration may be, it can serve only very partially. For at regeneration the "new life" is not grafted onto us in order to draw its life force from the old, evil nature; it arises in us to sink its own root, and to flourish on that renewed root through the vital sap provided for the new life by the Holy Spirit. The grafted, cultivated tree dies when you saw it off from the old trunk, and it can neither live nor flower without that old trunk and the root of that trunk. In the child of God, however, the new life is intended to be separated entirely from the old trunk at death and only after this to flourish in its full splendor in the holy atmosphere of the life of the saved. Therefore, even though we continue to consider the image of grafting remarkable and striking, we must not carry the comparison too far. It gives us an image of a wild and a cultivated life in one and the same plant, miraculously intertwined while nevertheless maintaining their distinct character, but it does not explain the mystery of the one self in its twofold life in God's child. For when it comes to that, it is precisely the reverse of what it is in the grafted tree.

Nor can we permit the attempt to solve the riddle by viewing the new §5
birth as introducing a new entity or substance into the soul. A child of God is not equal to a sinner + *x*. On the contrary, he himself is changed. He was *a*; he became *b*. Only, *a* is not suddenly gone, and *b* does not break through all at once completely. Rather, *b* begins by being very small, while *a* still grows appreciably. After this, *b* gains and *a* decreases. And finally, in death, *a* is cast off completely, and nothing but *b* remains. Were we to say that the "seed of God" is a certain entity inserted into our soul by the Holy Spirit, this would lead us automatically to see in sin a kind of poisonous bacterium that was inserted into our soul by Satan. Sin would then dwell in us as a separate being, and the seed of God as a second separate being, and everything would in fact occur outside our person. It would become the process of a disease and medication that did not touch our person, our self. The prophets and apostles, and in their wake the Reformed fathers, therefore have continually taught that sin is not an entity, but a transformation of the power that God created for good within our soul into its opposite. But consequently, it has also always been our confession that the new birth cannot be the insertion into the soul of a new component, but a working of God in our soul through which what became crooked and distorted by sin is set aright again. It was confessed so beautifully at Dordrecht in 1619:

> But when God accomplishes His good pleasure in the elect, or works in them true conversion, He not only causes the gospel to be externally preached to them, and powerfully illuminates their minds by His Holy Spirit, that they may rightly understand and discern the things of the Spirit of God; but by the efficacy of the same regenerating[4] Spirit He pervades the inmost recesses of man; He opens the closed and softens the hardened heart, and circumcises that which was uncircumcised; infuses new qualities into the will, which, though heretofore dead, He quickens; from being evil, disobedient, and refractory, He renders it good, obedient, and pliable; actuates

4. *Regenerating* is taken here in the sense of the continuing renewal of life.

> and strengthens it, that like a good tree, it may bring forth the fruits of good actions.[5]

The only expression to which exception might be taken here is that he "*infuses* new qualities," but this too is merely apparent. For a quality is never an entity or a constitutive element, but rather nothing but a state, a shape, a form of the entity that already exists and is already present. But even so, this change of us and in us remains a mystery, of which it was so rightly confessed at Dordrecht: "The manner of this operation cannot be fully comprehended by believers in this life. Nevertheless, they are satisfied to know and experience that by this grace of God they are enabled to believe with the heart and to love their Savior."[6]

All that remains for us, if we are to explain sanctification further in its connection with civic righteousness, is to point to the distinction in every sphere of life between the center and the periphery—or in plant life, to the distinction between the life in a seed and life in the fully grown plant. We do not comprehend this in its application, but it at least gives us a notion of a point from which the action of life emanates and of a broader sphere in which the action of that life operates. The point of departure, then, is small, hiding invisibly, and yet it dominates all the rest. That periphery, that sphere of life is broad and manifests itself in the visible, but is dominated by the force that works its way up from the hidden seed. And this distinction enables us to conceive of how a change can occur in the seed, in that one point from which the action springs, without any noticeable change occurring as yet in that broad periphery. But as that change in the center gradually is completed, it gains in strength and begins to manifest itself in the expressions of life as well, and thus the change or renewal is also noticeable in that broad periphery.

---

5. *Canons of Dort*, III/IV.11.
6. *Canons of Dort*, III/IV.13.

CHAPTER THIRTY-NINE

MORAL GOOD IN THE UNREGENERATE

Can a fig tree, my brothers, bear olives, or a grapevine produce figs? Neither can a salt pond yield fresh water.

JAMES 3:12

The great challenge in forming a correct perception of the condition of a regenerated individual is that he gives the impression of being something that cannot exist, according to the Apostle James: a fountain that yields both sweet and salt water [Jas 3:11]. There certainly are good works in him, at least works in which we cannot discern any blemish, but there also are so many sins in the life of the born-again individual, yet not in the sense that he gives the impression of being someone who generally walks the straight path and only occasionally makes a misstep. The Reformed churches confess, rather, that no one in this life gets beyond a small beginning of true obedience; that in this life the children of God struggle with evil until the very end; and that until the grave, the prayer accompanies us, "Forgive us our sins, and lead us not into temptation, but deliver us from evil."[1] Not §1

1. See Heidelberg Catechism, Lord's Day 16, Q&A 14; Lord's Day 44, Q&A 114; and Lord's Day 51, Q&A 126.

until death itself comes and cuts off all our communion with the world does the stimulus for sin end, and nothing is at work any longer in the child of God except the stimulus that comes from the Holy Spirit, who was given to him at regeneration.

In contrast to this confession of the Reformed churches stands the claim of others that a child of God already can attain "perfect holiness" in this life. Any claim like this is based on a misunderstanding, however. For the question of whether someone is perfectly holy depends not on what others discover in him, but on what God's holy eye sees in him, and no one knows that judgment except the individual himself (at least to the extent that there is no self-deception involved). In the meantime, experience shows that when someone's piety becomes more fervent and his conscience more scrupulous, his search for recourse in the cross of Golgotha will increase. Some men in the pulpit have even dared to claim that they did not remember ever having committed a sin in the past three or more years, but this claim was based on a very superficial concept of sin and stood little higher than the standard declaration heard so often among people of the world: "I am beyond reproach. There is no one who can say even the slightest negative thing about me."

We therefore do not deny at all that now and then a few men and women have been seen who had received uncommonly beautiful gifts from their God and who radiated very powerfully the light of the Spirit through a pure, devout walk; fervent surrender and devotion; and alluringly beautiful self-denial. But the only basis on which the conclusion was reached that they therefore were holy was by comparing them with the imperfection of others. They would have been judged differently had they been held up against the holiness of *God*. Without further elaboration we therefore hold fast to what Paul exclaimed: "Wretched man that I am!" [Rom 7:24] and to John's declaration that "if we say we have no sin, we deceive ourselves, and the truth is not in us" [1 John 1:8], in which this holy apostle includes himself, as is evident from the plural *we*.

Thus we start from the fact that a regenerated individual already gives the impression of being a fountain in which we alternatingly find fresh and salt water—the salt water most often, the fresh more rarely. For it remains, after all, the same single self; it is and remains the same person who at one time denies himself in love, and at another time denies love through selfishness. We must admit that what is holy in God's children often expresses itself weakly, and in general they are not all that different from the ordinary children of the world (at least if we do not incline toward the despairing notion that in an entire local church there are at most ten or twelve genuine children of God together with hundreds and thousands of hypocrites—not in the world but in the best of churches). If we do not fall into this negative view and if we charitably assume that the number of God's children is much, much greater, then we must agree that a comparison between these blessed people and the children of the world, in business and trade, in commerce and concourse, on average does not show the great difference that we would expect.

Anyone who has ever made such a comparison in relation to saved and unsaved persons who work in the same office, in the same trade, and so on, can reach virtually no other conclusion than that the people of the world were better than expected, and that blessed people were worse than expected. There was a distinction in certain things, such as church attendance, reading Scripture, praying, observing the Sabbath, and refraining from gambling and amusements. But when we compare both groups in terms of their business, their everyday commerce and interactions, their conversations, their deliberations, their temper, their anger, their conceit, and so on, then we cannot help but be struck that the difference was far less than we suspected. And although we may say without exaggeration that, generally and proportionally, confessing Christians do not lag behind (indeed, in some things they are even a step ahead of the others), yet everyone who gives honest thought to this point senses that this difference definitely does not correspond to what we expect when we know that the people of the world are still in the kingdom of darkness, whereas regenerated persons have been transferred to the kingdom of light. It must be acknowledged, and we emphasize this, that in trade and business, in conversations and considerations, some people of the world display greater scrupulousness and show greater benevolence than many others whom, to be charitable, you do not doubt to be children of God. It is not rare that the children of God are put to shame by the children of the world. And when it nevertheless is certain that in these children of God the self has been regenerated and that this regenerated self not only "does not sin but cannot sin," then everyone senses and feels that there is only one way out of this dilemma, and this way out must lie in the very different relationship between the working of common grace, which goes out to all, and the working of particular grace, which works exclusively in the children of God.

§2 It is generally presented as if common grace works only in the unregenerate, and as if the good that manifests itself in believers is the fruit of particular grace. But it takes little effort to see that this does not hold true. For on that assumption, common grace would not infrequently produce more and better fruit than saving grace, and each of us who felt ashamed by the gentler temper, the broader generosity, or the more tender mood of the unbeliever then would have proof that what has the power to improve life is not saving grace but common grace. But apart from this, it is clear as day that common grace works through all kinds of particulars that influence the converted as well as the unconverted. Descent and birth are at work in both. Upbringing had an influence on both. Both are influenced by their environment, their business, their lot in life, what they read, the spirit of the age, and so forth. We cannot think of the converted as standing outside of or being excluded from all of this, and there is no sense in thinking that all this would stop having an impact on him from the moment of conversion onward, leaving only the working of saving grace in him. Even if we could totally separate him from his environment—indeed, segregate him from the world—he nevertheless would continue to carry the continuing effects of the former influences of common grace in his person, his memory, and his education. We therefore must abandon this entire construal. It is not valid to explain all that is good in the believer only on the basis of the grace received as a covenant child, and precisely for this reason we cannot and must not ascribe the evil that is manifest in him, without further qualification, to a decline in the grace received as a covenant child.

If we want to understand this matter clearly, we will have to acknowledge that there are two kinds of grace at work in the believer; both particular grace from the seed of God that is in him, and common grace that he has in common with the people of the world. In the believer we are not dealing with one but with two grace factors, and because his own nature is also operative in him, his behavior must be understood as a complex of three kinds of working: first, of his nature; second, of the grace he received as a covenant child; and third, of common grace. Here we must keep in mind that his sinful nature still receives stimuli from the sinful world outside him as well as from the demonic world below him. And only where this is rightly understood can it be grasped how extremely complicated it is to explain and judge the condition of a child of God in his life here below, after his conversion. We will never succeed in this unless we start from the condition in which he found himself before his conversion and then think specifically of an adult person and not of an as-yet-unaware infant; equally, we must not think of the adult individual as a scoundrel or criminal, but as a common individual in a civilized society. The error commonly committed in all such considerations is that these differences in the life of the individual are not clearly taken into consideration, and furthermore, various relationships connected to this are confused. In an unaware infant it is different than in an adult, and the signs of conversion are also quite different in a coarse drunkard than in a civilized, respectable man. When we nevertheless speak of conversion in general and then transfer to an adult what only occurs in an infant, or demand the same signs in an upright, honorable man as those that occur in the conversion of a scoundrel, then we will reach the wrong conclusion each time. Even preaching loses an enormous amount of power on account of this generalizing, which it would regain immediately by more carefully illustrating particular cases and pointing this out more emphatically.

If we inquire in this spirit concerning the condition prior to regenera- §3
tion, not for humanity in general but specifically for an adult and upright man, then we learn that he is "dead in sin and trespasses" [see Eph 2:1] but that there are nevertheless some "remnants" or "sparks" of the good in him, and that he, supported and strengthened by "common grace," is capable, not of any saving grace, but of what is called "civic righteousness." This raises numerous questions, the most important being how someone who is dead can still continue to perform activities, and how the arresting of sin by common grace can lead to sin not only failing to occur or being lessened, but doing something positively good, albeit only in the sense of civic righteousness. When a young child lies in the water and is in imminent danger of drowning, and a totally unconverted person jumps in after the child and saves the child at the risk of his own life, was this man "completely incapable of any good and prone to all evil" when he did this?[2] Certainly not, you would say, yet this is what all Reformed Christians confess. Such an apparent contradiction requires an explanation.

The Catechism provides this by declaring *good* to be only what is done from true faith, in conformity with God's law and to his glory. But this too requires explanation. "Sin is lawlessness" [1 John 3:4], says the Apostle John, using a word that literally means "something that is not in conformity

2. See Heidelberg Catechism, Lord's Day 3, Q&A 8.

with God's law." This must be understood to mean that God as Creator has given ordinances for all things and for all relationships. For nature he did this in what are called the laws of nature, for each creature as concerns its life functions. God has ordained how our respiration will work, how our blood will move through our blood vessels, how our food and drink will be transmuted into the blood, and so forth. If all these things function in accordance with these ordinances, then we are healthy and the life of our body is good. In entirely the same way, God also gave his ordinance for what is called our moral and religious life. That life also has its law, and all that takes place in conformity with that law or that ordinance is good, and what does not happen in conformity with that law is sin, because it is different from the will of God. Because saving the [drowning] child is not against, but in conformity with, God's ordinance, we neither can nor may come to any other judgment than that such an act was good, and because that act required a high degree of courage and self-denial, it is in all respects deserving of praise, and we applaud it.

Such a deed that is in itself good can occur in various ways. When a spider spins its web, it never makes a mistake. The web is always good, because it is always spun in accordance with God's ordinance. Yet this is not any merit of the spider but the stimulus of its instinct, since it cannot do otherwise. The spider itself did not spin the web from its own impulse, however, but from the impulse of its instinct. So too, there is much in what we humans do in which we ourselves are not the conscious actors at all, but to which we are driven by our nature. This can be the case even in the deeply tender love of a young mother for her newborn infant, which is apparent from the fact that entirely the same love, sometimes even stronger, can be found among chickens and cats and in general among many animals.

Thus we also see that if a child lies in the water, and there are three or four bystanders, then one might jump into the water without a moment's thought, a second one might hesitate over whether he should, the third one might feel that he must do it but flinches, and the fourth might know that something like this would be impossible for him. Does this mean that the first one lives on a much higher moral plane? Certainly not. Such an act is not infrequently performed by a man who in other respects lives on a very low plane, and among those who hesitated or could not bring themselves to jump we not infrequently find excellent men and women. This shows that such an act, which in itself is always good, can definitely not be credited to that person as good. For it is possible that it was more the impulse of his nature that took action than he himself, and that it therefore was not a moral triumph at all. At this point then the nature of the man is what is at work, a nature that he did not give to himself, but that God gave to him. In this way many things occur in life that are undoubtedly in conformity with God's will, and thus good, without the man who did it having performed a good act. If it is to be credited to him as good, then he himself must have willed it thus, not as an animal under the impulse of a certain instinct, but having *willed* to act as *human being* and having *acted* in obedience to God.

Obedience is the mark of every morally good deed. Obedience means personally acting—and wanting to act—in conformity with the will of God, in conformity with the ordinance of God. A train or a horse or a courier can go from Haarlem to Leiden, and when the train, horse, or courier does this, it is a good act on the part of all three, but it is not therefore an act of obedience on the part of all three. The train is pulled by steam power, the horse is guided, but only the courier walks out of obedience to the person who sent him. The question is therefore not only whether an act as such is in conformity with God's law, but also whether it is done in conformity with that law out of obedience. And even that as such is not sufficient. We can obey reluctantly. Travelers in a stagecoach who are ambushed by robbers on a deserted road and commanded to step down and lie flat on the ground, will obey if they see no possibility of resisting. But who would claim that there is a moral good in such obedience? When we obey out of fear or because we are outnumbered, we are not intending to obey. Assume that someone will obey God's ordinance "You shall not steal" [Exod 20:15] out of fear of judgment, or out of fear that his act will become known; he does obey God's ordinance, and he acts in conformity with the law, but this is not in any way obedience in the moral sense. Obedience must be rooted in the conviction that it is good as God demands it and that only God has the right to command; this then is faith—faith in God's wisdom, faith in God's sovereign ordination, faith in God's love. §4

Finally, it is not enough to believe that God's ordinances are best for us; there must be more. God's ordinance requires moderation in the use of food and drink, and the result constantly teaches us that such an ordinance is best for us. If we remain moderate in the face of the temptation to excess lest we feel sick the next day, we have not only practiced moderation but have also done it from obedience, believing that that obedience was best and safest—yet the ultimate goal was our own well-being. This is why there still must be more. It is God's ordinance not to put our life at risk.[3] But when our confession of Christ threatens us with persecution, even death, then everyone honors the martyr who, when necessary, puts his life at risk and in the end climbs the gallows. It had to end this way because it was best for God's cause. And therefore the good is truly good, in the objective as well as the subjective sense, only if it is (1) in conformity with the law, (2) done from obedience, (3) done from obedience rooted in the faith that God's ordinance is best, and (4) that it is best, not for our temporary well-being, but best for the glory of God and therefore also for our eternal well-being.[4] Taken in this sense, the unregenerate person is "incapable of any good" and always inclined to corrupt what seemed to be good. Indeed, he is dead to what is essentially good. Within him nothing exists or dwells through which he would be able to work himself up again to the good in this high, noble sense. And this not only is the case now, but it remains the case (unless God intervenes), and he therefore ends up in eternal death.

§5 But this definitely is not to say that such a person is not alive. We see before our eyes that he still lives. Even in hell, all the wretched still live. From this it follows that in the unconverted, all kinds of powers certainly function, albeit only partially in the direction ordained by God. Sin and death are not the absence of functions; to the contrary, they are strong activities. Satan is entirely given over to sin and death, yet an uncommonly strong power and activity proceeds from him—but these powers and activities go in a direction radically contrary to what they should. If no common grace had entered paradise after the fall, man would have found himself in the same condition as the fallen angels. After a brief process he would have become absolutely sinful and incapable of being saved. But it is different now. The reversal of the power at work in him, moving now in the opposite direction, did not fully persist but was arrested by God, and God's common grace is still continually at work to partially redirect in the right direction all kinds of powers and activities within him that, if left alone, would head entirely into sin. This is not his merit, for the impact that came from his self would have driven that activity in the entirely wrong direction instead. But God intervenes, and through his common grace he partially arrests the change of direction, thereby ensuring that the activity ends up to a certain extent in conformity with God's will.

3. See Heidelberg Catechism, Lord's Day 40, Q&A 105.
4. See Heidelberg Catechism, Lord's Day 33, Q&A 91.

When the wind is directly south, a ship that set out on the North Sea from our coast could float only northward if left to itself. But when a rudder has been put behind the ship and the helmsman turns that rudder, that same ship does not end up going north, even though the wind remains southerly, but it lands on the English coast. What the rudder does for the ship, common grace does for sinful man. The sinful impulse would take him directly to absolute sin, but common grace deflects him, and thus the outcome for him is civic righteousness. Yet what propels the ship to England is not the rudder but the south wind. And in the same way, what brings sinful man to civic righteousness is not the propelling power of common grace, but the life at work from himself. Only, even as the rudder arrests the straight movement to the north and deflects it, so too common grace deflects the power that comes from sinful man and that propels him in the wrong direction, and redirects it according to God's ordinance. But all this happens in such a way that it is only due to the rudder that the ship gets to where it should be, and so too it is only due to common grace, and not to the sinner, that civic righteousness comes about. The ferry that crosses the river attached to a chain (a so-called cable ferry) can serve as an illustration of the same thought: the water's current would carry the ferry away, but that same propelling power of the water is nonetheless what brings the ferry to the other side when resisted.

If we are not mistaken, then we have an answer to that challenging question—namely, if common grace does nothing but arrest sin, how can it nevertheless lead to something positively good?

CHAPTER FORTY

TWO KINDS OF SELF

That is why many of you are weak and ill, and some have died.

1 CORINTHIANS 11:30

§1 We came to the following conclusion concerning the unregenerate: (1) the same powers are still at work in him that are given by God to man as belonging to his nature; (2) the depravity of his nature consists in the fact that as sinner he constantly wants to make these powers operate in the entirely wrong direction; (3) consequently, the effects of these powers would never be anything but completely evil as long as another power did not arrest this deflection in the wrong direction; (4) common grace brings about this arresting in a varied spectrum of ways, and due to this arresting, all kinds of manifestations of life still end up in sometimes very gentle and scrupulous civic righteousness; but (5) however much objective good still comes about in this way, the subjective self can never be blameless, since whenever the power proceeding from him yields good results, this always happens against the will of that self.

We must add something to this last point to avoid confusion. People may ask, "How would an unconverted individual always, at every point, want to do wrong? And would every good outcome in his life happen against his will and intentions? But we neither can nor may look at it this way! Aren't there many excellent persons among the people of the world who are faithful in doing their duty, assiduous in completing their task, devoting themselves with dedication not only to what brings them profit but also to what results merely in loss of time and strength, as well as loss of money? Must all of this be denied? And without falling into sin, can we declare all this to be from the evil one, albeit with regard to the intention of the self and not to the result?"

We fully appreciate the force of this reservation and do not wish to evade it. What we have explained concerning common grace, however, prevents the disparagement of the many forms of civic righteousness, but it continues to denounce and reject as sinful the first impulse of any act that emerges from the unregenerate self. Now we readily admit that this last statement has an element that shocks us when we first hear it. It therefore requires some explanation.

To begin with, it is impossible for anyone who holds to the Word of God to abandon the absolute position. "Dead in sin and trespasses" [see Eph 2:1] is *dead*. If we are all "by nature children of wrath" [Eph 2:3], Paul included, then there is no conceivable virtue, in the fundamental sense, in us as sinners. Every exception we allow here overturns the entire notion. If the sinner is not dead to the extent that he still practices civic righteousness, and is dead only to the extent that he does conspicuously evil things, then hundreds and hundreds of persons are still as good as fully alive in their unconverted state, with at most a spot of gangrene here and there, or the odd spot that festers. Then we change the nature of regeneration, such that it does not remain a gracious re-creation of the whole person but [becomes] an excising of a spot of gangrene. In other words, we then have suddenly slid from the Christian position to the world's position, which still considers sinful man to be in the main intact, good, and unscathed, suffering only from an occasional wound that calls for healing. Sin is then not a deadly illness, but something incidental that affects a certain part of our being. And in some people who live very circumspectly and honestly, this incidental defect is sometimes so small that we can understand when, at their grave, it is eloquently proclaimed how good and how excellent they were.

We therefore cannot and must not abandon the absolute position; otherwise, we ourselves will move immediately from the testimony of holy Scripture to the conceit of the world. But this does not explain the matter. We have maintained our position, but not explained it. For it cannot be denied that many an unconverted individual wills many good things with his will. They often persevere with an uncommon force of will in a good cause. Therefore we need to employ a second distinction here. Our first §2 distinction was that there is within us a center from which the working of our life proceeds outward, and a periphery where that working manifests itself. We presented that emanation of this life from the center as the radiating outward of lines, and judged that sin redirects these radiating lines in an entirely wrong direction. The lines are then to be thought of as crooked, bent lines. When they come out of the center, they all tend through sin toward the left, but at some point along the line, common grace bends them again to the right so that they are straight again. Initially we could not go into more detail about this distinction without losing all clarity and transparency in the presentation. But now we must add a second distinction that touches on the center itself.

We understood this center to mean our self at the center of our being, and in contrast to the external manifestations of our life, it is a single entity. But when we consider this center as such, it is striking how we must distinguish between, on the one hand, our inclinations, our mind, and our will, and on the other hand, the self that works in these three: *I* am inclined, *I* think, *I* will. Inclination, will, and thought find their integrating point in the self. This shows that here in the center of our being itself we must distinguish between the core within the self and the various movements or functions of that self. Once we grasp this clearly, we immediately see how only this self, as innermost core, remains what it is, but by contrast, the movements of inclination, thinking, and willing undergo a measure of influence from common grace.

Test this yourself by taking three or four thin copper wires, twisting the ends together, and spreading the wires in various directions. At the point where they are joined, bend them to the left with your left hand; halfway along the wires, bend them with your right hand to the right. Then you will feel how the pressure exerted by your right hand not only bends the wires to the right, but also exerts some pressure on the lower parts of the wires, which you can clearly feel with your left hand. Naturally, the same is true for common grace. When common grace grasps the line at an arbitrary point and bends the rest of the line to the right, a tension is produced, a pressure downward that can never touch the core of the self but does have its effect on the inclination, the consciousness, and the will. And this explains how the unconverted can undergo the influence of common grace that reaches his inclinations, his consciousness, and his will.

But the outcome shows that, no matter how far this goes, it never transforms the self, and this transformation of the self can actually be the fruit only of re-creation and rebirth. For even among the most excellent of these persons, the result is not that they bend toward God, but that they always bend away from God. And even though it is not possible to decide this on the basis of a single individual, because most individuals express themselves so little, it in any case is beyond doubt that the direction in which these eminent citizens of the world collectively move increasingly leads to pulling them and their environment away from the Scriptures, to alienating them from the church of Christ, to straying from the confession of the living God, and to finding the highest ideal in the glorification not of God but of man. And in this way, on the one hand, we can appreciate all the good that is found in the world, but on the other hand, we maintain rigorously and strictly our confession that to the extent that common grace cannot make complete headway—that is, with regard to our self as the core of our being, the first impulse of the sinner always remains not to direct his life's expressions toward God, but to turn them away from him. And this is precisely what the Catechism means when it says that there exist in the self an incapacity to do any good and a constant inclination toward all evil. Everything relating to this that either is better than we might expect, or does not manifest itself externally, proceeds not from the self but from common grace.

All this serves merely as introduction to the main issue that we now §3
investigate—namely, the situation of the born-again individual. In order to understand the born-again individual, we were obliged to ask ourselves what transpires in the soul of the unregenerate individual. We cannot understand an illness without knowing what the healthy individual is like, but we cannot bring any healing without knowing the situation of the sick person. We have seen the situation of the sick person. Now we ask the question of what alteration, what change, is brought about in such a sinner by regeneration.

It is quite simple when we take an individual who dies immediately after regeneration. For then regeneration does nothing but set right the self that had been wrong. That self had turned away from God and existed in unbelief. Now it has been turned back to God and therefore exists in faith. And nothing else is to be added, since death removes such a person from the outward periphery of life. In this case we have nothing to do with the lines that went from the self to that periphery: death severs all of this. The self has been totally liberated in death. And if the self has been turned toward God through rebirth, then after death it is turned toward God with its inclination, thinking, and willing, for none of those three undergoes any influence any longer from those lines that extended to the periphery of this life. Those have all been severed. Death is "a dying to sin and an entering into eternal life."[1]

But the matter is quite different, of course, when the regenerated individual does not die immediately after regeneration, but continues to live. For then she continues to be connected with the periphery of life. The lines that ran from her *self* to that periphery definitely react to her person. And what was produced in the core of her self cannot immediately reach the periphery. Indeed, the dominance of the periphery of life is then so strong that until death the born-again *self* is neither able nor in a position to achieve anything more than a "small beginning" of perfect obedience, according to our Catechism, which in this respect so perfectly reflects the truth of Scripture.[2] This is an expression that, translated into our metaphor of lines and wires, means that our reborn self is capable only in very small part of making even one single line proceed in the direction God has willed, with a totally perfect movement, from the self to the outermost periphery.

§4 Does this change anything in the innermost core of the self? Definitely not. It can be in only one of two [states]: either turned toward God or turned away from God. It can exist either in faith or in unbelief. There is no third option. The self was turned away in unbelief, but regeneration was precisely that act of God that turned the turned-away self back to God again. And in that turning back, God also permanently fixes our self in place. It is then impossible to turn away again. A born-again person cannot choose against God again. There is the perseverance of the saints. Thus if we renounce the inclination, the consciousness, the will, and also the entire periphery of life and the lines that proceed from the self, and focus exclusively on the hidden self of our being in the deepest core of our personality, then what was dead has been brought to life again, what was sick has been healed, and what lay under God's wrath has been put under the radiance of God's pleasure, and this self is completely holy.

This is what the apostle has in view when he says that anyone who is born of God does not continue to sin—indeed, *can* no longer sin—because the seed of God abides in him. That most hidden, innermost self is entirely holy and thus without sin. In fact, it has been cut off from all sin. It is

1. Heidelberg Catechism, Lord's Day 16, A 42.
2. Heidelberg Catechism, Lord's Day 44, A 114.

incapable of falling again. It is inclined to all good now, incapable of all evil. It is as holy as it can become in all eternity. It has received eternal life from God. It is this reborn self in which the Holy Spirit dwells, with which the Holy Spirit has fellowship, and that receives its impulse only from the Holy Spirit. Indeed, we must add that it is this self in the most hidden core of our life of which the apostle says: "I no longer do this myself, but sin that dwells in me" [see Rom 7:17, 20]. All kinds of sin still proceed from him; that sin therefore must still be in him, or else it could not proceed from him. Yet that sin no longer springs from his deepest self; rather, it proceeds from something entirely different. Before God all born-again persons are holy, and together they are called "the saints who are at Corinth," "the saints who are in Thessalonica," and so on.

If this starting point is fixed, then in the second place the question arises as to how this holiness with its radiating beams is fractured as soon as it seeks to express itself from the deepest self, not upward to God, but outward to the world. For there are two kinds of movement that proceed from this self: the one is entirely mystical and goes directly to God, and the other goes to the world. We can also call them the vertical movement (which moves upward, to God) and the horizontal one (which moves outward, into the human life).

In that connection, we must pay attention first to the consciousness. Not everything that lives in the self therefore lives immediately in the consciousness of that self. In the newborn child, even before birth in fact, the self is present in each human being. But this definitely does not mean that we can say that we find self-awareness and self-consciousness in the infant before or immediately at birth. Even in an infant who has lived for several months, human consciousness is still entirely dormant, and we can say that only at an adult age has this consciousness fully developed. But even then, it absolutely is not true that the entire self of this self-conscious human being is present in the person's consciousness at every moment. We sleep one-third of our life, with our consciousness entirely at rest. During a very large part of our waking hours we think only of the one thing we are busy with, while all the rest is dormant. At most we can say that there are some spirited moments in our life when we have a large part of our self vividly in our consciousness.

There is more. A man of fifty knows himself better than a young man who is a quarter-century younger. There is progress, there is development, there is maturing in our consciousness as well. While the deepest self in our being remains the very same, the consciousness progresses, becomes richer in content, and learns to understand itself better. It is therefore contrary to all reason and life experience when we refuse to pay close attention to this distinction between consciousness and self. This distinction is even the basis of all pedagogy, and whoever neglects this distinction simply is not to be counted among the thoughtful.

§5 But it also follows from this that in re-creation a distinction must be made between the regeneration of our self and the conversion or reversal of our consciousness. The Greek word used in holy Scripture for conversion is *metanoia* (that is, a transformation of our consciousness), followed by *metastrepsis* (that is, a change in our walk), and both this transformation of our consciousness and this transformation of our walk of life are entirely distinguished from our being born of God, from our rebirth. There are superficial people who firmly maintain that rebirth cannot be hidden, that whatever lives must manifest itself in life, and so forth. But all such statements are casual expressions of unthinking persons. What we remember of the infant before birth, of the human being in his sleep, and of the maturing of our consciousness, shows the opposite. It absolutely is not true that a change in our self immediately, in the same moment, is followed by a related change in our consciousness. These are different matters that can diverge considerably in terms of chronology. When John the Baptist lay in the cradle, he knew nothing of what had already happened to him in his mother's womb. That change in consciousness is therefore a second act of God that can follow immediately after the transformation of the self, but it also can occur considerably later. And only then does conscious faith arise from the capacity for faith.

The same is true, of course, of the inclination and the will; we need not argue these separately. The self can be altered without any change having yet occurred in a person's consciousness, inclination, or will. Even as the seed germ lies in the earth for a short time before there is any observable sprouting, so too the "seed of God," as the apostle calls it [see 1 Cor 15:38], can be hidden within our self without any working proceeding from it. This working will most certainly follow, but not automatically and not immediately. If we place a seed germ just beneath the surface of the soil, and if the soil is half frozen so that no moisture gets to it and no sun shines on it, then the seed can lie under the earth for weeks without anything happening. So too the seed of God begins to work only when the soil of the heart is made soft and experiences the warming activity of grace. But even when this germination begins and perseveres, so that stirrings toward the good arise within the person's inclination, consciousness, and will, this most certainly does not yet mean that all those inclinations are immediately sanctified, that the whole consciousness, the entire will, is transformed toward the good.

On the contrary, each of these three movements of the self has a broad sphere, and only very gradually does the re-creation in those three spheres penetrate from this reborn self. Each of us can trace within himself how only very gradually a wrong inclination is silenced to make room for a better inclination. We ourselves know how we continue to carry for many years untrue and incorrect notions in our consciousness that only very slowly make room for true notions and conceptions. Similarly, it is no secret to us that we still have to struggle continually to restrain our will, which is already partially inclined toward the good, from evil on all kinds of other points. As completely as the re-creation of the self is accomplished at once, so imperfect does the transformation of our consciousness, our inclination, and our will remain throughout our life. It is supremely important to grasp clearly what the cause of the latter is, because only then can we understand how there can be two kinds of self in us, and how we can speak of an old and a new man. There is our essential self, hidden deep in our being, but there is also the self as it can differ quite considerably from what lies hidden within our innermost being. It is therefore perfectly understandable that a born-again person, speaking out of his consciousness, confesses, "I have sinned," while, taking into account his inner being, confessing equally decisively, "My *self* did not commit that sin, for *I* can no longer sin."

CHAPTER FORTY-ONE

THE TWOFOLD WILL

For I know that nothing good dwells in me, that is, in my flesh. For I have the desire to do what is right, but not the ability to carry it out.

ROMANS 7:18

§ 1 Although it is impermissible from a Christian standpoint to speak of two persons dwelling together in the born-again individual, we nevertheless must affirm the presence of a twofold *self*. When Paul says, "If *I* do what I do not want, it is no longer *I* who do it" [Rom 7:20], then it is settled that two kinds of *self* are distinguished here. The one self *does* act, while the second self in fact does *not* act. Let us see how we can further analyze this twofold self in which both selves simultaneously speak. Up to this point, we have pointed to only one distinction between the two—namely, that the reborn self can still remain dormant while the unregenerated self still remains active. But this one distinction cannot suffice. Even if the reborn self penetrates the consciousness through conversion, it does not yet in any way control our whole conscious life. The one who comes to conversion, and thus to true faith in Christ, now knows and confesses "what [God] has done for my soul" [see Ps 66:16]. He confesses to having gone from the kingdom of darkness into God's marvelous light. He now knows that he was dead and, behold, he lives. When it comes to a direct expression of faith, he is certainly conscious of the fact that the self out of which he speaks is the reborn self. He will say, "I *was* dead but now I *have* eternal life." But this does not mean in the least that this awareness of faith has therefore permeated his *whole* consciousness. In entire segments of his life, his consciousness does not spring directly from the life of his soul but arises from a whole world of facts, notions, habits, and the environment to whose domination and rule he is subject. He does not yet perceive that his faith requires an entirely different perspective for all these things as well, and he continues to live in those earlier perspectives without realizing how they must change.

Let us take an example. When at the beginning of this century no political group had yet arisen in the Netherlands that derived its political convictions from faith principles, there nevertheless were many people who came to conversion and knew very well within their deepest self that they had gone from death to life. But this did not yet result in any way in their coming to a proper political perspective. On the contrary, hundreds of these persons have lived and died without ever having perceived the demands of faith for government, and in spite of their rebirth and conversion they continued to cling to political notions that were rooted in unbelief. Even now there are countries—for example, Switzerland and France—in which people of Reformed theological conviction have not yet gained sufficient insight into this distinction in terms of political perspective. The consequence, then, is that the reborn self speaks from the hidden depths of the soul while in the political realm the self that says, "I think such and such," remains part of the unregenerated self.

Another example may clarify this difference. When the church of Christ first went out into the world, the sons of Abraham maintained a Jewish view of ceremonial service to God. And this could not be otherwise. They grew up with these views. They observed special days. They could not live without circumcision. They avoided unclean foods. They stood in sharp contrast to the Gentiles. Only those who were incorporated into Israel as proselytes could be saved. Then when many of these children of Israel converted to Christ, it was natural that the faith principle that had been implanted in them should bring the requirement that they let go of all these Jewish notions and adopt true Christian beliefs about these various matters. To put it differently, their conversion to the Christ required that they move with their whole conscious life from the "ministry of shadows" to the "ministry of fulfillment."

But even though this was the indisputable demand of the principle of faith, they nevertheless did not do so. Their conscious life did not come along very quickly. It lagged behind. And so we see the phenomenon of men who sincerely believed in Jesus, but nevertheless remained entrenched in ceremonies that had their fulfillment in Christ and thus had been abolished. For this reason we frequently see in Paul's epistles, especially in the epistle to the Galatians, Paul's battle with those individuals who had not yet matured, particularly in situations where the Jews used their conviction to lead people away from Christ again. With Peter we clearly see that this phenomenon did not only occur among a few uneducated people; he went so far astray that Paul had to publicly chastise him [see Gal 2:11–14]. This phenomenon is even more apparent before Golgotha when we hear Jesus' disciples, who were reborn, continually weary the Lord either with their Jewish questions or with their as-yet unpurified consciousness. Clearly, then, we see the two selves: the reborn self that affirms, "We have believed that you are the Christ, the Son of God" [see John 11:27], and the unregenerated self that says, "Lord, this shall never happen to you," so that Jesus even is compelled to say, "Get behind me, Satan" [see Matt 16:22–23]. There is therefore no doubt that after conversion, the self can still speak out of the old consciousness on various issues into which the faith principle has not yet penetrated.

§ 2 This leads to a third distinction with regard to the person's consciousness—namely, that of the vacillation between spiritual peaks and valleys. Our spiritual state is not constant. On the one hand, we know moments of high spiritual intensity, in which all that is less holy recedes and the light of faith shines forth again and again from our reborn heart into various domains of our lives and into our whole environment. After attending the Lord's Supper, after a visit to a glorious deathbed, or after a mighty spiritual struggle, we are filled with such a clarity that we see everything in a higher light. But there are other moments in our lives: times of obfuscation, times when the light of faith has simply become a smoking wick of a candle and when mist seems to surround us. On those occasions things appear dark and somber in the twilight of our sinful existence. This difference in spiritual sensitivity is a factor as well. As a result, on one occasion we might see more clearly the more stringent demands of our faith and have a proper perspective, but on other occasions we might lack this light and thus remain stuck in ordinary, more egocentric thinking that is not rooted in genuine faith. The reason is not that we wish this—we shall return to the matter of *the will* in a moment—but rather that we have grown accustomed to seeing it this way and only this way, since in such moments the mists clouding our vision are too thick for the light of faith to break through.

In this connection, then, a twofold self will be manifest within one person. A person might open the Bible and read it with the family and afterward pray, and in that prayer he will truthfully say, "O Lord, I know that you are the source of light." But that same person will then go and talk about matters at the office, or about a sick person, or about a friend, but in a way that shows he is hardly seeing things in the light of Scripture; he is seeing things according to the flesh. We can see this vacillation or duality even in people who are dying. On one occasion someone will depart from this life in the full light of God's countenance; on another occasion, a child of God might die and be overwhelmed with thoughts that mirror this world. And yet that should not lead us to conclude that the latter is *not* a child of God. Is it not often the case that moments of spiritual ecstasy in the Savior alternate with irritability or even selfishness within the same person on his or her deathbed? But enough about this. It is simply to point out abundant evidence that our reborn self definitely does not always permeate our consciousness thoroughly. Given this distinction, it doesn't need to be argued further that a self *can* speak from a partially darkened consciousness—a self that is *not* the expression of a reborn heart.

In addition to distinctions in our consciousness, we also find in ourselves § 3
differences in terms of our will, and in this context we must also focus, practically speaking, on the manifestation of the will. In Romans 7 Paul does not only speak of two kinds of *law* that he finds in himself (that is, two forms of life and thus two kinds of consciousness), but he also speaks of two kinds of *will*: a will of the reborn self and a will of the flesh. We can illustrate this most clearly by considering a large ship that is moving ahead with rapid speed but must suddenly stop and move in reverse. In the movement of the ship we can see the working of two kinds of "will." On the one hand, there is the "will" of the helmsman who calls to the engineer, "Full speed astern!"; and on the other hand, there is the "will" of the ship to speed ahead. What the helmsman *says* does not actually happen. He called for the ship to go *in reverse*, yet the ship still goes *forward*. What, then, is the will of the ship? Of course, the ship's will is nothing more than the will of the helmsman as it existed previously. Previously his will was to call, "Ahead!" The ship obeyed this will, but now his second will, which is to call for the ship to move in reverse, is incapable—at least for the time being—of reversing the continuing effect of his prior will. For Paul, the "flesh" is like the ship. Before his conversion, Paul was steering full speed in this flesh, moving in the opposite direction from Christ; this was his previous "will." But now,

as someone who is converted, he commands his reborn "will" differently. Yet, as with the ship, in the flesh the momentum of his former will, of his old self, is still active, and thus he now does what he now *does not will*, so that now it is not "he himself" doing it; rather, it is the momentum of the flesh—that is, the sin that still impels and works in him.

This state of affairs is incomprehensible if we take "the will" as the whim of the moment. Perhaps someone might also use the illustration of a pair of scales. The needle might be pointing straight up, in the neutral position, yet it is the manifestation of our will that determines whether the needle moves somewhat to the left or to the right. Perhaps we move it to the left, but we also could have moved it to the right. At any moment we could go either way; it lies within our power. This undoubtedly is how many people envision the use of the human will. But such a conception is misleading, for the will is a capacity in us that *develops*, and at any given moment it is entirely dependent on the entire past that lies behind it. We can observe this simply from the fact that one person might have a strong will, whereas another person might be virtually without a will of his own, vacillating back and forth. This tendency, of course, is linked to the person's predisposition, upbringing, and past. The one person exercises his willpower, while the other does not. Furthermore, our will constantly comes into contact with other wills, including the will of our family, the will of public opinion, and the will of the world.

To use another analogy, we do not speed along like a solitary wheel, rolling by ourselves; rather, we roll along together with other wills, together, like wheels under the very same wagon. Therefore, even though our reborn self forms the starting point of our will in a proper direction, this momentum in the right direction surely will not necessarily carry over immediately into all areas of our lives. Along the spectrum of exercising our will, we can observe entirely different influences being active, and all too often the impulse that goes out from our "reborn self" is simply too weak to overcome those other influences. Perhaps the impulse or intention of our will is indeed good, but that impulse is unable to persevere, and in fact those other influences from the past that were still affecting us continue to gain the upper hand. The result is that our will, which perhaps starts with the right intention, often ends up veering off in a wrong direction when it comes to external aspects of our lives. When the famous "Sea Beggars" took the city of Brielle in 1572, the initial impulse of their will was noble, yet when that will expressed itself in the reckless murder of Roman Catholic priests, it ended up being terribly sinful in its implementation.[1] But this is our experience as well. Thus, in this connection we must make a distinction between the first impulse that goes out from the will of our reborn self, and the direction in which that will might veer off when it is implemented under quite different influences in real life.

Paul speaks of being "of the flesh, sold under sin" [Rom 7:14]. That language expresses the point exactly. Between our reborn self at the center of our being and the outside world lies our "flesh," which refers to everything in our lives that has been formed under the influences of sin committed by self and by others. Our deeds, then, are consequences, outcomes, and expressions of the will that indeed arise from the self but have to pass through that broad sphere of "the flesh" to manifest themselves. And in that "passage" these deeds encounter all kinds of obstacles and opposition; consequently, [our will] finds ultimate expression in our lives in ways very different from how it was intended. The "flesh"—that is, the whole "in-between" sphere through which intention must pass—is too strong for us, too mighty, too overwhelming. We are "sold" under it, to use Pauline language. Set free at the core of our being as children of God, we are at the periphery of our lives still slaves of sin. What does the self want? Does it want the good, or does it want sin? The answer, alas, is *both*, depending how one views it. If we understand the will as deployed by—and under the influence of—reborn self, then of course the will wants the good and *nothing but* the good, since what is born of God *cannot* want anything sinful, since the seed of God has been sown within. If, on the other hand, we understand the self to manifest itself in the outer periphery of our lives as we live them in the world, then the will can be understood as directed toward what is sinful, with the ability to achieve it.

Now, if this explanation is sufficient to explain the *twofold* will, then we § 4
may draw out its implications. Life can be awakened in us without there being any apparent impact on the will. Spiritual reality may have begun to impact the will, leading to conversion, but at that point it may influence only part of our will. Also, through variations in the degree of intensity, spiritual reality might on one occasion powerfully seize the will and on another occasion have only little effect. This would help explain certain apparent

1. The *Watergeuzen*, or Sea Beggars, fought against Spain during the Eighty Years War. The capture of Brielle was the beginning of the liberation of the northern part of the Netherlands, which led to the founding of the Dutch Republic.

contradictions that are found in spiritual life, things we do not understand about ourselves. At times people might elevate themselves, despite the fact that the initial impetus of the reborn is so strong that it breaks through every resistance. At other times they might be listless, with the regenerate will reacting so weakly that they succumb to the very first resistance they encounter. But most of this should be sufficiently clear based on our previous discussion of the different levels of human consciousness. We need not go into any further detail at this point. It is enough to clarify that the reborn self *always* wants to do the good, while the self that wills will continually vary in terms of how it responds to our "peripheral" life; sometimes that may go in a contrary direction, which makes it seem as if there are *two* selves that exert their will, when in fact there is only one.

But more needs to be said. Sometimes the reborn self expresses itself through the will and through actions in a way that simply cannot be explained even in this manner. Here I am referring to what our Confession has in view when it says that the elect, even after their conversion, sometimes experience a terrible fall, without necessarily falling away, as the tragic examples of David and Peter illustrate.[2] In the case of such actions, and of those that are less severe in nature, there exists no *intention* of the will to do good; the will is simply deflected sideways, as it were, by the influences of the world, our sin, and Satan. These are actions and expressions of the will that were intended for evil from the start. In order to understand these, we must call upon [the image of] the felled tree. If a heavy tree trunk, with its many branches and limbs, is cut down so that the felled trunk lies dead on the ground, then not infrequently a branch will sprout from the felled trunk, as if the tree in fact were still alive. This, of course, is nothing more than the "aftereffect" of its former life. In its huge trunk are still to be found all kinds of juices, and as long as the supply of those juices lasts, sprouting will continue. This is precisely how we might understand the reborn sinner. The trunk of his old life has been felled, but there are still present so many residual effects—past expressions of the will—that, [though they] will soon come to an end, for the time being they have not yet lost their effect. It needs to be reiterated that such sinful effects do come from the "self," but not from the "self" that has been regenerated.

2. See the Canons of Dort, V.4.

On occasion a family might receive a telegraph message about a distant family member who has passed away, and yet the postal service still could deliver two or three letters from that deceased family member as if he or she were still alive. The letters were sent before the actual death occurred and continued [on their way], arriving in apparent contradiction to reality. Something similar is at work here as well. With our conversion we certainly are not suddenly rid of the other self. The expressions and effects of that self continue to work over months and years, even if the older self has long since died in the center of our life and been buried with Christ. This explains why expressions of the former self and the former will still manifest themselves in the "periphery" of our lives. It therefore is a matter of course that God's child pray, be on guard, and do battle against this inclination, and that the church provide support through preaching, the sacraments, discipline, and communion of the saints. But that is not our present emphasis. What occupies us in the present discussion is not the question of how we can avert this evil inclination, but rather how its manifestation can be best explained. Hopefully, this has been made clear, not in the sense that there are two human beings within our single person, but in the realization that there is a distinction between the *essence* of our self (even when it can be understood as latent in the core of our personality before we were born) and the *consciousness* of our self (by which that personality manifests itself externally). If the two were always one and wholly congruent, then immediately following rebirth our entire consciousness and every aspect of our will—everywhere and at all times, in a universal sense—necessarily would be completely holy. But this is not the case. We are faced in our earthly lives with a process that involves very slow transitions. And this is the reason our self can be different in its essence and in the way that it works and expresses itself *externally*.

One final analogy: imagine a child born of a purely Dutch father and a purely Dutch mother who, after both parents died, was sent by his family to live in England or France at a very young age. The child may never have learned to speak a word of Dutch and is shaped by a consciousness that is completely English or French. This, however, does not diminish in any way the fact that the child, in his or her *essence*, is Dutch and would find only in the Dutch language—his mother tongue—that which fully corresponds to his nature. This example, which distinguishes between the *essence* of a child and the *language* in which the consciousness of that child expresses itself, also serves to illustrate our main point. A similar distinction, but on a spiritual and much more serious level, exists between the reborn *essence* of the self, which will express itself in holy language, and the *consciousness* of the old self (that is, a consciousness that initially knows nothing other than the language and experience of the world).

CHAPTER FORTY-TWO

IT IS GOD WHO SANCTIFIES US

Now may the God of peace himself sanctify you completely,
and may your whole spirit and soul and body be kept
blameless at the coming of our Lord Jesus Christ.

1 THESSALONIANS 5:23

We have tried to explain how our reborn self can exist entirely holy in the core of our being and nevertheless express itself in our conscious life as wrong and distorted. We also have explored how to understand that the impulse of the will in the essence of our being is straight as a plumb line and that nevertheless the will, as it manifests itself in daily life, is askew and crooked. The comparison of a black person who works in a limekiln with a white European who works in a coal mine makes this distinction fully transparent. If the two were to meet and look in the mirror, the black person covered with white chalk dust and the white European who crawled coal-black out of his mine, then based on what they see in the mirror, they might claim that the black person is less black than the European. But the black person knows full well that he is black, even though his appearance is somewhat white, and the European says with full conviction, "I am white," even though we see him standing coal-black before us. And when this same § 1

European laborer, who looks black, says to the black person, "I really am white," comes home, and his child jumps up to him and wants to throw her arms around his neck, then the father will say to the child, "Wait a minute, sweetheart, for *I am black.*" Are these then *two selves* in this man, a black self and a white self? Of course not. It is one and the same self that at one point claims "I am white" and later acknowledges "I am black"; which of the two he says depends on the context. When the black person disputes the hidden whiteness of his skin, he says decisively, "Not true, I am wholly white; there is not a black spot on me." But to his child, who would get dirty if she embraced him, he acknowledges, "I am totally black."

And this is how it is with the reborn man. In contrast to the man who challenges the work of God in his heart, he will boast: "I am holy and *cannot* sin." But in contrast to his brother, and on his knees before God, he will confess, "Wretched man that I am." And this not because there are two *selves* in him, one self from the old Adam and another self that belongs to the child of God. Rather, it is because the very same person speaks one time from his hidden essence, and another time about the form in which he manifests himself before the world. We are entirely glorified internally, yet we defile all the gifts of God that we touch.[1]

We need not explore this point any further. Suffice it to say that the "dangerous doctrine" of the two selves has been elucidated, and thus it should be sufficiently clear how the self in our hidden essence can be entirely sinless, and yet in actual life we nevertheless can and *must* kneel down before our God with the plea for forgiveness. In this connection, we have demonstrated the link between consciousness and will. It is therefore superfluous to treat the matter of human affections separately, even though our Forms of Unity mention the affections in addition to consciousness and will. They state,

> Man was originally formed after the image of God. His understanding was adorned with a true and saving knowledge of his Creator, and of spiritual things; his heart and will were upright, all his affections pure, and the whole man was holy.

---

1. Although the comparisons involving skin color here do not seem to necessarily imply any value judgments, elsewhere Kuyper does write from a decidedly Eurocentric perspective. For more on Kuyper's racial judgments, see *CG* 1.12.10n4; 1.41.2n3. See similar instances in *CG* 1.61 and 1.62. At the very least, such comparison indicates the consciousness of skin color as a relevant point of contact both for Kuyper as well as for his intended audience.

> But, revolting from God by the instigation of the devil and by his own free will, he forfeited these excellent gifts; and in the place thereof became involved in blindness of mind, horrible darkness, vanity, and perverseness of judgment; became wicked, rebellious, and obdurate in heart and will, and impure in his affections.[2]

In addition to mind (or consciousness) and will, the Canons thus say that "all his affections" were "pure" and then they say separately that the human person is "impure in his affections" as a consequence of sin. We therefore must certainly pay attention to those inclinations or tendencies, but this definitely does not mean that they are on a par with consciousness and will. By this I simply wish to observe that in his consciousness and will man is active, but in his inclinations he is passive. That which inclines or impels us does so automatically and unintentionally, and the action of the will, if it functions, goes against that inclination and tries to remain straight. Human inclinations, therefore, are a part of created human nature and thus a part of every human being. Fully apart from the matter of sin, human inclinations toward one thing or another are per se nothing but affections that God has put in us by nature.

By way of illustration, one boy, as he grows up, by nature will be drawn to the sea and perhaps not rest until he is a sailor; another young man, by contrast, has an insurmountable aversion to water and the ocean in particular, feeling that his heart goes out to the mountains. Of these two individuals, both of whom tend to be artistically inclined, one will perhaps gravitate, quite naturally, toward the world of sounds, while the other will be inclined toward a world that expresses itself in—let's say—painting. Practically, that means that the one is inclined toward being more "active" and "practical," while the other perhaps tends toward being more quiet, contemplative, and reflective. The one feels an inner inclination toward what is profound and mystical, while the other tends to respond to what is clear in terms of external phenomena. Socioculturally we might even say that one or another inclination is more pronounced in different nations. Yet, at the practical level we might say that this difference in inclination dominates our relationships with various people in our own environment,

2. Canons of Dort, III/IV.1.

which is why as human beings we speak of sympathy for one person and antipathy toward another.

At the bottom of these inclinations, then, lies nothing more than the specific attraction that the one or the other force might exert upon us. Even as a plant flourishes better in one environment than in another, so too our being as humans flourishes better in one environment than in another. The effects of this, of course, are not the same for all; it is different for each individual, and it is this endless variety of inclinations that gives us the rich multiplicity in life. For there are indeed general human inclinations that distinguish human nature from that of other creatures, but these basic inclinations of our human nature differ in all kinds of ways—for example, in degree of strength, in preference of choice, and in their merging and intertwining. It is from these specific measurements and proportions that each individual's aptitude, disposition, and character arise. As long as the original harmony of God's composition of these various inclinations is not disturbed, these inclinations are pure and remain in balance, without the one negating the other. But if, through sin, human beings are pulled from God's design, then this harmony, this correct relationship, this balance is lost. Subsequently, the inclination toward the flesh becomes more pronounced and distortion sets in, resulting in *normative* distortion, whereby all inclinations within become impure. While such questions about human inclination should doubtless be a part of any discussion of regenerate nature, the very fact that they are an abiding aspect of our consciousness operating volitionally (however small the distortion may be), requires a separate discussion that is too far afield of our present concerns.

§ 2 Summarizing our findings up to this point, we can state the following conclusions: (1) The very first impulse that comes from the reborn self, in the hidden core of our being, is by nature good, holy, and pure, even when it does not always penetrate even to our dimmest consciousness. (2) This initial holy impulse seeks to penetrate into our consciousness and our will, but as is it is by no means always capable of conquering and overcoming the opposite working that still affects the consciousness and the will from the past; thus, we may conclude that while the first impulse is certainly holy our consciousness and our will manifest themselves in many ways that are unholy. (3) This action of our reborn self, one that is already broken, must move along the guide wires of the whole of organic life in which we are enmeshed and bring about some influence to the good and some bending of the misguided lines. It does so but is not therefore capable of straightening these guide wires along their full length and fully reintegrating them. (4) The line along which the reborn self lifts itself up to God is a different matter, because this line runs not horizontally but vertically and allows for immediate fellowship with God, which is what we confess by means of the indwelling of the Holy Spirit. (5) Finally, all this leads to the result of an apparently quite contradictory existence, in which the self at one time testifies to be a holy and redeemed individual yet, at another time, confesses to be burdened with sin and sinking in sin—one who both glories in spiritually lofty things and yet also confesses sin that supposedly was not desired or intended. The result is the feeling, or the awareness, of both an "old man" and a "new man" who struggle within. Stated the other way around: a "new" person created in Christ Jesus to do good works that God has prepared us to walk in, whose whole desire is to keep all the commandments of God, is juxtaposed with an "old" person who is continually prevented from obtaining anything more than a small beginning of this obedience in the "new" life.

If the matter were left to us, there would be neither progress nor advance in this understanding of human nature, and what we confess as "sanctification" would be, quite simply, inconceivable. But this is not the case. "Now may the God of peace himself sanctify you completely," Paul prays for the church at Thessalonica, "and may your whole spirit and soul and body be kept blameless at the coming of our Lord Jesus Christ" (1 Thess 5:23). According to Paul, this is how an act of God, a steady gift of grace, infuses or enters the life of the soul. Our reborn self stands powerless against evildoing that has crept into our consciousness and our will, as well as against the organic coherence of life through which we must work our way in order to come out into the life of this world, but God now intervenes with his strengthening and sanctifying grace to expand the sphere in which the reborn self might rule, and to weaken the opposition of the unregenerated sphere of life around and within us.

We therefore may distinguish a twofold working of God here. On the one hand, there is a working to strengthen the reborn self, not in its core but in its own consciousness and the sphere of its will; and on the other hand, there is a working to weaken the opposition in the organic coherence of life. Both of these workings reinforce one another. They are designed for one another, to the extent that they result in the reborn self coming to a clearer consciousness—that is, to a stronger will for the good and to a purer manifestation in life. But even though both of these can be reconciled, and even though both contribute to sanctification, they nevertheless are different in nature. That is to say, the working of God's grace aiming at our salvation, that inwardly strengthens the reborn self and brings it to clearer consciousness—as well as a stronger force of will for the good—is entirely personal and particular. By contrast, the other working, through which God breaks the resistance that manifests itself through the aftereffects and impact of sin from external influences, has a more general character; such "grace" elevates the character of temporal life but has nothing to do with eternal salvation. Thus, we might say that the first action is a working of *particular* grace, and the second is of *common* grace.

§ 3 Failure to grasp the distinction between these two properties of grace has repeatedly led to a misunderstanding of the entirely unique character of sanctification; in fact, it has led, at bottom, to sanctification being seen as little else than an attempt on the part of those who confess Christ to improve themselves morally: we then made ourselves "holy." Now pay attention: we can find many noble unbelievers who pay close attention to their walk of life and who are virtuous—people who not infrequently make such remarkable progress in righteous living that they put to shame many a child of God—and this causes a dilemma for us. Understanding the nature of sanctification in this way has mistakenly led to a jettisoning of the need for faith in the process of sanctification. As a result, the thesis ultimately was accepted that Christian doctrine did not matter as long as people led a decent, sober, and moral life. The "Christian social virtues," which were formerly part of our national education law, could be disengaged from their foundation—namely, our confession of the Son of God. This sort of moralism was the result of just such a false notion.[3] For this reason, it is quite necessary that a corresponding confession of our fathers also be restored to its rightful place—namely, that we confess boldly and firmly that sanctification is not a matter of *improving ourselves* but rather that it is an act and working of the Holy Spirit within our hearts. God, not man, is the one who works sanctification. He *works* on us.

This truth should be grasped immediately when we note the absolute meaning of "holy." A garment that has become dirty can gradually be made clean. After it is first washed in water and detergent, much of the dirt will

---

3. On the autonomous character of even "Christian social" or "civic" virtues, see Abraham Kuyper, *Our Program: A Christian Political Manifesto*, trans. and ed. Harry Van Dyke (Bellingham, WA: Lexham Press, 2015), 8.I.76n4.

already have disappeared. A second washing will make the remaining stains fade. A third washing must also attack those [faded stains]. And by this time we will have succeeded in getting the garment completely clean. Yet, this is not how it is with the saint. The defiled and inwardly totally dirty human heart cannot be first made one-tenth holy, then two-tenths, and so on, until it arrives at being ten-tenths holy. Nicodemus thought so, but Jesus disagreed with him (John 3:1–21). To become holy from being unholy, the very root of life must be transformed. What is necessary is a radically new beginning of life. And therefore, only the new birth avails here—namely, the birth that comes from God. But once that has occurred, the new that has been born *is* holy—not three-fourths, not one-half, not one-fourth, but suddenly and entirely.

Between holy and unholy there is a sharp line of demarcation, a line a hair's breadth wide that is barely measurable. Everything to the left of that line is unholy, and everything to the right is holy. If we stand to the right after first having stood to the left, then we have been *transposed*—transposed "out of darkness into his marvelous light" [1 Pet 2:9]. We did not first come out of the darkness into the twilight and then, after having wandered for a long time, at last be able to recognize and greet the light from afar. No, we first stood thoroughly rooted in the dark night, and now suddenly we stand in the light. "Holy" means standing in the realm of God and no longer in the realm of sin. "Unholy" means to still live in sin, no matter how virtuous and decent we are, and therefore apart from God. This means that either our soul is bonded with God or it is not. If that bond is absent, then there is no "faith" operative and we are still in the realm of the unholy. But if that bond is there, then electricity vibrates, so to speak, along that "bonded" line, which means that the *grace* of God moves toward us and, by *faith,* moves from us toward God. Thus, we make no headway by holding to some sort of theory of gradual cleansing. The concept of holiness does not allow for any gradations in its application to the individual. All members of Christ's church who are not hypocrites are therefore, without distinction, called saints [holy ones] by the Apostle Paul. In that sense Jesus said to Peter, "The one who has bathed does not need to wash, except for his feet, but *is completely clean*" [John 13:10]. And another time, "Already you *are* clean because of the word that I have spoken to you" [John 15:3]. This is why Jesus did not institute repeated washing, as was the custom among Israel, but rather introduced the one bathing with the water of baptism, and this is why the Christian church firmly confessed that baptism could not be repeated.

§ 4 Holiness and moral improvement, alas, have nothing in common. Moral improvement is the pruning of the branches; holiness, by contrast, is the grafting onto a wild tree of an entirely different life. Moral improvement can be the result of upbringing, but even the best upbringing cannot sanctify the child in his or her growth. Both the unregenerated and the spiritually reborn, of course, can undertake self-purification of heart and character, but the greatest self-control and the most earnest attempt to discipline oneself can never make *holy* what is unholy. The Neo-Kohlbruggeans, who were entirely blind to the work of common grace and to the real working of the Holy Spirit within the human heart, in fact set aside sanctification as being included in faith.[4] They were correct to the extent that they raged with a seemingly righteous anger against making sanctification seem to appear to be a gradual process on which the sinner, after coming to faith, *worked himself*. But we must insist that sanctification is an act of grace toward us on God's part, not a work of man performed on himself. When Scripture admonishes, "Strive . . . for the holiness without which no one will see the Lord" [Heb 12:14], it does not mean, "Do your best, exert yourself to improve yourself morally, for only the one who completes this will see the Christ in glory." Rather, striving for holiness means seeking an intimate fellowship of faith and love with God and Christ, so that God's sanctifying grace may manifest itself powerfully in us. Any other notion leads to despair. If, by analogy, holiness were a garment that we ourselves were to weave, and that had to be finished before we could enter heaven, then only a gray-haired old man could imagine finishing this project, whereas all those who stopped (weaving, that is) in the middle of their life would be prevented by God himself from perfecting their holiness. Then they would be utterly lost. We cannot stress enough the absolute character of holiness. Either we are holy or we are not holy. A man who is born again is holy and precisely for that reason cannot sin, insofar as the holy seed remains in him. A wild vine that has been grafted onto a "true" or cultivated vine [see John 15:1–8] does not gradually go from one state into the other; rather, in its grafting it suddenly ceases to be a wild vine and becomes at once a true vine.

---

4. Kuyper refers here to followers of Hermann F. Kohlbrugge (1803–75), a prominent Reformed pastor in Germany who opposed Modernism and Ethical theology. From Kuyper's perspective, these "Neo-Kohlbruggeans" overemphasized particular grace to the derogation of common grace.

Understood in this way, our rebirth itself is our *sanctification*. The person who is reborn *was* unholy and then *became* holy. When Paul writes to the church at Corinth, "But you were washed, you were sanctified, you were justified" (1 Cor 6:11), we can deduce from his placing justification *after* sanctification that sanctification here refers to the rebirth itself—including, of course, its aftereffects. We can assume here two possibilities. On the one hand, since everything within God's work is organically related and constitutes a unity, we can sum up that whole work of God under *rebirth*, under *conversion*, or under *sanctification*; or we can distinguish all three. This explains why, on some occasions in Scripture, regeneration refers to all that God does in us, and is complete only when we die, while on other occasions it may refer only to that first act of God through which new life enters us. In the same way, conversion will refer on one occasion to the whole work of God to bring us from sin and misery to holiness and glory, and on another occasion only to the act by which God brings us to conscious faith. So, too, the term *sanctification* will refer sometimes to all that God has wrought in us, from our rebirth to our death, whereas at other times it will depict only that specific act of God through which he causes the implanted life of holiness to penetrate into our various spheres of living, and by which he separates us from all that is sinful when we die. We only understand sanctification in this latter sense, and we are using it only in this sense here, because only in this particular sense does it touch on the theme of common grace.

CHAPTER FORTY-THREE

SELF-PURIFICATION

To equip the saints for the work of ministry, for building up the body of Christ, until we all attain to the unity of the faith and of the knowledge of the Son of God, to mature manhood, to the measure of the stature of the fullness of Christ.

EPHESIANS 4:12–13

§ 1 We have thus far eliminated the mistaken conception that the redeemed of the Lord are made holy by degrees. Anyone who is born again is holy in his or her innermost being, not in part but entirely, not conditionally but for eternity. Adam was also holy, but with a holiness that could be lost. The redeemed, on the other hand, cannot become unholy again. No one can pluck him from the hand of the Father [see John 10:29]. But this must not lead one to suppose that a reborn individual may remain as he was at the moment of his rebirth. Following conversion, one must be purified through struggle. One must not stand still but go forward. holy Scripture clearly speaks of growth, indeed of a growing up "to *mature* manhood, to the measure of the stature of *the fullness of Christ*" [Eph 4:13]; we may call this sanctification. Our salvation is not a consequence of this growing in Christ; for whether a redeemed person dies immediately after being incorporated into Christ or after sixty or seventy years of life, one's salvation is the same. In truth, if God does not take us away but leaves us in this life, this continued life has a purpose, and this purpose is that we "may proclaim the excellencies of him who called you out of darkness into his marvelous light" [1 Pet 2:9], through our person, our life, our word and work. It is inconceivable for someone to say, "If only I will be saved." The truth is that we do not exist for ourselves, but for God, and the duty of growth has been imposed upon us. For indeed, the Holy Spirit works directly in this growth, but he also works indirectly, as is apparent from what immediately precedes the words from Ephesians 4:11 (quoted at the beginning of this chapter)—namely, that God has appointed apostles and evangelists for the *perfecting of the saints* [see KJV]. And it is in this indirect way that we are called to act. And since we are now no longer dead but alive in Christ, we must collaborate in our own purification through waking, praying, and contending.

In this context then, there are three factors at work in our growth: (1) the Holy Spirit, (2) the ministry of the Word, and (3) we as redeemed selves. It is of no help to claim that a tree is passive in the growth process. For the Apostle Peter says emphatically, "Grow in the grace of our Lord and Savior Jesus Christ" [see 2 Pet 3:18]. It is indeed a matter of course that our spiritual growth happens through faith (that is, through the power of God's grace), but this does not deny the fact that we also must purify ourselves and must ourselves grow up. Paul says, "Put off your old self, which ... is corrupt through deceitful desires, and ... put on the new self, created after the likeness of God in true righteousness and holiness" [Eph 4:22–24]. And we must do this, not only by believing through faith what we cannot apprehend ourselves but also by putting off sin practically. For this reason Paul continues: "Therefore, having put away falsehood, let each one of you speak the truth. ... Be angry and do not sin; ... give no opportunity to the devil. Let the thief no longer steal. ... Let no corrupting talk come out of your mouths," and so on [Eph 4:25–29]. All of these admonitions are practical victories that we must achieve in our life's struggle with sin, the world, and Satan.

So, we must not let ourselves be led astray into thinking that it would be sufficient if we simply "believe" without some sort of practical response. Certainly, faith is sufficient, and nothing but faith is necessary—as long as by "faith" we mean a faith that does not slumber but is living, a faith that dominates our whole person and all that we do. The fact remains that in our regeneration we were changed from an unholy person to a holy person; yet, at the same time we must grow up, make progress, and purify ourselves as long as God grants us life, so that we may proclaim by this the excellencies of him who called us, and may cause the light that has been kindled in us to shine in such a way that because of it, others may glorify our Father who is in heaven [see Matt 5:16].

§ 2 This needs particular emphasis because the belief that we are holy through what God *did* in us and *maintains* in us so easily leads to a neglect of the "watching and praying and striving," the "growing up in Christ," and the continual "cleansing of our soul." And also because, out of reaction to this, others then perceive that growing up in Christ as a kind of moral improvement, thereby undermining the very foundations of holiness that comes through regeneration. Careless Christians who neglect issues of the conscience and remain as they were in the past are to blame for the fact that this Arminian tendency repeatedly rears its head in the church of Christ. But if it has been established that self-purification also has been imposed on the child of God, then the need arises as to how we understand and distinguish the ongoing work of the Holy Spirit from self-purification. "May the God of peace himself *sanctify* you completely," Paul writes to the Thessalonians [1 Thess 5:23]. Even after God has made us completely holy through regeneration, that same God nevertheless still continues to sanctify us. And this sanctifying work that God performs in us is something very different from our self-purification, even though, of course, we surely could not accomplish that self-purification apart from the power of God. This work is accomplished as a "second cause," which always presupposes God as the first cause. Let us therefore first examine how this sanctifying that God continues to accomplish in his saints is to be understood, and then how this differs from self-purification.

Since Scripture itself uses the image of a growing tree, we would clearly benefit from considering this image. Notice that a tree branches out *underground* as well as *aboveground*. And between these two lies what we might call the *life center* of the tree. From that life center, the roots have sprouted downward, while shoots, and later the branches, have sprouted upward. We thus can think of a plant as consisting of three parts: (1) the life center, (2) the roots that spread out in the soil, and (3) the branches that spread out aboveground in the air. Applying this image to man, we might say that the first, the life center, is our hidden *self*. The roots, by analogy, are the inner development of our being, through which the "life juices" from God flow while the branches are the manifestations in the world of who we are. The life center can be said to have been made holy through regeneration, while the roots spread out in the sanctifying process that follows, and the broadening of the branches represents self-purification. This is a simple but transparent image that illustrates the distinctions we have been discussing up to this point.

Let us assume, by way of further elucidation, that, even as the human person was originally good yet became a sinner, this plant as well, which has grown to maturity, becomes wild after once having been cultivated. The plant was, we may presume, originally a noble grapevine, and as such had grown with roots *beneath* the soil and with broad vines *above* it, but then over time it became wild and turned into a wild vine. Or, to take the image from Isaiah 55, what was a myrtle became a thistle. This, of course, does not really happen in the plant world, but if we want to be able to apply the image of the tree to people, we must start with this obvious assumption. There stands a plant that was formerly valuable but became wild in the life center, wild in the roots, and wild in its branches. The plant has degenerated in nature so that it is of no value. But now the gardener intends to restore the tree again; he does not accomplish this by grafting, because then all that lies below the graft would remain unrestored, but rather by restoring the tree from the inside to its original condition. Assuming that he could do this, it would not benefit the tree if he started with the roots or tried to restore the branches. To make that wild plant wholly useful again, there is only one means, and that is to begin with what is hidden, the life center, and to renew this life center [so that it is] noble once more. If the gardener succeeds, he will have a plant that is restored in its core but still wild in its roots and wild in its branches. § 3

This is precisely the situation of the fallen sinner whom God regenerates, who has been renewed at once and is now holy in his life center, which is to say, in his hidden self where the sources of life lie. This individual is not yet sanctified at the root level, nor in terms of the "branches" (the life manifestations). To continue this process of restoration, the renewing force from the life center needs to be directed toward the root until that root is entirely renewed and has become the bearer of new life. Applied to ourselves, this means that the same God who regenerated our self and sanctified us now, in the second place, sanctifies the hidden root of our being by repeatedly [giving] new grace. This is not a work of God that, like regeneration, began and was completed at a single point in time; rather, it is one that continues until our death and is only completed when we die.

But the renewing of the *branches* is quite a different matter. The roots hide in the soil, but the branches manifest themselves in broad daylight. In the same way, the roots of our inner life are hidden in the mysterious soil of the Spirit, but the branches constitute the manifestation of ourselves in and to the world in a manner that is seen by everyone. In the strictest and fullest sense, it is impossible to revive that grown trunk and those branches. Such a thing simply does not happen. The trunk and the branches might be spared for as long as necessary to complete the working of the life center at the root level, but once this goal is reached, the trunk is cut down with its branches, and an entirely new plant must sprout from what has been salvaged.

Accordingly, we confess that in this life we can manifest only a small beginning of this new life in us, and when we die, God will annihilate all manifestations in our lives that are impure and give us a newness of shape and character that is eternal. But even though we know beforehand that all we have accomplished in our unregenerate life will perish one day, we must be mindful in the present of the fact that the wild tree needs to be pruned as much as possible, so that the sap of the new life may rise as high as possible and flow into the wild branches. The whole process of pruning, removing [harmful] insects, and allowing the sap of life to flow is, one might say, what constitutes our self-purification. In this way, then, it is something quite different from our sanctification, which God himself accomplishes in us. For God's sanctification works on the root, and that root does not perish in death; rather, it remains and passes over into eternity. This is an enduring good. Self-purification, by contrast, is what is done to the branches and the trunk, if you will, for the renewing of our character and our life's expressions. This process, of course, remains patchwork; it does not undergo a total renewal until our dying day, when we are liberated from the body of death—that is, when we die completely to the sinful life and retain our spiritual essence. However, for the perfection of this essence we receive a new, more glorious existence in eternity.

§ 4 At this point, let us leave aside our discussion of the renewing of the life's center through regeneration and the inner sanctification that God increasingly brings about at the root of our being. Let us instead focus on the self-purification of the branches and the trunk. This requires us to take into account factors other than only the "life sap" that rises from the center of our being. After all, the growth and increase of both trunk and branches are dependent on the *environment* in which the tree has been planted: the air, the wind, the rain, the sunshine, harmful insects, and external forces arising from humans or animals. What the environment is for the tree, the surrounding world is for us—but not the world frequently understood here as the realm of evil—that is, the world in its actual condition. After all, we were not simply removed from this visible world at our rebirth; rather, we remain, with eternal life in us, placed in a world and in an environment that at present still lacks that eternal life. Our self-purification, therefore, must occur in the midst of a world that is *not* consistent with our inner, holy existence. This matter, of course, is different for infants who go from the cradle directly to the grave; but those who reach adulthood and continue to live, exist as inwardly renewed plants in the midst of an environment that is not conducive to the renewed plant. And that world, that environment which issues from that unsanctified nature, is continually in contact with the Christian; in fact, it is a seed that we as believers all still carry within us. Scripture calls the realm that still adheres to us "the flesh," but that realm is homogeneous with the world outside us, so that we can simply say that we have to accomplish our self-purification in a world that adheres to us and surrounds us.

If the world that adheres to and surrounds us had been left entirely to the development of its own evil principle, self-purification would be literally impossible. The Christian could only protest, only attempt to leave the world, but any sort of purified character, purified existence, or purified life would be unthinkable. In this case, we would have to be separated from our flesh and leave this evil world. Self-purification could consist only in suicide, the absolute break with an absolutely evil flesh and an absolutely evil world. But (for the sake of the argument) even if this suicide were disguised as a self-sought martyrdom, it would be a self-purification that ended in sin, to the extent that martyrdom might be our experience only through someone else's coercion. But this is *not* how the condition of the world in and around us functions, and the world owes it to common grace that it is not absolutely evil but rather, in many respects, still relatively bearable. Common grace arrests the development of the principle of evil in the world, surely at certain points more than others. In point of fact, from this, as we showed on the basis of the earlier image of the cable ferry, people happen to absorb various customs and developments of life that display a measure of civic righteousness, beauty, and harmony. As a result, the world around us is partly good and partly evil. In light of this mixture, self-purification becomes possible, or to put it more accurately, self-purification is made possible by God.

Broadly speaking, life experience shows us that in many respects believers approach self-purification in the same way as the more virtuous among unbelievers. And we grant that the most pathetic thing about this is that many a child of God is put to shame by the more-virtuous individuals who § 5 are unbelievers. And let it be said: having a scrupulous conscience, developing a firm character, detesting what is base and lacking in virtue, controlling passions, leading a moderate and upstanding life, and so on, are altogether marvelous things that the child of God strives for in his or her self-purification. At the same time, it needs to be said that these same things—albeit in a different mode (about which I have more to say later)—are things in which many unbelievers excel; indeed, they are virtues that radiate among the unconverted. And surely we must grant that if we carefully read the ethical admonitions of the New Testament in which the apostles recommend and develop precisely this notion of self-purification and virtue, we can scarcely deny that these exhortations generally exhort readers to a walk of life that as such is also recommended and aspired to by more-virtuous unbelievers.

By way of example, simply recall what we quoted from Ephesians 4 [at the beginning of this chapter]: put away falsehood, be angry without sinning, give no opportunity to the devil, do not steal but instead labor, let there be no corrupting talk, and so on. We can only admit that not a few unbelievers detest these things as we do and try to guard against them—granted, surely not all, but at the same time we must level the same complaint against believers. In truth, there are many people who do *not* believe in Christ and nevertheless support this sort of virtuous approach to life and in fact put it into practice. So, in reality, we are dealing here with the possibility of a renewing of our being and a cleansing of our life that arise from human capacities that are not exclusively the domain of Christian believers; rather, they indicate a domain in which many unbelievers participate as well (and, quite honestly, not without good results). This, quite simply, corresponds with the facts as we observe them in life—facts we must face, precisely in order to understand that we bring dishonor upon the name of the Lord if we let ourselves be surpassed and shamed in these areas of self-purification. If unbelievers can accomplish such great things without the highest spiritual impulse, to what high aims should we then exert ourselves? Take, for instance, generosity, as but one example. Can we deny the fact that not infrequently a virtuous unbeliever can part more willingly and cheerfully with his money than a well-to-do believer? The point to be emphasized is this: we err if we think only of particular grace in connection with self-purification. Particular grace is involved, without question, as we shall see in a subsequent chapter, but not solely. The general sphere of self-purification is different, for it belongs to the realm of *common grace*.

CHAPTER FORTY-FOUR

THE CONDUCT OF BELIEVERS IN THE WORLD

In the same way, let your light shine before others, so that they may see your good works and give glory to your Father who is in heaven.

Matthew 5:16

The fruits of our discussion up to this point are exceedingly important. § 1
We can now see clearly the distinction between the twofold process a sinner undergoes when he or she returns to life. On the one hand, there is a direct act of God, who *once and for all* destroys in the core of a person's self *all* consequences of sin and of sinful straying. God's act makes the dead self alive and the sinful self holy. This occurs in such a thoroughgoing and pervasive way that there is no possible falling back into sin, so that the reborn individual *can no longer sin*, since the seed of God is resident within him. This direct act of God is not extended over time, is not tied to any preparation, does not use any means, and is in no way dependent on human beings whatsoever. It is the sovereign God who, in accordance with his eternal counsel, accomplishes this act at the appropriate time in each of his elect, and accomplishes it in the same way in all of them. This

act of God is therefore exclusively an act of *particular grace*. After this first foundational act, this act of re-creation, all kinds of subsequent acts follow in order to maintain what has been newly created (Eph 2:10) and to bring it to further sprouting and development; the reborn self most definitely collaborates in all this.

All kinds of forces come indirectly into play as means that God uses and lets his child use. But, in the main, the *impetus* that causes the plant with its flowers and fruit to grow upward continues to come from that same *particular grace*. In this sense, then, it is God who not only regenerates but also converts us, and who also grants us faith, sanctifies us, and will one day glorify us. But all this together constitutes one holy work whose aim is not this earth but heaven, not this life of struggle but the life of glory. In this sense it makes no difference whether God concentrates these various workings in a single point of time in the case of someone who dies immediately after conversion, or in the case of another whom God has appointed to walk this earth for many years in the glow of the higher light.

But in addition to this direct act of God—which, although it can be divided into acts of re-creating, maintaining, and developing, is ultimately *one single act*—there are acts of self-purification, which neither add anything to nor detract anything from our rebirth. Such self-purification does not add the tiniest bit to our eternal salvation but only strengthens us, as long as we are here on earth, enabling us to glorify the name of our God by demonstrating a godly life. This naturally is a mixed work—that is, a work accomplished within and to our person, in which God anticipates, supports, and inspires us; in which other children of God support and help us; but in which the impetus for the main action must always come from us. We must cleanse ourselves. "Cleanse your hands, you sinners, and purify your hearts, you double-minded," it says in James 4:8. It is striking that they who must purify themselves are addressed here as "sinners" and not as "believers," even though these same persons were told shortly before: "Of his own will he brought us forth by the word of truth, that we should be a kind of firstfruits of his creatures" (Jas 1:18). The difference, then, is that they are not addressed here in their hidden standing before God, by which they are holy and perfect, but rather in their standing as people who still live in the world and nevertheless are called to proclaim in the world the virtues of him who has called them to his marvelous light [see 1 Pet 2:9].

We are not at all claiming, of course, that there is no inner and necessary connection between self-purification and our hidden life before God, even when it might appear so. On the contrary, we hold fast to the conviction that living in the world, struggling in the world, and intermingling with the world is not a *means* to salvation but a *consequence* of salvation, and that its aim is not to add something to the work of Christ but to glorify God in this life. The Heidelberg Catechism expresses it in this way: our striving manifests a life of gratitude, which expresses what we have been describing.[1] Gratitude expresses the *motivation* for our actions and nothing more, yet it does not indicate what this action leads to and what our ultimate aim is. Why do I show gratitude when I purify myself? The answer is not merely because it gives me satisfaction. Although this does in fact occur, it is not our ultimate motivation. If we wish to express gratitude, it must be intended not for ourselves but for God. And we experience the latter only if our attempts at self-purification lack any motivation of being saved through it, so that we intend only to proclaim the virtues of him who called us. In this way we let the light that is in us shine forth, so that people might see and glorify our Father who is in heaven. For this reason, then, when it comes to our self-purification, we must never say that we don't care about what people think. For Christ himself says to us that this is *precisely why* we should do it. And only when people see it can our Father in heaven be glorified through it. But this implies that self-purification cannot be accomplished by the direct working of particular grace; rather, its working out is based on *common grace*.

This reality is necessarily so if only because it is a self-purification that is to be observed by unbelievers. For they must see our good works and be able to glorify God because of them. That is not the case with the direct working of the Holy Spirit. The world is simply incapable of observing what grows directly out of saving grace. The Lord Christ himself continually pointed out to the disciples that the world does not and cannot see the Holy Spirit and therefore cannot appreciate his workings. Only believers can do that. Only the one who has the Holy Spirit within has an eye that is open to the things of the Spirit. The person who is still merely "natural" does not see the things of the Spirit of God. And Jesus spoke as decisively as possible to Nicodemus about all that belongs in a narrower sense to the kingdom of God: "Unless one is born again he cannot [even] see the kingdom of God" (John 3:3). If spiritual things that are a direct product of particular grace belong to the kingdom

1. Heidelberg Catechism, Lord's Day 32, Q&A 86.

of God (as all Christians acknowledge), then it directly follows that when we are told to let our light shine before the world so that the world might see it, this is not referring to spiritual life in the kingdom of God. If people are capable of seeing it, and are to glorify God in heaven because of what they observe in us, then this *must* refer to things that are within their reach, things that fall within their horizon, things that they can judge to be good and praiseworthy, based on the discernment at their disposal. Here we are necessarily distinguishing between mystical stirrings and manifestations in common human life that are within everyone's reach—manifestations that, up to a point, command the respect of unbelieving people.

§ 2 Now, if this is the case, we begin to sense how different a perspective this provides for our understanding of the self-purification of believers. The need for self-purification does not drive us from the world to our prayer closet so that we might accomplish this work alone in secrecy with God. Rather, the reverse is true: we are driven from our prayer cell out into the world to stand there as a witness for our God. Certainly, it is the case that we do witness through our words; confession is always a duty. But we are not speaking about *that* confession here. And in this context "being a witness" refers to the whole manifestation of our person—our manner of acting, our conduct, and our whole lifestyle. And that lifestyle, that personal behavior, that manifestation in the eyes of others, must be a *commendation*, not of ourselves, but of the God whom we confess. By nature, the world is set against God. But when others see our walk and how our lives appeal to people's consciences, they *cannot* resist acknowledging that this God has decent, honest, and virtuous men and women in his service. And in the same way that we might, say, honor the military general of our enemy opponent, were he to appear with an army of courageous and virtuous soldiers, so too the world would have to honor our King because our lives are evidence that he has called to himself such a beautiful army of faithful, courageous servants.

It is imperative to underscore what we are *not* saying here. We are *not* implying that Christians should passively accommodate the world in order to curry its favor. On the contrary, the world would not appreciate this tendency in us. Rather, it must be clearly evident through our lives that we are not of the world, and that we do not honor the world but Christ as our King, and that we have engaged in battle against that world, having been enlisted into the King's army. But in the midst of that battle we must come across to others as robust and courageous, presenting ourselves as virtuous and decent, so that our opponents are attracted by the appeal of our courage, our amiability, and our virtuous tendencies. In this way they should ultimately envy Jesus, so to speak, for the fact that he has been able to win them for his kingdom. In the army of the Christ, discipline must bear such excellent and abundant fruit that the world, with all its hatred toward God and his Christ, nevertheless must come under the allure of his people; even in spite of itself the world must acknowledge the excellence of this King.

It needs to be emphasized that the self-purification of which we are § 3
speaking has nothing in common with the so-called spiritual affectation that is sometimes exalted in certain mystical or hyperspiritual circles. Walking around with a certain "holy" demeanor ends up eliciting from the world a rather strong repulsion. Even though it might mislead the average person for a while, the more mature Christian will see right through the conceit of this "spiritual affectation." After all, this sort of intentionally pious manner, mode of dress, tone of speech, and so on, has never been able to make anything more than a fleeting impression in the church of Christ. Covering a grimy and cracked wall with white plaster was never authentic and therefore could never last. But we should be mindful of the fact that all religious movements and all preaching that have viewed self-purification as occurring in the secret closet rather than in front of the world (that is, not in connection with common grace but exclusively as a fruit of particular grace) almost always, out of necessity, end up forcing the individual in the direction of spiritual pride, which is the death of all true godliness. In this perspective, a virtuous, honest, and faithful life in the world is nothing but what any person can achieve. The child of God then begins to pay attention only when something specifically "spiritual" is at play. Only what is overtly "spiritual" is of any value. And because this specifically "spiritual" inclination tends to express itself in certain external forms, it can do nothing but express itself through "spiritual" speech and in certain outward manifestations such as a dignified posture or appearance, (spiritually) overstrained verbal expressions, curious dress, and in a dour facial expression or an occasional forced "sweet" smile.

But things look very different when we take Scripture seriously and begin to understand that we must let our light shine *before others*, that *they* may see and glorify God because of it. At that point we realize that it is in the very nature of things that we must function in a realm that the world itself can examine—a realm that the world itself understands, where it is capable of judging, and where it will (and must) acknowledge us if in fact that realm lies open to all and if we do in fact manifest a power and enthusiasm that surpass the world's. Thus, the point of emphasis concerns our life in the world and not a closed-off spiritual life that exists, fenced off, alongside our other life; we live our lives as human beings among human beings. Our regeneration has re-created us as human beings. It has not taken us out of the world of people and magically created a pure quasi-angelic existence that now suppresses our human personality. On the contrary, we have been reborn as *human beings*. We are becoming children of our God as *human beings*. And thus we are to glorify our God among human beings as *human beings*.

§ 4 To reach this goal, we are well aware of the path before us. It is no secret how the world operates: people simply cannot leave the Christian alone; we don't have to do anything to get the world's attention. And wherever people are gathered, in their own circles, you typically will find an agenda, and that agenda is likely the following: let's see whether we can find something to criticize in those Christians. The world criticizes us as a matter of course; it will do so severely, sharply, and incessantly. The world does this in every corner, in every sphere, and in every social context. And if the world is able to find any Christian believers whose walk doesn't match their talk; who are careless in their personal life; who don't pay attention to their families, who let their businesses slide; who are not exactly honest in money matters responsible in handling financial obligations; who aren't upright and decent in their behavior; who are awkward in their dealings with people, or who are moody or prickly or tend to get angry—and perhaps also are guilty of even more serious things—then howls of derision will be heard because of such hypocrisy. And, of course, the world's shouts of derision are aimed first and foremost against us, but in reality they are aimed against the God of our confession, at which point the world says to itself: "Why should we exchange serving the world for serving the God of Christians? Now you see for yourself what so-called Christianity offers."

Jesus' admonition, "Let your light shine before others, so that they may see your good works and give glory to your Father who is in heaven," refers entirely to the world as it is, psychologically as well as anthropologically. Jesus knew that the world continually looks with an eagle's eye at God's redeemed, and that the glory of his Father, which was everything to him, would suffer bitterly if those who confessed his name did not live honorably in the midst of this world. And yet the truth is that the godly are always inclined to deflect this profound thought of Jesus, neglecting the realm of common grace (which is *the only realm in which the world can judge*) and attempting to inflate themselves spiritually in a false and unhealthy manner externally, through their appearance or certain actions that are perceived to be "spiritual." We cannot overstate the danger in this. Suppose that a Christian becomes an officer, or notary, or mayor, or member of a board. If we ignored the realm of common grace by simply withdrawing into our little one-sided world of "spirituality," we might imagine that we were acting in a specifically "Christian" manner if, being present at any of the above functions, we stood up and spoke sharply and decisively on behalf of one or another special Christian interest. But we would be forgetting that each child of God, according to the measure of his gift, must focus in the first place on the "natural" aspects of his position at work or group membership in such a way that he shows more diligence, displays more dedication, is more competent, and is able to accomplish more than someone else who is far from Christ.

It is true that the child of God must also bear witness. Of course. He must also take a stand for particular Christian interests. Not to do so would be cowardly. But this is most assuredly not all that it means to "let your light shine" as a mayor, or as a notary, or as an officer, or as a member of some board, and to do so in such a way that people see it and glorify God because of it. God's children do this precisely when they let their light shine at the office, through their occupation, in their actions as board members, and when they show that they can perform their tasks with excellence. Moreover, this applies to everything that we do. It applies equally to the civil servant, the store manager, the maid, and the average laborer. As Christians, all of these must be more virtuous and more productive than others. People must notice in everything we do that there truly is a power at work in us that is simply lacking in the world. In this way we make ourselves attractive to people's consciences. This is what it means to "let our light shine" in the exceedingly practical matters of life and in spheres of living that the world can judge. In these spheres we must command the world's respect. The impulse in us to do so must be steady and unremitting if we are to manifest ourselves in all spheres of life in such a way that we do not bring disrespect on the name of our Lord but rather compel the world to glorify our God and our Savior.

But let us not misunderstand the notion of "glorifying" either. In the § 5
proper, strictest sense, the world will *never* glorify our God and our Savior. On the contrary, it always opposes him. However, the world can be inspired

to have awe before this God. Many a father who himself is not a Christian believer nevertheless wants his child to be raised in the faith because he sees that children and young people from believing circles generally become less immoral than children and young adults in worldly circles. Well then, for the world's part, this is its way of glorifying God. When people prefer having Christians in the office because they are dependable or because they are "as honest as the day is long," then God is being glorified in and through that Christian office clerk. When people say, "Those religious maids are a nuisance with all their going to church, but they surely do work hard. They are excellent cooks, and they usually are available when you need them," then God is being glorified in such people. For then the world acknowledges, in spite of itself, that a power is operative in life as a result of faith, and that such power has a moral and useful impact on life. Young men's groups are at their best, not on the basis of how they dress or how they look, but when the groups propel them out [into the world] to be the first in skill, dedication, faithfulness, and diligence—each in his business, occupation, or work environment. And all this, in turn, rests on the fact that, in terms of its conscience, the world cannot free itself from Christ. This is why the world is glad when it sees a Christian stray and fall, insofar as that hollow confession has the effect of smothering the voice of the world's own conscience. At the same time, that same conscience is also awakened and stirred whenever the world encounters a Christian who inspires admiration and commands respect. For then the world senses that in that Christ there is a power, and from that Christ a power goes out, against which the world inevitably hardens itself in the only way it knows: in a sinful manner.

CHAPTER FORTY-FIVE

A NECESSARY AND DANGEROUS DUALISM

Since all these things are thus to be dissolved, what sort of people ought you to be in lives of holiness and godliness.

2 PETER 3:11

To the extent that we can differentiate in spiritual matters by distinguishing one operation from the other, we may conclude (1) that in regeneration God has made our self, at the core of our being, entirely holy all at once; (2) that he also sanctifies us afterward by causing the new life to spread from that reborn center into the roots of our being; and (3) that through his Word and Spirit he stimulates and incites us to purify ourselves in the branches. It is not as if the last operation could add anything to our salvation, nor is this indispensable for eternal life. Rather, the light we receive should radiate from us, and God may be glorified through this in the eyes of the world. But precisely because of the last [fact] it follows that this self-purification must be active primarily in the realm of common grace, since "the world" can participate only in this realm, and only in this realm, in spite of itself, can "the world" come to the point of appreciating and respecting Christians. § 1

All that flows from "particular grace" annoys the world, since grace is "a stumbling block to Jews and folly to Gentiles" [see 1 Cor 1:23]. Jesus could never have said that "the world" would glorify the Father in heaven because of particular grace. The world can come to glorify the name of the Father only in its own arena, and what is operative in this arena is not particular grace but common grace. Particular grace, we might say, digs a trench between Christianity and the world; only common grace offers a common sphere. All commonality between us and the world ceases where particular grace enters. It is only in the realm of common grace that we can find contact, collaboration, and shared judgment with the world. This is true even to the extent that "the world" judges and evaluates the significance and value of the Christian religion exclusively on the basis of its significance for that common sphere.

The atheist might find the Christian religion "a good thing," a "useful phenomenon in history," even something necessary for the masses; religion thus is viewed as an aid—a first step—in helping people progress from primitive conditions to more humane and civilized conditions. But the atheist holds this view of Christianity only to the extent that it increases moral sensitivity, brings order and regularity to domestic life, promotes honesty and "good faith" in social contacts, tempers the fire of human passions, curbs sensuality, fosters moderation, and elicits charity and sympathy toward the suffering. The atheist, therefore, considers himself elevated far above Christian religion. In his eyes, in terms of the civilizing and development of wider culture, the Christian church is something like a kindergarten for beginners and a correctional facility for people who are as yet unbridled and impetuous. The atheist might consider himself at present to be in the much more sophisticated school of freemasonry or of pessimism. But this does not contradict the fact that he considers the kindergarten indispensable for those who are less sophisticated (and alas, these are the great masses), and he sometimes is even prepared to condescend and make a financial contribution to the kindergarten.

§ 2 This attitude can be seen most clearly in how missions has been perceived. The perception of the unbelieving world basically went through three stages: first the period of malice, then the period of indifference, and now it has entered the period of appreciation. The conservatives were malicious, the classical liberals were indifferent, and the progressives are appreciative. Of course these three successive stages could be identified in the official documents of the government, the parliamentary debates of the States General, and the reports of the officials of the Dutch East Indies. In the period of malice, Christian missions was considered a dangerous intruder: the simple native population, especially on Java, lived quietly, was passive, and found in Islam exactly what it needed for religion. Islam was not so bad at all, and for such a simple Indian population it was much more suitable than Christianity with all of its foolish dogmas. If a mission began to operate among such a population, it caused nothing but discord and division; it could incite fanaticism among the Muslims and therefore had to be considered highly dangerous. Consequently, missions was obstructed in every manner possible. The men who went out on such a mission were harassed and reviled, and every possible means was used to make their lives unbearable. This angry period came to an end when the Dutch East Indies ceased to be treated officially as a source of profit.[1]

At that point the liberals replaced the conservatives and rejected those missionary harassments: the freedom of all should be respected. They themselves did not expect that Christianity would benefit the natives very much. Furthermore, the mission was powerless and small, but it was dependent on the friends of missions themselves. In no instance should the government and those in official positions oppose missionary activity in a small-minded fashion. The freedom of conscience should be defended in the Indies. Due to this less austere way of thinking, missions has gradually expanded, and outside of Java and Madura in particular, it gradually has become of no small importance.

As a result, it became possible for the fruit of missions to become generally more recognized in the life of the people on a somewhat broader scale, and in this way the judgment of the "unbelieving world" entered its third phase; namely, that of appreciation. Now it virtually is a standing contest to see who will write and speak most appreciatively about missions. Even the government followed this tack, and under its inspiration the perspective and approach among officials in the Dutch East Indies have turned around completely: they are pleased with missions now, and they appreciate and value missions. They even want to encourage missions. Some of these unbelievers have even given money to missions out of their own pocket. In fact, the government has already shown in more than one way that it is not at all disinclined to support missions using public funds in matters of education and medical help.

---

1. That is, with the dissolution of the so-called Batig slot, the colonial cultural system imposed by the Dutch focused on generation of revenue for the Dutch government.

This demonstrates literally what the Savior said: "Let your light shine before others, so that they may see your good works and give glory to your Father who is in heaven." For if the world is to see this light, it must be a light for which the world itself has an eye, and this is simply the higher light that shines upon the realm of common grace. For this reason we have continually urged that missions test its mettle in this arena as well. It is not, of course, as if missionary work in the realm of common grace, in education and medical help, could ever take the place of the call to eternal life. Rather, missions understood this way commends itself to the world, in order to be accepted and able to be all the more devoted to the work of conversion. This is why, in the political arena, this author also has resisted every effort to ask the government for direct help with the evangelization of the Dutch East Indies. The work of the government lies entirely in the realm of common grace, and for this reason we have maintained a strong position vis-à-vis the national government only if we asked for its support in *this* arena and compelled it to acknowledge that missions is of major significance in *this* arena as well. The Salvation Army, for example, owes its strong growth to observing the same rule. And the Christian church as such would certainly gain greater respect in the eyes of the world if the church's diaconal work were more strongly developed.

§ 3 Therefore, if we hold strictly to the principle that we cannot compel the world to give God reverence except in the arena and in those things of which the world itself also has a part (which is to say, those things about which it can form a judgment and by which it can measure what is worthwhile), we nevertheless must guard at this point against a very serious danger that has crept into the Christian church in an incredibly destructive manner. The knowledgeable reader might have guessed already that we are referring to the rise of the Ethical movement.[2] The emergence of this highly questionable movement can be explained only from the desire to show the truth of the Christian religion to the world through deeds. The people from whose heart and head this movement came were all sincere men who took umbrage at the barrenness of Christianity for daily life. They were men who reached for the powers of eternal life, were averse to abstract dogmas,

2. After his conversion in the early 1860s, Kuyper came to see the danger that theological modernism posed to vibrant Christian faith. In this respect, he was especially critical of the modernist Ethical theology associated with figures like Friedrich Schleiermacher (1768–1834) and Albrecht Ritschl (1822–89).

and imagined (entirely in good faith) that Christianity would conquer the world like magic if only it were shown that Christianity resulted not in words but in power. All that is true should legitimate itself by bearing the fruit of a moral life.

What they believed and confessed should, in fact, bear an ethical character, and the contest with the world should not be waged merely by setting thesis against thesis, principle against principle, dogma against dogma, and association against association. Rather, the contest should be undertaken by demonstrating through their actions that those who follow Christ surpass those who reject Christ in terms of self-denial and self-renunciation, honesty and good faith, humility and serving love, and moderation and mastery over passion and lust. The intent of these men was noble, of course. Their outlook did have an influence, and our heavenly Father was glorified—and not infrequently, either—because of the light that radiated from these men. We might even go so far as to say that many confessional and legalistic persons who spoke high-sounding but hollow words against this Ethical movement would have had better standing before their Savior and would have come further along in godliness if they had allowed themselves to be corrected by these ethical champions and, being inspired by that zeal, to be kindled in their own hearts with such zeal. At the same time this does not contradict the fact that these sometimes-harsh confessing Christians were entirely right in one respect: the Ethical movement knew how to work its "magic" in the *branches* but failed to see how, under its spell, the *root* of the tree was being cut off.

Thanks to the light that is shed on these matters by way of a broader understanding of common grace, we can see with sufficient clarity now the fundamental error of the Ethical movement. The movement's fundamental error is that it failed to distinguish between particular grace and common grace. The movement sought refuge in the manifestation of common grace and ultimately underestimated and reduced the meaning of particular grace; in fact, in its own circles it brought that meaning close to extinction. Again and again it tended to deny all that belongs to particular grace, because, in its limited understanding, particular grace merely divided and individualized. Instead, it attempted to develop all of its strength in the realm of common grace, where the world could praise and value the movement. The result was that such individuals constantly cast an inviting glance toward Modernists and looked with a suspicious and distrustful eye toward orthodox believers. As one of the leaders of this movement, since deceased, once told this author personally some thirty years ago: "We don't expect anything from the orthodox anymore; we are finished with them, but we will bend as far as possible toward the Moderns. We still have good expectations from them."[3] Indeed, when this author had left Modernism and entered the kingdom of God's Son, none other than the late professor de la Saussaye stated in a publication that he saw in the present author's transition to faith the confirmation of what he had always maintained, namely, that the new recruits for the army of Christ would come from the Modernist corner.

In such circles, the workings of faith in the realm of common grace were accorded the authority to evaluate the genuineness and truth of the content of particular grace. In the first generation of these enlightened thinkers, this went rather well, because the people belonging to this first generation still had been raised in orthodox circles and still had brought with them certain firm convictions and insights. However, by the second generation one clearly notes a downward movement, just as water always seeks the lowest path. And it is remarkable how, after a very short time, the young Ethical theologians actually came to surrender literally everything that was still associated with the realm of particular grace. Where the transition from the first to the second generation was already so rapid and alarming, who could say what the transition in the phase ahead, from the second to the third generation, would be? At present, there seems to be almost nothing left to give up that has not already been surrendered. For them, common grace (which they misconstrue) has become literally their be-all and end-all. Nothing pertaining to special grace has survived. These individuals still play with electricity, as it were, but they no longer want anything to do with the battery from which that current flows. All that remains for them is the conviction that any awareness of sin must be denied; consequently, there is not a single conceivable reason why they will not slide with Modernists into the seductive waters of evolution. The result is a Christ who came forth from humanity, reacting to the humanity that came after him, only

3. This presumably would have been around the time Kuyper became a pastor in Utrecht (ca. 1867). Jan Jacob van Oosterzee (1817–82), whom he identifies with a moderate theological persuasion, was a professor at Utrecht at this time and was deceased by the time these articles on common grace were originally published. Kuyper may also be referring here to Daniel Chantepie de la Saussaye (1818–74), who was a pastor in Leiden from 1848 to 1862, and whom he mentions by name in the following. For Kuyper's interaction with de la Saussaye, see "Confidentially," in *AKCR*, 57.

to be surpassed later by an even more highly developed humanity, indeed, even more highly developed in the ethical realm. Alas, the criticism of Jesus' ethical pronouncements has already begun.

But however resolute our protest against this fundamental error, to the extent that we foresee its danger and have a clear picture of what the ethical implications of this development are, we don't wish to dwell on this. That is because in its early development the Ethical movement had been provoked, at least in our firm opinion, by the false dualism that crept into the church and among believers. The fact that the church, in its orthodoxy, maintained its own unique character was its honor, its duty, its strength. The church must remain church and not devolve into a collegial association. The confession of that church should courageously be proclaimed over against the "catechism" of the world. Holy Scripture must remain the holy oracle that clearly shows the contrast with the thought world of unbelieving multitudes. Grace must stand over against sin, and rebirth over against the self-betterment. The chasm between belief and unbelief cannot and must not be bridged. In this respect our periodical has always supported confessional Christians,[4] and in fact it has even spurred them on to fight even more courageously and persistently to defend what is sacred and to act vigorously for their protection, if need be. § 4

But what we have denounced from the beginning is the false notion that the link with everyday life should be severed on this account, as if the Christian religion was not called to the life of society, the state, and science, for example. What we therefore have not continually resisted is the subjectivism of human experience, since we could not imagine a saving grace apart from the mystical communion with Christ generating love in the human heart again. Nor have we ever resisted a certain degree of breaking off contact with the world. Rather, in the footsteps of our forefathers, we have extended that breach into areas such as dancing, gambling, and the theatre. We have never resisted the rigors of a separate upbringing; instead, we have demanded that the nurture of Christian children be specifically Christian in terms of providing them an education. But what we have always opposed, and what we will continue to oppose as long as God grants us life, is taking particular grace as sufficient while completely neglecting the broad arena of common grace, [the arena] in which our

4. The church newspaper, *De Heraut*, which Kuyper edited and in which these articles on common grace originally appeared.

contact with the world must be maintained—in which we must engage with greater effort in the contest with the world and in which we must win our laurels to the honor of the Christ. "Scrupulous in their faith, but sloppy in their walk" has been the serious indictment that, because of this false dualism on the part of many Christians, has been leveled so constantly against believers, and, sadly, so often with good reason. Believers may have glorified God in their sentiments, in their family, or in their associations, but they completely forgot that they had to be "a city set on a hill," the "salt of the world"; they forgot that they had to radiate light so that the world, seeing that light, might glorify our Father who is in heaven. As long as people were "safe for eternity" themselves and enjoyed themselves spiritually, that unhealthy dualism made them indifferent to the honor of God in the midst of the world. Not all people [had this attitude], of course, and perhaps not even most people. Nevertheless, this unhealthy phenomenon has progressed further than many suspected, and that has diluted our strength and undermined our influence.

In light of this, from the very beginning we have engaged in battle against this unhealthy dualism. This has not failed to meet with resistance, of course. What has been bent and crooked does not easily allow itself to be straightened again. And because of our convictions, have we not even been branded pantheists by others? For that precise reason, it was necessary that the fundamental error from which this unreasonable and dangerous resistance sprang also be expounded doctrinally, and with that goal in mind, we have embarked upon such a detailed exposition of common grace. In fact, this was the very point on which our Reformed confession deviated from the Anabaptist practice of shunning, and therefore a false dualism had to be conquered on this very point. Dualism remains—and indeed, must remain—until the day of the last judgment, on which all things in heaven and on earth are brought again under Christ as the one Head (the *anakephalaioun*).

But it must be understood that the realm of particular grace does not exist simply in opposition to the evil realm of sin and unrighteousness. Rather, God through his common grace has also called into being an intermediate realm of civic righteousness, and it is in this realm that his redeemed children must contend with the world for his honor. Otherwise, the grand lie creeps in, and people begin to deny the many virtues that actually can be observed in unbelievers. Consequently, people cease to value a pure and godly walk for themselves, as long as people only settle for vague stirrings of peace in their hearts. In the absence of behavior, character formation, and a walk that commands the respect of the world, people are going to seek salvation in a pious lifestyle and demeanor, and in artificial spirituality. The only result to be expected is that spiritual pride will drive out humility, which is certainly not the least of the Holy Spirit's graces. In this way the life of faith suffocates because it isolates itself, and instead of commanding the world's respect by reason of the powers of the kingdom that are at work in us, we make ourselves and our circle a mockery before that very world.

As proof of our argument we might refer specifically to the many con- § 5
cluding admonitions in the New Testament epistles that urge continual self-purification precisely by means of laying aside all manner of vice and making a habit of developing various virtues. As they are listed and broadly enlarged upon in the epistles, they are almost always confined to the realm of living in which we see unbelievers excel too. It of course is not as if the life of faith consisted only of this, or as if that contest with the world in the realm of common grace were the *whole* of our Christianity. The ten volumes of *De Heraut* show otherwise, so no one can honestly accuse us of this sort of perversion. But everything has its place and its order in the Christian life. In this exposition of common grace we are not dealing with the mysteries of the life of faith, but exclusively with the effect of the light of faith in the realm of common grace, and only according to this criterion should our account be judged. If among our readers—older and younger alike—there are those who, no matter how firm and assured they stand in their faith, can acknowledge that until now they have never found and understood their proper calling in that broad field of common grace, let them not harden their consciences. May zeal and desire awaken in their hearts, in order that they might make up for lost time, not resting until on the basis of our walk and conduct as well, our Father who is in heaven may be glorified *by unbelievers who stand outside our circles.*

CHAPTER FORTY-SIX

THE ORDINARY AND THE EXTRAORDINARY

So that you may walk properly before outsiders and be dependent on no one.

1 THESSALONIANS 4:12

§ 1 We all are familiar with the contrast between the *ordinary* and the *extraordinary*, with the vast appeal that the extraordinary usually has for us. The ordinary does not stimulate, but the unfamiliar, the extraordinary, fascinates. By virtue of creation this appeal of the extraordinary lies in our nature itself, to the extent that it expresses the need for something to be desired in the midst of the ceaseless, monotonous course of things. Through the Sabbath, our human life follows the rhythm of the divine life, and the Sabbath is in fact the recurring extraordinary day in contrast to the six ordinary days that precede and follow the Sabbath. Whenever the Sabbath recurs, we experience the day as elevating; all people—whether young or old—enjoy the fact that it is Sunday again. In point of fact, we would not regret it if, now and then, a weekday were to fall out; but if a Sunday dropped out and our workdays ran together for two weeks straight, it would give a sense of exhaustion and fatigue. We would not like to miss Sunday, even if it is only the idea or the feeling that we would miss. This alone shows that the contrast between the ordinary and what disrupts the ordinary is woven into our human nature. As a consequence of sin and the curse related to sin, the pull toward the extraordinary has even been strengthened, although from an entirely different source of motivation. Seen in this way, our life is sensed to be below par.

What this means is that, if it were not for sin, the level within and around us would be much higher; we have regressed. But even though we live at a lesser level, the "memory" of the level on which our life *should* be experienced has not been erased from our spirit. Deep within lives the realization that we should be disposed to higher things, that the development of our sensibilities should be greater, and that we should be able to stretch our wings, as it were. Living in the valley, so to speak, being homesick for the mountain top, we look up subconsciously again and again, and occasionally we actually do climb some distance upward. That is, we do have experiences of higher enjoyment and greater joy, of higher intensity of life, higher zeal, and higher inspiration. There are days when the blood flows more rapidly through our veins, our pulse beats more strongly, the color of our face is more intense, the glow in our eyes has a stronger spark, and we can't help but laugh. On those occasions we do indeed live more richly, inhaling something of the high mountain air and experiencing how the extraordinary speaks to an otherwise unsatisfied need of our hearts.

This is not only true when our soul exalts in pleasure and joy. In serious times, when life becomes tense and our fears and struggles cause head and heart to tremble—and this might occur through trauma affecting our own lives or our families, or from enormous upheavals in the affairs of our country or other nations—there nonetheless lies within those tensions, even though they wound us, something that speaks to our hearts more than the everyday routine of the ordinary. In addition, we also can distinguish between two kinds of impulse that make us yearn for the extraordinary. On the one hand, there is the need, created in us, for a rhythmic life, a life in which the ordinary flow is interrupted by a Sabbath rest. But on the other hand, there is an inner desire, due to sin, to repeatedly reach a higher level after having sunk far below the level where we should be. Here it would be superfluous to offer examples, since everyone knows well from experience and from the simple enjoyment of their own children what that greater enjoyment of a higher and richer life means as a result of the extraordinary. Being able to go outside on a glorious summer day, being able to travel without being confined, experiencing the birth of an infant, passing an exam in our studies, or experiencing an engagement or a wedding or even a birthday—these are all experiences that beckon us to the path that otherwise so often leads us through our own fog and mist.

§ 2 This inclination of the human heart quite understandably has its effect in the spiritual realm. We live *below* our proper level. But notice that grace through Christ is there precisely to bring us back to our proper place. Everything directly related to this life of grace thus stands on a higher plane than ordinary life. It is the extraordinary that enters our life through the miracle of our rebirth, through the miracle of Christ's presence, and through the miracle of the Scriptures. There is therefore nothing strange in the fact that we find ourselves inclined to value what is overtly "Christian" over ordinary life that is "Christianized." As a result, we typically think that we can give ourselves wholly to the Lord only by becoming a minister of the gospel, as if someone who goes into missions is a better Christian than the father of a Christian family who has an ordinary job. Or perhaps we think that someone who devotes herself to nursing occupies a holier position than someone who devotes herself quietly to keeping house. We deceive ourselves into thinking that time devoted to one's occupation is really wasted time, as if the real work of a Christian begins only in the arena of Sunday school, church meetings, and Christian associations. The spiritual and monastic orders tend to be based entirely on this sort of mind-set. The life of the world and the "spiritual" life are understood subsequently to be two separate spheres: the first sphere is viewed as the earthly, the everyday, the very ordinary; whereas the second sphere is viewed as the heavenly, the elevated, the extraordinary, and the truly valuable.

In this way a vow of poverty, chastity, and obedience involves saying goodbye to the earthly, ordinary sphere of life and being taken up into the elevated, spiritual sphere. I thereby backdate my death, as it were. That is, I anticipate a transition from one sphere into another; however, in reality this transition occurs only when I die. But through taking such a vow I make that transition now, saying farewell to the world, wanting to be dead to the world, and walking around on earth as some sort of "higher" being who actually is no longer of the earth but nevertheless stays here—whether to complete the dying to the world or to bless this world with spiritual and heavenly gifts. At bottom, such a notion is based on a fundamental mind-set, a mind-set that prefers the extraordinary over the ordinary and strengthens the contrast between life in the world and the spiritual life by opposing them to each other in an absolute sense.

This tendency manifests itself differently, of course, among Protestants, but ultimately it has the same effect among us, as clearly demonstrated by the quasi-monasteries and quasi-orders that are emerging at present in the Episcopal Church of England. The Salvation Army, for its part, derives its appeal to many a youthful heart from the same feature. Helping at home, doing mundane work around the house, and so forth, have simply come to be viewed as too tedious, too dull, too ordinary. But appearing on the street with a "hallelujah bonnet" and a "hallelujah cape,"[1] being gawked at by everyone, and going from meeting to meeting for the purposes of Christian performance, praying out loud, singing, or preaching—this seems to offer the sort of excitement in which the youthful soul revels. And even when the hunt for the extraordinary doesn't take on such overt forms, we notice, for example, in typical Methodist goings-on something of the same thing. These types have neither eye nor ear for ordinary life, but rather a preference for spiritual conflict, spiritual excitement, and for what bears an overtly "spiritual" mark. In fact, the temperance movement derives its inspiration from that sort of spiritual inclination. This inclination tends to be found less frequently in its more active form among us Reformed Christians—in fact, we may safely say *too* infrequently—but this same inclination can also be found in our midst in other ways. For example, it might manifest itself in wanting to display a spiritual appearance, in praying often and long, in displaying a demeanor and attitude that exhibits something "extraordinary," or in what our spiritual fathers viewed as an artificial legalism, which ultimately devolves into a legalistic arguing about rule upon rule and statute after statute. First this is applied to oneself, and later it becomes a standard that can be used to judge the behavior of others.

We must be careful, however, with how we approach this problem. Many § 3
who become aware of the unscriptural nature of neglecting the ordinary and who yearn for the extraordinary easily swing to the other extreme and end up banishing everything that is considered "spiritual." We then find in our midst men and women with whom we can't even have a spiritual conversation, people who systematically avoid everything spiritual, people who show no sign of spiritual hunger, and those who consider themselves to be "Reformed" only when they have eliminated with the passion of the ancient Israelites—and we must note the irony here—the last grain of Methodist

1. Names of typical elements of the Salvation Army uniform.

leaven from their heart and home, until finally, nothing remains but ordinary worldliness as people in the world know it. These are the enemies of any spiritual revival who, at their best, act equally as unwisely as those who pursue a life with nothing but revival.[2] One sense of the term *revival* refers to being awoken from slumber. Even as in life a tendency toward sleep and slumber overcomes our spirits, so too revival will always remain necessary and must be gratefully accepted as a gift from God to stir us awake continually, to open our eyes again with a clear vision, and to make us go through life with care and sobriety.

This is why it is foolish to want nothing but revival. Indeed, it is necessary to be awakened in the morning after we have been asleep, even if the alarm may sound a bit harsh. But if the alarm were to continue to sound in our ears once we were thoroughly awake, had risen, and had gone to work, it would be an annoyance and hinder our work. This is why it is so unreasonable and absurd to let life be consumed by revival, since every revival must be followed by a pattern of waking until sleep is once more upon us, after which we again will need an alarm (that is, revival). But simply because it would be foolish to let the morning alarm sound all day long, we must not imagine that revival itself is superfluous. We imagine this only because we love a peaceful sleep and dread awaking and getting up. We experience a healthy lifestyle to the extent that we realize that every period of sleep must be followed by a "revival"—that is, an awakened and alert period of work. Or, to put it in broader spiritual terms, as often as Christianity "dozes off," the admonition "Awake, O sleeper, and arise from the dead, and Christ will shine on you" [Eph 5:14] must resound again across the land, and it must resound as long as it takes until Christianity is "awake" once more. But then the sound of the morning alarm must be silent (if we may press the analogy further), to make room for the singing of the psalm of life.

This truth, applied to the contrast between our intrinsically spiritual life and our life in the world, means that we sin if we seek the spiritual life exclusively in the "inner chamber" while neglecting the world. But we sin equally by imagining that we have a calling only to the world and thus are released from nourishing our spiritual life. On the contrary, those who go into the world without nourishing their spiritual life very quickly become utterly worldly. Only those who return continually to God's presence to be

2. Here and in what follows, "revival" is used to translate the Dutch term *réveil*, which is also the proper name for a nineteenth-century Dutch revival movement.

anointed anew with fresh oil can go out from that presence into the world to glorify their God there and to bless that world. This reality needs to be emphasized clearly and distinctly in order to safeguard God's children from the great danger that, in order not to be one-sidedly spiritual, they might make a complete turnabout in the direction of a total lack of spirituality. For before they themselves even suspect it, they become children of the world. Each day we must go out into the world again with our lamp to let our light shine in the world. But if we don't repeatedly fill that lamp with the oil of holiness, and light it with eternal light, that lamp will bring shame on both us and the name of our God, rendering us incapable of causing any ray of light to shine in the world. If we are to be effective in the world, it is certainly imperative that we continually advance in the knowledge of truth, continually sanctify our souls, unremittingly seek fellowship with God in Christ, feed ourselves with the Word, and strengthen ourselves through the fellowship of the saints.

Once we have understood this, we will be able to clearly grasp the fact that arrows do not exist simply to be kept in the quiver; at some point they need to be placed on the bowstring. All spiritual exercise and all spiritual enrichment exist for the purpose of increasing the Christian's strength, but that strength must at some point be *demonstrated* in battle. Exercise is always a means to an end; it can never be the end. But if we exercise, anoint, and enrich ourselves spiritually, and then subsequently isolate ourselves, it would be similar to a thoroughly equipped and well-trained army that isolates itself behind an impregnable wall while at the same time abandoning the country to the enemy. Before we go out into the world with a view to demonstrate effectiveness in the world, therefore, it is necessary that we allow our intrinsically Christian character to be etched ever more deeply on our entire being, so that being a Christian is no longer a mere outward appearance but something natural. In short, we must spiritually equip and exercise ourselves.

At the same time, our calling is not merely to seek the extraordinary, to allow our Christianity to be wholly consumed by the extraordinary, or even to pursue our work in the realm of the extraordinary. Rather, we must continually condescend from the extraordinary down to ordinary life in order to demonstrate in this ordinary life our spiritual superiority. We do this with a threefold motivation: first, to glorify our God; second, to bless the world; and third, to steel and harden ourselves for the battle against Satan. And we must accomplish this task not as if we are in a foreign region where we have to show images of a higher world by means of a projector. Rather, we must act in that world while recognizing *God's* world in it, and we must do so among people in whom our own nature dwells. We do this in an environment that is sick and bleeds from its wounds, but that nevertheless is a part of us and from which we neither can nor may separate ourselves without committing the sin of spiritual pride.

What we have just stated needs particular emphasis. Spiritual pride is the sin that stands waiting at the door of the heart of every believer when, because as God's children we have received grace and are sanctified, we sense that the unconverted world is far beneath us. We then tend to approach that poor world like some wealthy individual by throwing our spiritual pittance at our feet. And this is precisely what hardens the heart of the world toward us. It effectively severs any fellowship between the world and us. We then become aliens to the world, neither given any trust nor able to bless the world. Christ operated very differently. He came to the world, went out into that world, and became like us in all things, with the exception of sin. And this is precisely how we should go about it. We shouldn't approach the world as a schoolmaster would his students or as a physician encounters his patients in a hospital; rather, we should engage a world that is the world of our own family, the world of our own flesh and blood and common lineage. We should approach the world as a world in which we recognize and rediscover God's own handiwork, albeit damaged—a world that God loved to the extent that he gave to it his only Son. Therefore, we too must love the world, and love it in such a way that we give ourselves. And we do this not through artificial means as if to seduce it but rather because of our deepest convictions and because we feel a sense of solidarity with the world. We also do this in the knowledge of the world's transformation, convinced that the aim of every work of grace is to wrest the world from Satan and establish it again *as glorifying our God* who has ordained and created it, and who has maintained it in spite of its degradation. God does the latter through his common grace. Only where particular grace operating within us leads us to discover God's common grace in the world, by which we honor and accept it gratefully, is a harmony achieved that our faith needs in order to live in this world as a child of God.

§ 4 In the end it comes down to this: we do not walk away from our own circle of human involvement and our occupation, but we remain in the order and location to which God has appointed us in life. In that calling and in that vocation we do not bury our talents but, using every means possible, we make the most of them. We remain diligent in our daytime tasks, and we make sure that we have the highest standards in terms of the quality of our work, particularly when compared to others. We take our relationships with all people seriously, and we never let our influence on them be used for evil but always for good. We show genuine sympathy through our friendliness and the way in which we engage others, which arouses in others a like response. We practice thinking less about ourselves and more about others. We help where we can in terms of our deeds, giving counsel, our time, our money, and our encouragement. We purge our attitudes of all that is irksome, irritating, or unpleasant, and we seek to develop our character in ways that accord with holiness. We don't excuse anything in ourselves when it comes to honesty. We are resolutely fair in our judgment; we submit our desires to the guidance of the Holy Spirit; and we tame our passions, thereby attempting to live moderately, justly, and godly in this present world and in this way being a "letter of commendation" of Christ to the consciences of people [see 2 Cor 3:3].

From all this it will be apparent how many aspects of the common grace of God are incorporated into our entire lives. Take, for example, an African tribesman who worked for many years to conquer his neighbors and, where there was conquest, massacred them. Even after he has converted to Christ, he will continue to feel the desire to stick his spear into the ribs of an enemy. By contrast, we who have never known or participated in this kind of brutality, but who by God's common grace understood the morality of killing in a context of relative peace and order and never have killed anyone, will never know *that* particular temptation toward bloodshed. And in a less extreme example, take a person redeemed by the Lord who has come out of circles in which dishonesty and lying were routine: even after conversion, that person will continue to feel a much stronger temptation toward small deceptions and untruths than someone who grew up in circles where every lie was condemned and every dishonesty denounced, regardless of how worldly that person might be.

The great variation in the "distribution" of God's common grace thus would seem to cause self-purification to assume a very different character for one individual over another. We might even say that, as a rule, self-purification basically goes up and down with the lowering and rising of the waters of common grace. Christians who seem to have the benefit of having experienced common grace to a very high degree and therefore seem to raise self-purification to a very high level sometimes look down with indignation on other Christians who seem to lack this benefit and whose self-purification seems to have remained on a lesser level. But this is misguided. It is misguided because, even though they would seem to be supported by a much stronger impact of common grace and to have advanced so much further, in truth they do not stand on a relatively higher plane than the others. Yes, they may have advanced further, but it definitely does not follow that they have developed a greater strength of faith. To illustrate, someone who comes inside to escape a mild summer rain with only a few wet spots on his clothes does not have any right to look down on the person who comes in from a downpour with soaked clothes.

But from all of this we may conclude how utterly important it is to enrich the treasure of common grace in our circles. This is particularly the case as we devote ourselves with great care to bringing up the next generation. For a brief period, our system of education was inclined to see as its main goal—indeed, virtually its only goal—a "leading of our children to Jesus." Now, we would not want to minimize this aim at all, of course. But one can see that this would end up going off the tracks if it were understood as making our entire educational system subservient exclusively to particular grace, and if we forgot that the school is one of the chief instruments precisely for enriching people with common grace. It is not as if the two are opposed to one another. Nor must we conclude that the witness of the Christian teacher's presence is silenced. We grant that a school is not a Christian school if the Word and prayer are not there, if it does not promote the knowledge of the truth, if the sound of Jesus' call does not go out from it, and if the particular grace that flows from baptism does not make itself felt there. But all this does not deny the fact that common grace comes from the same God from whom our baptism comes, and that a school must earn its honors specifically in the realm of common grace.

Not only that, but everything that applies to nurture in school applies to nurture at home as well. Domestic nurture entails two streams of life that derive from God: the stream of his saving grace as well as the stream of his common grace. Only the person who understands this will be able to help his child with self-purification as the child grows, facilitating spiritual development and strengthening the possibility that the child in time will truly function in the world in a way that honors God and Christ. And let us not limit the concept of nurture to small children only. Living together in the home must have a pedagogical effect on all, and the parents do not understand the power of family life if they fail to sense that as they nurture their children they are continuing to nurture themselves, and in fact are being partially nurtured by their children. The entire family life, the very manner in which family members relate to one another, should seek to elevate the tone of cultural life as we participate in an ever-richer "distribution" of common grace within the culture. As long as we realize that an even greater portion of common grace is at work in other families, it should provoke within us a holy zeal to experience even greater grace. This should be our longing, not out of a desire for vain self-exaltation, and not viewing it as something that stands independently alongside our religion. We should desire it because all common grace flows from the same God from whom our eternal salvation also flows, and because obtaining more and more of God's grace is the natural fruit of the love for God that dwells in our hearts.

CHAPTER FORTY-SEVEN

COMMON GRACE AND GOD'S PROVIDENTIAL ORDINATION

O LORD, our Lord, how majestic is your name in all the earth! You have set your glory above the heavens.

PSALM 8:1

§ 1 If we have succeeded in our attempt to elucidate the meaning of the doctrine of common grace for our confession of Christ as well as for its bearing on the Christian life, and in a manner that has been more comprehensive than most treatments, then we must now deal with the subject of God's providence. Redeemer and redeemed find in the Triune God their deeper unity, and at the same time it is in and through God's providence that the unity between particular grace and common grace is assured. This fact of their unity, it must be emphasized, is of great importance. However much clarity we achieve by correctly and clearly distinguishing between particular and common grace, there always lurks the danger that a *distinction* ends up becoming a *separation.* The result in our thinking is that both workings of grace end up as two series of independent actions. But this must not be. Such a separation might lead to a duality in our hearts, in our lives, and in our confession, and it can ultimately undermine the foundations of our self-awareness and our moral existence. The trajectory of our argument so far therefore demands that we now go back directly to God himself and reestablish the overarching unity of the two kinds of grace within his providential ordination.

We have all the more reason to do this because, in common parlance, God's providence is most often applied to what happens outside of saving grace. People may not be interested in spirituality, but they hold on to "providence." In fact, they apparently cannot do without it and think it is fairly easy to understand. We find, for example, many well-to-do people in this sort of frame of mind, people who feel that it is appropriate to thank God for special success in business, for an enterprise that succeeded exceptionally well, or for a risk that paid off well. They began small but gradually earned significant money, and they think that God must be acknowledged for this. Sometimes the fear of losing what they have might overtake them, and where else can they find security against that except in the benevolence of God? Or perhaps they think that it is only God who can help their children through the world. After all, we are constantly in danger of illness, accident, or even death, and such people might not understand how others continue to live without some "faith" in a God who watches over the world. As far as they are concerned, the motto "Faith in Providence" could be emblazoned in gold letters on every street corner.

But we also find among the less fortunate of the world quite a few who believe in providence. People who have known great disappointment and for whom everything has gone wrong, people who still have to struggle with adversity, people with mounting cares who sometimes even lack the bare necessities, such people also continue to carry in their heart the hope of finding happiness. Of course, they would like to have it here and now, but this apparently is not always possible, and there is little chance that their fate will change. And yet a ray of hope is shed on their existence when they hold on to the prospect of someday being the Lazarus in Abraham's bosom [see Luke 16:19–31]. Perhaps they settle for the thought that everyone's fate must turn, so they reason that one portion of humanity is happy here and will be doomed in eternity, while another part suffers here but will rejoice after death. And they don't think it through any further. In the end, such people don't entertain thoughts of guilt and redemption. They don't take into account the possibility that there are exceptions to the rule. They only know generally that there is a measure of truth in this balance. And in this way these poor souls find in the confession of a providential God a certain antidote to the pessimism that otherwise would overwhelm their hearts.

In this way we can see that such belief in providence is divorced from saving faith on a fairly broad scale; and by some people it is even set in opposition to it. But there is no denying that a similar tendency also can be found among those who have trusted in Christ for their salvation. Such people definitely believe in heavenly and eternal realities, and because of this, one has a Savior and believes in these profound mysteries. But there are also earthly, ordinary, and very human realities that stand apart from those heavenly realities and have nothing to do with them. It is because of those things that one maintains an ordinary "belief in providence." It is possible to hear about a profound, spiritual faith on Sunday in church, but in practical terms a vague "belief in providence" is useful in domestic and everyday life. Moreover, by seeing things this way, the false split in our existence is carried through into the realm of faith; indeed, it penetrates our very view of God himself. As a result, people live two kinds of life: the one natural and ordinary, which we have in common with all people; and the other spiritual, which proceeds from regeneration, known only by those who have been born again. Requisite for the latter are the doctrines of the Christian faith, with their great mysteries, whereas in the case of the former people rely on that simple "belief in providence," which everyone can understand. Corresponding to our true spiritual life, we have Christ himself, with all that belongs to the mysteries surrounding his incarnation, resurrection, and ascension; affecting this natural life, we hope, is the moving confession of a Father who only resides in heaven.

But the more deeply initiated Christian would not create a divorce between confessional realities of the faith and a God of providence who resides in heaven. As it is, the Catechism teaches us to understand the words "Our Father who art in heaven" differently and in a proper sense.[1] At the same time, many believing Christians, who in fact take their faith seriously but are not used to thinking deeply about spiritual things and consequently often do not probe the mysteries of the faith, tend to view these two realms as separate domains. As a result, the confession of "Our Father who art in heaven" is generally understood as one's external lot in life. This separation, at least in the minds of some, is undeniable, which is clear evidence that we

1. See Heidelberg Catechism, Lord's Day 46.

are dealing with a distinction that resembles that of particular and common grace. Indeed, this belief in providence in part touches on the life we have in common with all people—that is, a life that accrues from the moment of our physical birth—whereas only saving grace refers to the spiritual life that accrues from the reality of our second birth. Furthermore, the fact that our Confession also distinguishes between these two lives shows that this distinction is based on clear scriptural truth, and that error results when what was only intended to be *distinguished* ends up being entirely *separated*.

In order to counter this inclination, we must emphasize the fact that in the holy Scriptures both the realities of saving grace and the things related to belief in providence receive equal emphasis. If we look closely, [we see that] entire books of holy Scripture are devoted almost exclusively to the affairs of the present life. Although we do not deny, for example, that in the books of Job, Proverbs, and Ecclesiastes spiritual reality shines through and, on occasion, is wonderfully conspicuous, it nevertheless is quite clear that the subject matter of these books and the revelation that they contain are largely concerned with the natural realm and not the sinner's salvation. They do not focus on God's mercy shown to guilty humanity, but on his grandeur in creation and his governance of the children of man. No matter how deeply the Psalms exhibit the spiritual life, we all are aware of how the Psalms constantly extol the omnipotence of God and his glory in the work of creation. And we are well aware that there are psalms devoted to this theme almost in their entirety, reminding us—sometimes with only a single word or single verse—of an even higher order of things. It scarcely needs to be said that the prophets of the Old Testament continually move in the context of the nations around Israel, which fall entirely outside of sacred space. § 2

And even when we move to the New Testament, we find our Savior continually engaged with the things of this earthly life when he heals the sick, feeds the multitude, or points his listeners to the lilies of the field and the birds of the air in order to exhort people toward a quiet acceptance of their external lot in life. Of course, when we come to the New Testament letters, we must acknowledge that the matters of saving faith get the lion's share of attention. At the same time, even apostolic literature is filled with all kinds of admonitions and consolations aimed not merely at the spiritual life but at the ordinary earthly life.

For this reason, we can hardly claim that we have nature to remind us of belief in providence on the one hand and the Bible for the purpose of saving faith on the other. On the contrary, holy Scripture focuses on both in equal measure and in indissoluble interconnectedness—a fact that must be emphasized all the more in light of the fact that current preaching in general could lead so easily to the opposite conclusion. In much standard preaching, the attention of the congregation is almost exclusively focused on those statements of holy Scripture that relate to saving faith. If we selected a sampling of texts used for preaching taken from a hundred or so churches, we likely would find that 90 percent of those texts belong to this latter category. Scriptural texts that focus more broadly on "providence" are chosen only by way of exception, since most congregations are accustomed to this one-sidedness anyway, to the extent that people might be disappointed and dissatisfied if the central focus on saving faith did not receive sufficient attention. In the past, people guarded against this one-sidedness by preaching through the whole of Scripture consecutively. Nowadays preaching from the Catechism helps somewhat, although we can say that we generally get the impression in church that the opening of the sacred Word is really the opening of a portion of Scripture dealing almost exclusively with the matters of *saving* faith.

§ 3 In actuality this is not the case; however, it is not superfluous to offer some measure of clarification before we continue with our present line of thinking. To begin, let us consider Psalm 148:

> Praise the Lord! Praise the Lord from the heavens;
> praise him in the heights!
> Praise him, all his angels;
> praise him, all his hosts!
>
> Praise him, sun and moon,
> praise him, all you shining stars!
> Praise him, you highest heavens,
> and you waters above the heavens!
>
> Let them praise the name of the Lord!
> For he commanded and they were created.
> And he established them forever and ever;
> he gave a decree, and it shall not pass away.
>
> Praise the Lord from the earth,
> you great sea creatures and all deeps,

fire and hail, snow and mist,
  stormy wind fulfilling his word!

Mountains and all hills,
  fruit trees and all cedars!
Beasts and all livestock,
  creeping things and flying birds!

Kings of the earth and all peoples,
  princes and all rulers of the earth!
Young men and maidens together,
  old men and children!

Let them praise the name of the Lord,
  for his name alone is exalted;
  his majesty is above earth and heaven.
He has raised up a horn for his people,
  praise for all his saints,
  for the people of Israel who are near to him.
Praise the Lord!

The concluding words of this psalm are explicit in underscoring particular grace in relation to Israel, and the use of the covenant name, Lord, indicates sufficiently that the work of particular grace is not lost on the writer. But the rest of this majestic hymn moves entirely in the realm of nature. It speaks neither of a Mediator nor of regeneration or election, but rather describes with energy and force the great acts of God in the realm of creation. This serves not merely as a reminder of the past but also as a reminder of the profound way in which God, on a regular basis, should be given honor and glory.

Chapter 8 in the book of Proverbs, more than any other chapter of this rich book, speaks of the spiritual realm, and some have noted, certainly with justification, that through the extolling of wisdom being done here, the eternal Word is being glorified. Even if this is the case, it is evident here that the subject is almost exclusively the mediating of creation and not of redemption. As evidence thereof, consider the following (vv. 12–31):

I, wisdom, dwell with prudence,
  and I find knowledge and discretion.

The fear of the Lord is hatred of evil.
Pride and arrogance and the way of evil
    and perverted speech I hate.
I have counsel and sound wisdom;
    I have insight; I have strength.
By me kings reign,
    and rulers decree what is just;
by me princes rule,
    and nobles, all who govern justly.
I love those who love me,
    and those who seek me diligently find me.
Riches and honor are with me,
    enduring wealth and righteousness.
My fruit is better than gold, even fine gold,
    and my yield than choice silver.
I walk in the way of righteousness,
    in the paths of justice,
granting an inheritance to those who love me,
    and filling their treasuries.

The Lord possessed me at the beginning of his work,
    the first of his acts of old.
Ages ago I was set up,
    at the first, before the beginning of the earth.
When there were no depths I was brought forth,
    when there were no springs abounding with water.
Before the mountains had been shaped,
    before the hills, I was brought forth,
before he had made the earth with its fields,
    or the first of the dust of the world.
When he established the heavens, I was there;
    when he drew a circle on the face of the deep,
when he made firm the skies above,
    when he established the fountains of the deep,
when he assigned to the sea its limit,
    so that the waters might not transgress his command,
when he marked out the foundations of the earth,
    then I was beside him, like a master workman,

and I was daily his delight,
    rejoicing before him always,
rejoicing in his inhabited world
    and delighting in the children of man.

Here, too, the deeper meaning is most assuredly not being ignored, and these stirring words definitely have import for saving faith. Yet in verse after verse the text shows how the eye of faith is being directed here not primarily toward the mysteries of salvation, but—at least primarily—toward the greatness and wisdom of God in the natural life that is based on creation.

This phenomenon is even more apparent in Ecclesiastes, although § 4
we need not offer extensive evidence of it. In the case of Job, what needs emphasis is the glorious self-revelation of God when he himself speaks to Job out of a whirlwind. Many today would hold to the interpretation that those who admonished Job were correcting him by means of a sagacious argument about the origin, nature, proportions, and consequences of sin, as well as of the means of grace that have been ordained to overcome sin, even the sin of unbelief. And not knowing anything about the book of Job, if we knew only that God himself had answered from a whirlwind, without knowing what God said, we would hardly imagine anything else except that God addressed his servant Job, at least first and foremost, in the realm of *spiritual* life. But we read something entirely different in Job 38–41. In four marvelously beautiful chapters the Lord God himself speaks to Job to reveal his glory. And about what does God speak in addressing him? He speaks about creation, about the ordinances of nature, about the stars in the firmament, about the lion, the horse, the peacock, the hippopotamus, and so on. In fact, let's simply refresh our memory with what God says about the horse:

Do you give the horse his might?
    Do you clothe his neck with a mane?
Do you make him leap like the locust?
    His majestic snorting is terrifying.
He paws in the valley and exults in his strength;
    he goes out to meet the weapons.
He laughs at fear and is not dismayed;
    he does not turn back from the sword.
Upon him rattle the quiver,
    the flashing spear, and the javelin.

> With fierceness and rage he swallows the ground;
> he cannot stand still at the sound of the trumpet.
> When the trumpet sounds, he says "Aha!"
> He smells the battle from afar,
> the thunder of the captains, and the shouting.
> [Job 39:19–25]

Now, imagine a preacher who visits someone in Job's condition, and in the presence of many believers he begins to speak to him about a constellation of stars, about wild animals, and about a horse. How would people respond? Everyone would likely say that this was not the message of a "preacher," that it doesn't do any good to trouble a man who is in torment with such mundane things. Rather, they would say it was the duty of this preacher to point out the depths of sin and the riches of grace in Christ. And yet, God does not do this. In fact, he speaks to Job exclusively about the works of creation, not in passing but at length, and it is all the more striking that the Lord does not add anything to this glorification of the created order. It is this preaching—and only this preaching—about the omnipotence and glory of God in creation that, in the end, gets through to Job. In fact, it accomplishes what all his friends' talk had not been able to accomplish, with the result that Job humbles himself in sackcloth and ashes.

§ 5 Now let us place alongside Job the following section from the Sermon on the Mount:

> No one can serve two masters, for either he will hate the one and love the other, or he will be devoted to the one and despise the other. You cannot serve God and money.
>
> Therefore I tell you, do not be anxious about your life, what you will eat or what you will drink, nor about your body, what you will put on. Is not life more than food, and the body more than clothing? Look at the birds of the air: they neither sow nor reap nor gather into barns, and yet your heavenly Father feeds them. Are you not of more value than they? And which of you by being anxious can add a single hour to his span of life? And why are you anxious about clothing? Consider the lilies of the field, how they grow: they neither toil nor spin, yet I tell you, even Solomon in all his glory was not arrayed like one of these. But if God so clothes the grass of the field, which today is alive and tomorrow is thrown into the oven, will he not

> much more clothe you, O you of little faith? Therefore do not be anxious, saying, "What shall we eat?" or "What shall we drink?" or "What shall we wear?" For the Gentiles seek after all these things, and your heavenly Father knows that you need them all. But seek first the kingdom of God and his righteousness, and all these things will be added to you.
>
> Therefore do not be anxious about tomorrow, for tomorrow will be anxious for itself. Sufficient for the day is its own trouble. [Matt 6:24–34]

No one disputes, of course, that the import of these moving words truly leads to the kingdom of God, and that these words bear some relationship to the spiritual realm. But after simply conceding this, we also must clearly acknowledge that the words themselves do not directly address the spiritual realm; rather, they are occupied almost exclusively with nature and the created order. The listeners are pointed to this realm of nature by means of plant life and the animal kingdom. What's more, Jesus describes these two aspects of nature by using poetry in a delightful way. It is true, of course, that human life is addressed in his use of animate nature, and the conclusion, of course, is drawn that we may surrender into the hands of our Father in heaven all those things in our natural life that frighten us, and do so with a quiet and unperturbed heart.

In this connection we might also point out that our Savior generally uses the same approach in his rich parables. Unfortunately, the parables are often rendered "unnatural" by people attempting to see spiritual depictions in them, and by interpreting every detail of every image in spiritual terms. However, this is illegitimate. It is precisely such impropriety—in this case, let us call it an exegetical impropriety—that renders absolutely meaningless the lesson taught by Jesus when we commended the "dishonest manager" [Luke 16:8]. But if we look at the parables as we should, as scenes that Jesus took from everyday life, and if we simply understand them as a mirror of that everyday life in which sin happens to be present, then it becomes apparent that in these parables our Savior is explaining to us the deepest mysteries of life by returning to the themes of creation, nature, and human everyday life. In short, the parables speak to both realms of common grace. A field, weeds, a mustard seed, yeast, and so on are all quite ordinary phenomena in the natural life. A child who takes the wrong path while his brother remains well-behaved and stays at home, laborers in the field and disputes about their wages, the leasing of a vineyard and problems with the collection of the rent—these are nothing but normal circumstances drawn from human life. And Christ points us to such circumstances, not once but repeatedly and continually, in order to educate us precisely in the knowledge of the deep mysteries of the kingdom.

The kingdom, Jesus wants to say through his parables, is not something strange that is tangential to this world. The kingdom is, as it were, reflected in ordinary life. The realm of particular grace finds its reflection in the realm of common grace. Between the two realms there is a certain shared identity, and all similarity is based on that identity. It is precisely these similarities that the Lord uses in his parables to explain to us the mysteries of the kingdom. Wherever tapestries from nature are found in his teaching, we may understand this to be normative. Hence, nature is in accordance with the ordinances of God, and the God who thus determined these ordinances is the same God who calls us into his kingdom. Moreover, when the parables involve a human being, human actions, and the expressions of the human heart, then the reader may conclude, in one form or another, that the parables are depicting human nature. And man is created in God's image. Therefore, we can know God based on the image of God, since we as humans are the ones who bear the divine image, however wondrous that might be.

CHAPTER FORTY-EIGHT

THE COUNSEL OF GOD

Remember the former things of old; for I am God, and there is no other; I am God, and there is none like me, declaring the end from the beginning and from ancient times things not yet done, saying, "My counsel shall stand, and I will accomplish all my purpose."

ISAIAH 46:9–10

We generally do not find among believers a clear and discerning insight § 1
into the essence of the doctrine of providence. Divine providence constitutes a very small portion of their religious reflection, and, as was argued previously, because preaching rarely delves with any depth into this doctrine, it is understandable that most people are satisfied with a superficial understanding of the topic, not taking into account the important issues that are governed by it. For the sake of clarity, we must initially delineate the contours of the doctrine. Perhaps it will not sound so strange if we preface our remarks with the comment that the confession of divine providence has actually more of a pagan than a scriptural origin, at least in the way that many people understand it. Holy Scripture never speaks of "providence" by that name, and Genesis 22:14, which often is cited in support of this absence,

does not substantiate the notion.[1] In the first place, the Hebrew language does not have prepositions before verbs, so that *provide* (from the Latin *pro* + *vide* = before + see) is a notion that could not be expressed in the original. The two words rendered "provide" in this verse both mean simply "see." Second, this is not about an event in ordinary life but about a miraculous action in particular grace. For the entire incident serves to test Abraham's faith in a manner symbolically connected with Golgotha. And third, a provision occurs here, not in the fuller sense in which the Heidelberg Catechism explains providence as "the almighty, everywhere-present power of God, whereby, as it were by His hand, He still upholds heaven and earth with all creatures," but rather in the sense of providing in a special case of distress.[2]

With that said, however, it does not follow from the absence of the term in holy Scripture that we must therefore refrain from using it. If this were so, we also could not speak of God's "Trinity," or of a "sacrament," and so forth. Holy Scripture is not given with a view to spell out concepts for us in great detail. Rather, it intends to impart the substance or content of our faith, a rich and full revelation showing the essence of reality. It falls to the church, which has received the Scriptures, to incorporate the richness of this content into its cognitive consciousness and to confess it in words and concepts that are intelligible. Scripture gives revelation, but theology arises through the church's reflection on this revelation. In this intellectual work, the church (understood here in its function as an organism) makes use of what has developed both cross-culturally in ordinary human life and in the course of human consciousness under the governance of common grace. This is why the Christian church, in its confession and in its theology, uses so many terms and concepts and why so often a term is not found in Scripture but derived from elsewhere. Anabaptists as well as Methodists have tended to dispute our right to do this, being under the misapprehension that we simply have to parrot Scripture without any further intellectual effort. But against this, the Reformed position has always maintained that we are called to much more strenuous work than a mere parroting. Rather, we are to incorporate into our consciousness the content of the revelation, translating it into the thought form of our human reflection. It is not enough that we simply place the gold ore from this gold mine, as it

1. "So Abraham called the name of that place, 'The Lord will provide'; as it is said to this day, 'On the mount of the Lord it shall be provided.' "
2. Heidelberg Catechism, Lord's Day 10, Q&A 27.

were, in front of us. Gold ore only displays its full splendor after it has been melted and gracefully wrought.

Therefore, we find no objection as such to using a term of non-Christian origin to depict the doctrine of providence; just the same can be said for the doctrine of the sacraments. But when we use this term, we must seriously guard against the danger of adopting pagan notions and then mixing them with the content of revelation. The task before us is precisely the opposite: to analyze the content of Scripture as clearly as possible in constructing doctrine, and through this analytical process to exclude all that is unchristian and foreign. The church through the ages has indeed done this, and when, for example, we read in the Confession and the Catechism or in systematic theology and prayer books what has been taught and confessed concerning the doctrine of providence, we are left to acknowledge that indeed nothing but scriptural content is expressed. However, the situation is entirely different with the more popular, common understanding of providence that still persists. For in that common understanding, held by most people, the concept of "pro-vide" in the sense of seeing ahead and the providence of God is seen as consisting primarily in God's seeing ahead of time what distress we will encounter, what inconveniences we will undergo, and then taking measures so that when the actual moment of distress arrives, the distress will be taken care of. § 2

This of course is something entirely different from "the almighty, everywhere-present power of God, whereby, as it were by His hand, He still upholds heaven and earth with all creatures."[3] The former implies that the world follows its course outside of God, as if, from this course, all sorts of troubles come, and God, watching from afar, now intervenes and provides in the case of trouble. He does this, not by intervening only at the moment the trouble arrives, but by already arranging things beforehand, so that the remedies are already present when the distress arrives. When heavy weather comes and storms rage, a traveler crossing the ocean by ship can be amazed at how the captain of the ship is prepared for everything, how he has everything on board that seems necessary to brave the danger, and how, through this foresight and action, the captain saves the ship and brings it to a safe harbor—the same, it is thought, is true of God, our marvelous Savior, who on the sea of life appears to have foreseen all

3. Heidelberg Catechism, Lord's Day 10, Q&A 27.

dangers and all eventualities and appears to be surprised by nothing, having taken everything into account, down to the last details, and therefore is able to save us.

Alas, this is quite simply contrary to the entire conception that holy Scripture gives us concerning the relationship in which God stands to the world and the world to God. The world does not float along independently, following a course of its own, and God is not a God who sees from afar and sees ahead, noticing the danger that will threaten and implementing his measures to ward off the danger. Much to the contrary: the world is not for a moment outside of God's immediate sphere of action; all that happens in the life and affairs of the world is linked to his eternal ordination. Thus, if we wish to speak (however mistakenly) of providence in the sense of seeing ahead, then we should understand that this "seeing" occurred in the decrees of God—that is, in his eternal counsel. All that relates to this understanding must then be subsumed under the doctrine of the decrees of God, not the doctrine of providence. In other words, providence is not a determination of what will happen, but rather the execution of what has already been decreed. "My counsel shall stand, and I will accomplish all my purpose" [Isa 46:10] expresses a proper understanding in Scripture that serves as the foundation of this doctrine. And if in retrospect it appears that we have been truly provided for in all things, then this is only because in fact all things are "known," ordained, and arranged beforehand through God's eternal counsel.

A proper Christian confession, therefore, depends entirely on the acknowledgment of the eternal counsel of God and on the conviction that God does not abandon his counsel but rather executes it to the end. Without a doubt, if this were understood from the outset, there would not be a doctrine of "providence" as widely understood; rather, we would speak of the maintenance and governing of the world, or we might express it in different words. In any case, the notion of providence would remain subordinated under the decrees, where indeed it belongs. When we trace what has been discussed in systematic theology about this doctrine, we readily discover that the notion of "foreseeing" or "seeing ahead" is absent. The entire discussion is about the maintenance and governance of all things instead.

§ 3 The fact that this erroneous belief has persisted in the perception of most people is due in no small measure to the fact that the counsel of God was viewed too narrowly and exclusively as the counsel of God for the salvation of sinners, and the decrees of God [were viewed] too narrowly as predestination. In the thinking of many, it is as if the counsel of God contains nothing but a list of the elect, or at most it is thought to include our reception of divine grace. What Scripture calls the book of life [Rev 3:5; 13:8], for example, is then thought to be virtually synonymous with the counsel or the decrees of God. If we add to this the typical understanding of the book with the seven seals [see Rev 5:1], it is generally assumed that these extraordinary events are to occur in order to decide the life-and-death struggle between the kingdom of God and the kingdom of Satan. This is basically how most people perceive the counsel of God, and not otherwise. Now, it is not as if, when questioned, people would fail to acknowledge a degree of certainty about other things based on the divine decree from eternity, but these other elements seem unrelated in their thinking. The mundane things of life are mentally separated from the spiritual realities of the kingdom, and as a result people tend to arrive automatically in their thinking at the untenable position that the decree of God is confined almost exclusively to this single, spiritual context.

Consequently, as a matter of course, people have a certain need to find for everything else in life a place where these mundane things can be subsumed and located so that they stand at least in some sort of a relationship to God. This place ends up being the doctrine of "providence." That means, of course, that God perseveres in his counsel with respect to his kingdom, but as it involves everything else in life beyond this, he is thought to have these matters in his power as well, "holding them in his hand," as it were. Hence, God's providential decree consists in his governing and ordering those other things with wisdom. And, as broadly understood, this providential decree then finds its core and center in his arranging and ordering all these elements according to so-called special and very special providence, the good as well as the bad, in order that they benefit his elect. But the decree of God is taken in a much too narrow and limited sense, with the result that the providence of God is imported in order to supply what is lacking. It is as if our salvation is affected by God's counsel, outside of his providence, whereas our ordinary life is ruled by his "providence," apart from his counsel. Both end up standing alongside each other as two sources from which the provision for our life flows: the counsel of God as the source for our eternal salvation, and the providence of God as the source of our weal and woe in this earthly life. But this sort of thinking is precisely how we fall into a dangerous dualism whereby our faith diverges along two paths and the unity in God's decree is no longer recognized.

§ 4 The starting point for a proper understanding of the providence of God must therefore be the confession that the counsel and decrees of God are all-embracing, that the eternal counsel of God encompasses all things, and that nothing can be named or imagined—regardless of how large or small—that is not included in and does not proceed from the decrees of God. There is undoubtedly a variance of perspective within this counsel of God; that is, one aspect of those decrees may be much more prominent than another and more dominant in the context of the whole than another aspect as it relates, for example, to a particular person or a particular situation, yet *nothing* may be excluded from that counsel of God. World history is not concerned with whether a single starling or sparrow falls dead from the trees during hot weather, and yet the death of that worthless bird cannot take place apart from the will of God, and that will of God cannot work other than by deriving from his decree [see Matt 10:29]. It likewise is of little significance when two African warriors pull a tuft of hair from each other's head, and yet Jesus teaches us that God has numbered even the hairs on our head; this necessarily includes the hair of those two warriors [see Matt 10:30]. We use these two examples not because we want to be irreverent but only because Jesus himself uses them to clearly state the reality: there is nothing that happens apart from God, and there is nothing that we may exclude from his decretive will—that is, from his eternal counsel. Anyone who suggests or argues otherwise immediately breaks the necessary and organic connection that mutually exists among *all* things, misunderstanding the unity of God's creation and devaluing it to the level of a tool assembled from individual parts or a mechanism such as we humans make.

We should pay all the more attention to this difference between an assembled mechanism and an inwardly coherent organism, because in the past this difference has been overlooked far too often. At the same time we should gratefully acknowledge that especially in the present century there is evidence of greater insight into the essence and the significance of "the organism." For what God accomplishes and what humankind is able to accomplish cannot be distinguished any better than by means of precisely this contrast. We humans make bouquets of flowers; God makes the flowers grow. Now, what is the difference between the two other than the fact we pick flowers and combine and arrange these flowers in a certain order of size and color, and tie them together with string, yarn, or wire? We cannot make a bouquet if we don't first find the flowers. We cannot do anything beyond collecting or bundling the loose flowers together. And when the bouquet is finished and pleases the senses, it only takes one or two days before that same bouquet wilts and soon becomes so deformed and foul smelling that we remove it from the room and throw it in the garbage.

But God makes flowers *grow*. He does not put those flowers together from leaves and stems and pistils as we do when we manufacture artificial flowers; he creates them in such a way that they develop from a bud, the bud sprouts from a stem or stalk, the stalk shoots up from a germ, and the germ arises from the seed—the seed that he has prepared from an earlier flower and that he also has prepared organically. And when that flower later has completed its period of blooming, it bears fruit, and that fruit contains new seed. From that seed yet again God cultivates new flowers, while in the meantime with the arrival of spring, new buds appear on the old stem. Now, we humans could never do this—neither the gardener, nor the florist, nor the nurseryman—or even something remotely like it. Humans can determine which flowers they want to see grow in their garden, and they can crossbreed various kinds of flowers too, but they are powerless when it comes to the processes of growth and blooming. That comes only from nature, and what is the source of nature other than the omnipotent power of God? Our work, as it were, always remains "assembling" things, at least as far as what is visible; only in the spiritual realm has God imparted to his image-bearer something of the glory of the organic. The thinker and the singer think and sing organically, not mechanically, and in such a way that they can think and sing only if God, the Source and Creator of all that is organic, works organically in their thinking or imagining.

But if the organic is therefore the unique hallmark of the activity of God, § 5
then it goes without saying that we utterly misunderstand the glory of the counsel of God if we view that eternal counsel as a string of separate, individual decrees. Yet this is what people so often do. Thus, the counsel of God as it concerns the doctrine of election (to use this most profound doctrine as an illustration), is understood as a long list of unrelated names. All the elect appear on this list, one below or alongside the other. But by contrast, holy Scripture teaches that the elect are members of one body, that they belong together under one Head and constitute one entity, and that all the elect come from one and the same human race and are incorporated into the one Christ, intended to be one living vine with him and standing as members of the same body in one mutual life relationship. We sense, then, that we cannot exclude from the counsel of God the corporate element—this unity of the body, this unity in Christ, this belonging together and being one.

Both elements belong to the counsel of God: namely, that these individual, specific persons are the elect members of the body, and that together they will constitute one body. Both the entire body and the individual members of that body must therefore be established in God's counsel. And to further the organic analogy, because a body does not come into being by the mere assembly of its members, but rather grows from the root and seed, those individual members as well as the body of Christ itself must have been organically conceived and predetermined in God's counsel. Believers are "elect" indeed, but elect in him (that is, in Christ) who is eternal.

If this is true in the spiritual realm, then it applies, of course, in the nonspiritual realm as well, and in the link between the non-spiritual and the spiritual. We simply may not confess that the decrees of God account for the soul but not for our body. The profound difference between the masculine and the feminine among human beings demonstrates this, as does ethnicity: the body of a Khoi, for example, differs so drastically from the body of a European that no one can say that God is "indifferent" in how he has prepared the human soul to indwell a human body. No one would deny that much depends on our body. Nor would we claim that although both our soul and our body are predetermined as such, the connection and cohesion between the two are somehow a matter of divine indifference. As evidence, simply ask anyone who is deaf or blind from birth how such a "small" defect as deafness or blindness dominates the whole development of that person's inner life. The same is true of the family into which we were born: who can deny the degree to which past generations of our ancestors affect our own inclinations and habits? This applies not only to our immediate surroundings but also to the environment in which we have been placed. An Eskimo, for example, is exposed to entirely different temptations than someone who lives in a large metropolis. In many respects, the conflicts in rural areas are quite different from those in the office or at the stock exchange or in our commercial centers. In short, the interaction—the connection—between us and our environment does not have boundaries but extends everywhere. There is literally nothing that cannot exercise influence, and those influences are exercised by the smallest as well as the largest things.

We already have pointed out that the physical cause of many people's deafness can rarely be determined, and yet that same rule is at work in all spheres. The Syrian who killed Ahab did not aim at him, even when his arrow penetrated Ahab's heart [see 1 Kgs 22:34]. What determines the point where the arrow penetrates? One millimeter to the left or to the right on the bowstring makes a difference as wide as ten men when shooting from a distance. In addition, the variability of the wind causes deviations to the left or to the right. Yet, life and death were in the balance—and in this case, the death of an important person, for Ahab was king. Also at stake was the redemption of God's people, insofar as Ahab was the opponent of Jehovah and his people. Therefore, we are not permitted to conceive of any decree involving Israel other than one that also determined what kind of wind would blow on that day, in that hour, and in that spot, as well as how strong that wind would be blowing.

But this is the case in all things. Nothing is so small that it cannot have far-reaching consequences. When lots are cast, the tipping of the dice in a container can decide a man's life or death. Although that lot is cast by human hands, how it ends up falling is the Lord's doing. This is not an ad hoc decision on God's part but rather a decision that was foreseen and intended from eternity and now comes in this form because it had been foreseen this way. Our conclusion, then, is this: nothing—nothing in heaven and nothing on earth, nothing in the universe, nothing in nature, nothing in the plant kingdom, nothing in the animal kingdom, and surely nothing among human beings—can be excluded from the counsel and decrees of God. As for human beings, nothing with respect to their soul, their body, their lot in life, their gender, or even the entire history of humanity may be excluded. This leads to the inexorable conclusion that the entire realm that often is considered to be the "providence of God" must be included within God's counsel with just as equal decisiveness as the decree concerning our spiritual salvation. For in God's decrees, not only the results but the causes as well are determined. This simply cannot be otherwise, since the results require and presuppose their causes. And if this is so, then it follows that the providence of God can never simply mean a looking ahead to future afflictions from within time, since this aspect is already included in the divine decree. At the very most it can refer to not merely a "fore-seeing" but a providing, to the extent that the nature of the decree is such that everything requiring maintenance inheres in that very decree itself.

CHAPTER FORTY-NINE

TRANSCENDENCE AND IMMANENCE

And yet this was a small thing in your eyes, O Lord God. You have spoken also of your servant's house for a great while to come, and this is instruction for mankind, O Lord God!

2 Samuel 7:19

§ 1 Following the preceding argument, it is undeniable that any "seeing ahead of time" of what is to come may not be ascribed to the providence of God as popularly understood; rather, it belongs to the *decrees* of God. The whole notion needs to be set aside that the affairs of the world run by themselves, and that, as a result, they repeatedly break down as a consequence of sin, but that God, seeing beforehand what is coming, now hastily takes measures to prevent the threat. To the contrary, everything is fixed in the eternal decree, and in that decree everything *has been* seen beforehand. Moreover, in that same decree all the means by which everything comes that must come are also planned and assured. It is unthinkable that the order of creation should be disturbed contrary to the divine decree. Equally unthinkable is a restoration of the original order in which the entire plan and every means for implementing that plan is not included in the decree. Therefore, after the decree a *second* foreseeing is simply impossible. All that can, and certainly does, come afterward is the fact that God omnipotently executes his decree that has been established from eternity.

Thus, if any sense of "seeing ahead of time" is eliminated from the concept of providence, we should not conclude that in his decree God has "seen" future things beforehand, as if they were observed by him as being outside themselves. Past generations have continually struggled with this distorted understanding of the "knowledge of God." To cite a contemporary application, the Arminians tend to embrace this way of thinking, in order to maintain their belief in "foreseen faith." The implication is that election did not take place in order that the elect would come to faith; rather, it is thought, long before the persons were born, God saw who would accept faith and who would reject it. The conclusion was that he elected only the former on the basis of their faith, which he foresaw. This, let it be said, is a monstrous notion, and our Christian forefathers always maintained in contrast, on the basis of God's Word, that God's knowledge comes from his decree, not from his observation of things. God "decrees" his purposes just as a general knows how his troops will march: not because he scrutinizes and studies them, but on the basis of the battle plan he himself draws up and the command he himself has issued.[1] Here we might add an additional observation: "seeing what will happen" makes sense for a prophet because he sees what God shows him in his counsel. However, from the divine standpoint this is an idle and meaningless thought when we fail to consider God's counsel, for outside that counsel there is simply nothing in the future, nothing that is or exists under any form or name whatever; and wherever there is nothing, no one, including God, can observe what is not there.

We also must recognize that the whole secondary notion of seeing a matter beforehand—and on this basis taking measures beforehand so that when the moment comes the "provision" is ready—should be abandoned once and for all. Even when we grant the fact of the decree of God, it does not involve "seeing" distresses "beforehand" in order to prepare the necessary measures for provision. On the contrary, it is the reverse: the final goal has been set by God himself, and all the means have also been directed by him to reach that final goal with certainty. In some ways, the term *providence* obstructs a proper understanding of the concept, but since the term has become so entrenched in our vocabulary (with no better term to replace it),

1. See Canons of Dort, I.9.

it behooves us to warn against any distortions that people would associate with the term. What we call providence is nothing but the implementation of the decree by means of maintaining and governing all things.

§ 2 At the same time, we must not be oblivious to the fact that, from our human perspective, everything is in a state of constant change, and in terms of our own finite awareness there is something profoundly reassuring in holding on to this notion of a fatherly care that accompanies us. In relation to spiritual reality, everything has two sides, and everything can be presented in two ways: how it manifests itself from God's side, and how it manifests itself in our human awareness. Holy Scripture itself reminds us of this duality, for example, when it speaks of a divine "repentance." On one occasion we read that "the Lord regretted that he had made man on the earth, and it grieved him to his heart" [Gen 6:6], yet it firmly states elsewhere that God "is not a man, that he should have regret" [1 Sam 15:29]. This is a contradiction, the skeptic will say, and the enemy of Christian faith will use such examples to lead the unreflecting, wavering, and doubting person astray.

Yet we should not think it unnatural or impossible that these two statements, which seem so apparently contradictory, should be contained in the same scriptural text. Here is yet another example of viewing a matter from two perspectives: God's perspective and man's perspective. When we place ourselves (and we say this reverently) in God's position, then his counsel is unchangeable, his being is unchangeable, and it is foolishness to speak of God "regretting." But, on the other hand, if we speak as human beings from our perspective, then when we first hear of the threat of God's wrath and feel ourselves restored by the judgment being turned away and by mercy coming, as human beings we have no other way of expressing it than by saying that God "regrets" or "repents" of the evil that he announced he would bring upon the people.

Even in the relationship between an earthly father and his child we can find the same contrast. If a child does not want to do what is good, the father will realize that in order to turn the child away from his evil scheme, as a final measure he must employ a very serious threat. He does not use this threat so much with the intention of implementing it, but rather in the quiet confidence that the threat alone will have the desired outcome and make its implementation unnecessary. But then isn't he toying with his child? No. If his child does not change his behavior, then it *will* indeed get that far, and it is precisely the seriousness of the fatherly word that accomplishes the desired outcome. The fatherly anger does touch the child's heart. The child turns around, and the father's anger is defused. We see God dealing with his people in this way (and in no other). He treats his people entirely in the manner of an earnestly disposed father. First, he exhorts, and if that does not help, he becomes angry and threatens. But when that flaming anger and the threat it produces have turned the heart of the people, then God relents and turns once again in mercy toward his children, and in this sense it is said that God "regretted" or "repented" of the evil that he had threatened to bring upon his people.

We dare not think that it would be safest to set aside and banish this human perspective and only keep the divine perspective, for this would mean giving up an essential and indispensable element of God's revelation in terms of its *pedagogical* character—something that more than one Reformed Christian has been guilty of doing all too rashly. Just as someone who attempts to converse with a foreigner has to transpose his own thoughts into the other's language in order to be understood, and just as when speaking with a small child you must express yourself in a way understandable in the child's world, so too it is with God: in order to deal with us human beings, he had to approach us and deal with us using human categories. This is condescending goodness, but no less a condescension of his love, which is indispensable if it is to have any impact on us. No one understands, the Apostle Paul observes, what is in man but the spirit of man that is in him [1 Cor 2:11]. It is not God who is limited, but we. Divine realities can have an effect on us only when they are communicated to us in a meaningful manner. And the fact that God *can and does* deal with us in such a way is evidenced by the fact that he himself created us as humans and thus devised human nature for us and realized human nature in us.

Approaching us in human fashion is therefore not approaching us in a form that is alien to him, but rather in a form that he himself has devised and decreed for us. Nothing would have had a more devastating impact on our spiritual life than if God had laid open before us the "book" of his decrees. In reading what it had decreed, we would have lost all courage, our resilience would have vanished, and any growth or development in us would have simply been aborted. For this reason, the truths of God's eternal counsel have been deliberately hidden from us. From our perspective, then, our whole future is *uncertain*, notwithstanding the fact that it is totally certain and fixed with God. And now in the midst of that uncertainty, God comes to us with his command, his exhortation, his threat of punishment, and his promise of reward in order to stimulate and develop us in accordance with our human nature. And God does all this just as essentially, intentionally, and seriously as we ourselves would when speaking seriously with a small child. This is true even if we express ourselves in words we would not use with ourselves or with others.

§ 3 In all of this nothing else is at work other than the antithesis—which for us seems irreconcilable—between the eternal in God and the temporal in our human existence. God is, whereas we become. His name is Jehovah, that is, "I am who I am; I will be who I will be." In him there is no change or shadow of turning (Jas 1:17). It would amount to abandoning the Triune God and giving ourselves to the most dangerous form of pantheism if we were to think of a change, a "becoming," a process in God's being. But this is not our nature. We don't remain the same even for a moment. We change continually. Our life is one of continuously "becoming." In fact, a continual process is what our existence demands. This "being" of God and this "becoming" of humans, this eternality of God and this changing, temporal nature of humans thus stand directly opposite one another. No bridge can be built here. We cannot imagine an eternally unchanging *being*. For our part, we lack the capacity to put ourselves in the position of the eternal God. But God, who himself created time, in his revelation to us can move for our sake from the eternal into the temporal, making himself known to us in all kinds of manifestations.

Meanwhile, reminders of the eternal and unchangeable character of the divine Being must be injected into human experience, so that we may fear and honor him as Jehovah, as being who he was, is, and will be. But in his dealings with his people, the Almighty continually steps out of the eternal into the temporal and changeable; he adapts himself to our human nature and speaks and deals with us as if he were a human being. We experience a condescending goodness of God that ultimately culminated in the incarnation of the Word, when God himself appeared in human form among us and as a man spoke and dwelt among us humans. It therefore is an error if we set aside this important aspect of Scripture as being simply an imperfect Old Testament notion. We are dealing here not with a mere notion or construction but with ultimate reality. God *has* dwelt among human beings in this manner, and in this manner he still dwells with those who are his. The truly instructive force of this revelation affects our soul only when, in this way, we understand scriptural commands or exhortations and take seriously the threat of punishment or an exhortation or the prospect of reward, allowing them to affect and dominate our behavior.

If we now transfer this understanding to the doctrine of providence, what we said at the beginning of this chapter becomes intelligible: from the standpoint of human awareness, the notion of One who cares for us and sees everything beforehand, of a Helper who takes care of everything, is richly comforting. The knowledge that we are in the hand of God, who will make everything "turn to my good; for He is able to do it, being Almighty God, and willing also, being a faithful Father," gives rest to our heart and is the source of our vitality.[2] This is not because we want to set aside the counsel of God, as if we would want to make his decree uncertain, but because in *our* consciousness our life is not lived on the basis of these decrees. Certainly, we firmly know that in those decrees—and in those decrees alone—lies the foundation on which our entire existence rests, and we heartily believe that one day it will become manifest how our whole life has been nothing but the implementation of the program for our personal life that had been determined from all eternity in those decrees. But we *do not operate* on this basis, we must not *want to operate* on this basis, and we *cannot operate* on the basis of this, for the very reason that we do not know this program for our life. It resides in God. It is in his book, and we cannot read in the book of his counsel.

Thus, when each new day dawns, we do not think, "It stands in the decree that I will spend today in this way, and so this is how I will act." Rather, knowing nothing of the content of the decree, we begin to think about our task, to work out what we have to do, to set our duty before us, and to act accordingly, albeit with a mixture of all kinds of influences and circumstances. If we wanted to act on the basis of the decree, we would simply have to give up and do nothing. After all, who can build on the basis of sealed specifications? We therefore conduct our real life every morning, afternoon, and evening, not as something flowing to us from the decree, but as something arising out of the promptings of our heart, from the pressure of circumstances, and from the voice of conscience that speaks to us. Looking back, we are able to confess that, in this way, it was fixed and decreed in God's counsel, even when God did not work it in us directly from that counsel. He implements his counsel by causing all kinds of promptings,

2. Heidelberg Catechism, Lord's Day 9, Q&A 26.

stimuli, influences, and calls of duty to affect us, but for us these various factors represent the only motivations underlying our actions. Therefore, it is not at all accurate to say that this is merely a human notion. On the contrary, this is how human reality subsists. This is how we exist. This is how we pass from one day to the next. In this way, and no other, we know life. We simply know nothing of what is included in God's decrees about our life from year to year; indeed, even about the day of our death we know nothing until the decree has been implemented.

§ 4 Is it, then, as a result of sin that we sealed the book of God's counsel on our behalf? Is it possible that God originally intended for us to live on the basis of a direct knowledge of the decrees? And is it only because of the consequences of sin that the book of the decrees was closed to us, so that now we wander around in uncertainty as a result of our own guilt? By no means. The probationary command given to Adam already proves the contrary. At that time there was no sin yet, but even in that sinless state Adam did not read his future from the decree; rather, he himself wove the thread further under the rule of divine command. The decree is thus hidden from us, not by mistake, nor as a consequence of our sin. On the contrary, this was God's will for us from the beginning. It is part of the decree itself that the decree should remain hidden from our understanding until it had been implemented. God himself, who created us, has therefore ordained our human nature in such a way that, apart from any knowledge of the decree, we should continue our life day by day, from past to present. This occurs by the urging of our hearts and our minds, and the resilience of our wills. In all of this we are guided by God's commands and exhortations, his threats and promises, and this proceeds in the context of all the circumstances and under the impact of all the influences that are part of his decree. It is therefore no accident that it is this way, and no illusion on our part; rather, it *is* and *must* be this way because he, the Lord, has ordained it to be this way over us.

From this reality it follows that we cannot enjoy the providence of God practically in our life except as a power that sustains our life, watches over our life, looks after our whole life, and prepares us for its outcomes. Our prayer each morning is the ever-recurring expression of faith in that faithful, all-caring love of our Father. We are and remain human, and therefore it is impossible to survey our entire life each morning. Each morning we stand before a piece of our life, most immediately before that small piece of the one day that is opening up before us. So we focus our attention on the demands of that single day, on what awaits us and will come before us, and on what weighs us down and causes worry for that particular day. And in the moment, sensing our impotence to direct everything and to provide for ourselves in everything, we reverently bow down to invoke the help of Almighty God in whose hand we are held, who is ever powerful to save us in every distress. This is the radiance of the love of God that spreads over our whole lives; this we enjoy, in this we rest, and in this we rejoice, for it brings us comfort and allows a lasting peace to penetrate our soul. The person who is to be truly pitied is the unbending intellectual who has lost the childlike ability to be trusting in God in this manner.

It needs to be emphasized that what we have argued concerning the error of the common notion of God's providence is in no way intended to remove the reality of divine comfort from our lives. Much to the contrary: precisely through our attempts to underscore the human element in providence—something that is willed by God himself—we restore a sense of depth and certainty to the profound and comforting character of this doctrine. At the same time we eliminate any sophistry inherent in the decrees that would rob us of this comfort. We are and remain human beings, incapable of enjoying the glorious things of our God other than in a human manner—which is to say, in human form and in human language. What Jesus said of the lilies of the field and the birds of the air to prove to us that we should not worry about tomorrow confirms this in the most literal sense [see Matt 6:26–34].

However, we must never forget that this is a *human interpretation*, and § 5
we must never allow ourselves to think that this represents divine reality either; yet this is the error into which people have fallen. By analogy, if a wise man converses with a small child in a childlike way and with childlike language, no one would conclude that this wise man himself thinks in this way, talks to himself in this way, or sees himself in this way too. We must constantly keep in mind that we are dealing with an interpretation, and in order to perceive him properly we must return from our interpretation of him to his own original mode of being. Therefore, when in systematic theology (or dogmatics, as it is called) we speak of the "work of God" and think of this "work" as "sustaining and governing," we must anchor our interpretation in the divine nature. If we do otherwise and continue to argue from the standpoint of our human experience, we create a human image of God that is entirely in conflict with his being and his work. Of course, if we had not received any revelation of the knowledge of God, we would of necessity need to go about it in this way, and indeed those who

lack this revelation do go about it in this way. But such revelation has in fact been given to us. God has communicated to us something of the majesty of his holy way of acting. He has enabled us to understand something of the depth and immutability with which he carries through with his holy will in all that takes place among humankind. Since this is the case, we no longer need to derive our knowledge of God strictly from our human interpretation of what he does; rather, we stand under the obligation to consult what he himself has revealed to us about his eternal actions. Where our personal life is concerned, we cannot penetrate the decrees of God, because the guideline is his revealed, not his hidden, will. But when we are dealing with the knowledge of God and speak about his eternal acting as it springs from him, then we must not bypass his decrees but rather in every exposition of providence always return to the decrees that lie behind it and constitute its animating force.

Viewing the matter theologically, we must reconcile God's immanence and his transcendence. To be concerned with God's immanence is to view his impact in our lives, and this always occurs in accordance with human nature. As such, our heavenly Father addresses us according to our need as his children, and we delight in his fatherly faithfulness. But this same Father who is present every day of our life deals with us as his beloved children. He is and nevertheless always remains the transcendent God—that is, our Father—yes, but he also is the one *who is in heaven*, in order "that we might have no earthly thought of the heavenly majesty of God."[3] We therefore transcend our own lives, with their vicissitudes, when we ascend to that exalted divine perspective from which the whole can be surveyed as one grand unity. At that point, all human form, all "earthly thought," falls away, and that infinite majesty opens up before us—a majesty that created all, sustains all, rules all, and thereby directs all things to their appointed end in accordance with his eternal counsel. If, in our understanding of the Father in heaven, we look past the faithfulness and love of "our Father," our lives become barren, our hearts cold, and our future dubious. But conversely, if the fact that God is our Father causes us to forget that he is "in heaven," then we fall into a sickly faith that is influenced by sentiment and fragmentation, a faith that effectively blocks the path leading to glorious worship in which the true knowledge of God alone is enjoyed.

3. Heidelberg Catechism, Lord's Day 46, Q&A 121.

God is and remains "our Father," but one who is "in heaven." Although the words "your will be done" direct the eye of the soul to God's revealed will, they are preceded by "hallowed be your name," in order that the majesty of God not be clouded by the mists of our human existence.

CHAPTER FIFTY

PROVIDENCE AND CREATION

Your faithfulness endures to all generations; you have established the earth, and it stands fast.

Psalm 119:90

§ 1 We may say with certainty, then, that the ordination of all things that looks ahead and foresees lies within the decree of God, and that the so-called providence of God, properly understood, is an implementation of the decree that looks back to that decree and actualizes it. Nevertheless, the term *providence* covers only a part of this implementation and not the whole. Rather, the implementation of the decree, we may say, consists in three parts: (1) creation, (2) providence, and (3) eternal life. We deliberately state it this way in order to draw sharp boundaries and to make it clear what, as the church understands it, does and does not fall under the concept of providence. This broader concept is then circumscribed and delimited on two sides. On the one hand, it is circumscribed by what lies ahead, what is beyond this earthly life. In the doctrine of providence, on the other hand, eternal life and the kingdom of glory are never dealt with; only the work of God that precedes the re-creation of the world presents itself for discussion. This delimitation, if you will, is arbitrary, to the extent that the "maintaining and governing of all things" also continues in eternal life.[1] But because the discussion of what belongs to this doctrine has always been aimed, in practical terms, at our existing circumstances, and specifically at situations in which sin continues to spread insidiously, all manner of disturbance, resistance, and misery follow. It is thus quite understandable that the kingdom of glory would be discussed under the rubric of the doctrine of the last things. We will return to this subject in the next chapter. Nevertheless, this demonstrates anew how entirely subjective our understanding of providence tends to be. This understanding, which remains very much alive in the church, is oriented almost exclusively toward our human perception of the development and unfolding of reality.

Even though it is taken for granted by people that the "maintaining and governing of all things" continues without end as long as things exist, it needs to be emphasized that this maintaining and governing bears an entirely different character as long as human struggle and resistance continue; it will obtain an entirely different character one day, when the kingdom of eternal peace has appeared. Then all human conflict will come to an end, and all existence and life will automatically continue harmoniously. By way of analogy, we might understand this theological concept similarly to how the helmsman on a ship hardly displays anything of his helmsmanship as long as the ship is floating on a smooth sea with calm winds, but seems to display his skill most when storms arise and bad weather persists. When life seems to run peacefully, calmly, and smoothly, we tend not to notice what we call God's providence, even when it continues to exist in a deeper sense. God's maintenance and preservation are there, to be sure, but they are implicit in the course of everyday life itself. However, when the affairs of men and nations reflect abiding conflict and turmoil, providence seems to manifest itself as a force that is even greater than the force of the seas;, when this occurs, it adopts forms that we can notice and admire.

In fact, we end up automatically distinguishing between two kinds of periods in our own lives as well as in the life of the world. We take notice of periods when life takes its usual course (that is, when nothing unusual happens), and we take notice of periods when great upheaval, distress, and unrest are present. As soon as we make this distinction, we seem to acquire a far deeper impression of God's providence in those periods of upheaval.

1. See Belgic Confession, Art. 12; see also Heidelberg Catechism, Lord's Day 10, Q&A 27.

And by God's providential ordination in those uncommon periods of struggle and upheaval, we are moved to worship. Although we know that in eternity as well the "almighty, everywhere-present power of God" will not only continue to function in full force but be even richer, it is nevertheless better that in the present life we adopt the common understanding of divine providence in the sense of God preserving our present world and governing it in such a way that all things will one day culminate in the kingdom of glory.[2]

§ 2 But if what has just been said constitutes the boundary of what lies ahead, beyond this earthly life (a subject to which we will return), there also is a boundary that lies in the past, and here the boundary is creation. Within the decree, we must reiterate that all three realms—creation, preservation, and the final goal—are united, even when in our experience they are distinct. Creation is the bringing into being of something, and providence the preservation of all things, while the ultimate goal is making things correspond to their eternal destiny. Creation and providence therefore must be neither confused nor mixed together, and what we call providence begins only where creation is completed. The distinction between the two, however, is more easily stated than clearly perceived and determined. For it is not the case that things came about through creation and now continue to exist on their own, so that henceforth God has nothing more to do than to repair any possible damage and provide what is necessary. In that case, something could be attributed to the world that the world simply does not possess: an independent existence apart from God. It would then be analogous to a master builder who has built a house (in this case, the universe) and subsequently has nothing to do with that house until something goes wrong, at which point he intervenes to make repairs. As it is, such a house would remain what it was, with or without the master builder. And if the master builder died, the house would outlive him and someone else would perform, just as well as he, whatever is necessary to repair any damage.

However, this is not how it is with the world. If God has created the world, it is not conceivable that there should be a single moment when the world would have an independent existence apart from him. The world is not a mechanism that has been "put together" in human terms; it is an organism that exists only through the powers that indwell and stand behind it. But

2. Heidelberg Catechism, Lord's Day 10, Q&A 27.

those indwelling powers are not powers that the organism possesses in and of itself, nor are they powers arising outside of God. Rather, all the powers that are at work in this organism of the world and that cause this world to continue to exist are *God's powers*. By way of illustration, a poet who has a song in his head but has not yet written it down or sung it in front of others possesses that song only within himself; the poet can only recite it publicly or sing it for others. That song, in the end, dies when he dies; it can be heard—that is, it has life—only when the poet utters the words. This is how it is with God's world. The whole world and all that it contains possesses nothing—neither within itself nor outside of itself—in terms of a fixed point on which it rests or a power through which it exists and operates apart from *the power of God*. Imagine that God the Lord, for a single indivisible moment, were to cease to work his divine power in all that exists. At that precise moment, everything would not only sink and perish, but would in fact suddenly and immediately cease to exist. In the same way we too—with our physical lives, our souls, our minds, our hearts, our senses, and everything around us—continue to exist only because Almighty God sustains from moment to moment every drop of blood, every nerve, every power and force in existence, thereby affirming our whole being and keeping it alive.

Looking at the matter from this perspective, we can say that God contin- § 3
ues to do what he did when he created all things; that continuation means he has preserved what he created. Even as in the hour of creation he willed things to come into being, and in his omnipotence realized this will, so too God continues to will the same. Now it is the same omnipotence that makes this will of his a reality. So it appears that the distinction between the creation and the preservation of all things is much less than people usually imagine, and in fact it was the failure to perceive this link that resulted in distinctly non-Christian deism, which falsified the root of true religion.[3] In a deistic framework, the separation between creation and providence is made so wide that what has been created is taken as an independent entity, over which God exercises a measure of supervision and which he supports when it is likely to topple or collapse. That feeling of independence alongside and apart from God concentrates itself most strongly in our human

3. Deism is a form of theism associated with the Enlightenment that generally affirms a divine but uninvolved creator of the universe. For deists, God designed the world and set it in motion, but beyond this, he is not active in the world.

consciousness. We humans begin to feel as though we are independent beings apart from God. We become like one party standing in opposition to another party, and consequently our egotism cannot rest until we have turned things on their head and made ourselves the center of reality, so that in the end God appears to exist *for the sake of human beings*. Pelagianism and Arminianism have been the unfortunate transmitters of this false notion, and we may still insist that the root of all sin lies precisely in this misunderstanding of human nature; it is as though human existence were an independent existence in relation to God. Even worldliness and sensuality, which so often accompany sin, are nothing more than an expression of the same basic thought.

Subsequently, we fortify ourselves in opposition to God when we view this world as *our* sphere and this earth as *our* domain. God has his heaven, and we have this earth, and a bartering ensues in which, after death, God allocates to us a piece of his heaven, while we, in exchange, give God during our earthly life a piece of this earthly life, as it were. And then, of course, a somewhat businesslike mind-set governs in this sacred realm as well, by which we attempt to purchase as large a piece of heaven as possible by sacrificing as small a piece of this earthly life as possible. But, at bottom, this entails a difference that is not secondary or nonessential; rather, it truly involves the basic relationship in which we stand with respect to God. Only two basic relationships, we may conclude, are conceivable. The first is that we owe our origin to God, but for the rest of our lives we are on our own, placing ourselves in relation to God as a party with equal rights, bargaining and bartering with him. This is one possibility. The other is that we not only owe our origin to God but that we subsequently exist from moment to moment only through him and for him, so that we stand with all that is ours under his sovereign authority and exist only for his glory. The first basic notion is the source of all sin; the second is the starting point of all true religion. The difference between the two becomes readily apparent: the more we enter into this latter mind-set (by denying ourselves increasingly before God, in the awareness that we have no other existence apart from being in his hand and living from, through, and for him), the more fervent, authentic, and impassioned our religious faith becomes.

§ 4 But—and we must not lose sight of this possiblity—we can also go to the opposite extreme and in fact dissolve any distinction between creation and providence by denying not only any independent existence in ourselves, but also any independent existence in the hand of God; this is the sin of an unhealthy mysticism and the mortal sin of pantheism. At that point, we either identify ourselves with God or identify God with ourselves; the latter and the former, in fact, stand on the same line. Quite properly, we do not wish to countenance an independence that we would possess in ourselves in contradistinction from God. However, this then might be carried to such an extreme that in the process we deny our independent existence in and through the will of God so that we do not have *any* independent existence. This amounts to not having a real existence, only an existence in the thought, will, and power of God. Consequently, nothing of all that is can exist outside of God, for outside of God there is nothing. All that exists is God in essence, and because God is not outside his being, we, and all that we possess, are in fact included within God's being. Consider the ramifications: whether something in God's nature, an undulation in God's thought, or a movement of his will, there cannot exist any such thing as moral responsibility, sense of guilt, or obligation toward God, neither for us nor for anyone else. Consequently, what presents itself to our mode of thinking and our wills is only a generic "pull" of the will of God. And what we call "love for God" is not a love that proceeds from heart to heart, but only the warmth of the sense of self in God, just as in our physical bodies individual blood cells chase after other blood cells and thus are thought to have "love" for one another.

Here lies the danger of false mysticism, which is extremely seductive because it expresses self-rejection and self-denial before God in such a fanatically exuberant manner. The truly God-fearing person, however, will reject it as being outside of God's will. Alongside this sort of mysticism stands the conceptual error of pantheism, which does not allow us to be absorbed into God's being but rather absorbs God into *the being of the world*. God then is everywhere, and everything that exists is God; he is all in all that exists. Thus, nothing exists that is not God. God is all, and all is God. And as the all goes, so goes God. As the all changes and is continually becoming, so too God is continually developing, changing, and becoming. There are never two distinct entities; there never exists my own self and God's self. Ultimately my own self becomes God himself. And in this way, all moral responsibility disappears, and there can no longer be sin or duty. What is is good, for all that is is God. The absurdity of pantheism can be expressed in this way: God is good, and when Christ died on the cross of Golgotha, and when in Rome Nero became a brute and destroyed himself in infamy, then of course that Christ was good, for that Christ was God, but so too was Nero to the extent that God was also in Nero. Mind you, Nero was not partially good but entirely so, and for this reason Nero had to be as he was because *God is good in all things and in all people.*

§ 5 In this way we can see how appallingly great the danger is if our theological foundations are distorted in even the slightest way. Theological belief is like two lines that initially lie so close together that they seem to coincide yet deviate a tiny bit and then gradually veer off in opposite directions, the one a bit to the left, the other a bit to the right. We only have to extend those lines farther and farther to soon observe how they diverge: first one foot, then ten feet, then a mile, soon a thousand miles, and finally they are an infinite distance apart. Two sets of rails may converge at the train station and form one set, but one set that leaves the station may extend to Madrid whereas the other leads to Moscow. The same applies theologically as well. If we deviate a mere fraction from the correct starting point, it is inevitable that we will leave the path of truth altogether. Anyone who understands creation as if God had given us an independent existence in ourselves ends up in Pelagianism and finally in deism and atheism. Conversely, anyone who understands creation as having given us no independent existence at all lapses into the distortions of mysticism and pantheism. We believe properly when we hold fast equally to both truths: first, that creation definitely gave an independent existence to things outside the being of God; and second, that this independent existence outside the being of God is possible only because it rests from moment to moment in the will and the power of God. The entire difference arises from making a sharp distinction between the being of God and the power of God. Creating is bringing about something outside the being of God, but in such a way that it exists and continues to exist only through the power of God. For this reason the Heidelberg Catechism, with precison and clarity, describes providence as the "almighty, everywhere-present power of God."[4] After all, the distinction between creation and providence lies in precisely this very difference. Creation causes things to come into existence outside of God, while providence causes the things that exist outside of God to *persist* outside of God, albeit only through God and his power.

We can express it differently by saying that creation orders itself only according to the decree and is tied to nothing but that decree, whereas

4. Heidelberg Cathechism, Lord's Day 10, Q&A 27.

providence is tied to *two* things: to the decree and also to creation. Creation itself is an independent act, determined only by the decree; providence is a dependent act, insofar as it is determined by the preceding creation. It is therefore wrong if we depict providence as a continuing creation (as people often think). In this view, things came into being in the first moment, through God's will and word; and in each moment thereafter, if God intends the same thing again, these things first cease to be but each time come into being again anew. Of course, we do not notice this, simply because these transitions from moment to moment occur so rapidly that we can detect neither division nor transition. But such a view is utterly mistaken, since it would destroy the continuity of things. Nothing, then, would ever *be*; everything would only *become*. The result is that we would end up in pantheism.

Now, we might consider this a somewhat trivial matter as it concerns material entities, but with respect to spiritual life this would amount to the total undermining of moral responsibility. My "self" today would not be the same as my "self" of yesterday. The "self" that sinned yesterday would not be any concern of mine. I myself would exist only for that one indivisible moment, only to perish again immediately, and in that one indivisible moment there would not even be time to sin. Providence, therefore, must not be understood as an ever-renewing creation. Providence must remain tied to creation, be posited as dependent on creation, and have the "calling" of preserving what came into being in creation. Creation provides the *coming into existence* of things; providence entails their *being in existence*. Only in this manner is the world real, with an unfolding of history in that real world, and only in this manner does historical humanity manifest itself in that world as one coherent race, within which there exist actual morally responsible personalities.

A further truth follows from this, one that generally is not perceived § 6
clearly enough: if the coming into being of things is creation, and providence is essentially causing existing things to continue to exist and develop, then it follows automatically that nothing is ever added to what was initially created, and nothing is ever taken away. If something were added, then providence would be a supplemental creation; if something were subtracted, providence would not be the continuation of what came into existence in creation. The phenomenon of "miracle" must never be understood, therefore, in the sense that by means of a "second creation" something is supposedly added to creation that did not exist beforehand. As it stands, modern physics has helped to underscore this reality, and we Christians can be

grateful for the confirmation of something that follows directly from our Christian confession.

Everything depends on whether God's work is complete. If the work of creation had been waiting for later additions, then this work of God would still be incomplete. But that contradicts holy Scripture, which, in the first place, teaches us that God's work is complete and, in the second place, testifies emphatically that after he had created all things, God looked upon his handiwork and saw that it was *good* [see Gen 1:31]. Moreover, it utterly contradicts the organic notion of creation to imagine that something was added to it. A whole consists of its parts—*all* of its parts. Creation as a whole, therefore, consisted of all of its parts. And in this whole there is no room for adding new elements, since every place and every aspect in creation is taken up and occupied. Consequently, nothing can be taken away either, for taking away something would mean removing a part, and removing any "organ" at all from this wider organism would inevitably destroy the integrity of the whole. Therefore, no additional creation, later creation, or second creation is conceivable, and if the organism is thought to be disrupted, the only conceivable option is *re-creation*. For this reason re-creation must never be thought of as the introduction of a new element, but only as a restoring of those elements that existed but became distorted.

This creational reality excludes the counterargument that plants and animals perish while new plants spring up and new animals are born. The creation narrative clearly teaches that God created plants and animals "with their seed." What, we may ask, does the word *seed* mean? Only that the germ of the existence of everything coming afterward was already given in the creation. This is precisely the "miracle" of creation: it not only calls into being certain species of life but also puts within those species the germ and potentialities of all that would emerge later. Material substances change—for example, in the metabolic process. However, a change of substance is not an adding of substance. All that we see before us now in the plant and animal kingdom consists of two components: the organism and the matter that causes that particular organism to germinate and develop. That organism was contained in the germ, which came from the seed, and God created that seed from the beginning. Hence, as for the material substance of plants, flowers, and animals as they now exist, it is the same material substance that was a genetic part of a whole past sequence of plants, flowers, and animals. It has its genesis in original creation itself.

Only in humankind, can we admit, is there an element that might require further explanation, in order to do justice to the confession that the soul of each individual human being is created by God. But we must note here as well the definitive statement of Scripture—namely, that we were all included in the body (that is, the "loins") of our forefathers. The human race does not consist of a collection of beings who came into being separately; it coheres organically, so that one human being is generated by and born from another. We err badly, then, if we understand this creationism[5] in such a drastic and sharp sense, to the effect that one human came into being independently of another. Be that as it may, we must acknowledge that Reformed theology has confined itself to placing these truths side by side without necessarily reconciling them. On the one hand, we confess that our souls did *not* come from our father and mother, but rather from the creating hand of God. On the other hand, we confess that we were already in Adam, not only physically but also in our spiritual being, because we, being "in Adam," sinned "in him" and consequently bear our guilt for that by which we, being "in him," rebelled against God.

Put this way, both truths seem to stand unreconciled alongside each other. The one seems to preclude the other, and Reformed theology will need to be prepared to bring further clarity on this seeming lack of reconciliation. It is not our task, at this point, to attempt this reconciliation, for such would require an extensive—and entirely separate—study that simply cannot be undertaken here. For our present purposes, it is sufficiently clear to conclude in this way: as far as our own persons are concerned, we were already reckoned *in Adam*, and therefore we have not been added to creation but belong in this creation from the very beginning.

---

5. See *CG* 2.28.4.

CHAPTER FIFTY-ONE

BOUND YET FREE

And the LORD said to Satan, "Behold, all that he has is in your hand. Only against him do not stretch out your hand." So Satan went out from the presence of the LORD.

JOB 1:12

§ 1 At this point, two things are certain. In the first place, by firmly tightening the bond that binds providence to the divine decree, we restore three things to what we are aware of by faith: the steadfastness of the order, the progression of the ordination, and the governance of divine providence. This permits us to dispense with the wrong notion that providence is a kind of *deus ex machina* that follows us on our path through life, leaving us to ourselves as long as things go well and intervening suddenly when danger threatens or distress comes upon us. This deistic tendency, which repeatedly surfaces in the church's thinking, undermines the essence of Reformed thought and life and therefore needs to be eradicated root and branch. Second, it is equally true that in the vicissitudes of life we must be able to transpose this eternal and immutable character of God's providence from the eternal into the temporal, drawing from the wider picture that speaks to the needs of our lives at that moment. This will allow us to enjoy at each moment of our lives—and in a very personal way—our companionship with God, as it strengthens our souls and provides comfort. Because this companionship is in truth a personal interaction with our

God, it should by no means be viewed as the product of our imagination; rather, it is something anchored deep within the soul as God has ordained it in our lives, and by it he preserves and guides us through his providence.

This interaction with God is no figment of our imagination; rather, God wills and has ordained that we develop differently than the rest of his creation—differently, for example, than plants and differently than animals. In humankind God has placed another "self" in addition to his presence, and even when we might deny that God influences that self and bears upon it in a hidden physical manner, it is certainly the case, as is confirmed by holy Scripture, that God both as Sovereign Lord and as Father enters into negotiations with a person's self and influences it in a *moral* manner. This occurs, specifically, by God's revealing his ordinances and by his motivating through reward or punishment, depending on whether or not we comply with those ordinances. Thus, a person experiences self-determination, unlike a star in the universe that continues along its path without consciousness and agency, moved only by God's omnipotent power. A human being's movement is a *walking on his own*, either toward glory or toward destruction; however, this movement always occurs in such a way that a person's own self as "second subject" participates in the relationship, whether that takes place alongside of or in opposition to God.

This process is not mere appearance but rather represents ultimate reality. For in this way it has pleased God to ordain man's mode of existence. In his interaction with human beings, then, God does not accommodate himself to us; rather, he accommodates himself to the mode of existence that he himself has determined for our human self. If we could separate our *inner* life entirely from our *external* life (as Modernists attempted to do), this would not have much of an impact on the very notion of God's providence, since by far the greater part of God's "providential care" would be understood as limited almost exclusively to our *external* life. But holy Scripture does not permit this sort of separation, nor do our consciences seem to permit it either, given the fact that the conscience is normally moved to remind us automatically of our sins. To a sinless life belongs glory, while to a life in sin belongs curse. In light of this wisdom saying, the command "Honor your father and your mother, *that it may go well with you*" [see Eph 6:2–3] is not an ethic of happiness that prefers sin but rather an ethic that refrains from sin for the very purpose of prospering externally. At the same time, it *is* an indication of the indissoluble connection that God himself has established between inner integrity and external greatness. Therefore, our moral struggles are always mixed with the thirst for happiness and an aversion to curse and misery. It is written that even our Savior became obedient unto death, and that because of this he was exalted above every name [Phil 2:8–9]. For this reason it is beyond doubt that this inclination of our hearts occurs not only at a lower level of our moral development but at the highest level as well. This indicates, then, that it is part of our nature itself and consequently cannot be the result of sin; it must have been created in us by God.

Consequently, in our human experience, God's providential ordination over our external lot in life expresses itself through the moral struggles of the soul before him under whose ordinances we stand and against whose commandments the self continually rebels. If this moral struggle is not properly comprehended but viewed only as a series of isolated decisions that our self encounters, then inevitably, we will constantly either fear or await divine wrath or divine favor in connection with these unrelated incidents in our inner life. And precisely this is the reason why the "decisions" of God regarding our external lot present themselves to us in equally isolated measure, insofar as we know that our moral decisions, whether they be for or against God, exist only in isolation from each other. If we build our experience of God and our confession of faith on these subjective experiences alone, we will certainly err. For then God's eternal character will be lost on us as a consequence of *our* being tied to—and limited by—the temporal. But if, on the basis of Scripture, our confession of what is eternal and enduring in God's providential ordination, by virtue of his decree, is irrevocably and immovably firm, then this "humanizing"—if we may put it this way—of God's providence in our own life experience is nothing but the rendering of the eternal in the temporal, as required by the very human mode of existence that God himself has willed and continues to will for us.

§ 2 In an absolute sense, this human mode of existence is moral in nature. That is, it was moral in paradise, and it will be moral for eternity, both in the kingdom of glory and in the place of outermost darkness. Whether morally good or morally evil, it will always be moral in its essense, even when some would regard it in a neutral sense. In contrast to the material character of the life of plants or animals, the moral character of human existence will last forever. In hell it sinks to a minimum, but even in hell it is never completely eradicated; otherwise, there would be no awareness of the worm that does not die [Mark 9:48]. In the kingdom of glory it certainly is not superseded but rather only raised to its utmost perfection. Because there will no longer exist any struggle then, the moral life in *the full freedom of the children of God* will fully unfold. But regardless of how firmly we hold to this reality, it does not remove the fact that, experientially, we do not know moral life apart from sin. What life was like prior to the appearance of sin seems to give us the impression that the moral life would have run its course on its own; and when we imagine ourselves in the kingdom of glory, we similarly cannot imagine that there would be any need for God's providential governance. At that point, in terms of our own awareness, everything will run on its own. In a state of glory—that is, where no disturbance is to be feared or can occur—what we subjectively refer to as "God's providential care" is not located in or confined to any place or sphere of activity. For as we observed previously in our discussion, providence fulfills for us the role of the physician who comes to restore the sick and to forestall mortal danger. Where sickness neither exists nor is conceivable, nothing remains for the physician to do.

Taken in an extreme sense, this interpretation would be incorrect of course. Providence, which we understand as the preservation and governance of all created things, does not begin with sin, nor does it end when sin has been destroyed; rather, it begins in the context of creation and never ceases to be. A cessation of providence would entail the universe sinking away into nothingness. Understood in absolute terms and viewed from God's perspective, providence therefore must be conceived in our confession of faith as something that extends from the moment when creation was completed—or, if you will, from Genesis 2:1 onward—into all eternity. To illustrate, a person is not a "horseman" only when he is riding his horse and controlling the horse with reins, spurs, and riding crop. The perfect mastery of the horseman over his steed remains even when nothing can be observed of the horse's resistance or struggle. In fact, such mastery is demonstrated when that noble animal has become, as it were, one with its rider, obeying its master habitually and with such compliance that there is no "handling" of the horse or pulling on the reins at all. In the same way, we might say that the providence of God does not manifest itself only in keeping a tight rein on this recalcitrant world or confounding the nations in their raging and frenzy. Rather, the providential mastery of God over his entire world also shines in its full splendor when no shadow of resistance can be found, when at long last there no longer will be any need for "pulling on the reins." At that point, the highest level of freedom experienced by God's children will be on display by the very fact that they progress to eternal glory in a perfected manner in the "harness" of God's ordinances.

But even if this is ultimate spiritual reality according to the confession of our faith, it does not wholly correspond to our own subjective life experience, to the extent that life experience is contextualized in the sphere of human sin. We may experience blessing and hope, and we may find comfort and joy in conceiving a future life in which all struggle is past, but that life without struggle does not yet exist for us in actuality. And even though the more mature among God's children may have periods in their lives when they overcome their struggles for a moment and seem spiritually able to drift along, as it were, with the wind and tide at their back, their lives nonetheless remain entangled with the life of the sinful world. Their lives do not stand as independent entities; rather, they are interconnected with a sinful world that is in flux. For this reason, even when we admit there are periodic spiritual "oases" in their own spiritual existence, Christian believers can have no other conception of God's providence than that of a providence that struggles with a disturbed world with a view to preserving and sanctifying it. Therefore, in the present life, the notion of God's providence that we acquire from our own experience begins only with our awareness of sin and ends with the last judgment. It is at this point that God's providence bears directly on common grace; in fact, it is inconceivable for even a moment without common grace. This is not the case when in our confession of God's providence we think in strictly absolute terms, for then providence seems to continue to exist in a straight line, even beyond the point at which common grace ceases to be at work. But providence most assuredly is at work in our subjective experience. In looking at providence from this perspective, the Heidelberg Catechism adequately demonstrates how the church has understood providence in a limited sense.

§ 3 Consider, by contrast, the Belgic Confession, which speaks to the question of divine providence in absolute terms:

> We believe that the same good God, after He had created all things, did not forsake them or give them up to fortune or chance, but that He rules and governs them according to His holy will, so that nothing happens in this world without His appointment; nevertheless, God neither is the author of nor can be charged with the sins which are committed. For His power and goodness are so great and incomprehensible that

> He orders and executes His work in the most excellent and just manner, even then when devils and wicked men act unjustly. And as to what He does surpassing human understanding, we will not curiously inquire into farther than our capacity will admit of; but with the greatest humility and reverence adore the righteous judgments of God, which are hid from us, contenting ourselves that we are pupils of Christ, to learn only those things which He has revealed to us in His Word, without transgressing these limits.[1]

Note the particular language of this confessional statement, which expresses spiritual truth in *absolute* terms. It begins at creation and is tied to the decree. It speaks from the vantage point of God's perspective—or, if you will, "theologically"—to the extent that it does not allude thus to our fragmented earthly experience. The Heidelberg Catechism, on the other hand, which relates to our *subjective* experience and leaves aside the absoluteness of divine providence, focuses exclusively on the human condition; we are embroiled in sin and misery. The answer to question 27, "What do you understand by the providence of God?," states:

> The almighty, everywhere-present power of God, whereby, as it were by His hand, He still upholds heaven and earth with all creatures, and so governs them that herbs and grass, rain and drought, fruitful and barren years, meat and drink, health and sickness, riches and poverty, indeed, all things come not by chance, but by His fatherly hand.

And when it further asks about what advantage this knowledge is to us, the answer is given from a subjective perspective as well:

> That we may be patient in adversity, thankful in prosperity, and for what is future have good confidence in our faithful God and Father, that no creature shall separate us from His love, since all creatures are so in His hand, that without His will they cannot so much as move.[2]

God governs things in such a way that "fruitful and barren years, meat and drink, health and sickness, riches and poverty" come to us by his

---

1. Art. 13.
2. Heidelberg Catechism, Lord's Day 10, Q&A 28.

fatherly hand. This statement alone is evidence that the Catechism focuses on our human condition, one that is entangled in sin. For neither barrenness, nor sickness, nor poverty, nor any part of our misery can exist in paradise or in the kingdom of glory. Here it is exclusively our present situation of struggle that is in view. This is even clearer in the second answer, in which *adversity* stands at the beginning, and in which life is presented as being threatened steadily and continually by the evil powers that are intent on our ruin and would destroy us now if God did not keep them in check. This does not mean, of course, that the Catechism would deny that providence is tied to the decree. This is clear from answer 26, which states as directly and sharply as possible that God "upholds, and governs by His eternal counsel and providence," all things; both aspects are mentioned in one breath. But when it comes to the further explication of providence, the Catechism drops the eternal aspect entirely and takes only the *subjective* side of the issue, discussing it only in connection with our situation of sin and misery.

§ 4 Understood this way, providential ordination is inseparable from common grace; indeed, it depends on it. We can go even further and say that the formulation of the Catechism (namely, that "all creatures are so in His hand, that without His will they cannot so much as move") implies the entire doctrine of common grace.[3] According to Jesus' own testimony, the devils and demons, if left to themselves, unfettered and without restraint, would murder as they began with committing murder in paradise [John 8:44]; moreover, they would not have let themselves be stopped in the destruction that they had begun. Had they even been able to "so much as move" according to their evil impulses, the poison of sin would have dripped into our race, and the misery they brought into this world would have brought about complete destruction with lightning speed and irresistibility. They would not have been able to cease from their activity until they had rendered the human race and the world compliant to their own devilish nature and the sphere of outer darkness. But an unbridled freedom is precisely what they lack. They can only move according to their own will and impulse to the extent and manner that God wills. Without his will, the Catechism declares, they cannot so much as move. In principle, therefore, common grace is rooted in the "bridle" that God puts upon the devils and demons. The powers

3. Heidelberg Catechism, Lord's Day 10, Q&A 28.

of darkness were not denied power or influence over the human race, as evidenced by the fact that the glory of Christ's wrestling with Satan, his suffering, and his conquest cannot be explained apart from the demonic "ruler of this world." Jesus' supreme moral test had to be intensified by demonic powers in order to reveal the supreme glory of his holy existence.

But even though God has intentionally permitted a contact between demonic existence and ours in ways that proceed through the centuries and affect the entire human race, never for one moment have the powers of darkness been given free rein in this. Irrespective of their strategies, they have not been able to so much as prevail against God's will. This is not only true of the initial point at which the demonic world made its first attack on our human race; it is true until the end of time. The powers of darkness, if we may put it this way, are on a leash, and they cannot move a hair's breadth forward unless God lengthens the leash. However much they seek our woe, they cannot harm us further, not now or ever. And even though we do not penetrate this mystery, the end result will clearly show one day, as was demonstrated at Calvary, that God never "lengthened the leash" further than necessary. This was done to demonstrate the virtues of the ultimate conflict, by which the richest victory for our moral existence was verified.

But this interpretation of spiritual conflict does not necessarily relieve § 5
us of the anxiety arising from the thought that God *might* release demonic powers. To put it more practically: what would become of us *if* God were to give the powers of darkness free play one day? We immediately sense that, if that happened, we suddenly would cease to exist. If Adam already succumbed, even though he was in the state of perfect righteousness, what resistance could we offer in our broken, undermined nature? No opposition, no struggle, no fighting would even be possible, and as slaves of sin we quite simply would become Satan's prey. And if sin is followed by curse, and if from this curse misery has been poured upon this world, then what could prevent the general disorder of our external existence, if we consequently were left to the influences of demonic powers without any resistance and without the governance of God?

Here we can grasp how the starting point of common grace lies in the rule of God over the devil and the demons who oppose God's purposes, and how this rule rests in God's omnipotence itself, which determines that not a single creature can so much as move without his will. The power with which God does or does not allow demons to stir and move also determines the measure of his common grace. To the extent that he allows them greater "leeway" and lets them be, common grace might be thought to "shrink"; and to the degree that he keeps them under "tighter control" and reins them in, common grace might seem to expand. At bottom, providence depends to such an extent on common grace that in the absence of the latter (at least, viewed in the subjective sense), no providential ordination of God would be manifest at all. We would have been annihilated while still in paradise. Immediately after the fall, a complete ruin would have followed, and the sobering reality for those who continually turn away from God and who now await the last judgment would have occurred immediately. paradise would have transmuted at once, not into a world under the curse, but into a place of utter darkness. The reason there is now an intermediate state between paradise and the last judgment—that is, between creation and consummation—is due only to fact that God did *not* give the demonic powers free rein but always kept them in hand, so that without his will they could not so much as move a hair's breadth further than God allowed in their attempts to destroy the human race. And it is this intermediate state from which both our human understanding of God's providence and our understanding of common grace are born. From this understanding it follows that the two are inseparable.

CHAPTER FIFTY-TWO

GOD'S WORKING THROUGH MEANS

For he will command his angels concerning you to guard you in all your ways.

Psalm 91:11

Based on our argument thus far, common grace not only interacts indirectly with providence but is encompassed entirely by God's providential order and hence arises from it. If Reformed theology is to develop along proper lines, then common grace—to the extent that it currently is not widely embraced—should be treated primarily under the doctrine of providence. The present discussion will not develop this connection any further. How to correctly organize the various aspects of the truth in dogmatics confronts the scholar as such an extremely difficult and complex problem that it is highly doubtful whether the fundamentally correct and altogether sound arrangement can be achieved in any other way than through very gradual transitions from a previously inadequate and imperfectly arranged order. In any case, it is impossible to do justice to this challenging theological question while writing at a more popular level. We therefore will limit ourselves to pointing to the inseparable link between common grace and providence, and it must be reiterated that we are limiting the notion of providence to the preservation and governing of all things from the fall until the last § 1 judgment. We are not denying, as we have attempted to emphasize, that providence was at work before the fall and continues after the last judgment. Rather, the effectual working of providence manifests itself to us only under the double sign of curse and redemption, of wrath and grace. If we leave the work of particular grace out of consideration here, given the fact that it is frequently discussed separately under the doctrine of Christ and the salvation of sinners, then it is particularly common grace that finds its "home" in the context of divine providence. And, as we observed, it can be fundamentally linked to God's providential governance of the spirit world as well. Only because devils and demons "cannot so much as move" apart from God's will is it possible to arrest the continued working of sin and misery, and thereby make common grace possible.[1]

The general theological assumption here is that our human life is closely connected with the life of the spirit world, a connection that is even closer than is commonly noted. Every one of us can acknowledge this connection at the fall in paradise, and we can concede that on occasion satanic influences are at work upon us. But for most people, the influence of the spirit world upon our lives is something resembling a closed book. The Roman Catholic Church has recognized this influence in terms of the soul's experience, but it conceives of it as something located in some context between the Savior and the Christian's soul. Given the manner in which this understanding tended to undermine the unique honor of the Christ, the Protestant Reformation correctly repudiated the veneration of angels and the invocation of the intercession of angels. But it did so without replacing the wrong notion about the influence of the spirit world on our life with a more correct notion. On occasion, the theologians who followed would discuss the doctrine of angels separately and specifically, acknowledging and teaching variations on the doctrine that might address the human need, but this has never seemed to lead to a basic reorientation. Consequently, this important doctrine rarely has received attention in catechetical classes, and only extremely rarely is it addressed in preaching. As a result, this important doctrine has disappeared virtually without a trace from our consciousness as Protestant Christians. This is all the more remarkable given a very different perspective presented in Scripture, particularly the

1. Heidelberg Catechism, Lord's Day 10, Q&A 28.

priority in Jesus' and the apostles' teaching devoted to the influence of evil spirits as well as good angels.

This topic is discussed in greater detail in the volume *The Angels of God,* § 2
and for particulars we refer the reader to that volume.[2] Nevertheless, it behooves us to offer at least a partial analysis of this doctrine here, particularly as it applies to common grace. What is indisputable is the reality of a twofold working that proceeds from God: one of those workings does not make use of intervening means, while the other operates with and through the use of means. This twofold operation is already made clear by the contrast between creation and the preservation of all things. With regard to creation, the rule applies that "what is seen was not made out of things that are visible" [Heb 11:3]; or in Pauline language, God "calls into existence the things that do not exist" [Rom 4:17]. Because of this *immediate* working the psalmist exults that God "spoke, and it came to be; he commanded, and it stood firm" [Ps 33:9], and, "By the word of the Lord the heavens were made, and by the breath of his mouth all their host" [Ps 33:6]. In this vein, we need not think of either emanation or evolution with regard to creation. To create is to call into being with a word of power—without any intervening means—that which was not before. This is not a *creatio ex nihilo* in the strict sense, since nothing can ever proceed from nothing, and to that extent *ex nihilo* is a misnomer, occurring nowhere in Scripture. Creation comes not from *nothing*, but from the *omnipotence of God*. What is actually meant by *creatio ex nihilo* is that creation was a calling into existence not out of something that already existed but solely out of the omnipotence of God. As the writer teaches in Hebrews 11, it was a creation "by the word of God" and not from something that already existed. It is, therefore, very clear that in creation we are dealing with an absolutely *immediate* working of God's omnipotence.

Equally indisputable is the fact that, in addition to these immediate activities of God, there are other mediated activities—that is, activities in which God makes use of already-existing things to achieve his purpose. It is precisely this manner of working that constitutes God's rule in providence. For providence is in the first place preservation, and preservation presupposes something that already exists. We are not arguing that there are not also immediate activities in God's providence. On the contrary, the

2. Abraham Kuyper, *De Engelen Gods* (Amsterdam: Höveker & Wormser, 1902).

fundamental powers animating all that exists never rest on anything but the omnipotence of God. We might say that these fundamental powers are the foundations on which the entire edifice of the universe rests, and it goes without saying that these foundations themselves cannot rest on anything except directly on the omnipotence of God. We also can agree that in all organic life, an inner, driving force is at work in the core of life that cannot be anything but an immediate working of God's omnipotence. Ultimately, all human inquiry always runs into a mystery that defies any further investigation of the matter of cause and effect. That mystery supplies us again and again with the conviction that, ultimately, in the deepest structure of all creation, a force is at work that must be the immediate power of God. And what especially should not be overlooked when we move from visible to invisible reality and attempt to consider the inner spiritual life in terms of a person's genius or talents, love, regeneration, or sanctification is the clear teaching of holy Scripture. That teaching reminds us that we stand before the immediate working of God in the life of the soul—a working that ultimately finds its zenith in the indwelling within us of God the Holy Spirit.

§ 3 But even if, in this light, we are not prone to limiting the immediate activities of God's powers to creation, it is undeniable that in the common governance of God's providence those activities are usually mediated. Hence, the false notion that God is less majestic in his mediating activities needs to be utterly rejected. It must be rejected, since this false notion still holds many of us back in our thinking. In order to combat this, we need only point to Christ as Mediator. There does exist a view of divine operation that prefers to take into account only the direct activities of the Holy Spirit—a view that, in fact, tends to diminish the intermediary place of the Son—and in the Greek Orthodox Church this has been emphasized so strongly that the Church refuses to accept the procession of the Holy Spirit as also being from the Son.[3] But this is not how the Holy Spirit is presented to us in Scripture. There we find the continual affirmation that all of the Holy Spirit's work is tied to the Son. Jesus himself stated that the Holy Spirit "will take what is mine and declare it to you" [John 16:14].

This reality deserves to be emphasized all the more because in our knowledge of the natural world, so many things at one time appeared to have no intervening means, but now they seem to occur through distinctly

3. This refers to the so-called *filioque* clause of the Nicene Creed, which is not affirmed by the Orthodox Church.

intervening means. There are, for instance, many illnesses that in times past were thought to infect our bodies directly by God; later it appeared that God, in allowing a given illness, made use of all kinds of microscopic foreign elements called bacteria or microbes. Or to use another example, consider how people changed in their understanding when they viewed a flash of lightning as a spark of fire hurled through space directly and immediately—until, that is, they observed for themselves on the peaks of mountains, walking among electrically charged particles in the clouds, how the flash of lightning was formed from elements that first were separate. Now we are better informed, having studied and learned about the phenomenon, and now we grasp the origins of lightning.

This sort of process of learning about creation continues unabated. Again and again we discover how all kinds of phenomena that initially were attributed to the immediate working of God in fact have various sorts of intervening means by which God accomplishes them. If, regrettably, people have become accustomed to underestimating what happens through mediation, as if God's majesty shone only in the immediate, then the result is that the revelation of God's majesty is diminished. In this way the influence of religion itself is lessened by the increase in our knowledge of nature. The end result is that some people become fanatical about natural science while closing their eyes to the majesty of God, while others, wishing to uphold the glory of their God, end up resenting natural science as if it were black magic from the evil one. If, however, we clearly see that both God's immediate and his mediate activities are equally majestic and sublime, and that it has pleased God to glorify himself in both, then all conflict between religion and our expanding knowledge of nature vanishes. This helps us to begin to see the activities of God in a different light as we observe certain phenomena; we begin to see more accurately and clearly.

Here, of course, the question arises as to whether outside of the broad § 4
field that the natural sciences investigate there is a second, deeper realm in which God makes use of intervening means that are entirely different from those that physics can measure. What is the role of spirits or angels in their proper calling before God? It is important to affirm that both the spiritual and the physical realms are involved here. Taking Scripture into account, we cannot deny that a certain influence from the spirit world does in fact impact our spiritual life. The petition that Jesus put on our lips through the Lord's Prayer already demonstrates this: "Lead us not into temptation, but deliver us from evil" [Matt 6:13]. Jesus himself was tempted by Satan in the

desert. Of Peter, the Master explicitly stated, "Satan demanded to have you, that he might sift you like wheat" [Luke 22:31]. The apostles point out to us in various ways that our struggle is not with flesh and blood (that is, with people), but with the "spiritual forces of evil in the heavenly places" [Eph 6:12]. Scripture teaches us that even after the finished sacrifice on Golgotha, Satan still "prowls around like a roaring lion, seeking someone to devour" [1 Pet 5:8]. And when in Revelation the final climax is portrayed, part of that description is the dreadful prediction that Satan will once more be let loose with full power; only thereafter will he be bound forever and cast into the lake of fire. As for the good angels, Scripture teaches us that they are spirits destined to serve, sent out for the sake of those who will inherit salvation. Jesus pointed out that the children possess the glory that their angels behold every day before the face of their Father in heaven. And Paul declares that the heavenly realm is occupied with the manifestation of the spiritual life in the church, even as Jesus affirmed that they shout with joy in heaven for every sinner who repents. We are told in Revelation that the good angels continue the battle against evil spirits with and under Jesus and that one day they will participate in the final struggle.

As such, it would be difficult to accept that evil angels exercise such far-reaching influence while the good angels stand by idle and helpless. But once evil angels are undeniably shown to be the cause of much that is sinful on earth, and if it follows from this that it lies in the nature and the destination of the angels to be instruments of God in his governance of the earthly realm, then it would also follow that the good angels are instruments in the hand of the Lord as well. Whatever power the fallen angels may exercise on earth, the story of Job already teaches us that this influence can never be exercised except in the service of God, with his permission, and in accordance with his will. The doctrine of angels therefore must be understood in the light of the providence of God. For from all this it is apparent that both good and evil spirits are instruments through which God executes his will.

§ 5 If this is true in the spiritual realm, then on the basis of Scripture we cannot deny that these spirits exercise a measure of instrumental influence in the material realm as well. More than once a story is told about such influence in both the Old and New Testament. Just think of the angel who slew the Egyptians; the angel who destroyed Sennacherib's army; and also, in the New Testament, the evil spirits who touched many bodies and who made the pigs hurl themselves into the Sea of Gennesaret. Jesus' statement that at his prayer the Father could send more than twelve legions of angels to assist him also points to the material power that could be exercised by these spirits. This makes it evident that in exceptional cases such an external action did in fact proceed from these spirits. In fact, this makes it entirely probable that the extraordinary has its basis in the ordinary, suggesting a certain angelic instrumental working that in God's order operates in the material realm as well. Thus, for example, we encounter the cherubim as bearers of God's omnipotent power in revelation.

At the same time, neither psychology nor physics, considered to be the "pure" means of empirical analysis, is able to measure this working of the angelic realm on our spiritual and material existence, since the latter transcends the boundaries of human ability. This reality is confirmed for us on the basis of Scripture (that is, divine revelation), and once we are anchored in this foundation, we can make sense of the experience of our souls. However, it is impossible to arrive at an explanation or analysis of this influence by mere human categories. We can identify attempts to do this in the past, and spiritualism tries in part to realize it at present; however, this is on a par with divination, against which God's Word warns us so earnestly, commanding us to be satisfied with what has been revealed to us. We must not attempt to push back the curtain that hides these mysteries. But what we can and must do is to establish that psychology as well as the natural sciences, for their part, must acknowledge that once they have done all of their exploration, they too encounter mystery beyond a certain point. When we penetrate to the very foundations of life and all that exists, there is ultimately always a point beyond which we can go no further with our investigation and must acknowledge the inadequacies of the searching mind. Honest psychologists and honest researchers in the natural sciences readily admit that their research goes to a certain depth and that as soon as they try to go deeper, the extent of human knowledge simply becomes inadequate. Precisely when we encounter the most profound problems of life and existence, we can go no further; we stand before a curtain that hides the mystery of life. The two elements for which we have been arguing, then, fully fit together. On the one hand, scriptural evidence points us to the hidden instrumental activities from the spirit world that continue to stand before us as a mystery; on the other hand, the empirical evidence stemming from disciplines such as psychology and the natural sciences confirms with equal measure how all human inquiry ultimately encounters a mystery that limits the boundaries of further exploration.

§ 6 From these reflections the conclusion automatically follows that the mediated realm of God's governance appears to be much, much broader and extensive than we might have imagined, and that we therefore step completely outside the truth if we underestimate even minimally this mediated working of God or put it on a lower plane than his direct working. This conclusion also suggests that we must not imagine common grace as something that works directly, since common grace entails the instrumental service that the spirit world renders in general. When we see in paradise that the fall was brought about by means of a seduction coming from the spirit world, it becomes clear that arresting the continuing working of this evil had to occur automatically as soon as God the Lord bound and reined in the influence of those evil spirits upon this world. This is in contrast to the state of righteousness, when the working of these spirits was permitted in full force, because in that state man stood in a much stronger position. But as soon as man was weakened in his spiritual being, with the result that nothing else could be anticipated other than that he would succumb to sin, God can be understood to have reined in the working of the evil spirits, reducing their power and thus ensuring that inner and outer ruin would not continue with utter devastation. It is God who raises his shield to protect human beings—fallen and broken in their strength—against what amounts for them to the irresistible and superior strength of the demonic world.

In this connection it also becomes clear that the first intimations of common grace lie outside the material realm—namely, in the spirit world. Intending to prevent our ruin, God arrests (not entirely but partially) the source from which the soul's poison flowed in our direction—that is, to the extent that Satan's spiritual influence on our life is no longer utterly destructive. We leave open the questions of how this occurred (and still occurs) and whether God fortified the counterweight of the operation of his angels, or whether he was simply preventing the manifestation of the power of evil spirits from stirring and moving in such a way that they would have definitively ruined us. Both options are conceivable, and both may have been, and may still be, true at the same time. But whatever the case may be, we should not view this restraint of destructive demonic power as taking place solely in the spiritual realm. If the instrumental service of the angels (those that are good as well as those that are evil) continues in both the spiritual realm and the material realm, then the curse, and all that is contained in this sobering concept, is also connected with mysterious activities from the angelic realm. And the act by which God arrested the continuation of this evil working means not only that the burden on the life of our soul is relieved, but also that our outward life is relieved of having to bear the effects of the curse.

CHAPTER FIFTY-THREE

THE SPIRITUAL FORCES OF EVIL

For we do not wrestle against flesh and blood, but against the rulers, against the authorities, against the cosmic powers over this present darkness, against the spiritual forces of evil in the heavenly places.

EPHESIANS 6:12

Our train of thought has been as follows. Already from the Lord's Prayer it appears that an activity emanates into this world from the fallen angels. This must also be true of the angels who did not fall. Therefore, these countless spirits are instruments God uses as he governs this world. Furthermore, this instrumental use by God of these spirits cannot be limited to our spiritual nature; rather, it also necessarily affects the material part of creation—after all, the material realm is organically related to the spiritual. Our soul has not been inserted into the body as we insert our body into our clothing; rather, there is an integrity, a unity of the body so that it stands in direct relationship to the soul. As for common grace, we must conclude that its starting point consists in the fact that God is pleased to arrest or rein in the fateful influence of evil spirits; this is true with regard to ruin as well as to curse, and to sin as well as to misery. And at the same time God was pleased to strengthen across a very broad spectrum the resistance of the angels who had not fallen.

It is clear that we are unable to define in more detail the manner of this influence and its differences in degree. All of this is shrouded in mystery for us. But no matter how impenetrable this mystery may be to our inquiring minds, it surely remains true that every Christian who still prays the Lord's Prayer and in this wonderful prayer beseeches the Lord to "deliver us from evil" acknowledges the very fact of that influence [Matt 6:13]. Furthermore, in all of Scripture we find confirmation of this influence, from the side of both the evil angels as well as the holy ones, and this occurs in both the spiritual and the material realm. Seeking to deny this mystery amounts to an indefensible inconsistency. It is simply undeniable that Christ as well as his apostles, and consequently all of Scripture, point repeatedly to God's instrumental use of these myriad spirits. This was so before the fall, it has remained so since, and it will remain so until the end. On this basis, we cannot but acknowledge this instrumental ministry of angels to be a very important factor in the whole of providential care, and specifically in the execution of the *order of grace*. In relation to *particular* grace we see this in what Scripture says of the good angels: they are "ministering spirits sent out to serve for the sake of those who are to inherit salvation" [Heb 1:14]. As for the demons, we need look only at the significance of Jesus' temptation for the sake of our salvation. Consequently, there is no doubt at all that this same instrumental use of good and evil spirits takes place to a much greater degree in the common grace that is woven into the whole of God's providential order from the fall until the last judgment. It still needs to be emphasized, however, that wherever influences from the spirit world are sensed, these influences must be understood as having existed previously because they function on a deeper spiritual level.

However, we must warn against the *abuse* of this revelation of holy Scripture, an abuse that consists in human attempts to identify in even greater detail and definition the various activities and influences from the spirit world, especially as they apply to our own internal and external life. This tendency, let it be said, is fully pagan and not Christian. "Spiritualists" do this sort of thing. They will attempt to tell you about the working of the spirit world, down to the smallest detail. Quite boldly they attempt to identify these activities to us and delineate them further. And then they seek to exorcise the evil spirits by all kinds of magic spells and charms. To this end, they wear amulets, talismans, and so on, and they ascribe to such necklaces or medallions a measure of protective power. Among some peoples, this even goes so far as attributing to their own priests the power to seize these spirits and render them harmless. This entirely misplaced understanding of the spirit world flows from the single fundamental error that people view these spirits as working in their own power, unaided, rather than as instrumental spirits who can do nothing outside the divine order. Even the objection that in Scripture such personal applications are mentioned continually—for example, that Jesus personally struggled with Satan, that Jesus spoke of how Satan wanted to sift Peter, that Paul said that Satan harassed him, or, conversely, that a good angel delivered Peter and later Paul and Silas from prison—all this does not prove anything to the contrary. We are not permitted to do what Christ and his apostles were free to do simply because they did it. For Christ and the apostles, the curtain that remains hanging impenetrably before us was pulled aside. Based on the testimony of Christ and his apostles, we are given to know only that in general these influences and activities from the spirit world affect our internal and external life. As a result, we must pray against the influences of Satan and his powers, and we may pray to God for the influences of the good spirits.

§ 7 We would even go a bit further and emphasize that we must never imagine these influences of the spirit world to be exclusively *personal* in nature. On the contrary, the entire view of Scripture leads us to believe that these influences first and foremost relate to the general nature and orientation of the spirit world. The contrast between various influences upon our person and the general orientation of the angelic spirits should be sufficiently clear. In our world with the varied contexts in which we are placed, there are certain powers or influences that we call customs and common practices, public opinion, vogue, zeitgeist, the spiritual temper of the times, and so forth. These surface in our common language, in our discourse, and in reigning ideas; they end up finding their way into general literature, into maxims and "catch phrases," and ultimately even into jurisprudence and the law. All together these constitute a wider set of general presuppositions that govern our life. And beneath these general presuppositions stand other unseen powers that determine the movement of angelic powers, not throughout the entire cosmos, but over only a specific nation, a single province, a single city, or, even more narrowly viewed, over a particular sphere, a single family, or a single business, for example. And as long as they operate, these general and less general powers influence the opinions, dispositions, perspectives, and ways that most people think. Of course, there are always people who swim against the stream, succeed in bringing about a change in the general opinion, and thereby provide access to other influences.

But these are isolated individuals and they are the exception rather than the rule. Far and away most people, by contrast, are *not* original but purely the product of their environment. They do not speak out of their own consciousness but merely as an echo of broader opinion. When the zeitgeist changes, they also change. If they are placed in a different intellectual atmosphere, their viewpoint also changes. But by and large their abiding wish is to be representative of their contemporaries, so that in any discussion of public opinion, the essence of their argument is that "everybody says this," or "this is how everybody sees it," or "it would be a miracle if everybody else were wrong and you were right." We see this tendency even in the political realm. In a city like Rotterdam, for example, a spirit rules that seems to cause the great masses of the common people to move always in the direction of one particular newspaper; however, in Utrecht or The Hague, by contrast, an entirely different spirit dominates. Thus, it would appear that a great multitude of people is dependent on the spirit dominant in their particular town or circle of influence, and it is that "dominant spirit" to which we refer when we speak of the "general orientation of the spirits."

It is perfectly clear that all kinds of observable factors also bear on the shaping of this general orientation. This even applies to a variety of material factors, particularly as it concerns various schools of thought and opinion, people, what is in print, as well as events and circumstances. But we err if we think that demonstrable factors exhaust the matter, providing us with a complete explanation of why and how the spirit world is oriented like this. Standing behind and informing these observable factors is also a collective force that is closed to any sort of examination and has its roots in the way the spirit world mysteriously influences human social life. The apostolic testimony of Scripture makes it very clear that we as Christians do not do battle with people whom we encounter—that is, with people of flesh and blood—but rather, in the final analysis, with principalities and powers of darkness. And although we have no really clear understanding of this dimension, we are able to say something about it—namely, that there is both a personal and a communal aspect to this reality. We are both individuals as well as members of a race, a family, a household, and a particular circle of friends. Hence, a distinction should be made between two contexts in which the influence of the spirit world can occur—that is, between our personal lives and our shared life, what today we call our social life.

"Nominalists," of course, want nothing to do with this understanding.[1] They can acknowledge nothing except individuals or separate entities, allowing for neither any community nor any other connections than those that are simply the sum of all these individuals and parts. But as Christians, and particularly as Reformed Christians, we have always stood—and still stand—squarely against this nominalist tendency, which at its base is Pelagian. We recognize that in terms of the development of intellectual and spiritual thought, the communal has priority, existing prior to the individual, who springs from the communal.[2] For example, sin does not first begin with a few thousand people who then form a race; rather, the human race exists first, and from that race collectively individual persons emerge. Thus, the church does not come into existence simply because there is first a number of believers who join together to form a church; rather, the church exists first, and in that church believers are born and reborn, and through them the church is manifested. If this is true regarding the human race and the church collectively, then it stands to reason that the same basic principle applies everywhere. We consequently acknowledge in all realms that human community, which establishes the social context for all of life, furnishes the spirit world with a point of contact by which it operates among us.

It would be difficult to argue that Satan pays much attention to most people in terms of personal attacks or temptation. He knows full well that far and away most people run with the crowd, and that if he succeeds in merely injecting a modicum of his poison into the stream of human society, the large majority of people will imbibe this quite readily. Why then would he bother to persecute them personally? In general terms, there are only relatively few who have within themselves the power to live independently and influence others; thus, in order to negate them, he must attack them personally. It is therefore remarkable that, when the Lord Christ finally

1. A philosophical position that holds that only individual entities actually exist and that any common or shared extramental realities exist only in name.

2. The conceptual connection between nominalism and Pelagianism here lies in the functional denial of the organic connection between an individual and others. Pelagianism denies the Augustinian formulations that affirm that all human beings were somehow "in Adam" and that the human race has such a communal, corporate, or federal identity.

appears in person, Satan makes his attack as personal as possible—far more personal than with any of the disciples For example, nowhere is it stated that he attacked Nathanael or Matthew, of the twelve disciples; rather, he attacked Peter and Paul. The petition in the Lord's Prayer is therefore in the plural: "Lead *us* not into temptation but deliver *us* from evil" [Matt 6:13]. The use of the plural here is not in reference to resisting personal temptations; rather, it concerns the resisting of collective evil influences that can proceed from Satan to the entire community of Christians or to our entire race. We may surely admit that each one of the elect will become a target for him sooner or later, and this explains why people who earlier in their lives laughed about Satan begin only *after* their conversion to take these satanic and demonic influences seriously.

Understood in this way, the significance of common grace perhaps § 8
will be clearer now. It is precisely in the general orientation of the spirit world that we see a clear difference between one century and the next, and between one continent and another. The general orientation of angelic spirits might be viewed as operating at a very low level in Africa among certain native tribes; perhaps at a somewhat higher level in the heart of Asia; still higher in China; even higher in India; and so forth. But the manner in which the spirit world operates in each of these cultures cannot be compared to how it operates, say, in Europe and America.[3] Even when we in Europe might complain bitterly about the general nature of demonic activity because we continually see and experience its harmful effects, it nevertheless would be a miracle of grace if we could succeed in making the situation in Africa and Asia the same as ours. This comparison could be extended even further. We complain in our country, but some people in France and Spain would do anything if the general tone of society there were anything near what it is here. And even in a much more restricted sense, we complain bitterly in our own circles about the overall spiritual tenor of Christianity in general and of the Reformed Church specifically. But if our entire nation could be imbued with the moral earnestness that is prevalent in some of our circles, the moral fiber of our nation would be uncommonly strengthened.

At bottom, we are able to see that there are considerable differences of degree in terms of the nature and activity of the spirit world, and in this

3. For more on Kuyper's racial judgments from his Eurocentric perspective, see *CG* 1.12.10n4; 1.41.1n3. See similar instances in *CG* 1.61 and 1.62, among others.

way we can well imagine a thermometer able to show us how "warm" or "cold" the general "temperature" of the spiritual world is. In one nation the thermometer would register below the freezing point, in another it would register at the freezing point, and in other nations it would register with gradually rising temperatures of different degrees. Even as the thermometer goes up and down depending on how the cold or warmth in the atmosphere impacts the mercury in the thermometer, so too among various people groups the general nature of spiritual activity rises or falls depending on the spiritual "atmospheric conditions" that press upon the very sensitive life of the soul. These influences emanate from the spiritual world, whether positively or negatively, and they press upon us with greater or lesser force and intensity. This struggle, of course, is in God's hand. His is the power to let the influences of either the demons or the holy angels be dominant; his is the power to make the degree of intensity of these spiritual influences weaker or stronger, as he pleases. If God were to let the spiritual influence from the demonic world impact us and our lives with full force in an unhindered way, then suddenly a quite literally *hellish* situation would break upon us. The very fact that this terrible condition does not occur is due only to the fact that it has pleased God to restrain that influence and in part even to negate it through the influence of his holy angels.

As best we understand this phenomenon theologically, there is no uniform order in this. After the fall, God did not fix the atmospheric influences from the demonic world at, say, ten degrees above the freezing point, so to speak, and then let this particular spiritual atmosphere be prevalent throughout every century and in every part of the world. On the contrary, the spiritual atmosphere that emerges due to common grace ranges, just as the "thermometer" of natural life ranges over a variety of temperatures and conditions. When the flood occurred, we might conclude that this "atmosphere" fell to its deepest point, whereas, by contrast, in the days of the Protestant Reformation it climbed very high. There is no arbitrariness in play to be assumed here, as if God were toying with our human existence; rather, all of human history evinces a fixed order—an order that mirrors God's wider purpose. Again and again he makes the atmospheric temperature drop or climb as necessary for that spiritual atmosphere to cause the history of the world, in all its complexities, to follow such a course as is foreseen in his counsel. The ultimate result accords with the divine intention, and according to his intention he arranges the specified means, the principal means being the regulation of the spiritual atmosphere in which our lives are lived.

Viewed accordingly, it is always God the Lord who executes his counsel by setting the ratio between the cold that comes from the demonic world and the warmth that emanates from the influence of God's holy angels, in the proportions that God himself wills. But no matter how low the spiritual temperature may go as a result, as long as the temperature does not go below the freezing point, common grace is always still at work. At present, that common grace is definitely still working in the heart of African culture and among the Chinese, even when this common grace seems to manifest itself much more strongly in so-called Christian nations. To the extent that generally Christian ideas still hold sway on the unbelieving masses in "Christian" nations, this phenomenon can be ascribed solely to common grace. But if in the present the influence of Christian thinking recedes, it can be ascribed to a gradual withdrawal of that common grace, which—although it does not wholly depart—very noticeably declines in terms of its intensity.

What holy Scripture calls "the outer darkness," a realm where there § 9
will be "weeping and gnashing of teeth" [Matt 22:13], is nothing but the condition that comes about when the spiritual "atmosphere" descends completely to the point of "freezing" or below. At that point, all working of common grace ceases. The sun of this grace then disappears behind mists so dense that not a single one of its rays can break through to foster life and preserve it from death and doom. Yet, this would have been the deserved reward for our original rebellion against the living God. It would have been punishment, yes, but a punishment that would have consisted in nothing but the logical consequence of our defection, with rebellion as the automatic consequence. Sin is an opening up of the human heart to the atmosphere of the demonic world and a closing of the heart to God. If God had permitted all positive influence of the spirit world to be cut off and the demonic realm to work on us unhindered and with full intensity, then hell would have become the universal condition here on earth. The very fact that this did not come about is something we owe only to God's intervening via common grace, by which he both binds evil powers and releases the influences of good. This is another way in which we observe our mixed life in terms of its varying degrees of moral awareness. To use Jesus' language, the sun remains the symbol of this, insofar as it rises over the bad and the

good, being common to all. Where the sun breaks through, life sprouts; where the sun goes into hiding, death comes, as it were, automatically, the result being that life dies off and a shroud hangs over the whole of nature. And once the moment has come (if we may extend the metaphor) when in a certain place on earth the sun never has broken through again, "outer darkness" would reign there in the sense of permanent death.

If it is this way in the visible world with the sun, which is perched on the earth's horizon, it is no different with the "sun" of common grace. Where this sun breaks through, life sprouts again. One could argue that this is less so in what we might call our spiritual Greenland or Novaya Zemlya,[4] more so where the sun sends its rays more liberally and mildly, and greatly so where the sun of righteousness breaks through the clouds in radiance. In any event, in spiritual terms it is certainly true that where the sun of our God's common grace goes into hiding, life becomes weak, impoverished, difficult, and rigid, until it finally manifests only the image of spiritual death. And if one day the point is reached where the sun of divine grace withdraws altogether, with not a ray of its precious glow breaking through the firmament any longer, then for those experiencing it, nothing but death remains—an eternal death in which the dominion of the evil is absolute.

4. Novaya Zemlya is an isolated Arctic archipelago in northern Russia.

CHAPTER FIFTY-FOUR

THE MANIFESTATION OF GOD'S WRATH

For the wrath of God is revealed from heaven against all ungodliness and unrighteousness of men, who by their unrighteousness suppress the truth.

ROMANS 1:18

Looking at Scripture, we can determine how the binding of the evil spirits' influence is brought about only in the general sense that it is *controlled spiritually*. Even though there is also mention of the "iron fetters" with which the demons are bound, this is obviously not to be taken in a literal sense.[1] Since an immaterial spirit cannot be put in chains, the phrase *iron fetters* is to be understood aphoristically, as indicating that demons are powerless in their spiritual bonds like a prisoner who lies chained in his dungeon. Both from Job (where it refers to the demonic realm), as well as from Psalm 103 and elsewhere (that is, where it refers to the angels of God), the sole § 1

1. The reference to the binding of angels with iron fetters comes from 1 Enoch 54:3, which describes the preparation of "iron fetters of immense weight." See also Jude 6: "And the angels who did not stay within their own position of authority, but left their proper dwelling, he has kept in eternal chains under gloomy darkness until the judgment of the great day."

impression we get from Scripture is that God rules the spirit world, as one who executes authority over subordinates. The external coercion of spirits is naturally excluded; force can be exerted only upon their spiritual being. And even though it is not revealed to us in Scripture more specifically how this happens, we have abundant examples of demons' spiritual activity among men. The demons do not "obey," of course: they do not submit willingly to the authority of the Lord. Not to them, but only to the good angels are the following words applicable: "You his angels, you mighty ones who do his word, obeying the voice of his word" [Ps 103:20].

This willing obedience that renounces its own will in order to submit to God's will is absolutely alien to the evil spirits. In an absolute sense, they are and remain enemies of God who constantly rebel against God, ready and inclined at any moment to resist God with all their power and might. When they nevertheless do what God wills them to do, it is not willingly, but forcedly, with a force that paralyzes their willpower and breaks their capacity to resist. What we see here is comparable to what is seen among people whenever a strong personality exercises power over a weak one, or when abusive authority is exercised by one person over another. Another example might be the spiritual violation done by one person to another by means of mesmerizing or hypnotizing. If such an oppressed person later were to successfully escape the influences of someone who had violated his will or consciousness, then such a victim would surely acknowledge, "He had me totally under his power and influence. It was as if I were paralyzed, powerless, and utterly passive before him. He could do with me whatever he wanted. And all this was done against my will."

What we are dealing with here, then, is a general spiritual phenomenon that could be called vexation or violation—that is, one spirit penetrating another in order to subject one to its will. We human beings with bodies know very well what it means when in a fight or a quarrel someone grabs the other by the throat, throws him to the ground, and then subjugates him so that he can't even move a muscle. Here we are speaking of bodily harm, to the extent that a disagreement between two embodied humans results in physical violence. Similarly, attacks can also take place in the spiritual realm, yet these are wholly spiritual in nature. In the spiritual realm there exist means of attack that can go so far as to totally disarm and enslave the spirit that is attacked. We see clear evidence of this in those who were "demon possessed" in Jesus' day. Those individuals referred to in Scripture as "possessed" had been seized in their spirit by evil spirits. These demons had lodged in their spirit, as it were, and gained full domination of those individuals' souls. On occasion, the demons even speak in and through the possessed individual, so that when the possessed person later is free again and able to speak for himself, the difference is clearly audible. From one and the same mouth came simultaneously the words "What have you to do with me? ... I beg you, do not torment me," and later, "Lord, deliver me" [see Luke 8:28, 38]. The first was spoken by the evil spirit, of course, and the latter by the person who had been possessed by the evil spirit. In many respects, the lessons here are instructive. And although we are prevented from a more detailed analysis of precisely how this takes place, it should be clear that one spirit can and does interfere directly in the being of another spirit. We even observe this at two levels in the case of those who are possessed. The demon interferes in the soul of the possessed individual, and then later Jesus attacks the demon and casts him out of the possessed person.

If God is the Father of the spirits, so that all that is spirit owes its life, its nature, its powers, and its capacities to God alone, then we need no further proof that God himself—albeit in a much more majestic way—can intervene directly in the being of every created spirit and do it "violence." That violence, in fact, is of such severity that, no matter how unwilling and rebellious the spirits are, they are forced to do what God wills, and in nothing are they able to go beyond what God allows. Satan had a strongly aroused desire to harm Job's life, of course, but God did not allow it, so then Satan *could not* harm Job. Satan equally desired to attack Peter in such a way that he would lapse totally, but when Jesus prayed for him and in answer to that prayer the Father intervened, Satan was rendered powerless to the extent that Peter did not succumb entirely. The demons and devils, we may conclude, are incapable of *moral* obedience. They do not have that capability. They are absolutely evil, and for all eternity they are never capable of doing God's will voluntarily. When they nevertheless "obey" and restrain their evil influence where God purposes to diminish that influence, it is therefore not a voluntary act of the will on their part, but rather a yielding to the *spiritual violence that God does to them*.

The origin of common grace, therefore, lies definitely in a direct act § 2
of God. It is he who through such spiritual violence done to the demons ensures that their unholy influence upon the human race and human beings does not transgress certain boundaries. It is utterly important to keep this clearly in mind. In the case of *particular* or saving grace, we may conclude that if evil sprang from the root of a sinner's being but did not flow into

him from Satan, that sinner would be utterly unsavable and impervious to salvation. Absolute evil can only be damned; it cannot be set aright. Thus, if man had already found himself in this terrible condition, there would have been no possibility of salvation. The fact not only that there is salvation, but that thousands upon thousands and even millions upon millions have already been saved and now shout with joy before the throne, is due precisely to this reality: evil had deeply penetrated them, but the root of this evil always lay in Satan and not in them.

Now, this very fact has considerable importance for common grace. For if the sinner were absolutely bad in and of himself, common grace would have no other effect than preventing the sinner from doing evil, or keeping him from pursuing evil to the furthest extent his evil nature wanted. There could never be a "good deed" that was performed by the sinner in his unconverted state. For evil that is tempered or restrained can only produce evil. If something that is completely evil is restrained, nothing happens. But if it is only partially restrained, then nothing but evil is produced by what remains. However, it is of course entirely different if the sinner is not evil in and of himself but rather is "inspired" to do evil by a power outside of him. At this point we recognize that more needs to be said—and later will be said—about how evil takes root in the sinner. Suffice it to state a general principle here, however: the tendency toward evil in human beings will increase when they are more strongly inspired to evil by Satan; conversely, that tendency will decrease when this inspiration weakens. If the spiritual violence with which God restrains the demons prevents their evil inspiration from proceeding in full force to the human race and to individuals in the human race, then it follows that due to this act of God, the evil that stirs within the human heart takes on a less intense character.

Of course, the motivation behind the sinner's life can never be thought of apart from this evil source of inspiration, since the sinner's heart remains hostile toward God. And far from coming to faith, that person persists in unbelief. But in the life of the human soul there exists not only that heart-of-hearts "center" from which either faith or unbelief springs; there exists a wider periphery as well. For example, when the inclination toward evil inspiration is strong, it radiates from that "center" so strongly that it penetrates to the outermost perimeter, as it were. At that point, there can no longer be even the weakest manifestation of "doing good" or a "virtuous act." But if God reins in demonic powers so that their inspiration is reduced to half its strength, then that inspiration also radiates with half strength to the perimeter. In this case it might be assumed to become so weak at the perimeter that it is barely noticeable. "Good deeds," alas, seem to be produced from man's nature then—deeds that can pass the test of civic virtue, even when we must acknowledge that they are never completely flawless, and hence never "good" in the absolute sense. This would explain the otherwise inexplicable fact that our depraved nature still produces things that are "righteous" in the sense of civic virtue. And what we attempted to illustrate in an earlier chapter with the metaphors of a sailing ship and of the cable ferry finds an analogy here too. In that earlier discussion we were confined to the use of an illuminating metaphor, because the context of that discussion did not yet require allusion to the demonic world. But now that we have found it necessary to deal with this important point, it is hoped that we have obtained some insight into the notion of civic virtue apart from recourse to the earlier metaphor.

Scripture teaches us as decisively as possible that our fall and the deprav- § 3
ity of our nature did not stand in isolation but rather came about in connection with—and as the consequence of—an influence from the spirit world. Holy Scripture teaches us that the connection between our life on earth and the world of evil spirits still continues and will continue up to the end of human history, when Satan and his power will finally be cast into the lake of fire. From this it naturally follows that the same Satan also had to be active in the salvific work completed by Christ, and that he still seeks to work among the redeemed of the Lord, so that they must pray daily, "Deliver us from evil" [Matt 6:13]. And if this is the case, then without a doubt, we must take into account the same influence of Satan as it relates to common grace. We therefore err when we limit our explanation of common grace to our earthly, human life. Our insight into the essence and working of common grace can only be clarified when we place the starting point of common grace where the starting point of our moral depravity lies, that is, not in man, but in Satan; not on earth, but in the spirit world. Any understanding of common grace that does not address the starting point would ultimately prove to be pointless. To use a crude example, plastering does not help when the wall is peeling because there is a leak in the roof. In order to stop the peeling, we must go to the roof to stop the leak. In the same way, it would not help us if, in our understanding, common grace were to restrain all the eruption of evil in our heart. Here, as well, the "leak" comes from below, from the demonic world, and this is why God had to intervene in the demonic world in order to restrain evil on earth.

§ 4 The same reasoning is to be applied to the curse as well. The withering of paradise into a wilderness with thorns and thistles is not an external, mechanically imposed punishment, but rather an organic consequence of the decay in the spiritual realm. To some extent, we can still see this in human nature. Sorrow not only gnaws at the heart but also ravages the countenance. Inner suffering has outer effects, sapping the body. And more than one individual has turned gray overnight from mortal fear. There have been countless unfortunate individuals who have been so terribly seized by the suffering of their soul that their health and vitality never recovered. Many of these ended up in the grave. Among many "insane" persons, the effect of the soul on the body is terrible. This condition, mind you, does not occur because another suffering is added mechanically to the life of the soul; rather, this physical suffering is caused organically by psychological suffering—that is, the suffering of the soul. The same applies here as well. The human heart is the spiritual core of the entire world, and this entire world is organically related to man and his human existence. Because this is part of God's design for human creatures, it follows that God created the world in this way. In the human person is lodged the factor that determined how the world had to be in order to be suited or tailored to human beings.

Given this organic relationship, the world seems to go "up" and "down" with human performance. When human beings shine in their original, created righteousness, then paradise flourishes on earth. When human beings are reigned by sin, then the earth withers under the curse. And to this we may add that when humans one day flourish in full glory, the world will shine in full majestic radiance as well. This reality accords with the theological principle that humans and the world share in the same fate, which can be explained only from the fact that the deepest cause determining the human condition is simultaneously the deepest cause determining the state and condition of the world. Thus, if the starting point of determining our spiritual condition lies in the spiritual realm, then the power that determines the rotation of the world around its pivot, whether to the left or to the right, must come from that same spiritual dimension too.

This leaves us with three possibilities. The first is that the spiritual realm is darkened completely, and then external life darkens to the "outer darkness," with hell as the result. The second is that the spiritual realm "clears up" completely, resulting in the external world also "clearing up" in a way that makes life more like heaven instead of hell. The third is that the spiritual realm is darkened only *in part*, with the result that twilight is capable of piercing the darkness in external and cultural forms. This would yield the "mixed" condition that, in the present, we observe on earth all around us—a condition of curse tempered by common grace. Without common grace paradise would have turned into hell immediately after the fall. Now, thanks to common grace, this hellish condition has been ameliorated and postponed. This state of affairs remains, and hell will break through only when, at history's consummation, common grace is withdrawn forever.

The "dial," if we may express it graphically, that must be turned to make this world hell, heaven, half hell, or half heaven, lies in the spiritual realm. The dial originally was set at "paradise." One day the dial will set at "hell" for those who are spiritually lost. But in the interim, between the fall and the day of judgment, that dial points to the setting "tempered." That is, it indicates that we now endure a condition on earth that at times is capable of bringing upon us the most terrible pestilences, storms, volcanic eruptions, and floods; yet, at other times this condition yields the enjoyment of the most delightful displays of nature, of a world that entices us through its opulence, and of a sun that invigorates us and gently warms us with its rays. Continuously, every day and every night, God's providence is first and foremost glorious, to the extent that it exercises its reign over the spirit world. This exercise has the effect of tempering the evil inspiration of Satan toward the human race and individual human beings. At the same time, there is an equally important—and parallel—working of God on those forces of the spirit world that determine the general condition on this earth, a working that the curse does not remove but limits.

In order to understand this properly, we must take into account *the wrath* § 5
of God. This wrath is not, as with us humans, a surging fit of indignation or bitterness, but rather a steady working of his holiness. "The wrath of God," the Apostle Paul writes, "is revealed from heaven against all ungodliness" [Rom 1:18]. There can be no sin in the spiritual realm or on earth without at the same moment an awakening of the wrath in God's nature against that sin; this reality continues as long as that sin exists. When we hear of something abominable, our wrath is kindled for a moment, but soon we receive new impressions and other impulses, and the feeling of wrath vanishes from our soul. But with God that wrath continues and cannot be taken away unless the sin itself is taken away. This wrath, therefore, never vanishes from that part of the earthly realm where sin continues in perpetuity by which we mean the realm of the demons and the realm of unconverted dying humans; hell is nothing other than a condition that

lies continually under the full effect of that wrath. God's pleasure rested on paradise, when he saw that it was good. But as soon as sin entered, God's wrath rested upon the earth, and that wrath will continue to rest upon it until one day the new earth comes, on which there will be no sin. Even though common grace tempers that wrath, it never leads to a neutral territory on earth where neither wrath nor grace is active. This serves as an important reminder: in moral matters, God is never neutral. And regardless of whatever place or condition we may imagine as being possible, such a situation will always be the result either of the wrath of God or of the preserving agency of his grace. But this is precisely how particular grace and common grace can be distinguished. Where particular grace enters, wrath recedes entirely in order to let nothing but grace rule, so that no child of God suffers punishment any longer but only undergoes discipline as a child of God. In the realm of common grace, however, it is always wrath that orders everything. Common grace does not remove this wrath; it only softens and alleviates its effect.

At this point in our discussion, we are prevented from addressing further the fact that the alleviation of God's wrath through common grace can be explained only through particular grace. Suffice it to say that everything is about Christ—a fact that itself must be clearly understood. Just as in the spiritual realm common grace does not remove the poison of sin from the center of our soul's existence, so here on earth common grace can never produce *true happiness* in the center of our being. Those who are not converted to life remain children of wrath. And no matter how much the level of our human development has risen, we need only read what the daily newspapers report about the chaos and conflicts among the nations to realize immediately that the agitation of the waters of life does not cease. They simply cannot come to rest. And the fact that they *cannot* find rest is only because God's wrath does not cease. "The godless have no peace" [see Isa 48:22]. God's wrath continues to reverberate. Even believers, as long as they are still in this life, experience this, not necessarily in their personal lives but in the social life they still have in common with the world. But they also experience it in the realm of their consciences as soon as they slide from their spiritual state back into the life of the world.

But it is also true that by grace the wrath of God is restrained in part so that it does not overwhelm us. God's providential order is precisely what variously regulates this restraint of divine wrath. This regulation occurs in different ways—perhaps more strongly when pestilence, war, or natural disasters frighten the nations, wreaking destruction on all sides, but perhaps as well on other occasions, during periods of prosperity and relative happiness. Within this variation of divine "regulation," a necessary distinction is assumed between various nations, families, and individuals, since it is evident that the wrath of God does not proceed uniformly over all; rather, it manifests itself in very different ways and to very different degrees in the lives of all people.

CHAPTER FIFTY-FIVE

SECOND NATURE

Now if I do what I do not want, it is no longer I who do it, but sin that dwells within me.

ROMANS 7:20

§ 1 God's providential order, therefore, brings about the initial working of common grace for our benefit: the reining in of demonic spirits in the unseen world and the equipping of the holy angels with more authority. But even when, in our discussion, we have found it necessary to return to the subject of angels and demons, it needs to be emphasized that the working of common grace is not limited to the spirit world; its influence is also felt existentially and directly in human living. It is true that we experience the influences of the spirit world, but that does not make us machines or blind instruments that incline toward good or evil depending on whether angels or demons move us one way or the other. On the contrary, we have our own independent existence upon which the influences from the angelic world indeed have an effect, but without destroying our own integrity. We remain morally responsible persons. It is necessary to emphasize this all the more because there are not a few Christians who would prefer to imagine it to be different and who visualize little except a field on which the demons and angels battle with each other. They may acknowledge that they indeed have fallen into sin, but this does not bring them to a sense of guilt or self-mortification. After all, how could they help it if the demons decided to choose their heart as the place to manifest their evil power? The demons did not ask them for permission to do this, and they did not give the demons permission. The devil simply forced his way into their hearts and thus performed his evil work. And, of course, they were powerless against such a mighty force as the devil. As a result of this sort of reasoning, human responsibility is left out of the picture. At this point nothing remains but a funnel into which either the demons pour their evil or the good angels pour their good. The soul, then, no longer exists independently.

Having elucidated the working of common grace through the spirit world, then, we must let the requisite light shine on the second working of common grace that takes place directly in our human lives. This working is tied to our "habits," an infelicitous translation of the Latin word *habitus*. Indeed, our nature has been created by God in such a way that what we do or experience leaves behind a certain trait, a certain impression, within us. Through this impression we become accustomed to doing or experiencing something, and as a result of this process our nature begins to cooperate. Take the simple example of going up or down stairs. To a child who is just beginning to do this, those stairs look like a mountain, and the child teeters with difficulty to make it up and down two or three steps. And perhaps the same applies as well to someone from the heart of Africa, who has never seen a house with stairs and does not know what is happening to him when he suddenly must go up the stairs and gets dizzy when he goes down again from the top of the stairs. In any case, after the child goes up and down a few times, his eyes, hands, and feet gradually get used to going up and down. Over time the child grows fully accustomed to doing this so that any hesitation disappears and the child's nature cooperates, even without being aware, and eventually a boy of ten or twelve goes flying up the same stairs, no matter how high, and slides down the banister without thinking of any danger. He no longer calculates where to put his foot or how high to lift his foot to reach the next step. All that marvelous work of lifting the foot up and putting it down or bending and straightening the body is automatic, effortless, and without a problem.

And so it is with all things that belong to the normal activities of our lives. Reading is complicated work, and so is writing. At first it is laborious, but gradually it proceeds more fluently and quickly. And it does not take long before our eyes fly across the page, allowing us to catch the main ideas without paying attention to the individual letters. Similarly, we compose and write without the question even arising of how we must write a given letter of the alphabet. It is as if our eyes read automatically and our hand writes automatically. In the end, this is nothing but the result of getting used to it, of acquiring the habit, so that the function occurs automatically for us. Such a function becomes, as it is often said, "second nature" to us.

§ 2 We cannot stress this "second nature" enough. It is actually somehow miraculous how this acquiring of habits, this "second nature," gradually becomes a force in us. This force can even work in our sleep. There are people who wake up every morning at precisely the same hour or half hour and never have to be called. What is it that awakens them? It is not the conscious self that initiates their waking up while they are sleeping when, for example, they must depart for a trip early in the morning and thus need to get up at, say, four o'clock. At that point, something deeper in the self, even in their sleep, works so precisely that they wake up exactly at four o'clock. This is not true of everyone, of course, but there are those who can do this without fail. Such a tendency has nothing to do with waking up at a specific time, day after day. Anyone accustomed to waking up at a fixed time eventually never thinks about it anymore; that person simply goes to bed without worrying about it, without consciously giving it even a moment's thought. Yet that person wakes up at exactly the usual time. What is to account for this? Not the "self," not one's environment, and not something that is external; it must be the person's nature. But not human nature in general; otherwise, this would apply to everybody. Rather, it is due to something special in that person's nature—something that at first was not present but now has developed as a result of habit. But however it may have begun, eventually it has become a real force in that person's nature, a force so strong that it is capable of waking the person from the deepest sleep at that particular hour. We could multiply similar examples ad infinitum, but we can dispense with an extensive enumeration, since the reader could supply any number of examples from personal experience.

We all know how difficult it is to break someone of a habit. But breaking a habit is nothing but getting rid of a habit that has become a force. Conversely, we can say that all of life, all upbringing, all formation of mind and character, indeed, all habituation in the use of tools or instruments (even if it is just something as simple as using knitting needles or even having good manners and being courteous) rests essentially on this innate quality that is part of our nature. Fully apart from our consciousness, when something has been internalized we can do relatively easily what at first we could only do with exceedingly great conscious effort. The knitting needles we just mentioned are strong evidence of this. Think of how much effort it would require of you if you try, just for the fun of it, to put ten stitches in a row neatly and evenly on the needle. And yet this very thing that almost ties your brain in a knot can be quickly accomplished by, say, a twelve-year-old girl without even looking; she can do it while talking with someone or even while walking. On the road to Scheveningen[1] you often encounter fishermen's children who are walking there. They are looking here and there at everything on the street, and they are arguing loudly with one another; at the same time, they are using both of their hands, almost as if they were a sort of knitting machine, working on some item or other, which in itself is rather complicated, and doing it well and quickly. Now, they are not thinking about it while they are actually doing it, and they are not calculating anything; it simply goes on as if it were automatic, and yet the knitting continues vigorously. In this example too, in fact, we can observe that nothing other than their "nature" is busy, and yet their "nature" has taken on a fixed quality that has become a force of habit in them.

The same "rule" might be observed to be at work in the body. For example, rat poison is a strong poison, and yet there are people in southeastern Europe who are habituated from their youth to ingest it and almost cannot do without it. They ingest a daily dose without any harm, a dose large enough to kill entire families among us.[2] On a smaller scale we see this in those who drink gin. At first, gin is abhorrent. No one who tastes it for the first time can do so without reacting strongly to the unpleasant taste. But gradually a person conquers that aversion, and eventually his or her "nature" gets used to it. And it does not take long before that person can no longer do without it. § 3

We can even say that the difference between an acute illness and a chronic illness is based on the same phenomenon. When an illness invades a healthy body for the first time, everything in that body reacts against the illness and tries to expel it. What we call a fever is often nothing but this struggle of the healthy nature against the invading enemy. The illness is at this point still "acute," and if the body succeeds in expelling this acute form,

1. A seaside district in The Hague.
2. Arsenic was commonly used as a poison for vermin in the nineteenth century, but it also was a component of various remedies in the nineteenth century and sold as having medicinal purposes. It is commonly found in some concentration in various foods.

then the nature of the body will remain what it was and not undergo change. This is almost always the case with an inflammation or a cold. Strong sneezing or sweating is often sufficient to chase away the inflammation entirely. But—and this is what we want to point out—such an inflammation can also become *chronic*; that is, the illness can bring about a change in the nature of our body, settle in it, and from that point, without any external cause, be generated from inside our body. In medicine a distinction is even made between primary, secondary, and tertiary forms of illness—that is, between forms of illness that newly originate in the body and others that originate from previous illnesses of a related nature. But whatever we want to call this change in the condition of the physical body, the issue remains one and the same. It always means that something that happens in us or to us leaves something behind in our nature, settling in it permanently and then beginning to function as a force of its own in our nature.

We can call this miraculous phenomenon in general the continuity of our existence. All continuity would be absent in our life if the impression or influence of one moment had no consequence for the further moments of our existence, and if, with each moment, all that preceded it were lost. No development, no progress would be possible. We would always remain the same, like a thermometer, which, no matter how much the mercury in the tube rises or falls, always remains the same thermometer and undergoes no changes in its nature. But God has created us so marvelously that there is continuity in our life; our life is not a series of beads that have been strung together but rather is like a swift-running stream or a growing plant. Because of this, the condition of our person changes unremittingly; it can bring us further ahead or, as the unavoidable flipside of human existence, it can set us back and diminish us. Initially we experience growth, but in old age we diminish. The same is true of plants and animals, since they mirror aspects of human existence; they display a similar phenomenon, albeit in a weaker and shadow-like form. The swallow still builds its nest as in the time of Noah, but an extraordinary difference separates the ark of Noah from a ship sailing in the Atlantic Ocean. Only in human beings do we observe this remarkable ability to change the make-up of our nature manifested in such a marvelously strong way. We might consider the difference between human and angelic beings. Nothing is said about any change in the angels. They are all at once good or bad, and they remain as they are. It is only in humankind that we see this mystery of habit, a process that can entail progress or decline. And that process always exhibits the same pattern: through habit or custom something becomes rooted in our nature that often is subconscious and independent of external factors, working on us automatically and within us independently.

The same is true of the moral life as it relates to good and evil. Without § 4
this property of our moral nature there could be neither indwelling sin nor indwelling holiness. In every living moment we would be either absolutely good or absolutely evil (in a Pelagian sense), and our free will could swing at any given moment, like a pair of scales, completely in one direction or the other. The balance of our moral life would rise and fall, depending on whether Satan or God was influencing us, and only later would the moral scales achieve any sort of equilibrium. But according to the law of continuity or of habit, this is not the case. Scripture speaks of *indwelling sin*, and in the moral realm indwelling sin is nothing but what in medical terms we describe as a chronic illness. Scripture depicts this as slavery or servitude to sin. The one who commits sin is a "slave" of sin: doing sin reduces our resistance to sin and our ability to react against it. As a consequence of our committing one sin, sin begins to get a footing in our life, fixing itself within us; it conquers our ability to react against it, and ultimately it eats into our nature so deeply that it comes to rule us. Whether we call this a force of habit, custom, or continuity doesn't matter—it always returns in the form of the same pattern: first, sin forces its way into our lives and then, subsequently, it becomes an independent force within us. This force in our nature eventually functions without any external cause and apart from our consciousness. People who have grown accustomed to lying lie again and again without even noticing it. This pattern of lying can even occur entirely apart from their consciousness so that, when it is pointed out to them by someone else, they will maintain obstinately that they did not lie. This is why sin has been compared to a cancer; cancer too can be lodged in us for a long time, entirely without our knowledge, and entirely of its own accord. Eventually, this force that sin acquires in our nature can become so strong that even if we try to react against it, our resistance remains useless and its power overcomes us, forcing us to sin and reducing us to despicable, entirely unholy slavery.

From the foregoing it will be clear that common grace most assuredly encounters within the human person a power that needs to be restrained and reined in if the process of evil in human lives is to be truly arrested. It is not as if this would render demonic activity as a matter of indifference. For a tuberculosis patient, it is not a matter of indifference at all whether we are in March, with its angry squalls, or in the gentler coolness of spring. The environment influences us in incalculable ways. But no matter how great this influence is, in our attempts to help the tuberculosis patient we cannot simply limit ourselves to dealing with the surrounding environment; rather, we must get at the tuberculosis that has afflicted the patient's body. It is the same way in the moral realm. If God is to bring healing by means of common grace to the patient ravaged by the "tuberculosis" of sin, then two things are necessary. First, the spiritual environment needs to be attenuated by God's constraint of demonic power; and second, God must counteract the indwelling "tuberculosis" of sin and not allow it to break out too destructively in our inner being. Here we are confronted by a second action of common grace that is aimed directly at our personal being. That is, God the Lord, in whose hand our inner life lies, intervenes in the life of the soul by restraining and partially disarming the evil power that has nestled itself as a "second nature" in us and threatens our eternal life.

§ 5 The influence of common grace to which we are referring should not be confused with the prevention of one particular sin, as, for example, when we read that God "kept [Abimelech] from sinning" with Sarah [Gen 20:6], or when the Lord freed Peter from Satan's sifting so that his faith would not cease [Luke 22:31–32]. This "incidental" protection from sin, if we may call it that, does exist, and it operates in unregenerate people like Abimelech as well as in regenerate people such as Peter. In fact, each of us can attest to this reality based on our own experience. The petition in the Lord's Prayer, "Lead us not into temptation" [Matt 6:13], clearly refers to such a divine preservation that keeps us partly through providential guidance and partly through spiritual strengthening—from a specific sin in which we would otherwise fall. But this is not the kind of preservation we are discussing here. We are not speaking at this point about an incidental restraint from one particular sin; rather, we are referring to the tempering of indwelling sin that has become an independent force in our depraved nature and the lessening of the severity of sin's "fever." Just as we measure fever by the degrees we read on the thermometer, whether it reads 100 or 104 or 107, we can also say that sin can stir within us with greater or lesser severity as measured by a spiritual thermometer.

Indwelling sin has a character that may be said to be partially general and partially particular. It is *general* to the extent that the contamination or "habitual nature" of sin has become a corrupting force in the root of our nature owing to our solidarity with Adam. It is *particular* because this general evil manifests itself differently depending on the person—perhaps through pride in one, perhaps sensual lust in another, and so on. Consequently, the seeds of all sin lie in our hearts. But not all seeds sprout in the plant kingdom, and not all seeds come up equally quickly or in time flower equally brilliantly; so too is the character of sin's seed within human nature. There are seeds of sin in our hearts that God subdues in our nature so that, thanks to common grace, they will not even *begin* to sprout during our entire life. There are seeds of other sins that he allows to sprout, but that only barely sprout. And then there are still other seeds of sin that will grow within us quickly and to a high stature. All of this happens, of course, in a mysterious way. It occurs as a providential operation of God in the hidden depths of the human heart, but it is no less real. Only once has common grace been entirely withdrawn: in the case of Judas, when Satan entered his heart [see Luke 22:3; John 13:27]. But for all others, not excluding one single person, no matter how deeply fallen and utterly broken by sin a person might be, that person's fallenness would be even worse if God had not restrained the power of sin that ruled within. This is the reason why the most deeply fallen person remains capable of salvation, and why we must never despair of the salvation of anyone.

As long as the spiritual environment has not become pitch-black, and a single ray of light attempts to penetrate the clouds of darkness, the possibility of bringing eternal life to an individual is never precluded. The fact that this possibility exists and continues to exist until the death of the sinner is something we owe exclusively to the glorious working of God's common grace, and specifically to the connection being discussed here of grace and habitual or indwelling sin. When the "thermometer" registers 113 degrees, as it were, then all hope is lost. What ensues at that point is death, which consists in the internal burning up of the person. But this is precisely what common grace will never allow to happen here on earth. For those who die outside of Christ, temporal death comes first. What follows—self-combustion as a result of the "fever" of sin itself—is the fire that will never be quenched.

CHAPTER FIFTY-SIX

THE TEMPERING OF THE CURSE

Thus says the Lord*: If I have not established my covenant with day and night and the fixed order of heaven and earth . . .*

Jeremiah 33:25

§ 1 We have argued thus far that there is a twofold tempering of the energy of sin. One occurs by the restraint of the spirit world, in order that the demons may not rage uncontrollably; the other is of such a nature that the restraining work takes place within human beings whereby the sprouting of indwelling sin in our lives that would become too strong is arrested. The petition "Deliver us from evil" applies to the first kind of tempering, while its counterpart "Lead us not into temptation" concerns the second one [Matt 6:13]. Yet with both kinds of tempering it is God's providential order in which the strategy of common grace is realized.

Having established this, we now must point out that a similar double tempering is also applicable to the consequences of sin as a result of the curse. Our existence always remains two-sided: it is both physical and spiritual, part of the visible and invisible world. These two sides of our existence always remain connected; they always stand in such an organic relationship that, alongside the effects in the spiritual, we must always keep in mind a similar working *in the material*. In our previous discussion of the spirit world, which utilized the illustration of the dial, we observed the influence of the angels not only in the spiritual but also in the material realm. The same applies here as well, even when we are dealing with the second kind of tempering—a tempering that stems not from the spirit world but directly from the material world. Using medical terminology, we might refer to the "secondary manifestations" of the root problem within. Those manifestations occur not only in the soul but also in the body, not only in the invisible realm but also in visible nature. This being the case, it is a matter of course that common grace tempers and arrests the influence of evil that has crept in, not only within us but also in our external lives. Up to now, too little attention has been paid to this, particularly with regard to the doctrine of the means as it relates to disease prevention or healing the pathogens that have already entered the body. In practical terms, believers are faced with all manner of related issues. To cite but several examples, think only of the question of healing exclusively through prayer, or whether health insurance is permissible, or whether lightning rods should be employed, or whether one should receive vaccination against cowpox, and so forth.[1] By taking common grace far too little into account, we lose insight into what governs these and similar practical matters. Consequently, people approach such issues with inadequate rationale and deficient arguments. Among believers this then leads to conflicting beliefs, and people end up choosing sides. For this reason it is important to clarify this aspect of common grace with some precision. Hopefully, it will become clearer how a path can be found that mitigates such disagreements.

In order to accomplish this, it is necessary that we distinguish at the outset between two kinds of divine order. God tempers the continued effects of sin's curse in our physical bodies in two ways: first, by working directly, without our cooperation; and second, by using us as a "secondary cause," as some have called it. It is, of course, only in the context of this second manner of tempering the curse that the use of *means* becomes a subject of any significance. Proper reasoning requires that we first reflect on the immediate or direct tempering in order to keep our line of argument clear. We have in mind, more specifically, the direct tempering of the curse that is brought about in nature, in life, and in the body in which we exist here on

1. For more on Kuyper's views of vaccination, see *OP* 16.II.204.

earth, not that which concerns the spirit world. Only then can we discuss the mediated tempering of the curse for which we ourselves must apply the means as God teaches us.

§ 2 With regard to the immediate influence of common grace, our thesis amounts very simply to this: there are "ordinary" or natural influences that work upon nature and upon our body. These natural influences mirror the curse to a stronger or weaker degree, depending on how God governs these influences through his providential order. By way of clarifying our argument, we begin by mentioning a study of Dr. R. Brück, published more than thirty years ago, in which he argues that the rise and decline of the nations has kept pace with the magnetic stream that gradually moved from place to place across the globe.[2] The argument amounted to this: it can be demonstrated by physics how the strongest undulation of this stream moved at one time under Italy, then under France, another time under England, and yet another time under Germany or Russia. Tracing the points in history at which this stream happened to be under these various countries in succession, the author claimed to be able to show that the undulations of the strongest magnetic stream always coincided with the highest period of flowering of each nation, and that as soon as this undulation decreased in strength, it was paralleled by the decline and deterioration of such a nation.[3]

Of course, we consider ourselves totally unqualified to judge whether this author's arguments concerning the flow of the magnetic stream are correct, although we must keep in mind that he is not a theologian but a physicist, and thus a specialist in the realm of science. In any event, especially striking is his comment that the strongest undulation of the magnetic stream was currently under Berlin, and that therefore Germany was now the country that awaited its highest period of flowering. This declaration was made more than thirty years ago (before 1870), and while it actually

2. Nicolas-Remi Brück (1818–70) was involved as a volunteer from Luxembourg in the Belgian Revolution of 1830. He later graduated from the Belgian Royal Military Academy and had a career in military service.

3. *Note by the author*: The title of this highly interesting work was *L'Humanité, son développement et sa durée*, 2 vols. (Paris: Librairie Internationale, 1866). It is based on his earlier work, *Électricité ou magnétisme du globe terrestre*, 2 vols. (Brussels: Delevingne et Callewaert, 1851–55). The work mentioned in the text also consists of two hefty volumes. Both works have been summarized in a superficial and rather imprecise survey entitled *Manifeste du magnétisme du globe et de l'humanité* (Paris: Librairie Internationale, 1866).

surprises us, it has been confirmed entirely by the evidence. This scholar's argument is worth noting only to the extent that it showed how the magnetic working is all-pervasive and how the stronger or weaker intensity of the magnetic stream can have a stronger or weaker influence on the manifestation of our human life, in both the spiritual and the physical realm.

We need not probe Brück's argument in any greater depth here. Our intent is only to get across the general notion that natural influences can actually be at work, both in the material realm and entirely apart from our will or our agency. These can affect a society's quality of life, contributing to an increase or decrease in human flourishing. We know from our own history how in our nation we have lived through a time of flourishing in the sixteenth century and early seventeenth century, a time when our nation not only was spiritually minded but seemed almost capable of achieving the miraculous. When we look back at the old paintings now and see the busts and statues of the men of that period, we get the sense that they were also physically much more dynamic, in spite of the fact that physical health was considered much less important then than it is now. When we realize how a condition such as our forefathers experienced signifies a considerable tempering of the curse, even bringing about a state of flourishing of truly rare proportions, we can appreciate how, in that period, the influence of common grace was strong in our country and how, in a later period, the influence of common grace would weaken.

Such influences are at work in all kinds of ways in nature and our phys- § 3
ical lives, and it is precisely in those natural influences that we must look for the direct effect of common grace upon our external life. A few short years ago, a professor at Leiden University pointed out how it was possible that influences from beyond our earth could have an impact on our globe as well. He even went so far as to attempt to explain the origin of life on this planet on the basis of such extraterrestrial influences.[4] This, of course, is a fantasy that he is welcome to hold, but in it lurks nevertheless an element of truth, to the extent that it is pure folly to think that no influence of any kind would impact our globe. Everyone observes this through the phenomenon

4. The ancient Gnostic doctrine of "panspermia," thus named because the seeds of life are said to be present throughout the cosmos, was revitalized in the late nineteenth and early twentieth centuries among scientists seeking to explain the origins of terrestrial life. The theory essentially holds that the building blocks of life on Earth were carried here from elsewhere in the cosmos by some mechanism, whether natural, such as comets or meteors, or artificial (that is, by some other intelligence).

of the sun, because we feel it ourselves. It is also clear with regard to the moon—so clear, in fact, that superstition has been built around these lunar influences. But even though this thinking has generally been perverted, it is certainly the case that the moon not only influences the tides but also influences certain dispositions in our physical lives. Why, then, would it be so bold to assume that similar influences from the rest of the universe can affect our planet, not only from the sun and stars that shine but also from other, as yet unknown, ethereal entities that might fill outer space?

To the extent that such influences do in fact exist, they all mirror, of course, a *general* character, and by their nature they can affect the air around us and the life of nature as well as our own blood—in short, our entire body. To a certain degree, the same can be said of the influences in the environment. And when we add to this various global influences, as noted above in connection with the magnetic stream, it should become apparent how all kinds of means are at God's disposal through which he can work in such a way that humans flourish to a greater or lesser extent—and fully apart from our agency and will. Viewed scripturally, through all of these influences God can work in such a way that we are aware of sin's curse and its destructive effects, whether to a greater or a lesser extent. What Scripture calls hell will also one day be realized through such general influences, even as the kingdom of glory, in stark contrast, will mirror the working of such general cosmic influences. But in anticipation of this, God holds these general cosmic, terrestrial, and environmental influences in his hand. To the degree that he causes these influences to function in one way or another, the curse of sin either breaks through more strongly and creates a wretched condition, or is restrained and thereby facilitates a relative state of flourishing health in our human existence.

§ 4 But in addition to these general influences through which common grace more or less arrests the inclination of life toward the curse, we also must take into account the various ways in which God's work is distributed. Specifically, earthly atmospheric conditions vary enormously; the difference between one region and another is very great—so great, in fact, that there are regions of the earth where human life simply cannot exist. Our own history tells us this about how some have had to spend the winter on Novaya Zemlya;[5] and whatever attempts have been made in the recent

5. Novaya Zemlya is an isolated Arctic archipelago in northern Russia. In the sixteenth century the Dutch explorers Willem Barentsz (ca. 1550–97) and Jacob van

past to reach the North or South Pole, the virtually insurmountable difficulties encountered were apparent again and again. Even though heroic human attempts at exploration will continue, no one intends to create in these polar regions a place where people might live. In these regions, we might say that death already reigns, and death in all of its dimensions. By means of sheer coldness, God has allowed the effects of the curse to be felt here in the extreme, as if to show us the greatness of his common grace by which he preserves us from the full impact of the curse in more hospitable regions of the world. And yet even in these regions something of his light still breaks through, for the odd polar bear, bird, or some creature still manages to exist. But imagine if this brief and weak radiation of light were to fall away. Then death would be complete there, and the blackest night and the utmost darkness would reign continually. Or we might imagine if God were to extinguish the furnace-like conditions of the sun, with the result that utter darkness would be the general state of the earth. This should produce within us a sense of gratitude that rises irresistibly heavenward from our souls, in the realization that God's common grace maintains the covenant of day and night [see Jer 33:20, 25], so that in certain regions of the globe a human existence that is both bearable and even enjoyable in many ways is made possible.

The desert regions, likewise, make a similar impression on us. In our country we are not familiar with wilderness areas per se, although perhaps in some drab areas of the Veluwe we can get some idea of a barren, bare region where the endless sand stunts all growth and all development. When we compare the Veluwe and the Betuwe,[6] even the names of the two regions seem to be suggestive of their entirely different environments, which bear significantly on the possibility of people living there. This impression is strengthened even further when we take the frequent allusions in Scripture to *desert* and *wilderness* and then ponder the fact that those vast regions of our planet are also inimical to life. Of course, in contrast to the polar regions, these huge expanses discourage life because of the overwhelming intensity of the sun's heat and not its absence. Now, if we add to this how

---

Heemskerck (1567–1607) were famously forced to spend the winter on the island. Barentsz died during the return voyage.

6. The Veluwe is a sandy region near the center of Holland (now in part a national park). The Betuwe is the fertile region between the Waal and Rhine Rivers. It is thought that Veluwe means "fallow land," and Betuwe "good land."

Scripture points us to the omnipotence of God that is able transform the wilderness into fertile land and make the desert bloom like a rose, as well as the reverse ("He turns rivers into a desert, springs of water into thirsty ground, a fruitful land into a salty waste" [Ps 107:33–34]), then we grasp some idea of the extent to which we should take into account these highly varied regions of our own planet as they mirror the means through which God regulates the impact of the curse around us. Those nations that find themselves in a moderate climate and on fertile soil particularly cannot be grateful enough that our lines have fallen in pleasant places (Ps 16:6), given divine providence. Neither history nor Scripture provides an explanation as to why one nation has been favored so greatly over another.

Here, too, we cannot but rest in the election of God. It was his pleasure to ordain it in this way, as Paul taught so clearly in Athens before the Areopagus Council; this pleasure is and remains unconditioned: "And he made from one man every nation of mankind to live on all the face of the earth, having determined allotted periods and *the boundaries of their dwelling place*" (Acts 17:26). When the Eskimo endures in his stern existence amid cold and deprivation and we in Western European countries, by contrast, are granted such opportunities for flourishing, no other explanation can be given than the unconditioned, providential order of the Lord. He causes it to be this way, and he does not give account of his actions. He remains our "potter" and we are like clay in his hand [see Isa 45:9; Rom 9:20–21]. But even apart from this, it is evident how these different geographical allotments mirror a more or less effectual working of common grace, which tempers both the cold of the curse by giving more warmth for life and its destructive force through a greater degree of human flourishing.

§ 5 But even further, in addition to the aforementioned general and diverse influences, we come now to a third kind of influence that is responsible for all manner of phenomena in nature. We refer simply to phenomena such as earthquakes, volcanic eruptions, tsunamis and floods, and not least, those pestilences in human life to which Scripture often alludes and that affect us profoundly at the social level. Here we need to speak cautiously about famine, since current news information has illuminated the problem considerably. At the same time, we should not forget that under English domination in India, thousands upon thousands have died of hunger; what's more, even in Italy in more recent times, terrible misery has been suffered as a result of lack of food. But even when we acknowledge that famine no longer possesses the evil character that it once had, it is nevertheless clear that in many nations a failed harvest or an abundant harvest typically results either in great misery or an enrichment of life, and that a failed or an abundant harvest is dependent on influences that generally fall outside of human agency and are determined only by God's ordination. Thus, the origin of disease almost always remains a mystery. For a long time, plague—that is, the "black death"—and smallpox raged here in Europe. Then came cholera. More recently influenza, seemingly quite harmless but in its consequences often so deadly, has manifested itself again without our being able to solve the mystery of its cause and disappearance. But this much, we may say, is certain: here, too, natural phenomena are involved. These natural elements, moreover, are governed and ordained by God. According to his providential counsel, these elements allow destruction and the effects of sin's curse to break through at one time and a tempering or mitigating by means of common grace at another time. Without common grace, pestilence and disease would rage ceaselessly. The fact that in the present they frighten us only temporarily and then leave us alone for a season is due to God's restraining and curbing of these influences.

Finally, to these three kinds of natural activities we add a fourth, one § 6
that touches on our own bodily existence. We tend to live with the mindset that a healthy constitution and a sound body are our own possession and fundamental right, and that the onset of suffering and evil only rarely disturbs this normal condition. This notion, however, is entirely incorrect. Essential health is enjoyed only by exception and only for a short time. Aside from particular acute illnesses, we constantly hear people all around us complaining repeatedly about all kinds of aches and pains, unpleasant sensations and indispositions, painful physical ailments, or discomforts that rob us of the full enjoyment of life. Even when most people experience a happy youth, sooner or later disease of some kind will befall everybody. And when we approach old age, then almost without exception we encounter various infirmities, until the body is simply wasted away and we descend into the grave.

But even in all this, there exist great differences in terms of *personal* allotment in life. Entirely apart from disease and illness, a so-called strong will and constitution—or, conversely, a weak constitution—fully aside from any hereditary tendencies, can be viewed as a specific allotment of God's providential order that bears significantly on our existence in the present life. For if all weakness and all illness (including all hereditary illness) derives from the curse—that is, from the misery that came upon the earth as a result of sin—then all relative health, all constitutional strength, all flourishing of any physical capacities, is nothing other than a fruit of common grace by which it pleases God to suppress and arrest any destructive forces related to these. We might even venture to say that deformity and "ugliness" in appearance are at some level the natural fruit of the misery that inheres in the curse, so that, in a state of eternal damnation, we can only imagine various figures, spatial configurations, or facial features to be strikingly repulsive and ugly. If a nation, a family, a household, or an individual displays a prouder, better, and more handsome appearance in terms of what is projected, then this too may be the fruit of common grace; this too might be attributed to God's unconditioned omnipotence, to the extent that some seem to have a richer allotment and some a more sparing one.

CHAPTER FIFTY-SEVEN

NATURE IS NOT IRRELIGIOUS

By the sweat of your face you shall eat bread, till you return to the ground, for out of it you were taken; for you are dust, and to dust you shall return.

GENESIS 3:19

Not content with the general confession that God in his grace tempers the power and the consequences of sin for everything that is human, we looked into the question of how this tempering takes place. For this purpose we have divided the providential working of God into two lines, one running through the angels and the other directly to us. The first point, that common grace extends through the angelic world, has been sufficiently discussed with regard to sin as well as the misery it causes. Then we discussed the immediate working of this grace upon human life, both as it arrests the sprouting of sin's seed and as it restrains the woes springing from the curse. What remains for our consideration then is the other operation of common grace, by which it lets us *ourselves* function as an instrument and uses us *ourselves* as the means. Thus, for example, God used Judah to keep his brothers from murdering Joseph. And God also let Isaiah have a cake of figs made to heal Hezekiah's boil. If, in both cases, God had allowed the evil to proceed, Joseph's brothers would have committed fratricide, and § 1

Hezekiah's illness would have taken him to the grave within a few days. Thus, in the one instance *sin* was prevented, while in the other the fruit of sin was tempered in the effects of its misery. But in both cases a human being functions as an instrument: Judah in the case of Joseph's brothers, and in Hezekiah's case the physician who put the cake of figs on the boil.

There is no disputing, then, whether God's grace uses human beings as an instrument. A mere mention of one or two illustrations from the biblical narrative demonstrates this. But we err if we think that the matter is settled by merely pointing to two such illustrations. To the contrary, this mediated action of common grace confronts us with one of the more important questions as it relates to practical matters. Here we refer to the *use of means*, as noted in the previous chapter through the examples of using medicines, purchasing insurance, using vaccines, employing the use of lightning rods, and so forth. For this reason it is useful to examine the teaching about means in a fuller context.

We should initially distinguish two things here. First, we may identify a use of means that is based on creation ordinances and hence founded on our human nature as such. Second, we may observe an intensified use of means that came about only after the fall. Common grace, of course, finds expression only in the latter. We might clarify this distinction with a helpful illustration. Already before the fall it was ordained as a requirement for human nature that humankind would maintain their physical life by being nourished: "You may surely eat of every tree of the garden" [Gen 2:16]. But after the fall this ordinance is made more stringent and therefore changed: "By the sweat of your face you shall eat bread" [Gen 3:19]. Common grace is expressed not in the former but in the latter. We point to this example only in passing, yet if we are to get clearer insight into this important aspect of our confession, we should probe the matter a bit further.

§ 2 When we ask how God's work in preserving and governing the world occurs, we quickly realize that it can only be partially understood as a direct working of God, apart from all means, and that by far the greater part of God's work occurs by means of something that already exists.

When a human being is born, much can be explained from the father's begetting, from the manner of conception, from how the pregnancy developed, and from how the mother gave birth. This applies not only to the physical process of birth but also to original guilt and original sin as well as various aptitudes for living. But in this process of a human being coming into existence there is one thing that is fixed: we confess that it involves a *direct act* of God. It is well possible that this truth has not been taken seriously enough by all too many in a general sense, and as a result the connection with father and mother, and thus with the entire family line, is all too often lost from view. It nevertheless is a good indication that Reformed theologians have always protested against the traducianism of Augustine by championing creationism.[1] They cannot resign themselves to the notion that a person's entire personality should be understood exclusively as the fruit of reproduction. The deepest origin of the human soul must be related directly to God himself. And even when they have often gone too far in this, neglecting the significance of the covenant on this point, their protest against traducianism has had a profound significance and has been rightly of holy intent; without this protest our Confession would surely suffer harm.

For those, however, who are relatively unfamiliar with such terms, we add here that *traducianism* refers to the doctrine that the human soul is the product of procreation, and that an individual's soul therefore derives from the life of the soul of the father and the mother. Conversely, *creationism* affirms that the human soul's existence ultimately cannot be traced to procreation but comes about directly through creation. It is true that on occasion the latter notion was carried so far that the soul was thought to be created by God in "unformed substance" (Ps 139:16) and not until several months after conception. In any case, the Reformed protest gained in significance when Lutheran theologians in particular began to espouse traducianism. And given the fact that since in our day among us the Ethical theologians virtually all incline toward traducianism, it is all the more important that, for our part, we offer resistance to this notion, which diminishes human nature.

But even apart from the direct influence of God in the creation of a human soul, it is clear that there are all kinds of influences surrounding the mystery of life that, based on nature, occur directly and without any means or mediation. Life itself simply defies our attempts to offer meaningful explanations; life is maintained through God's powers. In fact, all basic forces of nature can only be attributed to and maintained by God's direct powers. To mention but one example, no matter the extent to which astronomy succeeds in explaining the course and mutual relationship of

1. See Kuyper's earlier discussion at *CG* 2.28.4.

the stars in the universe, it nevertheless is clear that there must be a power outside and above the universe that has infused it with momentum, keeps it going, and prevents the whole from collapsing. What Isaiah says of him who calls the stars "all by name[,] by the greatness of his might and because he is strong in power" [Isa 40:26] remains palpable truth.

§ 3 However, even when we would not think of denying God's working apart from the use of means, as soon as we build upon these basic forces of creation and consider their interlocking and derivative consequences, virtually all of God's working appears to become *mediated* in nature. We can go even further and say that all activities of God that are traceable have such an instrumental character—that is, they make use of something that already exists. All that occurs directly escapes our observation. Only something in which we observe a certain regularity and a specific activity arising from a demonstrable cause can be an object of our knowledge. And as soon as we reach the limit of that knowledge and confront those forces and developments that do not point to a further cause or disclose a regular pattern, we then find ourselves in awe, worshiping and believing by faith. But at that point we simply cannot go any further with our inquiring mind; any further knowledge is simply beyond our grasp. As foolish as it would be to want to deny the real existence of these underlying basic forces, it would be equally absurd if, on the basis of our religious perspective, we wanted to close our eyes to the mediated and instrumental character of derivative forces.

It nevertheless is necessary to linger for a moment on this point, since faith always, and rightly, seeks to hold on to the very essential work of God's power, even as this power manifests itself through derivative forces and various means. It might be simply illustrated in the following way: Electricity accumulates in the air. Electricity is kept and stored, as it were, in the clouds. And just as a so-called Leyden jar, when properly charged, eventually shoots out a spark, so too do the clouds that are charged with electricity.[2] The child of God, of course, does not object to explaining the phenomenon of lightning in this way, since anyone who has ever stood on a mountaintop of three thousand meters or higher in the middle of a thunderstorm has been able to observe the initiation of lightning flashes in the clouds. The only thing the child of God would object to is that the

2. Invented in the eighteenth century, the Leyden jar is a glass-and-metal device that can store static electricity.

mediated character of this activity might lead us to forget the majesty of God that expresses itself in this thundering of the clouds.

When a poet writes his epic poem down on paper, one can say with technical correctness that nothing happens here other than that a steel tip is dipped in ink, and this steel tip glides across the paper making all kinds of lines and squiggles. To an extent, this is quite true. We can go even further and say that this steel tip is attached to a penholder, and this penholder in turn is gripped by two or three digits made of flesh that cause the gliding of the steel tip across the paper. And we can say further that these digits of flesh sprout from the extremities of a body that is internally activated by blood and nerves. But after all this has been said in great detail, can't people rightly dispute your focus on "means" and look beyond these directly to the poet and simply say, having bypassed blood and nerves, hand and finger, penholder and steel tip, that *the poet wrote his poem for us*?

The same is true here. Even though it is perfectly true that the flash of lightning comes about in the way described above, who would deny us the right to simply say (bypassing electricity, clouds, and so forth) that it is God who gave his voice to these clouds? Not only are we fully entitled to do so, but this way of expressing it is in fact much more accurate and intrinsically true. Granted, when we observe someone sawing wood, viewed literally it is not the man who "saws," but rather a series of sharp points that cut through the wood. These points are attached to a strip of iron, which in turn is attached to a handgrip, and so forth. But even though we know all this to be well and good, everyone nevertheless says, "*The man* saws through the wood," and anyone who responds, "No, not the man but this iron strip with steel points," would be ridiculed because of his literalism. Thus, faith does retain the fullest right to say of lightning, rain, hail, and so forth, that God does this directly. But it would err if it thereby denied that God makes use of the electricity and the pressure of the atmosphere to give himself a voice in the clouds. A sawyer who does not know what happens when he saws cannot sharpen the teeth of his saw. In the same way, the man of religious faith who refuses to learn about the instrumental nature of lightning and who, standing on a mountaintop in the midst of clouds that are alive with current, refuses to toss his metal ax as far away as possible, would only have himself to blame when the electricity shot in his direction and electrocuted him right there in the middle of the clouds.

No one, therefore, should see in our discussion about means even the § 4
slightest attempt to elevate the means themselves at the expense of God's

majesty. Here the word spoken to the king of Assyria is applicable—namely, that the ax should not "boast over him who hews with it, or the saw magnify itself against him who wields it" [Isa 10:15]. Equally true, it is the Lord who "would feed us with the finest of the wheat" (see Ps 81:16), and the wheat grows because the earth responds to the grain, while the heavens respond to the earth, and the Lord responds to the heavens (Hos 2:20–21). We are, then, fully in the right when we go directly from God to our daily bread in the Lord's Prayer, and at another time take into account all the intermediate steps involving the baker, the farmer, the soil, moisture, and warmth. But what the physicist must *not* do in observing many intermediate causes in the universe is to close his eyes to the God who links these various causes together. And what we as believers must not do is to ignore this chain of causes, for the simple reason that it is God who links all these causes together.

§ 5 When we first look at nature aside from humankind, it is clear that we initially must distinguish between two kinds of intermediate links. It is one thing to say that a seagull picks a fish out of the water or that a plant absorbs something from the soil. It is something quite different to say that iron absorbs oxygen from the air and oxidizes. Indeed, God does all of these, it is true. He feeds the gull, he makes the plant grow, and he oxidizes the metal. But although in all three instances the work of God is instrumental in nature, precisely how this instrumental working occurs is not at all the same in these three cases. The iron cannot contribute anything. As soon as it is exposed to air containing oxygen, it begins to oxidize unless protected by a layer of oil or grease. In the case of the plant, something of the plant itself is already at work. Not every plant is equally healthy and strong. For example, we can plant three chestnut cuttings in the same garden; the one will grow out colossally, the second will grow so-so, and the third will stay close to the ground. By contrast, the collaboration of the instrument itself becomes more pronounced in the case of the seagull, based on the action of the gull itself. The gull peers and spies from afar, darts as swiftly as an arrow, dives quickly, and suddenly grasps the thrashing fish with its beak. Even when the nature of these three chains of influence diverge, it nevertheless is clear that the work of God takes place in a mediated fashion in all three cases. The oxidation of iron is not an immediate working, but God brings it about with the help of the air. Causing the plant to grow is not a direct action of God, but God brings it about by letting the root draw substances from the soil, among other things. And so too, the feeding of the seagull does not happen directly but comes about through what God created in the bird and in the water.

Thus, all of God's work as displayed in the realm of chemistry, in plant life, or in the animal kingdom, for example, is mediated. God could have brought about all of this directly, as he did in creation. But no new creation of plants and animals occurs at present in the existing creation; God always and invariably uses existing plants and animals to bring forth new life. No plant can produce another plant apart from God, no animal can bear its young, and no bird can lay and hatch eggs without God and apart from his power. And, conversely, it is also part of God's providential order not to allow a new plant to spring up except from a plant that already exists, and in the same way to let no new, young lion come forth except from an already-existing lion and lioness, or let an eagle ascend except one that came from the eagle's nest built by eagles that had been hatched in the past. Of course, much more is involved, since a plant not only grows because of its roots but also because of the need to drink in oxygen, light, and warmth; similarly, the lion cub would have died after having been born if the mother lioness had not suckled her cub. We even read that the young ravens call to God and God feeds them [Ps 147:9]. But in general terms, it suffices to point out that the work of God's majesty in nature is manifested only in *connection* with what exists and with the *help* of what exists.

Is nature therefore "irreligious"? Or to state it with other words, is § 6
nature therefore a power set in contrast to God, while at the same time being partly dependent on him? By no means! For who has created in the plant that marvelous means of procreation by which the floating seed is taken and carried away on the wings of the wind and then deposited on receiving plants in other locations? It is God the Lord, and he alone. And far from reducing our adoration of God's work, the realm of nature makes God's work all the more glorious and rich. Or consider the work that we humans do in factories to make composite products; for this to occur, we must make each piece individually and then assemble all of those parts into a whole. We can make a clock, and then another clock, and we can do so endlessly. But humankind cannot make a clock from which a watch is automatically produced.

This is only to say that all human work is *mechanical*; only God works *organically*. And his majesty lies in the fact that in connection with creation he has once and for all time arranged things for human beings in such a way that one multifaceted stream of life would proceed from his first creation, throughout all of human history. God just as easily could have done it differently and created each plant and each animal anew. But that, it may be argued, would have been *less* rich, *less* divine. As he has done it within space and time now, then it is incomparably more majestic and marvelous—as long as we keep in mind that all resources that inhere in nature have been deposited in nature by him and are supported by him each moment through his omnipresence. In this vein it needs to be reiterated that it is not the case that God finished his work in creation and now lets nature work under its own power. Rather, from moment to moment it is he who, being omnipresent in each plant and in each animal, maintains all these capacities and makes them function.

This point is important, for it shows that the aversion many feel toward God's use of particular means flows from an error in their understanding of faith. They intend to say, of course, that God is manifested more gloriously in his *direct* working. But from what we have set forth above, it would appear that this is a misunderstanding and that God's majesty in his organic creation manifests itself most exaltedly in the fact that he does not repeat himself in endlessly creating again and again; rather, in what he initially created he miraculously and majestically hid all that he now uses as means to have his nature continue to exist in all of its splendor.

CHAPTER FIFTY-EIGHT

MAN AND ANIMAL

They neither sow nor reap.

Matthew 6:26

The preceding leads us to conclude that we must distinguish between what God does in or for us but without us, and what he does in or for us yet through us. When the oxygen in the lungs must stimulate our blood, then God does this, but apart from us—in fact even without our knowledge or awareness. But when that same blood must be fed through food or drink, then God does this as well, but he does it through us because we eat or drink. This applies both in the material and the spiritual realm. When Job says, "You have granted me life and steadfast love, *and your care has preserved my spirit*" (Job 10:12), the very last words express common grace watching directly over the life of Job's soul. But when David shouts with joy in Psalm 23, "The Lord is my shepherd; I shall not want," the very image of the shepherd assumes that the sheep of the flock know how to find food for themselves as long as the shepherd leads them to green pastures. The individual sheep itself does not know where there is a meadow with grass and nourishment; only the shepherd knows this. But when the shepherd has led his flock to this spot, the flock knows immediately that it is good and lush in that meadow. At this point the shepherd does not need to put the grass into the mouths of the sheep; the sheep will automatically graze, must grind it and chew the cud, and then convert it into suitable § 1 food. God could have arranged it differently, of course; he could have fed man and animals in the way he feeds plants, but he ordained it differently. He ordained that animals and humans would in large part collaborate in the work of their God.

In our discussion we need to begin by comparing humans and animals side by side. This is necessary only to appreciate how radically humans and animals differ. Jesus himself underscores this obvious difference when he said that the birds of the air differ from us to the extent that they do not sow and harvest. But we do not grasp the meaning of these words, or at the very least we walk right on by them, if we do not first have a proper sense of the ways in which humans and animals are alike. We previously alluded to the matter of eating and drinking. The animal, with mouth opened and body poised, stretches toward the food or drink that is about to be consumed, slurping the water or milk with tongue and lip. The point is that animal is involved in the process of consumption. Food and drink do not automatically flow into it. And yet even in the process of eating, the active participation of the animal is limited. The animal seeks its food, seeks water, and catches its prey, sometimes with remarkable cunning and agility, and sometimes even with a very great exertion of strength and even danger to its own life. By comparison, the cunning of a human being in catching an animal, as a rule, is generally based on this very trait—namely, seeking food and, when hungry, risking everything for the sake of finding that food.

To some extent (and continuing the similarities), we can even speak of a preparation of food on the part of the animal before the animal consumes it. Birds and apes peel any food that has a skin. Other animals tear and divide it to make smaller pieces. The birds chew and moisten it before giving it to their young. And the ant, the spider, and other insects even lay up a supply of food. In fact, it has been shown that the ant, for example, milks the aphid and mixes a drop of sticky liquid with other drops, lets them harden, and then carries them into the nest. While this is not the place to examine various traits of the animal kingdom in greater detail, we may conclude that God's pleasure and glory are evident in the animal kingdom by how he does not work apart from but often instead through and within the creature. The latter, we might argue, is much more ingenious. It displays a greater majesty. And those among us who think that God's majesty is reduced by using various means show that we really do not grasp what the animal world teaches us. Many people find it much more interesting to discover how an ant is fed than to learn how a perch feeds itself. But what matters is that we perceive that God feeds both, though in very different ways: the perch quite simply, the ant quite ingeniously.

But this is not all. § 2

The concept of *home* indeed has a place in the animal world. However, the notion of *clothing* does not exist, which is remarkable. The animal is clothed, and as Jesus observed, the plant and animal are even clothed gloriously, but God does this for the animal without the animal's active participation. A lion is born with its fur automatically. The birds have feathers. God clothes the sheep with downy wool. And God even clothes man by means of the fur of the animal.

It is entirely different with the notion of "home." A home is not common among animals and occurs only by way of exception. But when it occurs, God builds the dwelling for the animal through the animal itself. The fish does not know a dwelling place; the bird, however, does. A pair of birds has a nest, and the birds build that nest themselves. God teaches them this. When spring approaches, young birds that have never seen a nest being built spontaneously begin gathering straw, twigs, and feathers and use these to build a nest. They did not go to school for this, nor did they learn a craft. Neither do they let others build it for them. They build it themselves. And sometimes, as in the case of the swallow, they do this in a way that is elegant. Among aquatic animals the beaver is equally skilled in this regard, and among the insects the bee and the spider are just as remarkable when it comes to constructing their homes. In the animal world, the more the animal is left to its own devices, the higher the animal stands in this respect and the more God's greatness is manifest in its instinct.

We also notice God's greatness in the manner by which he equips animals to protect themselves or to fight. God himself has armed the animals. To some he has given a remarkable strong armor. Some even look as if they have plated armor, because of their heavy shoulders and thick skin. The venom gland that is found in some animals serves as a means of attack or defense. But consider as well the differences. There are animals that simply use their claws and teeth, but there also are those that do something themselves to strengthen their position. So, for example, the spider stretches its web and then goes on the lookout, and when prey comes it winds its cobweb around that prey, rendering it powerless. And sometimes in the animal kingdom we find—though by way of exception, not as a rule—a strange collaboration of the animal with God. Thus, for example, the chicken eats chalk and that helps to give the egg a shell. God makes that shell, but not as the bark on the tree that grows automatically; rather, the chicken itself collaborates in this process. If the chicken does not find calcium, it produces an egg without a shell, which is lost. Here, then, there is clearly collaboration. There are means God presents to the animal that the animal must use and in fact does use to accomplish God's aim. And the animal is so subject to God's ordinances—"obedient and willing," we might say—that the animal's failure to use the means and thereby to collaborate is simply unthinkable. Bees that do not gather honey when there are flowers in the vicinity simply do not exist.

Let no one say, then, "What does the animal kingdom matter?" For Scripture itself continually draws our attention to it, and in both the Old and the New Testaments the Holy Spirit points us again and again to the life of the animals, in order that we humans might become wise through them, and thus wise before God. There are all kinds of connections between our life and the life of the animals; one such connection is that of analogy. One of those connections, however, is not (as people are inclined to think today) that humans have come from animals; rather, it is in the sense that God has made the animals with human beings in mind. Indeed, the animal world already shows in vague contours what would later be manifested so richly and gloriously in humankind. This connection even goes so far that holy Scripture does not hesitate to ascribe a soul to animals—not, of course, a soul like that of humans, but an animal *soul* nevertheless. Is it not written of Adam that God brought the animals to Adam to see what he would call *every living soul* (Gen 2:19 KJV)? Does it not say in Genesis 9:4 that man should not eat "flesh with *its soul*, that is, its blood" [KJV]? And so too in Leviticus 24:18: "*Whoever takes an animal's soul*" (KJV)? It is therefore our duty to pay attention to the animal kingdom, and any preaching that never gets around to utilizing this part of creation is certainly remiss in light of God's revelation in Scripture.

§ 3 Having pointed to clear correspondences that exist between humans and animals, we must now focus on the far-reaching differences that have been established by God between the two. The chief differences can be identified as follows: (1) reliance on the use of means occurs in animals only in part, while in human beings it is all-encompassing; (2) animals must and do use means without using their own judgment, doing so instinctively, whereas humans as a rule exercise judgment and make choices; and (3) animals remain on the level at which they have been created, whereas humans continually progress in terms of their choices and appropriation of various means.

To begin with the last point, it is clear that today's swallow and the swallow of three millennia ago both build their nest in exactly the same way. An ants' nest today is exactly the same as that of 200 years ago. A spiderweb or a honeycomb today is still exactly as it has been for centuries. In this light it would be senseless to attempt any sort of exhibition of illustrations, since nothing would be demonstrated. Nor do animals advance in their techniques for preparing food or fending off their enemies. There exists neither progress nor development here. All remains as it was, unvaryingly the same, century after century.

Equally conspicuous is the second element mentioned above—that is, the absence or presence of judgment or choice. This is not to argue that animals lack all "choice." The location of the nest is "chosen," if we may say so. And in the pursuit of prey we can observe calculation in the animal, with the tiger calculating its leap as a prime example. But in most animals this choice is extremely limited, and its action is entirely unfree. We humans can ruin a textile we are weaving, but a spider cannot ruin its web. It makes its web impeccably artfully, in precisely the correct proportions; the length of the strands and the length of the attachments are always exactly what they should be. The web is perfect according to its kind. Precisely from this, then, we can discern that a mysterious power in the insect guides the spider in the weaving process. It is not trial and error and gradual discovery; it is an immediate and complete capability, without ever making further "progress." Viewed in this way, one might argue that the honeycomb and the spiderweb mirror far more clearly the divine mark when compared to what humans construct or weave. At the same time, however, it is precisely this that shows us that the animal is unfree and that an instinct drives the animal. The animal is more an automaton than the human. However, it is not an automaton like what we would assemble; rather, it is an automaton as only God can make it. This causes the capacity for judgment in the animals to recede entirely into the background. While there clearly exists a trace of "judgment" in some animals, this capacity also appears to be extremely limited and does not progress.

As for the third point of difference, it is clear that our dependence on the means that God lays before us for our use is the general governing principle for human beings, whereas it remains very much the exception in the animal kingdom. Anyone inclined to say, "This is how animals function, but human beings, who are superior to animals, receive directly from God," would completely miss the target. Contrarily, it might even be argued that the use of means demonstrates a more refined position—one that is only found in limited fashion among some animals but that is actually intended for human beings and fully deployed in human society. We might even argue that existing and developing through means is *the* characteristic trait of human life.

§ 4 We can find compelling evidence of this by contrasting human beings in a state of utter helplessness with animals in their state of being well provided for. Using a very crude example, consider together, for a moment, a lion and a naked, unarmed tribesman. The lion is far stronger, furnished in a splendid way, armed in an awesome manner to defeat any potential foe. In contrast to the lion stands a native, much smaller and weaker, in bare skin, and without any weapon provided by nature other than two hands with small, insignificant fingernails. Viewed in this way, the animal is superior to the human in every respect. The animal has been richly endowed by God, while this human being has found himself in the presence of a dreaded enemy. Yet this is only appearance, as experience has taught us differently. Eventually the strongest animal can do nothing against a man, because that man, with his brain and in his hidden inner life, has something the animal lacks entirely: the ability to reflect, invent, integrate, and move from one thought to the next. He thus has the capacity for ever-continuing development.

When we fail to take into account this quite distinct inner being of the human person, we cannot make sense of the various realms of creation. We initially observe a progressively upward movement. From the minerals we move up to the plants, and from the plants to the animals; even within the animal kingdom we observe a remarkable diversity—from the virtually oblivious crustaceans to the lion in the forest and the eagle that builds its nest on a cliff. But when we move from animals to human beings, there is not an upward movement but rather a decline. The human is much less strong, with a much less splendidly clothed body, and physically far less prepared to fight. In addition, the human is bound to this earth, whereas the bird wings through the air. Now, if we were to view it from this perspective we should place the minerals first, then the plants, after that the helpless human, and finally the strong and noble world of animals. But in doing so we realize that we pervert the natural order by failing to realize that animals do not stand above human beings but rather below. From this it follows that the primary criterion is not strength; it is the capacity for independent action and development, and here human beings obviously are superior to animals. And from this reality it further follows that the use of means—and, hence, dependence on the application of means—is not a deficiency that we must try to transcend; rather, it is the very reason for a higher development and the human being's superiority over the animal.

With this understanding, an entire notion collapses—namely, the § 5
assumption that being restricted to the use of means constitutes a deficiency, whereas any divine assistance or help apart from means is superior. God helps the plant immediately. God helps the animal only to a small extent by permitting it to collaborate. But in the case of human life, this assistance by way of means that human beings themselves must apply is the rule by which God operates. This is surely not difficult to understand. For if God helps us through the very means that we ourselves have to apply, then this gives birth to a collaboration with God. From that standpoint it is easy to perceive that this collaboration with God must decrease if the creature stands on a lesser plane, whereas collaboration increases to the extent that the creature occupies a higher place. An admiral of a naval fleet can let his chief officers collaborate in his war council, but for the average sailor, such collaboration with the admiral would be unthinkable. By the same token, minerals and plants are entirely unsuitable for such collaboration with God. In an animal, however, the beginning of such "collaborative process" at the most rudimentary level begins to manifest itself, although genuine collaboration with God can only be said to take place in human beings. The reason is precisely because only humans, as created in God's image, stand on a high enough plane to do this. "What is man that you are mindful of him?" [Ps 8:4]. But God has placed that same puny man over all of his creation and has made all things subject to him—not magically, but by granting him in his spiritual existence a power that, provided it is developed, far exceeds all other traits manifest among God's creatures.

Thus, a simple comparison of human beings and animals demonstrates fairly conclusively that the assistance of human life through various means corresponds to a higher form of life than the direct divine impartation. This very process suggests that there exists a correspondence beween human development and the degree to which human beings utilize various means that God has put at their disposal. God feeds the birds of the air directly, for they do not sow and do not harvest; they have no other food than what they find. Humankind, by contrast, is called to sow and to reap, and thus not to find but to prepare food and nourishment. And God clothes the lilies of the field directly as well, for they neither toil nor spin, yet Solomon in all his glory was not arrayed like one of these. But human beings are born naked and must toil and spin in order to prepare raiment for themselves from the wool of an animal or the fiber of a plant. In using this language, does Jesus intend to say that humankind should neither sow nor reap, and neither toil nor spin? Obviously not, for Jesus was speaking to people after the fall, to whom God himself had said that they would eat bread by the sweat of their brow.

But a root of evil that Jesus was combating lay in the fact that people, because they worked, thought that they had worked *alone*, forgetting that in their work none other than God himself was working. The end result was that they had set their work in contrast to God's work. People assumed that where they worked, God did not work, and where God worked, they did not have to work. The human tendency, then, is to sink and fall into passivity and, consequently, into worry and fear. This is one reason why Jesus reproves the people of his day, pointing them not only to something higher but also to something lower. The fact that the birds of the air could live without sowing or reaping mirrored a lower condition of these creatures, just as the fact that the lilies were clothed without toiling or spinning was a reflection of the same. Doesn't Jesus himself add, "If God so clothes the grass of the field, . . . will he not much more clothe you?" [Matt 6:30].

At bottom, human beings are not tempted and urged to desire a life similar to that of the plants and animals. To the contrary, human life has a much greater value to God—with one proviso: that a human being not say, "Because I sow and reap, spin and toil, I—and I alone—therefore feed and clothe myself." Because of his nature, the human being will understand and believe that in his sowing and reaping, in his toiling and spinning, *God* is the one doing the work. It is and remains God who feeds and clothes the human being; at the same time, God feeds and clothes the human through the higher action that becomes manifest only as the creature utilizes *the means* God has placed in the human hand.

CHAPTER FIFTY-NINE

INSTINCTIVE ACTION

Go to the ant, O sluggard; consider her ways, and be wise.

PROVERBS 6:6

The use of means beyond the merely instinctual that can be observed in some animal species is of such paramount importance because no Christian can deny that this peculiarity, this nature, this way of acting, has been put into these animals by God himself. It also finds confirmation in the fact that there can never be observed so much as a beginning of progressive development in the animal kingdom. Insofar as we can observe the world of animals, they act today entirely the same as they have for thousands of years. But among human beings, the development is so remarkable that if someone who lived during the war with Spain[1] were to rise from the grave, he would scarcely recognize Amsterdam as a city. By contrast, during these same three hundred years there was in the animal kingdom no trace of change in the manner of building, the manner of fighting, or the manner of life. This is as we might expect, of course, if the use of means were understood to be the invention of a species. For whatever a creature itself devises comes to perfection only gradually and step-by-step over the years. Since this is not the case in the animal kingdom, it serves as conclusive evidence § 1

1. The Dutch war for independence from Spanish rule, known as the Eighty Years' War (1568–1648).

that the use of means is not "discovered" or "created" by animal life; rather, it is a ready-made manifestation of the nature God gave them. If this is true, then it is not appropriate for human beings to want to be wiser than God and to disapprove of the use of means. In fact, we do not hesitate even to say that the animal kingdom serves to instruct us here on God's behalf.

This animal instruction (if we may call it that) relies on analogy or correspondence that in so many ways exists between human and animal life. This correspondence by no means suggests in the least that our race descended from the animal kingdom and developed progressively. It does show, however, that the Creator, from whose hand both animal and human life came forth, has called into being, not accidentally but intentionally, this partial correspondence. We cannot express this correspondence any better than to say that God created the animal *according to the image of man*. This assumes, of course, a significant distance. If we confess that God created man after his image, this distance is and remains no less so than the distance between God and his creature. By saying that the animal is created in or according to the image of man, we are not in the least placing animals and humans on the same level. But we are stating that there are traits of similarity, and that these traits did not develop accidentally but rather owe their emergence to the fact that the animal is made with human creation in view and therefore must bear some sort of correspondence.

The animal kingdom was not intended to exist in isolation alongside human life. The two were created to come into contact. And for this reason there should not only exist a certain accommodation in how humans make use of some animals, but there also has to be, generally speaking, a certain correspondence between the two worlds. This can be observed in physical or bodily growth and development as well as in behavior patterns and manners of existence. It it perfectly obvious that the horse is intended for human beings, to be ridden. If we had to design a riding animal whose height, girth, and other dimensions correspond exactly with human dimensions like height, weight, leg length, and so forth, we could not come up with a better design. But apart from such a special correspondence between form and dimensions of an animal and a human being, there is among animals a gradual ascent toward a more complete development of the body; in a few mammals this presents primarily a prototype—or if you will, a protoform—of the human body. Among some animal species, then, it is possible to see the exhibition of various traits or behavioral patterns that serve as faint traces of what characterizes human society, albeit in a much higher form.

One objection that can be raised, of course, is that animals were created before humankind; hence, it would be incorrect to speak of animals as created in the image of man. When a brilliant master builder has worked out for himself the plans for a palace that is to be built and has determined the specifications, then he can very well build a smaller building of similar style before he builds the palace itself. For him, it is not an issue of whether the palace has already been constructed in stone and wood or whether it exists as yet only as a blueprint. And it was exactly the same for God as creator, whether humankind already stood before him in paradise or existed only as a "blueprint" in the divine decree. God saw human creation from the perspective of eternity, and when we say that animals were created in the image of man, we are referring only to the order of the decrees. We do not mean that the image of the animal came first and only thereafter that of humankind. Rather, God first intended human creation, and basing his design and adaptation on the mold of this "image of man," he created the blueprint for the animal kingdom. In the mind of God, the animals did not come first, in order to derive from this the perfect image of man. Rather, in God's decree the goal of the kingdom of heaven was established first, with the chosen human race as its center. Nonhuman creation, then, was created with humanity in view.

But if this is the case, we as humans should find it instructive, and we § 2
should see important lessons in the animal kingdom. The issue is not that the animals stand on a higher plane and, as such, are our teachers; it is a matter of simply discovering in the animal kingdom all sorts of God's thoughts that serve as guidelines for our lives. In this line, therefore, we must explain that holy Scripture points us repeatedly to the animal world, and sometimes to our shame. "The ox knows its owner, and the donkey its master's crib, but Israel does not … understand" [Isa 1:3]. Being instructed applies especially to that marvelous little creature to which we drew attention in the previous chapter: the ant. It is generally quite striking that we find especially in the smallest of creatures such a rich revelation of God's order and omnipotence. In some respects, the ant, the bee, the caterpillar, the swallow, and so on, are much more remarkable than the ox, the lion, or the eagle. So, for example, Scripture tells us, "Go to the ant, O sluggard; consider her ways, and be wise. Without having any chief, officer, or ruler, she prepares her bread in summer and gathers her food in harvest" [Prov 6:6–8]. We learn, further, in Proverbs 30:24–25: "[Some] things on earth are small, but they are exceedingly wise: the ants are a people not strong, yet

they provide their food in the summer." The latter even states explicitly that these animals are among the *smallest* but nevertheless have an exceedingly high degree of *wisdom*: They "are among the smallest on the earth, and yet are exceedingly wise" [NAB].[2]

Previously we mentioned in passing what might be called the "dairy farming" of the ants.[3] We now want to highlight what Sir John Lubbock says concerning this phenomenon in his well-known work *Ants, Wasps and Bees*.[4] In Lubbock's study, which provided this author with first-hand informa tion on the investigations of this particular scholar, there are descriptions of entire cabinets full of drawers, and in each drawer under glass is an ants' nest whose movements are checked precisely. Lubbock is therefore not someone who has relied on second-hand information; rather, he has given all kinds of interesting reports of what he personally observed and discovered, as well as the results of other researchers. Concerning the "dairy farming" of the ants, or as he also calls it, the "honey preparation," we read the following on this matter in the work in question:

> It has long been known that ants derive a very important part of their sustenance from the sweet juice excreted by aphides. These insects, in fact, as has been over and over again observed, are the cows of the ants; in the words of Linnaeus, "Aphis formicarumvacca." A good account of the relations existing between ants and aphides was given more than a hundred years ago by the Abbé Boisierde Sauvages.
>
> Nor are the aphides the only insects which serve as cows to the ants. Various species of Coccidæ, Cercopis, Centrotus, Membracis, &c., are utilised in the same manner. H. Edwards and M'Cook have observed ants licking the larva of a butterfly, *Lycoenapseudargiolus*.
>
> The different species of ants utilise different species of aphis. The common brown garden ant (*Lasius niger*) devotes itself principally to aphides which frequent twigs and leaves; *Lasius brunneus*, to the aphides which live on the bark of trees;

2. This is how the text appears in the Dutch Bible.
3. A reference to the "milking" of the aphid.
4. John Lubbock, *Ants, Bees and Wasps: A Record of Observations on the Habits of the Social Hymenoptera* (London: Keegan Paul, Trench, & Co., 1882).

while the little yellow ant (*Lasius flavus*) keeps flocks and herds of the root-feeding aphides.

In fact, to this difference of habit the difference of colour is perhaps due. The Baltic amber contains among the remains of many other insects a species of ant intermediate between our small brown garden ants and the little yellow meadow ants. This is possibly the stock from which these and other allied species are descended. One is tempted to suggest that the brown species which live so much in the open air, and climb up trees and bushes, have retained and even deepened their dark colour; while others, such as *Lasius flavus*, the yellow meadow ant, which lives almost entirely below ground, has become much paler.

The ants may be said almost literally to milk the aphides; for, as Darwin and others have shown, the aphides generally retain the secretion until the ants are ready to receive it. The ants stroke and caress the aphides with their antennae; and the aphides then emit the sweet secretion.

As the honey of the aphides is more or less sticky, it is probably an advantage to the aphides that it should be removed. Nor is this the only service which ants render to them. They protect them from the attacks of enemies; and not infrequently even build cowsheds of earth over them. The yellow ants collect the root-feeding species in their nests, and tend them as carefully as their own young. But this is not all. The ants not only guard the mature aphides, which are useful; but also the eggs of the aphides, which of course, until they come to maturity, are quite useless. These eggs were first observed by our countryman Gould, whose excellent little work on ants has hardly received the attention it deserves. In this case, however, he fell into error. He states that "the queen ant" (he is speaking of *Lasius flavus*) "lays three different sorts of eggs, the slave, female, and neutral. The two first are deposited in the spring, the last in July and part of August; or, if the summer be extremely favourable, perhaps a little sooner. The female eggs are covered with a thin black membrane, are oblong, and about the sixteenth or seventeenth part of an inch in length. The male eggs are of a more brown complexion, and usually laid in March."

> These dark eggs are not those of ants, but of aphides. The error is very pardonable, because the ants treat these eggs exactly as if they were their own.[5]

Lubbock also reports that ants not only can manipulate others of their own, caring for them as if they are their own, but even more remarkably, they also have the capacity to have others *obey* them. By way of illustration, there are species of ants that go into battle against other ants, occupy their nest, take away the eggs, and drag them to their own nest. When these eggs hatch, the ants make these hatchlings their slaves and have them work for them. If this happens generation after generation, then such a "patrician" ant, with its slaves, eventually "unlearns" doing any work itself and ultimately gets so accustomed to this that when the slaves leave the ant alone, it will die of hunger. Here again we cite Lubbock:

> For the knowledge of the existence of slavery among ants we are indebted to Huber, and I cannot resist quoting the passage in which he records his discovery:—"On June 17, 1804," he says, "while walking in the environs of Geneva, between four and five in the evening, I observed close at my feet, traversing the road, a legion of Rufescent ants.
>
> "They moved in a body with considerable rapidity and occupied a space of from eight to ten inches in length, by three or four in breadth. In a few minutes they quitted the road, passed a thick hedge, and entered a pasture ground, where I followed them. They wound along the grass without straggling, and their column remained unbroken, notwithstanding the obstacles they had to surmount. At length they approached a nest, inhabited by dark ash-coloured ants, the dome of which rose above the grass, at a distance of twenty feet from the hedge. Some of its inhabitants were guarding the entrance; but, on the discovery of an approaching army, darted forth upon the advanced guard. The alarm spread at the same moment in the interior, and their companions came forth in numbers from their underground residence. The Rufescent ants, the bulk of whose army lay only at the distance of two paces, quickened their march to arrive at the foot of the ant-hill; the whole

5. Lubbock, *Ants, Bees and Wasps*, 67–70. Original footnotes omitted.

> battalion, in an instant, fell upon and overthrew the ash-coloured ants, who, after a short but obstinate conflict, retired to the bottom of their nest. The Rufescent ants now ascended the hillock, collected in crowds on the summit, and took possession of the principal avenues, leaving some of their companions to work an opening in the side of the ant-hill with their teeth. Success crowned their enterprise, and by the newly-made breach the remainder of the army entered. Their sojourn was, however, of short duration, for in three or four minutes they returned by the same apertures which gave them entrance, each bearing off in its mouth a larva or a pupa."
>
> The expeditions generally start in the afternoon, and are from 100 to 2,000 strong.[6]

As a third trait in the ant colony we should take note of something that is not mentioned by Lubbock but noted by others and that this author himself also has observed. For example, you can take a number of ants that are underway to their nest with food and are walking side by side and even helping one another, and throw them together in a glass jar. These ants then are suddenly so confused that they suspect treason or whatever may be the case, and they immediately begin to attack one another, biting each other's bodies and killing each other off with such ruthlessness that soon no more than two remain alive, and these two furiously bite and slash one another until they too die.

If we attempt to process these phenomena, it would appear that God him- § 3
self not only uses means in the life of the ants, but that he also puts things at their disposal so that they themselves must put to use various means. And not only that, he also gives them the power to put other creatures into their service so that they force them to use these means for the benefit of their masters. We thus find here in the animal kingdom something that comes very close to the multistage use of means that God has given to humankind. Let us identify these multiple successive layers. (1) There are direct activities from God both within and upon us that work without means; examples include our very life itself, which God maintains directly, as well as spiritual influences that go directly to our heart. (2) There are activities of God through means that God himself applies; for example, God uses our

6. Lubbock, *Ants, Bees and Wasps*, 81–82. Original footnotes omitted.

lungs in part to purify our blood and in part to feed it with new substances. (3) There are also activities of God through means that God has us apply ourselves; take, for example, the use of food, which God presents to us but we must take in ourselves. (4) And there are activities of God through the use of means that God not only has us apply but also has us prepare; an example of this is protection against cold by means of lighting a fire, by building a dwelling, by putting on clothes, and so on. (5) Finally, we can identify activities of God through means that we ourselves do not prepare but that have been prepared by other people or animals, which we then apply either alone or with the help of others; for example, if God intends to transfer our place of residence to another land, he does not literally pick us up and carry us through the air. Rather, he gives us the means of a sailing vessel that we must use but that has been prepared by someone else and that we use with the help of others.

There exist, then, definite distinctions in terms of the use of means at various levels. First are the means used without human agency. Then there are the means presented to us for our use. Then there are the means that we first must prepare ourselves before we can utilize them. This leads to the next level of means, which we first must invent ourselves before we can prepare them. The next level are the means not prepared by us but prepared for our use by someone else. Finally, there are means that are not prepared by someone else but that can be used only with the help of others. We observe here, then, a development that is much richer than what we can observe in the animal kingdom among, say, the ants, although it is one that nevertheless is already *foreshadowed* in the animal kingdom, where we also see a self-built and self-arranged nest; the liquid milked from other animals in order to prepare food; a careful raising and protecting of those animals that produce this liquid; and a forcing of other creatures, including ants, to work and collect food for those of their own species.

This multifaceted use of means is neither opposed nor rejected anywhere in Scripture but rather is always either assumed or commended. Where it is commended to the reader, we are specifically pointed in the direction of the animal kingdom in order that we may get instruction from these creatures that are well endowed with "wisdom." From this it follows that, in the use of means, we are dealing with an *ordinance* of God, and the person who does not apply these means or rejects them is in fact opposing God. From all of Scripture we get the impression that those species of animals that maintain their existence through the use of means are not looked down upon as inferior; on the contrary, they are given a prominent place as a more superior or, if you will, more refined and wiser sort that is presented for our learning. If, then, we find among humans this use of means so infinitely more richly developed, then in humankind this is not a *deficiency* but rather evidence of a superior position vis-à-vis the animal kingdom. The more richly and more detailed this becomes, the more human beings demonstrate their superiority and the further their development progresses. The use of means never diminishes human beings; it always represents the imperative condition for the fuller deployment of their power.

Let no one object that a countless number of means that we use are § 4
only the consequence of our deficient condition due to sin, and that these things were unthinkable in paradise or will fall away again one day in the kingdom of glory. While this is in part entirely true, these changes only concern the *kinds* of means, not the *use* of means as such. In centuries past, when someone wanted to send an important message from Northern Europe to the south, it often was necessary to send it by a separate courier and to employ and pay for a multitude of horses, saddles, and tack, a process that lasted week after week. Since then, the means necessary to transfer such a message have changed and been simplified again and again. Now we have even reached a point at which an action taking place can be conveyed by means of a cable that transfers the message from Amsterdam to Madrid in an hour. But even though the means are different, and even though they now work much more rapidly and simply, the *use* of means remains. Similarly, when an inexperienced speaker has to speak at a public meeting, that person will first write it out as a rough draft and then make a copy to be taken along and read. A practiced speaker does not need all of this; he or she processes the material mentally and delivers the speech without involving pen or paper. But even when the seasoned speaker's means are finer and quicker, the means of internal thought and preparation are every bit as instrumental as the use of pen and paper. In the end, even if we concede that a different use of means is suited to the sinless state of paradise and to the kingdom of glory, where the corresponding means are more refined and higher in nature, the use of means nevertheless remains and is even of a far nobler nature.

But now we turn to the condition of our sinful state, in order to determine what the use of means represents in the era of *common grace*, and how the Lord God, precisely *in* that use of means, has revealed and continues to work through such an important part of his common grace.

CHAPTER SIXTY

THE USE OF MEANS

And the Lord *God made for Adam and for his wife garments of skins and clothed them.*

Genesis 3:21

§ 1 If we may summarize our conclusions of the preceding discussion, it would appear, first of all, that God made two kinds of creatures. On the one hand, we observe creatures to which God did not give the access to means; on the other hand, we find creatures to which he did grant the use of means. Thus, for example, the cedar of Lebanon lives its plant life without consciousness, while the eagle swoops down from its eagle's nest, grasps the lamb as prey, and lifts it high into the air in order to feed its young with it.

In addition, we found that the use of means increases as the creature stands on a *higher* level. In the world of plants, the use of means is virtually unknown, but this use of means is common among animals, and the use of means is mostly strongly represented among the more highly developed animals. Especially in the case of ants, it is almost incredible. Holy Scripture, which does not point us to the ape but to the ant to bring the animal kingdom closer to our awareness, corresponds far more with the reality of nature than so many assumptions of contemporary scholars do. They tend to pay attention only to physical correspondences, whereas Scripture draws attention to the manner of existence and social behavior in the context of community or "society" as they are exhibited among animals as well as humans.

However this may be demonstrated, the rule is (and continues to be) that the use of means decreases the lower a creature stands in the rank of created beings. Conversely, it increases the higher the place of the creature is on the ladder of creation. This being the case, it follows directly that we may assume that in humankind, as the highest of all creatures on this planet, the use of means will be strongest by far. Based on the evidence, this indeed appears to be the case. Those who would disapprove or oppose this conclusion end up denigrating rather than glorifying God. They do not realize that their basic thinking goes against the entire order of God's creation. And they discern even less that by removing *all* use of means from our life they, by extension, would send us naked into the wilderness to die there of hunger or to fall prey to wild animals. Those who are most strongly opposed to the idea of any use of means in fact do not go that far in their opposition. They clothe themselves, they live in well-built and well-furnished houses, they eat prepared foods, and they allow themselves all the comforts of life. By doing this, they reveal their inconsistency.

An illustration may be useful in clarifying this point. At present, a new sect calling itself Christian Scientists is spreading in America, England, and Germany. When we enter their "church" on Fourth Avenue in New York City during a service, we see a broad platform in front of rows of pews, on which Chinese vases sit, overflowing and decorated with flowers. Behind the platform is an organ and a place for the choir. At the front of this platform there stand two lecterns next to each other. At the one stands a woman, at the other a man, each of whom does nothing but take turns reading aloud. The woman does nothing but read phrases from holy Scripture with a silver voice, while the man does nothing but read phrases from the *Book of the Christian Scientists*. There is relatively little singing, there is virtually no praying, and the intent of such a service is apparently to mesmerize the hearers by an impressive, authoritative, methodical, and solemn reading. What is the belief system of these Christian Scientists? It is expounded in the work of Rev. Mary Baker Eddy, entitled *Science and Health with Key to the Scriptures*.[1] The thrust of this text is summarized in a tract that is handed out:

1. Mary Baker Eddy, *Science and Health with Key to the Scriptures* (Boston: Christian Scientist Publishing Co., 1875).

When Mr. N. realized the state I was then in, he said to me: "You are adhering too closely to the letter, you must depend more on the spiritual. You must study the Science of Being, think not of healing disease but of *healing sin.*" I caught his meaning on the instant. I found I had been working in the wrong direction, by giving more thought to the physical than to the spiritual. My main, and only object, seemed to be to get healed from the so-called gout; employing the treatment through Mind, as if it were a drug. I thought only of my recovery from pain and lameness, expecting to be healed instantaneously, and wondering all the while why I could not arise and walk a perfectly healed man. To my surprise, I found that the understanding of the letter was only the human aid to prepare me for the understanding of the spiritual, and as it were, the stepping stone to spirituality, and that if I stopped at that point of progress I would never be permanently healed. *For the letter alone cannot heal.* My eyes were now opened. I realized that *fear, sin and mortal belief* were at the bottom of the difficulty. Destroy sin, and I would be free from all disease.

Then the question arose in my mind: How do I sin? I try to act right with all men, on all occasions. I don't think I am such a great sinner. I have no very bad habits. I don't get drunk, carouse and blaspheme. I certainly am better than most men! I try to follow the Golden Rule. Why then should I be compelled to pass through all of these years of misery? Do I bear the least malice against any man? I could not say No to that. Do I nurture any feeling of revenge, intending some day to get even with any one who had seemingly done me an injury? I could not exactly say No to *that.* Do I envy any man? Yes! Do I love all men? A *big No.* Would I push resentment so far as to take life? Certainly not. Do I try to control my appetites and passions? They control *me* oftener than I control *them.* Have I any other aim of life but to "Eat, drink and be merry, for to-morrow we die?" Well, when we get right down to bottom facts, and brush away the spangles that decorate our mortal life, that is about the way *most* people are living, including myself.

Thus I continued to question myself, until I found I was not half as good a man as I thought I was, and that I disobeyed

God's law every day of my life. I had not yet looked beyond the physical. Who am I? What am I? Am I a mortal or an immortal man? I *must* be one or the other? I know that both could not be real. Which was the finite, matter, body, who had a beginning, and will have an ending, or the infinite, God's idea, who never had a beginning, and never will have an ending? If the matter-body, without the mortal senses, cannot think, talk, move, or experience pain, it must be the mortal senses alone, and not the body that cause sin, sickness, pain and death. It cannot be matter, for matter is nothing without the mortal senses. It therefore must be the mortal senses, alias, the carnal mind, that cause sin. What is sin? Error, evil, the opposite of Truth or Good! Destroy sin to mortal consciousness, and Truth has no opposite. All will then be real, and there will be no sin, sickness, pain or death. How can we destroy sin? By declaring and realizing that God only is real; that God has no mortality; that He is omnipotent, omnipresent and omniscient; that He is All in All, and there can be nothing real beside Him, His idea and His eternal verities. All else is illusion.

Ah! But I hear you ask the same question that I did. What is meant by unreality? Is it possible for one to declare that he has no pain, that pain is unreal, a lie, when at the same moment he is apparently suffering its torments? I say Yes. Mortal mind can only hold one thought at one and the same instant. Pain is only a belief. If one should deny the belief and the existence of pain in thought there would be no pain during the instant of that thought. Now continue to hold that thought, of denial, and disabuse yourself of your own mortality. Transfer the thought to Spirit, for God is Spirit. Realize that you are the spiritual man, call one Spirit continually, keeping Spirit in the thought; and you will have no pain during the continuance of that thought. Spiritual thought will supplant the mortal belief of sin, sickness and death; and in proportion to the inflowing, and the holding of the Spiritual thought, will the mortal thought be destroyed. Sin and sickness will disappear, and we will become more and more spiritual, until we ultimately reach a state of perfect harmony, which is Heaven. Often, it may seem difficult to the beginner in Science, to take in and hold that

> instant spiritual thought, and to experience that instantaneous change from the unreal to the real. It can only be attained by persistent spiritual desire.
>
> *Persistent denial in words only, without the spiritual thought will not affect anything.*
>
> When I ceased to realize, that my only object in submitting to Christian Science treatment was to be healed from gout, and from that alone, employing the treatment as if it were medicine administered by a physician, I determined to seek the real cause of my trouble, and having found it, I became a new man. The Science of Being, that is the knowledge of my true existence as a spiritual, not a material, or mortal man had first place in my thought. Fear was destroyed, chemicalization[2] disappeared, and spiritual thoughts filled me. The existence of disease, passed into nothingness, and from that moment, God with all of his verities, became my all, and now the gout has been totally destroyed. *So it will be with you, when you give up the idea of wanting to be healed only from pain and lameness.* You cannot accomplish thorough healing, without a struggle. For old mortal thought will press his claims a thousand times a day, in almost as many shapes. Have your armor always on! Be prepared to deny in thought, the reality of sin and sickness. Deny the reality of your mortal existence. Declare in thought, that you being immortal, it is impossible *for you to experience sin, sickness, or death; for the purely spiritual man is eternal, and can never suffer the pangs of mortality.* Let these thoughts ever fill you, and you will continue to advance in spirituality.[3]

We discover here that a particular worldview lies behind this. We are told that our real being is *spiritual*, and that therefore all that is not spiritual is *unreal*. Such a paradigm derives from Fichte's philosophy.[4] By withdrawing into ourselves, we must reduce our body and all that belongs to our body to

---

2. *Note by the author:* In Christian Science this term refers to an increase in the intensity of the illness at the beginning of the treatment.
3. See John C. Schooley, "How I Was Healed: A Letter to an Enquirer," *Christian Science Journal* 12 (April 1894): 510–12. The English text in Kuyper's original is moved here from a later footnote.
4. Johann Gottlieb Fichte (1762–1814), a German philosopher and a founder of idealism.

nothing in our consciousness, so that pain becomes no pain, and no illness has power over us any longer. The author of this tract adds in a postscript: "Nearly two years have elapsed since the date of my healing, and during this time I have not taken any medicine nor resorted to any other material means."[5] We do not dispute that, in this manner, illnesses have indeed disappeared. We seem to have here the same thing that is operative in the healings at Lourdes in the Pyrenees.[6] At this point we note only that, among these Christian Scientists, the paradigm has been worked out in great detail and formulated most clearly. It is an attempt to bring us to such a strong spiritual concentration in the innermost part of our being that our soul obtains the greatest possible independence, and our dependence on the body is reduced to the smallest degree.

This is the polar opposite of those poor, feeble folks who are literally obsessed with their body and all its minor ailments and diseases; this causes them to suffer terribly, and their healing is hindered precisely because of this focus. All physicians acknowledge today that, in many illnesses, so much depends on what they call the "morale" of the patient. The patient can make much more progress when morale is high rather than low. It is known, for example, from Bismarck that there are men who can suppress the most severe toothache by means of their willpower.[7] Every preacher knows from his own experience how many ailments can be suppressed the moment he enters the pulpit. More than one preacher who entered the pulpit half-sick felt robust and even inspired when he left it afterward. So we would not deny for a moment the partial truth contained in this viewpoint.

In response, we would simply say here that anyone who considers this to be the truth must also abstain from food. If indeed only our spiritual existence is real and our bodily existence merely apparent and imaginary, and thus unreal, then it is as equally nonsensical to eat food as it is to take medicine. And if this is countered with the objection that the food that is eaten is not real either, that it is only "apparent," then it goes without saying

5. Schooley, "How I Was Healed," 514.
6. In 1858 a series of visions of the Virgin Mary were reported in a grotto at Lourdes, a village in the Pyrenees mountains in the south of France. Since this time a number of miraculous occurrences have been reported.
7. Presumably a reference to Otto von Bismarck (1815–98), a renowned German politician and chancellor from 1871 to 1890.

that the same also applies to medicine; it is therefore folly to want to fight any use of medicine that is unreal and has no real effect anyway. And if the argument is carried further by saying that it is precisely the illusory use of medicine that weakens the soul, then the same applies to the illusion that food is ingested. Precisely *this* must also be rejected, then, in order to attain to the state of the soul in which the body is totally denied.

But even if this applies to Christian Scientists, it does not apply to others who think similarly about medicines yet do so on the basis of an entirely different assumption that falls entirely outside Fichte's philosophical framework. These particular people judge that a distinction must be made in the present life between what flows directly from creation and what results from sin. What issues out of creation, they argue, is our "nature." What belongs to that nature must run its course. Eating and drinking are needs equally as natural as sleeping and breathing; surely no one can deny this. But it is quite different with physical deficiencies, maladies, and sickness. Those do not stem from nature but from the curse that came through sin. They are how the wrath of God is manifested. God brings these upon us because of our iniquity. Here we encounter, therefore, not a *natural* but a *spiritual* cause. That is, as long as we hold on to that spiritual cause, sin and sickness must also be understood as a consequence. And, therefore, it is thought that the proper right path to healing is not going to physicians but to the Great Physician alone, so that with sincere prayer we are loosed from the sin from which the illness sprang, and so that we can expect restoration of health from God's almighty influence upon our body *without* the intervention of means.

We now must scrutinize this very notion because it is related directly to the issue of *common grace*. For common grace means that God the Lord, out of pure mercy and apart from salvific grace, has ordained *common* means against the *common* misery, or if you will, against the *common* consequences of sin. But those who reject the use of means to combat illness and even call it sinful deny the existence of such a common grace. They are of the mindset that applying common means to combat the common consequences of sin is somehow going against God and attempting to avert his judgment upon us; in the end, this is an act of rebellion and reckless resistance. In this light, it stands to reason that their beliefs and our confession of common grace stand in principled opposition to one another. It is God himself who takes up the battle against the curse—that is, against all common misery that is a consequence of the fall. His common grace, in its essence and as it is intended, is nothing other than a combating of the curse in order to temper and mitigate it. And it is he himself who has devised and ordained the means to accomplish this.

Given this reality, it is then the calling of the child of God to act against that curse, like his Father in heaven, and in obedience to God to search for and discover the means that God has provided for this purpose, and when discovered, to apply them with care and diligence. Conversely, if it is true that God has willed the curse in such a way that, according to his order, it must bear down upon us unmitigated and unopposed, then the means that we apply against the common misery are nothing but human fabrications, or worse yet, promptings from the evil one with which believers then resist the judgment of God. In that case, it would be right for the child of God to reject all such use of means, to put them away, to resist them, and to submit passively to such judgment, unless it would please God to deliver that person as his elect child through a direct act of grace.

These two positions, alas, are diametrically opposed to one another. They do not allow for compromise. It is therefore of the greatest importance that we arrive at a lucid, clear solution regarding this matter. For the person who rejects the doctor and trusts only in God all too often gives the impression, even to those who themselves still use medicine, of possessing a *higher form of godliness*: the people who still use medicine perhaps would like to do the same, but they lack the faith for it and thus see themselves as deficient in godliness. This is simply unacceptable. If the rejection of medicine is more "godly," then we *all* must reject medicine, since godliness is the highest honorific title for the child of God. If, on the other hand, it appears that it is a duty imposed by God that we use medicine, and that he wills the use of means, then it is in fact ungodly not to use them, and whoever is guilty of this should therefore be rebuked for creating a "self-made religion and asceticism and severity to the body" [Col 2:23], thereby straying from the paths of the Lord.

In this connection we might identify Genesis 3:21 as an important marker: "And the LORD God made for Adam and for his wife garments of skins and clothed them." At this point in our discussion it would lead us too far afield to attempt a detailed exposition of this verse. We wish only to derive from this statement the fact that this act of the Lord shows that God himself taught humans to use *means* in the face of the common misery that is the consequence of sin. We have no interest, of course, in entering into a discussion at this point with those who do not believe what is written here or who interpret it metaphorically. We are dealing here only with those who with us accept and believe the narrative in the first chapters of Genesis to be a truthful report of facts that really did take place in this way. What follows then is that this statement is not only very important and instructive but even decisive. It is without question that in paradise any clothing or covering was inconceivable. God created the human person naked, not with the intent of covering various parts of the body but rather that they might be displayed. And this was indeed possible in a state of purity because every sense of shame was absent. "The man and his wife were both naked and were not ashamed" [Gen 2:25]. But immediately after their sin they were overcome by such a strong sense of shame that, even though the two of them were alone and knew that there were no eyes of a third person to see them, they immediately covered their loins with leaves. They were therefore the first ones to immediately use external means in the face of the common consequences of sin.

If God had not wanted this to happen, if it were impermissible and reprehensible, then we should be reading, "And the Lord God took away from their loins the leaves they had put on." But this is not how the text reads; rather, it says the opposite. In God's eye the leaves are inadequate. He knows that it is not only shame they will have to cover up, but also that as a result of sin the environment will affect them. The atmosphere of paradise, with its constant mildness, was affected. Elements such as chill and dampness would replace the balmy environment, and covering and warmth for the weak, fragile body would continually be needed for humankind's welfare. God does not say, "In the cold lies my judgment. That cold is because of sin. You must not combat the cold. You must not use *means* against it." No, far from it. Rather, God himself provides what humans must now use. Animals had their fur. God clothed the animals directly. But humankind was naked. And God now takes the fur of animals and drapes it around Adam and his wife. This is not, as is often depicted, as a piece of fur draped around the loins as a replacement for the fig leaf, but as a *ketoneth*—that is, as a garment draped around the shoulders, or a coat, as we still sometimes call it today [Gen 3:21].

This use of means, of course, involves clothing. This clothing had to serve as a covering against the elements and was thus a means that God provided for the human person, to be draped around the shoulders to combat one of the direct consequences of the curse. It needs to be pointed out that the nudists in Amsterdam in the sixteenth century did not grasp this at all.[8] But they were consistent to the extent that as they considered themselves to be elevated above the consequences of the curse, they rejected every means for combating the curse. Whatever the case may be, this much is certain: (1) cold and damp did not exist in paradise; (2) these elements came upon the earth as a consequence of sin and curse; (3) far from wanting man to submit passively to them, God himself took the initiative to combat them; (4) God himself thinks of the means and applies it; and (5) he instructs man at the same time how he must combat the consequences of the curse in the future. In this light, then, it is clear that from the beginning of human history on, according to the teaching of holy Scripture, the curse and the common misery are something to which we must not submit passively but rather that which we must combat with all means God places at our disposal for this purpose.

8. In the early sixteenth century, a variety of radical groups proclaimed the coming of the kingdom of God. One such group ran naked through Amsterdam, proclaiming the judgment of God on the city.

CHAPTER SIXTY-ONE

AGAINST THE CURSE

By the sweat of your face you shall eat bread, till you return to the ground, for out of it you were taken; for you are dust, and to dust you shall return.

GENESIS 3:19

§ 1 Following the fall, God made it clear that humanity should not be destroyed by the effects of the environment but rather was to seize and use various means to receive protection from dangerous elements that threatened from the atmosphere. This necessarily leads to the conclusion that it is not God's design to let evil overcome us; on the contrary, God's moral law constrains us to combat the miseries of life. God does not allow our use of various means of defense against the misery and suffering of life as if it were something that really should not be permitted but is only allowed for our enjoyment. In truth, the paradise narrative teaches us clearly that the use of means is imposed upon us as an obligation. We not only *may* combat the consequences of sin; we *must* do so. It is a demand, a command, and an ordinance that has been given us. Those who oppose this oppose the divine command.

This conclusion may be seen to derive from the skins that God himself draped on Adam and Eve after the fall. That act of God in itself contains an implicit command, even though it is not mentioned by the text that this clothing of man was accompanied by a spoken word. When God gives us an example, then, by its very nature, we must follow it. For Adam and Eve personally, following this example probably would not be a consideration in the near future, since such a skin virtually never wears out. But when their children were born and exposed to the same dangers of the environment, Adam and Eve would have acted contrary to God's clearly expressed will if they had not protected their children. Thus, implicit in the clothing of Adam and Eve was the precept, ordinance, and commandment that, wherever the effects of the atmosphere would threaten human health or life, human beings must defend themselves against this danger, which includes fighting the destructive forces of nature. For this, human beings must make use of the means that God has put in nature at their disposal.

Adam and Eve did not yet know that in nature there also were plants from which linen and cotton could be made, as well as the silkworm, from which one day silk would be spun. And the art of making thread from a plant and spinning this thread would be shown to man by God only after further developments. The only thing prepared at this point, as it were, was the garment with which God himself had clothed the animals. At the point at which the human person might have questioned whether it was permissible to kill an animal to take its fur as a covering, God's grace intervenes with an *action*, and the fur taken from an animal is placed upon the human. God had prepared that animal fur in order to cover the human person with it. And thus from the very beginning the human person has not been uncertain for a minute what is to be done in this situation. No matter how widely human knowledge increases, we continue to find humanity clothed with the skins of animals. And the general awareness that we *may* and *must* cover ourselves in order to protect ourselves from various effects of our environment is so natural—even irresistible—that even those who might argue vehemently in theory against the use of means end up presenting themselves well-clothed, thus offering conclusive evidence in their very person that at least on this point they deny their own principle.

What is important is that people seem to be more aware than ever before of the extent of the consequences of the curse. If people think only of certain illnesses or national disasters or personal accidents, then it is quite natural that they should apply their theory of having to remain passive under the punishing hand of God only to those kinds of manifestations of the curse. By doing so, they fail to see the inconsistency in their use of all kinds of means in everyday life while at the same time condemning their use in certain cases. But this is a thoroughly inconsistent position that cannot be defended for even a moment, either before the tribunal of holy Scripture or in the light of human experience.

The reason it is unscriptural is that holy Scripture points to the consequences of the curse after the fall, and in this context it does not speak of illnesses, nor of national disasters, but rather—even exclusively—of the general misery that in everyday experience bears down upon our human life as a consequence of the curse. "In pain you shall bring forth children" [Gen 3:16] is not an illness, nor a national disaster, but the common fate of women in the procreation of the human race. In the same way, the fact that the earth will produce thorns and thistles, and that man will not be able to get his food from the earth except by great effort, is not exceptional; rather, it refers to the very common condition of our human life, throughout the centuries, everywhere, and at all times. It is therefore a direct contradiction of the clear revelation of God's Word if we claim and maintain that this common human misery is *not* a consequence of the curse, and that the curse would manifest itself only in famine, pestilences, war, and so forth. It also needs to be pointed out—perhaps unnecessarily—that what we read about "the curse" in Genesis 3 is stated directly in words that God himself brings on humanity as judgment and punishment.

We will return to this later, but for now we wish to emphasize that a second factor—namely, our experience of life—contradicts this mistaken notion as well. Even if we leave human illness and national calamities out of consideration, can it be denied that the many kinds of misery and distress with which all people struggle have their roots in the general and universally experienced conditions of nature and society around us? The effects of the fall as they are expressed in *society* are particularly relevant and in our day come when we consider public outcry regarding social needs. But the effects of the fall are also abundantly clear in *nature* as well. For example, is it not real suffering when, century after century, the Eskimos languish under dreadfully cold conditions and scarcely can move about? And is it not widespread misery when fishing villages see the number of widows and orphans steadily rise due to factors directly related to fishing? In fact, the sacrifice demanded continually by the ocean when, even apart from storms, many perish at sea under normal conditions—is it not simply the result of the nature of things, even without interference from anything out of the ordinary?

Thus, it would appear that the question remains one and the same, in the case of ordinary as well as extraordinary consequences of the curse, whether God wants us to undergo these consequences passively or whether he requires and commands that we oppose and combat them with all the means he has put at our disposal. In that light, then, we may come to several conclusions: (1) God created human beings, in contrast to the animals, unclothed. (2) Clothing was not even an issue in paradise, insofar as the curse was absent. Even when God brought the animals to Adam and he observed them, the question "Why are these clothed and I am not?" doubtless did not occur to him; Adam feels only the lack of a counterpart. (3) The atmosphere in paradise must have been of such a nature that being unclothed did not bother man. (4) The situation after paradise became entirely different; elements such as cold, bleakness, wind, storm, hail, snow and ice, and even conditions such as dampness, fog, mist, and rain have all come upon us as manifestations of God's righteous judgment, and in a very serious sense as a punishment that lay embedded in the curse that would press down upon our life.

If in fact it were the case that we should remain passive under everything that mirrors judgment, punishment, and the curse and not oppose it, then humans should have let themselves freeze to death. But when we observe that God himself teaches us quite otherwise and himself shows us the very covering with which we should clothe ourselves, then it is quite clear, allowing no counterargument, that God condemns the passive yielding to the consequences of the curse. Very much to the contrary, he makes it our duty to combat the consequences of the curse by using all such means as he discloses and provides for us. Of course, God could equally well have given man a furry skin like that of the lion or the tiger. The hair on our heads proves this, and Esau illustrates the degree to which this possibly might have occurred. But God has not willed this. Man and woman would remain naked, and being naked, they themselves would have to take it upon themselves to cover themselves artificially by looking for clothing.

If some readers are inclined to deny the force of our argument because in their view the matter of covering with animal skins concerns only the issue of shame and not protection from the elements, then we want to ask in all seriousness what their evidence for this is. Surely they would have to agree that the Genesis narrative contains not a single word in support of their view; earlier, the text clearly identified shame to be the purpose in the case of the leaves that Adam and Eve themselves sought for covering. Additionally, as mentioned earlier, the Hebrew word for "garments" in Genesis 3:21 argues against it. The word used almost always refers to a coat of some kind, rather than a simple skirt. It is, to be precise, a garment that is draped around the shoulders. The same word is used for the garment of the priests and the Levites. In support of this view, the word used for "clothed" does not point to a "putting around the body's midsection"; it represents clothing in the wider sense. Anyone familiar with Hebrew will agree without reservation with regard to the use in the Genesis text of the noun *ketoneth* and the verb *labash*. On this basis we maintain that it is an entirely wrong interpretation to think here in terms of covering their shame. The text does not mention this at all, and the grammar being used here contradicts it.

But even if we were to concede (which we cannot) that this *could* be the meaning of the words, then our argument retains its force. The fearful sense of shame was unknown in paradise. Scripture emphatically confirms this. This sense of shame was therefore exclusively a consequence of sin. And the Lord does not will that we suffer this oppressive and heavy feeling passively. On the contrary, he demands that we oppose and combat it, and that we use a means of covering for this purpose. Sin, then, would consist not in the use of the means that are needed and provided for this, but rather a failing to use these means. No matter what we do, the fact that God himself put the animal skin around the shoulders of fallen humankind is conclusive evidence and an abiding lesson that God calls us to the use of means, and specifically to combat the consequences of sin brought upon us.

The same truth is evident as well from the command that man will eat bread by the sweat of his face. These words too should not be misunderstood. They do not say that man may eat only bread, or that one may not eat bread that one himself has not prepared by the sweat of his own face. The mere fact that little children need to be fed contradicts this. The sense of these words is quite different. Before the fall in paradise human creation lived from what nature spontaneously produced. Luxuriant vegetation featuring choice and noble fruits offered all that was needed for human nourishment. "You may surely eat of every tree of the garden" [Gen 2:16], was the word of the Creator that put his seal upon this noble food. After the fall it changed. The curse came upon this world, and the earth produced thorns and thistles. This, of course, does not mean that there were no fruit trees after the fall, but it does indicate that the food that was available in this way became insufficient and that the greater part of the earth from then on would produce all kinds of timber, but in wooded areas without fruit suitable for man. As soon as the human race expanded, there would be a shortage of food to sustain life. Hunger would plague human beings. For the animals there was grass, but there would be no endless source of food for humans, whose lives would simply sense an ebbing away. Famine would dog their steps, followed with death by starvation.

In theoretical terms, what would the human condition be in a situation like this? In such distress, a consequence of the curse would overtake each person. That distress would contain a judgment of God and constitute a justified punishment for each person's sin. By forfeiting paradise, human beings brought upon themselves a life of distress and misery on an inhospitable earth. Then the question arises, Did humans have to subject themselves passively to this punishment of God and, if there was no food, die of hunger? Or was it their duty to combat this hunger and, in order to do that, to use the means God put at their disposal? There can scarcely be any doubt about the answer to this question. Before Adam and Eve have thought for even a moment of that coming distress, while paradise still surrounds them, and their provision is still certain and assured—even in overabundance and profusion—it is God himself who points to this coming need and holds it before them, predicting it as a consequence of sin and curse, while at the same time pointing to the means at hand to escape the consequences of that misery. We might conclude that a treasure lies hidden in the earth. It contains all kinds of kernels and seeds from which all manner of plants can sprout, fully capable of stilling human hunger and nourishing the body. However, the earth does not produce this food spontaneously. It must be cultivated. Furthermore, the crops must be prepared so that the earth provides human beings with healthy and tasty food. Humankind does not invent this; it is God's ordinance. Out of grace God prepared it to spring forth in this way. But man will have to expend effort for it. It will entail hard, heavy, and difficult labor. And now God commands him not to shirk this exertion; rather, he *must* enter into combat with the consequences of the curse, and thus eat bread in the sweat of his face, thereby *saving his life* that was threatened by the distress and misery that flow from the curse.

We grant that this is not stated explicitly in Genesis 3:19. In paradise after the fall we find no debate or any proclaimed dogmas. There was judgment, there has been sentencing, and there has been action, with the first steps having been taken on the new path of life. But in and from all of this God's will and intent are expressed, and the great issue as to whether we must passively waste away under our punishment or carry on and combat the evil in which the punishment manifests itself is decided immediately. Anyone since Adam who does not apply every means available to protect his life against death is guilty of violating the sixth commandment. Adam himself is not allowed to give up. He must not give in to the thought of despair so as to simply fade away. Suicide is deeply entrenched in the human heart, as we witness all around us in ever-increasing sorts of ways. And this is understandable from Adam's perspective after the fall. But no living human being could ever be in a more painful situation than Adam was at that moment: being alone with one female on this entire earth, with God's wrath upon him, leaving paradise with the elements bursting forth against him, and looking at a desolate world without end. We fail to sufficiently imagine ourselves in such conditions. We fail to sufficiently appreciate the reality that Adam faced. We suffer too little with Adam's suffering, and we therefore do not feel what must have gone on in his heart. But when we think about what it was like to stand virtually alone in a still-desolate, untamed world, bearing the guilt of sin through which an entire world sank into curse, we might wonder whether the thought "O God, if only I were gone!" or "O God, destroy me eternally!" would have vexed Adam's heart. In that heart and at that moment, despondency and despair must have made suicide and self-destruction attractive.

And now God intervenes and says, "Not so. You shall not kill. You shall not let yourself be destroyed by distress and hunger. You shall live, but in order to live you will need to combat death and hunger; to this end I will let you discover the means. Indeed, you will have to exert yourself, exerting yourself until the sweat drips from your body. And in that sweat of your face you will eat bread, and live."

We are not denying that in that life of exertion there was an aftereffect of punishment. But even as a woman would suffer in giving birth to children and yet through that stress obtain the life of her child, so Adam would suffer under unremitting labor, yet through that hard work he would in turn obtain life for his wife, his children, and himself. We must therefore not get a wrong picture. The punishment proper was and remained *death*. "When you eat of this tree, *you will surely die*," Adam was told. And in what came after this, the curse of death did in fact have its aftereffect, but eating bread by "the sweat of his brow" was in itself *not* a curse; rather, it was grace, showing him the means to combat the curse.

CHAPTER SIXTY-TWO

REBUKE AND WRATH

And he stood over her and rebuked the fever, and it left her,
and immediately she rose and began to serve them.

LUKE 4:39

It became apparent from the paradise narrative how God the Lord himself, far from rejecting the use of means, demonstrated, taught, and commanded for humankind the use of means. Likewise, it became apparent how God obligated humans to use means, not only because of what flowed from human nature but certainly also for what was the consequence of sin and the curse. The elements against which the animal skins were intended and the hunger against which the sweat of his brow had to struggle were a result not of creation but of the misery that the fall brought upon man. § 1

But we cannot stop at this point. For if God himself brings misery *as punishment* upon man, and if God nevertheless teaches humankind to engage in the struggle against that misery and restrict it by all kinds of means, the natural question arises whether God is not in conflict with himself. His is the judgment under which we stand. His is the punishment that came upon us in the curse. If, in spite of this, God himself teaches us to engage in battle with all kinds of means against that judgment, against that punishment, and against that misery, doesn't this give the impression that God himself incites man to resist his verdict? This is the central question, the pivot around which this entire issue revolves. Those who are inclined toward passivity and who seek refuge in renouncing means do so out of fear of going against God. If they are struck by a fever, it is because God has sent them this fever; therefore they refuse to take quinine, because it would be resisting God to combat that fever. And, if they are to be delivered from the fever, then God himself must give them his grace and lift the punishment in response to their humble prayer.

Sin, they rightly judge, was rebellion against God. And if we are now being punished because of that rebellion against God, then the first condition for receiving grace is that we strictly refrain from all resistance to God and his just judgment. Thus, when they are struck by illness or accident, they consider it disobedient to do anything against it out of fear that they might rebel once again against God. It would be rebelling against his judgment now, even as in paradise Adam and Eve rebelled against his commandment. The question is therefore inescapable: Is the use of any means against any suffering that God sends our way actually doing battle against God himself? If this is indeed the case, then we should also conclude without reservation that we must desist, and we must undergo the most terrible sufferings passively rather than be understood as raising our hand against God.

In order to bring clarity on this point before the tribunal of holy Scripture, we begin by pointing to what is reported about Jesus in Luke 4:38–39. There we are told that when Jesus was in Capernaum, he entered the house of Simon the fisherman and heard there how Simon's mother-in-law was lying in bed, "ill with a high fever." Then, according to the narrative, Jesus entered the room where she lay and he "rebuked the fever." The result of this rebuke was that she was suddenly healed and could get up and prepare the midday meal. Pay close attention to what Jesus did. He did not say, "Nothing can be done about this." He did not urge her to resign herself passively to that fever. He did not call upon grace for her to be delivered from this fever. On the contrary, Jesus acts directly against the fever itself, as against any evil that must not be left to itself, and he does this by *rebuking* the fever. "Rebuking" implies that whatever is rebuked is guilty. Does Jesus rebuke the woman? Does he say, "This is something caused by your sin?" No, Jesus does not rebuke the sick woman but rather the fever that has her in its grip. The evil does not reside in Peter's mother-in-law but in the illness that came upon her. Here the fever is the evil power. That fever is the guilty entity. And this is why Jesus addresses the fever. Jesus rebukes the fever with a rebuke that implies, "You must not be there. You must go away from this woman. I command you to let go of this woman immediately." This is indeed what happened, and thus Peter's mother-in-law immediately became healthy.

We generally gloss over such statements; we read and see them as a particular way of expressing things, and we understand this particular text to say merely that Jesus healed the woman. But we must not read it in this way. It is neither by accident nor arbitrarily that the word *rebuke* is used here. This word was chosen deliberately, and therefore we must not rest until we correctly understand the word in its context.

We are all the more impelled to do this because the same word, *rebuke*, is also used elsewhere by Jesus. An example of this is Matthew 8:26, which describes a storm on the Sea of Gennesaret that came upon the boat in which Jesus and his disciples were sailing. Especially on larger bodies of water, such sudden storms can be extremely dangerous, given the violent nature of wind-generated wave activity. Even in our day, reports are heard of such storm activity that result in shipwreck, and almost always these shipwrecks are beyond rescue. Jesus' disciples, who were experienced fishermen, realized the mortal danger in which they found themselves. This is why they called out to Jesus, "Save us, Lord; we are perishing." And then, it is reported, Jesus came on deck, looked with clear vision into the raging storm and the wind-swept waves, and then, it says, he rebuked the winds and the sea. Here, too, the result of this rebuke was the immediate ceasing of the evil: "and there was a great calm."

This second story is even more remarkable than the first. When, in the first example, the fever is rebuked, we are dealing with a power that we can still sense carries something evil within it. Fever, of course, can be the result of any number of things that are wrong. We would even be able to make better sense of it if the rebuke had not concerned a common fever but rather a fever that actually had been contracted by evil and immoral living. But even in the case of a fever we sense that there is a certain evil element at work. But here, in the case of a storm, there is nothing like that. Here it does not involve something that deserves rebuke; rather, it concerns elements in the form of the winds that God allows to blow and that the sea has created. Wind and sea are both forces of nature that rage even if there is no ship on the sea and not a living soul is at stake. The immense ocean that separates Europe from America, and on the Pacific side, America from Asia, was not navigated for centuries by a single ship, yet there is no doubt that the same elemental forces, as they are called, churned up and influenced these waters during those centuries as well. We might therefore conclude, what is a storm other than the direct blowing of God's breath upon the waters? And if this is the case, why didn't Jesus beg the sea and the winds to be still, instead of rebuking them as an evil force for doing something they should not have been doing, and commanding them to let go of their fury? Yet, incredible as it may seem to us at first glance, the story leaves no doubt, based on holy Scripture's clear testimony: Jesus rebuked not only the fever but also the sea and the winds. From this it follows that Jesus considered that the sea and wind were a working of God's power that was "abused" by an evil and culpable force—a force that was both permitted and needing to be "punished." After all, how could Jesus, who was himself God, ever have rebuked the direct action of God?

We can save ourselves the trouble of tampering with the word *rebuke*. The Greek text uses the verb *epitimaō*, a word that generally does not allow another meaning. It is, however, a word with a double meaning to the extent that it can mean "to commend, to praise," as well as "to rebuke or chastise." This latitude, however, does not make the meaning any less certain in this instance. A very literal translation might be "to give someone what he deserves," and for this reason the same word can at one time mean "to praise" someone, if we are dealing with a person who deserves praise, and at another time "to rebuke" someone, if we are dealing with someone who deserves to be chastised. To know what it means here, we only have to ask ourselves, Did Jesus commend the fever because it deserved praise? We sense immediately that this is not possible, nor would it make any sense, given what follows: "immediately the fever left her." The conclusion, therefore, is obvious: Jesus rebuked the fever because it deserved to be chastised and had to depart.

It would make equally little sense to read Matthew 8:26 as if it said that Jesus praised the storm, for how could this have the result that the storm suddenly ceased? If Jesus had praised the storm as something that should be commended, the storm should only have increased in force. Here, too, there is therefore no doubt that the translation must remain as it is: Jesus rebuked the sea and the winds. At the same time, a closer look at the Greek word that is found in the text is instructive. It indicates that "to rebuke" means to give to the fever, to the sea, or to the winds what they deserved. Insofar as this leads to a rebuke, it is implicit that the fever, the sea, and the winds were culpable, that they deserved "punishment," and that Jesus meted out this punishment. This punishment, moreover, consisted in the fact that, because these forces had the power to bring ruin, Jesus forbade them to exercise that power. The fever could have destroyed the woman, and the storm could have destroyed the boat. But Jesus prevents them from doing this and imputes to them as evil the fact that they were trying to do this. He not only prevents, but he rebukes.[1]

The Greek translation of the Old Testament, the Septuagint, uses this very verb, *epitimaō*; however, there is a difference in connotation. Whereas Greek is a rational language and therefore conveys the sense of "to give someone what he or she deserves," in Hebrew, by contrast, given its ancient Near Eastern milieu, the verb translated by *epitimaō* carries the sense of anger or wrath. It expresses acting out of inner wrath against someone with fierce emotion and overwhelming awareness to thwart his intent. A notable example is 2 Samuel 22:16, where the rebuke of the Lord does not merely result in the cessation of something but rather in an utter laying waste: "Then the channels of the sea were seen; the foundations of the world were laid bare, at the *rebuke* of the LORD, at the blast of the breath of his nostrils."

We therefore have every right to say that holy Scripture, in the Old Testament as well as in the New Testament, knows of a rebuking and being angry that proceeds from God and his Christ against all destruction that resulted from the curse. The curse itself is a consequence of judgment and punishment on account of sin. But it does not follow that humankind therefore must be passively subjected to the consequences of the curse, since God and his Christ themselves are angry with the consequences of the curse; rebuke them; and disrupt, arrest, and oppose them. Only when we look at it in this depth can clarity be gained regarding the very important question of whether God wants us to passively undergo his external punishments or whether it is God's will, God's intention, even God's demand of the human race that we, as children of God and those redeemed in Christ Jesus, should rebuke any evil in the forces of nature even as God rebukes them, and that we should rebuke them as Jesus rebuked them.

At this point, the answer cannot for a moment be in doubt. Anyone who preaches that being passively resigned to the curse is part of the misery is

---

1. Here follows a lengthy discussion (omitted in this English edition) of the meaning of the Dutch word *schelden*. The SV uses *schelden*, a word that in the sense of "to rebuke" was already archaic in Kuyper's time. *Schelden* already meant in Kuyper's day "to curse, to swear, to vituperate." Kuyper argues that all occurrences of *schelden* must be understood in the sense of "rebuke," which is the preferred translation of most English Bibles.

preaching in direct opposition to holy Scripture; that person leads souls astray, resists God's ordinance, and one day, at the last judgment, will have to render serious account of the sin personally committed and by which others have been misled. If an epidemic breaks out among a people, it is God's demand that all, with every means available, combat and rebuke that epidemic as a great evil. The person who does not do this is guilty of breaking the sixth commandment and is accountable to God for murder, since his or her inaction would result in the epidemic claiming victims. This reality is confirmed very clearly by what the Old Testament teaches concerning the first symptoms of leprosy. To see it otherwise and to act otherwise is not only unhealthy but profoundly sinful. The reason we state this so starkly and severely is because we, as far as our words might reach, wish to reject any responsibility for those who are sick and might succumb through inaction. We would even add that ministers of the Word cannot be blameless if they do not preach this ordinance of God to the people clearly, convincingly, and without any trace of doubt.

We freely grant that this is not the end of the matter, and we are now faced with the question, But if we are to *combat* the curse and all its consequences, how can it be a punishment of God over us?

The next chapter deals with this question.

CHAPTER SIXTY-THREE

DEATH IS AN ENEMY TO BE OPPOSED

The last enemy to be destroyed is death.

1 CORINTHIANS 15:26

The result of our inquiry thus far has been that God wages battle against sin's misery in its full extent and that we, having been created in the image of God, are called to the same battle. This, in truth, is precisely the opposite of what so many believers with a misguided sense of piety attempt to embody. Our religious duty is not to passively resign ourselves to suffering and misery as a judgment of God that comes upon us. Rather, we are required to combat suffering and misery as a *common enemy*. In this God himself goes before us, and Christ himself understood it in the same way when he was on earth. Passive resignation is therefore no authentic piety, but rather sin, and among the children of God this truth must be proclaimed ever more clearly: suffering and misery are our enemy, against which we must arm ourselves and with which we must do battle. But, as we already noted, anyone who hears this for the first time bumps into a very serious difficulty and asks involuntarily how it is to be reconciled that, on the one hand, God brings suffering and misery upon us as punishment for sin, while, § 1 on the other hand, he himself battles against that suffering and rebukes that misery.

The solution to this difficulty will be made somewhat easier for us if we first pay attention to the reality of death. As to its essence, death is understood with certainty to have come into the world as a punishment for sin, and it is equally certain from holy Scripture that death is an *enemy* against which God stands. For it is clearly written that *death came into the world through sin* [Rom 5:12], which implies that if sin had not come, death would not have reigned. Any notion that death is natural and belongs to the nature of creation must be absolutely rejected on these grounds by anyone who acknowledges holy Scripture. From this it does not follow, of course, that the first human being would have lived endlessly on this earth; rather, the opposite appears to be the case. Paradise was certainly not the highest state of bliss. The coming kingdom of glory stands *above* paradise. But the transfiguration of Jesus on Mount Tabor shows clearly that our human nature can very well transition to a higher state *without dying*. And the Apostle Paul foretells that the children of God who experience the return of the Lord also will *not* die but be transformed, without dying, into a higher state of glory [1 Cor 15:51].

The fact remains, therefore, that death reigns on earth exclusively through sin. And not only that, but Scripture teaches with equal clarity that God has brought death upon this world as a judgment—that is, as a punishment for sin. The statement "In the day that you eat of it you shall surely die" [Gen 2:17] is conclusive evidence of this. Death, therefore, did not come into the world through sin in the sense that it flowed from living in the world as a consequence; rather, death was *threatened* before sin came, and in death lay a judgment of God: he would subject us to death as a punishment. The fact that this is no longer true for the Christian, and that those who share in Jesus Christ may confess, "For me, death is no longer a payment for sin but a gateway to eternal life," does not in the least cancel out this reality.[1] For by delivering us from death, what Christ has borne for us was precisely *punishment*, *judgment*, and *curse*. It is therefore incontrovertible: death is a judgment of God that has come upon our human race as punishment for sin and stands therefore on the same plane as famine, war, and whatever other misery God brings upon us as a punishment because

1. See Heidelberg Catechism, Lord's Day 16, Q&A 42.

of sin. The comparison continues in the most absolute sense. And the holy Scriptures witness with equal certainty concerning this death: death is an *enemy* of God against which God wages battle and that will be conquered by God's holy rule and annihilated. *The last enemy to be destroyed is death.*

We point this out with particular emphasis because there are many believers who remain in substantial doubt. Our previous argument was based chiefly on the expression "rebuking" a fever, "rebuking" the wind, and so on; and in the Old Testament, "rebuking" wild animals, the storm, the heathen, and so on. Based on that argument, the conclusion that suffering and misery are an enemy of God against which he enters into battle was only derivative. But here we do not even need such a derivation. For in 1 Corinthians 15:26 we read, quite literally and in so many words, that death is an enemy of God—an enemy that, although it will be the final one, will certainly be annihilated. Holy Scripture goes even further and prophesies in Revelation 20:14 that the terrible moment is soon to come when death will be thrown into the lake of fire. Much more could be said about this on the basis of the book of Revelation, but we will refrain from commentary at this point, lest we distract attention from the main point. For our present purposes, it is sufficient if we have demonstrated incontrovertibly that (1) death exists because of sin, (2) death has come into the world as judgment and punishment, (3) death is an enemy, and (4) therefore battle must be waged against death, a battle that will end in death's annihilation.

Let us now establish the link with what preceded. Between death and all other suffering there exists an undeniable connection. We see this in pestilence, famine, and war. It is death that kills people in pestilence. Famine strikes down its victims by death, as was seen recently in British India.[2] And when we consider that even in the nineteenth century the number of persons killed by war and its aftermath has exceeded far beyond five hundred thousand, there can then be no doubt that death is an ally of war. The same can be said about victims at sea. Most regrettable are the stories that reach us again and again of the hundreds of victims who have lost their lives at sea. But the same applies to all kinds of accidents: of fires that break out, of train disasters, or accidents on the rivers, or among those riding horses. In the Dutch East Indies annually, thousands of people are fatally bitten by snakes or mauled by tigers. In short, the broad range of manifestations

2. There was a famine in India in 1896–97 in which some five million people perished.

of the miseries that have come upon us because of sin makes it clear to everybody how, in all these things, death is at work; death celebrates its bitter and frightening triumphs.

But this misery extends even further. There is ever so much nameless misery that, although it is not yet *complete* death, nevertheless partially restricts life for us, burdening and oppressing us. Blindness causes us to walk around as if we were in the darkness of death. All kinds of chronic diseases and illnesses bring a half death upon us as human beings. And even when we look at more inward suffering, there too we sense a "shadow of death" that comes over us. Everyone experiences automatically what transpires when we confront mourning: it is as if death had stolen our hearts. But the same applies as well to other sources of sorrow: in all pain of the soul and torment of the heart, it is always as if the chains of death are wrapped around us, or as if a moral death has stricken us. All poets who have ever written about human suffering show in their poems that they have so deeply felt the link between inner suffering and death that they have interpreted for us the grief of our soul in the metaphor of death, each in their own way. Death in itself is nothing; death is the taking away of life. This can happen in an absolute sense, by which we die. But our lives can also be assailed partially, and the enjoyment of life can be taken away from us in part. All that breaks the strength of our lives, or causes the full enjoyment of life to be lost, is a beginning of death, a dying while we yet live. In any case, let no one say that this is merely metaphorical language. Whoever says this does not know suffering in its mortal terror. Just ask the unfortunate person who has struggled with suicide: for that person wasn't the "living death," by means of suffering and psychological torment, harder to bear than sudden death—that is, death in its full effect, death in its absoluteness?

These are the facts of human existence, and what Scripture teaches us about the rise of suffering and what human experience tells us cannot be otherwise. Only one thing was threatened when man rebelled against God, and that one thing was death. Only one judgment was mentioned before the fall, and that one judgment was death. No punishment for sin other than death is mentioned. And in that one, terrible word, "You will surely die" (that is, through the promise of eternal and absolute death) God Almighty epitomized all future revelation of his wrath. Nothing at all is said about any punishment beside or before death. "In the day you eat thereof, you will surely die," is the only threat of the Holy One, which epitomizes all suffering, all misery, and all eternal wretchedness. Death was the epitome and the summary of all that—both now and in eternity—could oppress or torture human life and being and existence, whether in soul and body. This is why such a concept of death could never refer exclusively to *temporal* death. For then God would have had to say, "In the day you eat thereof you will die, and *after your death you will be wretched for all eternity*." This is not at all what is said. Adam and Eve would die. Nothing else. Nothing is added, so that one word included eternal death as well.

If we are to understand death rightly, then we must therefore take death as a single concept in which the rays converge from two sides into one central point. Death encompasses all eternal wretchedness, and from the other side it encompasses all temporal suffering and common misery; temporal death is nothing but the transition that for the unregenerate leads from temporary misery to eternal wretchedness. As we have earlier argued at length, eternal death should have set in immediately after the fall. That this was suspended is due to common grace, and from this perspective our temporary misery can be best understood as *tempered death*. Temporary misery represents, as it were, the labor pains, the "practice contractions" in which death with a curtailed power makes us feel its working in advance. Death is the root from which all human misery sprouts. Death and misery belong to one family. All misery is a beginning of death, a foretaste of death, a first station on the long road whose end is death. No human misery, whether external or internal, is conceivable without bearing the imprint of death. Death is the one source, always welling up, from which all human misery springs. The spirit, the force, the inimical, demonic force of death is what operates in our suffering and in all of our misery. In other words, death is like the well-known mother plant from which hang all little plants of suffering and misery with their organic ties.

We flatly contradict both Scripture and experience if we both acknowledge, on the one hand, that death is an *enemy* of God, the last enemy that will be destroyed, but do *not* acknowledge, on the other hand, that all suffering and misery are a force that stands as an enemy in opposition to God. Suffering and misery are tied to death; they form a single whole with death and are inseparable from death. They are weapons death uses as long as it is prevented from giving us the fatal blow, to oppress and torture us and to make us feel something of its approach. "The snares of death encompassed me; the pangs of Sheol laid hold on me; I suffered distress and anguish" [Ps 116:3]—this is the painful awareness, the fearful realization we experience whenever our soul is heavy under the suffering of soul and of life. And this is why death is an enemy of God, an enemy that God repels and that God wills we resist. There can arise no doubt that our suffering and misery are also an enemy of God that comes to us as the anticipation of that one deadly enemy. At the same time, it also is certain that God works against suffering and misery as well, demanding that we, implacably, steadfastly, and with the courage of faith, enter into combat with *all* suffering and *all* misery.

In the old covenant we see how, as an enemy of God, death defiled and desecrated people. For this reason, the high priest of Jehovah was not allowed to bury his nearest relatives himself. Any contact with a dead body made a person unclean, and in order to become ceremonially clean again, an offering had to be brought. It could not be expressed more clearly that God abhors death and that death is an opponent of God. But this is taught not only about death; illness also made a person unclean before God and required atonement—think of leprosy. Wasn't leprosy a pestilence? Wasn't it a judgment? Wasn't it a punishment? Didn't it come upon the unfortunate individual from God? Undoubtedly. At the same time, it nevertheless made people "unclean"; that is, it was an evil power that came upon the afflicted, and that evil power had to be warded off and opposed. Israel's law, therefore, does not specify that the afflicted had to remain passive under God's judgment. On the contrary, both the afflicted and the priest were instructed to be most careful in combating leprosy. A passive Jew would have tempted God and trespassed his law. And in such an affliction a Jew could say that he stood right with God only when he saw in leprosy, even as in death, an enemy that should be combated with all means possible. Even the walls of his house had to be scraped.

Thus, our overall argument is confirmed when we look at it from the perspective of death. To surrender to suffering—that is, to resign ourselves to it and not to combat it but to sit still under it—is a sin; it is to play into the hand of the enemy. To do such a thing is to ally ourselves with a power that God views as an *enemy* in opposition to him and treats as such. Therefore, we cannot emphasize enough the definite word of Scripture: *the last enemy to be destroyed is death*. Death, of course, is not the first enemy: the first enemy remains Satan. But after Satan, the enmity follows two paths. The first is the spiritual path through fall and sin; this is followed by the external path through curse and death. And it is along this path of curse and death that all external suffering lies, by which we mean all physical misery that can befall us in this life or the life hereafter. The difficult question as to how both can exist—that misery is a punishment of God, and yet that we must combat misery with all our strength—can be resolved only by going back to the origin of death and misery in Satan. Only when we have clearly perceived that the ultimate origin of suffering lies not in God but in the devil can it become clear to us how the misery had to come upon us, and how nonetheless the battle against misery, no less than the battle against death, has been given us as our duty.

CHAPTER SIXTY-FOUR

THE UNHOLY CHARACTER OF ALL AFFLICTION

And Jesus rebuked the demon, and it came out of him, and the boy was healed instantly.

MATTHEW 17:18

§ 1 All misunderstanding about combating the evil that befalls us appears, therefore, to have its origin in the fact that we fail to see the *unholy* that is attached to all evil that befalls us—not occasionally and incidentally, but always and necessarily. Because suffering is so often a means to the sanctification of our inner life and so often stirs the prodigal son to go back to his father again, people have even sought in suffering in part something excellent, something precious, something to which we even must ascribe an almost *holy* character. In this way, reality has been turned into its opposite. Suffering has become something that we should not evade and loathe but something that seems almost desirable and attractive. Because so many people have had to confess with the psalmist, "Before I was afflicted I went astray, but now I keep your word" [Ps 119:67], any notion of the evil, the ungodly, the inhuman, the unnatural, and the perverse that would manifest itself in suffering generally has gradually come to be lost entirely. People of this mind-set have almost developed an aversion to joyful laughter; tears seemed inwardly beautiful. As a result, it was no longer understood that if all of life had remained holy, not a single tear ever would have fallen from the human eye. In the end, people have yielded to feelings instead of listening to God and his Word, and in this way the entire perception of the mystery of suffering has been distorted, with the result that a certain melancholy satisfaction with one's own suffering eventually triumphed in the form of a sentimental pessimism.

This has even gone so far that earthly suffering is not considered by some to be terrible enough; hence, they begin to increase their portion of suffering through intentional self-chastisement. Thus, we find pious people in the pagan world who withdraw from all of life's joys and all human interaction, retreating to some wild region in the forest and attempting to live there until their death, seeking to become entirely one with nature. And we can find other self-flagellating Christians who have perhaps locked themselves in a pit or climbed atop a cliff in order to make their share of suffering as great as possible. Not grasping that Jesus has borne *the curse*, people began to view the suffering on Golgotha as *beautiful* per se, without realizing how in this line of reasoning the cross of Jesus, rather than being a shame, was an honor and a privilege.

All this goes diametrically against Scripture, of course.

The holy Scriptures teach us that Jesus has borne our shame, the curse, and our punishment; and in Revelation, they declare a triumph over Satan. Scripture indicates that leprosy and other sicknesses had to be atoned for by means of atonement offerings. In effect, holy Scripture knows no other suffering than what is the consequence of *the curse*, and that curse bears within itself the hallmark of the "unclean" and the "unholy." Moreover, holy Scripture very clearly affirms in this curse, which is the mother of all suffering, an activity that is linked with a satanic, demonic force. Christ's entering into this suffering, his bearing of the curse, and his taking upon himself the shame, is therefore, according to the uniform testimony of holy Scripture, an incomparable revelation of God's compassion and all-surpassing love insofar as surrendering to the *unholy* goes so directly contrary to the urge and demand of the divine Being.

But we must realize what the nature and meaning of the curse is. When God says, "Cursed is the ground because of you" [Gen 3:17], it does not mean only that suffering will enter our lives, but rather that an unholy atmosphere envelops the entire earthly realm. "Curse" does not only entail suffering; curse is something evil in nature that carries wrath within itself. It is something in which rage speaks and something through which God, in accordance with his being, creates and maintains, or ruins and disrupts, all things. The knowledge that the curse rests on something or is attached to something, that it is hidden in something, produces in us a repulsive and fearful reaction—something that suggests to us that we are not dealing with the activity of God's love but with an unholy force. As long as the curse rests on something, that thing does not thrive. The prayerful supplication that arises each day from Christian believers for "God's blessing" has nothing at all to do with what we call *success*; it is only a supplication that the working of the curse may be arrested, that the curse may be lifted, and that the unholy may recede. Anyone who prays differently does not really understand the prayer for God's blessing.

The teaching of the laws concerning Levitical purity has a much more profound meaning in this respect than is generally thought. Those laws did not merely contain a symbolic shadow of spiritual cleansing; rather, they emphatically showed the means commanded by God to keep the memory of the curse alive and to place clearly before Israel's eye the abominable character of all suffering. What is more intimate than tending to the corpse of one's father with one's own hands? And yet the high priest was not allowed to do this. Death remained death. In all death there is curse; therefore, every corpse is unclean and every corpse has something unholy. You will never see redeemed Christians who live close to God trifle with a dead body; they feel a shudder when faced with a corpse, and they still have the sensation today that was kept alive in Israel through the laws concerning touching a dead body. But it is precisely in circles where the focus is emotional and characterized by a lack of understanding that the body is almost pampered; people assume that they show their love by "stepping over their feelings" and by being with a body as if it were still the living body. But fully apart from laws against touching a dead body, the laws for Levitical purity are an abiding lesson about the curse that, because of sin, rests on our entire life and relates to all suffering. Even when such a defilement had happened without the person knowing it, the offering for cleansing still had to be brought. At issue here was not the consequence of someone's act of the will; rather, it was the unholy character that resided in all the suffering of the world by virtue of the curse.

But there is more. It must be admitted that even those who definitely still have an eye for this unholy meaning of the curse err in turn by entirely arbitrarily limiting this meaning of the curse. For often the activity of the curse is acknowledged only in what is unusual, attention-getting suffering, or in suffering of an exceptionally painful character. The idea, then, is that our everyday life is good and normal, and that only now and then, by way of exception, the cup of suffering goes around, and we must consider the curse to be present only when that cup of suffering is filled with bitter wine. This perspective, however, is distorted. Everything that is manifest in this world but did not exist in paradise and is equally unthinkable in the kingdom of glory is a consequence of the curse that has come upon the earthly realm. Even a child's birth accompanied by birth pangs makes the mother unclean, and Mary the mother of Jesus also sought the purification offering. We therefore cannot limit the working of the curse only to death, sickness, pestilence, or life's disasters. The curse works throughout the existence of our entire life. Thus, for example, when the elements rage, the storms rise, the waves threaten with death and destruction, lightning strikes, the predator creeps about, the poisonous insect bites, fatigue overcomes us, hunger torments us, or whatever in this earthly life interferes with our claim to perfect well-being, perfect happiness, and untroubled joy—that is when we must confess that all of this would be unthinkable in paradise and equally unthinkable in the kingdom of glory, and that it therefore does not exist in this world in accordance with the creation ordinance but rather as a result of the activity of the curse. The entirety of this existence in human sinfulness implies that what is unholy and cruel will always and everywhere be attached. Our Catechism confesses rightly that Jesus bore suffering starting from the beginning of his incarnation, and in that suffering he bore the wrath of God. Christ did this for us, for he stood outside of all sin, but we bear the wrath of God starting from our conception, and all the days of our life, from cradle to grave, the *curse* bears down on our life, and therefore the *unholy*, that in which and *against* which God's wrath manifests itself.

Viewed this way, the issue that occupies us already begins to become more transparent. If all suffering—that is, all that disturbs our human existence—is a consequence of the curse, and if it would not exist without the curse, and if therefore the curse is still at work in all affliction, suffering, sorrow, and privation of happiness and joy, then it is salient to understand how *all* suffering is causally connected with sin and therefore has something unholy at its root. The fact that Jesus rebukes the fever, that God rebukes the wild animals, and that death is called an enemy of God that must and will be conquered already becomes partially understandable if understood in this way. Everything to which the curse attaches itself stirs up a sense of abhorrence within us as humans. How much more understandable is it, then, that everything that reminds even remotely of the curse is inimical to God. This is true even at the natural level. Vermin elicit our revulsion; we recoil by nature. The decomposition of a corpse has something repulsive; a skeleton is painful for us to look at. We recoil from pain. Seeing a wound is painful to us. Staying to watch a bloody operation requires self-conquering effort. Skin diseases and suppurating blood diseases make us involuntarily avert our eyes. The stink of pus that might emanate from internal or external abscesses involuntarily arouses our revulsion. There are some who can neither bear to view nor tolerate such intimations of the curse, who faint or vomit in their presence. Anyone who has ever seen a smallpox victim, black with pox over the entire body, knows how contrary the response is to what is human, and if—God forbid—the pestilence or plague were ever to return, so that the sight of this revolting misery became more common, we would see how deeply it would be felt again that in such abhorrent illnesses a malevolent force overtakes our human life.

This element surrounding death manifests itself so evidently in disease, in the decomposition of the human body, and in some kinds of vermin that everyone notices, senses, and feels it. If this were just as strongly the case in all other suffering, then there could be no misunderstanding. Everyone would immediately be persuaded of the truth that the curse attaches to all suffering, and the impression all suffering would make would be immediately revolting and repulsive. Yet this is not the case. Here too, just as in all of life, there is a general experience that can be interpreted with the ordinary senses, as well as a more refined experience that is observable to the eye that is prepared to see it. When a feral cat bites us, we see the angry head and the scratching claws, but when we receive a poisonous bite from a flying ant, we must take a microscope to discover the sharp points that gave us the bites.

The same applies here. The revolting, abhorrence-inspiring, curse-revealing character of suffering is so clearly manifested in the case of disease, for example, that everyone senses and notices it; human reactions are superficial and universal. But whereas smallpox will repulse us immediately, someone suffering from tuberculosis might even have something attractive—that is, when, on an occasional visit with that person, we do not come into contact with what suggests the beginning of decomposition—namely, soaked bed linens and the blood-colored feces. Our reactions to catastrophes in other realms confirm this point. In the face of potential destructive storms and even earthquakes, the possibility of a threat will likely appall us; in the case of a mild storm, which may have occurred for the first time after the fall, due to sin, the drifting clouds may charm us. The main point here is that we cannot judge the nature and character of suffering based on its weakest manifestations, but rather based on its strongest, since it is from these strongest manifestations that we gain the firm conviction that suffering is truly evil in nature, against the will of God, and unholy in character.

We therefore wish to maintain this conclusion in terms that are intelligible and comprehensible to all. What God created was perfect. From God's creation there flowed for man nothing but pure, undisturbed joy and happiness. No hint was conceivable in paradise of anything at all that could cause suffering. The turnaround came through sin and sin alone, and the essence of this turnabout for our state of happiness is *the curse*. This curse, therefore, is the expression pointing to the source of *all* suffering, *all* stain, *all* sorrow, *all* pain, *all* privation of full and true happiness. And because all suffering—and here we wish to note the comprehensive nature of suffering in general—without distinction or exception carries curse within itself, all suffering therefore is laden with something unholy, and in all suffering that unholy thing, that bearing of the curse, must be rebuked and combated to the death. Only in this way can it be understood that Jesus bore the curse for us beginning with his incarnation, and only in this way do we understand how we, overcome and overtaken by suffering, nevertheless must turn against it with all the resilience with which God has armed us and with all the means that he puts at our disposal by means of his common grace. Only along these lines will it become clear how we gain insight into how God both punishes us with suffering and nevertheless punishes suffering itself as something unholy.

It is significant in this regard to look at our Savior after he descended from Tabor, the Mount of Transfiguration. On that mountain Jesus momentarily was relieved of the unholy pressure of the curse that restricts our human life. He tasted paradise moments and had a foretaste of the kingdom of glory that is to come. The pressure to which he subjected himself for our sake, the pressure of everyday life, was lifted from him, and he shone forth his glory. But this was only a momentary respite. Soon the pressure of suffering would return again, even intensified with "his departure, which he was about to accomplish at Jerusalem" [Luke 9:31]. And what is the first thing Jesus encounters when he descends from Mount Tabor? A father who requests Jesus' compassion for his child, who suffers so bitterly from what we would call "falling sickness," or epilepsy. The man said it himself: "Behold, a spirit seizes him, and he suddenly cries out. It convulses him so that he foams at the mouth, and shatters him, and will hardly leave him" [Luke 9:39]. At the very moment when they bring the boy to Jesus, he is thrown to the ground and convulses before Jesus' eyes. And what does Jesus do? Jesus, we read, rebuked the unclean spirit and said, "Leave him," and the suffering ceased. In this case the pernicious nature of the "falling sickness" was apparently intensified.

When Jesus appeared in his earthly ministry, the powers of evil urged humans to resist Jesus more intensely; hence, we read of various "possessed" persons. What is apparent is that all such suffering is linked to the demonic realm, and in such illnesses an influence goes out toward the human being from the evil spirit world. This confirms our general conclusions. In all suffering lies something of the curse, in all curse is something unholy, and now this unholy aspect is further explained as something that has a certain link with the activities and influences from the world of the demonic. Thus, in the suffering that oppresses our human lives, we learn to see the "practice contractions" of death—that is, a manifestation of the curse and an influence from Satan. In this way, then, the evil, unclean, and unholy character of our human suffering is readily explained. It becomes quite clear that in suffering we are faced with a power that is inimical to God. It appears that God rebukes and combats suffering and ultimately will annihilate it. Thus our calling becomes ever clearer—namely, to consciously enter into battle against all suffering.

CHAPTER SIXTY-FIVE

CURSE AND CREATION

And he withdrew from them about a stone's throw, and knelt down and prayed, saying, "Father, if you are willing, remove this cup from me. Nevertheless, not my will, but yours, be done." And there appeared to him an angel from heaven, strengthening him. And being in an agony he prayed more earnestly; and his sweat became like great drops of blood falling down to the ground.

LUKE 22:41–44

We actually have moved one important step closer to solving the enormous question that has occupied our thinking. The character of all misery, which comes from sin, has taken on a form that is entirely different from how we commonly think about it. Generally, all misery and human suffering seem to be broadly considered as a punishment that has accrued to us from God, as an evil imposed upon us in retribution for our iniquities, as a visitation imposed upon us and our children for the evil perpetrated by us or our parents. Those who rightly understand the atoning and satisfying work of the Mediator then note that, for the redeemed of the Lord, this character of punishment has been canceled because Christ bore the punishment for us. As a result, for God's children all suffering has become chastisement rather than punishment; but even this conviction does not clearly § 1 penetrate the awareness of most people. And where this understanding of chastisement in terms of human sinfulness is acknowledged, in the case of phenomena such as major national disasters or pestilences it is thought that the redeemed of the Lord also need to undergo these as if they were a punishment that comes upon them from God.

Those who speak or think this way reveal that they fail to understand that "the Lord has laid on him [Christ] the iniquity of us all" [Isa 53:6]. Nor do they realize that something can be a plague, judgment, or punishment for the unconverted masses, yet not for the redeemed of Jesus. But apart from this, every one of us knows how, in devotional writings and in sermons (except those dealing directly with the substitutionary work of Jesus), this retributory character of sin's curse stands almost exclusively in the foreground. It has a sanctifying effect, to be sure, but sanctifying only to the extent that it manifests God's displeasure, in accordance with the *leitmotif* of Psalm 119: "Before I was afflicted I went astray, but now I keep your word." Our investigation does not at all deny this retributory character of misery as punishment; rather, it would appear to fully support it. However—and here we suggest an entirely new perspective—it would appear that the character of suffering does not lie exclusively in this. An entirely different feature can be noted in the character of sin's misery: a repudiation of the clear revelation of Scripture if this entirely different feature is ignored and not taken into our considerations as indispensable.

That second trait of the misery of suffering appears appeared to consist in the fact that suffering is a force, inimical to God, against which God works—a force that will be entirely destroyed only when, once death is slayed, "the last enemy" is annihilated. Furthermore, it appears to us that this character of suffering that is inimical to God has its origin in *the curse*, from which all suffering springs. Finally, however much this curse has come upon us under God's holy ordination, we are able to observe an indirect working of Satan in it that makes God's battle against suffering, misery, and death fully understandable. For the moment, we will not delve into the conclusion that follows from this—namely, that God's "beloved children" in obedience must therefore also engage in an implacable battle against all suffering, and all misery, and all death. Before probing this point more deeply, we must take a closer look at how to understand the fact that the same suffering comes upon us, on the one hand, in accordance with God's will as retribution, yet on the other hand, against God's will, as something against which his compassion does battle.

If we had been less Pelagian at heart and therefore less inclined to imbibe Pelagian notions about the order and governance of our God, this formulation of "according to God's will" yet "against God's will" never would have sounded like a contradiction to our ears. We then would have understood that God's actions, however much manifested in time, nevertheless are always *eternal* in nature and therefore should never be viewed individually or separately, but always in their totality and their original coherence. The latter understanding is what Calvinism has always intended and what we ourselves wish to embody. Nevertheless, in stark contrast, many assume that God acts on the basis of the demands of the moment and takes into account only the facts of the moment. Someone sins and continues to sin in spite of all admonitions. Then, God judges that this must be stopped, and he sends the obstinate sinner an illness in his home, slays one of his children, strikes him in his business affairs, or lets an accident befall him. And just as such a punishment appears to occur in chaotic fashion and without context, so too divine compassion then comes, and equally suddenly, with forgiveness setting in, so that this person's doom is averted. In this way God is seen as acting in accordance with options A, B, or C. Note the assumption here: it is always with each individual person or action separately, and each time, outside any context, according to the position of that individual at that particular moment. Of course, if this were the case, any battle against the punishment sent from God would simply be audacious and sacrilegious. When God strikes, who will strike back against the hand of God that strikes him?

But it is this very perspective to which fundamental objection is being registered, both by Scripture and by human experience. Let us be clear: it is not as if there is no partial experiential truth in this perspective; there most certainly is. But the mistaken position itself—that God's actions in the mystery of suffering should be understood separately and incidentally—cannot be maintained for a moment. Only note these three undeniable facts. First, consider the fact that the children suffer because of the sin of their parents, as God says he visits "the iniquity of the fathers on the children to the third and the fourth generation of those who hate me" [Exod 20:5]. Second, consider the fact that plagues come upon an entire city or an entire country, with the result that the innocent and the guilty undergo the same suffering. Third, take into account the well-known fact of all human experience, which Scripture continually and emphatically puts in the foreground: so often the godless flourish and have no adversity until their death, whereas the servant of God is a "man of sorrows" [Isa 53:3]. This seems to be a universal phenomenon. By way of example, an institution that seeks to promote the kingdom of God might struggle and later go under, whereas a den of iniquity sees money flowing as if it were water. It is wholly unnecessary to add anything to our argument here to expose the notion of *incidental* suffering as utterly untrue and untenable, and to show by contrast the universal character of suffering as the only correct perspective. Those who understand the mystery of Golgotha, furthermore, know how in fact every Pelagian notion of God's ordination in suffering either undermines the substitutionary nature of Christ's suffering or marks it as the cruelest form of caprice.

But if our argument has merit, then it follows directly that the root of all suffering must be sought in the curse and that the curse is directly linked to creation. The curse is not something in isolation. It is not a kind of poisonous substance that forced its way into the world, nor is it a kind of microbe that, created after the fall, was sent out into this world. The curse, like sin, is not something substantial but a deprivation, a *privatio actuosa*, as our forefathers termed it.[1] When a terrible railroad accident takes place, no new, unholy force falls upon the train from the outside; rather, the same force that first made the train speed along the tracks is precisely what now wrenches the same train into pieces and destroys it. The only difference is that the steam power that first worked in accordance with the orders issued by the engineer now goes against them. For the railroad management, the basic operating principle is nothing new; they knew it beforehand. They knew that once the steam in the locomotive comes to full power, that steam will destroy the train as soon as the train derails at full speed. But the point is obvious: the railroad management, in light of catastrophic scenarios, does not therefore say, "Dispense with steam!"; quite obviously, the train is inconceivable without steam. It is only the reality of steam that brings life to that otherwise immobile train. It does not matter whether that steam will later be replaced by electricity. A great propulsive

1. See *DLGTT*, s.v. "privatio": "*privation, deprivation, the loss of a positive attribute or characteristic*; specifically, the loss of original righteousness (*iustitia originalis*, q.v.) in the first sinful willing of Adam. The consequent absence or deprivation of that righteousness is not, however, mere privation (*mere privatio*) but, as sin, is an active opposition to God and to the good, termed by the scholastics *actuosa privatio*, an actualized or active privation, a *vitiositas*, an active corruption or viciousness."

force remains indispensable, and the point is that great propelling force will always turn into a destructive force as soon as the train slips off the track.

It is precisely the same situation with the great train of life that was set in motion at the hour of creation. In order to complete its course, that immense train of life also required an unknowable propelling life force. That glow of life, from which this propelling force would develop, is what God kindled in the hour of creation. But God did more. He also laid down the rails of his holy ordinances along which the train of life would have to move, and he entrusted man with its running, to see to it that the train would follow that God-laid track from moment to moment and not derail. This, it needs to be reiterated, was certain ahead of time: if the train of life derailed because of human negligence, and human negligence alone, then there would be no other possibility that same propelling force of life intended to direct our life's speed toward the final goal of its development immediately, in that same moment, would turn into a terrible force of destruction and devastation. This, in fact, is what happened. Humankind has allowed the train of life to slip off the God-laid track of his holy order, and immediately thereafter the life force that pushes everything ahead of it has turned into an immeasurable force of destruction. This turning of the propelling force of life into a life-destroying force (which is to say, a force of death and destruction) is what Scripture calls the curse. It is not something new, not something added, not something that, like matter, is created separately and sent to us. Rather, it is and remains precisely and entirely the same force that God brought into being within creation; but that force, intended to propel our life forward, became a force of death and ruin through the curse.

A railway accident can have a cause that neither the engineer nor the conductor can do anything to avert. But that was not the case here. The train of life that God sent on its way in creation simply could not derail except by the deliberate culpability of mankind to whom God had entrusted the running of the train. Mankind wanted to derail; otherwise, no derailment would have occurred. This is, in fact, how it happened. Satan deluded mankind into believing that the tracks laid by God were not the right ones, and he placed another, splendid set of tracks before the human imagination, essentially saying, "Switch to those tracks." Man made that switch and, alas, that was how the great accident happened. Then, suddenly, the curse began to work—that is, the propelling force of life itself became a destructive and destroying force. That curse, we may conclude, was clearly punishment.

Adam knew what would happen, for God had told him. And God also willed (and in fact he still wills) that as soon as the train of life left the track of his order, the forward momentum would be broken and destruction would set in. That is the creation order. Allowing something else to happen would have meant renouncing the divine majesty and surrendering his holy order to Satan or to man turned sinner.

God himself—and we say this reverently—cannot change this reality in any way, because God cannot deny himself. Here God is bound by his very being. The curse had to come. The life force that he had created had to mirror its opposite, and only when the train of life was ready again to glide along the track of his order could the force of destruction once again become a force for salvation and the curse be changed into blessing. Suffering, misery, and death must therefore have their working. Looking at it differently would mean alienating God from himself, annihilating the original order of creation, and preparing the triumph of sin. If we express it in this way, then we do not shrink from stating that the unparalleled love of God for his fallen world was "powerless" to prevent this terrible outcome. A love that would have wanted to prevent this would have saved the world from suffering, but such a love also would have robbed the world of its God. This is because a God who in this way destroyed his own, original order that flowed from his being and his wisdom would cease to be God; he no longer would have been able to save his creature with his eternal fellowship of love. God had to change life into curse.

But did this therefore preclude the working of God's mercy? Yes, if we reason that it had been God's order to resign himself to the accident that happened to the train of life through man's willfulness. But this was *not* God's will. The derailed train of life, alas, would be put on the track of his divine order again, and the same force that now brought ruin would become again a force that would bring the train of life, traveling along the entire route of God's calling, inside the gate of the holy Jerusalem. For this to happen, the curse had to be combated, the effect of the curse had to be arrested, and every means had to be applied to save the threatened life from certain death and ruin. This is the goal of both particular and common grace. Because God is God, the curse cannot fail to come; but also because God is God, he cannot cease to act against the curse, until one day the omnipotence of his mercy has destroyed the curse entirely. The curse must break out, but also, once it has broken out, it must be attacked, reined in, and one day conquered once and for all. And this explains both the fact that all suffering must come upon us in accordance with God's righteous judgment and the fact that God is our ally against *all* suffering, whom we call upon to be saved from suffering.

Thus, our own soul's experience puts its seal on this solution, for as God's children we live through both of these realities in our own souls. On the one hand, we experience in all suffering the justice of God that overwhelms us and casts us down. Yet, on the other hand, each child of God calls upon that same God as his ally in the midst of his suffering to do battle for him against that suffering and to deliver him from it.

Think of Gethsemane. Some people might ask, how could Jesus pray, "Father, remove this cup from me, unless it must be that I drink it" [see Matt 26:42]? This indeed would seem contradictory by conventional thinking. But we must understand that God is humankind's ally against *all* suffering, that suffering is inimical to the very nature of God, and that among all those born of a woman, our Jesus was the only one who had to combat that suffering by sinking into it to the ultimate depths—and then all contradiction disappears. "Father, let this cup pass me by" is the heart-rending lament of his soul with which Jesus turns against suffering in its dreadfulness, and only when he is perfectly convinced that suffering cannot be slain except by allowing it to come fully over him does he cast himself into the abyss of curse and death, allowing himself to sink into the depths of suffering. At the same time, in no way does Jesus resign himself passively to the curse and death. Here, curse and death remain until the end the demonic forces against which he turns. And only when, in the struggle of prayer before God, he sees how curse and death can be conquered and destroyed by sinking into them, does he put the cup to his lips and drink it down to the dregs.

CHAPTER SIXTY-SIX

DERAILMENT

Then the Lord *rained on Sodom and Gomorrah*
sulfur and fire from the Lord *out of heaven.*

Genesis 19:24

§ 1 As we have seen, we find in creation the explanation for two facts related to suffering. On the one hand, suffering is a necessity and flows from the will of God; on the other hand, suffering is nevertheless something that stands in enmity to God and consequently is combated by God himself and must therefore also be combated by us. Creation called into existence forces and powers that flourish for good only to the extent that they move along the path of God's ordinances. They necessarily turn into destructive and ruinous powers as soon as they deviate from the path of those ordinances.

We have attempted to illustrate this with the image of a train that derails and is destroyed by the same power that otherwise would have brought it to its destination. A train that derails must end in misery; in the same way, when the train of our human life derails, misery cannot fail to come. This image, meanwhile, portrays only in part the terrible truth we are dealing with here. A train that derails is and remains a human product, under human guidance. Once initiated, the forces of steam and of momentum over which the engineer must maintain control are forces of nature that do not spring from his will but to which his will is subject. In the case of a speeding train, therefore, it can never be said that the engineer or conductor has willed the destruction of equipment and of human lives if it derails. On the contrary, he does not will them, but they happen in spite of and against his will. Here a necessity rules that he did not call into being, but that controls him.

The Lord our God, by contrast, stands in an entirely different relation to the train of human life. When he assembled the train of our life and sent it on its way, there were no powers or forces to which he had to conform. Consequently, there also were no forces or powers that, in spite of him, would have had to destroy or bring to ruin the train of life if it derailed. God himself created all forces and powers of life. He himself called them into being, in such a way and in such an order as was required to permit the train of human life to reach, in the quickest and surest way, the destination that he himself had ordained. This raises the question of whether that course of our life could not have been ordered and arranged in such a way that even if derailment were to come, the destruction, ruination, and misery associated with suffering would have failed to occur. For of course, if God had willed it, it would have happened in this way: "My counsel shall stand, and I will accomplish all my purpose" [Isa 46:10]. Since the result appeared to be different, and immediately after the derailment bitter destruction and terrible misery followed, it is certain that this was God's will, that he has determined and arranged it thus and not otherwise through his own divine will. It therefore did not happen by accident or because God could not put it right; rather, it was God's direct will and intention that the train of our life had to destroy itself as soon as it slid off the divine tracks.

Moreover, we can never thank God sufficiently for the necessity of the misery and self-destruction that resulted from that slide off the divine tracks. You need only imagine what would have happened if the derailed train of life had continued safely on its way. It would have resulted in one endless deviation from the divine plan, one ever-mightier breaking out of unrighteousness, one incessant moving further away from fellowship with our God—in short, therefore, one continuous triumph of sin and Satan. It would have been a world, a human life, and a human heart that ultimately would have been without God for all eternity. All that God had created would have turned into one great hell, and hell would have turned into the only thing that existed. God's will that all derailment would and had to avenge itself in self-destruction was therefore fundamentally nothing but the will of God to maintain his decree and his ordinances, for he neither could nor would tolerate that another decree, resting in other ordinances, would force itself into their place.

The forces and powers that he, as God, called into existence were to function as he had ordained; if not, it should be felt immediately how those forces ceased to bless and instead brought destruction and ruin. In those forces a fire burned with which no creature should play. Through its glow that fire could have brought our life to development, but when it did not do this, that same fire also was also able to singe and scorch us. The will of God that the train of life, should it derail, would destroy itself, was nothing other than the will of God to remain God. He is the "I am who I am" [Exod 3:14], the expression of the all-glorious Jehovah in the creation order. That all-dominant law, that inexorable necessity, therefore serves to directly ensure both the honor of God and the salvation of man. Without that law, without that will, without that necessity, Jehovah would have withdrawn within himself, and our life would have become one entire hell. In case of derailment the forces and powers of life could and must not be brought to a standstill or be "unemployed," as it were. That would have been a revoking of creation. These needed to remain forces and powers, forces that manifested their functioning. They therefore *had* to turn into their opposite. What was created and intended to bless now had to result in calamity and misery.

Here too lies the judging and punishing, the retributive and avenging character of the divine law and divine will. The derailment of the train of human life could not take place in any other way than by an act of man, and that act could not occur except intentionally, willed consciously and purposely. This point calls for understanding. The divine intention was not in the least to have the train of life crash. Adam did not at all want the misery to come about. On the contrary, his intent was to let the train of life speed along even more smoothly and quickly, and to have it reach its destination even more perfectly. He did not believe that the derailment would lead to a disaster, and he thought instead that leaving the track would improve the progress of the train of life. God said that derailment leads to self-destruction. Satan said, "The track to which God has assigned you hinders you and holds you back. Leave those rails and glide smoothly across the fields. Only then will you see what progress is possible." Yet Adam took it to be true that those rails and those ordinances of God essentially did not serve to help him advance but rather hindered him and slowed him down. Then he said to himself, "I will leave those tracks. I will seek my way by myself, in freedom, on that level field." Thus, he indeed intentionally steered the train of our human life off the divine track; he willed and intended that the train would leave the track. He expected, of course, that from then on he would make much more rapid and better progress. And it was terrible disillusionment for guilty Adam when the accident happened anyway, and the whole train wrecked itself. Then he discovered in the depth of his soul that God really had spoken the truth and that he himself, standing powerlessly before this destructive train of life, could not put the train back on the divine track again, no matter how much he lamented and how great his heartrending remorse. He saw the wrecked train, and he saw those shining rails of God's ordinances before him, but no human power could put that train and that track together again.

There was therefore *guilt* here—the guilt of intent and the intent of moving away from God and opposing him. And therefore the destruction that immediately followed brought not only disillusionment but also a remorseful self-reproach. He feels the wrath of God. He undergoes a judgment. And the punishment strikes him in self-destruction. This is why he hides himself and, as the Confession expresses it so movingly, "he trembling fled from His presence."[1] Was this imaginary? Had God intended that self-destruction but not the attendant remorse or sense of wrath or judgment? This mistaken view is how it is often taught today. Under the influence of Ritschl's great name, this audacious view has become remarkably widespread.[2] Let those who declare these audacious words explain to us then how this realization, this feeling, this awareness in Adam's soul came about. It sprang from his *nature*, not artificially, but of necessity, even as it has echoed again and again, century in, century out, in the guilty human heart. This awareness is less pronounced in superficial people but is found with great seriousness among the best, the noble ones, those who live with sobriety such as in a David, an Isaiah, a Paul, an Augustine, a Luther, a Calvin. This intuition, then, has come from humankind's fundamental disposition and

1. Belgic Confession, Art. 17.
2. Albrecht Ritschl (1822–89) was a renowned German theologian. As the Reformed theologian Benjamin B. Warfield (1851-1921), drawing on the work of Otto Pfleiderer (1839-1908) on Ritschl, describes Ritschl's doctrine of sin and guilt, "There is no such thing as sin. What we call sin is merely ignorance. Our feeling of guilt is therefore an illusion." See Benjamin B. Warfield, "Albrecht Ritschl and His Doctrine of Christian Perfection: II. Ritschl the Perfectionist," *Princeton Theological Review* 18, no. 1 (January 1920): 45.

nature. And as surely as we withdraw our hand with shock and an acute awareness of pain when we accidently touch a burning oven (mistakenly believing that oven to be off), equally surely we feel a real awareness of the wrath and the judgment of God when, after committing a sin, we experience the self-disintegration in our being. And if this is the case, if this sense of guilt, remorse, and self-reproach is neither manufactured nor imagined but comes really from our human nature, then we may properly ask, Who has thus ordained, equipped, and created that human nature? And if we happen to confess "God did it," then how can we maintain that God himself intended our misery, which flows directly from sin, not as a punishment, not as an expression of wrath, and not as bringing judgment upon us?

From that single perspective God's will is therefore quite clear. God wills that leaving the track laid down by him and his ordinances should result immediately in self-destruction and misery. And God thus also wills that we will discern this misery as punishment, as a manifestation of his wrath and as a judgment that comes over us, and that we will thus taste self-disintegration in the very depths of our own self-awareness.

But let us now view the matter from the other side. Can we really say that self-disintegration, misery, and our sinking under the curse were God's true intention? Is this what he had in mind with his creation? Is this the reason why he called that creation into existence and, within that creation, also called his humanity into existence? Did he ordain and call into existence those forces and powers for this very reason? The answer is an equally decisive *no*. Certainly, God willed all this indubitably and surely in case the train derailed, but he did not dispatch the train in order for it to derail. On the contrary, the purpose of creation was that the train of creaturely life that he sent forth on its way would reach a specific destination, that this destination would overflow with glory, and that he would delight in the completion of that wonderful purpose. The misery, the curse, the self-disintegration obstruct this purpose. They represent the opposite of the goal for which God called all things into being. If this is where creation stops, then its purpose of creation is thwarted. Therefore, two things flow from that one creation. On the one hand, creation entails the principle that the derailment must result in self-disintegration. But, on the other hand, creation also indicates that self-destruction and misery are a fact and terrible reality that God must oppose, combat, and ultimately annihilate in order to bring what he has created to the goal he established. Creation is *real*, which is why the forces that creation called into existence are also real and why, if they should be misdirected, they must work destructively. But creation also has a *destination*, and because such self-destruction goes against that destiny, it goes against God, and for this reason death is called an *enemy*—an enemy that must be combatted and, ultimately, annihilated by God. Thus, it appears that what at first seemed to be incompatible is truly in holy harmony, and that both realities—God's will that self-destruction would result from derailment and the fact that such self-destruction is inimical to God and eventually will be annihilated by him—flow from that one act of creation. Both are *inseparable* from the nature of that creation when we properly understand creation to be a real act of God in which his holy will came to expression.

In this context we must look at what Genesis 19:24 says about the destruction of Sodom. We read there, "Then the Lord rained on Sodom and Gomorrah sulfur and fire from the Lord out of heaven." In this expression we have an indisputable evidence of the twofold working that proceeds from God. On the one hand, there is "the Lord out of heaven" from whom the destruction of Sodom and Gomorrah proceeds. But on the other hand, there is also "the Lord," the one who appeared to Abraham and said, "For the sake of ten I will not destroy it" [Gen 18:32]. Thus, the majesty of God wills and brings about self-destruction, but his compassion also goes against human destruction, even stopping it. Both represent a unity. We do not have here the working of two "Lords"; rather, both workings issue from the same Lord, with the same name, expressed in the same way. In this way it becomes clear that we have before us a revelation of the twofold will of God: both to permit sin with the result of self-destruction and to counteract this self-same destruction. Granted, it is Abraham who begs for Sodom to be saved. Yet who would want to explain this in any way other than that "a spirit of grace and pleas for mercy" [Zech 12:10] were poured out in his heart? § 2

But even apart from this, it was the Lord who revealed his will to avert the destruction of Sodom if there were still ten righteous persons in Sodom. And when the judgment on Sodom had proceeded anyway, it says explicitly that the Lord who expressed compassion ultimately permitted judgment to come, although it is said to issue from "the Lord out of heaven." This has been understood by commentators as involving both God as Mediator and God as Father, and undoubtedly in that contrast such a duality seems to be mirrored, even when Genesis 19:24 does not explicitly indicate this. Here we seem to have what some have called an "outgoing work" of the divine activity, which is understood to mean that all outgoing works are in common to the Father, the Son, and the Holy Spirit. To view them otherwise is to fall into the error of tritheism. But the text itself also requires this interpretation. For it is not the Lord, who appeared to Abraham, who wanted to turn the evil away from Sodom, and the Lord, out of heaven, who brought it anyway. Rather, the text says the converse: the Lord who appeared to Abraham and in whom compassion was revealed did himself rain down sulfur and fire upon Sodom and Gomorrah. This proceeds only "from the Lord out of heaven." It is therefore the Lord in his fullness who is acting, but whose workings are twofold as he manifests his will. On the one hand, he judges and punishes Sodom's sin with self-destruction, and on the other hand, he wills to resist, arrest, and prevent Sodom's self-destruction if he should still find in Sodom a sufficient point of contact for his compassion.

And if we conclude from this that the language being used here is only metaphorical because God knew beforehand that even those ten righteous persons would not be found in Sodom, we readily concede this possibility. But then it should also be noted that Scripture is given to us for instruction and comfort and that Abraham's appearance and example also have been transmitted to us for revelation, in order that by them we might be initiated into the mystery of God's acting. Precisely from what happened back then and what is narrated here we might gain important insight into all of God's general dealings, both with the entire human race and also with us personally. We therefore have not only the right but the obligation to take all such remarkable narratives in holy Scripture as having a deeper meaning. If we do this, we cannot reach any conclusion other than that the Lord who appeared here to Abraham and who, if possible, wanted to save Sodom, is distinguished from the same Lord from whom the force of destruction actually proceeds. Since it is the same Lord in both instances, it follows that a twofold will of God comes to expression here. On the one hand, there is a will that requires Sodom's destruction, and on the other hand, there is a will that wants to resist Sodom's destruction.

We trust that this resolves the issue with which we were faced. We now can proceed. God wills sin's misery, as punishment, as curse, and as judgment. At the same time, for God that misery and destruction of his own creation represent something that goes counter to the goal for which he brought us into existence. God therefore combats it as an inimical force and wants to annihilate it. The latter becomes *compassion*, because God loves, with an eternal love, his creation, his divine masterpiece, and, within that creation, humankind. It is therefore that love itself that urges God not to let this creation fall prey to the destruction, but rather to wrest it from self-destruction. The honor of God, which requires that his creation reach its goal, and the love of God, which has compassion on his creature, are here unified as one.

CHAPTER SIXTY-SEVEN

THE FLOOD AND THE ARK

I will destroy them with the earth. Make yourself an ark.

Genesis 6:13–14

§ 1 We now have sought to refute, solely on scriptural grounds, the common and prevalent notion that the suffering that God sends us is an evil to which we should succumb powerlessly and passively. Misery had to come and must come, because sin produces it automatically. But precisely for this reason misery, as well as sin itself, constitutes an alien force in God's creation, one that stands in enmity against God's original plan for the world. God therefore combats misery as well as sin; they are his enemy. Making common cause with misery therefore must be condemned, just as making common cause with sin [must be condemned]. Both oppose God's order and both must be combatted by those who love God. This combatting takes on its noblest and most elevating character among people when we are given the opportunity to combat, under the impulse of compassionate love, the evil of suffering *in others*. Indeed, pity, compassion, and mercy (which in various forms express a resistance to suffering) are attempts to challenge the dominion of suffering by warding it off, ameliorating it, and arresting its full effect. We therefore must hold fast unflinchingly the connection between *sin* and *misery*. According to God's secret counsel, misery is a punishment for sin, and who among the faithful to God has not in his or her own life and soul struggled with the pangs of conscience that punishment for sin involves? Given this reality, should a person, therefore, give in to sin and allow sin to overwhelm the soul as an inevitable, irresistible evil? By no means. To the extent that we are truly godly we will guard, pray, and fight against sin. At the same time it is also our calling from God to guard, to pray, and to fight the effects of sin, against the misery that seeks to overwhelm us and destroy others. We do this even in the knowledge that sin's misery and the evil associated with suffering definitely flow from the curse and follow us as punishment for sin.

Having established this point, we must now explain, in the interest of necessary distinctions, that this battle against sin's misery proceeds from the Lord our God in a twofold manner. He arrests the misery either directly himself or by means of man. Common grace always arrests. On the one hand, it arrests the working of sin, so that it might not break out so terribly in our heart; on the other hand, it arrests the working of sin's effects, so that it does not overwhelm us so dreadfully. Sin is arrested to make possible an upright civic life; sin's effects are arrested in order that human society might not be entirely cut off. Recall the experience in centuries past of plague and famine, how all of human society was adversely affected. The arresting of that sort of social development is always the work of *grace*. It always comes to us from the God who has compassion; and whether the arresting is done by God himself or through us, the gratitude and glory for it are always owed to him and never to us. The difference nevertheless is striking. When God arrests a hurricane at the very moment when a seafaring vessel would appear to have been engulfed, then he is the one who exercises this saving power without human instrumentality. But when we are shipwrecked and a passing ship picks us up, it is still the Lord our God to whom we owe our salvation, even when God achieved that salvation through people.

We must keep this difference in mind, because only in the latter case are § 2
we called upon as human beings to act ourselves. Take the matter of climate as an example. The earth can be generally divided into three large zones. There is a zone with ice-cold air, where the misery of freezing virtually cuts off all human life. There is a middle zone with hot air, where the misery of heat and insects makes all human life virtually unsustainable. But between those two extreme regions, in the north and the south, there also are broad zones with moderate temperatures. It is in those regions where most of

human life has flourished and the most significant human development has taken place. Humans do not add or detract anything from this. The Eskimo is powerless against the cold that causes everything to freeze. The native near the equator suffers greatly under the scorching heat. The fact that we who live in more moderate regions can flourish and work and remain fresh in spirit comes to us through God's sovereign grace.

But God does not stop at this level of grace. In his common grace he wills that human beings flourish. He wills that the sin in our hearts be kept from erupting so terribly, not simply through his own direct working but also through human beings opposing and combating sin by spiritual means. Moreover, he wills that we humans also strongly resist the effect of sin ourselves, and it is he himself who points out to us the means and places them at our disposal. This is manifested most clearly in the effects of the flood. That flood was true misery—in fact the most terrible expression of misery that had ever been suffered on earth until then. Its degree of wretchedness will be equaled and exceeded only in the horror following the day of judgment. The flood was a judgment and even bore the special character of a direct judgment. And in this way, the flood was also a punishment, for God ordained this flood to exterminate the godless.

This, of course, raises the question, Was Noah exempted from the misery of the flood because he feared God? This is how it is often—though entirely incorrectly—perceived. In the first place, all little children who were not yet able to make a choice for or against God perished in this flood. No one may say therefore that all those who perished in the flood perished because of their personal hardening against the Almighty. In the second place, not only Noah was saved, but also his wife and Shem, Ham, and Japheth and their wives. Can we then say that Ham was saved because of his personal godliness? No, we cannot. But what is more decisive than everything else is the fact of common misery sparing the godly while affecting only the godless is fundamentally contradicted by Scripture and refuted by all human experience. It is in part precisely those who fear God who suffer more and who often suffer more intensely. The Servant of God is a Man of Sorrows.

Everything therefore contradicts the notion that Noah's being saved from the flood was mainly intended as a reward for his godliness. There was a much higher and richer purpose behind his being saved. In view was the procreation of the human race, the preservation of God's church, and the upholding of the glory of God in the continuation of his plan for the world. As such, there would have been nothing strange if Noah's family had perished in the flood. That very same thing has happened again and again when terrible judgments struck cities and countries in which those who feared God also perished.

But what do we read in Genesis? The flood comes, God sends and ordains this flood, and from him proceeds the arrangement that will make this flood so lethal and murderous. Must Noah subject himself passively and powerlessly to that coming flood? Had the duty been placed upon him by God that he drown with his hands at his side, and watch his family drown? Scripture answers much to the contrary. Noah must prepare himself in order to defend himself and his family against the terrible effect of the flood. And as far as he is concerned, he has to take heroic measures to combat the misery with which the flood threatens him. He does not conjure up this task on his own. He does not begin, being intent on saving his life, to build an ark on his own initiative. In the heart of Asia, where Noah lived at the time, there may have been ferries and riverboats, but nobody knew about seagoing vessels. These had not yet been invented, simply because no one had ever sailed the seas. And yet what Noah would need to defend himself against that terrible flood was not merely a simple seagoing vessel, but a colossal, seafaring fortress that could resist the effects of an enormous flood. How does Noah arrive at the idea of building such a seagoing fortress, and where does the idea come from of building it in such a way that it will survive the flood? Holy Scripture answers that question by saying that God himself commanded, instructed, and enabled Noah to do this. For this is what the Lord said to Noah: "Behold, I will destroy the earth. *Make yourself an ark.*"

The term *ark* is significant here, of course. One might have spoken of a § 3
"ship." But even if small river vessels were already known at that time, people certainly would not have been familiar with seagoing vessels of larger dimensions. So a word would have to be chosen from ordinary life that would communicate the idea of something colossal. The word *ark* means nothing other than a large chest or box; in the tabernacle there also was an ark or chest, in which the tablets of the law lay. An ark is therefore a closed, moveable storage space, and this is precisely what that large, colossal Noahic ship was to be. It was not intended to travel from one place to another, but exclusively to accommodate Noah's family with all livestock in an enclosed and covered space during the weeks of the flood, to shelter them in such a way that later the large box could be opened again and

everything could leave it. Shipbuilding has reached a very high level of development today, so high perhaps that the question of how to build such a giant vessel would even be solvable. But even at that time the advice of the most skilled shipbuilders would have been gathered, and no one would have considered assigning the task to someone who stood entirely outside that profession. And yet at the time of the flood this profession did not exist as yet, and therefore Noah was a complete amateur. And yet he was able to complete the enormous task of building the ark in such a way that the ark could resist the destructive forces of the flood, so that later all living creatures would come out alive again.

This was possible only because God gave Noah the necessary, detailed instructions. What did Noah know about the kind of wood he had to use? What about the dimensions of length, width, and depth needed to make the finished ship seaworthy? What did he know of the means required to make the huge vessel watertight? What about the decks that had to be placed inside the ship so that the weight would be distributed evenly? In the end, the ark met the requirements in all these respects. But how? Not because Noah first tried one way, then another, but because God gave him all the necessary information. Thus, for example, Noah had to use gopher wood. The length had to be three hundred cubits; the width, fifty; and the depth, thirty. Three decks had to be fit inside. The entire vessel, moreover, had to be made watertight from the outside by means of pitch. The divine design and the outline of the plan were perhaps expanded further in instructions that have not been recorded for us. In any case, God himself used Noah, his strength of faith, and his insight to call into existence the means—indeed, the very instrument—on which depended the future of all humanity, the future of God's church, and the glory of God's name and his work of creation.

Beyond this, God utilized in the process the willingness and abilities of many men who would perish in the flood to help Noah with the work. The construction of such a seagoing vessel called for hundreds of hands. Nothing is more foolish than to imagine that Noah, Shem, Ham, and Japheth built it by themselves. Ask workers at any shipyard what four men can accomplish alone. There, wood is delivered to a shipyard cut to length and finished. But in Noah's case, the timbers and woodwork had to be prepared first, and for this trees had to be cut in the forest. Even today, even with our technology, using four men to build a wooden ship for inland or coastal navigation would be next to impossible. What, then, would four men have been able to accomplish toward a gigantic vessel in the days when everything still had to be done by hand and the first tools had barely been crafted? Bible illustrations show Father Noah and his three sons hammering away, but a builder—or even a person who thinks about it—knows better. Noah must have received assistance on an extremely large scale. For this reason the remarkable fact remains that God made the hearts of unbelievers and the ungodly around him willing to work on and complete the massive vessel that would carry the future of the world and the church, and this under Noah's leadership and according to the plan that God himself had given.

Noah prepared the ark *by faith*. This faith, however, focused not only on § 4
the reality of the approaching judgment and the certainty that the flood would come, but certainly on the divine mandate as well. Two things had never been seen before as yet. One was the flood; the other, the ark; and Noah grasped both of these by faith. He saw the flood and all its terror with the eye of faith, but he also saw with the same eye the completed ark, and through that faith in the ark as a means of salvation, the ark came into being. God's Word, and that word alone, was for him the guarantee of both the flood that was to come and the ark that was to be built. With regard to both, Noah stood on solid ground by means of that faith. Noah's building of the ark proceeded identically to Moses' building of the tabernacle. God gave the "blueprint" for each through faith, and thus both the ark and the tabernacle came into existence. Also, the building of the ark entailed nothing mysterious, and it was not built in some enclosed area. Everyone could see what Noah was undertaking, what he was building, and what he completed. That building in full view of everyone also gave forth a testimony, a call to salvation, a voice of admonition to do the same. But no one followed Noah's example. Some at least could have thought, "To be on the safe side, let's build a rescue ship like this too; if a flood does not come, no harm is done." But no, they let their hands hang at their sides, and the idea of taking precautionary and safety measures against the approaching flood seems *not* to have occurred to the ungodly; rather, it proceeded from God himself and found an entrance only with him who believed.

The evidence offered here, at bottom, has an absolute character. God brings the flood; he brings that flood as judgment and punishment, and the punishment will be awful. But by his ordination, this same God who brings this terrible flood upon the world at the same time arrests the destructive effects of the flood. Left to itself, the flood would have destroyed everything: the world, humanity, the church of God. And now the same God who brings about this judgment of the flood calls to this flood: this far and no farther.

That flood will overwhelm everything; nothing will be able to withstand its destruction, except for one block of wood, a wooden hull, against which the flood will not be able to do anything. In fact, the flood itself will have to lift up the ark, carry it, and set it down again safely on Ararat. In that ark, carried by the flood itself, will be salvation for the whole future. The Apostle Peter himself points to this when he says that Noah and his family were saved, not through the ark but through the water (1 Pet 3:20). The ark itself would not have saved if the water had not raised and lifted the ark, carrying it on its waves. The fact that ark and water together arrest the destruction of the flood, making possible the salvation of humanity and the church, issues not from humankind but from God. There was so little faith among humanity that we do not read of a single individual who secretly hid in the ark or asked Noah for permission to sail with him. Noah and his family entered alone, and it is not unlikely that his contemporaries jeered at him to boot.

§ 5 It is God who sets a limit to sin's misery here. The flood may go so far with its destruction, but no farther. The power of the flood will pound against the outside of the ark, yet behind that hull the future of the world will be safe. The Lord accomplishes this goal, not merely by restraining the flood, but through a means that he does not construct himself but that is constructed by man. God himself can act directly, for example, when he divides the Red Sea all the way down to the bottom, so that Israel can pass through safely. But God also can work indirectly, through means, to accomplish salvation. His common grace also can use human beings as an instrument to save other human beings, and this is the aim of every development in the arts and sciences, in agriculture and industry, in design and human relations. Therefore, in the particular example of Noah, it was necessary that God would arrest destruction by using a human instrument and teaching human beings to be attentive to precautionary measures. This fact itself is sufficiently explained in Scripture and is incontrovertible. From the ark issues one mighty summons from God to the entire human race: Before it is too late, be saved from the powers of destruction that will rage.

CHAPTER SIXTY-EIGHT

FINDING THE MEANS

They that seek the Lord *understand all things.*

Proverbs 28:5 (KJV)

Far from passively sitting on one's hands, godliness would seem to consist in the fact that God has placed upon us the obligation of unremitting activity in the use of means. Common grace is God's gracious arrangement to temper sin and misery in their deadly effect, and every human being—whether young or old, weak or strong, rich or poor—is called upon to make his or her personal contribution to that tempering of sin and misery. Everyone has to participate in this. All persons, without distinction, must put forth effort in this. In fact, every bit of life's energy must be applied to this. In fact, it can and must be said without exaggeration that every manifestation of human life, in this interim dispensation, is sufficient only to the extent that it is directed toward that arresting and tempering of sin and misery. Those who in their labor are guided and inspired by this thought have grasped the nobility of our calling. Those who have not yet chosen this goal still lack coherence in their efforts. It was frequently argued in the Middle Ages that sin corrupts the soul, and against this the church struggles in terms of the mystery of salvation. Moreover, it was argued that sin darkens the mind, against which the knowledge of learning struggles, and that sin destroys the body, against which medical science and hygiene struggle. § 1

Sin, we could add, lays a curse upon *nature*, against which human attempts to master nature struggle. In fact, we may insist that sin also disrupts *society*, against which the study of law and jurisprudence, for example, struggle. This is said only with a view to stress the importance of the university. It points to the nature of study that each of the five academic faculties undertakes and pursues, which can be understood as a struggle against sin and its effects. And to this extent it clearly demonstrates why the believer must not shun scholarship but rather must contribute to maintaining the life and purpose of the university. For it is precisely the university that is one of the most powerful means for opposing sin and its effects and for advancing the reach of common grace by probing the question of proper means.

But our argument extends much further, of course. Combatting sin and its effects through the means provided by common grace includes every kind of nurture and upbringing, every kind of clothing and covering, every means of promoting of health and good housing, everything that brings warmth amid the cold and light in the darkness, everything that promotes community and concourse among human beings and joins peoples together in fraternity. Agriculture, industry, shipping, commerce, every kind of industry and expertise, every kind of business and trade, everything that adds luster to life, that beautifies it, elevates its tone and ennobles it—in short, everything that the human mind can conceive and human hands can make always involves various means that common grace puts at our disposal. What we are arguing is quite simply that all human endeavors must always and everywhere be derived from the attempt to oppose sin and its effects.

Granted, it is always possible that these means can be in the service of sin when and where sin and its effects are considered in isolation—that is, where sin is discounted as long as we can escape its symptoms. Correlatively, it is also entirely true that not a few people oppose only those effects of sin of which they themselves are the victim, and in so doing they not infrequently increase sin's effects among others. Here, too, we encounter abuse, one-sidedness, and selfishness; we reach the essential nobility of life only when we engage in our part of the struggle against *all* sin and *all* of its effects for God's sake and from love toward our neighbor. This being the case, it nevertheless is the rule that the impulse of virtually all human activity is born from the urge to combat sin or its effects. Stated differently, virtually all expressions of human life consist in applying the means that common grace appoints for our use and puts within our power.

In this context, full emphasis should be placed on this "appointing" and "putting within our power." Common grace issues from God, and from God come all the means that we humans must apply to oppose sin and its consequences in curse and misery. But it is God himself who leads us to find the means and instructs us how to use them. And it is precisely the latter that is forgotten. The human inventor of the electric light and electric motor is extolled, but God, who led Edison to discover it, is passed over. This severs the connection between what we might call our higher and our lower life. This is exactly why Scripture again and again emphasizes that the beginning of all learning—the starting point for all of our knowing and our abilities—lies in the acknowledgment of God as the source of common grace, or, as it is put succinctly, in "the fear of the Lord" [Prov 9:10]. For this reason the proverb says, "They that seek the Lord understand all things." This, of course, does not mean that a godly man does not have to apply himself to studying; quite the opposite is true: the one who has God as the starting point has the best prospects of succeeding in study. Praying well is half our duty. § 2

And when we compare various people-groups and nations, don't we find that indeed those nations that are truly Christian—that is, where the knowledge of the gospel has penetrated and where God has been sought—gradually came to greater levels of understanding, and that conversely, pagan societies—that is, those people-groups that did not seek the Lord or have knowledge of the Lord—have sunk into relative cultural impotence and ignorance? Japan may imitate us now, but everything it imitates has been discovered and understood, not among pagans societies but among Christian nations where the Lord was acknowledged. We can even go further and maintain that inventiveness and the standard of human learning and knowledge are developed most strongly among those nations that, due to the Reformation, sought the Lord more fervently and diligently than the southern regions of Europe and America. It is therefore essentially an ungodly predisposition to be hostile toward learning and knowledge. We are not referring here to the question of wrong speculations or theories of unbelief; we are only confining ourselves to the issue of what enriches human learning or expands human knowledge and thus increases our power vis-à-vis nature. In the end, we may simply conclude that knowledge and learning are nothing but discovering and learning the mystery of the means of common grace that God has ordained and appointed for us.

Everything in this regard simply depends on the correct insight into the manner in which it pleases God to bring about that "appointing" and that "putting into service" of the means of common grace. There are two possible ways of achieving this. For example, I can give a child a math problem along with its solution, or I can provide only the math problem, so that the child must find the solution for himself. God did the former, so to speak, with Noah, when Noah had to build the ark. The latter occurred when the profession of shipbuilding eventually sought and found the rules for building a seaworthy vessel. Or, to express it in more general terms, every means of common grace and its use could either be revealed directly to us by God or be indirectly discovered by us. Both were conceivable. In paradise Adam found everything prepared and ready, and also in the kingdom of glory everything will be handed to us prepared and ready. This is clearly expressed in the new Jerusalem, which will not be built by us but will descend "out of heaven" fully prepared [Rev 21:2]. Similarly, at the marriage supper of the Lamb everything will be "prepared" and "made ready."

Indeed, even in our condition of sin's misery, examples are not lacking of divine provision through various means. In the wilderness, Israel lived for forty years as though from God's hand. God sent Israel the manna. He did not allow their clothes to deteriorate. God directed them to the spring from which they should drink. Wasn't Elijah fed by the ravens without any effort on his part? After all, this mode of existence is commonplace in the world of plants and animals. "Consider the lilies of the field, how they grow: they neither toil nor spin, yet I tell you, even Solomon in all his glory was not arrayed like one of these" [Matt 6:28–29]. God possesses power, and where he deems it necessary, he uses this power. In fact, *without* food God kept his Servant alive in the wilderness for many days.

§ 3 But God withdrew the norm of paradise after the fall, and in its place came another norm: "You will have your bread, but only by the sweat of your face" [see Gen 3:19]. In paradise *everything* was ready, whereas on the cursed earth *nothing* is. In life after the fall, everything needed to stave off death and distress had to be discovered or invented and employed by human beings themselves; this would occur under steady exertion, with much effort, by pondering and reflecting and then working. In this connection we pointed earlier to Isaiah 28, which speaks of agriculture. For agriculture as well, all kinds of things had to be invented: the manner of preparing the soil, the choice of seed, irrigation, weeding, the time for harvesting, the manner of threshing, and so much more. Has the farmer discovered this himself, or did God teach him? The answer must be that he discovered these things himself, yet only because his God instructed him. Isaiah states quite clearly: "For he is rightly instructed; his God teaches him" (Isa 28:26). But how? Did the first farmer receive a manual? Did God send him an angel to demonstrate everything? Did God give him an oral revelation? None of these things. God gave him the soil, a head to think with, hands to work with, and (besides these) a basic *hunger*. God stimulated him by means of this drive. God taught him to think about things. And thus he had to try things. First one thing, and when that did not work, something else, until finally one person found this and the other that, with the results confirming that this was the right solution. Subsequently, the one imitated the other, and it was passed on from father to son, and in this way agriculture expanded. In fact, in this manner God has gradually taught us successively over the centuries how to cultivate the land.

It therefore is thoroughly wrong when we imagine that nothing remains to be learned about such an occupation. God's instruction continues ceaselessly, and throughout the centuries he uncovers for us new forces, new means, new ways of doing things; the same applies to agriculture. Everything from the chemical elements in the soil to those in the air is related. We can learn to understand that connection only through working with the soil. But gradually that knowledge becomes refined. All newly acquired knowledge then has its application in agriculture and in the preparation of agricultural products, in order to make the soil produce more, to simplify the work, and to better prepare the particular crop. And in all this, the common grace of God is at work, which increases our power over nature, gives us a more bountiful and better harvest, and makes us enjoy the fruits of the earth in even greater ways. And even though it is a fact that pseudo-intellectual presumption sometimes proposes things that simply do not hold up, it is equally the case that those who are opposed to increased knowledge or better insight go counter to God. Through endless types of experiments God has taught us all that we now know, and through all kinds of experiments our knowledge continues to be enriched.

Those who are fundamentally opposed to this incur their "punishment" automatically in the fact that someone else will outstrip them and pass them by. And when this twisted way of thinking takes root in an entire people group or society, the simple consequence is that those of other nations will outdo us. In the sixteenth century, Dutch farmers really were the teachers of Europe. We were the most advanced, and our products garnered the highest prices. And if and when something of the spirit of our forefathers once again awakens among us, it will also necessarily manifest itself also in this way, that we allow ourselves to be instructed in more and better ways by our God—not only in the Heidelberg Catechism but also in the catechism of agriculture, in the catechism of industry, and in the catechism of commerce. For it is obvious that everything we have said about farming on the basis of Isaiah 28 is just as applicable to all the rest of human endeavor.

§ 4 To the perceptive person it becomes immediately apparent that it is indeed God who instructs us about all these things and that humankind possesses none of this from purely within. Such learning involves discovering and applying elements that man cannot call forth from his own imagination or simply dream up; rather, these are elements or forces that must be present in nature. What is not present in nature, and what is not contained in or operative in nature, may be imagined in the abstract, but it never leads to any concrete result or provides any sort of solution. Effectiveness, permanent results, and true gain come only if we discover something that is contained in nature as a force or relationship, something that can now be used and applied. Human beings cannot introduce anything into nature; they can only derive things from nature, since it is not humankind but God who causes it to be present in nature and who created nature. Furthermore, God does not bring those things into nature when we discover them; rather, he included them in nature from the beginning. What's more, we humans toiled for many centuries with extremely inadequate tools while all we needed for the advancement of our undertaking lay at our feet all along, as it were. But we are not aware of it; in effect, we are blind to it. And this applies not just to one individual, but to all people everywhere. And after human beings have stumbled along for centuries in relative blindness, then God grants to one person eyes to see the solution. This person sees it, grasps it, and expresses it. At that point, everyone hears and knows about it. And we call this a discovery or an invention, and God, who in his grace thus enriched us, is almost always forgotten, or worse yet, denied. Then science and learning begin to boast about their discoveries and put on airs as if they were the actual ones that accomplished this, even though with all their findings they could not create or produce anything; they could work only with powers that they had discovered as they had been created by God.

At the same time, it would be wrong to think that we are dealing here with the fruit of particular grace. Everything that enriches our knowledge of nature is intended for humans as humans—that is, for all human beings, for humanity in its entirety. There is no distinction here between godly and ungodly. God has even ordained it in such a way that sin can abuse even the very ordinances that God in his grace has supplied to man and then can turn them to its own advantage. By way of illustration, chemistry permits us to detect the counterfeiting of foods; the thief and the swindler make use of technology even as we do; and technical design gives the murderer a refined weapon that is all the more deadly in its aim. Alas, all of this knowledge remains common property of humanity, for good and for evil. It is and remains part of common grace, and in the day of judgment both the individual person and humanity collectively will be held responsible for whether and how they have used these treasures of common grace for the purposes of preventing the effects of the fall, or for whether they have abused them for the purposes of furthering sin's effects. God gives us all of these instructions for blessing, and we are culpable if we turn what has been intended as medicine into a form of poison and thereby intensify human misery.

But whatever our choices, God does not adapt his ordinances to human decision. Divine ordinance is and remains that all these treasures of common grace remain the *common* property of all humanity. These treasures are not the private property of the godly; they are not the special possession of those who belong to the fold of Christ. On the contrary, common grace and all its treasures extend as far as the human race extends. And in order to make us understand this better, and to preclude any misunderstanding on this point, we must emphasize the fact that it is by no means a rare occurrence when, in the case of cultural developments, God opens the eyes, not of one of his servants, but of *unbelievers* who reject him. In their own generation the children of the world often are richer in inventiveness than the children of light. Indeed, it is not at all unusual for the children of the world to be the first to use various inventions and discoveries to their own superior advantage, and for the disciples of the Lord to bring up the rear only much later to enjoy these same benefits. In many a barroom in our day, people sit with electric light and evenly distributed steam heat while in many churches people still suffer bitter cold when dusk settles upon the building during a rather late afternoon service. The people of God almost never take the lead in such things, at least not in Europe. It is as if God's truth as it applies in the realm of physics does not exist for the church. And this is almost exclusively the result of a one-sided focus on particular grace and of living as if, alongside and behind particular grace, no divine common grace existed in this world.

§ 5 We offer further commentary as evidence that it is God who instructs us about these things and to whose voice we must listen—namely, that there is coherence, progression, and upward movement in that instruction. People in different countries who knew nothing about each other and people from different centuries who never spoke with one another discovered each in their own way various truths, and yet in retrospect these things appeared to be related, arising in an orderly fashion and helping us advance. The nature of sin was to disperse human beings; in consequence, contact between various people groups was virtually broken off for many centuries. For example, just think of the time and effort it still took in the days of the Reformation to get a letter from here to Vienna, or of the physical danger to which one exposed himself when traveling from Amsterdam to Geneva. Correspondence from those days shows example after example. Nevertheless, association between peoples always involves an arresting and tempering of certain consequences of sin. And look at how, in gradual sequence, that association has become easier and quicker. Today we can travel around the world in as many days as were needed to travel from west to east on our small continent three centuries ago. And if you go back to the days of the Great Migrations, back then it took weeks for what might take only days in the sixteenth century.[1] One mighty postal connection today brings human communication for virtually no money to all the ends of the earth. And if it is necessary, and you have the money to make use of the world's telegraph network, you can communicate with someone on the other part of the world and you have your answer, all within a few hours.

Now all of this, of course, was already resident within nature in the days of Adam and Noah. Not a single force has been added. From the beginning of human history, every human and cultural development has been brought about by existing forces; our generation has moved in a gradual sequence from one step to the next and has discovered first one force and then another. We therefore must acknowledge one of two things: either this is the fruit of chance—that is, we must leave it unexplained (since

1. Kuyper refers here to a long period of migration within and into Europe during the latter days of the Roman Empire, from roughly the second to the sixth century AD.

chance is without sense or reason); or God ordained and intended it this way from the beginning and has led us in due course to find and discover it. But it is a matter of ingratitude and ungodliness not only when the man of learning forgets to give God the glory for all of this, but also when we, as God's children, do not eagerly seize, apply, and use what God led us to find and revealed to us. God reveals it and uncovers it for us to make our lives happier. What, then, shall we say of those who consider themselves godly if they ignore these good things of our God and thus exhibit in practice that they don't want to use them? It is an offense that is all the more serious, because history teaches us how the godly always end up having to accept these developments anyway, albeit not as a gift from our God but as something forced on them by custom, fashion, or historical progress—not as the fruit of common grace but as a mere outcome of common usage.

CHAPTER SIXTY-NINE

PRECAUTIONARY MEASURES

They cried out, "O man of God, there is death in the pot!" And they could not eat it. He said, "Then bring flour." And he threw it into the pot and said, "Pour some out for the men, that they may eat." And there was no harm in the pot.

2 Kings 4:40–41

§ 1 Thus far we have presented a thorough answer to the question of whether we humans are allowed to fight against the suffering, misery, and distress that befall us, and hence to employ for that purpose every measure available to us. We not only may do so; we *must* do so. Those who fail to do so fall short in the discharge of their duty, and their failure to do so becomes sin. Indeed, when illness befalls us, not combating that illness is and remains a sin against the sixth commandment. There is therefore nothing reckless in our language if—at the outbreak of some virus among men, animals, or plants—we speak of taking measures against it and even of taking measures to arrest and eradicate it if it has reached the proportions of a national disaster. In truth, choosing a weaker response could lead to a breaking down of resilience. In spite of the fact that God allows us to experience evil, and that he allows it as judgment and punishment, it nevertheless is *that same God* who himself combats the evil of suffering and wants us to do the same, armed with the means supplied by common grace.

Meanwhile, many are not yet convinced that it is permissible to take precautionary measures to prevent the very evil that otherwise threatens to overcome us. The objection they raise is that, by means of precautionary measures for the prevention of a sickness or other evils, human beings place themselves in a position of contravening God Almighty and of denying him his absolutely sovereign power to do as he wishes. In past centuries there were repeated epidemics of pestilence. Today measures are taken, notably in the eastern Mediterranean region, to quarantine whatever comes from Asia. Such actions, thank God, have been successful for many years in safeguarding Europe against new outbreaks of disease. Precisely this sort of attempt at safeguarding, it is then thought, is tantamount to a human being standing up and resisting God. No pestilence can come upon us except by God's ordination. Thus, it constitutes an attempt on our part to limit God's omnipotence when we attempt to prevent this pestilence from entering Europe by taking measures. It is as if we were saying, "Even if God wanted to bring pestilence upon Europe, we will take measures so that it does not happen." Such a frame of mind, it is assumed, makes a mockery of God's majesty, and consequently the position that tempts us to adopt such an attitude is condemned.

In response to this mind-set we simply note that even the mere thought that we could arrest God's omnipotence by human means must be condemned in no uncertain terms. What's more, any politician or medical expert who even entertains such a thought while considering his responsibilities profanes the living God and, in so doing, sins greatly. But condemning the sinful frame of mind and taking precautionary measures are two entirely different things. When the Pharisee and the tax collector both go to the temple and both pray in the temple, the frame of mind that brings each of them there is very different. We fully concede that there may be people, whether in government or sitting on medical committees, who think with a measure of presumption, "We will put an end, once and for all, to all this talk about God having anything to do with disease; we'll simply eliminate disease." And yet it is also true that this sort of extreme statement is by no means the only conceivable human reaction when such human measures are adopted.

There is quite emphatically no necessary connection between the nature and working of such measures and the reasoning behind why they are implemented. In fact, it is quite conceivable that a medical authority who took such measures and even prescribed them to others did not think at all about God and was acting only practically and professionally. Let's suppose that the threat of an epidemic is present. Medical authorities learn that in other countries some given measure (or measures) was taken. They investigate how these measures should be managed, and then they introduce them in their own country. The outcome shows that the evil was averted. This way of thinking is not likely motivated by faith, to be sure, and whatever people undertake apart from God will not experience his blessing. But even when we are not intending to absolve people from unbelief per se, it needs to be acknowledged that most people are not attempting to be audacious or intending to mock God's majesty. The person who acts in this manner is simply acting (at least as it concerns his consciousness) apart from God.

But a third possibility is also conceivable. It may well be the case that someone who undertakes such health measures intentionally invokes the light, wisdom, help, and guidance of one's God. It may be the case, in the end, that that person is undertaking various measures in full faith that God has been guiding, and that God has made it a duty to avert a particular evil in that particular nation. As a result, the person who has been praying in this way also will be grateful to God when those efforts succeed in any measure. And while there will be no obvious reviling of the Lord, there also will be no ignoring of God in unbelief either. Thus, let that person's godliness be applauded.

§ 2 In the end, regardless of people's motivation, in different situations the health measures of, say, quarantine and isolation work entirely independently of what the person who prescribes such measures thinks or how that person is motivated in acting. When three different statesmen in three different countries take identical measures to prevent the plague from spreading into Europe, with the one doing it in anger against God, the second ignoring God entirely, and the third doing it after having sought support in prayer, those measures themselves remain entirely independent of the three divergent mind-sets. And this is necessarily the case, since it is not a human person who brings about the effect of the measures, but God alone. If God had ordained the nature of the plague such that its poison entered the air and was blown with the wind from country to country, then any quarantine measure would be utterly useless. The poison would penetrate through every barrier anyway. The success of such barriers is therefore the result of the fact that the plague virus is communicated from object to object only by touch. Through this means, and only through this means, God himself has made it possible to prevent the spread of the plague. That, as a result, we are still powerless in the face of influenza, whose victims number in the thousands, can be explained only from the fact that with this illness the nature of the virus bears another character. But where the virus is transmitted from object to object by touch, it is God himself who calls upon us to note this and use it to our advantage, so that we can avoid the danger of contagion by avoiding touching.

The ordinances given to Israel by God himself for combatting and preventing leprosy make this quite clear. In many respects, leprosy has a character similar to that of the plague. Leprosy, along with the plague, belongs to those terrible scourges that under various names, including Black Death, sometimes have wiped out entire villages and towns, even devastating entire nations. Within Israel's borders, who brought leprosy? The answer must be *God*. It is he, and he alone, who makes dead and alive. Nor can it be denied that such a disease constituted the suffering and punishment of judgment. Recall that Israel was told explicitly that if they left God's covenant, they would also be visited by the pestilences of other nations. At the same time, when we ask who combats leprosy in Israel and who ordains the most stringent measures against it, prescribing every conceivable means against it to prevent leprosy, then the answer is also *that very same God*. It is God who sends the leprosy, and it is the same God who ordains the means to prevent it from coming. We can call this contradictory, and if that is the case, so be it, as long as we acknowledge and agree that Scripture reveals it to us in this way and not otherwise. Anyone who denies divine activity either in the origin or the prevention of leprosy deviates from Scripture.

Nor can we say that the precautionary measures for preventing an outbreak of leprosy in holy Scripture are superficial in character, or that they are mentioned only in passing. The laws covering this occupy all of chapters 13 and 14 in Leviticus, and they go into the smallest of details. First, the various kinds and degrees of leprosy are to be distinguished in detail, and the symptoms of each are to be noted. Not all forms of leprosy are the same. Failure to make these distinctions could lead to a faulty diagnosis, and for this reason the various symptoms are clearly delineated, as if taken from a medical manual, in order to preclude any mistake. Next, people are appointed who must officially act in this regard and who have authority over the affected person and his welfare. The affected person, it is true, is most unfortunate, but in a certain sense he also is a liability to the whole town and even to others. Because of this God appoints people who will be authorized not only to examine the suspected sufferer but also to limit his freedom and isolate him. In the case of leprosy, the priest who has to decide in this matter even has the authority to *shut him up for seven days* (13:26). After this the affected person must not go out unless he is wearing torn clothes. He must walk with uncovered head. He must cover his upper lip (13:45). And whenever he encounters someone, to avoid the danger of contaminating another, he must call out from afar, "Keep your distance. I am unclean." The next step taken is to ensure that the affected person's clothes, household goods, and even house will not become a source of infection. The decontamination must be as complete as possible; even the plaster must be scraped from the walls. Finally, prescriptions are given as to how the healed leper can be declared clean and what he must do to purify himself. What we observe here is in fact a complete set of hygienic regulations, prescribed by God himself, to forestall the spread of leprosy in Israel. And even though these laws apply only to leprosy, it is obvious that a generally valid principle is stated here: in human society we should be intent on taking any and all such measures to prevent and stop the encroaching or spreading of contagious diseases.

Thus, we are faced with the clear fact that, on the one hand, the leprosy came from God and was so intimately connected with sin that it even required an offering for cleansing to become clean again. On the other hand, the same God who sent the leprosy gives definite and strict commandments not only to oppose the leprosy and combat it, but even to *prevent* it where it has not yet broken out. On the basis of this we are justified in concluding that the flawed motivations by which precautionary measures to prevent suffering occasionally are taken in no way add to or detract from the legitimacy and permissibility of such measures. God himself will judge all that is sinful according to an individual's motivation, and we must never condone or excuse this sinfulness. But at the same time, God's intention that we must take various measures has been revealed so plainly and clearly that abstaining from or resisting these measures must be condemned as *disobedience*.

§ 3 Furthermore, opposing or rejecting such precautionary measures in the prevention of illness or other disaster springs from an entirely arbitrary and false distinction. The evil of suffering then tends to be divided into two classes: in one class are placed ordinary misfortunes, and in the other, extraordinary misfortunes. In this way it is thought that God's angry judgment is expressed especially through the latter category. The mistaken conclusion is then drawn that there is nothing wrong with taking precautionary measures against *ordinary* misfortunes, whereas it is wrong to do so in the face of *extraordinary* disasters such as the plague, cholera, smallpox, and so forth. The facts seem to verify this. The very same people who raise such strenuous objections against taking precautionary measures to combat, prevent, or inhibit various kinds of disease among people, animals, and plants are quite willing to take precautionary measures against common, ordinary misfortunes. In point of fact, no large ship heads out to sea without taking into account the possibility of storms and shipwreck; this is why every ship is equipped with gear and accessories such as life preservers, and lifeboats, in the event of the possibility of such dangers. Likewise, in every town and village there is a fire engine, equipped with hooks, ladders, and so forth. We put handrails along stairs that are somewhat steep, and in front of a low window we put an iron grate. When it begins to freeze, we put on warm clothing to prevent catching a cold. In places where the river could rise and inundate the land, a dike is built and a dike watch is set up with a fixed schedule of who will serve in the hour of need. In short, throughout our lives we are attentive to all manner of possible misfortunes that may befall us, and with everyone's approval, we take all kinds of precautionary measures to prevent the misfortune—or, if it does visit, to limit its destructive effect.

It would constitute unbelief to claim that those kinds of more common misfortunes do not come upon us from God, and yet at the same time to claim that God manifests his wrath exclusively in extraordinary disasters, such as when lightning strikes, an epidemic breaks out in our community, or an earthquake occurs. What is extraordinary in that event in truth is not even one-thousandth of what happens in a human lifetime. This sort of mind-set leads to our placing our lives outside of God and placing God outside of our lives, with the consequence that we only acknowledge now and then his almighty intervention in the case of especially surprising and unexpected misfortunes. Can anyone who truly understands the Reformed confession in its fullest sense ever be satisfied with such a misplaced division of life? Our strength lies precisely in acknowledging God's omnipotence in all things and honoring God's ordination in every event in our life. We must not say, "If the land is inundated, it is caused by heavy rains. But when lightning strikes, it is an act of God." In both rain and lightning his majesty is one and the same, and therefore there is no sense in saying, "We may build a dike against the flood, but putting a lightning rod on our house is impermissible." Either both are permissible or neither is. But calling for the one and rejecting the other is nothing but being two-faced and equivocal.

We remain superficial and fail to reflect on the arrangement of God's works at its foundation. Flooding is a destruction that comes from God because God has given one country a lower elevation than another one, he lets his abundant rain fall, and he lets the swollen rivers first freeze and then suddenly thaw. God does all this. The low elevation of the land, the torrential downpour, the initial freezing and subsequent thawing—all this comes from him, and when nothing is done from our side and no precautionary measures are taken, then the inundation will surely come and cause devastation among both people and livestock in a way that simply makes the lightning strike seem like nothing by comparison. But now we are capable of building a dike, thereby inhibiting the waters in their progress from destroying our fields. And not only are we permitted to do this; in fact we must do it. Anyone who does not do this falls short in performing our most basic duties.

We return to a previous example: when God accumulates electricity in the clouds and the possibility increases of a lightning strike that might endanger the lives of a family or their property, we are not only *permitted* but *obligated* to apply every means available to avert or at least mitigate this danger. It is none other than God himself who has included within nature this means to divert the lightning. It is, in fact, God himself who has enlightened the human eye to ultimately discover this hidden force and to invent the means. And when a dangerous bolt of lightning travels down along the metal rod and terminates in the ground, it is God himself who guides the lightning along that rod and who smothers the enormous spark in the earth. Humankind does not do this, and Satan does not do this; it is God. And whoever honors God's majesty in the lightning that flashes, yet does not honor the majesty with which God draws this flashing lightning to the rod, grounding and guiding it away, takes from God half the honor due him.

The residue of contradictory thinking in our midst might be viewed as aftereffects of the old Anabaptist leaven that divided life at every point into two realms, claiming one part for God but leaving the other to the world. This sort of dichotomous mind-set clearly betrays the theological orientation of our confession if the church, both in catechesis and in preaching, does not affirm the all-encompassing, all-permeating nature of divine governance. In so doing it ends up banishing any contrary notions from the Reformed landscape. We must not entertain even for a moment the idea that God would work through lightning *directly* and yet flooding only *indirectly*. We should be diligent to stay current in our knowledge of nature; with this knowledge we can be assured that, whether God lets the downpour happen or lets the lightning flash, he always makes use of the elements he himself called into existence when he wrapped the earth with an atmosphere as with a belt. And because any distinction between various kinds of disasters would appear to be untenable, we make a plea for taking precautionary measures against all disasters without distinction; we do this not at the expense of godliness but precisely in order to enter through the royal gate of true piety that glorifies God in everything. All disasters that threaten or occur come from God, in the same way that every way, hidden in nature, to prevent disasters does as well.

What's more, the discovery and knowledge of these means come only from God, since God himself opens the human eye to them. We must no longer withdraw half of life from God's honor. We must not imagine that science could do anything on its own, as if science in this way had forged a weapon to defy God or if it had somehow succeeded in rendering God's lightning powerless. Science has no power whatsoever, and there exists no force in nature that is not worked by God. And when science is prone to put on airs, as it were, boasting in having a power it does not possess and passing off God's power as its own, it is not appropriate for Christians to encourage that illusion in an ungodly and unwise manner. Rather, it then is our duty and holy calling to seize these remedies in all their fullness, to display them in all their saving and misery-arresting effect. And if they appear to be empirically effective, we must magnify the Lord, who in his common grace has conceived such marvelous means and put them at our disposal.

CHAPTER SEVENTY

SUFFERING AS SOLIDARITY

Or those eighteen on whom the tower in Siloam fell and killed them: do you think that they were worse offenders than all the others who lived in Jerusalem?

LUKE 13:4

§ 1 The Christian duty not only to combat the suffering that has come upon us but also, where possible, to avert through precautionary measures the suffering that could come upon us therefore must encompass both ordinary and extraordinary dangers that may threaten, whether these be disease, famine, lightning strikes, or whatever. None of these phenomena occur apart from God. All have their origin in his ordination. They always bear the character of sin's consequences and, therefore, of judgment and punishment as well. And any measures we take to prevent any kind of suffering work exclusively through powers that God himself has created, maintained, and led us to discover; the result is that any moral evil in these measures can lie only in our intention. Using drugs to make us insensitive to pain can be necessary and obligatory, but it also can become sinful if it is intended to numb our consciousness at a time that requires clarity of mind. We utilize this latter example only in passing but state the principle rule in its essence: we must fight against all suffering, and suffering that can be prevented must be averted by precautionary measures. When the danger of rabies arises, we must muzzle our dogs. When a cattle plague breaks out, we must quarantine our cattle. When we embark on a voyage at sea, we must take life-saving devices with us in case of a possible shipwreck. And we must place lightning rods on top of castles or towers in order to prevent a lightning strike. We must always see our enemy in the suffering that does or can visit us, and we must always arm ourselves against that enemy.

At this point we should stop and examine more precisely than is commonly done the punishing and judgmental character of suffering. For all too often we still harbor the notion that the portion of suffering that befalls person A is allocated according to A's personal guilt and that A, when he resists this suffering, is not unlike the person who is arrested and resists the policeman and, in order to remain a free man, even knocks him down. The idea here is that God, who is enraged and wrathful about A's guilt, wants to arrest and punish A. If A goes against this, he resists the power of the Lord and sins even more seriously than the one who resists a policeman, because in the case of disease or something similar it is God himself who wants to arrest him. We must not simply gloss over this commonly held notion. For nothing assails the first principles of godliness more seriously than resisting the powers placed over us. Resisting the police and the law means breaking down all security and safety in our civic life. If the police and the law no longer command moral respect, their powers and use of force must be continually expanded, their weapons must become increasingly more forceful, and they must be given ever-greater powers over the citizenry.

For this reason our forefathers regularly taught that such resistance is always against God himself to the extent that the government is his servant and acts on his behalf. Even for the sake of our faith we must allow ourselves at times to be persecuted by police and the law. We might bring complaints about them to God for being his unfaithful servants, but we must bear their unjust punishment for God's sake. If we were to hold that the suffering that God brings upon us is equal in nature to arrests and punishments by the law and the police, then the conclusion is clear. *Every* resistance to such suffering, *every* defiance of such punishment, *every* opposition to such a misery would render us all the more guilty. Although it is correct that an ordinary policeman acts on behalf of the government, everyone will sense that resistance among people becomes more culpable to the degree that the government acts more personally. Resistance against the mayor in person, for example, presumes more wickedness in the heart than resistance to a policeman whom he has dispatched. Yet, how wouldn't this guilt increase if God himself came to arrest us, not through public servants or through government, but personally and in our home, through illness or accident? In that case resistance would be direct rebellion against his majesty and should therefore be punished with the highest penalty.

§ 2 But this viewpoint is wrong. If God really intends to arrest us, resistance is simply unthinkable—there cannot be any resistance. God has determined the hour of death for each one of us, and which creature, by whatever means of resistance, could add a single hour to its span of life? Jesus himself asked the same question, albeit in an entirely different context. If it is truly God's intent to put us on our deathbed through disease, what power in the world could resist him? We can resist a police officer or even a mayor in a moment by force, because people are weak creatures like us. But who could actually resist God? Who could stand for even a moment when faced with his omnipotence? Could we have any power to resist him other than the power God himself gave us and maintains in us? We must never forget the first of the Twelve Articles of Faith: "I believe in God the Father *Almighty*." We should keep in mind that this denies the existence of any might or power unless that power comes *from him* and is maintained *by him*. If God intends to strike us down with a blow, that blow is always decisive and direct, and we lie prostrate before any thought of resistance might even arise within us. Any other notion is simply *unbelief*; it is to harbor human, creaturely thoughts about the Infinite One.

But even apart from this, there is an entirely different reason why we may not make such a comparison: earthly justice touches us at the personal level on the basis of certain facts and adjudicates these facts in a way that concludes the case. Say, for example, that someone commits a crime, and it is proved that he in fact did commit this crime, and he then gets three years in prison, after which he has paid his debt. After completing his prison sentence, that person stands once again as a free citizen before the law, and the law can no longer touch him. But the punishment of suffering that God sends us never bears this sort of character. All of God's judgments and punishments in this life always bear an entirely provisional character. After these provisional punishments have been borne or have passed, not a single human being stands free before God. God's decisive punishment comes only on the day of judgment, and because his punishments at that time will be eternal in nature, there can never be an evading of his punishing justice. The deferred character of all punishment and judgment here below is a direct consequence of common grace. Had common grace not come, then judgment and punishment in paradise would have taken effect in their final form immediately, and paradise would have sunk into hell, flooding us with eternal death immediately and forever. But this did not happen. A reprieve occurred. But the consequence of this reprieve is that neither the judgments of God nor his punishments here below bear a personal, finite, and final character. Rather, they had to assume the character of preliminary pains, or of prophecies of the eternal pains that await the condemned in the future. Moreover, it is precisely this postponing character that accounts for the reality that all suffering and misery simultaneously became *grace*, whose goal was to arrest sin, nurture us, and thereby simultaneously sanctify us.

In this way, suffering received a double character. Most certainly, judg- § 3
ment and punishment speak in the form of suffering, but it is also true that grace operates for the purposes of arresting sin and sanctifying us. All misunderstanding on this point arises from the fact that when two people argue about this, the one overlooks the judgment in suffering while the other overlooks the sanctifying character of suffering. For the Christian, only the latter remains and the former falls away, not because there is no punishing reality in suffering but because Christ has borne all punishment for sin on his behalf, and he himself now stands righteous before God. This has occurred "as if [he] had never committed nor had any sins, and had [himself] accomplished all the obedience which Christ has fulfilled for [him]." Our Catechism adds, of course, [that this is the case] inasmuch as he embraces "such benefit with a believing heart."[1] But this means that a "Christian at his best" can no longer bear punishment, because Christ already bore it for him. If, then, a godly man or woman understands his or her suffering as punishment and undergoes it as such, this neither demonstrates nor proves one's godliness; rather, it is evidence of the opposite—namely, one's lack of godliness. In reality it shows a lack of faith and an inability to truly embrace and apply the sufficient power of Christ's own suffering and death. If this is the case, then as "beloved children" Christians would see nothing but chastisement in their suffering and would not be able to look amid their suffering to Christ, who personally took on their punishment. It is simply an enigma how godly, believing Christians, who claim to believe in the atoning and sufficient power of Jesus' suffering and death,

1. Heidelberg Catechism, Lord's Day 23, Q&A 60.

can still speak of disease and illness as being inflicted by a punishing and judging God, even when they might answer question 60 of the Heidelberg Catechism in terms of complete justification by faith.

Of course, to the extent that we languish in our faith, let it slide, and hence no longer feel justified before God, the awareness and sense of punishment in suffering immediately returns. At that point it touches our conscience. We feel ourselves standing again under indictment before God. Our sins rise up against us once more and bear witness against us. We feel ourselves to be outside of Christ. We once again bear our own judgment. And in such a state of mind we once more undergo our suffering as a clear *punishment* that presses upon us directly. Note that this takes place solely in our own consciousness, since we let go of our faith. But what we must do subsequently is not succumb under our punishment but *rebuke our unbelief*, return from our unbelief to faith again, make our half faith whole again, and anchor our vacillating faith. If we do this, the result will be that as soon as our faith has returned, the fearful sense of punishment will immediately disappear, and we will feel like the chastised child in the hand of our chastising Father once again. The suffering becomes medicine for our soul. Our grief becomes an instrument for sanctification. The misery under which we are bowed functions for us as an outflowing from particular grace.

It cannot be emphasized enough that when national disasters occur, the pulpit has offered a decidedly uncertain—even all too often mistaken—response. We often heard talk of some sort of ban that rested upon the church, or of sin that was being visited upon the church, or of the fearful judgment of God that was hanging over its souls. People had to repent of their sins. Then God would be gracious again, and in this way the punishment of disease or disaster would be removed. It was obvious how people reached this conclusion. Having read what was said in the Old Testament about the national conditions in God's covenant people of Israel and how God dealt with them in the time of his special revelation, people applied the same to the church of the new covenant, in spite of justification by faith and the fact that the era of special revelation has ceased. But however much such preaching gripped the heart and was even desired, it was not sound. If at such a time we preach to an unbelieving crowd as, for example, Jonah did in Nineveh—that is, to people who are outside of Christ, or to a mixed group of people—then there is truth in what we preach. But it is misguided when this is applied to the saints who are in Christ Jesus. Redeemed people in Christ are free from punishment and have been removed from judgment.

And in the case of national disasters that touch the church as well as those outside it, precisely in the midst of the church is where faith must resound in order to rebuke unbelief and lack of faith.

Faith, in its fullness and power, must be rekindled and revived again, and the glory of Jesus' church must manifest itself in the fact that while others cringe in fear and dismay, God's beloved children are joyful and do not experience punishment; rather, they are being chastised by their dear Father in heaven, and they know themselves to be reconciled and secure. Buoyed by that glorious, inspiring thought in such times, the church of the living God must bring to other people the power of encouragement, love, and mercy to those who suffer. Moreover, because of their fresh resilience, people must find measures with which to combat phenomena such as disaster or disease, arrest it, and bring it to an end with God's help. This is what Calvin did when the plague struck Geneva. Encouraging and comforting the sick and combatting the evil of the pestilence through hygienic measures were the two strategies he used to keep the spirits high in Geneva.

In this dispensation, then, there is no final judicial act on God's part, § 4
and for those who stand in a full and strong faith, any punishing character of suffering has given way to that of chastisement and sanctification. And when we ask how this can be explained, the answer lies in the fact that suffering for the sake of sin does not revolve around the individual but the community—that is, the many, the human race collectively. When the tower of Siloam collapsed and crushed many, Jesus asked, "Do you think that they were worse offenders than all the others who lived in Jerusalem?" This pointed question of Jesus contains a solution to the whole issue. Certainly, there are also personal consequences of all kinds of sin. A drunkard destroys his own body, the lecher poisons his own blood, the sluggard will in the end suffer lack of food, the daredevil who tempts God is killed, and so on. There are an infinite number of forms of misery that demonstrably come from specific personal sins. But even in those situations the punishment for specific and demonstrable sins is not at all limited merely to the guilty person. The drunkard certainly does not destroy only his own body but, alas, he also undermines the happiness of his family, his wife's enjoyment of life, and his children's future. The lecher who poisons his own blood is all too often the reason why his children are born with all kinds of terrible illnesses. The daredevil who is killed all too often takes the means for supporting his wife and children with him to the grave. We are not even mentioning here the profound misery these wretched people

cause for father and mother, brother and sister, friends and relatives. In this light, it is virtually impossible to come up with one single personal sin that does not bring some sense of suffering to others in its wake, even though these others had no part in this sin.

Even when there may well be exceptions of a more personal nature, it is very clear that major disasters such as shipwrecks and train accidents, famine and pestilence, insurrection and war, and hurricanes and cyclones are not in any way connected in their origin with any specific sin; rather, they are shared consequences of the general disturbance that came upon all of nature and human existence as a consequence of sin and the curse. Why did so much more disease break out in our own nation in centuries past, whereas today we seem to be spared from them? Is it because people in the past were much more hardened sinners, but now we are much more godly as a people? Most everyone would concede that godliness was a much more powerful factor in life back then and that in so many ways we have declined in terms of godliness, earnestness, and virtue when compared to past generations. When twenty oceangoing vessels are traveling simultaneously back and forth between Europe and America, and a dreaded fog envelops everything, with two of the twenty colliding and sinking, does this mean that the passengers on the eighteen other ships were so much more godly while the passengers on the two were exceptionally godless? No one would dare make this argument, and far from feeling a curse in our hearts for those who perished, we are gripped by a profound sense of pity for them. Otherwise, we should abolish all lifeboat companies and say that no lifeboats may be put out to sea to rescue guilty people whom God wants to drown.

§ 5 This entire perspective, then, needs to be jettisoned. We need to clearly see and confess that the issue is not about a personal account that is being settled between God and the individual sinner; that personal settling of accounts will not take place until the final judgment. At that time "each will have to bear his own load" [Gal 6:5], as the apostle says. But here it involves a shared account, with the holy God on one hand, and the world taken as a whole on the other. Suffering, therefore, which comes not only upon people but also upon animals and plants (indeed, upon all of nature in its entirety) and upon our human race—that is, over tribes, peoples, and nations—touches everything in creation. It touches nations and also individual generations, families, and individuals, and it does so, for example, through hereditary illnesses and defects. This fact explains why it so often is precisely the case that the godless escape suffering whereas the godly do not. In this sense, being godless or pious does not make any difference for the effect of the curse. Didn't Jesus himself say that God "makes his sun rise on the evil and on the good, and sends rain on the just and on the unjust" [Matt 5:45]? This is a saying with such rich content, indicating beyond any doubt for every Christian that in the common disasters of life God takes into account neither faith nor unbelief, virtue nor sin; rather, he lets these ordinary, commonly occurring disasters come upon all sorts of members of the human race, entirely apart from their inner condition.

To this extent the pious have no advantage over the godless, but they also have no disadvantage. They share equally with the godless in God's bounty, and they suffer with the godless on an equal footing under God's visitations. What's more, added to this common suffering for believers is the fact that they have to bear abuse and oppression for the sake of their faith, that they see themselves excluded from all kinds of advantages and enjoyments because of the sin these things involve and are discriminated against in all areas of life. Thus, their portion of suffering is actually much greater; hence the great problem for Job, Solomon, and Asaph: How is it possible that the godless flourish and the godly servant of God must suffer so bitterly? But even though this greater measure of suffering for the godly is undeniable, the main point is and remains that all such suffering must not be viewed as a personal invoice and that any perspective based on this personal calculation is errant and confuses us. The world lies in the power of the evil one, and this is why the world lies in the midst of suffering and why we, as those living in that world, share in that suffering.

CHAPTER SEVENTY-ONE

THE VACCINATION AGAINST COWPOX (1)

Ask, and it will be given to you; seek, and you will find; knock, and it will be opened to you.

MATTHEW 7:7

§ 1 We come now to the subject of the cowpox vaccination. No single issue must be left undiscussed in the present context when that particular issue confronts us with a moral principle. It cannot be emphasized enough that the Reformed confession leads to a well-considered, unwavering practice in life. Up to this point our discussion has shown sufficiently how "sitting on one's hands" is not in accord with Scripture and therefore also not Calvinistic; on the contrary, it is diametrically opposed to Scripture and our Confession. Reference to the single statement of Scripture, "The last enemy is death" [1 Cor 15:26], already shows this. Only the coward quietly bows his head before an enemy, whereas the hero of God engages in fighting everything inimical to God (in this case, death and suffering). Any other conception paralyzes and weakens, and only the confession that summons us to resist suffering with every means at our disposal stimulates our resilience, awakens our courage, and inspires us with high enthusiasm. Indeed, all true nursing of the sick must be based on that outlook. But now another issue intrudes here, and it is the issue of the cowpox vaccination, coupled with our sincere love for those who have become entangled in this issue (whether in this nation or elsewhere), which demands that we calmly and quietly look at their reservation—or, let us frankly say, their *objection*.

The objection sounds something like the following: "I grant that I am obligated to defend myself when my life is threatened; that I must not knuckle under to suffering as long as I see even the smallest chance of averting or limiting it; and that I therefore must combat all distress, all suffering that threatens, all misery that is a harbinger of death and thus in enmity with God. But none of this suggests anything to justify the cowpox vaccination. The reason why I, and so many with me, oppose the vaccination so strongly is not that we want to surrender passively to the vicissitudes of life, but quite otherwise: specifically, that we consider it impermissible to introduce an evil, poisonous substance into a healthy body, in part because this in itself may endanger life, and also because, even if the worst does not materialize, it is thoroughly unnatural. When my child is struck by cowpox, then I certainly will try to deliver my child from that disease with all medical help available. But if my dear child is still perfectly healthy and there is no indication that God will ever visit me with this epidemic in my offspring, then it not only goes against all reason but also is a risky venture with regard to my child, and a defying of God's majesty, if at such a moment I high-handedly introduce the pox vaccine into the healthy blood of my child and boast that I am now protected against the pox."

We have tried to present honestly and fairly the objection that is still heard from so many people. In England, it is true, the battle against the vaccination was conducted on the basis of other objections. One can hardly claim that in that country the objections had a religious basis. But in our country they do. Some individuals in our country may oppose the cowpox vaccination on exclusively medical grounds. But as a rule the opposition in our country comes from the side of religious piety, and we add, *misguided* and *errant* piety. Our ardent wish, therefore, is that we may succeed in elucidating this thorny question in such a way that every misunderstanding may be removed, and that we might replace the wrong thinking on the part of many with the correct, genuinely Scriptural, and hence purely Reformed perspective and practice.

We are assuming here that our point of departure is acknowledged; § 2
namely, that the pox illness results from the curse and is a harbinger and portent of death and that, as such, it must be combatted as an enemy of God.

For this reason we will not return to this point. We refer anyone who still hesitates on this point to our preceding argument. We now wish to address only those who agree that it is our duty to combat the pox illness with all our might when it breaks out, but who consider it impermissible to take measures against it as long as the illness has not yet appeared—specifically, when it is a measure that introduces a toxic, poisonous substance into the healthy body. This appears to them to be both irrational and unnatural, and it is as if they say, "I will see to it that God cannot touch my child with the pox!"

In contrast to such thinking we wish to suggest that in ordinary life no one would consider it impermissible to take precautionary measures to prevent the suffering that can strike our child but that has not yet come. Just like the pox bacillus, the common cold can be fatal when it strikes. Anyone who is careless enough to expose himself to a draft when he is sweaty is in danger of catching cold. And once caught, a cold can easily turn into pneumonia, as is apparent every day. Pneumonia can take us to the grave more quickly than the pox. And just like the pox, pneumonia comes from God. Does anyone therefore consider it impermissible to avert the danger of catching such a cold by putting on warmer clothing, a scarf, or something else? Indeed, if a mother did not wrap her child decently when that child came back from a children's party sweaty and overly excited, having to trek through the cold air, wouldn't such a mother be accused of dereliction of duty?

The dreaded typhoid fever can be as deadly as the pox, and it has spread all too often through poisonous gases and foul fumes that came from the floor of a dwelling due to poor drainage of rotting substances. And here too we ask again: When typhoid fever comes, isn't it sent by God? But no one thinks it is improper to take the necessary precautions against poisonous gases seeping into his dwelling. In fact, doesn't the father of a family stand indicted before God and his child if he neglects to pay attention to this and does not avert the danger from his child? This sort of example could be multiplied indefinitely, but suffice it to say that in general, preventing the outbreak of a deadly illness, whether for ourselves or for family members, and taking extensive preventative measures are not condemned by anyone; rather, they are considered to be everyone's duty. A child who dies of pneumonia because the mother did not protect him against the cold as she should have, or a child who passes away due to typhoid fever because the father did not take adequate precautionary measures by purifying the drainage from his house—in both of these cases the mother and the father respectively are guilty of breaking the sixth commandment.

The first objection that was raised therefore falls away. Our child may show no trace of any pulmonary disease, yet we must take precautionary measures so that our child will not be affected by that deadly disease. In the same way, even when there is no trace of typhoid fever in our loved one, we nevertheless take precautionary measures so that the disease will not strike. By that same token it also is true that if our child does not yet have the pox, but it may strike, we are therefore obligated to take all precautionary measures available to us in order to ensure that our child will not be infected by the pox.

We deliberately insert a comment here about quarantining people suf- § 3
fering from contagious diseases. God clearly prescribes the quarantining of lepers in his Word; on this basis Calvin decreed the isolation of those suffering from the plague in Geneva. But many people have come to believe, by contrast, that it testifies to a weak faith if, in times of an epidemic, a person hesitates to enter the sick room where such contagious persons lie, and that a person displays the strongest faith when he pays no heed to the contagion and acts as if he is oblivious to it. In many a family of this kind all members of the household often are admitted daily to visit such patients. They also go without hesitation to visit others who have contagious patients in their home. They believe that they cannot get the illness if God does not send it, and when God sends it, we must not seek to avoid it. This is then considered "godly," yet it is in fact very *ungodly*. The godly person is only someone who serves God in accordance with his Word and not according to one's own notions and choices. If God clearly reveals in his Word that a person with a contagious illness (in this case, a leper) must be kept apart and quarantined, then this settles and decides the matter, and it is irrevocably certain that those who are truly godly must do the same in the case of other contagious diseases.

This duty knows only one boundary: the boundary of love. The contagious patient is not an animal, but a human being, and as a human being that patient has the right to physical and spiritual care. For each patient, therefore, caregivers must be sought to take care of him or her physically and bring spiritual comfort. And those who have been called to do this from God are under the sacred duty not to let themselves be deterred from discharging their duty through fear of danger. The mother who gives care and the teacher who comes to exhort and comfort do not have an exemption from being infected. In fact, the results of this sort of action are not infrequently the contrary. Time and again we hear how such nurses and comforters become victims of their act of charity. But they must be prepared to do this for God and for the patient.

It is analogous to what happens in the case of a shipwreck, when someone falls into the water or is in mortal danger because of fire. In an incident a few years ago, a Dutch ship encountered a ship in distress. The captain asked who would volunteer to attempt a rescue, and right away eight men expressed their readiness. These eight were lowered in a sloop, the sloop capsized, and all eight men drowned. Yet, another eight men volunteered to do the same. Did the second group of eight think that they were exempted from drowning? Not at all, but they were driven by a sense of duty and human compassion, and they were prepared to sacrifice their lives. Greater love has no one, Jesus says, than he who lays down his life for others [John 15:13]. In this light, a mother who hesitates to nurse children who are sick because of contamination or a pastor who hesitates when there are contagious diseases in his congregation is put to shame by these rugged seafarers.

It is precisely the deluded piety of passive people that is in very serious danger of falling short of the mark through dereliction of duty, and specifically, out of fear for their own lives. The present author once experienced this, even witnessing a very serious case of the pox. In that particular case, a childless husband and wife were affected quite seriously by the pox, and both eventually died. But those two sick people lay helplessly alone. The husband could not care for his wife, nor the wife for her husband. They needed outside help, and since they were poor, the deacons had to take care of their needs. But none of the deacons offered to help, and no one from the congregation could be moved either by love or money to take care of these unfortunate souls. The physician and the present author were the only ones to enter their house, until finally a Roman Catholic girl offered to take on the task and took their care upon herself. And if someone says that this Roman Catholic girl did this to earn a place in heaven, or to do a "good work," it made the profound impression upon the present author that Jesus would have preferred the piety of this girl who helped over and above a piety that left the sufferers to their lot. And it was precisely those people who stayed far away who, due to a sinful passivity, argued against taking precautions. Now, we do not wish to judge anyone in this situation. Some people, granted, are simply more courageous by nature than others. But on the basis of God's sacred Word we continue to maintain that in the case of a contagious illness, it is our duty to isolate the infected persons as much as possible and to avoid all unnecessary contact with them, including members of their household. On the other hand, we must maintain that we should deal with them without fear when it comes to nursing them and caring for them spiritually. This is the discharge of the high duty of love, because it is a *human being* who lies ill.

We proceed under the assumption that we now have addressed the first point adequately. Like the pox, all illness, contagious or not, comes from God, and yet it is our duty to take all available precautions against being infected by this illness. This is true in the case of any illness, even contagious illnesses, and there is therefore no conceivable reason why this definite duty would not also apply to the pox. It is one and the same God who sends us the pox and who at the same time obligates us, when necessary, to combat it so that its deadly power might be broken. And when it has not yet broken out, God also calls upon us and obligates us to take all relevant measures as may serve to prevent its outbreak. To do so is not to fight against God, but quite the opposite: it is to fight in the name of God, and at his command, against the terrible suffering that visits the human race through sin and the curse, and that still continually threatens us. § 4

At this point, nothing has yet been said about the nature of the means that is recommended to us in the cowpox vaccination. Thus, we now stand before the second objection: precautionary measures, even against cowpox, are fine, but they must be purifying means, not the dripping of a toxic substance into the blood. This second objection shifts the issue to an entirely different area, of course. For here two questions arise: first, whether there is an absolute distinction between good and toxic substances; and second, whether toxic substances have been chosen by God as a means for healing.

As for the first question, toxicology (as the study of poisons is called) has shown with increasing clarity that the concept of antibiotics is very elastic and relative, especially since the important studies of Orfila, Christison, Tardieu, Taylor, and others.[1] A poison for a human being is definitely not

1. See, for instance, M. P. Orfila, *Traité des poisons tirés des règnes minéral, végétal et animal, ou Toxicologie générale*, 2 vols. (Paris: Crochard, 1818); Robert Christison, *A Treatise on Poisons* (Edinburgh: Black, 1829); A. Tardieu, P. Lorain, and Z. Roussin, *Empoisonnement par la strychnine, l'arsenic et les sels de cuivre* (Paris: Baillière, 1865); Alfred S. Taylor, *On Poisons, in Relation to Medical Jurisprudence and Medicine* (London: John Churchill, 1848).

always a poison for an animal, and what is toxic to one human being is therefore definitely not always toxic to another. We can become inured to poison, as we can observe in the rat-poison eaters in Stiermarken and the heavy users of opium in India. Poison can even have a beneficial effect. Leaving bacilli from diseases aside for the moment, it can be said that the human body is not suited to ingesting all substances, and that there are substances that will destroy the human body when they enter it—for example, irritating poisons such as rat poison, copper, colocynth, bryony, and so on, which disturb the organic tissue; or narcotic poisons, such as opium, water hemlock, hemlock, and so on, which paralyze the nervous system; or septic poisons such as hydrogen sulfide, and so on, which cause a wrong fermentation process in the blood.

But it does not at all follow from this that poisons as such are something demonic or satanic. For example, atropine, however much it may be a poison otherwise, renders a service against morphine poisoning, and in addition to atropine, strychnine, morphine, mercury, and other poisons are swallowed virtually every day in all kinds of powders and medicines by our patients and bring them a measure of relief. This extends even further in homeopathy. Scarcely any poison exists that is not used in homeopathy. Aconite, bryony, belladonna, *Hyoscyamus niger*, nux vomica, and so forth, are known as poisons when taken by themselves, and we could almost say that homeopathy heals almost exclusively through poison. Therefore, we cannot say that we should never introduce poison into the human body. That would be true if the poisonous substances worked destructively always and under all conditions. But since this is not the case, and the destructive working often comes about only if we introduce the poison in large quantities and under certain conditions into the human body, an entirely different rule follows from this: poisons must not be administered to a human being in such a quantity and in such a way that they harm a person, but only in such a measure and in such a way that they benefit him. When it comes to vaccination, this raises the question of whether the inoculation administers the pox vaccine in such a way that it destroys or in such a way that it saves. If the former is the case, then it is not allowed; if the latter, then it is allowed. Only experience can provide the answer here.

§ 5 All well and good, it may be said, but pox vaccine is not a poison; rather, it is an evil bacterium (that is, a tiny animal that can reproduce exceptionally rapidly), and when introduced into our body, it can destroy the body. The question then shifts somewhat, although it does not alter the main point. Is it permissible for me to use a cat to get rid of mice or a dog to chase a wild boar? Or in general, may I combat a dangerous animal by using another or similar animal? Yes, of course. If we assume that there are indeed tiny microbes in pox vaccine, why would it be impermissible as such to combat one animal through another in the microscopically small animal world? We will not go into the theory here that has been advanced to explain the actual working of the cowpox substance. In providing reasons for its actions, medical science is still very much behind. It is still primarily experimental in nature. That is, it applies means as a result of observing the various effects through experiments, without being able yet to explain how the disease works. For the time being we therefore need only ask whether the poison of an illness in which such tiny microbes are hidden can have a healing effect, and we know in how many ways this question has already been answered. Think only of the serum used in the case of diphtheria. Some years ago, after a serious pulmonary illness, the present author, after initial healing, continued to struggle with coughing up blood, and whatever other means were used, nothing helped, until finally his homeopathic physician from Brussels sent him a preparation prepared from the sputum of his patients. He used the preparation for two days, and the problem cleared up. Leaving entirely aside the question of whether inoculation with the cowpox vaccine carries a danger of an entirely different nature, experience shows that this inoculation was performed on thousands of people without them getting cowpox from the inoculation. Assuming therefore that such malignant microbes are introduced into the blood indeed, experience teaches us through the verified results that these poisonous microbes did not multiply after the inoculation and that no cowpox resulted from them.

In the end everything comes down to the question of whether inoculation, or whatever other means, shows empirically that it reduces susceptibility to cowpox and also does not bring other serious damage to the body. This must be tested, researched, and determined experimentally. If the result of this research is unfavorable, it automatically falls by the wayside. But if the results of the research are favorable, then not only does nothing stand in the way of its application from the standpoint of faith, but it would be foolhardy—even immoral—not to apply a means that God has shown us for the protection of the life of our child. We are not advocating coercion on the part of the government. That would always be impermissible; the government has nothing to say about my body and the body of my child.

Therefore, we will always protest in the name of our civil liberties against any sort of government coercion.

But for our present purposes we are not looking at the matter from this perspective. Rather, we wish to lay it before the conscience of parents. We ask what the sixth commandment imposes on them as a duty for protecting the life of their child. And we would very much like to spare parents who still hesitate from the bitter regret that, sadly, we have seen in so many instances when they finally decide at their child's grave that they will let their remaining children be inoculated. In our opinion, this goal can be achieved when it is clear that the Word of God requires demands combatting all suffering and all illness—that is, when it is understood by God's Word even to be duty through precautionary and preventive measures. Moreover, it will occur when we understand that a poisonous substance as such is not absolutely evil, but can also serve in the process of healing. We will need to recognize that a marvelous connection very often exists between a pathogen and its cure; indeed, the very same pathogen can overwhelm and kill us, but when administered in very small doses and in a different manner, it prevents or bridles the evil.

This understanding, however, is dependent on correct insight into God's providential order concerning both the degree of human effort that God requires of us and how in his common grace he has provided the means to do this. This is why at the beginning of this section we cited the words of Jesus: the one who *seeks*, that one *finds*. These words are intended by Jesus as a spiritual principle; however, they also are given to us as material law. We will elaborate on this in the next chapter.

CHAPTER SEVENTY-TWO

THE VACCINATION AGAINST COWPOX (2)

Test everything; hold fast what is good.

1 THESSALONIANS 5:21

Our multipronged thesis concerning the cowpox vaccination is fairly straightforward. First, the cowpox is a terrible plague that can be fatal for us and for our children. Second, God wills that we combat and attempt to prevent this evil with every means at our disposal. Neglecting this duty can make us guilty of violating the sixth commandment, "You shall not murder" [Exod 20:13]. Third, whether the cowpox vaccination is one of those means is a question that depends entirely on its efficacy. Neither the fact that this substance as such is poisonous nor the fact that it is inoculated into the healthy body condemns it per se. Fourth, its efficacy can be demonstrated only by its results, whether it is able to prevent the illness without causing other illnesses. Fifth, if other means of a less radical nature lead to the same goal, the other means are to be preferred. Sixth, if the cowpox vaccination or whatever other means reaches the intended goal, then the effectiveness that occurs in this process comes from God, and we owe God thanks for it. Seventh, since the cowpox vaccination affects the body, and each individual must by rights remain master over one's body or over those of one's young § 1 children, we must combat any power that wants to impose the cowpox inoculation by coercion. And eighth, measures intended to protect third parties against dangers that affect them through our omission may and must be taken by the authorities, as long as such measures do not assault our body—even as happened in Israel at God's command with respect to leprosy.

What is in fact the heart of this entire painful issue? It comes down to whether the inoculation is indeed effective. What's more, we can add to this the fact that *no other, less violent means achieve the objective equally as well*. But whether we focus only on the first point or the second, ultimately it all comes down to research and experience. For God's Word, as we have observed, not only opposes the failure to apply means and precautionary measures, and thus also the failure to use antibiotics, but it also makes it our duty to combat and prevent this evil, both for ourselves as well as for our children. To the extent that many Christians have opposed or avoided for a long time the cowpox vaccination or some other preventive measures because they felt they were not allowed to make use of them for God's sake, they have been under an incorrect understanding of God's providential order and common grace.

§ 2 Only ongoing research and human experience can be decisive here, and the fact that these alone are determinative serves as a mirror of God's ways made known to human creation by means of common grace. As we argued earlier, God does not give the farmer a special revelation as to how he must plow, sow, harrow, weed, and thresh. The farmer must learn by trying. But as he constantly experiments with new ways and when through much trial and error he has learned the hard way, then it is true what the prophet Isaiah says about this process: "His God teaches him" [Isa 28:26].

Because this is such an important matter we must elucidate the point even further. The argument often is quite correctly made that "it is easy to talk about *learning by trying* when it comes to a field, but this involves my own body or the body of my child, and those must not be endangered by experimentation. Therefore the rule does not apply in this case." The seriousness and weight of this objection deserves our full appreciation. It is entirely correct that the human body may not be treated like a plant or a rock. It would even be far from superfluous to hang a sign in big, bold letters in each of our hospital wards, or at least in each operating room: "As you experiment, never forget that you are dealing with the body *of a human being*." We mention only in passing that the issue of animal vivisection should also be considered to some extent in this context.

But although we grant to this objection all due weight, it does not change the general rule, always and everywhere applicable, that in accordance with God's order we can become wise in all such areas of life simply by investigation and by trial and error. For this reason we deliberately began this chapter with the words from 1 Thessalonians 5:21, "Test everything; hold fast what is good." We do not employ this text lightly or artificially. We know full well that the holy apostle is dealing here not with material, but with moral or spiritual, phenomena. The context shows this. And yet it is preceded by "Do not despise prophecies." That is, do not shrug contemptuously when someone speaks words under a certain inspiration that are stirring. And it is followed by "Abstain from every form of evil." This is essentially what the Apostle John says in 1 John 4:1: "Do not believe every spirit, but test the spirits to see whether they are from *God*, for many false prophets have gone out into the world."

It is helpful to combine these two statements from 1 Thessalonians 5:21 and 1 John 4:1, since they express the same truth from two sides. To someone inclined to simply pass over all kinds of phenomena in the spiritual realm in an arrogant or dismissive manner, the apostle says to him, "Do not do this, but investigate and test everything and keep that which is good in it." But to someone who, on the other hand, is insufficiently critical and goes along with everything, the very same apostle warns this follower, "Do not do this, don't be too hasty, but investigate and test first whether this spiritual manifestation you applaud is from God." After all, it could be from the evil one, for many false prophets have hidden among the true prophets. In both cases, testing includes investigating (because without investigating we cannot form a judgment), but in the narrower sense testing obligates us to pass judgment on something. We must decide, and decide for ourselves in all things. To test all things is a task that is far from easy; it requires effort and can bring us into intense anxiety. But this does not discharge us from our obligation. We must not dismissively or arrogantly pass things by. We must take them into account, and ask ourselves and decide for ourselves whether they are presented to us for our use or as a temptation to be avoided. If new phenomena appear in the spiritual realm (for example, spiritualism, the Salvation Army, the healing of illness without medicines, and so forth), then Scripture requires that we not simply say, "This is all simply deception." Rather, we are to investigate them, become aware of them, and judge them with such a knowledge of the facts that we know why and to what extent we must condemn and avoid these phenomena. On the other hand, we do not simply go along with them because they are stimulating novelties; rather, we test whether they are from God or belong to the realm of evil, a realm characterized by false prophets who go out into the world. Thus, in no case should arbitrariness or laziness, arrogance or rashness ever lead us. Rather, we should make every effort to search all things, test everything, and finally decide for ourselves and for our children with clear perception and with knowledge.

Note well that this is the rule in the spiritual and moral realm. At first glance this surprises us, since in this area direct instruction and intentional revelation from God serve us. We have the holy Scriptures, and in the holy Scriptures we have all kinds of intentional and clear directions that demarcate a sharp boundary between good and evil. In this sphere of living we easily might be inclined to set aside our own investigative efforts and our own "experiments," as it were, and thereby disregard important lessons from experience. But in the spiritual realm too we must be careful not to do this, for even if God were to send us some sort of partial direct revelation, that revelation still would give us only general principles, and it would remain our task to apply these principles appropriately in every relevant case. In the church of Christ, then, we find continual instruction by the Holy Spirit that through the centuries brings us further and clarifies our understanding. This instruction by the Holy Spirit does not occur through mystical direct revelation; rather, it comes by way of the spiritual experience of believers and the investigations of theologians. Believers in general and theologians among them then test this in all kinds of ways and thus learn on the basis of the results which of those many ways leads to the goal and which does not. The next generation benefits from that experience. In this way being guided and taught by investigation, testing, trial and error, and experience, the Christian church comes ever further into the knowledge of the "straight paths of the Lord" [Acts 13:10]. It is therefore the fault and sin of those who themselves continually reinterpret holy Scripture anew that in their blindness they are oblivious to the Holy Spirit's instruction that comes by way of believers' experience through the centuries. They want to do everything autonomously and only according to their own insights, instead of benefiting from the experience of previous generations.

§ 3 If this is a general rule that applies to both the spiritual and the moral realm, then it follows that the same rule, *a fortiori*, continues to apply in the material realm or, if you will, on the level of our natural life, where diseases such as cowpox occur, and where the subsequent means and precautions against cowpox belong. It stands to reason that God the Lord would have informed us directly about the nature of this terrible illness and also about the effective means to heal or prevent it. God alone knows completely what cowpox is. God knows fully and absolutely its cause, its workings, and its consequences. And thus God also knows with absolute conclusiveness which means are present in creation to nip the evil in the bud, and also which means can arrest it if it breaks out. It is therefore understandable that we sometimes think, "Well then, if God knows all this, and he observes our suffering, why does God keep all this knowledge to himself, and why doesn't he share it immediately and directly with suffering humanity?" When we apply this to other illnesses, we immediately sense the desperation that is lodged at the heart of that question. The *cinchona* tree has existed since creation, and since creation quinine taken from its bark has had the same power to heal fever that it does now. God knew this, for he created this tree, and with his own hand he placed in it this power against fever. And yet for centuries God has visited fever upon human civilization and allowed human beings to suffer bitterly under those fevers, without revealing to them where the medicine was hidden. God has not willed to tell humans, but he has willed that humans should discover it for themselves.

The same applies to so many types of surgery that were done in the past. God knew how surgeries could bring about infection and death if measures were not taken to sterilize the area of exposed flesh. God knew that this infection and death were the result of not using disinfected substances. God saw those substances; humankind did not. Yet God did not point them out to human beings from the beginning but let them be discovered. Now we do possess this knowledge, and we can perform operations under antiseptic, precautionary conditions, with the fortunate result that infection and death do not occur. But we must remember that for centuries thousands upon thousands died from such operations. God saw this and knew that it could be prevented, yet he has let all these people die, willing that in due time human beings should discover this through investigation and experimentation. Recently a wealthy man in England gave five million guilders to advance research of this nature, and we must simply conclude that this wealthy and generous donor took the right path that God wants us to follow. What we call medical research, which also includes research into hygiene, is nothing but this process of investigating, trying, and testing, and we cannot be sufficiently grateful to researchers who continually help us move forward. It simply can no longer be denied that there are effective means against all kinds of suffering. No one will deny that God has known this. It nevertheless is certain that God has not revealed them directly to us. No other possibility remains therefore than that God wills that we discover them ourselves by seeking, find them by testing them, and become wiser through trial and error, through experience.

We cannot go into more depth here as to why God has ordained this way and did not give direct revelation concerning all these things of natural life. It is sufficient, however, if we understand that the rule that we only find by seeking, that by investigating we become wiser, and that we learn by experience and trial, is imprinted deeply in our soul as the rule established by God. This also means that we permanently abandon as erroneous the notion that we go against God's will if we search for the means. Job beautifully and poignantly portrays this searching, investigating, and exploring by man in the material and natural realm.

> Surely there is a mine for silver,
>   and a place for gold that they refine.
> Iron is taken out of the earth,
>   and copper is smelted from the ore.
> Man puts an end to darkness
>   and searches out to the farthest limit
>   the ore in gloom and deep darkness.
> He opens shafts in a valley away from where anyone lives;
>   they are forgotten by travelers;
>   they hang in the air, far away from mankind; they swing to and fro.
> As for the earth, out of it comes bread,
>   but underneath it is turned up as by fire.
> Its stones are the place of sapphires,
>   and it has dust of gold.
>
> That path no bird of prey knows,
>   and the falcon's eye has not seen it.
> The proud beasts have not trodden it;
>   the lion has not passed over it.
>
> Man puts his hand to the flinty rock
>   and overturns mountains by the roots.

> He cuts out channels in the rocks,
> and his eye sees every precious thing.
> He dams up the streams so that they do not trickle,
> and the thing that is hidden he brings out to light.
> (Job 28:1–11)

Does holy Scripture reject man's searching? On the contrary. God himself has placed dominion over all of nature, even over the lion and the eagle, in the hands of human creation. What is disapproved is only that arrogant and foolhardy human beings should become proud through these explorations, not honor God's wise order in all things, but rather imagine that all this is due to their own wisdom.[1] And as it applies to illness and pestilence, we may not sit still, but it is God's will and his way that humans should investigate whether God himself has put into nature certain powers and means to arrest such illnesses and to prevent these pestilences. Those who succeed in discovering such means therefore glorify the Creator and bring to light a long-hidden power from God's creation. And those who thus prevent or avert suffering perform an act of love toward their neighbor unto distant generations.

Perhaps someone will persist and say, "All well and good, but the fact § 4
remains that the cowpox vaccination has helped bring children to their grave, and experts claim that even if they do not cause a sudden death, these vaccinations not infrequently transfer the illness from one person to someone else and break the vitality of the inoculated body." We have an answer for this as well. In the first place, our publication is not a medical journal and as such does not wish or intend to publish medical advice for or against the cowpox vaccination. The only thing this publication concerns itself with is showing from holy Scripture what position we as good Christians should take in regard to such an issue, and then we affirm the following rule: "Test everything; hold fast to that which is good. Learn by experimenting. Find out what is and what is not effective. Choose the best from what is effective. And glorify your Creator and your God in all that

1. In the next verses Job points out that this searching and digging is not the way to wisdom; rather, "the fear of the Lord, that is wisdom, and to turn away from evil is understanding" (v. 28). What man finds by his searching and exploring is knowledge—but Scripture does not reject this searching, as long as the difference between finding knowledge and finding wisdom is recognized.

you have found and all that is effective. This is the path, even in the *spiritual* realm, and therefore *a fortiori* in material and natural life."

Second, such testing may indeed cost human lives, but this is not a fact that as such invalidates the rule. No one will dispute that it is God's will that we sail the seas, and yet how many human lives did it cost before we learned how to sail the seas? Building houses is a duty, yet how many human lives did it cost before we understood the art of properly constructing scaffolding for a building? We use horses and oxen, yet how many human lives did it cost to learn how to handle horses and to learn how to use horned cattle? In our small part of the world alone, we can still count in the hundreds those who each year lose their lives through accidents with horses or cattle. It therefore would seem clear that God's order for humankind in learning to know nature and in using nature certainly does not preclude loss of human life. What, then, is our basis for assuming that the preservation of human life will always be guaranteed in the process of researching that which can deliver the human body from disease and illnesses? If this sort of response is thought to be harsh, so be it, but we must acknowledge that this is precisely how things are. All the power that we presently exercise over nature, all the comforts of life, all the use of the natural things in which we presently rejoice have been acquired by research and experimentation that cost many human lives in earlier centuries. And as a rule, agriculture, factories, shipping, and commerce still claim the sacrifice of many human lives. We find it marvelous that we can easily light lamps by means of a match. That is fine, but let us not forget how many human lives the manufacture of matches alone claims.

Third, from what has been said it follows that it is nothing "unnatural" if discovering a means to stop, heal, or prevent illnesses and disease brings the sacrifice of human lives. Concomitantly, the cowpox vaccination as such certainly does not stand condemned because it has caused death or transmitted other illnesses now and then. Several other conclusions also follow from this. First, further research into discovering whether other, less dangerous means will lead us to the same goal, such as cleanliness and isolation, must be stopped. In this regard, just think of the laws concerning leprosy. Second, research must be continued to determine whether the inoculation is really effective and whether any derivative conclusions are correct. Third, research must continue to determine whether the harmful effects of the vaccination can be prevented with better treatment or more cautious application. Fourth, on this point each one must decide for himself, and the father for his child, so that no one may coerce us against our will. And, fifth, should the treatment be effective, anyone who would want to apply this remedy without invoking God's blessing and thanking God cannot claim the label of being pious. Rather, his actions in this matter would be entirely ungodly—that is, apart from God—and hence impermissible.

Our conclusion, therefore, is that in this instance our religious faith does not stand in the way of the application (that is, vaccination), just as it does not in the case of any other means that are claimed to heal, arrest, or prevent illness or disease. The only question that is decisive is whether it achieves its goal. Aside from this, everyone is obligated, to apply it with all caution if it is effective, and to reject it if it is not effective.

CHAPTER SEVENTY-THREE

INSURANCE

When he [Cain] built a city, he called the name of the city after the name of his son, Enoch.

Genesis 4:17

§ 1 Thus far we have attempted to shed necessary light not only on precautionary measures in general but also specifically on the vaccination against cowpox (always to the exclusion of the medical aspect of this issue). This raises the related issue of insurance.

Our times demand that this be discussed. As often as a newly emerging factor in life reaches such a rapid expansion and begins to represent such power, the question must be raised what effect this new phenomenon will have on Christian ethics. This is all the more necessary with respect to insurance because in our Christian circles two views have emerged. The one is infatuated with it, while the other rejects it as sinful. This dichotomy should not exist. We must not allow the impression that such an important matter can be decided simply by whether a person has a strong feeling for or against it. One's rule in life must not rest either on one's own pleasure and discretion or on the opinion of others. Our neighbor is not our ruler. God the Lord is king over our hearts and lives; he is the omnipotent one, and not we ourselves. Therefore, on the matter of insurance, we must ask ourselves only this one thing: does God command me to participate or prohibit me from participating? Or, in the absence of a specific scriptural command, does God nevertheless allow and permit it so freely that there can be no question of God "turning a blind eye" (let alone a question of it being sin), or is it simply a tool that he himself places at our disposal?

We initially respond by framing the difference as seriously as possible. Our purpose is neither to absolve the insurance industry nor to defend the thesis that in the final analysis it would be better if the insurance industry did not exist. Rather, we only wish to acknowledge that differences of opinion be allowed to exist at the present. We do not begin our discussion of this subject in order to promote the notion that in the final analysis it would be better if we were to abandon all insurance, or that because of our weakness it is such a small sin that our conscience may gloss over it. Nor do we say that there should never be insurance in a truly Christian society, or that, since the non-Christian world accepts it, we cannot very well do anything but "go with the flow." On the contrary, we detest all such give-and-take in the ethical realm. Straight paths must be drawn for our footpaths. Those straight paths must follow the divine track. And ultimately, in all disputes of this nature each of us must come to the conclusion that we can go on with a firm stride, without hesitation or vacillation.

If on any particular issue we come to the conclusion that such a new phenomenon is evil, that it is sin before God, then we may not in any way have anything to do with it. At that point, preaching and catechesis must earnestly warn against it. And then we must rebuke in the name of the Lord those brothers or sisters who have let themselves be lured into it. Conversely, if the result of our investigation is that we are in the clear before God by participating in the matter of insurance—indeed, that in many cases such participation in insurance is a duty imposed on us by God—then we must have the courage to defend that position, not surreptitiously but before the eyes of all, not sparing those brothers or sisters who still hold the wrong view as if in their resistance there lay a higher form of piety; rather, we must have the courage to explain the matter to them earnestly and tenderly. We cannot have both the wholly pious and the merely half pious. The full crown of piety must adorn us all. It also is unacceptable to have a narrow conscience on the one hand and to let the door of our conscience stand ajar on the other. If slackness creeps in, we must mutually and duly sharpen our consciences. We absolutely refuse to take the position that ordinary Christians, pious persons of the common sort, could participate in an insurance program if need be, but that someone who aspires to be very godly should abstain from it instead. This leads to a distinction between a "higher" and a "lower" form of ethical behavior that finds no support in God's Word. God's commands alone establish the rules of life, and those commands apply to all. In addition, being convinced of one's own piety, going about with a very pious demeanor and desiring to be perceived as extraordinarily spiritual, often is a reflection of pride and a mind-set that says, "I am holier than thou; get thee away from me." And since God gives his grace only to the humble, we must continually enjoin one another, spurred by love, to strictly abstain from pursuing such "hyperspirituality."

§ 2 At the same time we are very aware of the fact that when the matter of insurance emerged, it was viewed as distasteful by many ordinary Christians. And to those who say that this is what they always believed, we simply challenge them at this point, in light of our previous discussion, to search their own consciences and answer the question before God of whether they perhaps were more intent on insuring their house and furniture than on demonstrating genuine faith.

In the writings of our spiritual forefathers there is reference time and again to "assurance" and to being "assured"; however, in context these words always refer not to what is now called "insurance" or "life insurance" but to the assurance of eternal life. Conviction and certainty are what Reformed people wanted from the beginning. They objected to being tossed to and fro. This endless lack of foundations is precisely what they reproved in Pelagianism and Arminianism. But they applied that certainty, that assurance, that firmness in life in the first place to their hearts, to the life of their soul, to their eternal fate and to their relationship with the Most High. But when we look at our present generation with such a yardstick in hand, shouldn't we register the complaint that the assurance, the certainty, the firmness that we now look for has shifted almost exclusively to insurance for material needs and for the needs of wife and children who remain behind, whereas the question "Are you assured of your election to eternal life?" is likely to be answered by otherwise wonderful "Christians" with an uncertain shaking of the head. These types have "hope," and they sometimes dare to trust the love of God, but are they assured of their salvation? No, they cannot say that they are. Twenty years ago they had no assurance, and they still have none now, and twenty years from now the same will still be the case. In truth, in their dying they will pray and they will sigh, but they will remain strangers to the apostolic confession "We know that we have passed from death into life" [1 John 3:14].

Given this possibility, we acknowledge that being fanatical about material insurance must most definitely be rejected. Those who might fear that their household goods might not be insured in the event of a fire, yet whose family members would not be insured against the detriment of eternal damnation should a deadly illness break out in their household tomorrow (and thus have no insurance toward eternal life) may not say that they themselves stand in right relationship with God. Rather, they seem to be more attached to mammon than to God. This is a strong statement, yet perhaps not too strong. Some more-highly educated Christians look down upon other Christians in lower circles who are still hesitant to get fire insurance but do not rest until they have found the assurance of faith of eternal life. These more-highly educated Christians may do well to ask themselves whether those others in fact will precede them into the kingdom of heaven. We, for our part, have no intentions of writing in our publication (a publication that seeks in the first place God's glory and only in the second place occupies itself with social questions) a single word about the insurance industry that would take anything away from the necessity to assure oneself of one's election by God. Should insurance companies or the press want to involve themselves in this particular issue, then we expressly ask them to note clearly that the *Heraut*, after first pointing out the higher demand that all people insure themselves in terms of the eternal life, has addressed the question of "life insurance" in terms of our earthly existence.

As for the objections to obtaining life insurance that have arisen among § 3
many, we can reduce them to three. First, insurance has been seen as an attempt by human beings to resist the trials that God wants to visit upon us. Second, it has been thought that the life of faith would be undermined if every emotion of fear were gradually removed from life so that trust in God's fatherly care would decline. And third, the perception has been present that the insurance industry has put out a lure to eventually lead people in the direction of swindle, cheating, arson, and even murder.

Let us first look more closely at these three objections before addressing the matter itself. We immediately acknowledge straightforwardly that the first objection does not come out of thin air in the least. The reference often used in this regard is what is written about Cain in Genesis 4:17. After having fled to the land of Nod, east of Eden, Cain first of all "built a city." The translators of the Dutch Bible added a marginal note that Cain did this "for assurance, from the fear of his conscience, whereas the godly patriarchs lived in tents or huts." It will not do merely to dismiss this marginal note with a condescending smile. At the same time, this brief note is in fact too brief, and therefore untenable. For if what this note says were applied as a general rule, then it would follow that all those who founded a city or lived in a city, at least in a fortified city, sinned; and all those who fear the Lord should live outside the city. If rigidly applied, it would mean that even living in a stone house deserves disapproval, and only the Bedouins, who wander about in tents, or the settlers in America, who live in wooden houses or huts, are without blame. But this, of course, was not the intent of the note. When the translators wrote this note, they themselves were in the stronghold of Leiden, which in the seventeenth century was still fortified with walls, ramparts, gates, and moats against surprise attacks. In addition, they wrote this note not in a tent or hut, but certainly in a house of stone, well protected against rain and wind. But all this does not deny the fact that their marginal note contains an element of truth and that the opponents of insurance are not at all foolish when they apply this observation to the matter of carrying insurance.

A number of very knowledgeable professors among the interpreters of Genesis have noted, not only previously but also in the second half of our nineteenth century, that the report concerning the city that Cain built certainly indicates how the secular direction of Cain's view of life finds expression in this first construction of a city, and how the same line of thinking is developed in what is reported about Lamech, Jubal, and Tubal-Cain. Today it is still the case that the greatest concentrations of unrighteousness are found predominantly in the large cities, and that specifically mighty metropolises such as London and Paris, Berlin and Vienna, New York and Chicago are veritable hotbeds of all kinds of sin and iniquity. Of course, no one, we acknowledge, would say that everything is holy in rural areas. Much sin is committed on tenant farms too. Rural fairs are often outpourings of licentiousness. And the girls from rural villages who come to the city to be servants (similar to the conscripts into military service who move from villages to the city to be garrisoned) often show all too clearly how sin does not simply come from the city but from the human heart, and that the human heart is equally depraved in rural villages.

Yet even when this may be true, it remains an incontrovertible fact that in the villages there is still a stronger sense of dependence on God. In many urban circles, by contrast, there is a prominent notion that humans have everything within their own power and that God does not have to be taken into account anymore. Consequently, wickedness and licentiousness take on much more refined and audacious forms in the large cities. Dangerous dispensers of shamefulness may be found in rural villages too, but the breeding ground, especially the hotbed of wickedness and outrage, lies in larger cities and not in rural areas. Thus, there is indeed in Cain's attempts to build a city an attempt to go in the wrong direction and to steel himself against God. God's judgment had been, "You shall be a fugitive and a wanderer on the earth" [Gen 4:12], but Cain resisted this and attempted to evade the judgment by building a city. It was not a city such as ours, of course; nor was it a completely finished stronghold. But implicit in the biblical narrative is that he built the dwellings for his family together and protected them in one way or another with excavations and walls in such a way that he thought he could withdraw quietly and securely in his permanent city.

In this light, we may grant that it is not utterly foolish of the opponents § 2
of insurance to appeal to this marginal note. The reader may judge accordingly whether it can be denied that the majority of people take out all kinds of insurance from motives similar to Cain's. Isn't it the case that anyone insured against fire damage, crop damage, accidents, travel risks, damages from illness and death, even funeral expenses, all too often and all too soon gets into a frame of mind that he or she now no longer has anything to fear? Isn't it to be expected that such a person can quietly await anything that may come, and that this false sense of peace of mind and assurance silences the prayer for God's gracious help and preservation? To an extent it even might give a sense that humans no longer need to take God into consideration in their lives. One need only read or reread the writings and pieces in circulars and newspapers in which these manifold kinds of insurance are offered, and then evaluate everything written in those articles and circulars in the light of the glory of God and the fear of his name; it immediately becomes apparent that we have gained virtually nothing. The companies that recommend life insurance speak movingly about impending death and equally movingly about the fate that awaits those who become widows and orphans. Even at train stations they try to play on our feelings by means of moving images that point to dying and to those who remain behind, abandoned. But God remains on the outside, and it is always again humans who through their cleverness have found the means to take their fate into their own hands and safeguard themselves from all damages. It therefore must not be denied that the insurance business definitely has undermined religious faith and that in broader circles it has given rise to the sense that

a new means has been found to make human beings masters of their own fate and, in this way, to deprive God of his mastery over our destiny.

This is why we do not detract anything from this first objection to having insurance. Instead, we readily concede that, in the past, much prayer for God's honor was offered that now has been silenced. We only deny, as we will further demonstrate, that this undeniable fact might constitute for us a reason to reject insurance. Few people would deny that an unfettered use of holy Scripture can give rise to all kinds of heresy and even to all manner of moral aberration. Think only of the Mormons.[1] But it certainly does not follow that the unfettered use of holy Scripture must be abandoned. And here it is also quite conceivable that, even when insurance might retard prayer and result in a false human self-confidence, it does not follow in the least that insurance as such cannot be a gift of God but must be avoided as an invention of Satan.

§ 3 We may deal more briefly with a second objection, which is directly related to the first. Accordingly, it maintains that a person who is insured has less fear of life and therefore forgets to seek the fatherly care of our God. What is meant is that insurance takes the place of God. We begin to live and rely on our insurance policy instead of on the promise of our God. As a consequence, therefore, not only does the evil heart passively let go of the fear of God, but the active trusting of God, seeking God's favor, or seeking the love of God, also decreases. We agree only in part with this second objection. Perhaps we state it too strongly when we say that the person who rests in the love of God purely as a protection against possible danger is purely egotistical in his or her religious faith to begin with and that the essential knowledge and assurance of the love of God simply is not found in that person. The person who truly rests in the love of God with the whole heart does not seek God in the first place for gain, nor solely to avert harm. That person's concern is God himself, in the knowledge of what Asaph sang: "What would my heart, what would my eye / on earth desire beside thee?"[2] And we deny that a true child of God who rests in this sense in the fatherly love of God would ever set aside his or her love for God by simply taking out insurance.

1. Presumably, Kuyper has in mind here the practice of polygamy associated with Mormonism.
2. See Psalm 73, stanza 13, in *Het boek der Psalmen* (Amsterdam: H. Brandt et al., 1773).

At the same time, we do not reject this second objection entirely, to the extent that we concede that even for "the holiest men, while in this life," as the Heidelberg Catechism calls the very godly, the prayer for help always remains one of the factors of their religion.[3] The Psalms prove this abundantly. And surely it cannot be denied that in these "holiest men" this added stimulus loses something of its acuity when they are "insured" against all damages. In centuries past, the prayer to be kept from disaster throughout the night and accident was much more fervent than it is now. What we are denying is only that insurance should be disapproved of or avoided for this reason. In prior ages, when anything approximating a police force was still very inadequate and people were regularly put in danger of being exposed to crime, the prayer for protection during the night was undoubtedly much more fervent. But who would say that the police and law-enforcement officers therefore should be abolished?

This train of thought can be expanded even further. The sense of fear that drove people to pray in the midst of distress was much stronger in every respect in earlier periods than it is now. For example, one could not travel without risk of falling into the hands of robbers. In the Psalms we continually hear the cry of fear in the face of this terrible danger. It might arise from pits having been dug in the road, or traps having been set, or from miserable victims falling into the strong hands of brigands. Now we travel safely throughout an entire continent. In our railroad cars, with their silly partitions, we might be in danger on long journeys from a fellow traveler, but in America that danger no longer exists either. All cars are connected, and one can travel perfectly safely there. In the past there was no street lighting, and one could not safely walk the streets once darkness fell. Today, gas [lighting] has also removed that danger. When all roofs were still made of wood and there was no fire department, there was continual fear that an entire village or city could burn down. Today the fire department in our cities comes to our door at the first emergency notice. As long as there was no compass, a journey across the sea was an endless one in the face of mortal danger. Today the compass directs us safely. In short, the whole richer development of life has continually served to ward off danger, make life safer, and make human existence much more tranquil. And even when it cannot in the least be denied that the dangers of life in the past led

3. Heidelberg Catechism, Lord's Day 44, Q&A 114.

to increased prayer, and that the relative absence of danger in our present life has caused prayer to decrease, this would not lead anyone to say that the compass, fire department, street lighting, and so forth are all from the evil one, and that we should return to the time of robbery and murder so that we can become more pious again due to fear.

CHAPTER SEVENTY-FOUR

INSURANCE (2)

Bear one another's burdens, and so fulfill the law of Christ.

GALATIANS 6:2

The third objection points to the many kinds of sin—sometimes of a very gruesome nature—to which insurance has seduced people. For example, an individual insured his house or his household effects for a rather high amount and then personally set fire to it to enrich himself with the insurance money. An old insured ship was sent out to sea and, if at all possible, beached in such a way that it was broken up. Persons whose lives were insured for a large amount died a violent death. Even small funeral policies were so enticing that monsters in human form sometimes killed several people through poisoning or by other means in order to receive that amount of $300 or $400. Almost no insurance providers have escaped such offensive and scandalous abuse, and the facts that brought this to light lead us to hazard only vague conjectures about the many other evil practices that succeeded without raising a scandal and therefore never came to court. But precisely because of this sort of possibility, the facts of the matter have surfaced with even greater clarity. Such extreme cases have been carefully investigated, their nefarious character has been demonstrated, and they have been judged in a most convincing manner. This terrible register of sins can in no way be mitigated. It is entirely true that these cases occurred and do occur. And we hasten to add that we quite understand how § 1 a somewhat tender conscience, when its voice is sounded within a person whose imagination is easily stimulated, becomes so indignant when it hears the reports of such cases, that such a person does not want to hear a word about insurance, being mindful of the saying that we must hate "even the garment stained by the flesh" (Jude 23).

Yet it is doubtful whether this conclusion is correct, since it is based on the general thesis that a matter that leads to or becomes the cause of many horrors or crimes is objectionable for that reason per se and hence should be avoided. Of course, if this general thesis is accepted, then the conclusion follows immediately, since insurance contains this evil element, and even when these horrors are incidental, insurance encourages the thought of doing them and thus elicits them. But is this in itself sufficient reason, or at least a license, to condemn insurance as such?

§ 2 Take savings accounts as an illustration. Ask yourself whether saving our earnings (for example, setting aside extra income or setting aside a portion of our earnings for possible illness or for old age) should always be considered objectionable. We could also make this very point through many other illustrations, but let us look at savings, since saving money is most closely related to insurance. In the past, people saved and stashed away money so that if they died, they would leave the widow a few thousand guilders; in the same way, people now take out a life insurance policy in order to have a sum paid out to the widow all at once, or an annuity of, say, $50 per week. With saving money we confront similar issues. We must take care of our surviving next of kin, and if we don't do it through insurance, we will have to do it through savings. But hasn't saving money also led to misfortune, and hasn't it tempted and stimulated people to commit all kinds of sin? What else do those recurrent reports of burglaries, robberies, and murder at the homes of elderly and the sick communicate? After all, it was known that they had stored up and saved a small means, and knowledge of this one person's savings ended up tempting the other to rob and to kill. Of course, it is true that the saving was not done with the intent of inducing robbery and murder. Hence, in this sort of case we need to make certain distinctions.

Nevertheless, the fact remains that saving, especially such small amounts, year after year has led and enticed people virtually everywhere to commit homicide and scandalous robberies on isolated farms and even among relatives. It was the money that had been saved and about which people had heard that stimulated the imagination toward robbery and that led to murder, which was necessary to make the robbery successful. But fully apart from these horrors, isn't it a fact that this desire to save, once it has made itself master of our hearts, has tempted so many people to withhold from their wives and children even money for the daily necessities, to become attached to the money as such, and to stifle all nobler impulses of the heart? Indeed, aren't there many instances known where remote relatives intentionally took poor care of their ill family member, deliberately exposing them to dangers in order to hasten their departure from this earth and in order to plunder the victim through death?

Cannot the same be said of an inheritance—in fact of anything through which one human being can receive the blessing of mammon upon someone's death or by violently murdering another human being? Do we dare draw the conclusion from this that all forms of saving, all forms of inheriting, all kinds of legacies, and so forth, are therefore from the evil one and must be condemned? If not, shouldn't we acknowledge that the conclusion *cannot* be maintained that insurance must be condemned if only because it so often stimulates all kinds of sin before God and wickedness among people? Indeed, if a statistic were drawn up of the burglaries and murders occasioned by the knowledge that saved money was to be found, and if this statistic were compared with the murders occasioned by insurance, wouldn't it become obvious that moving away from individuals' savings toward participating in an insurance program has led to a quite considerable *decrease* in the number of murders? For our part, we would not hesitate for a moment to answer this question affirmatively, as long as the numbers are taken proportionally. For in contrast to the ten who in the past saved money themselves, there are now a hundred or more who have taken out an insurance policy. We therefore must wonder what percentage of murders occurred in the past because of savings, and what percentage at present because of insurance.

Here, too, we see again that we must not resolve such complex questions based on the impression of the moment. Here, too, we are dealing not only with use but also with *abuse*. For it is striking that all such cases as those to which insurance has led are not intended by the insurance industry, and they do not flow from its legitimate use but exclusively from the *abuse* of insurance. It is not the insurance as such that brings about the evil; rather, it is the sinful heart, the addiction to mammon that looks at the insurance industry, as it looks at all things, to see whether it can be turned into an instrument of sin. Marriage is holy and good, but who will deny that the sin that mammon fosters in the heart has repeatedly enticed people to abuse marriage as a means to gain mastery over a sum of money? And once this goal had been achieved, people robbed the original owner by means of extravagance. Or take the case of a woman who causes the demise of her husband, especially if he is elderly, in order to enter into a second marriage later, enriched by the first husband's possessions, and then indulges in wanton luxury with the money acquired—or, shall we say, robbed—through the desecration of marriage and through murder.

There is nothing in this world that sin does not assail, abuse, and turn into sin, especially where money is involved. Cheating widows, robbing orphans, embezzling funds, robbing even churches of their possessions, falsifying wills, using threats to profit from a will, extorting through slander, and so forth, together constitute a broad range of evil deeds to which "sin + money" has seduced and stimulated immoral people. What are the scandalous frauds to which commerce and even the stock exchange are daily inducements? Has shipping traffic developed anywhere without a pirate, so to speak, automatically turning up? In short, throughout the ages among all peoples, can we conceive of any action among humans where money was involved, or where money was in someone's possession, such that this money has not led to fraud, to cheating, to clever and ingenious ways of conning someone out of it, or to violent robbery and murder? Mammon has always appeared to be a demon to the sinful heart, and there is no force on earth that has incited more to wickedness, baseness, and all kinds of abominations. The guilt lies, then, not with saving money, nor with the right to inherit it, nor with commerce, nor with the stock exchange, nor with shipping, but with the heart of man; as Jesus said, "Out of the heart of man, come evil thoughts" (Mark 7:21). But if this is the case, we should not make an exception to this generally valid rule when it comes to insurance, and we should judge that the horrors to which people point are to be blamed not on insurance itself, not on the insurance industry as such, but on the sinful heart and on the worship of mammon; these are the guilty parties.

§ 3 At this point, have we successfully shown that the insurance business is not blameworthy and hence must be approved? By no means. There are still two things that must be investigated. First, we must consider whether insurance as such is an instrument permitted by the principles of holy Scripture, and second, whether the degree of good produced compared to the evil caused by insurance surpasses the degree of evil. The second point can be dealt with more briefly than the first. The advantages of insurance for human society are so immeasurable that the evil to which insurance has lured people barely deserves mention as far as the number of cases is concerned. All we have to look at is how much effort it takes, in the case of a fire not covered by insurance, to get the unfortunate victims, who lost with one fell swoop their household goods or the whole inventory of their business, back on their feet again. Is it possible to list all the people who in the past were permanently reduced in this way to the beggar's life?

And yet insurance against fire loss is by far not even the most beneficial. Much greater is the blessing that accrues to our human society from insurance against illness, accidents, old age, and death. The suffering that once was so common and yet today still occurs certainly has receded. For example, take situations in which a protracted illness has made the breadwinner bedridden, or in which a fall or accident made someone an invalid and incapable of working, or in which old age took away someone's ability to work. And there are still even situations involving widows and orphans who remain behind, helpless. These various forms of misery were and remain so immense that they have created and fed into the problem of poverty—with its attendant immorality and decimation of entire families—in the coming generation to such an extent that it is impossible to overstate the benefits of the creation of something like insurance. This creation already serves as a dam against the broad stream of wickedness and suffering that exist, and its benefits will grow even more as its scope increases.

Calls go up from all sides for pension benefits for the aged worker, and we too have continued to be emphatic about its need. The reason for this, quite simply, is that the salvation of the lower class from the deadly grasp of thoroughgoing poverty cannot be achieved in any other way. Poverty causes humankind to degenerate, it stimulates within the heart the urge to sin in all kinds of ways, and in its consequences it leads to all manner of sexual immorality, robbery, and murder on a far greater scale than insurance ever has. We must not allow ourselves to be misled by appearances. On the one hand, we should not exaggerate the forms of wickedness to which insurance might entice people, but on the other hand, we also should not close our eyes to the far greater scope of wickedness that poverty encourages in exceedingly diverse forms. Instead, we should carefully take stock of truth and fairness. If we do that, listing all of the crimes to which insurance has led or tempted others and then listing all of the outrages and wickedness into which poverty has caused whole generations to sink, then we will see that the book of insurance contains ten pages filled with positive entries, in contrast to one page with negative entries, whereas the poverty that results from being uninsured has almost no positive assets. At the same time, we could fill page after page with entries describing the ills that are caused by poverty. We therefore must not constantly stare one-sidedly at the obvious problems associated with insurance; rather, we must ask ourselves how much good and how many benefits stand on the other side of the ledger. And no less should we be thinking about the even worse problems listed in the debit ledger if human society should continue to struggle along without the benefit of insurance.

§ 4 Meanwhile, we readily admit, the ends do not justify the means. If the means as such were found to be evil, forbidden by God, and thus improper, we would be prohibited from using them even if the results of insurance were blindingly attractive. We therefore must now confront the central question—namely, whether insurance as such is a good or an evil instrument. Insurance must be understood as a creation *through which the financial loss that threatens our communal life no longer falls upon the individual affected but is spread equally over all*. We know very well that this definition is entirely accurate only so long as everyone participates in such insurance. What's more, we do not lose sight of the fact that there are losses that do affect everyone and that differ only in that they affect one person more readily or more forcefully than the next person. But in discussing insurance as such, we are viewing it in its most general and complete form, in order to both elucidate it and test it by the principles of the Word of God. In such a study it is not possible to look at all the different forms of insurance at the same time. We must therefore ask ourselves, What is the actual impetus, the actual purpose, of insurance in general? Only then can we focus on various forms of insurance as they relate to this general principle. We therefore stick with the definition given above.

Our life is threatened by loss on all sides. That loss might be the result of fire, of theft, of flood, of hail, of illness, of accidents, of old age, of death, or of something else. As a rule, loss does not strike everyone equally. One time it does, another time it does not. One time it strikes the one but not the other; it strikes the one perhaps sooner but the other later. It induces very painful conditions for one person, yet it visits another person less painfully. This produces an inequality, a greater loss experienced by one person than what another experiences. And now insurance functions to distribute this total loss, as it were, gradually and for all times over all members of society. And even though this grand goal has not yet been achieved by far, so that for the time being this distribution of loss occurs for only a relatively small part of humanity, it nevertheless has been demonstrated that this distributing of loss already can lead to a distribution that is in large measure appropriate. The ideal is and remains, of course, to calculate, on the one hand, the sum total of all expected losses, to translate that total into monetary terms, and then to distribute this amount to everyone, depending on each individual's position and resources. Only when this goal is reached will insurance celebrate its full triumph. At present, its results are only preliminary, and it is certainly not too bold an expectation that it will make giant strides along this path toward its perfection. But now it already has realized a part of this ideal, and we must look at what it has achieved thus far from this general and ideal perspective.

Is this general perspective defensible before the tribunal of holy § 5
Scripture or isn't it? And in this connection permit us to point back to the statement we placed at the beginning of this discussion: *Bear one another's burdens*. And note that this stands in contrast to what follows two verses later: *Each will have to bear his own load*. We must note that these two statements of the apostle are not aimed at *financial* damages. The context clearly shows the contrary; it is talking about a *spiritual* "burden" and "load" that is borne and weighs us down. If anyone is caught in transgression, verse one states, don't think, "That is his problem," but rather be concerned about that sinner and restore him. For it is not right to stay far removed from a brother's spiritual burden or loss; on the contrary, we must bear one another's burdens and thus fulfill the law of Christ, who bore all of sin's burden on the cross. This is one aspect of our obligation, but on the other hand, we must not arrogate ourselves over our brother, as if he were the only one who was overtaken by spiritual harm. On the contrary, we must not take pride in ourselves at all. Anyone who does so deceives himself. Here too each one has his turn, as it were. The brother who on this occasion fell into transgression now bears *his* load, but we have our turn at our own spiritual loss and will bear our own load. And if we do not have to bear such a load of guilt and spiritual loss now, we must not shirk our brother's load of guilt. What is not yet can still come.

Spiritual harm also can come to us individually. In this way we have to take over a portion of our brother's load, *keeping watch over ourselves lest we too be tempted* [see Gal 6:1]. The whole context, therefore, is summed up in this way:

> Brothers, if anyone is caught in any transgression, you who are spiritual should restore him in a spirit of gentleness. Keep watch on yourself, lest you too be tempted. Bear one another's burdens, and so fulfill the law of Christ. For if anyone thinks he is something, when he is nothing, he deceives himself. But let each one test his own work, and then his reason to boast will be in himself alone and not in his neighbor. For each will have to bear his own load. [Gal 6:1-5]

This section of Paul's letter is dealing with a *burden of guilt*—that is, of spiritual harm. It states that everyone is exposed to it in turn and that this burden must not be borne solely by each one individually, but rather *communally*. We are to be motivated by the spirit of participating love, as if moved by a premonition of what may await us or by what has already happened to us.

We are deliberately putting this rule of behavior in the case of spiritual loss in the foreground here, because a consideration of human suffering that is not rooted in a view of sin can never be satisfactory. Many directors of insurance companies may look only at material damages, but this does not deny the fact that all suffering springs from sin and that the character of this suffering is always determined by the character of the sin. If sin accrues to a separate account for each individual, then the account of suffering also stands alone for each human being and has nothing to do with the account of others' suffering. Conversely, if it appears that sin is not merely personal but also has a *communal* aspect, then the character of suffering also changes entirely. Then in the case of suffering and misery, loss of goods or life, we must not merely pay attention to the individual's share; we must also take into account the communal that then cannot be divorced from the suffering common to all of us. If sin is purely individual, then the suffering, the misery, or the loss suffered by each individual, each family, stands in isolation too. But on the other hand, if sin, guilt, and spiritual loss have what is called a *solidary* character, then it directly follows that sin, guilt, and physical loss must be understood as *solidary* too. This does not mean that personal responsibility in case of spiritual harm is therefore canceled, nor that personal responsibility in case of material loss is eliminated. In the human conscience each individual knows better than this, and every widow knows better than this when her husband dies, even if she receives an annuity. But it does tell us that both spiritual and material losses have two faces, two aspects, two sides. Each one has a double character. And we err if each person continues to worry in isolation when spiritual loss comes or is even merely threatened. Equally so in the case of material loss, we err when we lose sight of part of the truth if we think or say, "Now it affects him, and now he has to deal with it. Later it will be my turn, and when that comes, I will deal with it too."

It is against this individualistic, fundamentally Pelagian view that the words of Paul quoted above constitute a complete protest on behalf of the solidary nature of sin, even where spiritual loss is concerned. For (1) the guilt of sin is presented here as a *burden*, as a *loss* that must be borne; (2) that burden, that loss, will weigh down each one in turn; (3) we must take into account not only the loss already suffered but certainly the loss that may still come; and (4) it is acknowledged that in all such loss there is a "load that each will have to bear alone," even when, on the other hand, we too have a part—namely, to bear with and for each other. Insofar as this is possible, it appears that the main lines of all elements that are relevant in the case of material loss are included in this apostolic discussion of the spiritual burden or spiritual harm. However much we might wish and pray that it were different, sin continues to spread insidiously century after century; it threatens every heart, just as in the material realm all kinds of suffering continue to spread and threaten our enjoyment of life. At this point, then, the apostle posits the rule that we are not to stand alone individually but *to share in bearing one another's burdens*.

CHAPTER SEVENTY-FIVE

INSURANCE (3)

And after all that has come upon us for our evil deeds and for our great guilt, seeing that you, our God, have punished us less than our iniquities deserved and have given us such a remnant as this.

EZRA 9:13

§ 1 In purely accounting terms, there are not as many separate "accounts" as there are people on earth; all humans together belong to one spiritual partnership, and together we stand before God with one incalculable debit account. Behind this corporate account also lies a personal account for each one individually, and to this extent each one of us, as the apostolic word says, bears his own load. But in addition to this personal and separate account, we stand all together, as one great partnership, in debt to God; for this reason the same apostle says, "Bear one another's burdens" [Gal 6:2]. The final settlement of one's *own* load does not occur until the last judgment. Then "we must all appear before the judgment seat of Christ, so that each one may receive what is due for what he has done in the body, whether good or evil" [2 Cor 5:10]. We cannot deny that in this life three kinds of personal settlement already may occur. First, this occurs in times of special revelation, when God punishes someone's guilt directly through his lot in life. Think of Cain, Saul, or Judas. But this kind of direct retribution must never be transferred from the realm of special revelation to our ordinary life. When someone has committed a crime and perishes in a railway accident the next day, no one may say that this happened because of his crime. Such a direct link is applicable only when God himself says so, and this no longer happens, now that special revelation has been closed.

The second personal settlement, if we may put it this way for the sake of brevity, is entirely mysterious. An accident happens to us, or a painful suffering and bitter sorrow come, and suddenly our conscience awakens and the fear of God comes over our soul, and we live with the realization that God is visiting our sin upon us. But it does not follow in the least from this that this specific suffering is being placed upon us by God because of some specific sin or other. After all, isn't it fairly clear that these pangs of conscience are felt less the more evil one is, and more strongly the more godly one is? A coarser, spiritually duller individual will feel so little compunction when illness befalls him, and will so completely avoid mortification, that he will continue his evil ways and provoke God through blasphemous language, even on his sickbed and even on his deathbed. By contrast, when serious adversity befalls a God-fearing Christian, he immediately will be led to reflect on his sins, even if these sins are so inconspicuous in nature that an ungodly individual would not view them as sin at all. How could the notion of a direct settlement on God's part be sustained where it involves a pang of conscience that the ungodly, coarse person does not even sense and that grips us more the closer we move toward God? While we do not deny in the least the partial truth that is also contained in this mystical self-indictment, we do refute the opinion that our understanding in this connection always coincides with God's intention.

In the third place, there is a personal visitation that stems from grace. Suppose a sinful tendency churns within the heart of the Christian. In that person's heart there is an inclination toward evil on this particular point. One person may be inclined toward pride, another toward sensuality, a third toward avarice, and so forth. Every child of God prays against this: "Father, do not lead me into temptation, but deliver me from the evil one" [see Matt 6:13]. God hears this prayer in such a way that the one who prayed must pay a heavy price for the first minor slips on these paths of sin—a price that entails bringing bitter consequences in sin's wake. Perhaps a man has indulged in pride or passion and consequently loses his job. He sins with alcohol addiction and, because the next day he is incapable of performing his work, forfeits a good opportunity so that he suffers serious financial loss. He lets himself be guided by avarice, and a rich uncle who is a miserly type disinherits him. In this way we can observe that there are many instances in which the evil that befalls us certainly is *causally* related to our sin. Then, of course, there is personal imputation. But in the case of a child of God this is not a *punishment* for sin but *grace* leading to salvation. As we head out to sea and experience the sea's violent convulsions, God lets us suffer shipwreck in order that we might permanently relinquish surrendering to a particular sin. But all of this most certainly is not the personal final settlement. That will come only when Christ sits on the judgment seat and the books of conscience are opened.

§ 2 These thoughts need to be placed in the foreground when it comes to the issue of insurance, so that the notion will never take root in our thinking that the communal debt in which we stand before God might cause our personal account to be canceled. It is and always remains a double account: one assigned to each of us individually, and one assigned to the whole world collectively. We confess Jesus Christ as an atonement "not only for our sins but also for those of the whole world" [see 1 John 2:2]. There is nothing strange or unusual in this. When merchants conduct business, they are used to separately entering the accounting transactions of the partners collectively and the accounting transactions of each partner individually for his household. It has to be this way, since there are two kinds of life: the one that we have in common with all, and the other that we live privately for ourselves. And because great accuracy is important here, permit us to state it in this way: the life that we live with others is divided in turn into the life that we live with our family, the life we live as citizens of our nation, and the life we live with the whole human race. Thus, we share three kinds of guilt: As members of the human race, we share in the guilt of Adam. As citizens of our country, we share in the guilt of our nation. And as members of our family, we share in the guilt of the life of our whole household. There are, then, three kinds of common guilt, in contrast to which stand three kinds of communal suffering. We suffer under the curse together with our entire race, with our entire nation (for example, in case of war), and with our whole family (for example, when the head of the household loses his job). Any confusion when speaking about guilt and imputation, punishment and retribution, suffering and misfortune, stems exclusively from the fact that these various kinds of guilt are jumbled together and that these very distinct kinds of suffering befalling us are entered under one and the same heading.

Leaving aside for a moment the further division of common guilt that encompasses our entire race, our entire nation, and our entire family, we may still identify one large entity to which two kinds of guilt and two kinds of suffering belong. On the one hand, there is our personal guilt, incurred through personal sins, and on the other hand, there is the communal guilt reckoned to us as a consequence of the communal sins of our race, nation, or family. On the basis of God's Word we posit the rule that the former guilt (personal guilt) is not settled in the sphere of communal suffering and in the communal misery of our life, and unless it is atoned for by Christ, it remains until the final judgment. Conversely, communal suffering serves as punishment for communal guilt and thus does not affect us personally; corporately, however, it affects all those who belong to our human race, our nation, or our family. Two assertions, then, summarize our position. [T]he first is that in addition to personal guilt there is also a communal guilt. The second is that in the main, the suffering of this world is not directed at the personal but rather at that communal guilt.

The communal character of sin has always been confessed by the § 3
Reformed churches in the doctrine of original sin. They confess it in referring back to Adam. They confess it in the covenant of works. They confess it above all in the atonement through the blood of the cross. For it is a matter of course that only in connection with communion in guilt does the possibility arise that one person should bear the sin of all on the cross. Contemporary science confirms, much more than in the past, this ancient confession of the church. What is said today about atavism and psychological evolution points emphatically to the spiritual connection between one human being and another, between generation and generation, even to such an extent that, through misunderstanding, the judge's duty to assign retribution in court is liable to be undermined. In the Word of God this connectedness of guilt is held before us repeatedly. The Lord visits the sins of the fathers upon the children to the third and the fourth generation of those who hate him [see Exod 20:5]. The sin of David as national head is not visited upon him personally but on the nation. Ezra and Nehemiah, although not guilty themselves, make a confession of sin with and for the people as if they themselves were guilty. Paul teaches us emphatically that through the sin of the one, many have been condemned. And even though many in Jerusalem adhered to Jesus with a burning love, all Jerusalem was given over by Jesus to destruction and curse because of others' unbelief.

The world in its unbelief stands diametrically opposed to this perspective of sin as God has revealed it to us. The world is Pelagian. It is Arminian. And this Pelagianism is nowhere more clearly manifested than in the fact that each human being is viewed as an individual and that the organic connectedness between man and man is denied. The result is that the words "Am I my brother's keeper?" are spiritualized, and each human being individually and entirely privately is considered to have a separate account with God. In the end, there is no hereditary guilt, no original sin, no common confession of sin, no spiritual partnership. And once this false individualism has taken root in the general consciousness, it is a matter of course that Golgotha should become an irritant. The Pelagian heart cannot tolerate such a "blood theory." If I am guilty and Jesus innocent, then what does Jesus have to do with my guilt, and how can he bear it? In the past these savvy Pelagians did not understand that the apostle's words "Bear one another's burdens" referred to spiritual decay, and they still do not understand it.

§ 4 If this basic point that there is solidarity of guilt is certain, then it will surprise no one that the suffering connected with this solidary guilt also bears a *communal* and not a *personal* character. And yet, this is what so often is not discerned among Christian believers. We still frequently hear arguments like this: "I warned him so often that his life could continue like this, but he never wanted to listen. At that point, a person must bear the consequences. And look at the difficulties he has with his children. One child is dead, the other has broken his leg, and the third is mentally deficient." Then people conclude that this person did not walk uprightly. They observe that heavy adversity has struck this person, and they are immediately ready with their judgment that this adversity has struck him because of this wayward journey. And although such blame and judgment do not take on an equally harsh form in all people, it nevertheless is always that direct link between an individual's sin and his or her fate on which these reflections are based. We may apply this to ourselves as well: because we have so clearly forsaken some sin or other, we now are leading a much better life, and therefore we conclude that *prosperity* should now come. But yet the suffering continues; indeed, it becomes even worse. Where was God's justice? And continuing in this vein, more than one person has ended up sinking back into his old sin. Forsaking sin appeared to not help him escape from suffering.

Alas, this fundamental error—that the suffering of the world is personal and not communal—has confused people for centuries, ensnaring them in their judgment, dulling them to the cross of Jesus, and leading them to play around with their own sin. It is therefore so essential that we be permanently cured of this foundational error, because every perspective on our own life and that of others, and every perspective on Golgotha, remains falsified as long as we persist in this error. We know how people in the Old Testament struggled with this error too. Just read and reread Psalm 36 and Psalm 73. The soul has always been faced with how "the wicked have no pangs until death" and how the pious servant of God is "a man of sorrows." Job's bitter struggle revolves around the same question. But gradually, clearer light dawns. The suffering of the godly comes to be understood. The mystery of the cross begins to unveil itself. And when Jesus himself finally appears and puts it so starkly and decisively to his contemporaries, "Those eighteen on whom the tower in Siloam fell and killed them: do you think that they were worse offenders than all the others who lived in Jerusalem?" [Luke 13:4], then the matter is settled and his apostles can boldly go into the world to preach both the solidarity and the fellowship of suffering. For them, there is no longer a struggle. They acquire understanding; the matter becomes transparent for them. Suffering no longer offends them but attracts them. They love it for the sake of Christ, though never in such a way that they tolerate it sentimentally or allow the healthy pull toward happiness to erode. On the contrary, the bitterness of suffering remains acknowledged and is deeply felt, and everything in them thirsts after "the freedom of the glory of the children of God" [Rom 8:21]. Jesus' words were understood to mean that, here on earth, neither good nor evil is proportioned according to one's personal sin or personal guilt, but *God makes his sun to rise on the evil and on the good, and he sends rain on the just and on the unjust*. These words contain the clearest possible statement that the apportioning of happiness and misfortune here on earth is a *mixture* and is *not* administered according to someone's personal guilt or merit.

But we must always make a fundamental distinction here. There are two kinds of suffering that must not be confused; we prefer to call these *causal* and *noncausal* suffering. One who lives a wicked life and consequently becomes weak and ill and dies early has brought causal suffering upon himself. That is, the cause of his becoming ill and sickly lay within himself, in his misconduct. But if someone sleeps in a hotel bed where the previous night a profligate or diseased person slept, and he breathes in or comes in contact with various germs or a virus, then there is no sinful cause in him from which this evil of illness arises. And this is how it is in life. There are all kinds of suffering of which we know very well that we have brought it upon ourselves, that its cause lies in our own carelessness or recklessness, and that by avoiding sin we would also have avoided that evil. This is not

(§ 5 in right margin beside the paragraph beginning "But we must always…")

the kind of suffering of which we are speaking. When we break an arm or a leg in a railway accident, we ourselves were not the cause of the derailment. When influenza, cholera, or the plague breaks out and affects us or our family, we are not to blame for the epidemic. If a fire breaks out next door and our house burns down too, we have not started that fire. When hail destroys our crop, we did not cause that hail to come down. When a dike bursts and the water floods our land, we are not to blame for the dike finally bursting. When a steam boiler explodes in the factory and kills a worker, the surviving widow is not to be blamed for the disaster. And in the same way, when in the normal course of things the breadwinner in a house goes to the grave, it is not that widow and those orphans who have murdered him; on the contrary, they would have made every effort to prevent his death.

We thus must make a sharp distinction between two kinds of suffering. There is *causal* suffering, of which we ourselves were the cause through sin or carelessness. But there is also *noncausal* suffering, whose cause does not lie with us or in us but rather outside of us, whether in someone else's fault or carelessness, in the elemental forces of nature, or in the ordinary course of our human life. Jesus forbids us to trace our suffering to personal sin only with respect to *noncausal* suffering, but absolutely not with respect to *causal* suffering. When the tower of Siloam collapsed, it was not the fault of those who were buried underneath it. When Pilate mixed the blood of the Galileans with their sacrifices, the cause of their slaughter did not lie with them. For this reason Jesus also points to the elemental forces of nature: God "makes his sun rise on the evil and on the good, and sends rain on the just and on the unjust" [Matt 5:45].

We thus arrive at a sharply delineated concept of "communal guilt" and, in connection with it, "communal suffering." That common suffering is further restricted to all the disasters and adversities, suffering and dying, and such damage and loss that we have not brought upon ourselves through our own fault, but rather that come upon us in our ordinary existence because the curse rests upon that existence.

And in this way, we have also to confront the realm in which insurance operates; namely, those cases of fire, burglary, hail, flood, accidents, illness, and death—all disasters to which the good are subjected along with the evil, the just with the unjust. These are disasters in which no cause lies in personal guilt or in which personal guilt in no way bears an intentional character. Someone who starts the fire himself does not receive anything; someone who caused the accident is not included in the insurance benefit;

suicide is excluded. Insurance therefore intends to move only in the area indicated by Jesus: for example, either accidents or organic natural disasters in which any cause that deserves personal blame is precluded. This, in fact, is the realm that corresponds entirely to that of our *communal* suffering, which in turn is related to our *communal* guilt. We don't doubt for a moment that the insurance industry certainly has not always thought this through clearly and soundly to the present, and that this newly arisen power will have to undergo all kinds of refinements and improvements. But it is certain that from the outset, the ethical instinct has led to the distinction that all personally caused damages are not covered, in order to deal only with all such damages or disasters that in the normal course of life happen—or can happen—to each of us, whether we are godly or ungodly, moral or immoral, persons of honor or without honor, *because we are human beings*.

CHAPTER SEVENTY-SIX

INSURANCE (4)

Rejoice with those who rejoice, weep with those who weep.

ROMANS 12:15

§ 1 On the basis of what we have adduced up to this point, we now may proceed from the fixed thesis that there is a portion of suffering that comes upon us *communally* but nevertheless strikes only *a few*. This happens in such a way that those who are affected are no more guilty than those who are unaffected; in fact, sometimes they are even more virtuous and more godly than those over whose head and home the thundercloud passes without the lightning striking them. Consider this scenario: an epidemic breaks out, and of the 500 families in a village, 50 are struck while the other 450 are untouched. Those who are untouched typically would include those who mock and deny God's existence, whereas conversely, one might find the godliest families of the whole village among those who have been visited by disaster, and visited most heavily. In addition, an aged aunt who cares for neither God nor others and who is a scourge to family members lives with the family of a godly man and his wife who have six children, and illness strikes there. Both she and the father of the family fall ill, but death claims not her but him, and the stricken family remains, virtually without income and not knowing how to get rid of this "Xanthippe" who now acts even more badly.[1] All this unfolds in accordance with the reality that this sad suffering is not allotted individually and personally, but rather happens to all; it spares the one but strikes the other, without respecting the criterion of the innocence of the one and the guilt of the other.

Or we might restate the problem differently. Time and again there is a shipwreck on the sea of life, with most people being rescued, although a few perish. That separation among the passengers as to who will escape with his or her life and who will die does not occur according to personal sin but rather according to a mystery that lies entirely outside of human comprehension. The example is known of a man who in youthful enthusiasm went out to proclaim the gospel among the heathen but drowned, whereas a reprobate who went out to seek slaves for houses of ill repute was rescued even as he was cursing. It is precisely as Jesus stated it so plainly: in the case of such suffering God makes no distinction as to whether someone is godly or godless. Rather, God's rain falls on the just and the unjust [Matt 5:45] without distinguishing between greater or lesser guilt.

Perhaps the reader will find this explanation somewhat harsh, even frightening. Perhaps some will even wish to call this unjust. But anyone who has ever prayerfully looked up to the cross of Golgotha and the "Righteous One who bore for us the sin on the cross" [see 1 Pet 2:24] will need to be silenced and humbly confess that he or she stands here before a mystery that, viewed from God's perspective, can be nothing other than worthy of adoration, even though the impression it makes on us through our shortsightedness remains painful. And yet, this painful reality notwithstanding, we currently are allowed to see one bright ray of light fall upon that dark spot of the human soul, when the light of compassionate love appears before us. Human beings belong together; together we constitute humanity, with the entire human race hanging together organically. This is why there is solidarity of guilt and therefore also communal suffering. But organic solidarity does not end with shared guilt and suffering. It goes further. It takes on the form of conscious, felt, and self-willed soul fellowship. Thus, compassion awakens and blossoms with the fragrance of compassion and mercy. The sweet luxuriance of sympathetic love surrounds us. If this is true of others but lacking in us, then the apostolic word admonishes and

1. Xanthippe was the wife of Socrates in ancient Athens. She sometimes was described as harsh and argumentative.

rebukes us: "Rejoice with those who rejoice; weep with those who weep." On the more callous Romans this was imposed only as a divine ordinance, but for the more contemplative Greeks this mystery of participatory love is further unveiled, as it says in 1 Corinthians 12:26, "If one member suffers, all suffer together; if one member is honored, all rejoice together." And immediately thereafter follows in 1 Corinthians 13 the lofty hymn of the love that effaces itself and seeks the good of the other:

> Love is patient and kind; love does not envy or boast; it is not arrogant or rude. It does not insist on its own way; it is not irritable or resentful; it does not rejoice at wrongdoing, but rejoices with the truth. Love bears all things, believes all things, hopes all things, endures all things. Love never ends. [vv. 4–8]

§ 2 This, we should emphasize at this point, is said not about humanity in general but about the body of Christ: "For just as the body is one and has many members, and all the members of the body, though many, are one body, so it is with Christ. For in one Spirit we were all baptized into one body—Jews or Greeks, slaves or free—and all were made to drink of one Spirit" [1 Cor 12:12–13].

Three things must be noted here. First, the apostle derives his image not from the spiritual but from the material realm, from our body of flesh and blood.

> But as it is, God arranged the members in the body, each one of them, as he chose. If all were a single member, where would the body be? As it is, there are many parts, yet one body.
>
> The eye cannot say to the hand, "I have no need of you," nor again the head to the feet, "I have no need of you." On the contrary, the parts of the body that seem to be weaker are indispensable, and on those parts of the body that we think less honorable we bestow the greater honor, and our unpresentable parts are treated with greater modesty, which our more presentable parts do not require. But God has so composed the body, giving greater honor to the part that lacked it. [1 Cor 12:18–24]

By borrowing this image from the material realm, Paul shows us that he speaks here of a fundamental truth that pervades *all of creation* and therefore has meaning and validity for the natural equally as much as for the spiritual life.

Second, we must note that the body of Christ consists of human beings, with him who became man at its head. Moreover, in this holy body of Christ exists not a second humanity alongside the first one but rather the old humanity itself, which was first corrupted in sin and *now* appears before us reborn. A child of God is not a second man who dwells alongside the old man; rather, this is the old man himself, who with the same self was reborn as a child of God. And in the same way it is the same humanity, the same human race, that first ruined itself in sin and now stands before God, renewed in the body of Christ, sanctified and reborn under Christ as its head. The fundamental rule of life is therefore the same for the body of Christ and for the human race. For both it is this: when one member suffers, all must suffer. And to both it is said, "Weep with those who weep, and rejoice with those who rejoice."

We add a third comment: this suffering along with those who suffer is not limited to the members of the body of Christ under the new covenant; already in the Old Testament we see the ordinance "If your enemy is hungry, give him bread to eat" [Prov 25:21]. The ordinance of pity and compassion is nowhere in holy Scripture limited to our fellow redeemed. We must suffer along with those who suffer *as fellow human beings*. The law of participation in the suffering of others deliberately covers all human suffering for all human beings.

The fact that such an ordinance of joint suffering—that is, of sharing in others' suffering, sorrow, and distress—is a law of nature for the human heart, appears as well from what we observe under the dominion of common grace, among unbelievers and the unconverted. Undoubtedly, if there were no common grace at work, Cain's exclamation, "Am I my brother's keeper?" [Gen 4:9], would be everyone's immutable life slogan. Nothing would come but "hated by others and hating one another" [Titus 3:3]. Nothing but mortal enmity would rule. And when, in the case of a few reprobates, God allows his common grace to recede to such an extent that mocking one another takes the place of having pity on the other's suffering, then God shows us in that frightening hardening of the heart how it would be with and among all human beings if his common grace did not come to our aid and rescue us. On the other hand, we testify that, thanks to common grace, which extends to the unbelieving and unconverted, "suffering with § 3 those who suffer" still manifests itself gloriously and sometimes in a way that puts us to shame. The heroic acts of love during a shipwreck, on the battlefield, in hospitals at the sickbed, and in the case of a fire emergency or potential drownings still reconcile us again and again to the human race.

The compassion in cases of disaster and accident, in sickness and death, may not always go very deep, but it nevertheless honors the human heart in this way. Giving alms, supporting the needy, establishing all kinds of institutions to support widows and orphans in their burdens, caring for the blind and the mentally ill—all this flows from the one ordinance of God that the one who is not suffering should take upon himself in part the suffering of the other who is being affected by suffering. And when we notice, especially in our century, how our loving participation extends to entire classes of our society and how it is aimed at the improvement of their miserable conditions, and when we see how it is often unbelievers who take the lead in this, then who can hold back utter praise and honor for that common grace of our God that causes the law of participating in the suffering of others to function so powerfully even in the hearts of the unconverted?

The conclusion to be drawn from this is obvious. God sees standing before himself not individual persons but our human race. He sees that race having sunk into sin. Through sin the curse rests upon this race. And where this curse manifests itself in suffering, this suffering does not affect individual persons but the race as a whole, and it is only his grace that causes it not to come upon everyone equally but only upon a few in that mass. It should have struck everyone. That it strikes only a few is therefore neither harshness nor injustice, but only sparing grace. He who is struck has nothing to complain about. He who is spared must give thanks for undeserved grace. Here, therefore, everything hangs on the sense of guilt. If we take our place before God as if our nature were good in itself, as if no blame were attached to us, then God would seem cruel and harsh, because he visits the innocent with suffering. But if we stand collectively in guilt, and if we assume that it would not be an injustice if all were to die in the outbreak of an epidemic, then those who are affected can raise no complaints against God, and it is only sparing grace that the angel of death passes by many other families. But then as well, the one who is spared must never look down upon the one who is affected as someone who is befallen because he has sinned more, but only as one on whom the consequences of the guilt of all are visited.

And in connection with this God has established bonds between human hearts, emotional ties that make it impossible for us to remain cold, unaffected, and happy when we see the suffering of others. A mother who sees her child suffer often suffers more than the actual child. The spectacle of human suffering strikes us as painful. When we see deep mourning in others, we experience the fearful sense of mourning in our own soul. We cannot see a painful operation without it stabbing our own heart. When we walk on the battlefield after the battle, we feel our heart contract in sadness. This empathy is even so strong that he who himself is unhurt nevertheless sheds tears over the pain of others. This sense of empathy may be dulled in physicians, hospital attendants, undertakers, and gravediggers, but among the great masses this sense remains dominant. We would err if we thought that only sensitive people who are quick to weep have a monopoly on this love. There is a quiet and hidden compassion toward the suffering of others that is less loud and less quick to find expression but, precisely for this reason, often goes deeper and continues when the passionate weeper has already forgotten everything; this kind of person often contributes far more.

Thus, wound and balm have a common origin. The wounds that God apportions in this communal portion of suffering go back to the organic unity and solidarity of our race. Our race is organically one, and therefore jointly accountable, and this is the truth that finds expression in original guilt and original sin. Personal guilt certainly exists as well, but it is always preceded by communal guilt, and personal sin arises only from communal sin. Consequently, it is possible that common grace caused the curse no longer to fall equally upon each one individually and with full force, but rather spared the many while afflicting the individual with the communal burden of suffering. Of course, this would not be possible if everyone's suffering were experienced in isolation and did not affect the rest. But this is exactly what is not the case. Because we are all one body, all members suffer when one member suffers. Pathology shows this to be true even in the physical body. A serious illness not only causes us suffering in the affected organ but also draws all organs, which are more or less weakened, into what the Germans call so beautifully *Mitleidenschaft*, a "suffering along with." If our lungs are affected, our head, stomach, and intestines suffer as well. And this is how it works in the human race, viewed as a single body; hence, the balm that will flow into the wound of communal suffering has its origin in the same unity and solidarity of our race from which that communal suffering itself arose. Because we together are one race, the communal suffering can strike one of us in particular. But because we are together one race, this particular suffering will cause others to suffer along, and love will prepare a balm and bring comfort to the sufferer.

§ 4 We concede that this compassion also functions in the realm of personal guilt. More than one person has risked his life by jumping into the water to save the life of someone attempting suicide. Sacrifices of love are made between men and women even when they individually might not be worthy. For this reason, someone who himself is to blame for an accident nevertheless remains an object of compassion. The cross of Golgotha will never cease to enjoin us to suffer for and with those who bear personal guilt. But this involves an entirely different element that is too far afield of our present focus. We currently are focused on the topic of insurance, and we therefore limit ourselves strictly to the question of *communal suffering* because this, and this alone, constitutes the foundation of the whole system of insurance, as will become apparent. But we must make certain distinctions in addressing this "suffering of the community" if we are to clearly perceive the relationship between insurance and the community of suffering. Two things are particularly relevant for our purposes.

First, as already suggested, *personal* suffering is inseparable from all *communal* suffering. And secondly, there are both *monetary* and *nonmonetary* damages that communal suffering brings upon us. When we lose our own child through disease or an epidemic, we experience indeed a suffering with which others can empathize. At the same time, if we truly loved that child, there is a level of suffering beyond that, into which no one can enter, not even with the greatest sensitivity and compassion. There are widows who, when they lose a husband, know no deeper suffering than that which flows from the general loss of their husband. But there also are widows who cry within their soul because they have lost something that remains a mystery of the human heart and that no one else can experience with them as they shed their tears. No matter how much care a surgeon employs in performing surgery on us, we are the ones who suffer the pain, and what we experience remains our portion of suffering that none can bear alongside us. Thus, in all suffering there is always a portion in the face of which even the most tender love is powerless. For this special portion there is comfort with God, but only with God. The sharing of love can never penetrate beyond the communal part of suffering. The love of one person will be more sensitive, more penetrating, and therefore more comforting.

In particular, those individuals who themselves have known a similar kind of suffering will enter more deeply into this common suffering than others. Nevertheless, there always remains a portion of suffering that no human being can possibly reach, a wound for which only God has the balm.

Added to this, then, is the second distinction, between the *monetary* and the *nonmonetary* portion of damages that the communal suffering causes us. Virtually all suffering brings monetary loss as well: in the case of shipwreck, the loss of our possessions; in the case of illness, the loss of income and the expenses for physician and pharmacist; in the case of death, the loss of income and the funeral expenses. In short, there is almost no "communal portion of suffering" we can think of that is not aggravated and worsened by the accompanying financial consequences. For the woman who became a widow and remained behind, uncared for, it is difficult to lose her husband, but her misfortune is made immeasurably heavier through the fearful thought of how she will find bread for herself and her young children to be able to continue living. When in a heavy storm two or more fishing boats from one of our fishing villages perish, the whole village feels the misery and poverty that threatens each of the affected families. It is the same when famine breaks out, when a flood submerges the fields, or when a war dooms commerce and industry to joblessness. We are not talking here of sorrow of the soul in a narrower sense but of essential suffering in the common sense of the word, which almost always occasions expenses, diminishes income, or causes losses. And it is for this reason that in all suffering of this nature, we must always distinguish as a rule between the suffering that can be calculated in *monetary* terms and the suffering that cannot.

We should not respond by insisting that this is a materialistic argument, or that we insult suffering by bringing monetary considerations into play. Such might be easy to say for those of us whose income is more than sufficient and whose means are abundant. However, when we try to empathize with the harsh conditions of suffering that for the poor and less endowed flow precisely from those financial consequences of suffering, then authentic charity will bring us to the acknowledgment that we must see as a blessing *any* means that can ameliorate the effects of suffering for those who have experienced it. Few people appreciate the agony of the poor widow who has lost not only her husband as a human being but her husband as a father; most people only take into consideration the loss of the breadwinner. What's more, the need can become so pressing that she herself through the loss of her income is dulled to the loss of her dear husband. Therefore, if there is a means that can at least collectively bear the *financial* portion of her suffering, so that she is at least relieved of *this* fearful burden, then we not only rescue her from distress but also mitigate her pain and mourning, and we return pride of place to what never should have been pushed into the background: the loss suffered, not merely in her pantry but *in her heart*.

CHAPTER SEVENTY-SEVEN

INSURANCE (5)

It was distributed to each as any had need.

Acts 4:35

In the common suffering that befalls humanity because of sin and through sin, we therefore can distinguish three kinds of misery. First, there is a misery that no one can take over and in which no can participate, but which the victim must suffer personally. An example might be a person who ends up with both legs cut off below the knee in a railway accident. The terror when this happens, the searing pain as the legs break off, the terrible loss of blood, and the mortal terror and screaming in pain that follows are strictly personal and suffered virtually exclusively by the person to whom it happens. He may have sat in the same train car across from us as someone who was normal. Why the accident struck him and not his fellow traveler is a question that remains without an answer. Here is a suffering that likely could not be averted or prevented and that personally strikes the sufferer, and only that particular sufferer. § 1

There is, however, a second kind of misery in this accident in which love most certainly can share. When the victim sits helpless and powerless amid the wreckage, he must be sawed out, then lifted up with indescribable care, placed on a stretcher, transported, and later cared for at home or in the hospital. Shared love comes into action in all this in order to help, to support, to quench thirst, to take away fear, to spare the victim needless pain through great carefulness, to comfort, to cheer up, and to help him recover. Thus, up to this point we have identified two kinds of suffering: on the one hand, suffering that the victim must bear *alone* and *by himself*, but on the other hand, a portion of suffering that can be ameliorated by others *through love*, and in part even can be prevented. This sharing of love is an element that *cannot* be translated into money. Granted, money can buy good care, but money cannot buy the help and comfort that must be given during and after such catastrophes. As a rule, the first and best help is rendered by people who voluntarily rush forward to help, and in this help initially rendered there is also found something that is difficult to put into words, and therefore cannot possibly be bought with money: an amelioration of suffering before our very eyes that is done out of purely humanitarian compassion.

But in addition to these two elements of suffering we encounter yet a third—that is, the element of monetary loss. Before such a victim described above is restored to a normal way of life, the bills from the physician, surgeon, and pharmacist will have run high. And what is much more serious, the loss of both legs makes the man incapable of performing his previous work, and in the absence of any income, he stands helpless in the world with wife and children. And even if the victim has means of his own, he nevertheless loses—as, for example, a military officer would—his position through the accident that befell him. This is fully aside from any loss of normal income, even if he receives a pension or reduced pay; the result always means suffering financial loss.

Insurance, we grant, can do nothing with respect to the first element (namely, the strictly personal suffering). Nor can insurance take over the sharing of love as it concerns the second aspect of suffering. But what insurance *can* do, as its exclusive goal, consists in dealing with that financial loss, the third element in suffering. While it cannot take away the financial loss, since a loss in fact has occurred, it can spread the loss over all, victims and nonvictims, so that the loss loses much of its hurt and, hence, is virtually no longer felt. When fire breaks out in our house, whether through carelessness or an unknown cause, and we must flee with our family across the adjacent roofs, then we personally suffer fear and are exposed to a danger that no one can take away from us. This corresponds to the first element noted. Following such an ordeal, we are deprived of home and household goods for an extended period of time. Yet this corresponds to the second element, which can be ameliorated by friends or neighbors and the community. But now we suffer the financial loss of our house and possessions going up in flames; this corresponds to the third element. Suppose our house is worth ten thousand guilders and our household goods are worth three thousand guilders.[1] We have lost thirteen thousand guilders in value, and unless we are people of means, we suffer an irreparable loss. But if thirteen thousand families who live in the same city contribute one guilder each, then the loss we suffer is fully covered, and no one among us really feels the loss of one guilder. Beyond this, that one guilder is paid gladly if this payment of one guilder brings the assurance that, should their home and household goods burn tomorrow night, they too would receive complete indemnification. Thus, this third aspect of suffering, which consists exclusively of financial loss, can be removed almost entirely. *Some* loss will always remain. Along with our household goods we will lose souvenirs that are irreplaceable and cannot be indemnified. Perhaps, as well, papers that had great value to us will be irretrievably gone. But the actual financial loss (that is, the loss that can be calculated in financial terms) is taken as such from the victim, and he is thereby unburdened. We pay along with others, but if there are thirteen thousand participants, we pay only one thirteen-thousandth of the total amount.

Well and good, you might say. But does this mean that benevolence will disappear from this world as a result? There is certainly some truth in this. § 2
If insurance could be introduced in all realms of society and for all people as participants, there never again would be any advertisements in the newspapers calling for help for widows and orphans left behind by fishermen and other shipwrecked persons. All appeals of this nature would cease, simply because after each misfortune, after each accident, after every death from whatever cause, the full amount for reimbursing the financial loss would be available, and therefore no financial loss could be suffered except communally. We fully concede this much. Nor do we deny that the sometimes moving display of such a benevolent impulse does indeed bring honor to the human heart. But it is an entirely different question as to whether we must reject the notion of insurance because it may cut off this display of benevolence in the future.

Anyone who proceeds on this assumption must remember that in centuries past, human life was still infinitely more exposed to so many kinds

1. At the time of Kuyper's writing, thirteen thousand guilders roughly amounted to one hundred fifty thousand US dollars in 2016.

of loss and danger; recall, too, that this greater exposure to danger and to greater loss in the past called forth so many expressions of love and assistance that people today simply take for granted or have forgotten. Take, for example, hospitality. In the past, when travel was always dangerous and in most places people could find no accommodations, the rule of hospitality had to be prevalent as a holy ordinance to make fellowship among people possible. And in the same way, when people were in constant danger of holdups, burglary, robbery, and murder, friendship had to acquire a character that was the equivalent of goods and life, similar to entering into marriage. And there certainly was something beautiful in that hospitality, something considered holy, and there was something special in the kind of friendship that demanded the whole person and one's whole life, something that brought honor to the human heart.

But in a certain sense, both of these examples are no longer around, at least in civilized countries. We no longer invite an unknown person into our guestroom if he arrived shortly before midnight and asked for lodging for the night; we would either turn him down or ask money for his lodging with us. And we must also acknowledge that a friendship that in the past was considered a matter of honor by people is no longer found with that depth, that extent, and that character. The advance of civilization, improved safety, better communications, comfortable lodging, and so forth, have brought an end to these expressions, in terms of both hospitality and the kind of friendship in which one puts one's life on the line for a friend. In our present society there is no longer a place for this. Do we therefore say that hospitality and friendship in life and death were such a splendid expression of human love that it would be better if we got rid of the safety and comfort of life, to return to the "good old days," in which life automatically called forth such hospitality and such friendship? Nobody thinks this way. Granted, we sometimes may complain poetically about the loss and even nurse a nostalgic feeling for those more romantic times, but in the meantime everyone who knows God thanks his Father in heaven that together with wife and children he may live in times that are so much safer and quieter.

§ 3 Precisely the same applies to the matter of insurance. It is entirely true that insofar as insurance has not yet been more widely accepted, disasters occur now and then that cause misery and financial loss on a large scale, and it is equally undeniable that this sometimes causes expressions of benevolence that bring honor to the human heart. It also is true that this becomes superfluous as soon as insurance has spread the cost of such losses to everybody. Just like hospitality and friendship to the death, so too benevolence reaches its zenith in days of uncontrolled misery. We can even say that these expressions of human love shine all the more brightly to the degree that the condition of human life is more wretched and sad. When somebody falls in the water, we are given the opportunity to save him. But who would ever draw the ridiculous conclusion that it is a pity if accidents in the water no longer happen, since this prevents altruism from expressing itself? Better hygiene is certainly the cause that pestilences from Asia or other parts of the world sneak upon us less often now than in the past, and it also is true that physicians and chaplains and nursing personnel lack many opportunities to display heroic love. But who would think that it would be better to allow such pestilences to appear again in order that this heroism of love may shine again? Even though we thus agree wholeheartedly that insurance causes the realm and scope of benevolence to shrink, we vigorously deny that this is a reason to combat insurance.

Besides, when we look more closely at the benevolent impulse and its effects, we must soon acknowledge that here, too, not nearly all that glitters is gold. We will not even begin to speak of the bazaars, balls, and lotteries that are dedicated to good causes. The false appearances of all such festivities are apparent. Through all the cracks and crevices, hypocrisy peers out. But apart from this we know how uneven and how biased such collections function. For one particular accident, too much money comes in; for another accident in a lesser-known region, no one donates anything. Someone with a well-known patron sees a committee organized quickly for his need, whereas someone who is struck by disaster in a remote region corner, in relative isolation, ends up at the door of the deacons or is left a pauper. Benevolence that operates in this manner cannot act on the basis of good ground rules—that is, with equity and deliberation. Such an undisciplined benevolence is blind and operates haphazardly, and as a result it not infrequently even causes evil. It is the same as giving money arbitrarily at one's doorstep, which so often feeds pauperism. Conversely, a good diaconal ministry that receives money from everyone, and evenly distributes it after investigating the needs, does indeed cut off much labor of love for the individual, but in fact it functions better, bringing more benefit.

Added to all of this is that when it comes to public benevolence, so much forced enrollment occurs. People are afraid not to participate for the sake of decorum. People do not want to refuse to give, because their neighbor gave. And the act of giving itself, and joining such benevolence committees, is so often nothing but a means to be seen and appreciated by one's fellow citizens, or for young people to commend themselves and to gain influence. In benevolence, the fact is that a great deal of what is unholy is hidden, and again and again it has remained far removed from the ideal that it be done according to Jesus' rule: "Do not let your left hand know what your right hand is doing" [Matt 6:3]. It is precisely this *hidden* giving that is practiced least.

§ 4 We must not forget one further element—namely, that we cannot exercise benevolence without the other person having to accept our gift, and that in this accepting of a gift, not from God but from fellow human beings, there is always something that hurts human feelings. If necessary, we accept the gift from our fellow human being, but we do so as something that is painful for us but that God imposes on us. It therefore must be deeply regretted that the high and holy notion of the diaconal ministries in this respect has been so sadly falsified. At present, someone feels only partly humiliated when he or she must be helped by a private gift, yet that person feels deeply aggrieved when referred to the deacons. But this is entirely wrong, and according to the high ideal it is precisely this being helped by the deacons that should be least painful. For what is the aim of the diaconal ministry other than that we have to receive nothing *from fellow humans* but everything *from Christ*; this should not be problematic at all. The well-to-do members of the church give back to Christ something of what he gave to them. The deacons, as the servants of Christ, collect this and distribute it to *his* poor members. This is as noble and elevating as we can imagine. It involves precisely the sparing of our sensibilities as humans. Therefore, every diaconate that is not intent on sparing the human feelings of all poor brothers and sisters in all matters is simply unworthy of serving in such a holy ministry.

But apart from the work of the diaconate, it remains a fact that benevolence, even where it truly honors the giver, generally brings the danger of lowering the proper sense of the recipient's self-worth. Families who still have a sense of honor and are even minimally capable of doing so should therefore make the greatest sacrifices to help an unfortunate family member, rather than a family member having to request public benevolence. In fear and great need, a person may stretch out the hand to beg, for hunger is a sharp sword, but the gift as such wounds the sense of independence and creates a feeling of obligation that hurts. Those who are inclined to focus on gratitude that befits the person who is helped would therefore do well to pay closer attention to the effects of assistance on a person's sense of self-worth. Certainly, gratitude is an obligation, but we must never think or say that a society functions at its best when there is much to give, when much in fact is given, and where gratitude flourishes most abundantly. Indeed, it is truly wonderful when much is given in the context of great need, but society is much happier when there is nothing to be given because there is no need. And when people point to the words of Scripture, "*The rich and the poor* meet together; the LORD is the Maker of them all" [Prov 22:2], and deduce from this verse that both the need of the poor and the gift of the rich should always abide, then please point these abusers of Scripture to another saying of Scripture, "The poor man and *the oppressor* meet together; the LORD gives light to the eyes of both" (Prov 29:13), and ask whether they also want to protect *the oppressor* as someone willed by God. Ask them, as well, whether they would consider it going against God's will if the oppressor disappeared from this life.

The notions of poverty and benevolence that still dominate so many § 5
people's thinking are in so many respects false and diametrically opposed to Christian principle that they in fact go astray if they wish to argue against insurance on the basis of these false notions. In paradise opulence came before poverty, and in the kingdom of glory there will be neither lack nor benevolence. The dread of poverty and lack that overcomes us as the result of a disaster or accident is part of the misery that came into our life as the result of sin. And of course, where misery raises it head, it is wonderful that benevolence appears to mitigate and alleviate it. But who offers the better assistance: the friend who takes the man with the broken leg by his arm and helps him stumble along, or the surgeon who sets the broken leg so that the man no longer needs help from others? This is the same difference as that between the gift of benevolence and the payment from the insurance company. Benevolence supports us and keeps us standing where we otherwise would have stumbled and been unable to go on. But the insurance enables us *to walk on our own legs again*. All benevolence combined will not reimburse one-tenth of the collective financial loss; insurance is able to cover much financial loss and facilitate the removal of financial loss from the list of life's disasters.

Note the saying of Scripture that stands at the beginning of this chapter and takes us to the first Christian church. From the socialist side, this verse has led—entirely erroneously—to deducing the communist concept of so-called communal property. Communism wants a community of property *by compulsion*, as a rule of law, among all people. What is narrated in Acts 5:4, by contrast, speaks of a community of goods, not under coercion but as *a free-will offering*, not as a rule of law but as *rule of love*. This exists not for all people but for those who are *brothers and sisters* in Christ. Peter says explicitly, "If you wanted to give it, *did it not remain your own*?" [see Acts 5:4]. Nevertheless, there is something in this story to which we definitely must pay attention. The private benevolence that causes A to give something that B receives from him disappeared altogether from the church in Jerusalem at that time. A gave nothing to B, and B had nothing to receive from A. We cannot speak in this way of any sort of undermining of human self-worth. Everyone brought contributions, and these were distributed in Jesus' name to all, with only this one criterion: *as each one had need*.

This is precisely how the need was met, and for this reason, all private benevolence automatically ceased. At that time the concept of insurance was as yet unknown and thus immaterial. Along the path of his common grace God had not yet given people an awareness of this. But it is in this light all the more remarkable how, upon its entry into the world, Christianity immediately pointed to an ideal in which private benevolence ceases entirely because the need is removed through a common action of all. Something of this ideal is realized in the concept of insurance, and when it spreads its wings broadly and widely over our entire society, it will lead to precisely the same goal; and in cases of fire, shipwreck, illness, death, and so forth, it will make all private benevolence superfluous because it will prevent every financial loss and every financial need by means of a communal action.

CHAPTER SEVENTY-EIGHT

INSURANCE (6)

For everything there is a season, and a time for every matter under heaven: a time to be born, and a time to die.

ECCLESIASTES 3:1–2

Summarizing what we have found thus far, here is where we stand. Because § 1
of sin there is suffering on earth. In this suffering, even as in sin, there is both a personal component and a communal component. The communal part of suffering is cast upon humanity in such a way that it affects both the just and the unjust. God lets his sun rise over the evil and the good, and those upon whom the tower of Siloam fell were no greater sinners than other people. To the extent that this common suffering strikes the one and not the other, the demand to bear one another's burdens emerges. This is never possible to the fullest extent. When suffering strikes us personally, there is always some part of it that no one else can bear with us or for us. But there is the possibility—and therefore also the duty—to suffer with others, to share in their suffering, whether it be through love that comforts, through alleviating the wound, or through taking away the financial loss. Insurance serves only the last purpose. Insurance is powerless against suffering that is a direct result of personal sin. It is equally powerless against all suffering that touches the heart. Insurance is of a purely material nature. Its first question is always, Is there financial loss? If not, then it withdraws and does not occupy itself further with the suffering. On the other hand,

when financial loss is apparent, then it immediately stands ready to offer its services.

Was nothing done, then, to alleviate that financial loss before insurance came into the picture? The answer is yes, but in a very inadequate manner. There was giving. But this giving happened without rules or order. One person received far too much, another person too little, a third person nothing. Already in the Christian church in Jerusalem, the compensation for financial need and loss was made a communal matter for everyone. But this eroded over time. Even now there are generous givers who find it much more gratifying for their own ego to give their gifts directly to those who have come to be in need than to give to Jesus, so that he may distribute it through his deacons. All kinds of sins attach to giving, and giving reaches its target only in a very limited measure. Many give to make a display of the fact that they are giving. Others give if they get a dance party or some other kind of entertainment in return. There are also those who give to make others dependent on them. And always accompanying giving is the unfortunate effect that the person who has been visited by misfortune now also has to undergo the painful experience of having to be helped by public benevolence. This is always, to a certain extent, humiliating. We will have to bear this humiliation if God imposes it on us, but it should not be fostered by people. As a rule, accepting gifts harms the character and undermines a person's awareness of freedom and independence. Accepting gifts carries the sense of being dependent.

§ 2 This, then, leads to the question of whether a means can be conceived whereby we humans divide among ourselves the financial damages that flow from the communal suffering in such a way that each contributes according to his means without the one having to thank the other. And this is the question to which insurance supplies an affirmative answer. Insurance is always involved only with financial loss caused by communal suffering. It reimburses those damages completely. It distributes the cost of reimbursements over the masses. And it does this in such a way that those who benefit from it have only God to thank, and with respect to people, beneficiaries have the indisputable claim to indemnification. In such a case the ideal has therefore been fulfilled, and insurance accords with what Scripture teaches us concerning sin and the suffering that results from sin.

What enabled the insurance business—very imperfectly at first, but more accurately over time—to find the desired solution for this very difficult and complicated problem? How is it possible that in the past, insurance could not become a force in life, and now—even remarkably so—it has become such a beneficial force and continues to become so even more? The answer is, only because people did not pay attention to God's doings, at least not with the necessary carefulness. The insurance business emerged from a discovery that was nothing but what Solomon wrote thousands of years ago in Ecclesiastes 3:1–2: "For everything there is a season, and a time for every matter under heaven: a time to be born, and a time to die." These words express nothing but the core of the Reformed confession that nothing happens to us by chance, but all things come to us from the Father's hand. Coincidence does not exist. All that happens does so according to God's command. It is fixed beforehand. There is nothing that has not been determined in God's counsel. And if we only knew this counsel beforehand, we would be able to calculate precisely and accurately how many disasters, misfortunes, and accidents would happen in a given year. Then we could calculate precisely how much financial loss would result and how much each of us would have to pay to indemnify the victims.

Assume for the moment that in God's counsel it has been determined that in a given year, one hundred thousand fires will occur—the number is arbitrary—and that in each of these fires, the average damage would amount to ten thousand guilders. Then the total fire damages in that year would amount to one billion guilders. If we assume that there are about 300 million families in this world, then the damage distributed among all the families would require only 3 guilders per year per family. And furthermore, each victim would be entitled to a full payment of ten thousand guilders. In the Pelagian perspective that all events are isolated and that everything depends on man's free will, such a calculation is of course absolutely impossible. Pelagianism excludes any notion of insurance. The Reformed position, on the other hand, confessing that all things are foreordained, provides the basis for such insurance, and we are faced only with the question, *How can we come to know how much financial loss has been determined for a given year in God's counsel, a loss to be debited to humanity as a whole?*

Of course, here we encounter the very serious objection that God's counsel is determined but hidden from us. And let us not be too quick to respond that this is a shame, for otherwise, insurance would automatically proceed smoothly. On the contrary, alas, the reverse must be acknowledged—namely, that if God's counsel were not hidden, insurance never would have been invented. For our human heart is so sinful and egotistical that, if it were known beforehand that according to God's counsel a fire would never break out in our house, by far the most people would say in that situation (truly in the spirit of Cain), "Then I won't pay a cent for insurance, for I am insured by God's counsel. This will pass me by. It neither will nor can happen to me. And the others are no concern of mine. Am I my brother's keeper?" If we are to be helped, something entirely different has to happen. Then God's counsel would have to reveal to us how many accidents would happen in a given period, and how much total damage would result, but without it being revealed who would be affected by an accident and who would not. If this were the case—namely, that we could know that according to God's counsel the total financial loss due to accidents would amount to a given amount, without anyone knowing beforehand whether he himself would or would not be spared—then there would be a stimulus to say, "Let me contribute something to the total loss each year. I will do this faithfully if you assure me that if an accident strikes me, the damages I suffer will be reimbursed in full." And this is what the insurance industry does.

In this respect we must now acknowledge that God indeed has ordained it thus. God has done three things. First, he has ordained certainly and immutably in his counsel which communal suffering will descend on mankind each year and in all manner of forms, and also who will be affected. Second, he has kept hidden who in a given year will be a victim of suffering and thus who also will suffer loss. And third, God has revealed which suffering, in what measure, and in how many instances mankind as a whole will undergo each year, and what financial loss this will bring each year. This latter revelation is a mercy of God. It is a piece of his common grace. Without that revelation all insurance would be inconceivable. Through that revelation it has been made possible. From this it follows that to disdain the insurance business is to neglect this God-given revelation.

§ 3 Where do we find this revelation? Not in holy Scripture, of course. Holy Scripture reveals to us that there is sin; that because of sin there is suffering; that sin works in solidarity with original, inherited sin; and that suffering therefore contains a communal element. Holy Scripture also reveals to us that there is a counsel of God, and that in that counsel everything in our life is foreordained, even in such a way that apart from God's will not a hair on our head can fall. But holy Scripture does not give us the application in life. However, our Reformed confession emphatically says that we know God through two means: he reveals himself through Scripture and through nature. "For his invisible attributes, namely, his eternal power and divine nature, have been clearly perceived, ever since the creation of the world, in the things that have been made" [Rom 1:20]. The question, therefore, is whether paying careful attention to the creaturely life, as it is lived in natural fashion among people, will show us beforehand and reveal, not *which* people will be struck, but *how many cases* of suffering there will be, and how large the financial loss will be that is caused by these cases in a given year. And this is what humankind could have come to know centuries ago, for it has been implicitly revealed with greatest clarity by God in the life of nature. The obtuseness of the human person alone was the reason it was not seen, nor discovered, nor read from nature. And the Pelagian form of unbelief involving chance was especially what contributed century after century to this general obtuseness. It had been written clearly in nature by God. We only had to read it. And yet no one read it. We were and remain perceptibly blind.

Are there numbers in nature? Most certainly. This was partially known in times past as well. Take birth and death, for example. Solomon points out that these have their appointed time under heaven. It would have been conceivable, of course, that in a given village of three thousand inhabitants, in one decade no one should die, while a year later half of the inhabitants, or even the entire population, should die. Yet it was clearly observed that this is not how it is ordained in God's counsel, but that death takes place with a certain regularity. The undertaker knows very well that, apart from epidemics, the number of persons who die in one year remains more or less the same from one year to the next. Thus, the official at the registry office could very well see in his records that the number of births was also fairly constant. In our orphanages and homes for the aged, it also was clearly noticed that it was not the case that in one year ten times as many orphans suddenly would come as in a previous year, and the year following none; rather, taken over a given number of years, the number remained virtually the same. Nor did it escape attention that this number was much more constant in a very large orphanage than in a small village orphanage. A doctor also knew (again apart from epidemics) that his income would not be excessively large in one year and fall to nothing in the following, but that when comparing a number of years, he would have nearly the same number of patients year after year.

In short, people also knew very well in times past that not only births but also deaths and, similarly, all kinds of misfortune, did not reach one thousand in one year, only to go down to zero in the next; rather, in all these things under heaven *we can observe a certain regularity from year to year*. This generally was the impression under which people lived. At times special conditions might prevail through epidemics, famine, pestilence, or war, but in normal times and under normal conditions, no one doubted that one year would be roughly the same as the years before. How this was possible, the unbelieving world did not know. It ascribed all this to chance. What is more changeable than the many causes of human death: catching a cold, contracting a contagious disease, a bad medication, and so forth. Yet chance arranged it in such a way that everything came out by and large the same. Thus, everything was a matter of guessing, leaving people with a feeling of uncertainty. What was neglected was making careful observations and calculations.

§ 4 In our century, however, people have broken with this routine for the first time. The greater development of science made a principled break with Pelagianism and exonerated Calvinism. People did not come to a confession of God's counsel, but they did come to acknowledge that there is no chance and that everything follows *fixed laws*. For the Reformed, this was an extraordinary gain. Starting from that conviction, the men of this century have applied themselves to careful observation and recording. It came to be said, Let the government collect very careful statistics of all that happens in human life. Let them record not only who and how many people die, but also at what age, in which month and which week, of what illness they died, and so forth. In the case of an epidemic, let it be recorded how many victims there are month by month in each town and each village. Indicate the illness from which they suffer. Record also whether the dying persons are male or female. Preferably indicate occupation as well, whether married or single, widow or widower. In short, record *all* the details you can collect. Do the same with births, both legitimate and illegitimate, male or female. Then calculate the average lifespan for all those categories of persons. Make records of crimes, thefts and burglaries, of murders and suicides. Compile a list of blind and deaf people, of insane and mentally handicapped people. Make lists of cases of fire and shipwreck, of damaging hail and floods. Indicate on those lists what sums of money were lost through all those misfortunes in a given region or country over a period of years. In short: *keep records*. Note everything. Be informed about everything. And after that has been done for, say, twenty years, then look at the results to see whether these numbers show a certain regularity, a certain constancy, or conversely, whether these numbers are so hopelessly different and diverse from one year to the next that no conclusions can be drawn.

Well, this in fact has been done. It is the science of statistics. Believers have undertaken scientific investigation to discover whether there is a certain fixed law at work in the communal suffering that God sends man, or whether God sends us the evil of suffering without any pattern—in one way now, and in another later. And the result of that scientific study has been extraordinarily surprising. Statistics as a discipline has not nearly arrived at where it should be. The scope of its studies is still much too small. Of the 1.4 billion people on earth, at most 400 million have been studied with some care; in the case of 200 million at most, this has been done to the extent of gradually collecting more firm data on a somewhat larger scale. But a good deal of progress has been made. The results that have been achieved thus far show beyond any doubt that the regularity is certain and that the constancy of life's suffering can no longer be disputed.

In this regard, see especially Buckle in his *History of the Civilization in England,* who has drawn some interesting conclusions.[1] He has shown that there is little chance or "free will" in man (as it is often understood), but that rather the same pattern repeats itself, year after year. There is a fixed regularity, for example, not only in suicides but also in the way people commit suicide. Thus, for example, year after year a given number of suicides occur, and among these, a certain number by drowning, a certain number by hanging, a certain number with a gun, a certain number with a sharp instrument, and so on. And even if we assume that Buckle's figures are exaggerated, or at least that there currently are insufficient data to draw firm conclusions about all these details, we nevertheless can see with our own eyes this much in the annual figures that are published each year: even in our own small country, the data from a given year are in remarkable agreement with the data from the previous year. The number of children who are born may climb, but it climbs according to a fixed proportion, and we never see, for example, twenty thousand more children being born one year and twenty thousand fewer the next. It is the same with deaths.

Here, due to hygienic measures, we may see a *decline* in the numbers, yet that decline is uniform, and we don't see any enormous spikes anywhere. It is the same with gender. Boys and girls are born in almost equal numbers, and almost as many men as women die. This regularity and invariability even goes so far that, for example, the streetcar company in Amsterdam

1. Henry Thomas Buckle (1821–62) was the author of the unfinished *History of the Civilization in England*, 2 vols. (London, J. W. Parker, 1857–61).

transports the same number of passengers year after year, except for a fixed, steady increase over the years. What can be less certain and coincidental than choosing between boarding a tram and walking? And yet the results show here as well that there is no chance, that all people, consciously or unconsciously, year after year, are moved by the same motives to do the same things. This in fact is so consistent that across an entire country the number of passengers using the railways always comes out to about the same. Every public transportation company proceeds on the basis of this principle; otherwise, it simply would be impossible to organize such travel. In fact, every small business is based on this, whatever its scale. A healthy business knows on January 1 that in the new year it will take in a certain amount, give or take. A hotel is taken over based on the calculation that a certain number travelers will stay there every year. Poor service and more competition can bring change, but under normal circumstances every healthy business will bring in a certain fixed sum, and all this despite the fact that everyone senses that nothing more changeable is conceivable than the question of how many travelers must be in a city in a given year, and which hotel they will choose in that city. We sit in the train and we don't yet know a hotel at our destination. We ask a fellow traveler. The hotel he mentions is the hotel we choose. This is purely accidental, you might say. And yet the results show that even such small things are not governed by chance and that our entire human life, down to the smallest details, follows such a marvelous regularity that one particular year, under the same conditions, always remains equal to the other. For us Reformed people, this is nothing strange, but for those who are Pelagian in their thinking, it is an almost unbelievable discovery. For given this reality, what remains of their chance and their free will?

CHAPTER SEVENTY-NINE

INSURANCE (7)

By your appointment they stand this day, for all things are your servants.

PSALM 119:91

As we have seen, the accurate record of disasters, misfortunes, accidents, cases of illness, deaths, and so forth, shows that the number of these cases, and similarly the financial losses they bring, do not significantly differ from one year to the next. God the Lord shows us in this that he does not allocate this suffering arbitrarily, but he brings this suffering on people according to a certain fixed regularity, and this regularity determines not only the final total numbers but also the small details from which this final number is composed and drawn up. § 1

All of this flows, of course, from God's counsel. It is part of the ordinance of God that all that is to happen is foreordained. In the issue at hand, therefore, we must confess that year after year, in God's foreordination roughly the same number of disasters are set and determined with roughly the same financial consequences. But we can go further and say that a certain law necessarily governs this, a certain ordination. The Christian church has always confessed that God's decrees are established with wisdom. Wisdom is not a chaotic, purely mechanical assembly of all kinds of things that must happen; rather, "wisdom" implies that there is a divine thought at the basis of all that has been decreed and that with wisdom God has placed all these things in a mutual relationship. We therefore can rightfully say that the regularity manifested in all kinds of disasters is also the consequence and fruit of an ordination—hidden from us, of course—which determines why it must be this way in order to reflect God's wisdom. Even as ordinary laws of nature do not govern God's counsel but have been ordained and established by God himself with a wise strategy, so here too there must be laws that govern human suffering. They may be laws that we do not know, laws that we can only very partially infer from the causes of the facts, but their existence nevertheless appears clearly and surely from the constant character of the disasters of life.

The significance of such laws of nature must never be wrongly construed. They are not laws of nature but laws that govern, or reign over, nature—laws that God conferred upon nature so that nature might obey those laws. But even when viewed in this light, it still follows from our knowledge of the laws of nature that we must organize our lives and our behavior in accordance with them. If a law of nature teaches that as soon as it is released, an object that is heavier than air falls down until it is stopped, then we must not step from the roof of our house into the air, but we must go down more slowly, via stairs or a ladder. And so it is with every law of nature. Our knowledge of these laws governs our actions, entirely apart from the question of whether we understand such a law.

And so it is in the realm of suffering as well. Once it has been revealed to us through the facts that there is regularity in communal suffering, it follows for us that it is our duty not to act as if this regularity does not exist. We must take it into account and ask ourselves what action would be appropriate in light of God's revelation of this regularity. In the past we did not know this regularity, and we could not take it into account. The same applies to other laws of nature that were not known in the past but were discovered later. In his common grace God does not show us everything at once. Past generations were not acquainted with gas, steam power, electricity, the telegraph, and so forth. Although all those forces did exist back then, they had not been shown to us; we did not yet know of their existence and functioning. Therefore, past generations were not at fault because they did not use these forces. But now they are known, so that now, when a mother has had a stroke and is in mortal danger, if the father does not inform his child of this by telegraph so that the child may be able to see his mother still alive, he will be at fault with respect to his child. Now that these forces have been discovered, it is not our choice whether we want to use them; we are obligated to make use of them, as often as a higher law demands its application—in this example, the law of love.

And the same is true of suffering as well. In times past, people did not know about any regularity in the disasters of life. People could not gauge those disasters and the financial loss they cause. Everything was uncertain, up in the air. But now this uncertainty has been removed—not the uncertainty as to who will be affected (that uncertainty remains) but the certainty as to the final numbers. A sense of "regularity" has now been determined. It was always fixed, but without our knowing it; now it has been shown and revealed to us that there is a fairly fixed regularity to various kinds of disaster. From this it follows that we no longer may act as if we did not know it. That would mean closing our eyes to revelation that God has provided for us through his common grace. Now that this light is here, we are obligated to walk in this light. We must avert and ameliorate suffering where possible. This is the high duty of love. If it appears that this regularity in suffering enables us to act to ameliorate suffering, then we are called and obligated to do so. It is not up to our choice; rather, it is imposed on us. § 2

The suffering of poor widows who remain behind, poverty stricken, with their orphaned children, is terrible. If we can avert this suffering with the help of the notion of regularity in suffering, then it must be done. And the results show that this can indeed be done. It appears that here too, the number of annual cases can be calculated, and this number of cases brings equal financial losses. It therefore is possible to calculate beforehand how much has to be contributed to ensure that all widows and orphans can lead a reasonably carefree life. When a woman does indeed lose her husband, and the children their father, that loss cannot be compensated. But the combined loss of the breadwinner *and* the grinding poverty that otherwise comes along with death and mourning can be ameliorated. All those who are threatened in this manner unite to deposit a certain small amount each year, and from this small amount, which is not a burden to anyone, more than enough money is raised to take away the difficulties of obtaining a livelihood in cases where the breadwinner dies.

The same applies to all those disasters that bring financial loss in their wake. We are all exposed to the danger of fire. If all of us pay a very small amount each year, then more than enough money will be raised to indemnify the person whom it strikes. This would not be possible if there were no regularity in suffering. But this regularity exists, and now that we know it, we can calculate beforehand roughly how much the total losses will be over a given period of time. Then we divide this total by the number of participants and ask from each a small sum according to the value of his house and goods. And through our ability to discern the regularity of suffering we have discovered, we are claiming that all financial losses can be reimbursed to the victims. Our responsibility for taking care of our property and goods, the ownership of which does not belong to us but to our family, therefore demands that we act in this manner. Love urges us to do this as well, since the individual can survive only if many participate. We also are impelled to apply this means if we manage someone else's property as guardians or caretakers. But this applies to goods that are in our own possession as well. A shipowner who has invested his entire capital in one ship and lives on the income from this one ship along with his wife, children, crew, and their families, is not at liberty to send it out to sea without insuring it against loss in case of shipwreck. He is not the only one affected by a shipwreck; his family is deprived of income too, as are the families of the members of his crew, at least until they can find work elsewhere. If he knows that he can avert this danger by annually paying a specified amount, then he must do so, since this has been imposed on him as a noble requirement of love and of care for those who depend on him.

§ 3 Putting these various considerations all together, the issue thus boils down to this: (1) God in his common grace takes away from most people the disasters that should strike all of us, allowing them to visit only a few; (2) God permits these few to be visited by these disasters, not by chance but in accordance with a certain regularity as a result of his holy counsel; (3) God has gradually revealed this regularity of suffering to us; and (4) the knowledge of this regularity enables us to spread and apportion the financial losses of such disasters equally to everybody. And this equal distribution and apportioning is precisely what the Reformed confession demands.

Our guilt, our Confession teaches us, is a communal guilt. In addition, there is also a personal guilt, but in the first place this is a communal guilt. Because of this communal guilt, communal suffering is also imposed on us. This communal suffering affects us together. In this respect the same thing can happen to the just and the unjust. The men who were buried under the stones of the tower of Siloam were not more guilty than the man who walked past, saw it happen, but came away unscathed. We therefore are faced with the mystery that all such disasters befall us because of the guilt of all, and yet they strike only a few. And herein lies the motivation and the stimulus to lift, insofar as possible, the suffering from the few and to spread it across all. The fact that it is communal guilt urges and motivates us automatically to bear it communally. And despite the potential for various kinds of abuse, this is precisely what insurance enables us to do. It calculates the financial loss of the disasters that we can expect based on the regularity of suffering. It tells us approximately how many must participate in order to make the calculations concrete, and it calculates for us how much of this communal suffering each has to bear, so that all can assume the losses that affect a few.

The term *insurance* is a very unfortunate choice. Even as God let Solomon's § 4
temple be built by the Gentiles, so God has also let this "taking over by all of what affects only a few" be discovered by men who stood outside the faith. Thus, what God revealed to us in his love they attempted to make into a throne for human prestige. Man would now be insured, according to the evil intentions of some, even against God. The term *insurance* suggests an egotistical, unbelieving notion, and we would give anything to be rid of this unfortunate term. *Participation* would have been a much more attractive term, and it would have expressed the same thing. But this is the fault of believers themselves. They should have been the first to keep the matter in their own hands in order to claim the right themselves to give the infant a better name. But they did not. They kept their distance. They left this entire significant discovery to unbelievers. They did not have an eye for the work of God that was revealed here. It was similar to the days before the flood. Not Seth, but the unbelieving Jubal invented the lyre and the pipe [see Gen 4:21]. But who would say that for this reason no one may play the harp, or that for this reason we may not use an organ to accompany our psalm singing? And in the same way, this new invention has been discovered and named by unbelievers, but this does not mean that for this very reason believers have a license or excuse not to make use of it. Not Abel but Cain built the first city. May believers for that reason not live in a city? And as far as proper naming is concerned, is the term *sacrament* a less desirable term because it is derived from pagan life, and would this be a reason to oppose the very sacramental life of the church to which it refers? Or would it be reasonable, for that matter, once the term has been accepted in standard usage by default, to oppose the reality of the sacraments?[1]

One more point in conclusion. There is uncertainty in human suffering § 5
that most assuredly will ultimately affect everyone. Let us limit ourselves to this one point: we must all die. This is a certainty. But one person dies

1. The paragraph that follows has been omitted, in which Kuyper argues against a misreading of Job 12:6 based on the Dutch text.

earlier, while another dies later. This is the uncertainty in this certainty. And that is precisely what so-called life insurance is based on. Again, this is an unfortunate term, for no one's life can be insured. However, like it or not, we are stuck with that term, and we will not be able to get rid of it. What it simply means is this: assurance against the uncertain consequences of the uncertain and unstable aspect of death. And this touches on the question of *savings*. Is saving not much more reassuring and better than life insurance? We know that the men of the Society for Public Welfare have urged this saving of money; let it therefore never be said that it came from our corner.[2] But back to the point. If it were certain beforehand that a married couple had forty years of married life ahead of them, and that at least the husband would not die before his seventieth birthday, then saving should be the rule, and life insurance would be foolish. But this is *not* the case. The husband may live to be seventy or even eighty, but he might also die at age thirty-five. And at that point the children are still small, and he would leave his family helpless. Let us assume that he saves one hundred guilders per year; this would give him after forty years, including interest, close to eight thousand guilders, which would guarantee his wife an annual income of just over three hundred guilders after the children have left home. But if the husband dies after having been married only six years, then only six hundred guilders will have been accumulated and she will receive only twenty-five guilders per year and thus suffer want. This is the reason why setting aside money ourselves is not a good way to take care of our widow. Saving money, yes, but saving in mutual association with others must be the rule for most people. Faced with the uncertainty as to whether we will die young or old, with insurance we will live in the knowledge that our savings will *always* be effective and that our widow will always receive her three hundred guilders annually, regardless of whether we die in the first year of our marriage or do not go to the grave until we are seventy. Saving as individuals works only for those who become old. Saving together helps those who die young as well as those who die old.

We discover this principle by paying attention to the work of God. God causes a person to die—the one young, the other old. And careful attention

2. Founded in 1784 by the Dutch Mennonite Jan Nieuwenhuijzen (1724–1806), the Society for Public Welfare still exists today and is focused on the promotion of welfare broadly understood, especially through provision of educational resources and support.

shows that God follows regularity in this. It is not the case that only old people die in one year and only young people the next; rather, each year approximately as many old people die as do young people. No one knows who will die at an old age and who will die young. But we do know that year after year, God calls out of this life approximately the same number of people from the various age groups. On the basis of this, it has been calculated how many people's pension would have to be paid out already at age thirty, and how many at age seventy. Knowing this, we could determine fairly accurately how much each individual would have to pay in order to communally bear the financial burden for those who die old and those who die young. The person who dies young will have paid little, while the person who dies old will have paid much, more than he would have paid by saving privately; but he also has the enjoyment of living longer. Those who live longer then pay the pensions for the widows of those who die young. In this way loss due to suffering is borne communally.

A final comment. It would be good if all humanity were in solidarity § 6
and if *all* participated. Then the awareness of the communality of guilt and suffering would come to full effect. But God has so ordained it that this is not strictly necessary. Regularity is manifested not only when all are taken into account, but it applies also when we have a large number, say, one hundred thousand or even less. This could be otherwise, of course, but then insurance would not be possible unless all were forced to participate. But now, by contrast, the goal can be achieved (at least for many cases) if only a large number join, and by this means any country, any circle of reasonable size, can help itself.

This is as far as our discussion of insurance will go. We are satisfied if we have shown, hopefully with some clarity, that resistance, not to *abuse* but to the *legitimate use* of insurance, goes against both Scripture and the Reformed confession. We hope to have shown that what is involved here is rather the opening of the eye of the soul to a work of God in his common grace. And what is true of insurance is also true of science in general: viewed superficially, it leads away from God, but when we look at the root, it elevates the glory of his holy name.

It is not at all surprising that many devout Christians have looked with resentment at insurance. The reason for this is the human arrogance with which it often is presented and the pride with which statisticians come to its defense. Furthermore, this important subject has never yet been discussed from a decidedly Reformed perspective on the basis of principles and overall context. And although we readily concede that the explanation we have presented is also very incomplete, especially with regard to its application to the various branches of insurance, we nevertheless believe that our argument is consistent with the direction in which Reformed faith must move in this regard, and that more than one individual will give praise and glory to our God for his common grace, whose mercy shines so gloriously, not least in the regularity of communal suffering.

CHAPTER EIGHTY

SUFFERING AND GUILT

Do not forsake the work of your hands.

PSALM 138:8

With this discussion we come to the conclusion of our treatment of the connection between common grace and God's providence. But although certain so-called means and precautionary measures ended up occupying the largest place in our discussion, the connection in question is not limited to this. Rather, the connection between common grace and providence lies primarily *in the process of steady development* that "common grace" opened up for the implementation of God's providential ordination. Without common grace there would be preservation and rule, but no *divine government* in providence, for governing aims at reaching a chosen goal, like steering the ship and guiding it as it moves forward so that it finally reaches the harbor of its destination. The large place occupied by our discussion of the precautionary measures should not lead us to lose sight of the coherence of our discussion. After all, suffering occupies such a large place in our life that we should not give it short shrift in a discussion such as ours. Thus we encounter the false inclination to seek the essence of religion and godliness in our absolute dependence on and our impotence apart from § 1

God, but without doing so within the context of the rich covenant idea (as Bullinger already did).[1]

A dull passivity tended to grow in many Reformed circles, one that mirrored a false view of suffering and the Christian's response. That false passivity ended up donning the robe of an angel of light, as it were, and beguiled many. Not to be passive in the face of suffering was thought to be falling short in godliness. Here and there this view even infected preaching, so that in the end the battle cry of God against the suffering and its misery almost never rang out among our Reformed people. Imperceptibly we slid into an attitude toward not fearing suffering, of which the logical and practical consequence could be no other than this: "Do not set any guardrails along your bridges anymore, for all such precautionary measures are sinful, and if your child happens to fall into the water, do not attempt to save him, but wait to see whether the Lord will bring him back to dry land."

Of course, we are not saying that anyone ever spoke such ridiculous words. But this much is certain: if applied to the case of a child falling from a bridge into the water, the passive theological perspective would in fact lead to this conclusion. This dangerous way of thinking had even penetrated our circles so deeply that it was impossible for us again to shed light on the scriptural perspective without initially correcting some of those individuals who had been led astray in this way. In a sense it even took courage to discuss such a thorny topic openly and straightforwardly, without glossing over it. But this is precisely the reason why it could and should not have been done in a hurry or in a superficial manner. Although we hope to never evade an unscriptural notion, no matter how piously it may be framed, love nevertheless requires us to approach error that is interwoven with piety in a somewhat tender manner that is sparing of others. At first the conscience does not testify against an error that is interwoven with piety. Rather, something stirs initially in the conscience against someone who shows this error for what it is.

Care and attention are therefore called for, and for that reason we could take no other approach than first to show clearly how throughout Scripture suffering does not appear as a friend but rather as an enemy of God, against

1. Heinrich Bullinger (1504–75) was a leading reformer in Zurich associated with the development of the doctrine of the covenant in Reformed thought, of which his treatise, *De testamento seu foedere dei unico & aeterno* (Zurich: Froschauer, 1534), is a prime example.

which the Lord and his Anointed wage battle. Then we could show that an enemy against whom God does battle must be fought by us also—namely, with the weapons and means that God himself puts at our disposal. Seeing that death is inclusive of all suffering, referring to that single statement of Scripture that *the last enemy is death* [1 Cor 15:26] turns the passive notion radically into its opposite. But even so, the battle we must undertake against suffering and misery was wrapped up in so many other questions that it was impossible to reach a convincing conclusion without discussing each of these incidental circumstances. In the end, we could not escape the necessity of providing a better and healthier explanation of some well-known interpretations of Scripture that sound as if they would seem to support the theory of passivity.

But that task has now been finished, and as far as the battle against suf- § 2
fering is concerned, it remains only to identify a misunderstanding that arises for so many from their reading of the Old Testament. It is an undeniable fact that under the old covenant, under the rule of special revelation, the link between suffering and the guilt of the people—indeed, even of individuals—repeatedly assumes a direct character. The plagues that came over Pharaoh and ultimately caused his successor to the throne to die are a direct punishment for resisting the command that Moses and Aaron brought to him in the name of the God of Israel. When the prophet at Bethel is torn in pieces by a lion upon his return home, it is a direct punishment for his disobedience, because he had eaten bread when God had told him not to do so, whereas the old man who had lied to him and seduced him escaped the lion [1 Kgs 13]. When David held the census, the punishment follows in the pestilence. And so it goes throughout the Old Testament. When Israel adheres strictly to the service of the Lord, it is blessed, but when it leaves the service of the Lord, it falls under punishment and curse. And the means to escape suffering as a judgment of God is always presented as a return to the service of the Lord. "Put me to the test, says the LORD of hosts, if I will not open the windows of heaven for you and pour down for you a blessing" [Mal 3:10] is the *leitmotif* of all prophecy to Israel.

In what we read and not infrequently in what is preached that notion is transferred without further distinction to our current condition, and it is this concept of suffering to which many—especially among godly people—hold fast. But this should not be. If we take this approach, we lose sight of the unique character of the theocracy in Israel and the peculiar nature of special revelation, a serious error that then is transferred to the church and seduces even so many sincere people to apply to the church of the new covenant what in Israel was inseparable from the national church.

We could and should have been on our guard against this continuing error, for it was especially the Apostle Paul who emphatically identified the fundamental difference between the old dispensation and the new dispensation to such an extent that it was almost impossible for the serious reader of Scripture to fail to notice it. There is no longer any special revelation, there is no longer any nation with a theocracy, and we lack any means to identify the correct link between a specific sin and specific suffering except in cases where suffering arises directly *from* a specific sin. The person who gets drunk and has an accident in his drunken state knows that this specific accident is causally related to the particular sin of his drunkenness. But for the rest, we lack any particular indication from God. Consequently, none of us has the right to establish such a direct link, either for ourselves or for others, in any specific case. Such attempts are directly contradicted and judged by Jesus' clear statement that God makes his sun rise on the unrighteous and the righteous, and that those who were crushed under the tower of Siloam did not perish because of their greater sins. Those who, whether in conversations or in preaching, nevertheless transfer to *our* situation without any restriction this notion, derived from the special revelation of the Old Testament, must figure out how they can justify themselves before Jesus, whose divine authority they too acknowledge.

§ 3 But there is more. Under the old covenant it already was observed how, apart from this direct imputation of guilt in exceptional cases, quite another current ran through suffering, a current that was contrary to and in direct conflict with this. For according to the theory of the direct attribution of suffering to one committed evil or another, the result should have been that the godlier a person was, the less suffering that person would experience, and that, conversely, more adversity would come upon the one who lived less righteously. But the results did not show this; rather, they showed quite the opposite. Job is the example here, who was godlier than all others but nevertheless was pursued more bitterly than anyone by the most fearful suffering. In Psalms 37 and 73, in Proverbs, and in Ecclesiastes it is pointed out again and again how the godly servants of Jehovah are surrendered like sheep for the slaughter, and how it is precisely the godless who do not know any suffering or limitations until the time of their death. And we still see the same today. This is how reality is. A Christian school must be sold for demolition while a *bordello* is expanded. A church must be built with insubstantial, bare walls while a beer hall or dance hall displays its proud façade in Belgian bluestone before the eyes of all.

It is precisely as Job complains: those who provoke God have abundance and are secure in that abundance [Job 12:6], or as Isaiah exclaims, the godly servant of God is a *man of sorrows* [Isa 53:3]. If success is an indicator of *blessing*, then God blesses the godless, and judgment comes down especially hard upon the godly. We need think only of Nero, who unleashed an orgy of crime and excess while the disciples of the Lord were murdered in the arena. Thus, the two lines with respect to suffering—that of particular revelation and that of general revelation—certainly are already present in the Old Testament itself, and it is only superficial thoughtlessness if in conversations, lectures, devotional literature, poetry, and preaching the direct-link theory, which is *not* applicable to us, is applied to our circumstances, whereas the complaint of Job and Asaph, which does apply to our life, is lost from view.

What in fact is imperative is a full awareness and recognition of ancient thinking in this regard. We must no longer take as our point of departure that which flowed from special revelation once it had ceased. To the contrary, we must apply in our present-day life the entirely other theory, which equally, but in a quite different manner, does justice to the link between sin and suffering. In special revelation that link is direct: for *this* sin, one receives *that* suffering. But apart from special revelation, that link is interwoven with all of life: the guilt of *all* brings the suffering that should have affected *all* of us, but common grace now limits that to a few. We have not yet addressed the importance of this doctrine for the suffering of Christ; it is sufficient that we simply mention it, so that those with understanding among us may understand.

After warning those who love God's Word, and calling them back to the § 4
correct scriptural notion of suffering as it applies to us, we now finally pick up the general thread again to put into clear relief God's governance through common grace in connection with the goal that it envisions. For this governance does not only consist in the fact that in paradise after the fall, a measure of common grace enters the picture to arrest the full effect of ruin and thus to make possible human life on earth; rather, it also extends to an ever-richer allocation of this common grace that allows human life to continually *progress* and, thanks to this progress, bring it to ever richer and fuller development. For that reason, a distinction must be made between these two aspects of common grace. One aspect is the constant activity of

common grace that began in paradise after the fall and has remained to the present exactly what it originally was. Further, this constant common grace itself consists in two parts. First, it functions in such a way that God arrests the destructive power *in nature* so that it will not destroy the world all at once. And second, God arrests the destructive power of sin *in the human heart*, so that civil righteousness is possible on earth among sinners and heathen. This arresting of sin and misery throughout the whole world among all nations operates with differences in degree where individuals are concerned, so that one party is allowed to go much further into sin than another. But whatever the differences in degree, this first activity of common grace remains constant throughout the centuries and among all nations. Common grace is what leads to the *preservation* and *governance* of our human life.

Yet common grace could not stop with this first, constant function. Preservation and governance alone do not answer the question of the earth's purpose for existing and surviving a history of many centuries. If nothing remains except what already has been, then for what purpose does it remain? If life is nothing but a repetition of what went before, why is life extended? Then it is all the same whether this life lasts two, three, or twenty centuries. It remains as it was: an endless reappearing of what just disappeared. In short, there is then no divine *governance*. There is no guiding principle that leads to a specific goal. The ship has no direction but drifts about and bobs up and down on the water without ever making any headway.

This is why a second, entirely different activity of common grace is added to the initial, constant activity of common grace, which serves only to maintain what already exists. This second function permits our human life and the life of the whole world to go through a process, allowing it to develop ever more fully and richly, bringing it from less to more. This activity can and will come to an end only when that process has been completely finished. This is what makes the continued existence of the world throughout a succession of centuries understandable and transparent. If I have to climb a mountain that is four thousand meters high, and I ascend at a rate of two hundred meters per hour, then it is clear that I must be allowed twenty hours to reach the top. And in the same way, if our human life has to go through a developmental path of a million kilometers, and in each century it can make no more progress than a hundred thousand kilometers, then anyone can understand why it takes ten centuries to reach the finish.

These numbers are only for purposes of illustration, of course, since at this point we already have far more than ten centuries behind us. But these numbers nevertheless make it clear why humanity was and still is granted such a centuries-long existence after the fall. The long human history that remains absolutely meaningless and incomprehensible as long as we take into account only the *constant* activity of common grace suddenly becomes absolutely necessary and logical as soon as we also take into account the *progressive* activity of that same common grace. The *constant* aspect consists in the fact that God, with all kinds of difference in gradation, arrests and restrains the curse of nature and the sin of the heart. The *progressive* aspect, by contrast, consists in the other kind of activity, through which God, under steady progress, ever more abundantly arms human life against suffering and brings it inwardly to richer and fuller development.

Related to this is the fact that there is a profound difference in the nature § 5
of these two operations of common grace. In the constant operation of common grace, God acts outside of man. In the progressive operation, by contrast, man himself acts as an instrument of and collaborator with God. When Adam does not die immediately after the fall but death is arrested in him, that phenomenon is executed directly by God. And when sin is arrested more strongly in Abel's heart than in Cain's heart, that is a direct activity of grace in Abel's heart. Thus it was then, and thus it is still. God himself, apart from us, makes it so that the sun does not burn us up but warms us. No human being adds to or detracts anything from it. And in the same way, it is a fact that the seeds of crime lying at the bottom of our heart too did not germinate in us but did so in the heart of the murderer or the adulterer, and this fact is the result of a difference in the direct activity of grace in the heart of one person but not another.

But when it comes to the progressive activity of common grace, things are entirely different. Look at how man now feeds and clothes himself, lives and develops and occupies himself, moves from place to place, knows how to make all kinds of works of art, and decorates his life and makes it more pleasant and enriches it. When we note the immeasurable difference between this and the condition that still prevails among various tribes of Africa—a condition that was once our portion as well—then we are faced with a difference between day and night, and we can scarcely conceive of even a very weak comparison between these two radically divergent conditions of human life. The height at which human life has arrived was not reached in a sudden leap. Human life has traveled a very long road to get there, and on that long road the development, progress, and civilization that gradually were achieved were achieved as a result of human effort, human struggle, human inventiveness, human cooperation, and human ingenuity.

Of course God the Lord was at work in all of this, and in no area of life whatsoever was there any progress of even one fraction of a millimeter apart from and without God. Yet in this realm God the Lord never worked immediately or directly, never apart from man, but *always in and through man*. God created people for this, and God prepared them for their task. Of course God made them find what they found. But this does not deny the fact that along this long road we always find man working in God's work, and God working through man as an instrument. Nothing has ever been invented, or thought up, or brought to light that God had not put many centuries ago into nature around us and into man's nature. But it lay hidden. No one saw it. Nobody knew it. Steam has existed from the very first time that water was heated by fire, but no one saw the potential in that steam and what could be done with it. God saw it, but for many centuries man did not. But when the power of steam finally becomes manifest, it is *man* who discovers it and man who gradually learns to apply that steam.

And thus it is with all things. Nothing new is added in this world. All that now appears was in the world from the beginning—albeit covered, hidden, concealed. And this is God's plan, as shown in the history of mankind, that God lets man find first one means and then another, through which man is enabled to avert more and more suffering and make life continually richer and happier. God does not do this all at once. He gradually lets the light go up in the darkness. Sometimes there are even centuries when we seem to regress. In Asia Minor life was at one time much richer and happier than it is today. But taken as a whole, mankind continually has progressed and has received from God more and more abundant means for exercising dominion over all of nature, in accordance with the original creation ordinance. And that is why it does not suit and befit us to resist and scorn new means when God lets us find them, since this is nothing but resisting and rejecting what God gives us in his common grace.

Rather, it is the calling of each of us to ask ourselves constantly the question whether there are still other means and powers hidden and concealed in nature that await discovery and that God wants to bring to light through human effort and human struggle. Civilization, enlightenment, development, and progress are not from the evil one but from God. Only their wrong, immoral, and godless application is from the evil one, and we Christians must oppose this with all our might. But arriving at greater dominion over nature is a gift of God's grace for which we must thank him and for which we as God's children must exert ourselves. At creation God himself placed these rich seeds for majestic development in humanity, and it was God's will from the very beginning that these seeds would come to development in dominion over nature. Satan has wanted to arrest this development through sin, but God intervened with his common grace to bring humanity, albeit via a path of blood and tears, to that high and rich development.

CHAPTER EIGHTY-ONE

THE COURSE OF THE AGES

... the mystery hidden for ages and generations but now revealed to his saints.

COLOSSIANS 1:26

§ 1 In the section we just completed, we dealt with the connection between common grace and God's providence, and we observed how God has willed that humanity should go through a history. The world does not suddenly stop after the fall, but continues. Days, months, years, and centuries follow. The fact that these centuries follow one another ceaselessly is possible only through common grace. Apart from common grace, the unholy fire of sin and curse soon would have erupted in a conflagration, and human life on this planet would have been utterly destroyed. But thanks to common grace, this destructive fire remains in a state of subdued smoldering. The destruction that threatened was arrested. And only thus did it become possible that after paradise and after the fall a history should follow, and that an immense time period should open up that has continued for centuries without interruption.

Nevertheless, this succession of one century after another would have been entirely purposeless if it had served only to allow that which existed to continue existing unchanged. Regardless of how great the grace would have been merely to allow our race to *continue to exist*, human existence thus lengthened would not in itself have had a reason for being if it had been a repetition without end of a life like that of Adam after the fall. We can hardly conceive of the condition in which Adam passed his long existence after the fall—no fewer than nine centuries—but the heart of each of us would sink if it were imposed on us to continue living in such a situation, even if only for fifty years. But there *was* progress in Adam's life. Let us look at Adam's situation, not as it ultimately became but as it was in those very first years when paradise had just disappeared and he, alone with Eve and with a few as-yet helpless children, had to protect himself on the cursed earth against a nature turned into wilderness and animals turned feral, and when he had to wrest bread from the earth with his hands, without the help of any tools—any of us can realize how Adam's initial existence after the fall must have been bitter and desperately lonely. What purpose would such a meaningless repetition of human misery have served if *no* change had come in his situation, if it had *not* been followed by development and progress, and if the centuries that followed had brought nothing but ever-new pairs of humans, doomed to continue their painful existence in entirely the same condition?

No, if after the fall a *human history* was to follow, then something entirely different had to happen. The possibility had to be opened up for escaping the condition governing human life and evolving into another, more desirable condition. Only in this way did each century of human existence acquire a purpose, a task, a "calling." This greater purpose had to envelop the past and fold it into the future, purified and ennobled, enriched with new discoveries. And human beings realized that in each successive century the construction of "the building" of human culture continued as it had been begun in prior centuries. And when they recognized that the result was not a loose pile of stones that would fall apart again but that the combined labor of many centuries (expressing itself in firm lines, perpendicular walls, and a façade) remained in the end, then it became clear that this labor of the centuries had been guided unawares by an unseen Master Builder. And it was the unseen guidance that this Supreme Builder gave to the work of all those centuries that transformed the life of humanity in these centuries into a "history." Our forefathers confessed this from of old in the doctrine of God's decrees. In those decrees, everything was fixed and determined. Nothing could emerge in the course of the ages unless it came from these decrees and was in accordance with them. Anything that § 2 might have existed outside of these decrees seemed utterly unthinkable to them. For this reason, then, they confessed that the decrees themselves were not an expression of incoherent arbitrariness; rather, in those decrees the ultimate goal was designed according to the highest wisdom, and all things were directed as means toward that ultimate goal.

Hence, the decrees offered a complete program for creation as well as for the history that followed. As it stood in the decrees, things would come to pass as designed and in no other possible way. Or stated more accurately, the past had been determined, the present was determined, and the future would be determined as they stood in the decrees. At no point in his existence was God without his creation, without history, and without glorification, only to achieve in time the world he had envisioned through creation and through history. No, the decrees exist from eternity, and in those decrees God possessed from eternity the knowledge and the vision of his entire creation, of the whole of history, and of the entire glory that is to come. And the distinction between what is still in those decrees and what already has sprung from those decrees consists only in the same distinction that we see between the acorn from which the oak tree will sprout and the oak tree itself. The tie that binds history with creation binds the individual pieces of history into a single whole, and binds the course of all centuries into one coherent drama, is therefore not our deliberation, nor even our consciousness; it is solely God's consciousness in his eternal decree. What's more, our knowledge of history is nothing but a weak insight into the coherence that God has ordained for the course of history in his decree.

§ 3 The Reformed confession, which more than any other emphasizes the doctrine of the decrees, certainly did not consider this decree to concern only the election of those who would enter into life. Undoubtedly, the salvation of the elect dominates everything else in God's decree. But it is not the final goal, nor does it stand by itself. The ultimate goal always remains the self-glorification of the Triune God. Directly under this lofty ultimate goal comes the gathering of the elect, only because God himself has placed man as prophet, priest, and king at the head of his entire creation, and because humanity, thus privileged, could serve this self-glorification of Christ directly and fully only in these elect people, which we understand to be the body of Christ. But precisely for this reason, the decree of election is not to be considered even for a moment apart from *the whole* of God's decrees. The linchpin in the decrees, around which everything revolves, is election, but election stands in an organic connection with all the other content of those decrees. The calling of the elect stands in direct connection with the life of Christ's church; the life of Christ's church with the people of Israel; the people of Israel with the existence and history of the rest of the nations; the life of the rest of these nations with the existence of the tribes, generations, families, and individuals; this entire life of the nations with the development of humanity's knowledge and abilities; this knowledge and these abilities with the life of nature around us; and finally, this life of nature around us with the existence of the sun, moon, and stars—or, if you will, with the existence and course of the universe. Only *all things* together, as they were, are, and will be, constitute the content of the decrees of God, and only in that coherence does election have its high and rich significance.

But it is at the same time striking how common grace cannot be omitted from the decrees of God, indeed, how indebted the history of humanity is to the motif of common grace in the decrees. We leave out of consideration in this regard the question of infra- or supralapsarianism, but this much is certain: proponents of the one as well as proponents of the other acknowledge that the fall was included in the decree as fact.[1] No one from Reformed stock has ever taught that the fall occurred apart from the decree, nor that the decrees were later modified because of the fall. And if we take as our starting point the firm position that the fall is included in the decrees, then the sinking of this world into eternal doom—apart from common grace, which wards off this sudden collapse of the entire universe—can only follow in that same decree. The fall is followed by the entrance of common grace. But it needs to be emphasized that this occurred not as an arbitrarily inserted expedient, but rather as demanded directly by the ultimate goal of God's decrees. The self-glorification of God is the only motive for the universe coming into existence. Apart from God's seeking his own glorification

---

1. On infralapsarianism and supralapsarianism, see *DLGTT*, s.v. "supra lapsum": "Two basic views of predestination emerged from the development of Reformed doctrine in the late sixteenth and early seventeenth centuries: the supralapsarian view, sometimes referred to as full double predestination, and the infralapsarian view, frequently termed single predestination. Both views arise out of consideration of an eternal, logical 'order of the things of the decree,' or *ordo rerum decretarum*, in the mind of God. According to the supralapsarian view, the election and reprobation of individuals are logically prior to the divine decree of creation and the divine ordination to permit the fall." By contrast, "the infralapsarian view, which is the confessional position of the Reformed churches, places the divine will to create human beings with free will and the decree to permit the fall prior to the election of some to salvation."

there was no reason why creation came into existence. Nothing outside himself moved God to create, and that creation did not come into existence at all for the sake of people. Humankind is included in creation itself, and no matter how high the ranking that God assigned to it in creation, human creation is and remains included among the means. Humankind comes into existence in and with the world because God wanted to see the whole world consecrated to himself through human creation as a "priest," and because it is his pleasure to see his own image reflected in human creation.

But everything in this world—all that is related to this world and concerns this world—is subordinate to the only ultimate goal that God has set, which lies exclusively in his own self-glorification. Therefore, human self-glorification through pride and haughtiness constitutes the mother of all sin because all *human* self-glorification goes directly against the ultimate goal of all things: self-glorification belongs to God only, and never to any creature. Therefore, if the fall exists in the decree, then immediately contextualized in that same decree is not only particular grace but common grace, both of which are incorporated into creation as a powerful driving force. After all, if the fall had not been followed by common grace as well, the entire continued existence of the world would have withdrawn forever from the self-glorification of God. This would be unthinkable in the decrees of God, since what determines all God's decree and everything in the decrees is his intent to glorify himself.

§ 4 But would the entry of particular grace have been sufficient to prevent the thwarting of this ultimate goal of the ways of the Lord? Think about this question. Particular grace saves unto eternal life those who have been so ordained by God, in the connection willed by God with Christ as their Head. But in order to save unto eternal life people who became sinners, those persons had to be *born*. First, they had to *be*. And how, we might wonder, would the elect of God who lived or still live in our own century ever have come into being if, immediately after the fall, at the time when they ate of the tree of knowledge, Adam and Eve had experienced death, as had been threatened? Then neither Abel, nor Cain, nor Seth would ever have been born, and there would have been no human race. Therefore, there had to be a tempering of the death sentence, if only to allow the elect to be born and to make possible the continued existence of our race. As it is, this could happen only through common grace.

But this is not all. Once they were born, the elect also should be able to live as *human beings*, in their families, in their generations, in their tribes, and in their nations. As human beings, they had to find a nature around them that made human existence possible. The consequence of their spiritual salvation was not that they were suddenly taken out of the world. Although this might be conceivable as such, and although we must concede that God could regenerate his elect already in their mother's womb and call them to himself immediately upon birth (as is certainly the case with some of the elect), this could not possibly apply to all. For then our human race would immediately have become extinct. In order to bring all the elect to eternal life, many of them would have to live at least long enough to bring into existence new elect persons and, beyond having children, to raise them as well. Their existence on this earth would therefore have lasted at least half a century. And during those fifty years they would have had to enjoy a human existence in a world suited for that. This would have been inconceivable after the fall and under the curse if common grace had not been added to particular grace to temper the curse immediately, to rein in the eruption of sin, and to make human development possible.

We are mistaken, therefore, if we imagine that particular grace in itself § 5
would have been enough. Rather, particular grace, and specifically the implementation of the decree of election, would be utterly inconceivable if we stop at the fall, the death sentence, and the curse. It is precisely particular grace, which saves only to eternal life, that calls for common grace if it is to achieve its goal. In the doctrine of the covenants, the connection between the life of particular grace and the life of nature is sealed, and the misunderstanding that crept in with respect to this stemmed only from the fact that *nature* and *grace* were placed in opposition to one another in an inaccurate way. This contrast between nature and grace seemed to give the wrong impression that nature was still nature in its originally created state. Lost from view was the fact that the curse had come upon that nature and that nature under the curse of necessity sinks into ruin unless grace comes to preserve it. Thus, it was overlooked that nature itself as we currently know it has received grace. Not grace unto eternal life, but grace against the results and continuing effects of the curse. If now, after the fall, we contrast nature and grace, we may refer by this to nothing other than the grace-endowed nature that stands in contrast to particular grace, which saves unto eternal life.

But obviously this runs the risk of falling into misunderstanding. If we treat nature and grace as two mutually exclusive concepts, then we automatically get the impression that nature continues to exist apart from any grace and that grace has been and is extended only to God's elect. And this is absolutely untenable. Common grace is extended to nature, and particular grace is extended to God's elect. The contrast holds only with these qualifications. Much clearer and purer, therefore, is the contrast between creation and re-creation, a contrast with which we are becoming more accustomed today. What we call "nature" is all that finds its origin and laws in the original creation. All of this suffered under the curse that entered after the fall, but common grace warded off the deadly consequences of the curse and made possible and ensured the continued existence (albeit in a disconsolate condition) of what was the original creation. And in contrast to this, then, stands what belongs to "re-creation" and all that together constitutes the realm of particular grace. Particular grace not only arrests, but *it creates anew*. The redeemed life is "a new creation in Christ" [see 2 Cor 5:17]. He is "the new man" [see Eph 4:24; Col 3:10]. From this follows all of divine revelation. From this follows the Christ. From this follows all born-again persons, the church, and the body of Christ. We have here an altogether *new creation* and yet one that remains related to the original creation, for it is a *re-creation*. At the same time, this new creation cannot be explained solely from the old, inasmuch as it has its own character. The false construal of nature and grace derives partly from medieval theology; the contrast can still be used as long as we always note that nature, cursed in itself, persists only through common grace. From the Reformed principle we have a much more accurate construal of that which derives from *creation* and that which derives from *re-creation*. This distinction is owing to what is anchored in common grace and what proceeds from particular grace. In common grace, there is never anything new, never anything that cannot be explained from the original creation. In particular grace, by contrast, there is nothing that comes from creation; rather, everything is *new* and can be explained only from the new creation or *re-creation*.

§ 6 Before we get to the practical significance of common grace for our human lives in the final chapters, it is necessary that in our discussion of the doctrinal aspect of common grace we probe more deeply its relationship to particular grace. Although this relationship has been discussed several times in passing, which was unavoidable, clarity demands that we pay more deliberate attention to this relationship. Our point of departure here is found in what we stated earlier—namely, that *common grace* first of all unlocks a history, opens up a broad temporal vista, and causes a stream of events to flow into distant regions, or, to put it succinctly, brings about an unfolding sequence of centuries. If, as we have shown, this sequence of centuries cannot have as its goal *a repetition of always the same*, then in the course of these centuries a gradual change, modification, and transformation of human life must take place. Even despite periods of temporary darkening, this process necessarily brings ever more light and enrichment of human life and hence bears the character of ever-continuing development of progress from less to more, in the end mirroring a fuller flourishing of life. When we consider the distance that currently still exists between the life of an African in his village and the life of a family in our present European society, we can catch a small glance of the distance already traversed. At the end of each century it is thought that the progress during that century was so amazing that it is virtually impossible to envision still further progress, yet each new century shows us that new developments utterly surpass every earlier imagination. Just consider how much the nineteenth century changed, enriched, and simplified our human life!

Quite mistakenly, people in godly circles often were inclined to resist progress and the ever-continuing development of our human life. And, sadly, it must be acknowledged that precisely this sort of Christian, by withdrawing from that gradual development, has caused that development so often to take wrong turns in moral and religious terms. Those who are in Christ not only should not resist development and progress; they should be greatly supportive of it. Surpassing others, at least in this realm, would seem to be their proper calling. Calvinism in the sixteenth and seventeenth centuries provides a model: it took the lead and as a result dominated life. The fact that we currently must make room for unbelief under all manner of Anabaptist and Methodist influences is a fault of our forefathers—a mistake whose bitter fruits we are bearing at present.

Precisely for this reason it needs to be pointed out that the time span of § 7
the centuries that have elapsed since the fall in no way constitutes an empty time frame in terms of the decrees of God. The time span of centuries that lies behind us must have had a purpose and destination, according to divine decree. And that purpose can be grasped only if it is first understood that the ongoing development of our human life is included in the divine plan. Thus, the history of the human race that resulted in this development did not come from Satan, nor from humans, but from God. Those who repudiate this development and do not value it misunderstand the work of God in history. Scripture speaks of "the end of the age" [Matt 28:20], which does not mean that the centuries will simply cease one day; rather, they

are directed toward an ultimate goal, and all that lies in those centuries is related to that ultimate goal.

God stimulates humankind toward that development through distress, suffering, and human misery, among other things. This is why it is so thoroughly wrong to see in suffering only a judgment under which we must groan; suffering must be recognized continually as the enemy against which God calls us to do battle. But this is where the problem lies. The means to protect and defend ourselves against this suffering, means that only God can point out to us, have not been revealed to us by God all at once. Over the course of the centuries, God again and again has let us discover something new, something more, with respect to those means. Noah was more advanced in this than Adam, Moses more than Noah, and Solomon more than Moses; hence, through the process of progress we have become more advanced than our forefathers. It is not that something new has been created. All that God uncovered for us lay in creation from the very beginning, but we did not know it (or at least we did not see it), and God has used the centuries to lead us gradually to discover—in increasing measure—new things that might enrich our human life. Progress, therefore, can be measured by the fact that, down through the course of the centuries, God has facilitated the discovery of new things we had not seen before, even though they were there.

CHAPTER EIGHTY-TWO

THE CLOSE OF THE AGE

The harvest is the end of the age.

MATTHEW 13:39

Common grace has arrested the continued working of sin and tempered the effects of the curse, and this tempering of the curse still continues. Century after century, more and more misery is being overcome, and more and more suffering is being alleviated. We owe this ever-continuing prevention and alleviation of suffering to the ever-new means that God places at our disposal by revealing them to us. These means, applied in accordance with God's will, extend our mastery over nature and thus enable us to combat suffering more effectively. We humans are given a task in this that makes us instruments of divine mercy. The man to whom God showed the means to prevent sepsis after a serious operation was made an instrument by God himself to save countless of lives after surgery and to spare early bereavement on the part of those who would have mourned the death of their loved one. The continuing discovery of the means to combat suffering required *time*. In this light, we may say that century had to follow upon century. And this explains in part why the end of all things was deferred so long. § 1

But this awareness does not secure for us a clear insight into the course of the centuries. For this reason it has been said that *the number of the elect must be complete, and thus the end of the age cannot come before the last of the elect have been born and have been born again.*[1] And this is undoubtedly one of the first causes of the long duration of the centuries. The number of centuries is in proportion to the number of generations that must come and go upon earth, to allow all those destined for eternal life to see the light of life. And only then, in second place, comes the fact that the full development of common grace could not be manifested suddenly but only gradually, and why in the same way many centuries were needed to gain time in order that everything could be discovered. At the same time, no matter how good this sounds, it does not satisfactorily solve the enigma of the large number of centuries.

Someone might legitimately ask, Can we suppress the question as to why the "elect" have been apportioned by God over so many centuries? From Abraham to Christ almost as many centuries went by as from Christ to us, but just for the moment, compare the small number of believers in those first centuries with the large numbers that were added to the church after Pentecost. We are not forgetting Melchizedek, and we certainly are not saying that there could have been no elect outside of Abraham's family as well in those early centuries of the human race. We know that the tribes of Israel in the days of Solomon had grown into a large group of people. And even in the days of Israel's captivity, we find Israelites in the whole known world. But how does this bear on the fact that apostasy in Israel itself was frightful century after century, and that time and again only a small remnant remained faithful to Jehovah, and that a small group of faithful dwindled time and again into insignificance compared with the hundreds of millions who continued their disconsolate existence in Asia, Europe, and Africa, without the hope of eternal life? One might conclude that the number of elect who died believing in the Christ who was to come remained comparatively small. And, of course, who can suppress the

---

1. See, for instance, Francis Turretin, *Institutes of Elenctic Theology*, ed. James T. Dennison Jr., trans. George Musgrave Giger, 3 vols. (Phillipsburg, NJ: P&R Publishing, 1992–97), 3:42–43: "The conservation of the world depends upon the conservation of the church, since for no other reason does he sustain the world than to collect from it the number of the elect, of whom the body of the church is composed. Thus the church could not wholly perish without the world itself (which is preserved on account of her) perishing."

question as to why this could not have been otherwise? Why was the birth of the large multitude of God's elect postponed for so many centuries? And why couldn't the birth of those elect have been arranged in such a way that they could have been born all together in, say, ten centuries? If that were the case, then, as far as God's elect are concerned, every reason for the continuation of this dispensation would have dissipated many centuries ago.

We do not raise this question in the least to meddle in the work of God, but only to make clear that the number of the elect per se does not explain the protracted existence of this world. At present, approximately 1.5 billion people live on this planet, and in each century 4 billion are born and die. Why couldn't the number of children born have grown faster in earlier centuries as well? And why couldn't the number of elect in each new generation have been increased tenfold? It goes without saying that anyone can sense how much shorter the timespan would have been in order to complete the number of the elect. It is understandable that the elect are spread over the whole series of generations if we grant that the world had to have such a long duration *for another reason*, and it certainly is understandable that this number was greater *after* Christ than before Christ. However, then the cause of the long duration of this world in its present dispensation lies not in the number of the elect itself, but rather in something else, and that is what we must try to investigate.

The same sort of reasoning applies to the second element to which we pointed. After the fall, God has not suddenly, all at once, given our human race *all* the means to combat misery and to mitigate the curse. Even as of today this has not happened; more is yet to come. We understand—and readily grant—that this takes time. A time span of many centuries, we concede, was not too much for this to occur. And yet who can suppress the question in this context, whether it was necessary that it happen so slowly? Take again the example we used earlier: the advances in surgery. Why couldn't the means to prevent sepsis have been revealed already in Abraham's day? Why wasn't the means to arrest the fierceness of disease and pestilence known already in Solomon's day? Why wasn't the use of quinine to combat fever revealed already in the days of Jeremiah? How much untold misery would earlier discoveries have prevented? When missions now opens a medical ministry in Yogyakarta [on Java], the natives come by the hundreds and are delivered from a number of diseases through means that are unknown to them.

But we ask again, couldn't the knowledge of these means have been revealed centuries ago, even to distant lands and far-away peoples, in order to mitigate and arrest their suffering? Certainly, *some* time was needed to gradually derive the one discovery from the other. From one perspective, generations upon generations have languished in their unmitigated misery, while all these means were hidden in creation from the very beginning. It may sound beautiful in the ears of religious people to say that "centuries were required to make the number of the complete, and it required centuries for God to let us discover successively all these means for the warding off of suffering and for the affirmation of our mastery over nature." But at best, this only explains why a certain duration of time, a certain number of centuries, was needed; it does not explain why that duration had to be extended so long and why the number of centuries had to be extended so far. Our memory of human civilization now goes back sixty long centuries, and, as we noted, ten centuries would have been more than enough to allow all the elect to be born and to reveal to us the entire panoply of armor against suffering.

§ 2 Given this long duration of the world, attention therefore needs to be focused on an entirely different concept that comes to us in Scripture itself, when Jesus speaks of the "end of the age." The notion of an "end of the age" also occurs in the farewell words of Jesus at the institution of sacred baptism: "And behold, I am with you always, *to the end of the age*" [Matt 28:20]. That saying could have been understood simply as a reference to the end of this dispensation—that is, to the end of the centuries or, stated succinctly, *the end*. Then it would refer to nothing but that point in time when everything will be over. And it could be understood in the same way when the disciples ask in Matthew 24:3, "What will be the sign of your coming and of the end of the age?" We might even deduce from the disciples' question here that the expression "the end of the age" was current in their day, with no other meaning attached to it other than *the end*, taken as a point in time when this dispensation will cease and the world will pass away. But even if Jesus sometimes borrowed this expression from common usage, Matthew 13 nonetheless shows us that, just as with so many other words he borrowed from his contemporaries, he was infusing this expression with a quite different, and much more profound, meaning.

Our Savior did this, for example, on the occasion of the parable of the weeds. This parable speaks of a field in which seed is scattered. The seed germinates and grows. This growth continues until the grain is ripe. Then the time for the harvest arrives, and the wheat is gathered into sheaves. With this image of the field in view, Jesus says that the field is the world and the "harvest is the end of the age, and the reapers are angels. Just as the weeds are gathered and burned with fire, so will it be at the end of the age. ... He who has ears, let him hear" [Matt 13:39–40, 43]. This, as we see, sheds an entirely different light on this concluding point, for here the sense of closure is definitely not merely an indication of a point in time; rather, it assumes and incorporates a slow process of germinating, of growing, of ripening and getting ready for the harvest. Jesus himself points to that slow process in the parable that is reported to us in Mark 4:28: "The earth produces by itself, first the blade, then the ear, then the full grain in the ear." Here a process is portrayed that moves from *seed* to the *blade* to the *ear* to the *full ear*. Such a process cannot occur in one week, not even in one month. It requires a complete growing season. It may happen a bit more slowly in a colder climate and a bit more rapidly in a warmer climate, but the point is that it takes time. And by this we mean time not merely to fill up a particular empty space, but time that is necessary and indispensable for moving from the seed to the grain that is ready to be harvested.

Here, therefore, the term *end* mirrors a much richer concept. It is no § 3
longer the "end of the age" in the sense of simply the end; rather, the world itself is what comes to a close, and this is why it speaks of "the end of the world." The world therefore is considered as a living whole that begins as a seed or, if you will, embryonically, and goes from this stage of germination gradually to a second stage—that is, a stage of forming shoots. After this, the process continues. Then comes the initial stage of the ear, and in that ear the kernels gradually begin to form. Small at first, those kernels swell out to their full size. And when that full size of the kernels of grain is reached, the final process begins, in which they go from green and unripe to yellow and full maturity. This is the same concept used by James when he writes of "sin when it is fully grown" [Jas 1:15]. No one will understand this as referring simply to the time used up by sin; rather, everyone will see that it refers to the steady progress of sin, a sin that starts with little but gradually gains in strength and by degrees manifests its full nature, at last ending up with its sour fruit and yielding all its bitter consequences.

In similar fashion Jesus instructs his disciples, "Go and tell that fox, 'Behold, I cast out demons and perform cures today and tomorrow, and the third day I finish my course' " [Luke 13:32]. No one understands this text in the sense that Jesus' death would be mechanically attached to his life; quite to the contrary, Jesus' battle against the devils and their kingdom had to end up in his bitter death. When it says in Psalm 9:6, "The enemy came to an end in everlasting ruins," it is not referring to the point in time when the destruction will cease, but to a destruction that destroys everything, a completion in which all that stands will be leveled. Jesus himself is called "the founder and perfecter of our faith" [Heb 12:2], and whether we interpret this to mean that Jesus in his example has elevated faith to its purest pinnacle or that Jesus elevates our faith, through all its stages, to its zenith, in both cases it does not refer to a literal point in time; rather, it indicates a process that must extend through all of its stages. It is the same idea being mirrored in Daniel 11:36, where the text says that the antichrist "shall exalt himself and magnify himself above every god, and shall speak astonishing things against the God of gods. He shall prosper till the indignation is accomplished." These words as well do not point to a specific point in time, but rather to a manifestation of anger, of wrath, and of indignation that begins small, gradually builds, and ceases only when the whole process has been completed and its strength is exhausted.

§ 4 Here, then, we may consider ourselves on firm ground. Jesus himself says that "the world" goes through a process; that it must go through various stages or steps; that it can proceed only gradually from one stage to the next; and that it therefore must keep going until this entire process has been completed—that is, until it has reached its goal. This cannot happen in a single leap. The long course of this process must be traveled step-by-step, and only in this way can and will it finally arrive at its end; in that end it will have achieved its ultimate goal.

In the building of Solomon's temple, the first step was digging the hole for the foundations. In that hole the foundations were laid, and on those foundations the walls were erected and fronted by a façade. Then, on those walls the crenellations were built, and behind those crenellations the flat roof was constructed. In this way the building was completed. So it is with the building of the history of this world as well. The roof cannot come before the walls stand, the walls cannot be erected before the foundations are in place, and the foundations can be set only in the excavated space. No part of the process can be skipped. One step has to precede the next one; it is according to a fixed plan and specifications that one phase appears after the other. The completion of the temple does not mean the point in time at which the temple will be finished; rather, it indicates that every part that belongs to the building has been put in its proper place, so that nothing can be added and so that the whole temple, which has been finished, radiates in its full splendor. In the same way, the life and development of the world is a historical building process whose Master Builder and Artisan is God, and in that building process everything must occur gradually. The whole building process aims at the realization of a predetermined plan, and in accordance with the demands of that plan, one phase after the next must be completed, and all this is subject to the ultimate goal God had envisioned. In its completed state the gable is supported by everything that was built before, and nothing that was built before can be omitted if the gable is to be supported.

But even when the construction of a building might serve for us as a picture of such divine completion, we nevertheless must note that, in order to make the completion of the world understandable, Jesus draws an image not from the mechanical artisanship of humanity but from the organic activity of nature. "The earth," Jesus says, "produces by itself [that is, organically] first the blade, then the ear, then the full grain in the ear."

Here, then, we get the indication that such an organic process occurs in the life of the world as well. At creation God himself scattered seeds in the whole of the life of the world, seeds that were designed to develop. He has put those seeds in nature outside of us as well as in the nature of our human race. He causes those seeds to sprout. When they sprout, first the blade appears, and only then can the ear develop in that blade. And then follows the natural process: the ear swells to its full size, and that ear, green at first, ripens and turns yellow. This process, just like the process of all plants as they grow, requires a measure of time. In such an organic process nothing appears all at once; rather, there is a gradual activity through which the process continually moves from one stage to the next, as if automatically. There is always ongoing development, and that development leads to steady progress. And through that steady progress everything moves toward the final goal, until completion has been reached and the yellowed stalk with the ripened fruit bows before the sickle at harvest.

Note that this *completion* refers not only to the kingdom of God, but to § 5
the *world* as such. The *world* goes through a process of development, and through that slow process of development it moves toward its own completion—that is, to the end that God wills it to reach. Therefore, it is not only the kingdom of God that moves in this world while the world lies dead and still—no, this world itself moves toward a goal that is set for it. Even in the mundane picture of the weeds sown among the wheat, the weeds sprout and grow equally as well as the wheat. The weeds go through a

process too, and that process also occurs according to a fixed law that God has determined for its growth.

In this way we arrive at the clear insight that the centuries must continue for such a long period, not only for the sake of the elect, and not only for the sake of the means God uncovers for us in the struggle against suffering, but also for the sake of the development of the world itself toward its end. The centuries had to continue as long as required to bring the world from its beginning and from the first emergence of our human life to the point at which that whole process will be completed and the ultimate goal God had in mind for it will truly be achieved. Therefore, there cannot be a half century or a quarter century too many. There is no emptiness or stagnation. That which does not yet grow above ground is already active underground, in the sprouting of the seed or the strengthening of the roots. Not a year, not a day, not an hour is in vain. Throughout those centuries, God has ceaselessly continued his work in our human race, in the whole of the life of this world. Nothing has been without purpose; nothing is superfluous. It had to go as it did. It could not have happened otherwise. And the sign of the Son of Man will appear in the clouds only when that great and mighty work of God has been completely finished, and with that, the end of the world will come.

Any notion that the work of God was to be found only in the small part of our human life that we could call ecclesiastical life must therefore be abandoned. By that I simply mean that in addition to the great work of God in particular grace, there is also that entirely different work of God in the realm of common grace. And that work of God in common grace encompasses the entire life of the world, the life among the natives in Africa, among those in China and Japan, and among the Indians to the south of the Himalayas. There was nothing in all previous centuries—whether among the Egyptians and Greeks or in Babylonia and Rome—and there is nothing now among the peoples of any particular part of the world that was or is unnecessary; all of it is an indispensable part of the great work in which God has been involved to bring the world in its development to completion. And even though much still baffles us concerning the cause of the kingdom or the content of our faith, all of it nevertheless has significance, and no part of it can be missed. The reason for this is that it pleases God to bring about what he put into this world from the beginning. Therefore, he has chosen to persevere in this process in spite of Satan's wiles and in spite of man's sins, bringing it to full development so that the full life energy of his creation will become manifest in the completion of the world.

CHAPTER EIGHTY-THREE

THE MANIFESTATION OF THE IMAGE OF GOD

For he was looking forward to the city that has foundations, whose designer and builder is God.

Hebrews 11:10

Human life on this earth, as it has developed through the centuries, is far too inherently significant and important for there to be seen in it nothing but an incidental means and indifferent instrument for the sake of an entirely different goal. We must admit that the extending and stretching of our human race across so many centuries undoubtedly was also related to the large number of persons God had decided to create and, related to this, to the large number of elect individuals who would attain salvation. And there likewise is no doubt that in this development of our race there was a process that moved from the seed to the harvest. But no sort of explanation has yet provided us with any sort of satisfactory solution. § 1

Once the golden kernel springs from the ear of corn, the ear and the stalk have no higher value than that of straw for the stable, fireplace, or dung pit. On this view, the knowledge that the *beginning* is connected with the *end* by means of a slow process means that, theologically speaking, everything is subordinate to the decision that comes with judgment and the revelation of the kingdom of glory that follows. Then, human history and the human development that transpired on the way to that goal might be considered meaningless chaff that is dispersed on the breath of the morning wind of the coming dispensation. Thus viewed, then, our entire human life is necessarily viewed exclusively from the perspective of the coming glory, and everything that does not become part of that glory becomes worthless in our estimation. For example, humankind's skill in painting passed through a glorious development from the daubing of the ancient East to the art treasures of someone like Rembrandt, but when the last trumpet is heard, it is assumed that all these art treasures on canvas will perish in the world's conflagration. Or using music as an example, how great was the ascent, it is acknowledged, from playing the flute with the lips to the swelling of the richest organ sounds, and yet one day, everything that churches possess by way of organ treasures will burn like firewood in the conflagration, and the pipes will melt. If we therefore focus only on the final goal of this process that the world travels, and if we understand the exclusive purpose of this world process to be the salvation of the spirits, then we are not doing justice to the slow and yet exceedingly rich process of the development of our race.

We then fail to understand and perceive why this development, which after all came from God's decree and has been guided among all peoples entirely by God, took on such broad dimensions and branched out so richly and raised up such a densely foliated crown. The question cannot be suppressed as to whether a simpler development of life would have guided our race more safely. Adding to our befuddlement, it would seem as if refinement of life led through opulence to sinful development, and we discover again and again how those with a godly inclination withdrew from that richly developed life into their prayer closets, their cloisters, or their private circles through isolation. Painful human experience taught us again and again that this stream of progressively developed, refined, and enriched life did not always serve the preservation of the soul. Even among us Moderns we see something of this asceticism return, and in the battle against alcohol—to cite but one prevalent example—the same trajectory is distinctly present. If, then, we look upon the history of the centuries exclusively with a view to latch on to the end goal, not only does the rich development of our human life remain unexplained, but the strong suspicion even arises that this rich development *impeded* the attainment of the envisioned proper goal. Had the development been less fulsome, we reckon, the temptation to sin definitely would have been less. And yet in refined social circles we still encounter the most distressing godlessness, while at the same time we still find that those who most value God's truth are among those who seem to lack any sense of a more refined development.

Alas, we have not arrived at any sort of conclusion. The long course of history throughout many centuries is certainly related to the fact that all the children of human beings who together would constitute our human race had to be born. That long course of history most certainly had significance in terms of the number of the elect which had to become complete. It also is beyond dispute that by means of its long duration, this course of history has served to facilitate in ever-increasing ways innumerable means for opposing suffering as the enemy of man. We also readily admit that we are dealing here with a process similar to the process that links the seed and the ripe ear of wheat, which also moves toward a final goal. But even if we acknowledge and realize all of this, it still does not explain the enormous profusion and splendor of this human development. Or we might express it in different terms: although it explains history's long duration and extensive course, it does not explain the wealth of its branching, the richness of its colorations, and the refined and careful character of its many developments. Added to this is the fact that endless masses of people who exist at a very low level of development and happiness are born and then die. This remains an enigma in itself and always forces upon us the question as to why the number of the elect could not have been compressed into a few centuries. These, of course, are questions that one can skim over without further thought, but nevertheless they lie at the core of human development and give a measure of direction to that life; this is particularly true from a Christian standpoint.

With this in view, we now dare to state the claim that our thinking never § 2
comes to rest unless we assign an independent goal, an inherent goal, to the development of our human race. From this it does not follow in the least that we thus deny a certain necessary relationship between this life and the life to come, or between common grace and particular grace. A tree at the roadside very well could have been planted for the purpose of providing shade and at the same time serve to produce fruit or, later, to serve as firewood. There is what the Germans call "heterogeny of ends" [*Heterogonie der Zwecke*]: one thing can serve two goals at the same time. For example, military service can serve primarily to defend the homeland in the event

of war yet, at the same time, have the goal of strengthening the notion of discipline and order among the people. And in that sense we must confess here that the long course of the centuries and the rich development of our human race in that history both constitute an inherent goal and at the same time serve all kinds of other purposes. This long process most certainly serves to complete the number of the elect; it certainly serves to lead us through a process that has significance for eternity. And it does so much more. But all this does not prevent it from having at the same time an *independent goal* as well—namely, to bring to light all that was hidden in our race in terms of potential to the glory and praise of God's name. Only in that perspective does our worldview find its grounding.

God has created his image in our human race by giving our race his imprint. Every believer concedes this. But after confessing this wholeheartedly, we almost always fall into the error of applying this significant truth virtually exclusively to the *individual*; in fact, many go even further by taking this image of God to refer exclusively to our spiritual qualities. Some ultimately see literally nothing but those elevated gifts of wisdom, holiness, and righteousness that were Adam's portion in the state of rectitude. According to that perspective, the image of God is therefore now virtually entirely gone. A faint trace or faintly visible afterglow may still shimmer, but it has effectively disappeared, and virtually nothing of that divine image is still discernible within the human person.

This is understandable. Past generations of theology possessed a comprehensive understanding only in terms of "covenant" doctrine; otherwise, theology never looked at anything apart from the *individual*, and it viewed the individual only from the perspective of *salvation*. On that account, of course, the image of God had to be taken in its highest manifestation, and that highest manifestation—at least as it had once shone in the state of rectitude before the fall—*most certainly* was lost. But this nevertheless was a very one-sided perspective and, we should add, a perspective that stood in conflict with the revelation of Scripture, for Scripture always points to the connection between human beings mutually, to the unity and solidarity of our race, to the societal dimension alongside the individual dimension. Even our reconciliation through the blood of the cross, as a result of this one-sided perspective of the individual, has become a sort of "blood theory," against which some Christians rightly have protested. It is to Reformed theology's credit that it has always emphasized this social element by placing covenantal truth in the foreground and by challenging this one-sided individualism. We can see the deadly fruit of this one-sided individualism on display not in Calvinism but in Methodism. But even when we stand by this claim on the basis of history and the development of doctrine, there is no denying that Reformed theology also has failed to consistently do justice to the social element in its doctrinal structure. The doctrine of covenant is there, and in the doctrine of the church the multiplicity and solidarity of the elect in "the communion of the saints" have been maintained. But specifically in the doctrine of man and the *imago Dei*, the individual aspect has been consistently dominant; consequently, the doctrine of salvation has been developed almost exclusively in individualistic terms. This error was tempered somewhat in the days of Calvin and Voetius, but later it became the cause of the regrettable partial degeneration of our Reformed theology immediately after à Marck and since à Brakel.[1]

With proper justification, therefore, we pose the question here whether the creation of man in the image of God goes much further than hitherto has been confessed in individualist terms. The answer lies in the simple observation that the image of God is a concept much too rich to be limited to *a single human being*. Among parents and children we sometimes see how the facial characteristics and character traits of father and mother can be found spread among the various children, but without any one of them showing these traits in their fullness. How much more, then, must we suppose that the image of the Eternal Being, as humans express it, is much too rich and full to be imprinted upon only a single human being. Don't we get closer to the truth by saying that the bearer of the full, rich image of God is not the individual person but *our human race as a whole*? Christ is *the* image of the invisible God [Col 1:15], since in him all the treasures of wisdom are hidden [Col 2:3], but does this apply to any *one* of us? Up to a point we also can say that the image of God lay concentrated in Adam (as the head of our entire race) in terms of potential, but never in any sense other than that he bore our entire race in his loins. And isn't it then the case that the image of God is understood in its full length and width, in its height and § 3

1. John Calvin (1509–64) was the major reformer of Geneva in the sixteenth century; Gisbertus Voetius (1589–1676) was a prominent Reformed orthodox theologian at Utrecht; Johannes à Marck or Marckius (1656–1731) was a Dutch Reformed theologian at Franeker, Groningen, and Leiden; Wilhelmus à Brakel (1635–1711) was a leading figure in the Dutch Further Reformation.

depth, only when we look for it, not only in what is manifested by a single human being, but rather in the rich development of our whole human race?

This does not mean in the least that we deny or even weaken the truth of our having been created in God's image as individuals. Even as Peter says that the temple of God is built of "living stones" [1 Pet 2:5], each one in itself a miniature temple, it remains necessary to affirm here as well that each of the constituent parts of the human race bears the human type and that the human type can never be understood as other than the imprint of God's image. Our existence as humans, in soul and body, and equally our being human in the way we are, is governed in the most absolute sense by the image of God. Even as in the organism of the tree each part of the root, trunk, bark, leaf, flower, and fruit exists organically in itself, it cannot be otherwise: in the great organism of our human race, which reflects the image of God, each individual, each separate human being, must be created in that type of God. Moreover, even in our sinful degeneration we as individuals still continue to manifest the inverse shadow outlines of that image. We therefore confess that the truth of our creation in God's image as individual humans can stand unabridged and untouched. We do not detract anything from it: rather, we add to it by the requirement that our whole human nature, in both soul and body, in both the state of rectitude and the sinful state, must be explained on the basis of the image of God. We urge only that this type of the image of God also be applied to the entire human race as a whole and to the manifestation and development of our human life viewed as a whole. Only then do we realize that, even as the sea consists of individual drops yet leads us to look past those drops when we see before us the mighty waves that crest from an endless ocean, so too the endless mass of humanity presents to our imagination the immeasurable totality of human life that belongs to the image of God reflected in its fullness.

§ 4 With this observation, an unexpected ray of light falls on all of humanity as a whole. The image of God reflected in our human life requires the full expanse of human potential if it is to be able to reflect the full image of God. Or to put it in different words, the majestic image of God, reflected in and through human beings, is not limited to one possibility or one model that replicates itself endlessly; rather, it realizes an endless diversity in possibilities. It may be reflected—and indeed is reflected—differently in the man than in the woman, differently in a child than in a young man, differently in the young man than in the adult man, and again differently in the old man. It is reflected differently in the sanguine than in the phlegmatic temperament, differently in the person with limited gifts than in the gifted individual. And amid all this variety it posits endless possibilities and combinations of character traits that repeatedly bring into existence a different human being, and in each of these persons it brings to manifestation the one type in a constantly different manner. We don't know the number of possibilities, because we simply lack the power to analyze the image of God; yet, we sense how these possibilities are determined, and we sense the fact that the exceedingly great number of people born throughout history mirrors in the fullest way the image of God in *all* its diversity and wealth of variations.

Character is something that is so very wonderful, but only because it manifests and delineates an aspect of the image of God in a unique way. We do not notice this when we see a mass of people surging along plazas or streets, or when we see endless masses of people in a foreign nation, all of whom seem to be of a similar type. But the father of a family knows very well that each of his children displays his or her own type, and the school teacher equally notices the differences between one student and another. Even as there are no two leaves on a tree that are identical, so too there are no two people, past or present, who were or are entirely identical. Were that not the case, person number two would have had no reason to exist. A human person has a reason for being only if he manifests something in his generation that no one else has, and if this being different consists in showing some aspect of the image of God in a different manner. We obviously cannot answer the question as to when the human race will cease to procreate, but the answer cannot be arbitrary. God knows, and God has not determined it by the whim of a number, but rather according to wisdom. Our human race will be complete only when all possibilities of the reflection of God's image in our race have been exhausted. Then it will stop, and not before.

The societal aspect of the truth of humankind's creation in God's image has nothing to do of course with salvation, nor with our personal position before God. This societal element means only that in creating man in his image, God has put an endless number of seeds for the advancement of human development into our nature. These seeds can come to development only through the social connection between human beings. And viewed in this light, expansively widening human development obtains a significance of its own, an independent goal, a reason for being that is separate from the matter of salvation. If it has pleased God to reflect the richness of his image in our human race through that social multiplicity and fullness, and if he himself has placed the seeds for that development in human nature, then this resplendence of his image must be manifested. That is, this splendor must not remain hidden, these seeds must not wither, and humanity must exist on earth and develop so broadly and richly until those seeds have come to full growth. At that point, full human development will be displayed in a measure by which all the glory of God's image can be reflected.

Humans may have the enjoyment and benefit of this development, but it does not occur for their sake but for God's. At that point, the Master Artist and Builder will see everything that was determined in the plan of his decree standing before him in a glorious design. At that point, God will rejoice in that elevated human development. At that point, he himself will bring it forth. And then he will seek his own glorification in it. At that point, that rich development and cultivation of nature through civilization, enlightenment, and progress, through science and art, and through all kinds of business undertakings and industry will be entirely separated from that entirely different development in holiness and righteousness. In fact, that external development can even come openly in collision with the inner development toward holiness and become a temptation for faith. But the external development nevertheless must continue and come to its final completion in order to bring the work of God in our human race to full manifestation. It does not matter whether everything will perish in the great cosmic conflagration afterward. It has existed; it has shone before God's eye. Satan has not succeeded in thwarting the manifestation of God's magnificent work. And after this cosmic conflagration of the world, that same God will again reveal in his kingdom of glory the reflection of his image in our race, but in an entirely different manner: the outer will be in complete harmony with our inner development.

In this way, common grace operates according to its own purpose. It serves not only to facilitate the development of the human race as uniquely "human," to permit the number of the elect to be born, and to arm human beings ever more powerfully against suffering, but also—and independently—to make manifest in its fullest dimensions what God planned when he put this potential for higher development into our race, notwithstanding Satan's resistance and the problem of sin. Without the fall and sin, this rich development undoubtedly would have been different: it would have flourished much more quickly and would not have borne the fearful character of battle and struggle that is now an integral part of our human development. Without the fall, Eve still would have given birth, but without pain. And humanity without sin would have reached its zenith of development without the painful distress that so often has colored our centuries-long history with such a somber hue. But in the end, humanity does arrive; it rises from collapse and climbs to an ever-higher position. What's more, thanks to common grace, the foundational creation ordinance that was given before the fall—the mandate that man would achieve mastery over all of the created order—also will be realized *after* the fall. Only in this way, then, can we understand, with the light of God's Word, the primary meaning of the history of our race, the long course of the centuries, and thus the exalted significance of the development of the world.

CHAPTER EIGHTY-FOUR

THE TWO SPHERES OF LIFE INTERMINGLED

"I am the Alpha and the Omega," says the Lord God, "who is and who was and who is to come, the Almighty."

REVELATION 1:8

§ 1 Thus, the continued existence of this world after the fall, and the centuries-long continuation of the interim era before the kingdom of glory begins, have no mere incidental goal; rather, they possess an *independent* goal—or, if you will, an inherent goal. Surely, the world has endured so that the elect could be born and the church might find a place prepared for it, but this is most assuredly not the only reason. The continuation of this world through all these centuries was also inherently necessary. At creation, as the Master Builder and Artist, God hid a treasure in this world, and all of this splendid work of God had to become manifest and bring glory to his name. To use another image, there was a stalk with exquisite flower buds that had not yet opened; Satan tore them from the plant so that these buds might wither without opening, but God revived the stalk and the bud with the moisture of his common grace so miraculously that this flower could open even on its severed stalk.

In this work of God that had to manifest itself, we have focused on one comprehensive thought: the epitome of the whole of creation in humanity created in God's image. That image, whose main characteristics are expressed in each human being but that in its richness and fullness could be manifested only in *all* people together, necessarily had to be realized in the complete development of our race through its complete mastery of the created order. This in turn is entirely in line with the oldest creation ordinance: God created man in his image, and said, "Multiply and have dominion over nature" [see Gen 1:28]. This acknowledgment of the independent goal that the continuation of the world inherently possesses is of the highest importance, since without it our whole societal life would lose every other goal for its existence except a utilitarian one. This is particularly on display in the case of art. The work of Rembrandt has nothing to do with our eternal salvation, and therefore a dualist might say that the "five 'nots' " of Schortinghuis are as valuable to him as the entire collection of Rembrandt's masterpieces.[1] From this perspective neither a well-kept home, nor better apparel, nor better preparation of food is of any value, and the cell and habit of the monk, with a piece of bread and a jar of water, are not only equally as good but better. Acknowledging an independent goal, on the other hand, gives *everything* value and significance; then the impulse automatically develops, as it were, not only to expand existence but also to bring to expression something in life and to do so in an ever more expressive and fuller measure. It needs to be emphasized that this is not a subordinate point; rather, it is central to the Reformed worldview. It is a conviction that is close to the heart of Reformed people, as it well should be: it is God himself who, to the glory of his name as Creator, has made the bud blossom in spite of Satan's tearing it from the stem. We simply cannot overstate the importance of this belief. If we are not thoroughly persuaded of this fundamental truth, we cannot live this life in true Reformed fashion,

1. Wilhelmus Schortinghuis (1700–50) was a Reformed preacher who became especially known for his devotional work *Het innige Christendom* (Groningen: Sandaw, 1740) in which he formulated five "nots": I will not, I cannot, I know not, I have not, and I am not good. The goal was to make it clear that man cannot contribute anything to his salvation. He is considered a representative of the late phase of the Dutch Further Reformation (*Nadere Reformatie*).

and in spite of ourselves we then become infected with monastic notions or Anabaptist isolation.

§ 2 But this is not all. All of this would be fine and true even if God had assigned an entirely separate realm to each of the two workings of his grace, to "common grace" and to "particular grace." If it had pleased God the Lord—and we might express it in a way that hopefully will not offend—to have all the elect, and none other than the elect, be born, say, in Europe, and conversely, to abandon the field in Asia and Africa entirely to those who receive only "common grace," then two streams of humanity would have developed: the one absolutely alien to all that belongs to the life of the world, and the other total strangers to what belongs to the life of heaven. It is not at all impossible to picture this, for God the Lord himself comes to our aid with the great and mighty wilderness miracle. The great miracle of Israel's experience in the wilderness consisted in the fact that God himself provided for all the needs of life. The garments of the Israelites and their footwear did not wear out [Deut 29:5]; they ate the bread of angels, and God gave them water from his springs and clefts in the rock.

Thus, as such it would have been possible for God to have had all the elect placed in one corner of the world and to have relieved them in their isolation from needing to provide all common needs of life. In that case there would have been no worldly labor and no societal development. Among the elect in this corner, the world would have become one large monastic cell, and all of life among God's elect would have been one great tasting of heavenly enjoyments. This also assumes that the elect would never have had any children except elect children; that *all* these children would have been regenerated the moment they saw the light of life; and finally, that regeneration would have led immediately to a perfect work, with total suppression of any remaining sin. This of course is all quite different from what occurs in reality, but it nevertheless is something we can imagine. And of course such a single holy race, like Israel in the wilderness, would be sustained directly by God and would have virtually nothing to do with the development of societal life. It would have stood entirely outside of social development, confined to a life of anticipation, with lamps burning, in the forecourt of heaven, as it were. In fact, this sort of scenario approximates the ideal pursued by genuine Anabaptists, not unlike that pursued by the monks, but it is an ideal that neither the Anabaptists nor the monks could or can realize, because such a fencing off of particular grace within an enclosed realm has never existed. It is true, of course, that the Anabaptists *tried* to fence themselves off by isolation and the monks by means of the monastery walls, but their attempts have been unsuccessful. For worse than the white ant, sin gnawed through every protective fence and monastery wall.

If we reverse this thinking, it is possible to argue that the human societies in Asia and Africa would have developed entirely apart from the influence of particular grace, something we can imagine so much more readily because to a considerable extent it was indeed the case. But we must qualify this, because the story of the queen of Sheba clearly indicates that an influence went out from Israel to the nations. That influence became much stronger still after the diaspora of the Jews. And that influence still has no less of an effect in Islam. The presumption gains even more strength by the possibility that the development of the ancient Greeks, as well as that of the Romans, owed not a little to the higher and earlier development of Israel under Solomon and in the days of Isaiah.

But even when it is possible to make this sort of argument, no one can deny that a social advancement such as one finds in Chinese and Indian cultures has developed almost exclusively through common grace. And when we observe Japan currently adopting and imitating European societies, we should not overlook the fact that this imitation is limited precisely to that which is the product of common grace. In this light, then, the Japanese people remain a thoroughly pagan people, just like the four hundred million people living in China and the three hundred million in India. Though mission work may at present be making a heroic attempt to let the lamp of the gospel shine among these millions, it nevertheless continues to ignite mere sparks in the darkness, and for the time being, these peoples *as nations* are not in the least affected by it. We simply wish to note here, in view of what follows concerning this contrast, that the development of common grace, where it was *not* impregnated by particular grace, turned out to be very inadequate. The indigenous groups of people in China and India who enjoyed only common grace have not succeeded in developing the treasures of common grace beyond a half measure and deficient manner. The actual, full, and rich development of common grace must be sought exclusively in Europe and now in North America as well, where it did not exist in isolation but was borne and impregnated by that completely other working of grace that we call particular grace.

Now we come naturally in our discussion to the extremely complex and difficult question concerning the mutual relationship in which common grace and particular grace exist with each other according to divine ordination. § 3

The two are not each locked inside the walls of their own respective realm. They affect each other by intermingling *in the same realm*. Therefore, they come into contact with each other. They encounter each other in one and the same marketplace of life. They are continually interwoven. They are spontaneously interactive. We find both of them within one and the same human heart, in one and the same human life, family, generation, and nation. And all the seemingly insoluble problems that have divided the church for eighteen centuries spring from this indispensable interweaving. Even the great issue of the relationship between church and state, and that of the visible and invisible aspects of the church, spring from nothing but this interweaving and can find their correct solution only when we reach a correct determination of the relationship in which these two operations of God's grace exist with—and mutually inform—each other. All those who confess and love Christ would therefore act better and more prudently if they were to focus all of their energy on determining this comprehensive relationship rather than biting and devouring each other because of other derivative and less important doctrinal disputes, as they do now.

Not without justification, the cross of Golgotha has been called the midpoint of history—that is, the point at which all the lines from the past converge and from which all the lines toward the future receive their direction. Scripture refers to this when it describes God as the Alpha and the Omega. The *alpha* is the first letter of the Greek alphabet, and the *omega* the last. Saying that Christ is the Alpha and Omega therefore indicates that the entire series of developmental stages through which the human race or human history moves is governed by that one center—namely, the Christ of God. That entire series of stages comes from him and ends in him.

But in this general confession we have not yet arrived at a solution. For this truth that Christ is the midpoint of world history not only *can* be confessed but often is confessed in a sense that does not bring us one step further. It often has been understood in the sense that Christ embodies himself in the Christian church, that the result of all earlier history is the emergence of the church, and that after the emergence of the church, the history of Europe has been dominated entirely by the history of the church. At that point, in the interests of the small segment of our human race that for many centuries barely exceeded one hundred million, we lose sight of the much larger part of humanity that lived and struggled in Asia and Africa. Even in Europe, the entire societal life of our forefathers is then viewed as no more than an appendix to ecclesiastical life. This view, however, does not do justice at all to the independent ground for the existence of common grace.

This view, moreover, does not accord with holy Scripture. Rather, holy Scripture repeatedly points us to the interweaving of the life of particular grace and the life of common grace, and it also reveals to us at the same time how the conjunction of the two lies not in Christ's birth in Bethlehem, but in his eternal existence as the *eternal Word*. Granted, we find only hints of this in the Gospels of Matthew, Mark, and Luke, when we read in Matthew 13, for example, that what Jesus revealed in his parables were things *hidden from the foundation of the world*. But in the Gospel of John we see this truth sharply delineated immediately at the beginning. John does not begin with the Mediator of redemption but with the Mediator of creation. He begins with the perspective of common grace and only from there moves in the direction of particular grace. Later, in the apostolic letters, this connection repeatedly is taken up again, and in the Redeemer of sinners we are shown the Mediator of creation through whom all things have been created and in whom all things still have their existence—indeed, in whom the Wisdom of God dwells bodily. It needs to be pointed out that this does not occur in the New Testament as a brand-new revelation; rather, the New Testament clearly refers back to what was already revealed during the old covenant—for example, in Proverbs 8 and elsewhere—concerning the personal Wisdom who had been anointed from eternity.

The un-Reformed, half-hearted orthodoxy of the latter part of the eigh- § 4
teenth century and the beginning of the nineteenth century, while not denying this part of God's revelation, did not know what to do with it and thus deformed it. It did not push from Bethlehem back to creation; rather, it concentrated these divine balances of power of the eternal Word and the "holy infant Jesus" in Christ's human manifestation, taking delight in exhaustively applying with great sophistication the divine nature to the cradle of Bethlehem—that is, to the creaturely aspects of the Savior. In truth, however, that "baby in the manger" had created the world; through that "baby in the manger" the world was sustained; and accordingly God himself later died as Jesus on the cross, bearing the sins of the world he had created. This all transpired of course in what seemed a sort of magic performance whereby nobody could envision, let alone surmise, anything theologically to be wrong—that is, until people finally realized the danger of adoring the creature as *creature* as they stood at the manger, which constitutes an abomination to every Reformed heart.

People may want to think of themselves as fairly knowledgeable regarding their understanding of the Second Person of the Trinity in his incarnation. And they may be well aware that holy Scripture uses a variety of expressions to depict the work of Christ as the "Anointed One" and as the mediator of redemption. They may recognize how sacred realities are described concerning him that in their essence apply exclusively to the eternal Word. But what we are arguing is a different matter; we want to maintain the truth that the self of the Mediator always is and remains the same self as that of the eternal Word. Our spiritual forefathers did justice to this by the emphatic confession that at his incarnation the eternal Word, the Second Person, did not take on a human nature with a unique human self but rather adopted *our human nature*. Nothing in our thinking should be thought to contradict the complete identity of the self of Mary's Son and the self of the eternal Word in any way.

But it needs to be emphasized that the conclusion ultimately reached by the sort of semi-orthodoxy described above is arrived at by reversing the order theologically. That is, it did not start from the eternal Word in order to see his manifestation in the Baby of Bethlehem; it started from the manger as such, from the man Jesus Christ, and expressed about this man Jesus Christ things that may never be ascribed to the creaturely, not even to the man Jesus, but only to God, who is to be praised above all things forever. In this way, altogether false notions have been introduced into the church—magical connections between the divine and the human or notions that might persist in people as a result of their emotions rather than by thinking. But among those who were thoughtful and who sought theological clarity, these false notions produced revulsion, and this automatically led to an unleashing of protest from the side of the Ethical theologians, which in turn finally led to the Jesus of Schleiermacher and his school—a Jesus who is in fact *nothing but human*, and therefore a human being who embodied not God himself, but merely *the divine*, and at a later stage only the awareness, the feeling, the *consciousness* of the divine.[2] In this way we lost the God-man, and we were left with nothing but the perfect religious human being in Jesus. Finally, under Modernist influence even that perfectly religious

2. Friedrich Schleiermacher (1768–1834) often is identified as the progenitor of modern liberal theology. He emphasized religious faith as the feeling of absolute dependence on the divine.

aspect of Jesus was sold off. This Jesus was certainly very pious for his day, but the free, pious persons of our time are still more pious than Jesus.

We therefore must register a well-considered protest, not only against this Modernist notion, not only against the Ethical watered-down version, but also against the original error of the half orthodoxy that was the mother of all that followed. Once again our Reformed consciousness must be penetrated by the conviction that the work of creation and the work of redemption, and to that extent also the work of common grace and of particular grace, find their exalted unity only in Christ because the eternal Son of God is at the very foundation of both. Moreover, we do this because the Father with the Son and the Holy Spirit, as the Triune God, has himself established this starting point and therefore the very point at which both operations diverge. It is not "the man Jesus Christ" who has created the world; rather, he who created the world and still maintains it does so even while "the man Jesus Christ" simultaneously expresses the clearest yet most sublime mystical revelation for the sinful human heart. Christ does not enter God's plan from the outside, as a foreign element that was only called on for assistance because of our fall; rather, the very Son of God himself with the Father and the Holy Spirit established the plan for this world. His assistance is not called for by means of the decree and to implement that decree; rather, the decree is *his*, belonging to what is called the "eternal counsel of peace" [see Zech 6:13]. Indeed, he includes himself in that counsel and obligates himself to its implementation. It is just as essential in the decree of redemption that he obligates himself to the mediatorship of sinners as it is that he truly is the mediator of creation. He is not first the mediator of redemption who, in order to be that mediator, must also be admitted as mediator of creation; to the contrary, the order is that he is first the original mediator of creation, and thereafter and in addition also mediator of redemption. This order makes possible the consummation of all creation as decreed beforehand. Christ does not come into being as a result of or through the decree; he precedes it both in temporal and conceptual order. He is present in its very determination. Concerning all things as well as concerning himself, he establishes all that is required to make the origin and end of all things suited to the eternal, ultimate goal of all things, which is his own self-glorification with the Father and the Holy Spirit. § 5

And because the eternal Word is both before the decree as well as included in the decree, and because he maintains the unity of creation and redemption in his own person based on the decree, the redemptive work of particular grace cannot stand in isolation from and outside of the life of the world. Rather, because both creation and redemption issue from one decree and from one and the same self in the Son of God, they are and remain fundamentally one. They are distinct, even as the Son is distinct from the Father, but they are never separated, even as we must never separate the Father and the Son in God's triune Being. It is one and the same "Being" about whom it is written that through him all things have been created and are maintained [see Col 1:16–17]. Elsewhere we read that through him every soul must be saved, as many as have been called to life [see Acts 13:48]. This truth, then, makes it possible that the very same human being may enjoy both God's common grace in societal life and God's particular grace in the sacred realm.

It is one and the same person who is both a citizen of his country and a member of Jesus' church. It is one and the same world in which God both makes his common grace to shine and glorifies his divine mercy unto salvation. Thus, we may say that common grace must act upon particular grace, and particular grace must act upon common grace. Any and all separating of the two must be opposed with all of our being. Temporal and eternal life, our life in the world and in the church, religion and citizenship, church and state, and so forth, may not be separated. Rather, precisely so that it might not come to such separation, we must always clearly distinguish sharply between the two, and the proper course of our life depends on the accuracy of this distinction. We sense this immediately in terms of the various interpretations of Article 36 of the Belgic Confession.[3] We may not separate church and state, as the liberals demand; neither may we merge them into a single entity, as spiritual enthusiasts do. Both realms must exist in their intermixture. And precisely for this reason the identification of any sort of proper distinction between the two should be sought in the specific nature and calling of each of the two, which determines both the unique character of each sphere as well as the mutual relationship of the two.

---

3. Article 36 of the Belgic Confession affirmed of civil magistrates that "their office is not only to have regard unto and watch for the welfare of the civil state, but also that they protect the sacred ministry, and thus may remove and prevent all idolatry and false worship, that the kingdom of antichrist may be thus destroyed and the kingdom of Christ promoted." The disassociation of church and state was a contentious topic in Kuyper's time, and he argued for a revision of this aspect of the confession to better reflect a correct understanding of the Reformed view of church and state relations.

CHAPTER EIGHTY-FIVE

THE CONTACT BETWEEN THE SPHERES

And he is before all things, and in him all things hold together.

COLOSSIANS 1:17

In the preceding discussion we saw that in human life on earth after the fall there is an undeniable fundamental difference between two sharply distinguished spheres. We now face the question of whether these two spheres of human life are entirely separate or interpenetrating. One of these two spheres of human life encompasses all that comes from *common grace*, whereas the other encompasses all that belongs to *particular grace*. As we saw, life in these spheres has a different origin as well as a different purpose and goal. With particular grace, that goal is determined in the salvation of the elect, and more specifically in the kingdom of God or the kingdom of heaven. With common grace, on the other hand, that purpose consists in part in the elect coming into this world and facilitating an environment in which the church can function. However, in the most proper sense it consists in the realizing of what God Almighty put into this world at creation. The point at which both goals meet is the fact that through § 1 common grace as well as through particular grace, God has in view his self-glorification—albeit in very different ways. God seeks his self-glorification with common grace as the original Artist and Master Builder of the universe, whereas with particular grace God glorifies himself through the realization of the kingdom of heaven.

Here we face two possibilities. It pleased God to let those two spheres function either in such a way that they did not even touch and had nothing to do with one another, or in such a way that both spheres of human life intermingle. The former would have occurred if it had pleased God to let each elect individual die to both spheres at the moment of his regeneration. The second actually took place because most of the elect in fact continue to live on the earth after their regeneration. But it is fruitful to reflect for a moment on the first of these possibilities. This first notion is not entirely fanciful, for it occurs. And although it is difficult for us to determine whether someone dies precisely at the moment of his or her regeneration, the Reformed church nevertheless confesses in the Canons of Dort that there are infants who die so early that they in fact have not participated in life on earth; we may assume that these, if they have been born in the covenant, did not die as unregenerate.[1] Such an infant of, say, one year never read from the Bible, never heard of Jesus, knew nothing of salvation, and knew no love for the kingdom of heaven. Nor did that baby have any conscious participation in common grace or the life of the world. It is true that the child received food and care, but all this took place apart from any awareness or knowledge on the infant's part. This, then, represents a case in which the spiritual rebirth and the entrance into the kingdom of heaven remained unmixed with the sphere of worldly life. This applies in an even stricter sense if an infant dies *immediately after*, *during*, or even *before* birth. If we confess with our churches that in such cases, parents who live within the covenant do not have to doubt the salvation of their infants, then it follows that these cases are far from rare. As we will show later, the number of infants who do not reach age five is, relatively speaking, fairly large.

At this point we are not entering into the question of whether God also saves infants outside the covenant who die very early. The holy Scriptures give no direct indication on this point, and where this is lacking we should

1. See Canons of Dort, I.17: "Godly parents ought not to doubt the election and salvation of their children whom it pleases God to call out of this life in their infancy."

refrain from any definite pronouncement (although we do not deny in the abstract the possibility of such a salvation, and it would be a great relief since it appeals to our human sensibilities). But although we defer this question and limit ourselves to the children of Christian parents who die in infancy, even then the number appears to be considerable—so large, in fact, that there would not be such a great difference (as we will show later) between the number of the regenerate who since the beginning of the world came to conscious conversion and thus continued to live and, on the other hand, the number of the regenerate who died without having come to conscious conversion. We should break, then, once and for all with the notion that those saved infants represent only a very small number that barely counts, or similarly, in our dogmatic theology, if we merely are concerned with those who die at a later age—that is, after being converted.

Something else needs to be added. Not only the cradle but the death- § 2
bed as well has its spiritual mysteries. Calvin once wrote to a friend and brother who was overly jubilant about the murder of the Duke of Guise, since it freed the Calvinists of a dangerous opponent: "Brother, do not revile the deceased. Can you say whether at the very moment when the dagger entered his heart, the regenerating grace of God entered that same heart?"[2] Assuming that Calvin here was considering the most extreme possibility and deliberately trying to squelch ignoble passion with his words, it nevertheless shows that Calvin believed in the possibility that God could give grace to a person in the hour of his death, even though those who saw his death were not able to observe the signs and consequences. And in this respect it suits us to join Calvin in keeping God's omnipotence from being bounded or limited, especially in the spiritual realm. We Reformed people tend to differ from all other churches on precisely this matter: however much we accept God's mediate act as the rule set for us, we nevertheless always acknowledge that God the Lord in himself is not tied to any means, any age, or any circumstance, and that he remains capable of giving eternal

2. Calvin comforted the duke's mother-in-law, the Duchess of Ferrara, with a similar sentiment: "To pronounce that he is damned, however, is to go too far, unless one had some certain and infallible mark of his reprobation. In which we must guard against presumption and temerity, for there is none can know that but the Judge before whose tribunal we have all to render an account." See John Calvin, "DCLXIV—To the Duchess of Ferrara," January 24, 1564, in *Letters of John Calvin*, ed. Jules Bonnet, trans. Marcus Robert Gilchrist (Philadelphia: Presbyterian Board of Publication, 1858), 4:354.

life to a formerly dead sinner at any point in time that pleases him, through his Holy Spirit. Of course we are governed by the regulative ordinance that binds us to the means; however, God in his majesty is governed by no other rule than his own sovereign good pleasure and by no other limitation than his omnipotence—that is, no limitation at all.

Thus, even as we take into account the salvation of those infants who die in the cradle, we must keep open the possibility that even on the deathbed it can please God to animate a sinner to eternal life, even in the final breath. Beyond this it is difficult to be dogmatic, since we have no certainty on this point. When someone dies at an age of discernment without having confessed his Savior, we should not say that God has not saved him. But if the question is raised whether God's omnipotence would fall short of being able to do so, we must confess with equal firmness that God's omnipotence never falls short, since nowhere in Scripture is any condition imposed on man to perform any prior action to make himself worthy or suited for regeneration. The possibility that we initially posed (that is, of being immediately called into eternity as soon as regeneration occurs) therefore must certainly be present at the cradle and perhaps a possibility at the deathbed.

§ 3 If this is true, we can also imagine that it pleased God to make what is now an exception into a general rule. If this had happened, then each human being who was regenerated through the Holy Spirit would be taken from this life at that very moment. He would not have any further part in this life. Consequently, no group of believers would have appeared on earth. There would have been no confession of the Christ. A church on earth would have been inconceivable. There would have been nothing except *the life of the world,* without any Christian influence impacting the world. There would not have been any interweaving or intermingling of the kingdom of God and this worldly life. The kingdom of God would have remained *in heaven,* and to enter it, temporal death would have had to open the eternal gate for us. Both spheres would have existed in this scenario. Common grace would have operated widely and broadly across the entire world—but only common grace. And particular grace would have touched upon this world only obliquely when it regenerated the elect in a hidden manner, only to separate these elect from this life immediately thereafter.

However, this is *not* how created life unfolds. Granted, no one can say with complete certainty which of these two forms of grace is dominant among the saved, if only because no one can possibly know how many people still might receive grace on their deathbed. But it is quite obvious that multitudes of people, following conversion, still continue in this life in human society for years. These constitute a group of *confessors*, and it is from this group of confessors that *the church* emerges. So it is that in this entire group we see the sphere of particular grace come into contact with the sphere of common grace. This contact relates to (1) the individual person, especially with respect to his or her body; (2) family life and family ties; (3) societal life; and (4) the life of the nation, in terms of the state and international relations. In these four arenas they come into contact not only externally but also internally. Sometimes this even occurs to such an extent that they seem to become one. This prompts us to investigate further the mutual relationship between the two whenever they come into contact with each other. This investigation, as it turns out, is a highly interesting investigation because the most difficult problems of personal, domestic, social, and political life are dominated by this very relationship between common grace and particular grace. We only have to mention the relationship between church and state to show immediately how the solution to the most serious historical problems must be derived from a right and correct insight into this relationship between common grace and particular grace.

Throughout the ages people have tried to place a buffer between the two § 4
spheres, even where the two come close together, in order to forestall the actual touching of the two. However, it was always only a very small portion of believers who wanted to take this path, and those who took that path never reached their goal. Here we are not talking about the Anabaptists, for although their system has the same aim, it lacks consistency. They say they avoid the world, yet in their own group they try to impress others. They walk in the mistaken assumption that the world is only *outside* their home, and not *inside* it. They fail to recognize that they carry the world with them in their own person. A similar goal is pursued consistently in strict monastic orders. Not all monasteries do this, to be sure, for in most of them the rule of life is relatively light. Yet in the past there were—and still are—monasteries in which life is approached with such severity that separation from the world seems to have almost succeeded. Those who live in such a monastery environment close themselves off from the outside world with a wall, and then with a cell wall, and in that cell they sleep on what scarcely deserves to be called a bed. Moreover, they wear extremely poor clothing and take only the most meager nourishment. They try to pass the major part of their time in spiritual exercises, attempting to keep their thoughts from everything worldly, even occasionally avoiding any

contact among themselves, silencing their tongue, and chastising the flesh in order to bring it into submission. They withdraw as much as possible into the blessings of particular grace and banish everything that comes to us humans as blessings from common grace. Only the fakirs in India go still further, by not even taking shelter under a roof but living out in the open in any weather, preferably riveted to one location that they never leave. They even let the branches grow through their hair. And they do all this with no other intention than to keep the sphere of common grace far from them and to withdraw exclusively into the sphere of particular grace.

Yet even in the strictest monastic order this aim has never been fully achieved; indeed, this aim could never succeed. They take with them the body of sin, and in that body is housed the human heart, out of which come the issues of life. As Jesus declared, it is from the heart of man that all sin springs forth. Now, if we take the position that a sinful *impulse* is not sin, then there is no issue. But when we acknowledge that sin definitely consists not only in deed and word, but most assuredly lies in the imagination and in thought as well, indeed lodged behind the thought and in the very impulse of the heart, then we realize that such a "fencing off," no matter to what extreme it is performed, can never lead to a *hermitical* fencing off. This is all the more impossible because the sinful impulse leads not only to sensual thought but also to the spiritual sin of self-exaltation, conceit, haughtiness, and personal pride. It is precisely for those who lead such a life that there is no danger nearer at hand than taking pride in this "spiritual" way of life, in the sacrifices they have brought, and in their renouncing of the world. Rather than being banished by the cloister walls, this self-exaltation in fact is cultivated and promoted by the monastic life, all the more so because a mistaken notion of piety leads many people who live fully in the world to revere this kind of self-control and self-punishment as a higher form of holiness. Add to this the fact that not fulfilling one's task in the world, withdrawing from one's calling and consecration, fencing oneself off from all development of self-sacrificing love—in short, failing to do the good—are as much sin as doing evil, and it becomes very clear how this heroic attempt to avoid all contact with common grace while living in particular grace is bound to go awry. This contact between the two realms exists, and it exists for everyone who is human. It ends only when death delivers us from this body of sin.

§ 5 The cause of this dilemma lies in the fact that regeneration banishes sin from the deepest root of the *self,* but not the indwelling sin that is in our heart. At our regeneration we indeed undergo a fundamental renewal, but we are not sanctified in soul and body all at once. God created the first man holy in soul and body, but the same thing could not occur where *re-creation* was required and not *creation*. Creation is ex nihilo and therefore not bound to what already exists and to what already has come into being; by contrast, re-creation is so bound. Here the sin and the consequences of sin that cleave to us must be taken into consideration. Furthermore, re-creation does not aim at a *changeable* holiness (the kind that Adam possessed), but at a holiness that is sinproof—that is, one that cannot sink back into unholiness. This change cannot be affected *all at once* even when it strikes at *the center* of our being, our most deeply hidden self. It does not transform the body, because it is precisely the body through which we are in contact with the world outside us. The fact that the sphere of particular grace comes into contact with the sphere of common grace and is interwoven with it, so to speak, should therefore not be seen as an incidental circumstance, but rather as flowing from the nature of the sinner's regeneration. Precisely this is what makes every effort to escape from this world not only purposeless but also against the very ordinance of life. Jesus' high priestly prayer remains valid: "I do not ask that you take them out of the world, but that you protect them in the world" [see John 17:15].

Therefore, if there is contact with the world, we must look at its nature and its character. Arrows that are bundled together touch externally, and this is always the case with things that have an entirely different origin and are tied together by a bond that is applied from the outside. The same is true of all mixing, intertwining, and interweaving. Each of these three types of contact involves materials or things that have been brought together externally, and only through these means do they come together. Thus, it is possible that the sphere of common grace and the sphere of particular grace might approach one another from two entirely different directions and in this way make contact without any underlying prior interaction. But it is entirely different when two branches of *the same tree* become intertwined. Those two branches then have a common origin. They both have one root. Before they sprouted they both had one single life in the same trunk.

And when we consult Scripture, it is clearly revealed to us that only the latter comparison is applicable here. Doesn't the Apostle Paul write to the church at Colossae that the one Christ is two things at once: both the root of the life of creation and the root of the life of re-creation? For he states first that Christ is "the firstborn of all creation. For by him all things were created, in heaven and on earth. . . . And he is before all things, and in him all things hold together" [Col 1:15–17]. It could not be expressed more clearly that Christ is the root of creation and therefore also of common grace, since common grace ensures that everything did not simply sink into nothingness: "In him all things hold together." But then it follows immediately, in the second place, that this same Christ is also "the *head of the body*, . . . the firstborn from the dead" [Col 1:18]—that is, he is also the root of the life of re-creation or of particular grace. Both are expressed in terms that are reminiscent of one another: the root of common grace, for he is *the firstborn of all creatures*, and at the same time the root of particular grace, for he is the *firstborn from the dead*. There is therefore no doubt that, owing already to their origin, both common grace and particular grace exist in a very intimate connection, and this connection lies in Christ.

CHAPTER EIGHTY-SIX

COMMON GRACE AND THE SON OF GOD

In him was life, and the life was the light of men.

JOHN 1:4

The common root from which both common grace and particular grace sprout is thus clearly revealed in Scripture. That root is the Second Person of the Triune Divine Being. Briefly stated, the three members of the Trinity find their unity *in Christ*. Yet, our language in designating the Second Person of the Three-in-One, without further specification, could lead to misunderstanding. "Christ" means the Anointed One, a designation that communicates to us a Mediator who is united with human nature, and in whose nature he comes ordained to fulfill a service or task. This can never be absolutely predicated of God as God, and therefore also not of the Second Person of the Trinity. God as God is always *active* in the anointing, never *passive*. God does not *serve* but *rules*. Only the *creature* can serve. This is why, when Paul describes Jesus as the obedient servant of God (Phil 2:7–8), the incarnation stands in the foreground and comes first. He has taken "the form of a *servant*" but only after he "made himself nothing." And he became *obedient* (that is, he served) but only after "being found in human form." Christ, or the Anointed One, is therefore a name the Mediator bears only § 1 in connection with his incarnation insofar as he has taken on creaturely form. The name as such never refers to his being God, to his divinity. God anoints the creature whom he ordains to his service, and thus also the Holy Spirit anoints us to serve in the kingdom, but the Father is never anointed, nor the Son, nor the Holy Spirit.

However, this does not at all mean that, because of the absolutely wondrous uniting of the divine with the human nature in the Mediator, the name "Christ" cannot also be used when the activities are in view that do not belong to the sphere of human nature but are inherently divine. This can be true because the *self* in the Second Person of the Trinity as well as in "the suffering servant of God" is one and the same *self*. And thus the apostle could speak of "*one Lord, Jesus Christ*, through whom are all things and through whom we exist" (1 Cor 8:6), even though it is of course true that the world was not created by the *man* Christ Jesus but by the eternal Word.

Can we conclude from this that common grace and particular grace find their conjunction in the manger of Bethlehem? Stated differently, must we assume that common grace and particular grace are actually independent and have come into more or less accidental contact through the incarnation? If so, then the answer is certainly not. This might seem to us to be the case, but the question here is not how it seems to us. What alone is decisive is how it exists *before God*. Things exist *essentially* only to the extent that they exist before God. And the ancient prophet already introduces the Messiah as saying, "Ages ago I was set up, at the first, before the beginning of the earth" [Prov 8:23]. Thus it says here that the personal Wisdom is also ordained and anointed for service from eternity. God knows all things *by virtue of his decree*, and in that decree the Son is both mediator of creation and mediator of redemption from "before the foundation of the world" [Eph 1:4]. It is therefore clear that according to Scripture the mediatorship of redemption certainly does not initiate its activity for the first time at Bethlehem; rather, this occurs immediately after the fall. Everything we read about the Angel of the Covenant or the Angel of the Lord, and what Peter tells us in 1 Peter 1:10–12—namely, that the Spirit of Christ already worked through the prophets—indicates this. Didn't the Lord Jesus himself say that Abraham longed to see his day and that he saw it and his soul rejoiced in it? But this must never be understood in the sense that the Messiah *became* mediator of redemption for the first time after the fall. This mediatorship became *operative* from that moment on, but it had existed earlier. A military general functions as general for the first time when war breaks out, but this does not deny that he was appointed general by his king already long before this, such that he has been overseeing the general's staff. So, too, the mediator could not begin the work of redemption while there was yet no sinner and thus nothing to be delivered from the arms of death and sin. But long before that, he was appointed as mediator of redemption—that is, as God's Anointed—and the title belongs to him on that basis.

How far back does this appointment go? Did that appointment of the § 2
Son of God occur *after* creation, with an eye to the danger in which creation stood of failing through sin? Clearly not. It is as the Catechism affirms: the name Christ (that is, Anointed One) tells us that he was ordained and anointed from eternity by the Father to be our Prophet, High Priest, and King.[1] It is *from eternity*, before creation, and not thereafter. It also would be incorrect to understand it as occurring *after* the decree, as if a change or codicil were introduced later; rather, it was *in* the decree itself. If this decree is the reflection and imprint of God's sovereign pleasure, as he has intended and determined all things and their course from eternity, then it follows that (1) the Son of God never appears, nor can appear, in any other way than *as being simultaneously the Christ*, and (2) the mediatorship of redemption and the mediatorship of creation *coincide* in this decree from eternity onward. Of course, in our own thinking we make this sort of distinction, and we cannot conceive it in any other way than by distinguishing between the creation through the eternal Word and the redemption through the Anointed of God. However, that distinction, which mirrors the limitations of human thinking about the matter, may never be conceived or understood as a *separation* that supposedly would exist in the decree itself.

This of course also touches on the profound issue of sin and, therefore, also on the question of supralapsarianism. The unity of the mediator of creation and the mediator of redemption also dissolves if we view the original decree as representing the will and intention of God to create a world without sin, so that a change in that decree occurs because God now discerns, discovers in advance, or sees ahead of time that sin will come. In such a construal, creation and redemption are not one; rather, they become intertwined through something external. Viewed as such, sin enters from the outside into the decree and, having done so, ties the two together. We can maintain the unity of creation and redemption in the person of the

1. See Heidelberg Catechism, Lord's Day 12, Q&A 31.

mediator only if we understand that in his sovereign decree God is not determined by anything external but rather himself *determines* all things that are external to him, so that no sinful development would have been possible or conceivable if the course of our human race had not been determined thusly in God's decree. This is a conception that we humans in our humanity cannot reconcile nor ever will be able to reconcile, given the verdict rendered by our sense of guilt and our confession of God's most pure holiness. It is a conception that therefore must never be offered as a solution to all enigmas (the error of the supralapsarians), but at the same time it is a conception that must not be set aside whenever we probe deeply into the decree of God's sovereign pleasure.

For everything depends here on the question of the nature of the knowledge God has of the created order. Of course, Arminians of any stripe will say that God acquires knowledge of things by *observing* them, just as we do, including observing them with the foreknowledge of how they will be before they come to pass. This is how they arrive at the theory of foreseen faith and foreseen sin. But Scripture teaches us that this is not the case and that God knows all things that will happen because he himself has determined how they must happen. An architect knows how a house that he has designed is put together, not because he goes and looks at the building but because of his specifications and plan. If something is wrong with the foundation, he does not tear the house down in order to get to the foundation and see how it is arranged; rather, he checks his blueprint, which tells him how the foundation is arranged and how the house is built. So it is with God's knowledge. This Master Craftsman and Builder has first made his plan or blueprint in his eternal decree, and he has built according to that decree. If he wants to know how the building is put together, so to speak, he consults not the building itself but his own specifications or decree, from which he has the knowledge of how all things fit together. God does not *know* all things because this is how they are; rather, this is how they are because God *knows* them and *has known* them from eternity. Therefore, when we investigate what the relationship is between the mediatorship of creation and that of redemption, we must not ask how these two functioned subsequently in a mutual relationship; instead, we should ask how this connection was established by God in his decree. It goes without saying that it is not we who have created this relationship; it exists outside of us and cannot exist in any other way apart from *what God himself has established.*

Let us use the illustration of a sick individual who recovers without receiving any external medication—which in less developed nations is still the rule and among us is once more being recommended as a good rule by what is called "natural medicine." Wholly apart from the issue of the medication's benefit, it generally is acknowledged that it previously was quite wrong when, instead of allowing nature to run its course, the natural working of the sick body was hindered by an accumulation of all kinds of medication. In fact, sometimes these were collected and mixed together to an absurd degree. This reaction to excesses of the past proceeds from the recognition that when sickness comes, *nature* itself immediately sets to work to counteract the wrong influences or to expel the unwelcome substances. This healing working of nature is still shrouded in relative mystery, to be sure, and it is true that there are cases in which nature "falls short." At the same time, no one denies any longer the importance of natural remedies, and experts now are convinced that we shouldn't in any way hinder this response by nature but rather should take it as our starting point and promote it. § 3

What, then, is this reaction of nature against the sickness that has crept in? Is this working actually *something that is added* to the normal powers of our nature? Not in the least. It is nothing but the ordinary energy of nature that sustains us in normal times and keeps all processes in our body functioning well. And when illness disturbs the balance, it undertakes to deliver us from that illness. There are, therefore, not *two* life principles, the one serving to maintain our life in its normal processes while the other frees our life in abnormal cases from this abnormal influence. No, the life principle is a unity; it is one that comprises both the energy that ordinarily keeps our life functions operating regularly, and it also is the energy that in abnormal cases of illness undertakes to deliver us from this disturbance.

To a certain degree, this fact sheds a surprising light on the relationship that exists between the action of Christ as our Creator and the action of Christ as our Redeemer. Christ himself is the life source of our human race. The Apostle John emphatically states this when he says of the eternal Word, "In him *was life, and the life was the light of men.*" Our life is sustained, as far as its normal manifestations are concerned, through Christ. Doesn't the Apostle Paul say, "By him all things were created . . . and *in him all things hold together*"? We may compare this to the action that in normal times sustains and regulates the life functions of our body. But now this normal human life is disturbed; we become ill through sin. And behold, as soon as that disturbance becomes active, Christ, who sustains our creaturely life, counteracts this disturbance and delivers us from sin. The first corresponds to his mediatorship in creation, which of course encompasses the *maintaining* of things. The second corresponds to his mediatorship of redemption, which reacts against the disturbance. Those two are not separate. The one is not separate from the other. It is one and the same divine life energy that does two things, by functioning in our life through Christ: it maintains our normal life functions and works redemptively against sin. Redemption can come only through him by whom we have been created and in whom we have our existence. Both functions were necessarily united in one and the same Christ. Only through him by whom we were created and are maintained could we also be redeemed. Only the mediator of creation can be the mediator of our redemption too.

§ 4 This undeniable truth has its deepest ground, of course, in the divine order that exists for "the economy" of the divine Being, if we may put it this way. The world does not comprehend and understand the confession of the holy Trinity. It thinks that a *human* person is the proper model of "personality," and when the world then hears that the church of Christ confesses one single Being in three persons, it can understand this only to mean that this refers to three independently existing individuals: A + B + C. And on this basis it declares as nonsense and illogical that one would ever be three, or that three would be one. Looked at it in this way, the world is right. Three flowers are never one flower, and three houses are never one house. The church has indeed never confessed that these three divine persons *were one person*, but only that they are one Being. It therefore is quite erroneous to think initially of a human individual as a person and then to conceptualize the Deity according to three such persons. We should say instead that there is *one humanity*, and in this humanity there are many persons if we view "humanity" as a single being. Then the comparison would fit, at least to some degree: one "humanity" with many "persons" in it, and thus one Deity, one divine Being with a triplicity of persons.

But all such comparisons fall short because God is not made in the image of man; rather, humanity has been made in the image of God. In us, the "person" is therefore only a weak reflection of what "personality" is in God, and the limited nature of our person must never be transposed to the personality in the divine Being. This applies as well to everything involving created things. This is to say, with everything that occurs outside of God, these activities we observe are never isolated activities of the Father, or of the Son, or of the Holy Spirit; rather, all these activities of creation, preservation, redemption, and sanctification are activities of the one divine Being. The *Father* has created the world, the *Son* has created the world, and *the Holy Spirit* has created the world. The *Father* preserves us, the *Son* preserves us, and the *Holy Spirit* preserves us. And so too, the *Father* redeems us, the *Son* redeems us, and the *Holy Spirit* redeems us. This truth can also be briefly stated as follows: God the Father created us, God the Son preserves us, and God the Holy Spirit preserves us.

Even when we must never detract from this unity of divine action, we nevertheless should clearly distinguish between what is singularly the work of the Father, the work of the Son, and the work of the Holy Spirit. If in a moment of imminent collision the captain on the bridge steers his ship in such a way that he avoids the collision and can continue on his way unharmed, then *the whole man* did this. Nevertheless, we must distinguish among the sharpness of his vision with which he correctly calculated the distances, the assurance with which he gripped the helm and turned it in the correct direction, and the stoutness of heart with which he remained master of himself in such a tense moment. Head, heart, and hand, as it were, belong to his one being, and the gifted steering of his ship was the effect of his entire action. At the same time, in this process we may say that his head had a function other than his hand, and his hand had a function other than the stoutness and courage of his heart. And although we concede that this crude illustration can never be transposed without severe qualification to the divine Being (when we speak of God, no illustration is ever perfect, not even the illustrations used by holy Scripture), this illustration nevertheless gives us some sense of how in the divine Being, in the strictest unity of divine action, there nevertheless can be—and in fact is—a difference in the activities. And it is this distinction in activity that holy Scripture explains to us to some degree when it teaches that the origin of things is *from* God the Father, and that the existence of things *as they are* is *through* God the Son, and that the life *in* things is from God the Holy Spirit. "Yet for us there is one God, the Father, *from* whom are all things and for whom we exist, and one Lord, Jesus Christ, *through* whom are all things and through whom we exist" (1 Cor 8:6 emphasis added).

This truth anchors us in our faith. The origin is from the Father, whereas the manner of existence through the Son. It becomes clear, then, why the mediator of redemption is neither from the Father, nor from the Holy Spirit, but is necessarily from the Son. For what is redemption? Is it *bringing something into being*? Certainly not. Rather, redemption is only causing a change in *the manner of existence*. This flows automatically from the nature of sin. Death is not the destruction or cessation of a creaturely human being, since both the righteous and the wicked will exist forever. Sin and death simply bring about a change *in the manner in which we exist*. A sinner continues to exist, but he exists in a wrong mode; he does not exist in the way that he ought. Redemption therefore is not a new bringing into existence of what did not previously exist; rather, it is a causing to become what should have been previously. From this we can recognize that all redemption concerns the *manner* of human existence, not human *origin*. If Scripture teaches us that we come *from* the Father but that the manner of our existence is not through him but through the Son, then it necessarily follows that the entire work of redemption is concentrated in the unique activity that belongs not to the Father but to the Son. For that reason, not the Father but only the Son can be the mediator of our redemption.

Naturally, it is not as if the work of the Father or the Holy Spirit in that connection would be absent even for a moment or could be dismissed. How could the Son govern the manner in which things exist if the Father did not sustain all things in their existence, or if the Holy Spirit did not fan the smoldering life spark? But from clear teaching of holy Scripture it follows that, when we make the clear distinctions and investigate further the arenas in which each of the three persons performs the action of redemption, redemption can only be understood as proceeding from the Son, the eternal Word, *through* whom all things are created and from whom they therefore have received their *manner* of existence. It is in the coming into being of our self that our essence lies. And it is in the manner of our existence that the thought and intention of God can be seen to lie, of which we are the expression and embodiment. And the very imprinting of the thought of God on creation is what the Son does, for that Son is the *Word*, and what else is the *Word* but an *enunciated thought*? This is true, and the Son therefore functions as mediator of *redemption*; it goes without saying that both common grace and particular grace must find their higher unity in Christ, for *both* intend to react against the disruption that intruded into creation through sin and death.

CHAPTER EIGHTY-SEVEN

THE ELECT TO ETERNAL LIFE

Godliness ... holds promise for the present life and also for the life to come.

1 TIMOTHY 4:8

Thus particular grace and common grace flow from one and the same source in the Triune God, and in a more specific sense they find their unity in Christ, who is mediator in a twofold sense. He is mediator of *creation* as the eternal Word and mediator of *redemption* through the incarnation. But not only do these two streams of grace flow from one and the same mountain of God's holiness; we also must point to the fact that the waters of these two streams partially blend in the life of humanity throughout history. They do not rush forward side by side in two separate stream beds; rather, there is a variety of demonstrable connections between one stream and the other. Particular grace enriches common grace, and common grace appears again and again to be presupposed by particular grace. It is on this mutual relatedness that we now must focus attention. We do this in two parts. The first discusses the significance of particular grace for common grace, and the second treats the significance of common grace for particular grace. The first we will address now, and the second will serve to conclude this volume. § 1

As such, the ultimate goal of particular grace lies on the other side of the grave. Its goal lies in eternity, and viewed by itself, particular grace can bypass earthly life altogether if necessary. All particular grace serves to magnify the compassions and mercies of God so that after humanity has fallen into sin and curse, he nevertheless guarantees eternal bliss to a regenerated humanity. We can agree, of course, that this requires only a single contact with this earthly life: *the birth of the elect*. Once the elect have been born, particular grace is sufficient in itself to impart eternal bliss to them. In fact, this very thing *does* take place in those many elect who shortly after their birth and regeneration are called from this earth and transferred to their home in heaven. This occurrence is in no way a product of our imagination or something that our intellect invents. It is a literal description of what continually happens in this life: some elect individuals are born, are regenerated, and depart from this earthly life, never having known anything of this earthly life. This starting point, then, should not be lost from view. It is decisive and characteristic of the relationship that exists between particular grace and human life, which is the arena in which common grace is active.

§ 2 In this connection, we have already pointed out several times that the purpose of institutional churches on earth is not to bring the elect to salvation or to prepare them for heaven. Here we may develop this point further. It is commonly thought that conscious conversion is *the* means of entering into eternal life. One is born and baptized, one grows up, one comes under the preaching of the Word and in contact with the community of the saints; to that external calling is joined the internal calling, and in this way one is converted. After that conversion comes sanctification, and sanctification is the further preparation of our soul for entrance into eternal life. This is the common view, which we readily admit did not spring up for the first time in our day; rather, it entered the Christian church and became mainstream centuries ago. This was *the way*, it was assumed, and people simply knew of no other way. Consequently, baptism, catechism, preaching, sacrament, and the communion of saints were almost exclusively viewed and interpreted from this perspective. People did acknowledge that it was also conceivable that an elect individual could die too soon to move through this sequence, but this was viewed as an exception that was barely taken into account, and in that case God would provide what was needed in an extraordinary way.

But this was a mistake. In a time when people were far less accustomed to statistics, the number of persons dying at a young age was *greatly underestimated*. We can generally set the minimum age for conversion at fourteen, and the mortality tables show that almost 40,000 people annually do *not* reach this age, out of a total of approximately 90,000. In 1894 the correct figures were as follows: (1) stillbirths: 7,389; (2) younger than age two: 23,587; (3) between ages one and five: 10,246; (4) between ages five and fourteen: 3,858. Altogether 39,011, or almost 40,000. Above the age of fourteen, 50,235 persons died. If we therefore take age fourteen as the minimum age of conversion, then we cannot speak of a small exception, but of *almost half*. And if we assume that conversions before the age of fourteen do occur more frequently than we think, we can subtract the almost 4,000 who died between ages five and fourteen; the result then is 36,000 who die at age five or younger, compared with 54,000 between ages five and one hundred. And then it also appears to be that those who die early and are *un*converted are far from an exception and still constitute a number that heavily counterbalances the 54,000. In addition, no one speaks of conversion before age five.

It therefore would appear that previous commentators forgot to take into account the *reality* of life. Through their ignorance of statistics and their unfamiliarity with "real life," they created an entirely false picture of the facts. For if we confess with the Canons of Dort that believing parents do not have to fear concerning the eternal salvation of their children who die young, then this assumes *as a rule* that those children are elect and saved insofar as they were born within the covenant.[1] Conversely, many of those who die at a later age depart from us without ever having manifested any sign of conversion.

Even if it is assumed, therefore, that many who never showed any signs of spiritual life come to life at the moment of death, the confession of Dort always assumes that a higher percentage of the 36,000 who die before age five is saved than of the 54,000 who die at a later age. If we assume that this amounts to 85 percent of the 36,000 and 55 percent of the 54,000 (numbers that are a guess, of course, but are certainly not exaggerated), then the result would be 30,600 among children ages one through five and 30,800 among those who die after age five. Of course, these numbers are based on

1. See Canons of Dort, I.17: "Since we are to judge of the will of God from His Word, which testifies that the children of believers are holy, not by nature, but in virtue of the covenant of grace, in which they together with the parents are comprehended, godly parents ought not to doubt the election and salvation of their children whom it pleases God to call out of this life in their infancy (Gen. 17:7; Acts 2:39; 1 Cor. 7:14)."

the whole population and therefore should be reduced to the much smaller number of those incorporated into the covenant of grace, but this does not change the proportionality of the numbers. Hence, it would appear that if we take the Canons of Dort, on the one hand, and the mortality tables, on the other hand, the number of the saved who die before the age of awareness and the number of the saved who die after their conversion are fairly well in balance.

A doctrinal theology that does not take this into account and, in the face of the convincing data of real life, constantly continues to make *conversion* the rule and looks down on salvation *outside* of conversion as being a minor exception can and must no longer be our guide. On the contrary, doctrinal theology will have explained these weighty issues as they bear upon the reality of life only when it clarifies how these two ways of bringing persons into the kingdom—the one unawares at an early age and the other involving a conscious conversion at a later age—must be understood from a single higher perspective. Note well, we are not speaking here about preaching and admonition, for preaching and admonition address exclusively those who have *not* died before age five and as a rule must focus on the needs of those who live a longer life. But theology *cannot* limit itself to this. Doctrinal theology is not preaching, even though it must have a guiding impact on preaching. Doctrinal theology must investigate the difficult issues of life at their root and interconnectedness, and it therefore must not act as if it is concerned with only one half of those saved and as if it can ignore the other half as being an exception that hardly needs to be taken into account.

§ 3 But there is more to be said, because the objection extends even further. The assumption commonly used as starting point is definitely not only that the elect here on earth must come to conversion, but that in this life they must be sanctified for heaven as well, and that through sanctification they must be prepared for heaven. Accordingly, after conversion we begin weaving the garment of sanctification, and only when the garment of our sanctification has been completed are we prepared and outfitted for our entry into eternity. True, we generally do not dare place too much emphasis on the latter, at least not in Reformed circles, since according to our confession there is the "perseverance of the saints," and hence it should not be said that a saved person entered heaven unprepared for the higher life there. But for the present we must note that those who do not affirm the perseverance of the saints definitely do say this, and we shouldn't lose sight of the fact that Reformed preaching on this point often is inadequate.

In point of fact, among many people "conversion" is something of a rather uncertain and at times slippery notion. Someone who falls back into unbelief and reckless living after conversion all too often gives the impression that his or her supposed conversion was little more than appearance; in the end, sanctification is thought to be proof that the conversion was sincere and genuine. But if someone like this dies *without* having reached higher sanctification, then all kinds of uncertainties arise—and rightly so—concerning his or her state before God. At this point we recognize how the mortality tables present a witness against the less correct theological view. For if the matter were as it is presented, then a man who is granted eighty or ninety years of life would have the greatest chance to get ready for heaven. By contrast, the many who die between ages fourteen and fifty would be deprived of any chance to complete the work of their sanctification.

This possibility, added to the first objection, can lead us to the conclusion that any notion goes astray if it makes the salvation of the elect dependent on a longer life or seeks the real purpose of a longer life of the elect in their being brought to salvation. Those who believe this arrive at no solution and become entangled in insoluble contradictions. Anyone who is Reformed in heart and soul can never make the eternal salvation of God's elect ultimately dependent on anything other than regeneration. That person must view salvation as guaranteed absolutely and entirely by regeneration, rejecting any notion that regeneration might be dependent on a shorter or longer life. But from this it also follows that the lives of the elect in this world who live longer should have an entirely different goal than merely being brought to personal salvation. A life span that long is not necessary for mere personal salvation. In fact, it would be irreverent to consider a life span of this length with its definite requirement of conversion and sanctification as something incidental. Anyone who has received a longer life, having come to the faith, has the irrefutable call to sanctification.

But all this is the *result* of coming to faith, not the *means* of coming to eternal life. Eternal life flows from pure grace and only through an act of God. What's more, as Reformed Christians, we must double our efforts in this regard to stress the primary and foremost goal of the Christian's calling: the *glorification of God's name*. That calling, it goes without saying, falls away for those who are called out of this world by God prior to, say, five years of age. But if God lets us continue the pilgrimage here below until a later age, then the call comes unmistakably and irrefutably to each of us. That call is for us to repent of our unbelief and evil works, so that as participants in the covenant of grace we may bring God's church to manifestation on earth, and for the church to hallow God's name and have God's kingdom come through the consecration of every power and gift, not least through the sanctification of our lives and the demonstration of love and compassion.

When we view things from this perspective, everything falls into place and every objection is addressed without any compulsion. Grace then remains the work of God, and the life we are given belongs to him and to him alone. But this God, who brings us to life out of his own sovereign will, is also the one who determines our fate. It depends on him and only on him whether he will have us function here on earth as an adult or whether we will be called by him to a better homeland before we reach the age of discernment. If he calls us earlier, then the light of Christ will rise for us, not here but in heaven, and in the sanctuary above we will be initiated into the mysteries of Christ's sacrifice. Then we, too, will glorify God's name, not here on earth, but immediately among the saints above. This is the fate of our children who die young, who comprise, as we have seen, almost half of all those who are saved. But this same God decides with equally sovereign omnipotence concerning the other half of his elect, and he allows them to grow up and reach adulthood, by which they develop to an ever clearer consciousness of faith.

Holy Scripture is for this latter group but not for those who die young. Preaching is not for the former but for the latter group. The communion of the saints is not for those who die young but for those who live longer here on earth. The former could not repent; the latter must repent. For the former no sanctification on this earth is conceivable; for the latter it is commanded. All this is according to the definite rule that their continued existence on earth has no other purpose than that they confess their God in the midst of this world, that they magnify their God in conversion and sanctification, and that they manifest their God and his truth in their public activity before the world. If someone lives for thirty years, then that person is not required to do so in the same way as a man who lives for eighty years. Each of us is called to do nothing other than to sanctify and magnify God *in our person* during all of those years that God gives us here—nothing less, but also nothing more. In this way, everything coalesces into one perspective. The great and significant difference between the calling of the one and that of the other finds its natural limits of explanation, which should comfort us, so that no dark corners of mystery remain in this whole question of conversion and salvation. Nothing in the least is left unaccounted for.

It becomes clear, then, that this conclusion relates directly to the topic at hand. If the purpose of the church, the purpose of preaching, the purpose of conversion, the purpose of sanctification, the purpose of the sacrament, and the purpose of the communion of saints and of good works ultimately were *not* the glorification of God's name but rather the salvation of the elect, then all of this could bypass the world and thus bypass the realm of common grace. If this were so, then there would be an argument for believers setting up their own society somewhere in an uninhabited area, with anyone who came to conversion moving there, in this way withdrawing entirely from the world. Then all believers could simply live together in a secluded place. They would have escaped from the temptations of the world. Their fellowship could be full and intimate. Their whole life together could be a life of prayer, of love, and of sanctification. As a matter of fact, the original Anabaptists always had this notion in mind, even though they have never realized it. § 4

But if, by contrast, their own salvation unto eternal life and their preparation for heaven are not the ultimate goal of their longer life here on earth, but rather the glorification of God's name is, then all this is turned upside down. If human beings are to sanctify and glorify God's name, there must be an arena in which they do this and people for whom and among whom they do this. In this case, they must not withdraw from the world, because they are to bear witness to this world; they are to confess in this world; and they are to manifest the power of the kingdom in the life of this world. Indeed, the goal of their own lives that was ordained and granted by God lies precisely *in the world*. Wherever in that world God meets them with his common grace, it necessarily follows that the particular grace granted to them comes into direct contact with common grace. And indeed, the working of the one can never reach its ultimate goal without the working of the other.

In this way we see that we should view the relationship between the one grace and the other as not at all accidental or incidental, let alone external. Any contact with common grace, it should be said, is not derived *directly* from the fact of the longer life of the recipients of particular grace here on earth. This longer life was not required to bring the elect to eternal life. Half of the elect do not have this longer life; some of them already have their lives cut off by God himself before their fifth year. However, this longer life *is* needed to make manifest in this world the marvelous greatness of God's almighty grace. Those who live longer are called to this, each one § 5 individually and all together. This is why they must manifest God's church on earth. This is why they must confess. For "confessing"—the word itself says it—always means to declare God's truth, for his glory and toward *un*believers. Even when we concentrate the Christian's entire calling in this idea of *confessing*, it still follows that Christians cannot confess except in the world to the world and that this is precisely the purpose for which they continue to live after their conversion. The one person lives longer, the other shorter. That makes no difference, as long as they are not remiss in their duty and calling to confess God as long as they live.

One further comment is needed to avoid misunderstanding. Let no one deduce from the preceding argument that we are of the opinion that the church should not be stressing conversion and sanctification in its preaching and sacraments. Beyond question the church's ministry is to serve that purpose. It cannot be otherwise. Apart from this work of the church, those who live longer would never come to conversion and therefore never arrive at the confession and glorification of God's name. We therefore wish to counter any suspicion that we have overlooked this. But that is an argument for another time. The point here was only to indicate the significance of particular grace for common grace. And where this is concerned, we have come to the conclusion that insofar as particular grace is not restricted to regeneration but rather, in the case of longer life, also progresses to conversion, sanctification, and manifestation of the powers of the kingdom, it is not directed first of all to the salvation of the elect but to the magnification of the Lord our God in the midst of this world.

CHAPTER EIGHTY-EIGHT

THE PURPOSE OF THE CHURCH ON EARTH

So that through the church the manifold wisdom of God might now be made known to the rulers and authorities in the heavenly places.

EPHESIANS 3:10

The churches that administer the Word and sacraments are therefore not the instruments ordained by God through which the sinner receives the inner essence of salvation. Only the Father of the spirits can cause a sinner to be regenerated, in Christ, through the Holy Spirit. But things do not exist only in their inner "essence"; God wills that they also possess an outer *manifestation*. For human beings themselves, that manifestation is located in their consciousness; for other creatures in creation, it is located in the *outward* appearance of what lies hidden in their inner being. Thus, we are saying that the manifestation of what God has accomplished in us through his Holy Spirit can assume two forms: it can be appear as our own consciousness, and it can appear before the eyes and ears of others. The reason for this is that there are two realities: the present world and the kingdom of heaven that one day will develop into the kingdom of glory. Consequently, a regenerated sinner can awaken to consciousness either in this world already or for the first time in heaven. He can manifest to others § 1 what God has re-created in him either already here or for the first time in the invisible world above. If the regenerated individual dies as an infant in the cradle, then he does not awaken to consciousness, and he does not manifest his state to the eyes and ears of others. His portion lies only above. The awakening of his consciousness, in this case, occurs only in heaven, not here. And the manifestation of his life before others does not occur on earth, but only in heaven, and then in the kingdom of glory.

Those who continue living on earth, on the other hand, already reach awareness here on this earth of their inner reversal, in faith, in altered intentions, and in the improvement of the will (conversion); as a result, they bring to manifestation before the ears and eyes of others what God has done in them. This lasts until God also calls them home, and then their consciousness, which had fallen asleep, will awaken again in heaven; at that point, they will reflect what God wrought in them first in heaven and then in the kingdom of glory. In the case of both experiences, we find (1) the work of God for the regenerating of the life of their soul, (2) the awakening of the consciousness of this rebirth, and (3) the manifestation of this rebirth before others. The difference is only that those who die early do not come to this awakening of their consciousness and to this manifestation before others until they enter heaven, whereas those who live longer have the same in a dual form: first here, and then after death, on the other side of the grave.

That manifestation of what God has wrought in them, specifically that manifestation already here on earth, is closely connected with the entire work of revelation that God established in this world after the fall in order to maintain justice and truth in the entire world of created things, and this is what we wish to emphasize. To bring some clarification, let us ask ourselves this question: After the fall, couldn't God have limited himself to regenerating the souls of the elect through the hidden working of the Holy Spirit, and after that rebirth simply have transferred them directly to heaven? Think carefully about this question. On the one hand, it posits something very attractive and alluring. There would have been no special revelation here below, no suffering of believers, no struggle on earth, no coming of Christ here below; there would have been no need of a cross on Golgotha. We would have neither Scripture, nor sacrament, nor any visible church. Nothing would have occurred except God's bringing to life the dead souls of his elect, and after having been brought to life, they immediately would have been redeemed.

Someone might ask what then was missing. The answer must be that along this path the *reality* of things in the created order would have been absent; that is, God's justice and truth would not have become manifest in the reality of all creation. But God has created *a world*. In that world, his justice has been violated, and his truth has been reviled. And therefore in this same world, in this real life of created things, that justice had to be restored to honor, and that truth had to be led to triumph. This *could* happen only if, in this same world, God revealed his wrath upon the horror of sin, placed himself in enmity against it, and engaged in battle against the suffering that sin had brought, in order to bring to manifestation his truth and justice to us, in his Christ, in his incarnation, through his death on the cross, and resurrection—and indeed, through his holy Scripture, through the sacraments, and through the visible church. A false mysticism denies this, or at least it has no eye for it. It would merely be content with "Christ in us" and consequently would close its eye to "Christ outside us." And precisely this is what we must oppose with all our might on the basis of God's Word. There is not only God in his *Being*, but also in his *name*—in his revelation in the midst of the real life of created things—and it is for this name of the Lord of lords that the entire outward manifestation of believers and the outward manifestation of the church on earth came into existence, persevered, and must continue persevering.

To some extent, this was understood by those who attempted to make § 2
regeneration dependent on conversion. They attempted to link the internal call to the external call, and they tried to establish a firm link between our salvation and the church with the holy Scriptures. Their only mistake was in seeking to explain the necessity and indispensability of the church, Word, and sacrament in terms of the soul's coming to life. That is not how the necessity is, or can be, grounded, since God the Holy Spirit is sovereign in the work of regeneration, and he cannot be bound to any particular means in it. But the necessity and indispensability of the church, Word, and sacrament do follow from the fact that God's justice and truth must become manifest in the reality of this same world that violated and reviled them. This applies not only to those who live longer but just as much to those who die young, for their atonement depends on the reality of the work of redemption too. Although their consciousness does not awaken until they are in heaven, their reconciliation there as well is necessarily anchored in the objective substitutionary work accomplished by Christ here on earth.

In heaven they, too, find their Savior in our flesh. They, too, find Christ in the sanctuary above, administering *their* salvation. And their gratitude rises eternally before the throne for what God has wrought through and in Christ here on earth for the sake of their redemption as well.

Let us firmly confess that God's work is twofold: (1) the revelation and triumph of his justice and truth in the reality of created life, and (2) the regeneration of those who were dead in sin. If that is true, then it is clear that that revelation of God's justice and truth must occur here on earth both to the children of men and to the created spirits above. Concerning the latter, we do indeed read in Ephesians 3:10 that *through the church the manifold wisdom of God might now be made known to the rulers and authorities in the heavenly places*. The entire passage reads as follows:

> To me, though I am the very least of all the saints, this grace was given, to preach to the Gentiles the unsearchable riches of Christ, and to bring to light for everyone what is the plan of the mystery hidden for ages in God, who created all things, so that through the church the manifold wisdom of God might now be made known to the rulers and authorities in the heavenly places. This was according to the eternal purpose that he has realized in Christ Jesus our Lord, in whom we have boldness and access with confidence through our faith in him. So I ask you not to lose heart over what I am suffering for you, which is your glory. For this reason I bow my knees before the Father. (Eph 3:8–14)

Note Paul's ending: the apostle bows his knees before that God "from whom every family in heaven and on earth is named" [Eph 3:15], referring to all created spirits. And he tells us that the church on earth has the calling to make manifest "the manifold wisdom of God" not only to the created spirits here below but also to the spirits above. Here, then, lies the calling and the purpose of the church of Christ that functions in this world. That calling and that purpose are to make manifest the manifold wisdom of God, which is mystically hidden in all of life. This is to be displayed before the elect who continue to live here after their regeneration, to bring them to actual faith, conversion, sanctification, and fellowship with God. It is to be displayed before the angels and the demons so that they may observe God's glory and majesty. And it also is to be displayed before the unbelieving world here in order that people might either convert or harden themselves before God, thereby confirming the world's judgment and condemnation.

Here then lies the significance of how particular grace, in majestic work, § 3
and common grace intersect. Broadly understood, the entire revelation of what the Triune God does on behalf of redemption *for* us, both *outside* of us and *in* us, becomes a powerful factor in that same world in which common grace operates; this factor has far-reaching consequences for the life of the world preserved by common grace. It is an influence so far-reaching that we can safely say that common grace achieves its goal only through this influence. The simplest way of stating this is as follows: wherever common grace is missing the factor of particular grace, it languishes and leads only to inadequate results. Conversely, wherever the factor of particular grace exerts influence upon common grace, and to the degree that it influences common grace more powerfully and intimately, to that degree common grace reaches its full and ever-richer development. In order to get a clear picture of this, we need only compare the activity of common grace in China, to take but one example, with the activity of that same grace in a country like ours. In China, common grace drifted on its own power and was not impregnated and enriched by particular grace. In our region of the world, the factor of particular grace began working eleven centuries ago. The result is that during all those centuries, there was only common grace in China, and in our countries there was common grace along with particular grace. The difference in result is that in China common grace came formally to a rich development, but concretely it remained on a *low* level. By contrast, in our country a more developed point of view over time has been adopted, even by the unbelieving segment of society, which, in a civil and cultural sense, towers above that of China in many cultural spheres.

This illustrates the need to distinguish between three different scenarios: first, the situation of a nation in which *only* common grace has been active, like China; second, the situation of a society in which both common grace and special grace have been active, as in our country; and third, the situation of the church of Christ as such, in which particular grace dominates life and consciousness entirely. But here things become complicated. There is a considerable difference between pagan countries and Christian countries; or Roman Catholic countries and Protestant countries; or even further, Lutheran and Reformed countries. In addition, we tend to use the language of a Christian society, Christian art, Christian government, and so forth. In our country this is understood for the most part in a confessional sense, which means that all these manifestations of life have been bound to a particular Christian confession. The sum total of this confession amounts to this: either all of life was related in some form or fashion to the church, or the church was equated with the state. But note that this stemmed from the fact that people had no proper conception of common grace. People knew only of *nature* or natural life—that is, life as it grew from the sensory root; and alongside it was the life of "grace"—that is, life as it blossomed from the sacred root of regeneration. As it was, people took into consideration only two rather than three factors: only sinful natural life and the life of grace. They failed to distinguish between sinful natural life, life proceeding from common grace, and life proceeding from particular grace.

If we correct that mistake, we may affirm the following: (1) life proceeding from particular grace is found only in the church, and this is the distinguishing characteristic of Christ's church on earth; (2) life springing almost solely from sinful natural life exists only where the influence of common grace remained very weak; and (3) life outside the church could enjoy a higher level of flourishing only where particular grace influenced common grace through the church's instrumentality and thereby brought it to full development. In this way, the life of the church, life outside the faith, and the so-called Christian life come to stand side by side. The church is better and purer to the degree that it lives more fully, more richly, and more purely, and this is true both objectively (in terms of its essence) and subjectively (in terms of its consciousness). Countries or cultures in which virtually no particular grace seems to have penetrated and common grace consequently continued to languish we have tended to call "pagan," while those in which particular grace has influenced common grace through the instrumentality of the church we usually refer to as "Christian."

§ 4 We will return to this distinction in a moment. But for our present purposes, to speak of a "Christian nation," a "Christian society," "Christian art," and so forth, does not mean that such a nation consists of elect, regenerated, and converted people, or that such a state and society have been transferred into the kingdom of heaven. This never has been the case at any time or in any place. Even within Israel, the masses were always apostate and idolatrous, and the "faithful" were always a minority in the land. Rather, to use such terminology simply means that in such a nation or state the influence of particular grace in the church and among believers has such an impact on common grace that through this common grace the land reached its highest development. The adjective *Christian*, therefore, does not say anything about the state of the soul of the inhabitants of such a country; it says only that public opinion, the national consciousness, dominant views, the shape of morality, and the nation's laws and customs clearly reveal the influence that the Christian faith has exerted upon them. This is owed to particular grace, but it is revealed in the realm of common grace—that is, in ordinary civil life. That influence also leads to important developments in public justice and public life such as the abolition of slavery, the improvement of the position of women, the maintenance of public decency, honoring the Sabbath, concern for the poor, and even elevated social manners, by which human existence is improved from its deteriorated state.

This viewpoint would not be held by those who think that Christ came § 5
to transcend the position of Sinai by ushering in a higher form of morality. Such people imagine that a lower morality existed prior to Christ and that the essence of Christianity consists in revealing to us a higher morality. We encounter this sort of thinking among those who stand outside the faith and therefore do not understand the essence of Christianity. If we properly understand the true nature of Christianity, we know that Christ did not come to abolish the law and the prophets, but rather to fulfill them. That means, of course, that God has never lowered or raised the moral bar, so to speak; rather, his moral standards always have been the same position. This means that the only goal of Christ's work is to destroy the works of Satan, which has the consequence of fortifying human nature and human society in such a way that they may more fully approximate their God-ordained destiny. To more fully approximate this is not to suggest that we as humans can gain salvation and eternal life; rather, it simply means that human life here on earth opposes God's commandment less strongly. Therefore, the Christian character of a nation or a state has nothing at all to do with the sacred observance of the law for salvation. Then the keeping of the law would have to proceed from a *genuine faith*, and this is not present in the nation, nor in the country, nor in the state (as such, taken as a whole). Then the state would have as its aim *God's glory*, and nothing of such a purpose can be discerned in that strict sense. Then it would have to be conformed to God's law in all its parts, and it appears that the state can barely fulfill, even inadequately, a few parts of it.

Therefore, we must abandon entirely this confessional notion, which misunderstands Christianity as a moral instrument of a higher order, and we must frankly admit that a Christian nation, a Christian country, a Christian state, and so forth, means nothing only that the powerful factor of particular grace has penetrated the life of this nation, this land, this state, as it survives under common grace, owing to the activity of the church, and that thanks to the penetration of this factor, the development of common grace in this people and this country has come to be of a much higher level. And from this it automatically and simultaneously follows that the Christian imprint impressed on such a nation, country, or state will necessarily bear a confessional imprint, not in the sense that it is bound by *any external bond* to a specific faith confession, but in such a way that it will manifest a certain affinity with the principles, the way of thinking, and the insights that are presupposed or placed in the foreground by a specific confession.

This occurs because particular grace influences common grace through the instrument of the church (both organic and institutional), and because the church stopped speaking with one voice after the Reformation. Until the time of the Reformation the church was one. True, the schism with the Greek and other Orthodox churches occurred before that time, but at that time the East was not considered. The great historical stream of human life was flowing in Western Europe, where there was only one church, "*the* Christian church," and this explains why at that time people could speak in no other way than of a Christian nation, a Christian state, a Christian society. But then, as a result of the Reformation, distinctions arose between the Roman Catholic Church, the Lutheran Church, and the Reformed Church, each with its own confession, its own principles, its own way of thinking. It therefore *could* not have been otherwise than that under common grace the life of the peoples and states had to adopt a different form and a different shape, depending on whether common grace received its enrichment from a Roman Catholic, a Lutheran, or a Reformed perspective. It is quite obvious that societal life displays a different form in Spain than in Norway, and in Norway again different than in Scotland. The results in all these countries have come about through particular grace infusing common grace and helping it reach a higher development. We may pass a harsher judgment on Spain when comparing it with Norway and Scotland, but Spain might be viewed as relatively "holy" when compared with conditions in Persia or Afghanistan. The difference is that in each of these countries the same particular grace has influenced common grace, but this has occurred through the instrumentality of *a different church*—hence the divergent results. In part these results are "purer" in one country than in another, but in part they are merely *different*.

CHAPTER EIGHTY-NINE

CHRISTIAN CIVILIZATION

And he made from one man every nation of mankind to live on all the face of the earth, having determined allotted periods and the boundaries of their dwelling place.

Acts 17:26

The significance of the activity of Christ's church for the general human development of our race—that is, the significance of particular grace for common grace—cannot easily be overestimated, given what we have argued. Wherever the cross of Christ is spread, the level of human development rises visibly. Missionary reports tell us again and again of the great changes that take place among small tribes or on remote islands as soon as the gospel was accepted and could permeate human life. But still stronger is the turnabout that occurred in Europe itself as people groups who were advancing from Asia accepted Christianity and not only built new states on the ruins of the once-mighty Roman world empire and its far-flung provinces but made an entirely new social order flourish. It will be worthwhile to dwell for a moment on this significant historical fact. § 1

The condition of human life as it exists in various continents on this earth still shows by and large four striking varieties. These can be broadly distinguished as African, Asian, Levantine, and European-American. As concerns Africa, we readily admit that the outer fringe of that continent consists, as it were, of an embroidery of alien elements of higher civilization, but the true, original Africa, stretching in the endless interior from north to south and from east to west, occupies the lowest level of human development. Common grace is certainly at work among the black population inhabiting this continent, but in a very limited sense. For example, there is still cannibalism, and there are fetish worshipers. Apart from a few folk songs, a few songs about heroism, or love songs, there is no significant body of literature among them at all. They usually wear no clothing, and they live in huts. Their fixed occupation is to go out to murder and plunder among the neighboring tribes after every harvest. Slavery is an integral part of tribal customs.[1]

On a much higher level than these African tribes stand the peoples of the Asiatic type, specifically the Indians, the Chinese, and the Japanese, and in the past this was also true among the peoples of South America and Central America, specifically the Peruvians, Aztecs, and Toltecs. Among this group of peoples, who to the same degree remained deprived of the light of special revelation, we find traces of a refined, elaborate civilization. Among these peoples a society is developing on a higher plane. They have a written language. They have an extensive literature. They are developing an artistic sense. There are thinkers among them. The pleasures of life among them are refined. Rich inventions increase the powers at their disposal. Yet their development appears to rise only to a certain level, at which point they seem to move forward no further. And as soon as they come into contact with more highly developed peoples, they have no other choice than either to imitate their way of life while surrendering their own attainments, or in their powerlessness to let themselves be dominated by those peoples. The former is the case with Japan, the latter with India and China. And in both these types of human development, the African as well as the Asiatic, it is clear in all kinds of ways that their development remains restricted to their own borders and that they produce virtually no benefit for the development

1. These sections are some of the clearest articulations of Kuyper's hierarchical judgments concerning human development. For more on Kuyper's racial and cultural judgments from his Eurocentric perspective, see *CG* 1.12.10n4; 1.41.2n3. See similar instances in *CG* 1.61 and 1.62.

of our human race as a whole. As a people group they rise to a certain level, but for the stream of human life as such they bear little fruit.

The Levantine development, which as such also stands outside of Christianity (even though the Christian church came out of Israel and thus out of the Levant), must also be distinguished from the two preceding types. The Levant is considered to include what in the ancient world was called the East. The Levant in the broader sense is thus the part of Asia that goes from the Asiatic highlands down to the Mediterranean Sea, along with Greece, Italy, and the northern coast of Africa. This region was home to the Babylonian, Egyptian, Greek, and Roman civilizations successively. Israel lay in the midst of this region, but it was isolated from the Levantine life as such. The Christian phase, which continued especially under the Byzantine emperors, was replaced by Islam from the seventh century on. And from that moment Islam became and remains the governor of all life in the entire region, while only Italy joined the European stream. In all these stages, the Levantine life has seen a much more elevated development than what is found either in the African or Asian type. And not only this, but it can be that in all these stages this Levantine development has actually borne fruit for the general development of our race. Islam may be languishing at present, but the crescent of Islam certainly still has vitality; in any case, it is undeniable that Islam has had a far-reaching influence during the Middle Ages, not only on history but even on the development of Europe. We thus may safely say that common grace has worked with a very uneven degree of strength: weakest in African life, somewhat stronger in Asian life, but most powerfully in the life of the Levant, among the Babylonians, Egyptians, Greeks, Romans, and Muslims. § 2

But no matter how high human life already may have existed in these various stages of development of the Levantine maturation of our race, it nevertheless is as clear as day that a much higher level of human development has been reached today in Europe and America. In Europe this development increased in strength as the main stage of European life shifted from southern Europe to northwestern Europe. Elsewhere, and in a different context, we recently expressed it in these words:

> In China it can be asserted with equal right that Confucianism has produced a form of its own for life in a given circle, and with the Mongolian race that form of life rests upon a theory of its own. But what has China done for humanity in general,

> and for the steady development of our race? Even so far as the waters of its life were clear, they formed nothing but an isolated lake. Almost the same remark applies to the high development which was once the boast of India and to the state of things in Mexico and Peru in the days of Montezuma and the Incas. In all these regions the people attained a high degree of development, but stopped there, and, remaining isolated, in no way proved a benefit to humanity at large. This applies more strongly still to the life of the colored races on the coast and in the interior of Africa—a far lower form of existence, reminding us not even of a *lake* but rather of *pools* and *marshes*. There is but one world-stream, broad and fresh, which from the beginning bore the promise of the future. This stream had its rise in Middle-Asia and the Levant, and has steadily continued its course from East to West. From Western Europe it has passed on to [America's] Eastern States and from thence to California. The sources of this stream of development are found in Babylon and in the valley of the Nile. From thence it flowed to Greece. From Greece it passed on to the Roman Empire. From the Romanic nations it continued its way to the Northwestern parts of Europe, and from Holland and England it reached at length [also America]. At present that stream is at a standstill. Its Western course through China and Japan is impeded; meanwhile no one can tell what forces for the future may yet lie slumbering in the Slavic races which have thus far failed of progress.[2]

This strong and striking difference between the preceding three types and the European type of human development can be explained mostly from the fact that European life has been well nurtured by the influences proceeding from the church of Christ. This certainly is not the only explanation. Undoubtedly, the aptitude of the peoples who elevated Europe to such a height was suited to a high development. Their capacity was greater. Yet even with this greater capacity they never would have climbed to their present high state had they not shared in the blessing of Christianity. This

2. Kuyper quotes here (in Dutch, with emphasis and brackets added) from his Stone lectures of 1898, published as Abraham Kuyper, *Lectures on Calvinism* (Grand Rapids: Eerdmans, 1999 [1931]), 32–33.

appears convincingly from the fact that these same peoples who at one time lived in Asia had *not* climbed to a higher level of development, and they even remained far behind the Levantine people in their development. The great turning point in their life and its development dates its beginning from the moment they came into contact with Christianity and the church of Christ became manifest in their midst. From that moment on we see entirely new capacities begin to develop in all areas of their life, and it is under the influence of these new capacities that a better and higher social order manifests itself. It is one that puts a truly human stamp on the whole of society, expands man's power over nature to an almost limitless extent, performs miracles in the areas of science and art, and finally develops a power that brings all other continents under its scepter.

If this establishes the fact that the Christian religion—that is, the embodiment of particular grace—has been the means to bring common grace to its most powerful manifestation, then the question arises as to how we must understand this effect of particular grace on common grace. It is customary to call the result of this effect "Christian" and then to speak of a Christian civilization, Christian society, Christian government, and so forth. But we sense immediately that, as we have briefly indicated, the word *Christian* has an entirely different meaning in these phrases than, for example, in the expressions *Christian church, Christian literature, Christian school, Christian press, Christian theology, Christian singers*, and so forth. This is because in the two series of expressions, the word *Christian* is used in terms of a different contrast. When we speak of Christian nations, a Christian society, and so on, this marks a contrast with pagan nations, pagan society, Islamic states, or Islamic society. But by contrast, when we speak of a Christian press, Christian school, Christian singers, and so on, then we are indicating a contrast with the liberal press, the neutral school, unbelieving singers, and so on. In the first instance, we are emphasizing the unique character of the European states and nations in contrast to those of Asia and Africa. In the second, we are not thinking of Africa or Asia, but of the Netherlands and distinguishing in our own country between the groups of those who defend their confession of Christ and those others who live out of what people call secularism or humanism. The first contrast, therefore, is not confessional; only the second one is. Or we could say that when we speak of a Christian state, a Christian society, a Christian civilization, and so forth, we have only common grace in view as it has been permeated by the gospel; but, on the other hand, when we speak of a Christian school, a Christian

§ 3

press, Christian singers, and so forth, we are referring to particular grace as it chooses to use the things of ordinary life.

We sense that this is correct when we ask ourselves, Can someone be a citizen of a Christian state, live in a Christian society, be part of a Christian civilization, without personally confessing Christ? The answer is definitely in the affirmative. The facts show and prove it. Many people who are averse to any confession of Christ are even prominent leaders in such a Christian society. But if we ask whether someone can be a Christian singer, Christian teacher, and so on, without personally confessing Christ, then everyone will sense the impossibility of this. It is clear, therefore, that "Christianized" common grace does not depend on personally belonging to Christ; by contrast, fully developed particular grace always remains inseparable from it. Yet until now, these two distinct meanings of the word *Christian* have been mistakenly confused. The thesis has even been promoted that the "Christian" school was the "best run" school. And it is from this confusion of the two notions of "Christian" that the endless confusion between the life of common grace and that of particular grace has sprung, under which we still suffer. On the one hand, people tried to tie down everything confessionally—state, society, popular culture; on the other hand, people tried to abolish the Christian church and to separate it from its confession, so that as national church it bleached what was fermenting among the people. Thus, we see the attempt to put the label *Christian* in its specific meaning as a stamp on common grace, and we also see the attempt to deprive the word *Christian* of its specific sense even in the realm of the church. Didn't the entire church ultimately have to be subsumed under the state in Rothe's teaching?[3] The cause of this endless confusion can also be described another way: the church tried to draw the world within its confessional circle, whereas the world tried to make the church equal to itself.

§ 4 We therefore direct our readers' attention especially to the fact that they can never come to a clear insight into the correct relationship between church and world, between the communion of saints and society, and thus also between church and state, unless they take the trouble to clearly think

3. Richard Rothe (1799–1867) was a Lutheran theologian of the German idealist school. Rothe believed that the earthly communities of the state eventually would arrive at such perfection that the church and state would become congruent and the church would wither away in favor of a Christian state, which would be both a religious and moral society.

through the enormous difference between these two meanings of the word *Christian*. The term *Christian* as it is applied to the entire nation, the whole of society, the entire state, and so on, stands in contrast to what is pagan or non-Christian. When applied to a narrower group within the population, within society, or within the state, the term stands in contrast to neutral, unbelieving, nonconfessing entities. In fact, it is with this distinction in mind that we can find the solution to the difficult problem described by Article 36 of the Belgic Confession ("The Civil Government"). As we noted earlier, this does not at all mean that the word *Christian* in both contexts cannot allow us to distinguish between Greek Orthodox, Roman Catholic, Lutheran, Reformed, and the like. Much to the contrary. Even as a tree does not communicate anything beyond its genus, calling the tree an oak, a cedar, a birch, or the like does; in the same way, it is impossible today to identify a "Christian" development in any country without understanding that development as the fruit of activity of the Greek Orthodox, Roman Catholic, Lutheran, or Reformed churches. Society in Spain has a face very different from that in Russia; it manifests itself differently in Pomerania than in Bavaria; and it takes on a different form in the Netherlands and in Scotland than it does in Switzerland and Denmark. We will return to this distinction at the end of the volume as we conclude our discussion of common grace. For the moment, however, what remains to be discussed is how we should envision this influence of particular grace on common grace.

Let us, then, pay attention to the following. In the first place, those who confess Christ constitute a group in the midst of a nation, from whom a serious call to duty sounds forth unceasingly to the nation. That call to duty issuing from the people of the Lord works on the conscience. And in this way, the activity of the conscience that Paul describes in Romans 2:13 is stimulated and sharpened by this exhortation, this call to duty from those who confess Christ. In the second place, believers elevate domestic and societal life to a higher level through their example, and God grants his effectiveness and his influence to this work. In the third place, believers in Christ also work in the public arena in order to proclaim what they understand to be true. They do this on the basis of the greater light that they have received. And thanks to this threefold influence, there emerges in the midst of the nation and its social life a force for combating unrighteousness and restraining sin. Although it is a fact that believers allow sin to continue in their personal lives, where it can still stir and rage in secret, this sense of "conscience" does not allow sin to hold its ground in the national conscience—that is, in public opinion and in the broader cultural ethos. In this way common grace is given a tremendous support precisely at the center of national life. This is the *moral* influence that proceeds from particular grace to the life of the nation as a whole, an influence before which unbelievers and scoffers ultimately must yield as well. And when the government, supported and pressed by this, finally expresses and codifies this higher moral life in its laws, then this influence ascends from public opinion directly to the life of the nation, putting a Christian stamp on society as such, whether it be a Roman Catholic, Greek Orthodox, Lutheran, or Reformed stamp. In a metaphorical sense we may call this a "Christianizing" or a "baptizing" of the nation as a whole, always keeping in mind, however, that this has nothing to do with the personal conversion of individual citizens and the personal application of the sacrament of baptism.

To this moral influence a second thing is added—namely, *the blessing of the Lord*. God loves his people as the apple of his eye, and he therefore extends his blessed influences in exceptional measure over those nations in which the church of his Son has come into existence. To those nations he gives the healthiest climate, the best-situated land, the greatest dominion over nature. He makes them into the best stock. He endows them with the richest talents and the most noble gifts. He enriches them with wealth and the most far-reaching inventions, and he thereby enhances the best opportunities for these nations to enjoy a comprehensive, undisturbed, and continually progressing development.

In summary, we may express it in this way: common grace intends a twofold restraint, the restraint of sin and the restraint of the curse. Particular grace helps to raise the activity of common grace to the highest level in terms of both. In connection with the arresting of sin, we see the *moral* influence of particular grace, and in connection with the arresting of the curse, we see the *providential* influence of particular grace.

CHAPTER NINETY

THE COMPLETION OF COMMON GRACE

Nor do people light a lamp and put it under a basket, but on a stand, and it gives light to all in the house.

MATTHEW 5:15

The fact that the presence of the church of Christ in a nation also will gradually exert a noticeable influence on the moral tenor of that nation and on its entire civic development will not need further proof after all that we have adduced. It is clear that particular grace influences the working of common grace. But while we can simply affirm this, it is something quite different to realize the *manner* in which and the *degree* to which this influence is exerted. In the final and practical part of our treatment of common grace we hope to shed the necessary light on this. To summarize our discussion up to this point, we first discussed the historical aspect of common grace, then next its doctrinal or dogmatic perspective. With this our doctrinal discussion comes to an end, leading to a discussion of the significance of common grace for the praxis of our life in civil society. This naturally includes considering the special influences that common grace exerts in the areas of domestic, civil, societal, and political life. But before § 1 concluding the present section on doctrine, a brief comment on how this influence on common grace is to be explained is in order.

In very general terms, we ask our readers to note the fact that a people's religion always and everywhere puts a particular imprint on a people's morals, customs, laws, and way of thinking (even if this religion has nothing to do with the gospel). There is therefore nothing strange in the fact that the Christian religion also exerts a similar influence where it is present. This fact warrants no further discussion. Religion always is and remains the expression of what is central to human existence. No matter how counterfeit and darkened the religion of a people may be, we always find expressed in that religion the central, dominating, and fundamental beliefs of that people. These deeper fundamental beliefs then, in turn, are related to the nature and character of the nation, and equally to its historical past—indeed, to the soil on which it lives and the climate in which it breathes. For this reason alone, it is so annoyingly foolish when from the liberal side the claim is still made that the salvation of the future must be sought in the separation of church and state, of religion and nation, of spiritual and civil life. And it is more incomprehensible how even other Christians—here we refer to kindred spirits in the faith—can suspect us, Reformed Christians, of agreeing with such an absurd notion. The difference between us and these other Christian believers concerns only the *manner* in which Christian faith, the church, and spiritual life influenced the nation, the state, and civil life.

In our (the Reformed) opinion, the others fail to pay sufficient attention to the differences among the three concepts of nation, state, and government. There need be no doubt that unanimity will be reached on this point. For people of all persuasions—whether the secularist or the Christian—people are generally agreed as to the importance of religion for the nation's values. But secularists in this country were intent on changing the Christian character of that fundamental conviction that fundamentally opposed them. For this reason we can fairly clearly identify two periods in their battle against Christian movements. In the first period they denied religion the right to exert any influence on *public* life, and in the second period they sought to strengthen that influence. The difference between these two periods can be explained from the fact that in the first period, the influence of the old-time religion still opposed them, whereas in the second period, modernized religion supported them.

It is no less striking that, historically, the Christian character of a nation always manifests itself practically in a specific form. This is not necessarily due to Christendom as such; rather, it flows from the general law that each human being and every people-group has something peculiarly its own that distinguishes it from other people-groups. This distinction is not limited merely to differences between one people and another; it goes much further. In the Netherlands, the provinces of Friesland and Zeeland are each of a distinct Reformed type, even to the degree that the unbelieving part of the population of these provinces has developed almost exclusively in opposition to the very traits that characterize the Reformed community. At the same time, what a broad difference exists between the specifically Reformed communities in Friesland and Zeeland. And an equally broad difference, for that matter, can be observed between Reformed believers of the province of Gelderland and those of South Holland. These differences, in fact, can even be refined further when we move from provinces to specific regions within those provinces. A Reformed person in the Betuwe region lives differently than a Reformed person in the Veluwe region, even though both are inhabitants of the one province of Gelderland. An equally sharp difference exists between the clay region and the sandy regions in Friesland, between the Kennemerland and the Gooi in North Holland. This difference can also be observed in several cities. Utrecht and Amsterdam have always shown a variegated character among the Reformed Christians as well. We can even say that the various districts of these cities vary, such as the residents of the so-called Jordan neighborhood in Amsterdam and those who live along the canals. § 2

But this was nothing peculiar to Reformed life, and we freely admit that the self-determining spirit of the Reformed life promoted independent development. In fact, the same might be said of the Roman Catholics in our country as well as those who live in the regions south of the rivers and those north of the rivers. Along these lines, moreover, American Catholics are very different from Spanish Catholics. In truth, one can find similar differences present in virtually any Christian church, albeit less sharply defined. But this is no different from the way variations manifest themselves among Jews, Muslims, and those who are not religious, for that matter. Polish, Russian, French, and Dutch Jews definitely are not cast from the same mold. The Muslims in Persia stand in sharp opposition to those nearby in the Middle East. The Buddhists in India, China, and Japan diverge in all kinds of ways. And even the pagan religions of Babylonia, Egypt, Greece, and Rome certainly could not be equated.

History shows, as does the present state of the people groups and nations just mentioned, that religion—however greatly it may vary in form—has exerted a far-reaching influence on domestic, national, and religious life. There is an interaction between national and religious life. This interaction is continually kept alive by the fact that this difference in fundamental conviction displayed in a particular culture or society finds its roots in differences of genius, character, and history. In that sense, therefore, it is entirely correct to say that the nation of the Netherlands is not secular but Christian, and not Roman Catholic but Protestant, not Lutheran but Reformed, and to the extent that we historically distinguish Calvinists as the most consistent type, it is definitely *Calvinist*. This being true, we nevertheless should keep in mind that this Reformed "national type" has not shown itself to be sufficiently strong to assimilate the entire population. For example, in the southern provinces the old Roman Catholic type has maintained itself, whereas in the northern provinces secularism always seems to lurk, especially among the cultural gatekeepers; here secularism never fully disappeared and at present has been revived again with great confidence. This gives rise to issues of justice and law, inasmuch as government must act as government per se; that is, it must utilize *coercive power*. In this context Reformed thinking emphatically denies that with sword in hand, the servant of God, the government, may let one segment of the population dominate another. It is on this point that people with conflicting views will need to engage in battle. For we must continue to set forth demarcations and limitations that concern the nation, the state, and government. If this is not done, the endless confusion of language will continue and we will make no progress.

§ 3 Further clarification on this point concerning pluralism must wait until the next volume on common grace. Our present concern is to deal specifically with the question of whether the effect of particular grace on common grace extends merely to the very natural effect of religion upon the nations and people groups or whether another factor should also be considered in this connection. If there is not another element factored in, then we may understand religion's effect on culture not in theological but in foremost ethnological terms. This is to argue that religion's effect on society would be something derived not from doctrine or theological dogma but from the "law" of a nation's customs. And the latter is definitely *not* the case. Paganism,

Islam, and even later Judaism all have had an effect on common grace at various times and in various regions of the world, and they in fact still do, but none of them has had the power to strengthen common grace to such an extent that it could come to full development. An essential, enduring, and complete development of common grace can be detected only where particular grace has permeated common grace—that is, where the Christian church arose among the nations and in cultural life. If we draw on a map of the world those regions in which common grace operated with varying degrees of difference, using the different colors of black, brown, gray, and white, we will get white areas only where the sacrament of holy baptism could be prevalent, not outside of it.

Even if the "religion" of human ingenuity, with its falsified idolatrous or godless forms, contributed *something* virtually everywhere to strengthen the capacities of common grace, we nevertheless observe that any sort of strengthening that is enduring and leads the human race to a higher level in fact exists exclusively in regions where so-called Christian nations are found—that is, in those nations where the church of Christ arose and the other religions fell away and where the common social life was influenced by fundamental Christian belief.

This is explained by the fact that both of God's acts of grace spring from the same source. Both are concerned with maintaining God's honor in opposition to Satan's designs. In particular grace God functions as the victor over Satan for the *eternal* existence of things. In common grace he acts as the victor over Satan for the *finite* existence of things. The terminus of the working of common grace is located, therefore, in the day of judgment. Particular grace has no terminus but continues into all eternity; we can discern a terminus only when its convicting character comes to an end and the *last enemy* is annihilated. This is nothing but the relationship between the Noahic and the Abrahamic covenants. The Noahic covenant is the covenant of common grace, whereas the Abrahamic covenant that of particular grace. Every form of covenant making involves establishing a mutual binding or a mutual being bound in fidelity, in order to engage a common enemy with joint forces, vanquish that enemy, and enjoy the fruit of victory afterward.

Consequently, both the Noahic and the Abrahamic covenant are oriented toward each other. The Abrahamic covenant is unthinkable without the Noahic. Both are related through their unity of origin, similarity of motif, and commonality of ultimate purpose, all of which are anchored in maintaining God's honor in the face of Satan's opposition. The one covenant does not exist disconnectedly alongside the other, nor does the one only accidentally come into contact with the other. On the contrary, the one is ordained and destined for the other. Together they constitute two complementary parts of a single plan. They are the two basic parts of one and the same divine decree. The Abrahamic covenant is inconceivable without the Noahic covenant as its natural and indispensable presupposition; conversely, the Noahic covenant cannot rise to a higher level unless the Abrahamic covenant grants the Noahic covenant its influence. The covenant of common grace assumes the covenant of particular grace, even as (and no less than) the covenant of particular grace assumes the covenant of common grace. The fact that for the sake of clarity we have pointed to the covenant form is not something incidental. All religion bears the character of a covenant, and only to the extent that it bears the character of a covenant is it a true religion. As Heinrich Bullinger has already noted, religion itself is the covenant and the covenant is the religion, which means that not a single relationship between God and man can ever be understood correctly and completely unless it be understood as a mutual covenant relationship and therefore rest upon religious faith.[1]

§ 4 Although it requires no further argument that particular grace exerts influence upon common grace, powerfully promotes its development, and only thus leads it to its highest level, we nevertheless must guard against misunderstanding. All too often this is understood to mean that the part of the arena of common grace in which the influence of particular grace could be discerned should be incorporated into the sphere of particular grace as well, and that all Christian nations, all Christian national customs, and all Christian societal forms therefore belong to the arena of particular grace. But this thinking is mistaken. There are four arenas to be distinguished. First of all, there is the arena of common grace that has not yet received any influence from particular grace. Second, there is the arena of the institutional church, which as such derives entirely and exclusively from particular grace. Third, there is an arena of common grace that is illuminated by the light shining from the candlestick of particular grace. And

1. As Bullinger put it, "The covenant of God and true religion are one." See Heinrich Bullinger, *Common Places of Christian Religion*, trans. John Stockwood (London: Tho. East and H. Middleton, 1572), Book 2, Chapter 8, p. 43v. This is a translation of Bullinger's *Summa Christenlicher Religion* (Zurich: Froschouer, 1556).

fourth, there is an arena of particular grace that has made the particulars of common grace serviceable to it.

China presents an example of the first arena. There common grace works to no small degree, but particular grace has not yet caused its influence to impact this gigantic empire, to such a degree that Chinese life has not yet undergone a change as a result of it. In our own European context we need only think of the broadly developed arena of sports, which exists only because of the influence of common grace and not some higher norm. The second arena manifests itself in the institutional churches that limit themselves to performing their own task, relinquishing all usurpation. We find abundant examples of the third arena in all the Christian countries of Europe and America, where we find all kinds of customs, common practices, morals, and laws, domestic as well as societal, that betray very clearly the influence of divine revelation, and that nevertheless are followed and implemented also by the wider population that at the personal level wishes to have nothing to do with faith or conversion. Finally, the fourth arena is to be found wherever the church manifests itself as an organism—that is, wherever personal followers of Jesus allow the life of common grace to be dominated by the principles of divine revelation within their own group. In that sense we have in mind examples such as Christian art, Christian schools, a Christian press, Christians involved in science, and so on. But here "Christian," as we noted before, possesses an entirely different and much more specific meaning than when we speak of a Christian nation, a Christian people, Christian states, and the like.

Thus, when in our thinking we envision side by side life in China, life in the institution of a Christian church, the life of unbelievers in a Christian country, and the life of believers in Christ outside the institution of the church, and when we take these forms of life not individualistically but in their societal and organic context, then the four distinct arenas lie clearly before us. Concerning the first arena of life, Scripture says that "the whole world lies in the power of the evil one" (1 John 5:19). In Scripture the second arena is called the church with its offices. The third is described by Scripture as the part of the world that is illuminated by the light shining from believers. And the fourth corresponds to what Jesus calls the three measures of flour that are completely leavened by the leaven of the gospel.

Nevertheless, there is great danger of confusing the latter two arenas in particular; in fact, this happens constantly. We may even say that most people do not understand the difference between the two images Jesus used (namely, that of the light that shines forth and that of the leaven). Preaching almost always fails to distinguish the two as well, although this may be because there is relatively little preaching on these fundamental concepts that were taught by Jesus as recorded in the Gospels. After all, it is easier to preach from the apostolic letters. There we find derivative and applied concepts, whereas in the Gospels we receive fundamental concepts from Jesus' lips that require further elaboration. The distinction is nevertheless clear. When the kingdom of heaven is compared to a mustard seed that later will shelter all kinds of birds in its branches, then all those birds remain alien to the nature of the grown tree. But when the leaven has leavened the flour, that flour has been changed in its nature by that leaven. The first image is therefore based on purely external contact, and the second image on inner relatedness. The sower sows seed that mixes with substances in the soil and in the air, and from these the seed produces fruit. Salt does nothing but arrest spoiling. The same also applies the light that shines out into the world. Consider in this regard Matthew 5:14–16, "You are the light of the world. A city set on a hill cannot be hidden. Nor do people light a lamp and put it under a basket, but on a stand, and it gives light to all in the house. In the same way, let your light shine before others, so that they may see your good works and give glory to your Father who is in heaven." As such, the world does not climb up to the city, and the city does not descend into the world. Both remain distinct and separate, but the light from the city shines into the world. The candle and those who are in the house remain two separate entities, but those who are in the house catch the light with the eye's retina. In the same way, believers radiate light for people, yet even therein those believers who radiate the light and those people who catch it remain two distinct kinds of persons. The distinction we have posited thus appears not to have been made arbitrarily; it is grounded in Scripture itself.

CHAPTER NINETY-ONE

THE INFLUENCES OF COMMON GRACE ON PARTICULAR GRACE

And Jesus came and said to them, "All authority in heaven and on earth has been given to me."

MATTHEW 28:18

In the concluding chapter we still must look briefly at the counterpart to the previous chapter: the significance of common grace for particular grace. In essence, the elements of the Lord's Supper have symbolic significance in this regard. The bread comes from the promise implicit in the judgment that came upon Adam: "By the sweat of your face you will eat bread." And only after the flood, living in the Noahic covenant of common grace, the second primogenitor of our human race is said to have cultivated wine. We leave out of consideration the question of whether this must be understood in the sense that various kinds of fermented drink were used before the flood but that the pressing of wine occurred first with Noah. At this point we are merely drawing attention to the fact that the elements of the Lord's Supper are not simply products of nature, but rather products of nature that have been *processed* by man: not wheat but *bread*; not grapes but *wine*. § 1

And it is precisely the characteristic feature of common grace that it not only preserves the products of nature in the face of the curse, but that it also preserves human culture or development in the face of the breakdown that sin brought in its wake. Therefore, we can even say that materially the elements for the Lord's Supper would be entirely absent if common grace had not arrested the curse.

Nevertheless, we attach much more importance to the symbolic meaning of this taking of the fruit of common grace into the holy sacrament of particular grace. This expresses that the covenant of particular grace is spiritual in its starting point and core, but it equally expresses that, if received in its comprehensive sense, the covenant of particular grace also encompasses the world of visible things. What's more, the symbols of the Lord's Supper also point to this, which is indicated by what Jesus himself said to his disciples after instituting the Lord's Supper: "I tell you I will not drink again of this fruit of the vine until that day when I drink it new with you in my Father's kingdom" [Matt 26:29]. Every attempt to interpret this saying of Jesus spiritually has always failed and is bound to fail. In the cup that Jesus held in his hand while speaking there was not spiritual wine but actual wine, and when Jesus says that he will drink it with his disciples one day again, but then drink it *new*, this statement permits no other interpretation than that Jesus is referring to the coming kingdom of glory, when a new earth will be spread forth under the new heavens. The elements of the Lord's Supper therefore pointed on the one hand to the blood that Jesus would shed, and on the other hand especially to the new conditions in the kingdom of the Father that was to come. And because this kingdom of glory will be the fruit not of common grace but of particular grace, the bread and the wine certainly include the symbolic indication that particular grace is not restricted to the spiritual realm; rather, it also truly lays claim to the world of visible things.

§ 2 Taking this as our starting point, we now can show that in everything particular grace *is* reality and *seeks* reality; in this way it could not have followed its course apart from common grace. For common grace is precisely what maintained and still maintains the reality of things in opposition to curse and death. We sense this most centrally and sharply in the incarnation of the Son of God. Firmly believing that this incarnation was real and no mere appearance or spiritual manifestation is indeed the core of Christianity to such an extent that the Apostle John sees the antichrist in anyone who detracts anything from the confession that Jesus has come *in the flesh*—that is, in true, natural reality. He became a partaker of flesh and blood, and this flesh and blood that he assumed from Mary is the same "flesh and blood" that was created in paradise and, after the fall, passed in sacred succession from Eve to Mary and from Mary to Jesus. Therefore, we must not say, "Of course Jesus had a body, too, but his spiritual being was the main point," for with the incarnation of the Word what matters most is the flesh and blood. That had to be present. All the centuries led toward the incarnate Christ. Hence it becomes obvious that this would *not* have been the case without common grace. It is common grace that preserved our human race and kept flesh and blood in readiness for the Word that was to become flesh.

From this center, the lines to the complete perimeter are easily drawn. All of particular grace is manifested in people. All of special revelation comes about by means of human beings as ordained for this purpose by God. Almost all miracles move in the realm of visible things. God's elect are conceived and born in the way of all flesh. A powerful part of the ministry of benevolence consists in material offerings and in alleviating physical suffering. In short, no matter how spiritual particular grace may be at its core and starting point, it always manifests itself in visible reality, penetrates visible reality, uses it as instrument, and is incapable of fulfilling its task without the world of external phenomena. If, then, it is certain that this world of external phenomena either would no longer have existed at all or would have degenerated into chaos without the intervention of common grace, then this also demonstrates that particular grace cannot exist apart from common grace for even a moment. It also demonstrates how the great work of God's grace in Christ presupposes the fruit of common grace as it touches all things.

But this truth, which can be briefly summarized by saying that without § 3
common grace the church would not have found a place to stand, is only one side of the matter.

The reality of things that are visible not only serves to make the manifestation of particular grace among sinners possible; it also has the purpose of itself being made suitable by particular grace. At first we do not discern this. The initial effect of particular grace is, rather, to turn us away from the world of visible phenomena. The recent convert is afraid of the visible world, and he only feels himself safe and at home in the spiritual. Throughout the centuries the tendency has even arisen to turn permanently away from the visible world after one's conversion, and the monastic notion as well as Anabaptist withdrawal aims to demarcate particular grace sharply from the arena of common grace. Nor must we hide the fact that the Lord's providential governance generally does not crown conversion with external prosperity. From the world's perspective we are not rewarded with external improvement when we decide to follow Jesus. The lot of the godly involves much suffering. And the sharper this opposition between the world and particular grace became manifest in the course of history, the more harshly the world cast out those who confess Jesus. Persecution testifies to this. No stone was left unturned to make the world of visible phenomena unbearable for God's children. We therefore must acknowledge that particular grace not only begins with acting *spiritually*, but thereafter, sometimes until the day we die, it makes the condition of the child of God worse rather than better in the things of the world. Here Christ himself remains the standard. His cross is the sign. And only from the hour of the resurrection can it be said that in Jesus the visible celebrates its triumph.

But even though this is the starting point, and even though for many, until their death, the world of visible things continues to belong to the realm of what Paul calls "this body of death" (so that he can ask, "Wretched man that I am! Who will deliver me from this body of death?" [Rom 7:24]), this contrast between the arena of particular grace and that of common grace nevertheless is only temporary. One day this course of things will reach its turning point, and then the re-creating power of particular grace will also claim the entire arena of common grace, including our body as well as this entire world. And then our body will be glorious, like Jesus' body after his ascension, and this earth will outshine the sun in its glory. Common grace therefore renders this service, by which it preserves and maintains the world of visible things during the long period of time when particular grace retreats more into the spiritual. This occurs until the moment arrives when there is no more sin to arrest and no more curse to temper—a time when the whole of God's creation, delivered from Satan's power, once again belongs to him in glory.

§ 4 This was already intimated in the dispensation given to Israel, and if we do not pay close attention to this intimation of a higher glory for Israel, we will not understand the Old Testament. Canaan held a different and higher meaning for Israel than our own land does for us. Jerusalem was something entirely different for an Israelite than Amsterdam is for us. And Zion, on the mount of Jerusalem, had a significance for the Israelite that cannot be compared to that of any church or plaza in our land. This exceptional significance was ceremonially expressed in the law of Levitical purity. Because of this the land itself (that is, the actual territory) bore in part a sacred character. Anyone crossing the borders went from holy to unholy territory. After the conquest, Canaan had an entirely different significance than either Edom or Egypt or even Babylon. The reason for this was that the physical land was for Israel a symbol of the kingdom of glory.

Especially in the seventeenth century, Christians—primarily in England but also here—were generally in the habit of calling heaven "Canaan," of viewing the crossing of Jordan as the image of the transition from life to death, and of understanding Zion as one with the throne of God's glory. Consequently, they spoke almost exclusively about Zion above. Since then, the rise of chiliasm has further weakened this insight into the symbolic—and in part even typological—meaning of the land of Canaan, of Jerusalem, and of Zion. Having lost sight of the difference between an identical and a symbolic reality, the notion was allowed again to gain entrance that the Jews had to return to Canaan, that Jesus would again appear in Jerusalem as king, and that the great vision of Ezekiel would be fulfilled only when, in a crassly physical sense, the land of Canaan again had dominion over the world. This notion of identical reality contained much that made it attractive, of course. It required no thinking. Everything was meant literally: [As for] Canaan, well, you reach it when you disembark from the boat in Jaffa. Jerusalem is a city that now can in part be reached by train. And Zion is that mountain at Jerusalem now built full of randomly scattered buildings. You can render practical help by taking Jews there. Zionists have even established a bank for this purpose. And if it were to reach the point now that some three or four million Jews could move to that spot on the Mediterranean, then the ultimate goal would be reached, Jesus would return, and the triumph of the kingdom of God would begin. It is too bad that the unconverted Jews understand this quite differently and are focused on nothing else than erecting the ancient temple again, so that even now large pillars for that new temple lie ready and waiting in Italy.

However, we will not end our discussion with this criticism of what § 5
might be called Capernaism,[1] which fortunately is gradually blowing over. We also must point out that the physical nation of Israel—including soil, capital, and temple—did in fact have a *symbolic* reality that is often wrongly

1. By "Capernaism," Kuyper means to refer to an excessive literalism or materialism. See John 6:22–59.

overlooked in Capernaism—a symbolic reality that even exists in the spiritual realm. As it says in Psalm 24, stanzas 2–3:

> Who shall ascend the hill of God,
> stand in his holy place, and laud
> the Lord who lives and reigns forever?
> He who withstands the wicked's lure,
> whose hands are clean, whose heart is pure,
> who keeps his oaths and does not waver.
>
> Rich blessings shall be his reward,
> and vindication from the Lord,
> who is the rock of his salvation.
> Such are all those who seek his face.
> O God of Jacob, God of grace,
> from you is all their expectation.

And in Psalm 15, stanzas 1–3:

> Who, Lord, may live on Zion's height,
> within your tent, your holy dwelling?
> He who does what is just and right,
> whose walk is blameless in your sight,
> all falsehood from his ways repelling.
>
> He who keeps slander from his tongue,
> who does no wrong to all those near him,
> nor will on them discredit bring;
> who scorns the vile, while honoring
> those who obey the Lord and fear him.
>
> He who keeps oaths at any cost,
> who seeks no interest for his lending,
> nor takes a bribe to harm the just.
> He'll stand unshaken, richly blest
> with grace and favor never-ending.[2]

2. The Psalms texts are from *Het Boek der Psalmen, nevens de Gezangen bij de Hervormde Kerk van Nederland in Gebruik* (The Hague: Hendrik Christoffel Gutteling, 1773). For the English, see *Book of Praise: Anglo-Genevan Psalter* (Winnipeg: Premier, 2010).

Or, finally, when we read Ezekiel 18:5–9:

> If a man is righteous and does what is just and right—if he does not eat upon the mountains or lift up his eyes to the idols of the house of Israel, does not defile his neighbor's wife or approach a woman in her time of menstrual impurity, does not oppress anyone, but restores to the debtor his pledge, commits no robbery, gives his bread to the hungry and covers the naked with a garment, does not lend at interest or take any profit, withholds his hand from injustice, executes true justice between man and man, walks in my statutes, and keeps my rules by acting faithfully—he is righteous; he shall surely live, declares the Lord God.

At this point, we should not understand this to mean that "eternal salvation" is being attributed to these people, for then salvation would be the fruit of an unreproachable walk and thus depend on merit. Ezekiel shows clearly that something else is needed, replacing the heart of stone with a heart of flesh, and being sprinkled with the water of the Spirit (Ezek 36:25–27). The prize that was held out as a prospect is therefore not eternal salvation but long life in the land of Canaan, part of which was enjoying in that Canaan the good of the land: grain, wine, and oil. The resurrection of Israel is even depicted as a reawakening of the Jews who passed away in Canaan. In this context dying makes such a melancholy, painful impression, because by dying an Israelite left Canaan, lost his temple on Zion, and in the grave was no longer able to praise his God. Later biblical commentary even concluded from this image that in the Old Testament there was not as yet a belief in immortality.

All this becomes entirely understandable as soon as we make a sharp distinction between two things: the personal salvation of the elect of the Lord, and the symbolic glory and holiness, indeed, even Levitical purity with which the "righteous" were clothed in their earthly life. But we see immediately that the elect among Israel had no other way to salvation than we have; they were saved only through regeneration and coming to Christ. In addition, there also is the symbolic meaning that remained entirely within the boundaries of this life and had nothing to do with salvation. And although it seems repeatedly as though these two flow together, this is simply because among the symbolically righteous only those people displayed the full symbol who, thanks to their personal turning to God, brought uprightness into their *external manifestation*. This is why there always is such a special emphasis precisely on that uprightness.

§ 6 It is particularly in this symbolism of what was joined together in the whole of Israel's external life—a symbolism that diverges with the coming of Jesus—that we find the conjoining of the *internal* and *external* working of particular grace. In the church of the new covenant it is the spiritual that has priority, whereas the external is parlayed to the return of Jesus. In the meantime, it is only common grace that ensures the continued existence of the visible realm. But although particular grace will break through gloriously in all things visible only by means of the regeneration of the "new world" of which Jesus spoke in Matthew 19:28, the initial breakthrough of the powers of particular grace in the visible realm nevertheless is already present. The church is concentrated spiritually in the institutional church, but the church itself is an organism. This means as such that believers with their talents, their gifts, and their relationships and influences in this world already constitute a unique sphere of life that can gloriously manifest the powers of the kingdom.

By this we are not referring to what we discussed earlier: the fact that particular grace supports and strengthens common grace. That occurs among the unbelievers and elevates their life to a higher level. Rather, what we are indicating here is the sphere of Christian living that extends as far as—and to the extent that—the organic movement of our Lord's church expands into all of life. And in that organic circle of the church's influence, this heightened form of human life manifests itself in a manner that foreshadows the coming kingdom of glory. This does not always occur, given the fact that a false spiritualism all too often hinders it, but it does occur at high points in history. Our own country has experienced this during the sixteenth and seventeenth centuries, a time when the "Zion of God" shone so gloriously in our nation. That considerable radiance did not consist exclusively in the fact that the institutional life of the church was perfectly healthy; in fact, much was even lacking during this period. However, because the saints of God contributed in substantial ways to the life of our national culture, the nation's cultural life indeed stood at an exceptionally high level both morally and socially.

BIBLIOGRAPHY

Anslijn, Nicolaas. *De Brave Hendrik, een leesboekje voor jonge kinderen*. Leiden: Du Mortier en Zoon, 1809.

Augustine. *The Confessions*. Translated by Maria Boulding. Hyde Park, NY: New City Press, 1997.

Bellarmine, Robert. *Opera omnia*. Vol. 4, *De gratia primi hominis*. Naples: Josephum Guiliano, 1858.

Bensdorp, Th. "Dr. Kuyper over her katholieke leerstuk der oorspronkelijke gerechtigheid." *De Katholiek* 110 (1896): 23–60; 300–329.

Bomberger, J. H. A., trans. and ed. *The Protestant Theological and Ecclesiastical Encyclopedia: A Condensed Translation of Herzog's Real Encyclopedia*. 2 vols. Philadelphia: Lindsay & Blakiston, 1860.

Book of Praise: Anglo-Genevan Psalter. Winnipeg: Premier, 2010.

Bratt, James D. *Abraham Kuyper: Modern Calvinist, Christian Democrat*. Grand Rapids: Eerdmans, 2013.

Brück, Nicolas-Remi. *Électricité ou magnétisme du globe terrestre*. 2 vols. Brussels: Delevingne et Callewaert, 1851–55.

———. *L'Humanité, son développement et sa durée*. 2 vols. Paris: Librairie Internationale, 1866.

———. *Manifeste du magnétisme du globe et de l'humanité*. Paris: Librairie Internationale, 1866.

Buckle, Henry Thomas. *History of the Civilization in England*. 2 vols. London: J. W. Parker, 1857–61.

Bullinger, Heinrich. *Common Places of Christian Religion*. Translated by John Stockwood. London: Tho. East and H. Middleton, 1572.

———. *De testamento seu foedere dei unico & aeterno*. Zurich: Froschauer, 1534.

Calvin, John. *Letters of John Calvin*. Edited by Jules Bonnet. Translated by Marcus Robert Gilchrist. Philadelphia: Presbyterian Board of Publication, 1858.

Christison, Robert. *A Treatise on Poisons*. Edinburgh: Black, 1829.

Christlieb, Theodor. *Protestant Missions to the Heathen: A General Survey of Their Recent Progress and Present State throughout the World*. Translated by W. Hastie. Calcutta: Thacker Spink & Co.; Edinburgh: David Douglas, 1882.

Dennison, James T., Jr., ed. *Reformed Confessions of the 16th and 17th Centuries in English Translation*. 4 vols. Grand Rapids: Reformation Heritage Books, 2008–2014.

Eddy, Mary Baker. *Science and Health with Key to the Scriptures*. Boston: Christian Scientist Publishing Co., 1875.

Hanson, J. W., ed. *The World's Congress of Religions: The Addresses and Papers Delivered before the Parliament*. Chicago: Monarch, 1894.

Heinrich, Johann Baptist. *Dogmatische Theologie*. 10 vols. 2nd ed. Mainz: Franz Kirchheim, 1881–1900.

Heldring, Otto G. "Hoe de overgeërfde regtzinnigheid onzer dagen in strijd staat met de ware leer der Hervormde Kerk." *De Vereeniging: Christelijke Stemmen* 18 (1864): 525–533; 668–674.

Het Boek der Psalmen, nevens de Gezangen bij de Hervormde Kerk van Nederland in Gebruik. The Hague: Hendrik Christoffel Gutteling, 1773.

Jacobs, Henry Eyster, and John A. W. Haas, eds. *The Lutheran Cyclopedia*. New York: Charles Scribner's Sons, 1899.

Kuyper, Abraham. *Our Program: A Christian Political Manifesto*. Translated and edited by Harry Van Dyke. Bellingham, WA: Lexham Press, 2015.

———. *De Engelen Gods*. Amsterdam: Höveker & Wormser, 1902.

———. *Lectures on Calvinism*. Grand Rapids: Eerdmans, 1931.

Lubbock, John. *Ants, Bees and Wasps: A Record of Observations on the Habits of the Social Hymenoptera*. London: Keegan Paul, Trench, & Co., 1882.

McKim, Donald K. *The Westminster Dictionary of Theological Terms*. 2nd ed. Louisville: Westminster John Knox, 2014.

Orfila, M. P. *Traité des poisons tirés des règnes minéral, végétal et animal, ou Toxicologie Générale*. 2 vols. Paris: Crochard, 1818.

The Psalms and Hymns: With the Catechism, Confession of Faith, and Canons, of the Synod of Dort, and Liturgy of the Reformed Protestant Dutch Church in North America. Philadelphia: Mentz & Rouvoudt, 1847.

Renan, Ernest. *Vie de Jésus*. Paris: Michel Lévy Fréres, 1863.

Schooley, John C. "How I Was Healed: A Letter to an Enquirer." *Christian Science Journal* 12 (April 1894): 510–12.

Schortinghuis, Wilhelmus. *Het innige Christendom*. Groningen: Sandaw, 1740.

Strauss, David Friedrich. *Das Leben Jesu, kritisch arbeitet*. 2 vols. Tubingen: Osiander, 1835–36.

Tappert, Theodore G., ed. *The Book of Concord: The Confessions of the Evangelical Lutheran Church*. Philadelphia: Fortress, 1959.

Tardieu, A., P. Lorain, and Z. Roussin. *Empoisonnement par la strychnine, l'arsenic et les sels de cuivre*. Paris: Baillière, 1865.

Taylor, Alfred S. *On Poisons, in Relation to Medical Jurisprudence and Medicine*. London: John Churchill, 1848.

Turretin, Francis. *Institutes of Elenctic Theology*. Edited by James T. Dennison, Jr. Translated by George Musgrave Giger. 3 vols. Phillipsburg, NJ: P&R Publishing, 1992–97.

van der Woud, Auke. *Koninkrijk vol sloppen: achterbuurten en vuil in de negentiende eeuw*. Amsterdam: Prometheus, 2010.

van Oosterzee, J. J. *Geschichte oder Roman? Das Leben Jesu von Ernst Renan vorläufig beleuchtet*. Hamburg: Rauhen Hauses, 1864.

Vree, Jasper, and Johan Zwaan, eds. *Abraham Kuyper's* Commentatio *(1860): The Young Kuyper about Calvin, à Lasco, and the Church*. 2 vols. Leiden: Brill, 2005.

Warfield, Benjamin B. "Albrecht Ritschl and His Doctrine of Christian Perfection: II. Ritschl the Perfectionist." *Princeton Theological Review* 18, no. 1 (January 1920): 44–102.

ABOUT ABRAHAM KUYPER (1837–1920)

Abraham Kuyper's life began in the small Dutch village of Maassluis on October 29, 1837. During his first pastorate, he developed a deep devotion to Jesus Christ and a strong commitment to Reformed theology that profoundly influenced his later careers. He labored tirelessly, publishing two newspapers, leading a reform movement out of the state church, founding the Free University of Amsterdam, and serving as prime minister of the Netherlands. He died on November 8, 1920, after relentlessly endeavoring to integrate his faith and life. Kuyper's emphasis on worldview formation has had a transforming influence upon evangelicalism, both through the diaspora of the Dutch Reformed churches, and those they have inspired.

In the mid-nineteenth-century Dutch political arena, the increasing sympathy for the "No God, no master!" dictum of the French Revolution greatly concerned Kuyper. To desire freedom from an oppressive government or heretical religion was one thing, but to eradicate religion from politics as spheres of mutual influence was, for Kuyper, unthinkable. Because man is sinful, he reasoned, a state that derives its power from men cannot avoid the vices of fallen human impulses. True limited government flourishes best when people recognize their sinful condition and acknowledge God's divine authority. In Kuyper's words, "The sovereignty of the state as the power that protects the individual and that defines the mutual relationships among the visible spheres, rises high above them by its right to command and compel. But within these spheres ... another authority rules, an authority that descends directly from God apart from the state. This authority the state does not confer but acknowledges."

ABOUT THE CONTRIBUTORS

Jordan J. Ballor (Dr. theol., University of Zurich; Ph.D., Calvin Theological Seminary) is a senior research fellow and director of publishing at the Acton Institute for the Study of Religion & Liberty. He is the author of books including *Covenant, Causality, and Law: A Study in the Theology of Wolfgang Musculus* (Vandenhoeck & Ruprecht) and *Ecumenical Babel: Confusing Economic Ideology and the Church's Social Witness* (Christian's Library Press), as well as editor or co-editor of numerous works, including *Church and School in Early Modern Protestantism* (Brill) and *Law and Religion: The Legal Teachings of the Catholic and Protestant Reformations* (Vandenhoeck & Ruprecht). In addition to working as a volume editor on *Common Grace*, he is also a general editor of the Abraham Kuyper Collected Works in Public Theology.

Craig G. Bartholomew (Ph.D., Bristol University) is the Director of the Kirby Laing Institute for Christian Ethics at Tyndale House, Cambridge. Formerly, he was Senior Research Fellow at the University of Gloucestershire and recently the H. Evan Runner Professor of Philosophy and Professor of Religion and Theology at Redeemer University College in Ancaster, Canada. He is also adjunct faculty at Trinity College, Bristol, and an Anglican priest. His academic background is in Old Testament studies and hermeneutics. He has edited and written many books, including *Beyond the Modern Age*

(IVP Academic, co-authored with the Dutch economist Bob Goudzwaard) and *Contours of the Kuyperian tradition* (IVP Academic).

J. Daryl Charles (Ph.D., Westminster Theological Seminary) is Affiliate Scholar in Theology & Ethics at the Acton Institute. He also serves as a contributing editor of *Providence: A Journal of Christianity and American Foreign Policy* and *Touchstone*, and is an affiliated scholar of the John Jay Institute. Charles is author, co-author, or editor of 15 books, including *Virtue amidst Vice* (Sheffield Academic Press), *The Unformed Conscience of Evangelicalism* (InterVarsity Press), *Retrieving the Natural Law* (Eerdmans), and *Natural Law and Religious Freedom* (Routledge). He is also the translator (German to English) of Claus Westermann's *Roots of Wisdom: The Oldest Proverbs of Israel and Other Peoples* (Westminster John Knox Press). Charles has taught at Taylor University and Union University and was a 2013/14 visiting professor in the honors program at Berry College. Has served as director and senior fellow of the Bryan Institute for Critical Thought and Practice, as the William E. Simon visiting fellow in religion and public life at the James Madison Program, Princeton University, and as a visiting fellow of the Institute for Faith and Learning, Baylor University.

Nelson D. Kloosterman (Th.D., Theological University of the Reformed Churches [Liberated], Kampen, the Netherlands) is ethics consultant and executive director of Worldview Resources International, a service organization whose mission is to produce and provide resources designed to assist in understanding and applying a Christian worldview to responsible living in a global culture. He has served as minister and professor for more than thirty years and has translated dozens of works on Reformed theology and ethics.

Ed M. van der Maas (Th.M., Dallas Theological Seminary) is an editor and translator. Among his translations are several volumes of the *Korte Verklaring* (*Bible Student's Commentary*) and *Concise Reformed Dogmatics* (Van Genderen and Velema). Ed has worked for several Dutch publishers and was also the associate editor for the *New International Dictionary of Pentecostal and Charismatic Movements*. Until his retirement he was senior editor at HarperCollins Christian Publishers/Zondervan in Grand Rapids, Mich. A native of the Netherlands, Ed lived in the United States for more than forty years before returning to his European base.

SUBJECT/AUTHOR INDEX

SCRIPTURE INDEX

Old Testament

New Testament

Pseudepigrapha